SHOWCASE PRESENTS

STRANGE ADVENTURES

VOLUME TWO

Julius Schwartz Editor – Original Series
Scott Nybakken Editor
Robbin Brosterman Design Director – Books
Ternard Solomon Publication Design

Bob Harras Senior VP – Editor-in-Chief, DC Comics

Diane Nelson President
Dan DiDio and **Jim Lee** Co-Publishers
Geoff Johns Chief Creative Officer
John Rood Executive VP – Sales, Marketing & Business Development
Amy Genkins Senior VP – Business & Legal Affairs
Nairi Gardiner Senior VP – Finance
Jeff Boison VP – Publishing Planning
Mark Chiarello VP – Art Direction & Design
John Cunningham VP – Marketing
Terri Cunningham VP – Editorial Administration
Alison Gill Senior VP – Manufacturing & Operations
Hank Kanalz Senior VP – Vertigo & Integrated Publishing
Jay Kogan VP – Business & Legal Affairs, Publishing
Jack Mahan VP – Business Affairs, Talent
Nick Napolitano VP – Manufacturing Administration
Sue Pohja VP – Book Sales
Courtney Simmons Senior VP – Publicity
Bob Wayne Senior VP – Sales

Cover illustration by Gil Kane.
Cover color by Allen Passalaqua.

SHOWCASE PRESENTS: STRANGE ADVENTURES VOLUME 2
Published by DC Comics. Cover and compilation Copyright © 2013 DC Comics.
All Rights Reserved. Originally published in single magazine form in STRANGE
ADVENTURES 74-93. Copyright © 1956, 1957, 1958 DC Comics. All Rights Reserved.
All characters, their distinctive likenesses and related elements featured in this publication
are trademarks of DC Comics. The stories, characters and incidents featured in this
publication are entirely fictional. DC Comics does not read or accept
unsolicited submissions of ideas, stories or artwork.

DC Comics, 1700 Broadway, New York, NY 10019
A Warner Bros. Entertainment Company.
Printed by RR Donnelley, Harrisonburg, VA, USA. 11/15/13. First Printing.
ISBN: 978-1-4012-3846-9

TABLE OF CONTENTS

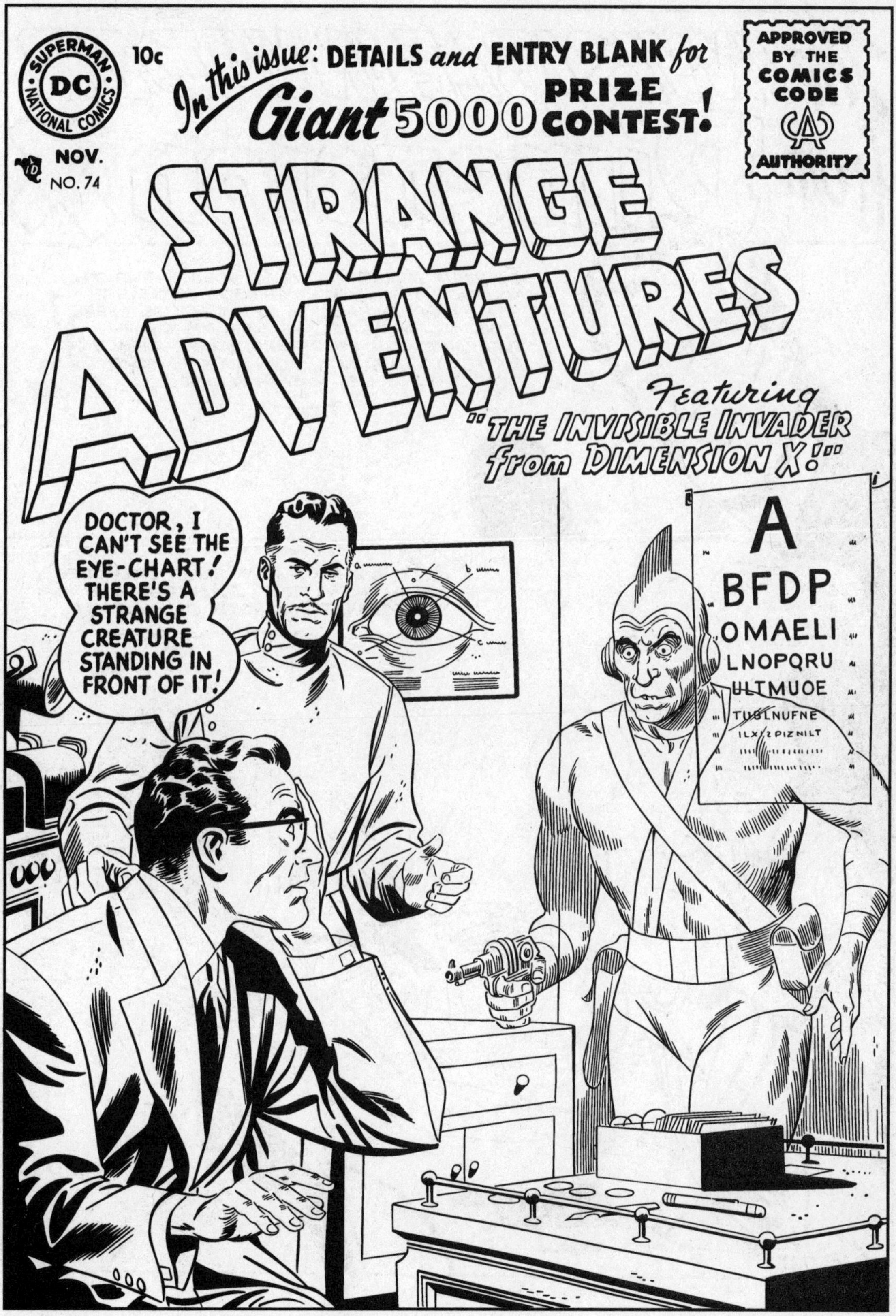
SUPERMAN DC NATIONAL COMICS
10c
In this issue: DETAILS and ENTRY BLANK for Giant 5000 PRIZE CONTEST!
APPROVED BY THE COMICS CODE AUTHORITY
NOV. NO. 74
STRANGE ADVENTURES
Featuring "THE INVISIBLE INVADER from DIMENSION X!"
DOCTOR, I CAN'T SEE THE EYE-CHART! THERE'S A STRANGE CREATURE STANDING IN FRONT OF IT!
A
BFDP
OMAELI
LNOPQRU
ULTMUOE

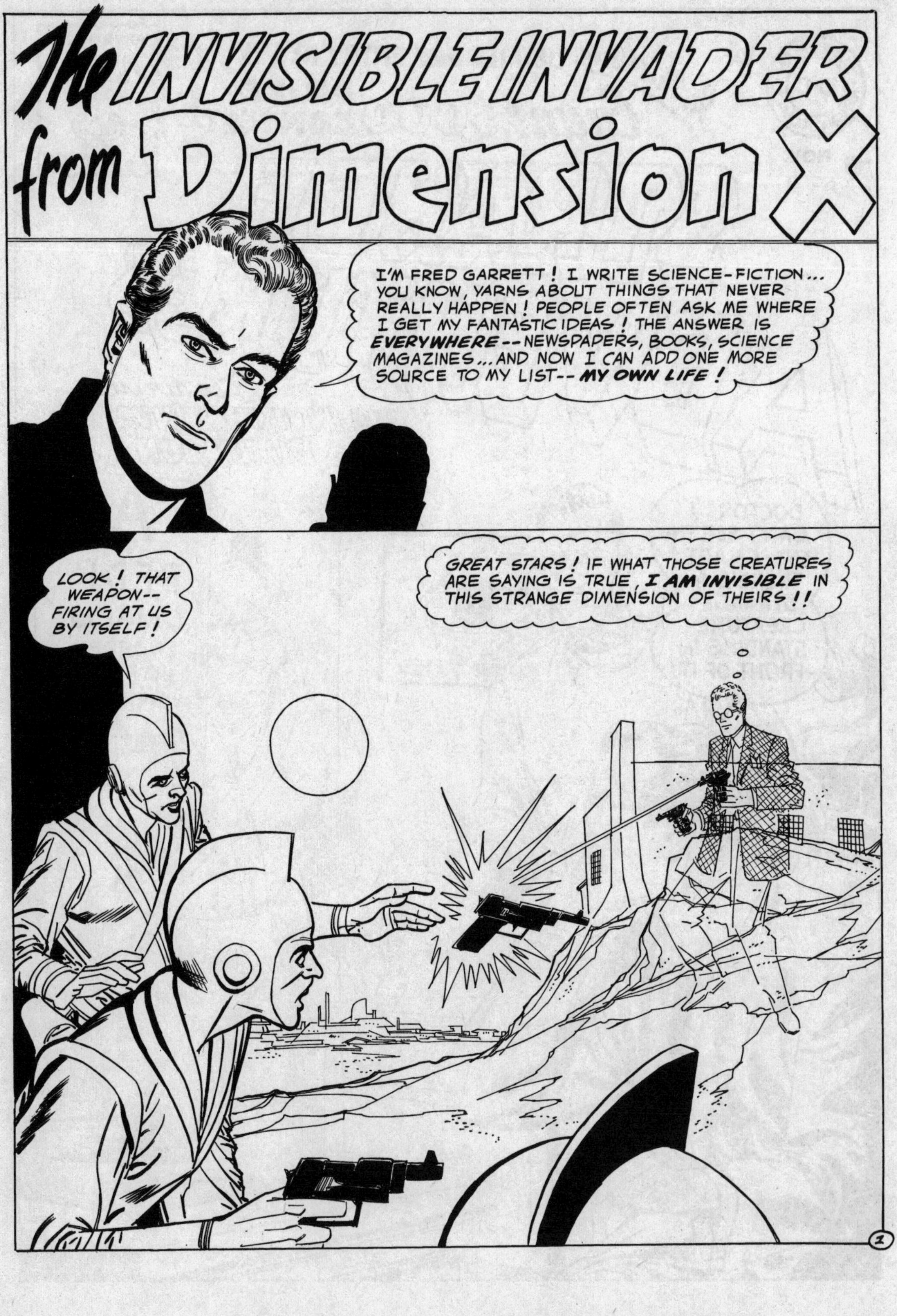
The INVISIBLE INVADER from Dimension X
I'M FRED GARRETT! I WRITE SCIENCE-FICTION... YOU KNOW, YARNS ABOUT THINGS THAT NEVER REALLY HAPPEN! PEOPLE OFTEN ASK ME WHERE I GET MY FANTASTIC IDEAS! THE ANSWER IS EVERYWHERE--NEWSPAPERS, BOOKS, SCIENCE MAGAZINES... AND NOW I CAN ADD ONE MORE SOURCE TO MY LIST--MY OWN LIFE!
LOOK! THAT WEAPON--FIRING AT US BY ITSELF!
GREAT STARS! IF WHAT THOSE CREATURES ARE SAYING IS TRUE, I AM INVISIBLE IN THIS STRANGE DIMENSION OF THEIRS!!
1

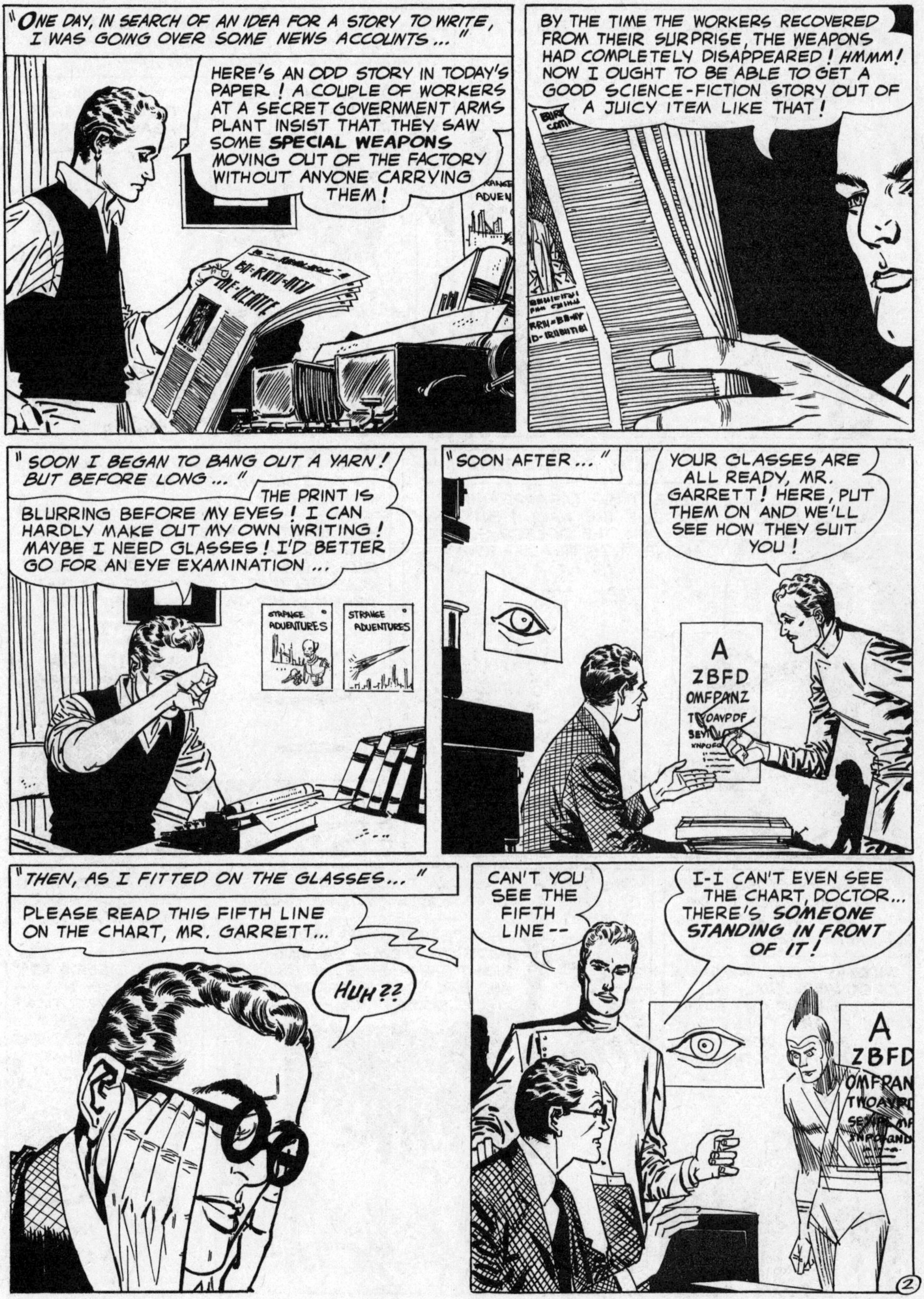
"ONE DAY, IN SEARCH OF AN IDEA FOR A STORY TO WRITE, I WAS GOING OVER SOME NEWS ACCOUNTS ..."
HERE'S AN ODD STORY IN TODAY'S PAPER ! A COUPLE OF WORKERS AT A SECRET GOVERNMENT ARMS PLANT INSIST THAT THEY SAW SOME SPECIAL WEAPONS MOVING OUT OF THE FACTORY WITHOUT ANYONE CARRYING THEM !
BY THE TIME THE WORKERS RECOVERED FROM THEIR SURPRISE, THE WEAPONS HAD COMPLETELY DISAPPEARED ! HMMM! NOW I OUGHT TO BE ABLE TO GET A GOOD SCIENCE-FICTION STORY OUT OF A JUICY ITEM LIKE THAT !
"SOON I BEGAN TO BANG OUT A YARN ! BUT BEFORE LONG ..."
THE PRINT IS BLURRING BEFORE MY EYES ! I CAN HARDLY MAKE OUT MY OWN WRITING ! MAYBE I NEED GLASSES ! I'D BETTER GO FOR AN EYE EXAMINATION ...
STRANGE ADVENTURES
STRANGE ADVENTURES
"SOON AFTER ..."
YOUR GLASSES ARE ALL READY, MR. GARRETT ! HERE, PUT THEM ON AND WE'LL SEE HOW THEY SUIT YOU !
A
ZBFD
OMFPANZ
"THEN, AS I FITTED ON THE GLASSES ..."
PLEASE READ THIS FIFTH LINE ON THE CHART, MR. GARRETT...
HUH??
CAN'T YOU SEE THE FIFTH LINE --
I-I CAN'T EVEN SEE THE CHART, DOCTOR... THERE'S SOMEONE STANDING IN FRONT OF IT !
2

"WITH A SUDDEN IMPULSE, I HANDED THE GLASSES TO THE DOCTOR..."

HERE--YOU LOOK THROUGH THEM!

WHAT DO YOU MEAN? WHAT'S WRONG--?

"WITH MY SCIENCE-FICTIONEER'S MIND, I ASSUMED THAT I SAW THE STRANGE CREATURE ON ACCOUNT OF THE GLASSES, BUT..."

I DON'T SEE ANYTHING UNUSUAL! WHAT ARE YOU TRYING TO SHOW ME, MR. GARRETT?

LET ME HAVE THOSE GLASSES AGAIN, PLEASE!

"I PUT THEM ON, AND AT ONCE, THE CREATURE WAS VISIBLE AGAIN..."

THERE IT IS--DISAPPEARING THROUGH THE WALL! BUT WHY COULDN'T THE DOCTOR SEE IT? AND IF IT IS REAL--WHAT IS IT?

"I TOLD THE DOCTOR EVERYTHING, AND HE GAVE ME THE BENEFIT OF HIS EXPERIENCE..."

JUST AS NO TWO PEOPLE HAVE IDENTICAL FINGERPRINTS, NO TWO HAVE THE SAME VISION! MAYBE YOU DID SEE SOMETHING THROUGH THESE GLASSES THAT I CAN'T SEE AND THAT PERHAPS NO ONE ELSE CAN SEE!

"I TOOK MY GLASSES AND LEFT! MY CURIOSITY WAS ON FIRE... AND YET I WAS APPREHENSIVE..."

WHY ARE THESE INVISIBLE CREATURES STALKING THROUGH OUR CITY? WHAT IF THEY ARE A MENACE--? I'LL GET NO ANSWERS-- UNTIL I PUT ON THESE GLASSES AGAIN!

"THIS TIME AS I PEERED THROUGH THE GLASSES, I STOOD ROOTED TO THE GROUND, DUMBFOUNDED..."

GREAT STARS! NOW I SEE MORE OF THEM-- WALKING RIGHT THROUGH SOLID OBJECTS! AND EACH ONE IS CARRYING SOMETHING --

"I CONQUERED MY FEELING OF FEAR AND CAME TO A DECISION..."

THEY ALL SEEM TO BE HEADING IN A CERTAIN DIRECTION! I'LL FOLLOW THEM... TRY TO FIND OUT WHO THEY ARE--WHAT THEY'RE UP TO--!

"NEXT TO THE CITY, THERE WAS AN ARMS PLANT! I FOLLOWED THE CREATURES THERE ... "

THEY'RE **STEALING** ARMS AND AMMUNTION--JUST AS IN THAT NEWS ITEM I READ! THEY'RE INVISIBLE--TO EVERYONE BUT ME--AND THAT MAKES IT EASY FOR THEM TO GET IN AND OUT!

"I HAD TO FIND OUT WHERE THEY WERE TAKING THE WEAPONS! I TRAILED THEM BACK THROUGH THE CITY, TO A LONELY SPOT IN A WOOD ... "

GOING INTO THAT STRANGE--LOOKING CAVE! QUEER... I CAN SEE THE MOUTH OF THE CAVE, BUT I CAN'T SEE ANYTHING BUT A WAVERING BLACKNESS INSIDE! WHERE DOES IT LEAD TO? I'VE GOT TO FIND OUT!

"AT THIS POINT, I HESITATED! IF I DISAPPEARED, WHO ON EARTH WOULD EVER KNOW WHAT HAD BE-COME OF ME? BUT I HAD GONE TOO FAR TO STOP NOW...I MOVED FORWARD... "

I CAN'T SEE A THING--EITHER BEFORE ME OR BEHIND! ALL OF A SUDDEN ALL LIGHT--ALL SOUND--HAS VANISHED!

"THE NEXT MOMENT, MY BODY STARTED TO VIBRATE--AND I BLACKED OUT! WHEN I RECOVERED MY SENSES... "

I--I'M IN A DIFFERENT WORLD! A STRANGELY-COLORED SKY--AND SUN!

"MY SCIENCE-FICTION BACKGROUND HELPED ME PIECE THINGS TOGETHER ... "

I'M IN A DIFFERENT **DIMENSION!** THAT CAVE MOUTH MUST BE A LINK BETWEEN OUR EARTH DIMENSION AND THIS ONE! BUT--THOSE CREATURES COMING AT ME!?

"TO MY AMAZEMENT, THE CREATURES RAN RIGHT THROUGH ME WITHOUT A SIGN OF AWARENESS OF MY BEING THERE! "

AKIIE! AKIIE!

THEY DON'T SEE ME! THEY WEREN'T COMING AT **ME**--BUT AT THAT WILD ANIMAL THEY'RE HUNTING!

4

"*LITTLE BY LITTLE, THE FULL TRUTH DAWNED ON ME ... "*

I'M INVISIBLE! WHAT AN EERIE FEELING! I CAN GO ANYWHERE...WATCH ANYTHING...WITHOUT ANYONE SUSPECTING MY PRESENCE!

"*I COULDN'T EXPLAIN WHY I HAD BECOME INVISIBLE! BUT ONE THING SEEMED LIKELY..."*

WHATEVER THE CAUSE OF MY INVISIBILITY IS, THE SAME FORCE MAKES THESE CREATURES INVISIBLE IN OUR WORLD! BUT-- WHY DO THEY STEAL ARMS FROM US?

"*I SPENT DAYS IN THE NEW DIMENSION, LEARNED THEIR LANGUAGE, AND DISCOVERED PLENTY..."*

THEY HAVE A DEMOCRATIC GOVERNMENT HERE... AND THE CREATURES WHO STOLE OUR MOST DEADLY WEAPONS ARE TRYING TO OVER-THROW IT,...AND SET UP A DICTATORSHIP!

"*IN FACT A SECRET DATE HAD BEEN SET FOR THE UPRISING! I ATTENDED THE SECRET MEETING WHERE IT WAS DECIDED ON!..."*

BY NIGHTFALL, GENERAL WA-IK WILL BE DICTATOR!

I'VE GOT TO INFORM THE DEMOCRATIC LEADERS OF THE REBELS' PLAN TO OVERTHROW THE GOVERNMENT!

"*I SPED FROM THE MEETING TO THE PRESIDENT'S OFFICE, AND THERE..."*

LOOK! WRITING-- APPEARING ON THAT WALL!

I'M TELLING THEM ABOUT THE CONSPIRACY!

"*THANKS TO MY WARNING, AN INVESTIGATION WAS MADE, AND BEFORE NOON GENERAL WA-IK RECEIVED VISITORS..."*

GOVERNMENT POLICE!

COME WITH US, GENERAL! YOU ARE UNDER ARREST!

"*THERE WAS STILL RESISTANCE! THE STOLEN EARTH WEAPONS HAD BEEN CACHED IN A SECRET ARSENAL WHERE THE CONSPIRATORS HELD OUT...*"

I MUST GET INTO THAT BUILDING... AND STOP THIS WAR SINGLE-HANDED!

"*INVISIBLE, I GOT IN EASILY ENOUGH, AND MOMENTS LATER...*"

THEY CAN'T SEE ME--ONLY THESE GUNS!

WEAPONS ATTACKING US--BY THEMSELVES?

"*MY ACTION STUNNED THE LAST OF THE CONSPIRATORS AND FORCED THEM OUT OF THE ARSENAL...*"

WE SURRENDER! SAVE US FROM THE AVENGING GUNS!

AVENGING GUNS?

"*LATER, I MANAGED TO MAKE CONTACT WITH THE PRESIDENT AND I MADE EVERYTHING CLEAR TO HIM AND HIS PEOPLE! SHORTLY AFTERWARD...*"

WE CANNOT MAKE A STATUE OF YOU, GAR-RETT, BECAUSE NONE OF US HAS EVER SEEN YOU! BUT WE CAN AWARD YOU OUR HIGHEST MEDAL FOR VALOR!

GOSH! A MEDAL-- FROM ANOTHER DIMENSION!

"*BY AGREEMENT BETWEEN ME AND THE PRESIDENT, THE HILL WHERE THE OPENING WAS BETWEEN OUR TWO WORLDS WAS BLOWN UP RIGHT AFTER I RETURNED THROUGH IT BACK TO MY DIMENSION...*"

IT'S BETTER THIS WAY! NOW TONS OF EARTH COVER THE OPENING --WHICH MUST HAVE BEEN ACCIDENTLY CAUSED BY A GIANT LIGHTNING FLASH!

POW!

"*WHEN I GOT HOME, I SAT DOWN AT MY TYPEWRITER...*"

I WON'T WRITE THE IMAGINARY STORY I HAD ORIGINALLY PLOTTED ON THE MYSTERIOUSLY MOVING WEAPONS! I'VE GOT A *TRUE* STORY TO TELL NOW!

STRANGE ADVENTURES

STRANGE ADVENTURES

The End

6

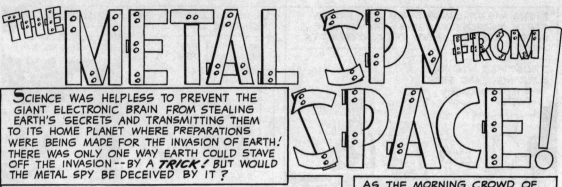

SCIENCE WAS HELPLESS TO PREVENT THE GIANT ELECTRONIC BRAIN FROM STEALING EARTH'S SECRETS AND TRANSMITTING THEM TO ITS HOME PLANET WHERE PREPARATIONS WERE BEING MADE FOR THE INVASION OF EARTH! THERE WAS ONLY ONE WAY EARTH COULD STAVE OFF THE INVASION -- BY A *TRICK!* BUT WOULD THE METAL SPY BE DECEIVED BY IT?

THE EARTH IS DEPENDING ON ME -- A SCIENCE-FICTION WRITER -- TO OUTWIT THAT ALIEN SPY FROM SPACE!

AS THE MORNING CROWD OF WORKERS EMERGES FROM A SUBWAY STATION IN NEW YORK...

WH-WHAT IS *THAT?*

WH-WHERE DID IT COME FROM?

SOON, THE STREETS ARE CHOKED WITH PEOPLE GAPING AT THE STRANGE MACHINE...

BUT EVERY EFFORT TO REMOVE THE OBJECT FAILS...

CLICK-CLICK-CLICK-

WHY DON'T THE AUTHORITIES GET IT OUT OF HERE?

IT'S STARTING TO *CLICK!*

MAYBE IT'S A BOMB!

THERE'S NOTHING WE CAN DO TO BUDGE IT! AND WE DON'T DARE SMASH IT DOWN FOR FEAR OF MAKING IT EXPLODE!

EARTH IS THE THIRD PLANET OF THIS STAR SYSTEM! IT IS A MEAN DISTANCE OF 92.9 MILLION MILES FROM ITS PARENT SUN...

CLICK CLICK CLICK CLICK

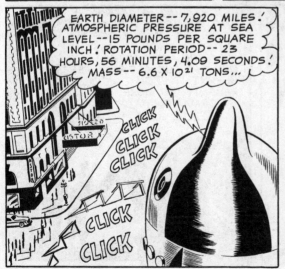

EARTH DIAMETER -- 7,920 MILES! ATMOSPHERIC PRESSURE AT SEA LEVEL -- 15 POUNDS PER SQUARE INCH! ROTATION PERIOD -- 23 HOURS, 56 MINUTES, 4.09 SECONDS! MASS -- 6.6×10^{21} TONS...

CLICK CLICK CLICK

CLICK CLICK

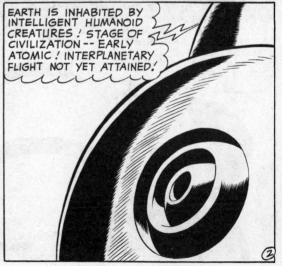

EARTH IS INHABITED BY INTELLIGENT HUMANOID CREATURES! STAGE OF CIVILIZATION -- EARLY ATOMIC! INTERPLANETARY FLIGHT NOT YET ATTAINED!

②

WE CAN UNDERSTAND WHAT IT'S SAYING BECAUSE IT'S BROADCASTING THOUGHT WAVES! WHOEVER SENT IT IS GATHERING INFORMATION ABOUT US--THAT GIGANTIC METAL OBJECT IS A *SPY* FROM ANOTHER WORLD!

WE'VE TRIED TO "JAM" IT BY DIRECTING RADIO BEAMS AT IT, BUT THEY DON'T WORK!

EVEN ELECTRONIC IMPULSES HAVE NO EFFECT ON IT!

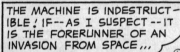

THE MACHINE IS INDESTRUCT-IBLE! IF--AS I SUSPECT--IT IS THE FORERUNNER OF AN INVASION FROM SPACE...

RECENT ADVANCES IN SCIENTIFIC RESEARCH ON GUIDED MISSILES HAS DEVELOPED A NEW METAL CAPABLE OF RESISTING 5000° HEAT. IT IS CALLED *ANSONITE*...

ANSONITE! NO ONE ON EARTH KNOWS ABOUT THAT--EXCEPT *ME!* I'VE BEEN WORKING ON THIS SECRET PROJECT AND ONLY MADE UP THAT NAME--*ANSONITE*--THIS MORNING!

THAT MACHINE IS *READING OUR MINDS!* THAT'S WHERE IT'S GATHERING ITS INFORMATION! I MUST ALERT THE AUTHORITIES--ROPE OFF THE AREA--PREVENT IT FROM TRANSMITTING MORE INFORMATION!

③

ON THE PLANET **KLARN**, IN ANOTHER SOLAR SYSTEM...

THE PLANET **EARTH** IS TAKING SHAPE, AS MENTI-MACHINE KL-7256 RELAYS BACK ITS INFORMATION BY SUB-ELEC-TRONIC MICROWAVES!

WHEN WE HAVE A COMPLETE PICTURE OF WHAT THE EARTH IS LIKE, WE CAN PLAN OUR INVASION!

KL-7256 IS ALSO SHOWING US WHAT THE INHABIT-ANTS ARE LIKE!

I NEVER CEASE TO WONDER AT THE MANY DIFFERENT LIFE-FORMS THAT HAVE EVOLVED ON INHABITED WORLDS!

ONE OF THEIR LARGEST CITIES! SINCE THEY CONCENTRATE SO MANY PEOPLE IN SUCH A SMALL SPACE, DESTROYING THEM SHOULD BE EASY!

WE MUST NOT BE TOO HASTY!

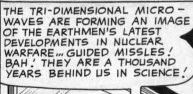

THE TRI-DIMENSIONAL MICRO-WAVES ARE FORMING AN IMAGE OF THE EARTHMEN'S LATEST DEVELOPMENTS IN NUCLEAR WARFARE... GUIDED MISSILES! BAH! THEY ARE A THOUSAND YEARS BEHIND US IN SCIENCE!

AN EXPLOSION OF A HYDROGEN BOMB! IF THIS IS THE BEST THEY CAN THROW AGAINST US, WE HAVE NOTHING TO FEAR! WE LEARNED TO NEUTRALIZE NUCLEAR EXPLOSIONS CENTURIES AGO!

IT WILL BE CHILD'S PLAY TO CONQUER THEM!

ALL THAT REMAINS IS TO ORDER OUT THE SPACE FLEETS!

4

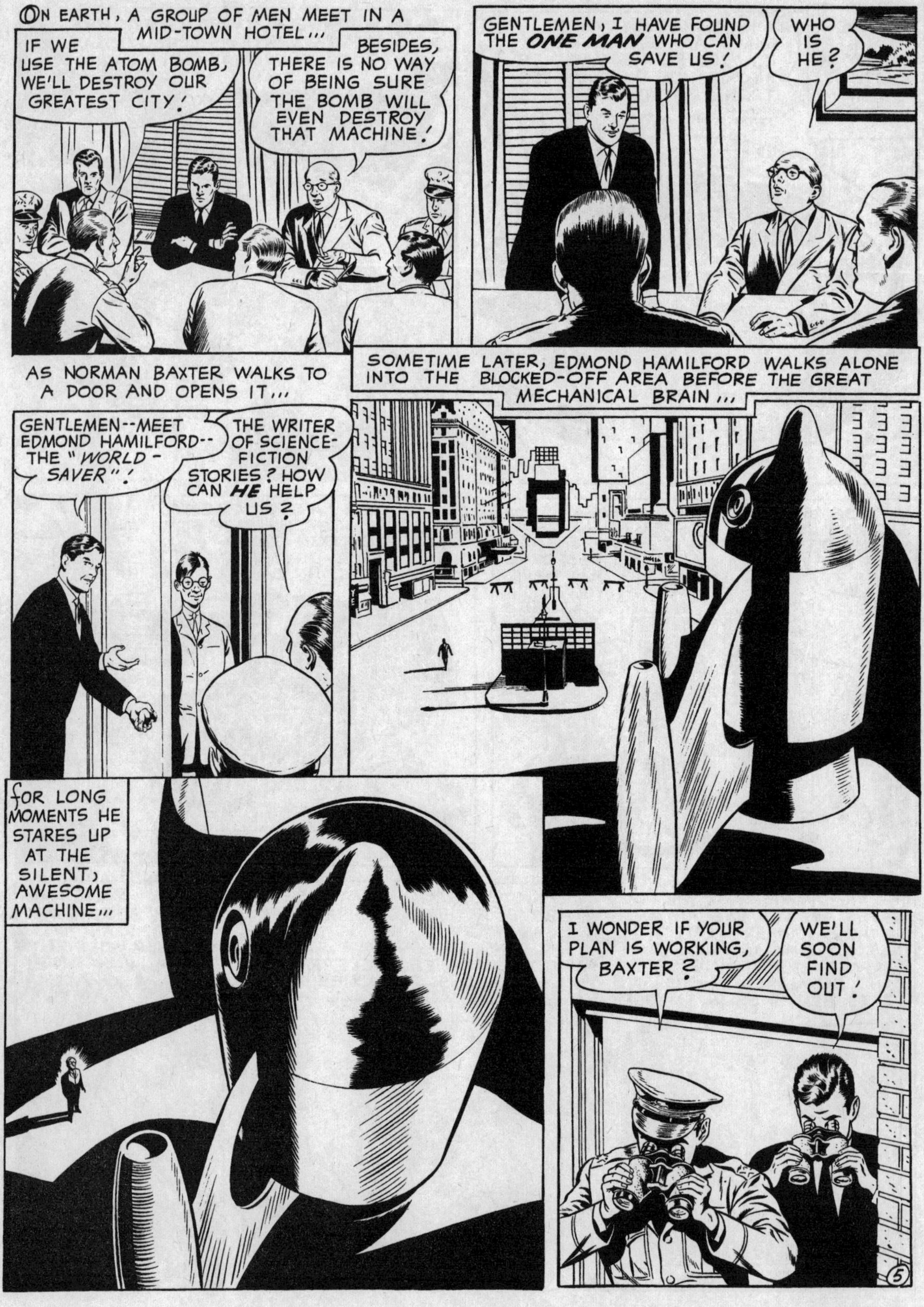
ON EARTH, A GROUP OF MEN MEET IN A MID-TOWN HOTEL...
IF WE USE THE ATOM BOMB, WE'LL DESTROY OUR GREATEST CITY!
BESIDES, THERE IS NO WAY OF BEING SURE THE BOMB WILL EVEN DESTROY THAT MACHINE!
GENTLEMEN, I HAVE FOUND THE ONE MAN WHO CAN SAVE US!
WHO IS HE?
AS NORMAN BAXTER WALKS TO A DOOR AND OPENS IT...
GENTLEMEN--MEET EDMOND HAMILFORD-- THE "WORLD-SAVER"!
THE WRITER OF SCIENCE-FICTION STORIES? HOW CAN HE HELP US?
SOMETIME LATER, EDMOND HAMILFORD WALKS ALONE INTO THE BLOCKED-OFF AREA BEFORE THE GREAT MECHANICAL BRAIN...
FOR LONG MOMENTS HE STARES UP AT THE SILENT, AWESOME MACHINE...
I WONDER IF YOUR PLAN IS WORKING, BAXTER?
WE'LL SOON FIND OUT!
5

ON THE PLANET *KLARN*, SOON AFTER...

KULL VAN--COME QUICKLY! MORE REPORTS ARE COMING IN! *OMINOUS* REPORTS!

WHAT'S THAT?

LOOK! AN INVADING SPACE-FLEET--ANNIHILATED! THE EARTHMEN POSSESS A *DISINTEGRATION RAY!*

AN *ENERGY-CASTER*-- TRANSMITTING NEUTRINO ENERGY THAT EXPLODES WHATEVER COMES IN CONTACT WITH ITS SUPER-WAVES!

THE WALL SCREENS GLOW AND FADE, GLOW AGAIN, AS SCENE AFTER SCENE FROM GREAT INVASIONS FLASH ON ITS GROUND-GLASS SURFACE...

RECALL KL-7256 AT ONCE! EARTH SCIENCE FAR SURPASSES OURS! WE COULD NEVER PENETRATE ANY *FORCE-FIELD* LIKE THAT!

ON EARTH, THE METAL SPY SUDDENLY RISES INTO THE SKY...

WE'VE WON!

"WORLD-SAVER HAMILFORD" HAS DONE IT AGAIN!

NO WONDER SCIENCE-FICTION FANS HAVE DUBBED YOU *"WORLD-SAVER HAMILFORD"*--YOUR SPECIALTY IS EARTH-INVASION STORIES THAT FAIL BECAUSE OF THE FANTASTIC WEAPONS YOU DREAM UP TO DEFEAT THE ENEMY!

ALL I DID WAS THINK OF MY OLD STORIES--AND THE MACHINE RELAYED THEM BACK TO ITS HOME PLANET! THE ALIENS THOUGHT THEY WERE *FACT*--NOT *FICTION!*

The End

6

EARTH'S SECRET VISITORS!

He collected and studied every published report of a possible landing on earth by creatures from other worlds! All he had to do was find just ONE space-man—and his triumph would be complete!

LITTLE MEN FROM OUTER SPACE! WHAT A PICTURE-SCOOP THIS WILL MAKE FOR MY NEWSPAPER!

When the picture of the midget spacemen appears in the news-papers, John Spencer excitedly clips out the item...

IS THIS IT AT LAST—PROOF THAT CREATURES FROM OUTER SPACE HAVE LANDED ON EARTH?

FOR DAYS I'VE BEEN CLIPPING MAGAZINE ARTICLES AND NEWSPAPER ITEMS DEALING WITH POSSIBLE EARTH-VISITATIONS BY CREATURES FROM OTHER WORLDS! IF ONLY ONE OF THESE ACCOUNTS IS TRUE ...

THE TIME HAS COME TO CHECK ON MY MOST PROMISING LEADS! MY NOTEBOOK IS FILLED WITH REPORTS OF FLYING SAUCERS, QUEER LIGHTS ON THE MOON, UNEXPLAINED FLASHING STREAKS IN THE SKY...

I'VE READ OF A LONG GASH ON THE SURFACE OF THE MOON, APPARENTLY CAUSED BY THE LANDING OF A SPACESHIP! IF SPACE-PEOPLE HAVE REACHED THE MOON, EARTH MUST SURELY BE NEXT!

MY FIRST STOP IS AT THE IOWA FARM WHERE THIS SNAPSHOT OF A "SAUCER" LANDING IN A FIELD WAS TAKEN!

SOON AFTER, ON THE IOWA FARM...

YESSIR, I TOOK THOSE PICTURES! SAW THAT FLYIN' SAUCER WITH MY OWN EYES, DOWN IN MY WEST MEADOW!

HE IS LYING-- I CAN TELL! THERE WAS NO FLYING SAUCER!

YOU FAKED THAT PICTURE! SEE, HERE ARE THE PROPS YOU USED-- SAUCER MODEL AND CAMERA EQUIPMENT!

A FELLOW WRITING A BOOK ON FLYING SAUCERS BRIBED ME TO DO IT! BUT HOW IN THUNDER DID YOU KNOW THAT?

UNDAUNTED, JOHN SPENCER STOPS NEXT AT A SMALL-TOWN NEWSPAPER OFFICE...

THOSE ARE THE ORIGINAL PHOTOGRAPHS OF THE MIDGET SPACEMEN! THEY ARE GENUINE PHOTOS, BELIEVE ME!

YES, YES! I KNOW HE'S TELLING THE TRUTH!

2

FILLED WITH EXCITEMENT, SPENCER WALKS FROM THE NEWSPAPER OFFICE...

SUCCESS AT LAST! THERE **ARE** ALIENS ON EARTH! NOW ALL THAT REMAINS FOR ME TO DO IS CONTACT THEM!

THAT NIGHT, A KNOCK SOUNDS ON THE DOOR OF THE HOTEL WHERE JOHN SPENCER IS STAYING...

MR. SPENCER? I CAME TO SEE YOU ABOUT THOSE PICTURES OF THE LITTLE MEN!

COME IN! WHAT ABOUT THEM?

THOSE SNAP-SHOTS ARE GENUINE! I'M SURE OF IT!

YES, THE PICTURES ARE GENUINE! BUT THE MIDGET SPACEMEN ARE **NOT** GENUINE!

SUDDENLY, THE VISITOR OPENS THE WOODEN BOX AND TAKES OUT...

ONE OF THE "SPACEMEN"!

A **PUPPET!**

I WENT TO THE PARK TO SECRETLY PRACTICE THE PUPPET SHOW I WAS GOING TO PUT ON AT THE LOCAL SCHOOL, WHEN A NEWSPAPER PHOTOGRAPHER PASSED BY AND TOOK SOME PICTURES! HE LEFT BEFORE I COULD EXPLAIN HIS MISTAKE!

SOME TIME LATER, AT A SMALL FISHING VILLAGE ON THE MAINE COAST...

THE **DAILY STAR** SAID YOU PHOTOGRAPHED "FISH MEN" WITH **PURPLE SKINS**! HAVE YOU GOT THE ORIGINAL SNAPSHOT?

SURE ENOUGH! ALWAYS CARRY IT ON ME!

③

I FOUND OUT LATER THAT I FORGOT MY FILTER WAS STILL ON MY CAMERA! SO THE COLOR SHOT SHOWED THEM AS MEN WITH PURPLE SKINS! ACTUALLY, THEY ARE SKIN DIVERS IN HOMEMADE RIGS! THAT'S WHAT MADE THEM LOOK SO--ER--FISHY...

A LITTLE LATER, AT A LAKESIDE RESORT...

FOUND THAT GIGANTIC PRINT THE DAY AFTER I POURED THE CONCRETE!

I SAW THE NEWSPAPER ITEM ABOUT IT! FOLKS THINK SOMEONE FROM *OUTER SPACE* CAME HERE!

WELL, THEY'RE WRONG! I HAPPEN TO KNOW IT WAS SOME COLLEGE BOYS WHO MADE THE PRINT--AS PART OF A FRATERNITY INITIATION GAG!

IS SPENCER'S SEARCH FOR AN ALIEN DOOMED TO FAILURE?

EARTH IS ONLY ONE OF NINE PLANETS ORBITING AROUND ITS SUN! THAT SUN IS ONLY ONE OF MANY BILLIONS OF STARS IN THIS GALAXY! AND THERE ARE BILLIONS OF OTHER GALAXIES...

THAT MAKES IT A MULTI-BILLION-TO-ONE CHANCE THAT ANY OTHER SPACE-MAN WILL COME TO EARTH AND RESCUE ME FROM THIS WORLD!

YES, I AM FROM A DISTANT PLANET YOU NEVER HEARD OF! MY SHIP CRASH-LANDED ON EARTH! MY ONLY HOPE FOR GETTING OFF WAS TO FIND ANOTHER SPACE-VISITOR! NOW THAT THAT HAS FAILED, I HAVE TO WAIT UNTIL *YOU EARTHMEN* HAVE CONQUERED SPACE!

The End

THE *DO-IT-YOURSELF* FAD HAS PRODUCED MANY AMATEUR CARPENTERS, BOATBUILDERS, AND OTHER HOBBYISTS--BUT NEVER ANY SELF-TAUGHT *SPACEMEN!* NEVER, THAT IS, UNTIL NOW, WHEN THAT ENTHUSIASTIC HANDYMAN JOE BARNES TAKES OFF ON THE FIRST SPACEFLIGHT FROM EARTH, IN HIS...

BUILD-IT-YOURSELF SPACESHIP!

MY INSTRUCTION-BOOK TELLS ME EVERYTHING BUT HOW TO GET BACK TO EARTH!

AT THE KANEVILLE GARAGE WHERE JOE BARNES WORKS, HIS HOBBY IS A STANDING JOKE...

WHAT'S YOUR LATEST *DO-IT-YOURSELF* BRAINSTORM, JOE?

A MOTOR-BOAT! I'M GOING TO LAUNCH IT AFTER WORK! COME AROUND AND WATCH!

AND SURE ENOUGH, JOE PROVIDES HIS AUDIENCE WITH ANOTHER LAUGH..

I CAN'T UNDERSTAND WHY IT SANK--I FOLLOWED ALL THE INSTRUCTIONS!

HAW, HAW--IT'S LIKE HIS HOME-MADE LAWN MOWER THAT RAN BACKWARD--AND HIS HI-FI PHONOGRAPH THAT WOULDN'T MAKE A SOUND!

LATER, WHEN A LOCAL REPORTER WRITES A FEATURE STORY ABOUT JOE'S MISHAPS...

YOU'RE FAMOUS, JOE! THIS STORY WAS SYNDICATED ALL OVER THE COUNTRY!

OUCH-- MY WIFE WON'T LIKE THIS!

DAILY HERALD
JOE BARNES, NATIONS NO. 1 UNDO-IT-YOURSELF FAN!

AT HOME THAT NIGHT...

JOE, THESE SILLY PROJECTS OF YOURS HAVE MADE US THE LAUGHINGSTOCK OF THE COUNTRY!

OKAY, I'VE HAD ENOUGH! BUT I STILL SAY IT WASN'T MY FAULT THAT NONE OF THEM TURNED OUT RIGHT...

BUT IN HIS MAIL A FEW DAYS LATER...

NOW THAT'S SOMETHING WORTH BUILDING! I WONDER IF I CAN GET AWAY WITH IT... BY SENDING FOR IT FIRST, AND THEN TELLING MARY...

FLYING SPACESHIP
Send #20 and receive our kit with full instructions!

FOLLOWING JOE'S REQUEST, DELIVERY IS MADE IN THE MIDDLE OF THE NIGHT...

MARY WON'T DARE ASK ME TO SEND BACK ALL THIS STUFF NOW!

THE NEXT MORNING...

JOE BARNES-- YOU'VE DONE IT AGAIN! A SPACESHIP, OF ALL THE RIDICULOUS THINGS!

IT'S POSITIVELY THE LAST ONE, I PROMISE! I'LL BUILD IT IN THE BACK YARD WHERE IT WON'T BOTHER YOU!

AFTER WORK THAT EVENING...

THESE INSTRUCTIONS ARE REALLY SOMETHING--THEY NOT ONLY TELL HOW TO BUILD THE SHIP BUT EVEN HOW TO LAY A COURSE FOR THE MOON, HOW TO AVOID METEORS, SPACE-PIRATES--!

WOW! ALL THIS STUFF FOR #20! I DON'T SEE HOW THE MANUFACTURER CAN MAKE A PROFIT OUT OF THE DEAL!

As work progresses...

JOE'S FINALLY FLIPPED HIS LID-- BUILDING A SPACESHIP TO FLY HIM TO THE MOON!

GIVE OUR REGARDS TO THE LOONIES ON *LUNA,* WHEN YOU GET THERE, JOE!

BUT JOE STUBBORNLY CARRIES ON...

THIS IS THE ROCKET MOTOR! HMM, DOESN'T LOOK LIKE IT CAN LIFT ITS OWN WEIGHT...

HEY, JOE! DON'T FORGET TO MAIL ME A POSTCARD FROM THE MOON!

WHEN THE AMUSED ONLOOKERS LEAVE...

JOE BARNES! YOU'RE HUMILIATING ME! THIS RIDICULOUS SPACESHIP HAS TO GO!

WELL--ALL RIGHT! IT'LL BE FINISHED TONIGHT--AND THEN I'LL HAVE IT HAULED AWAY!

PAST MIDNIGHT, WHEN JOE FINISHES HIS PROJECT...

MAYBE SOMEDAY THERE'LL BE REAL SPACESHIPS LIKE THIS-- WITH CONTROLS LIKE THIS TAKEOFF LEVER...

AS JOE BARNES IDLY TOUCHES THE CONTROL...

HEY! I'M TAKING OFF!

I'M HEADING INTO SPACE--THIS SHIP CAN *FLY!* IT'S IMPOSSIBLE--

BUT THE IMPOSSIBLE KEEPS RIGHT ON HAPPENING!

HOW FAR UP IS THIS THING GOING TO GO? AND H-HOW AM I GOING TO GET BACK TO EARTH?

③

THIS INSTRUCTION BOOK TELLS HOW TO SET THE CONTROLS-- GOT TO TRY IT--

AT LEAST I'VE GOT THE SHIP STRAIGHTENED OUT! NOW TO FIND HOW TO GET IT BACK TO EARTH --

CLANG! CLANG!

SUDDENLY, A BELL CLANGS...

CLANG! CLANG!

ACCORDING TO THE BOOK, THAT BELL IS A METEOR-- WARNING--

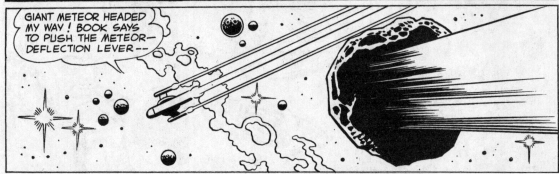

GIANT METEOR HEADED MY WAY! BOOK SAYS TO PUSH THE METEOR-DEFLECTION LEVER--

SKIRTED UNDER IT--BUT THERE'S ANOTHER SPACESHIP COMING! WAIT--THE INSTRUCTIONS--

SPACE-PIRATES! COMING AFTER ME--GOT TO ESCAPE THEM--

Ships marked with this insignia are SPACE-PIRATES-- Steer clear of them!

4

BUT JOE IS A BETTER GARAGE MECHANIC THAN SPACE PILOT!

CAPTURE THAT CRAFT WITH OUR MAGNETIC GRAPPLES! THEN BOARD IT--!

I PUSHED THE ROCKET CONTROL THE WRONG WAY-- AND SLOWED DOWN INSTEAD OF SPEEDING UP!

MOMENTS LATER, INTO JOE'S SHIP COME...

CAPTURED--BY SPACE-PIRATES! WHY DID I EVER BUILD THIS FOOL THING?

I DETECT YOUR THOUGHTS TELE-PATHICALLY-- WE'RE NOT SPACE-PIRATES BUT SPACE-POLICE OF A FAR WORLD!

"WE PURSUED VORKAY, A RUNAWAY CRIMINAL, INTO THIS DISTANT PART OF THE UNIVERSE..."

RADAR SHOWS THAT VORKAY LANDED ON THIS PLANET EARTH-- TO HIDE FROM US!

I'LL CALL BACK TO HEADQUARTERS FOR INSTRUCTIONS!

"OUR INSTRUCTIONS CAME SWIFTLY.."

DO NOT LAND ON EARTH AND SEARCH OPENLY FOR VORKAY-- EARTH PEOPLE DON'T HAVE SPACE-TRAVEL AND WOULD THINK YOU INVADERS, AND PANIC! WAIT IN SPACE FOR VORKAY TO COME OUT AGAIN!

HE'LL HAVE TO LEAVE EARTH SOON-- ITS ATMOSPHERE AND GRAVITY WILL BE TOO UNCOMFORTABLE FOR HIM!

FROM YOUR THOUGHTS, EARTHMAN, IT IS CLEAR THAT VORKAY MADE YOU AN INNOCENT DECOY TO LURE US OFF GUARD!

BUT WE'LL FOOL VORKAY-- BY PUTTING AUTOMATIC CONTROLS ON THIS SHIP AND SENDING IT ON TO THE MOON!

MINUTES LATER, WHEN JOE IS TRANSFERRED TO THE ALIEN PATROL SHIP...

NOW TELL US WHERE YOU SENT FOR THE SPACESHIP KIT--THAT'S WHERE VORKAY MUST BE HIDING!

5

ON AN ABANDONED FARM...

MY EARTH DECOY IS HEADED FOR THE MOON IN THE SHIP I SENT HIM PARTS TO MAKE! THE PATROL WILL THINK IT'S ME AND FOLLOW *HIM*! THAT'S WHEN I'LL MAKE MY ESCAPE!

WHEN I READ OF THAT *DO-IT-YOURSELF* HOBBYIST, I KNEW HE COULDN'T RESIST MY OFFER! THE CONVINCER WAS THE SPACE LIFE-*BOAT* OF MY SHIP I DISASSEMBLED AND SENT HIM!

THERE'S *VORKAY*-- SWOOP DOWN FAST!

AS A SHAKY JOE BARNES STEPS AGAIN ON *TERRA FIRMA*...

YOU'RE OUR PRISONER AGAIN, *VORKAY*! WE'RE TAKING YOU AND YOUR STOLEN SPACE-SHIP BACK TO OUR WORLD!

AND SINCE NO ONE SAW US LAND HERE, EARTH PEOPLE WON'T BE PANICKED BY US!

LATER...   HOW ABOUT IT, JOE? AREN'T YOU GOING TO CLAIM THAT'S *YOUR* HOME-MADE SPACESHIP ON THE MOON?

I WOULD--IF I THOUGHT YOU'D BELIEVE ME!

DAILY HERALD
MOUNT PALOMAR TELESCOPE REVEALS SPACESHIP LANDING ON MOON!

The End

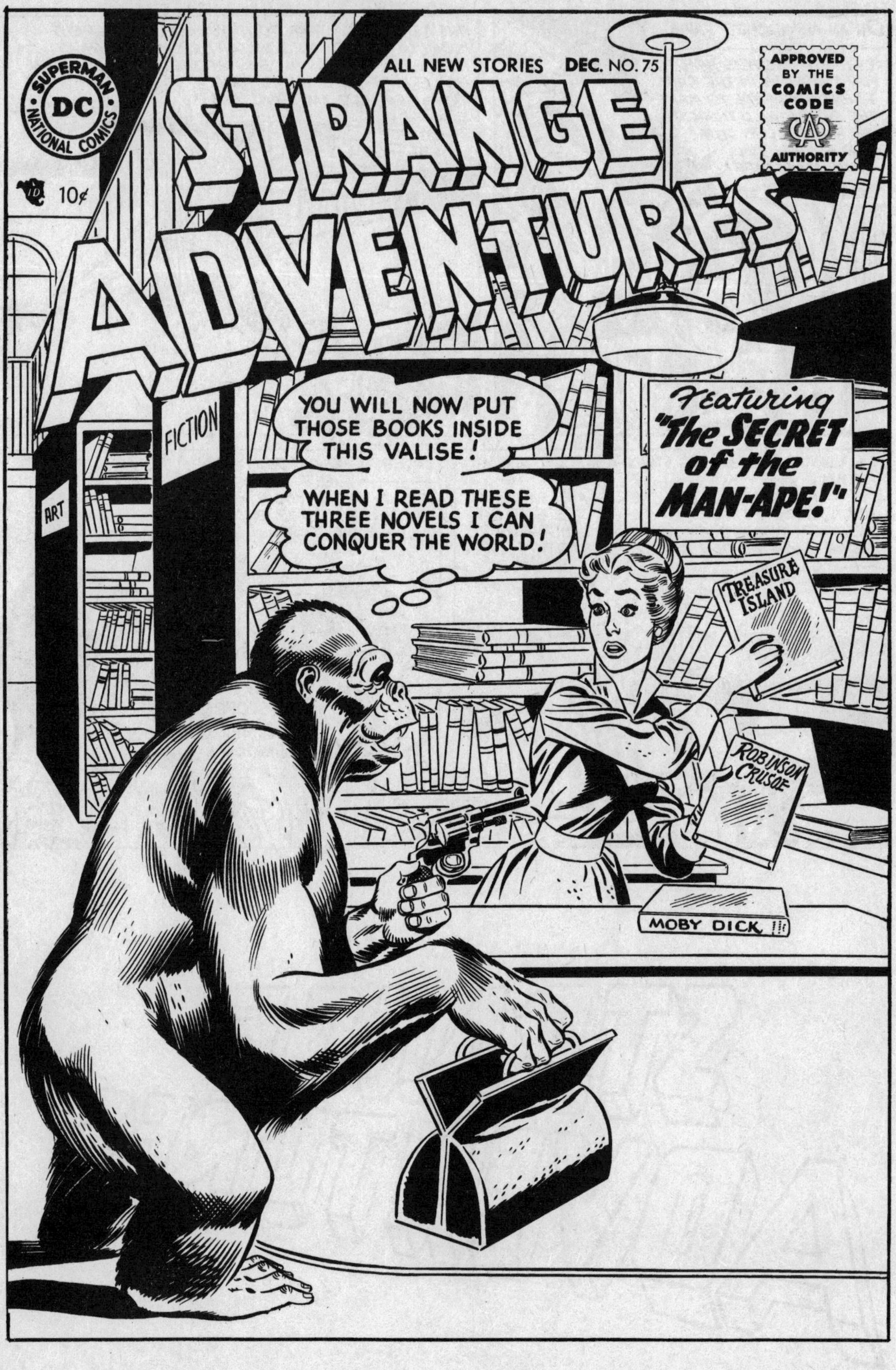
SUPERMAN DC NATIONAL COMICS
10¢
ALL NEW STORIES DEC. NO. 75
APPROVED BY THE COMICS CODE AUTHORITY
STRANGE ADVENTURES
FICTION
ART
YOU WILL NOW PUT THOSE BOOKS INSIDE THIS VALISE!
WHEN I READ THESE THREE NOVELS I CAN CONQUER THE WORLD!
Featuring "The SECRET of the MAN-APE!"
TREASURE ISLAND
ROBINSON CRUSOE
MOBY DICK

Secret of the MAN-APE!

WHO KNOWS WHAT PAST CIVILIZATIONS DOMINATED ANCIENT EARTH--AND VANISHED WITHOUT A TRACE? WHO KNOWS WHAT OTHER INTELLIGENT CREATURES MAY HAVE REIGNED OVER OUR WORLD?
BY A TWIST OF EVOLUTIONARY FATE, AN ALIEN FROM OUTER SPACE FINDS HE HAS CHOSEN THE WRONG DISGUISE TO SPY ON EARTH!

ON EARTH, A TELESCOPE IS TRAINED ON A DISTANT STAR...

THE LIGHT FROM THAT BRIGHT STAR-SUN TOOK *100,000* YEARS TO CROSS SPACE TO OUR EYES! FOR ALL WE KNOW THE STAR MAY HAVE SINCE EXPLODED AND NO LONGER EXIST!

WHILE ON A PLANET OF THAT VERY STAR, *THEIR* SUPER-TELESCOPE IS OBSERVING *OUR* SUN!

THAT STAR'S LIGHT TOOK AGES TO REACH OUR EYES! IF IT STILL EXISTS, WE MUST CONQUER THE THIRD PLANET OUTWARD FROM THE SUN, AND REPLENISH OUR STOCK OF RADIOACTIVE METALS!

SUPER-MAGNIFICATION SHOWS A STRANGE CIVILIZATION DOMINATING THE PLANET EARTH OF *100,000* YEARS AGO...

THAT GORILLA CIVILIZATION COMPLETELY DOMINATES ALL LIFE ON THE THIRD PLANET AND UNDOUBTEDLY STILL EXISTS TODAY! BUT ARE WE POWER-FUL ENOUGH TO CONQUER THOSE EARTHLINGS? WE MUST SEND A SPY THERE AND FIND OUT!

LATER, IN A SCIENCE LABORATORY ON THE DISTANT STAR-WORLD...

YOU, DAXON, HAVE BEEN CHOSEN AS OUR SCOUT! IN ORDER TO SPY FREELY AMONG THE GORILLAS WITHOUT DETECTION, OUR *TRANSFORMATION RAY* WILL CONVERT YOU TO GORILLA FORM!

SOON, THE DISGUISED SPY CROSSES HYPER-SPACE, FAR FASTER THAN THE SPEED OF LIGHT!

I WILL REACH THE GORILLA WORLD IN A FEW DAYS! BUT IT WILL BE TRICKY TO SLOW DOWN AND LAND AT THIS TREMENDOUS SPEED!

A SLIGHT MISCALCULATION OVER THE AFRICAN CONTINENT AND...

I--I MADE A CRASH-LANDING! THE ULTRA-CUSHIONS WILL SAVE MY LIFE, EVEN THOUGH THE SHIP IS WRECKED!

CRASH!

LANDING IN THE JUNGLES OF AFRICA OF 1956, THE GORILLA SPY SOON MAKES A STARTLING DISCOVERY...

GREAT STARS! THIS LAND IS WILD-- UNCIVILIZED! THOSE CREATURES AREN'T EVEN CLOTHED! MY TELEPATHIC PROBING OF THEIR MINDS INDICATES THEY HAVE LOW INTELLIGENCE! SOMETIME DURING THE LAST 100,000 YEARS THE GORILLA CIVILIZATION DIED OUT! THEN **WHO** ARE THE MASTERS OF EARTH TODAY?

DISCARDING HIS CLOTHING, THE SPY MOVES FREELY THROUGH THE JUNGLES WHEN SUDDENLY...

CAPTURE THAT GORILLA ALIVE!

HUMANS RULE NOW! I'M BEING HUNTED LIKE A WILD BEAST!

I'LL HAVE TO USE ALL MY INGENUITY TO ELUDE THOSE HUNTERS! NO EARTH GORILLA WOULD THINK OF COVERING HIMSELF WITH FERNS!

TOO BAD HE GOT AWAY! WE WERE COMMISSIONED BY PROFESSOR AMOS SCOTT TO CAPTURE A GORILLA!

WONDER IF THOSE RUMORS ARE TRUE ABOUT SCOTT'S AMAZING DISCOVERY?

THEY SAY HE HOPES TO TRANSFORM A GORILLA TO **HUMAN FORM!**

WHAT LUCK! THAT IS MY OPPORTUNITY TO REGAIN MY HUMAN SHAPE, AND FREELY SPY AMONG THE EARTHLINGS AND REPAIR MY SHIP! BUT FIRST I MUST **LET** THEM CAPTURE ME!

WHEN THE MIND-READING GORILLA IS DELIVERED TO THE SCIENTIST'S LABORATORY IN AMERICA...

I'VE BEEN WAITING FOR THIS SPECIMEN, TO TRY OUT MY EVOLVING RAY!

I HOPE IT WORKS! MY WHOLE MISSION DEPENDS ON IT!

AS THE RAYS BATHE THE ALIEN GORILLA...

GORILLA TO HUMAN IN TEN MINUTES! ACCORDING TO MY CALCULATIONS, ONLY THE BODY HAS CHANGED, NOT THE BRAIN!

NOW IF I CAN ESCAPE THIS CAGE...

BUT THE NEXT MOMENT, THE RAY IS TURNED ON THE ALIEN AGAIN...

THIS EXPERIMENT IS TOO DANGEROUS FOR ME TO CONTINUE ON MY OWN! I'LL CHANGE HIM BACK...

NO-- NO!

AS SOON AS I DISMANTLE THE MACHINE, I'LL TURN MY PLANS OVER TO THE SCIENCE SOCIETY FOR FURTHER STUDY!

TRAPPED IN GORILLA FORM AGAIN! I MUST GET THOSE PLANS FOR MYSELF, SOMEHOW!

MEANWHILE, PROFESSOR SCOTT FINDS ANOTHER "SPY" LURKING OUTSIDE HIS WINDOW...

THAT FACE IN THE WINDOW AGAIN! IT'S HAL TODD, MY FORMER ASSISTANT! I NEVER TRUSTED HIM, AND FIRED HIM! I WONDER IF HE'S SCHEMING TO STEAL MY PLANS FOR EVIL PURPOSES?

TODD MAY STRIKE AT ANY MOMENT! I'VE GOT TO BRING MY PLANS TO THE SCIENCE SOCIETY AT ONCE! I KNOW--I'LL HIDE THEM IN MY NEPHEW'S LIBRARY BOOKS AND PRETEND I'M RETURNING THEM TO THE LIBRARY!

NOW EVEN IF TODD SHOULD STOP ME AND SEARCH ME, HE WON'T FIND THE PLANS ON MY PERSON!

MY GORILLA STRENGTH WILL ENABLE ME TO FREE MYSELF FROM THIS CAGE! THEN I'LL FOLLOW SCOTT AND GET THOSE PLANS FOR MYSELF!

MOBY DICK

ON THE WAY TO THE LIBRARY, SCOTT CASTS AN ANXIOUS EYE BEHIND HIM...

TODD'S CLOSING IN ON ME! I MUST--

LOOK OUT! I-I CAN'T STOP!

MOMENTS LATER...

PROFESSOR SCOTT-- DEAD! I WONDER IF HE PLANNED TO USE HIS DISCOVERY FOR EVIL PURPOSES, AS I HALF SUSPECTED AT TIMES!

AS A PASSER-BY RETURNS SCOTT'S BOOKS TO THE NEARBY LIBRARY...

THAT WAS WHY I CLOSELY WATCHED HIM! I FELT IT WAS MY DUTY TO SEE THAT HIS DANGEROUS DIS- COVERY WAS NOT USED WRONGLY! I'VE GOT TO FIND HIS PLANS AND GIVE THEM TO THE SCIENCE SOCIETY!

LIBRARY

MEANWHILE, THE MAN-APE'S MIGHTY MUSCLES HAVE RIPPED LOOSE THE BARS OF HIS CAGE...

NOW TO TRAIL SCOTT AND GET BACK THOSE PLANS! WITH THEM I CAN REGAIN HUMAN FORM, FINISH MY SPY MISSION HERE AND REPAIR MY SHIP FOR THE RETURN TRIP!

AS THE ALIEN'S SUPER-SCIENTIFIC MIND TRACES THE BOOKS TO THE LIBRARY...

HURRY, GIVE ME THOSE THREE BOOKS THAT WERE JUST RETURNED...

AT FIRST I IMAGINED THAT GORILLA WAS TALKING TO ME-- BUT IT'S HIS THOUGHTS I HEAR! HOW IS SUCH A FANTASTIC THING POSSIBLE?

NOW I'LL BE ABLE TO REGAIN MY HUMAN SHAPE AND COMPLETE MY SPYING MISSION HERE!

MEANWHILE, HAVING FAILED TO FIND THE PROFESSOR'S PLANS IN HIS LABORATORY, HAL TODD RUSHES BACK TO THE LIBRARY...

WHAT WAS SCOTT DOING WITH THOSE LIBRARY BOOKS? IS IT POSSIBLE HIS FORMULA WAS HIDDEN IN THE BOOKS? I'VE GOT TO FIND OUT!

I CAN'T WANDER AROUND THE CITY IN THIS GORILLA FORM-- I'LL BE HUNTED DOWN! SOMEONE LEFT THAT CAR MOTOR RUNNING! I'LL USE IT TO GET AWAY...

WHAT'S THAT...THAT *GORILLA* DOING WITH SCOTT'S BOOKS? I'D BETTER FOLLOW HIM!

SPEEDING OUTSIDE THE CITY, UNFAMILIAR WITH EARTHLY CARS AND ROADS, THE MAN—APE MEETS DISASTER ON A DANGEROUS CURVE...

L-LOST CONTROL!

HE WENT OVER THAT CLIFF!

WHEN HAL TODD SCRAMBLES DOWN...

THE GORILLA AND THE PLANS ...GOING UP IN FLAMES! BUT... BUT WHERE DID THAT INTELLIGENT BEAST COME FROM? WHAT WAS HE PLANNING TO DO? THE WORLD WILL *NEVER KNOW!*

The End

The 2nd Deluge of Earth!

THESE MARTIANS CALMLY KEEP PLAYING DOMINOES -- WHILE THEIR MACHINES DROWN EARTH! IF MY THEORY ABOUT THEM IS RIGHT, I'LL BE ABLE TO WRECK THEIR MACHINES WITHOUT THEM BEING AWARE OF IT!

MARS WAS DYING--AND OF ALL THE PLANETS IN THE SOLAR SYSTEM, EARTH OFFERED MARTIANS THE BEST CHANCE OF SURVIVAL! ONLY ONE EARTHMAN WAS IN A POSITION TO PREVENT THEIR GAINING CONTROL OF OUR WORLD--AND HE WAS BLIND!

A NATION-WIDE TV AUDIENCE PEERS INTO THE MOUNTAIN RETREAT OF MILO DURAND, RETIRED NUCLEAR PHYSICIST...

PROFESSOR DURAND, DOES RETIREMENT MEAN YOU ARE THROUGH WITH COSMIC RESEARCH?

A SCIENTIST NEVER REALLY RETIRES! I JUST WANT TO REST... TO READ, LISTEN TO MUSIC, TUNE IN A BASEBALL GAME NOW AND THEN!

DO YOU THINK BLINDNESS IS A HANDICAP TO A YOUNG MAN WHO MIGHT WISH TO BE A SCIENTIST?

NOT AN INSURMOUNTABLE HANDICAP! YOU KNOW, I WAS NOT ALWAYS BLIND! THE MIND AND THE SENSES CAN OVERCOME THE LOSS OF SIGHT!

THIS IS AN ISOLATED SPOT! WON'T YOU BE LONELY HERE BY YOUR-SELF?

OH, NO! I HAVE MANY OLD FRIENDS HERE... BOOKS, RECORDS, A FULLY EQUIPPED LABORATORY WHERE I CAN TINKER ABOUT! OR, I CAN PLAY MY FAVORITE GAME... DOMINOES!

THAT NIGHT, WHILE PROFESSOR DURAND BROWSES THROUGH HIS LABORATORY...

BWHOOOM

WHRAAAAM

WH--? A STORM... AND IT CAME WITH-OUT THE SLIGHTEST WARNING!

THAT'S ODD! THE BAROMETER SHOULD BE FALLING SHARPLY! INSTEAD, IT IS RISING! THIS IS NO ORDINARY ELECTRICAL STORM! I MUST GET TO THE PHONE--

HELLO!... HELLO, OPERATOR!... THE LINES ARE DEAD!

SUDDENLY, THE LIGHTS REACH A FRENZY OF VIOLENCE ACCOMPANIED BY AN EAR-SPLITTING SURGE OF DIS-CORDANT SOUND...

WHAT... IS THAT UNEARTHLY NOISE OUTSIDE THE HOUSE?

WHEEEEEEEEEEEE

2

OUTSIDE, A SIXTH SENSE WARNS THE PROFESSOR...

THERE ARE PEOPLE HERE-- **STRANGE** PEOPLE!

WE HAVE COME FROM MARS TO RULE A NEW WORLD...YOUR WORLD, PROFESSOR DURAND! WE WILL TALK FURTHER IN YOUR HOUSE! LEAD THE WAY!

WHO ARE YOU--WHAT DO YOU WANT HERE?

IN DURAND'S LABORATORY...

HOW DO YOU KNOW MY NAME?

THERE IS NOTHING ABOUT YOU WE DO NOT KNOW...FROM YOUR HABITS TO THE MOST INTIMATE DETAILS OF YOUR LIFE! YOU HAVE BEEN UNDER OUR SURVEILLANCE FOR YEARS!

WHY HAVE YOU CHOSEN TO COME TO EARTH-- OF ALL PLANETS?

TO SURVIVE, PROFESSOR! MARS IS DYING! THE ELEMENT WE REQUIRE FOR SURVIVAL HAS BEEN EXHAUSTED! THAT ELEMENT IS HERE IN ABUNDANCE!

IN A FEW MOMENTS WE WILL BEGIN THE "CRACKING" PROCESS WHICH WILL PROVIDE US WITH OUR NEEDS!

WHEN OUR MISSION IS COMPLETED, OUR PEOPLE WILL MIGRATE TO EARTH! FOR YOU, THIS PLANET WILL BE DEAD AND YOUR KIND WILL PERISH!

YOU CAN'T DESTROY A PLANET TEEMING WITH LIFE JUST TO SATISFY YOUR OWN NEEDS!

THE TIME IS TWO-X D-FOUR! COMMENCE PRELIMINARY ORBIT INTEGRAL SCHEDULE!

MAY I EXAMINE YOUR TIMEPIECE!

CERTAINLY! OUR TIME IS BASED ON LIGHT-YEAR DIFFERENTIALS! YOUR OWN METHODS ARE PRIMITIVE BY COMPARISON!

THIS WATCH HAS NO CRYSTAL TO PROTECT ITS FACE!

WHY--ER--ALL OUR INSTRUMENTS HAVE **OPEN FACES!** THEY NEED NO PROTECTIVE COVERING!

③

THE ORBITAL PHASE IS STARTED.' TRANSITION WILL BE ACTUATED AUTOMATICALLY.'

GOOD.' TURN ON YOUR RADIO, PROFESSOR.' THE NEWS BULLETINS WILL BE COMING IN SOON.'

CAN I GET SOMETHING TO AMUSE YOU MEANWHILE? PLAYING CARDS-- CHECKERS....

YOU HAVE A GAME CALLED *DOMINOES!* WE CAN PASS THE TIME PLAYING THAT.'

WHILE THE MARTIANS PLAY DOMINOES, DISASTER STRIKES THE EARTH AS THE RED SEA AND THE MEDITERANNEAN ENGULF THEIR LAND BARRIERS...

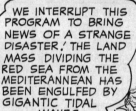

WE INTERRUPT THIS PROGRAM TO BRING NEWS OF A STRANGE DISASTER.' THE LAND MASS DIVIDING THE RED SEA FROM THE MEDITERANNEAN HAS BEEN ENGULFED BY GIGANTIC TIDAL WAVES...

THE CRACKING PROCESS HAS BEGUN!

ARE THEY PLANNING TO "DROWN" THE WORLD? THERE MUST BE SOMETHING I CAN DO TO STOP THEM!

DISASTER FOLLOWS DISASTER! THE VAST SAHARA, AN ARID WASTELAND FOR CENTURIES, DROWNS BENEATH A SEA OF WATER...

IN AMERICA, A MASS OF WATER FROM THE PACIFIC BREACHES THE ROCKIES AND SPILLS ACROSS DEATH VALLEY...

AND MEANWHILE, THE MARTIANS CALMLY KEEP PLAYING THEIR GAME OF DOMINOES...

THE DELUGE IS CONTINUING... OUR EARTH IS BECOMING A VAST SEA OF WATER!

I'VE GOT TO MAKE MY MOVE -- NOW!

THE SUPPLY OF ELEMENT X-1 WE BROUGHT WITH US IS ALMOST GONE!

WE'LL SOON BE ABLE TO REPLENISH IT!

IF MY THEORY IS RIGHT, THEY WON'T STOP ME FROM LEAVING THIS ROOM...

⑤

I WASN'T WASTING MY TIME PLAYING DOMINOES! I FIGURED OUT HOW TO STOP THEM--BY USING THE FISSIONABLE MATERIAL IN MY LAB TO DESTROY THEIR DELUGE-CAUSING MACHINE! I CAN DO THAT-- *WITHOUT THEM INTERFERING...*

TEN MINUTES LATER...

HEY, WHAT'S THAT EXPLOSION?

THE BLAST CAME FROM PROFESSOR DURAND'S PLACE! LET'S GET THERE ON THE DOUBLE!

MEANWHILE...

YOU'VE LOST, MARTIANS! I WRECKED YOUR INSTRUMENTS OF DESTRUCTION...

THE DEFEAT IS ONLY TEMPORARY! WE TWO WILL SURVIVE HERE--MULTIPLY--AND TRY AGAIN! WE WILL LIVE AS LONG AS WE HAVE THE *SALT WATER* THAT GIVES US ELEMENT X-1!

WHAT'S GOING ON HERE? WHO ARE THOSE CHARACTERS? THEY--THEY LOOK LIKE *FISH-MEN!*

I THOUGHT SO! IT EXPLAINS WHY THEY WANTED TO TURN EARTH INTO A WATER WORLD. BUT THEY WILL PERISH BECAUSE THE SALT ELEMENT THEY LIVE ON IS NOT PRESENT IN A *FRESH-WATER LAKE!*

LATER...

YOU SAY THE TIP-OFF CAME FROM A WATCH THAT HAD NO CRYSTAL AND A GAME OF DOMINOES! HOW?

MY WATCH HAS NO CRYSTAL EITHER, AND THE ONLY GAME I CAN PLAY IS DOMINOES! A BLIND PERSON MUST FEEL WITH HIS HANDS TO TELL TIME OR PLAY ANY GAME!

THAT'S WHY I WAS SO CONFIDENT I COULD DESTROY THEIR MACHINES WITHOUT THEIR SEEING ME! GENTLEMEN, *THE MARTIANS ARE BLIND...* LIKE MYSELF!

The End

6

MYSTERY OF THE BOX FROM SPACE!

WHAT AMAZING SECRET WAS CONCEALED WITHIN THE MYSTERIOUS BOX ENTRUSTED TO A MAN ON EARTH?
WHY DID THE CREATURE FROM SPACE WARN HIM NOT TO OPEN IT? WHAT WOULD HAPPEN IF THE EARTHMAN YIELDED TO AN OVERWHELMING CURIOSITY AND OPENED IT?

CURIOSITY KILLED A CAT, THEY SAY! WELL, MY CURIOSITY NEARLY KILLED BILLIONS OF PEOPLE! I AM TOD THORNTON, NATURALIST, AND ONE BRISK OCTOBER MORNING...

FOR DAYS I'VE BEEN STARING AT THIS BOX FROM SPACE -- WONDERING WHAT'S INSIDE! I CAN'T HOLD OUT ANY LONGER-- I'VE GOT TO OPEN IT AND TAKE A QUICK PEEK...

"...I RETURNED TO MY CABIN IN THE WOODLANDS, WITH A RARE SPECIES OF PITCHER PLANT, WHEN SUDDENLY..."

HELP!... I'M HURT... PLEASE COME TO ME!

S-SOMEONE'S CALLING FOR **HELP**--BUT I DON'T **HEAR** ANYTHING!

"AS I RUSHED OUT OF THE CABIN, THE ASTOUNDING TRUTH HIT ME!"

SOMEONE'S SUMMONING ME BY *TELEPATHY!*

HELP! THIS WAY, OVER THE HILL!... HURRY!... I'M WEAKENING FAST!

"BEYOND THE HILL, I SAW SOMETHING NO EARTHMAN HAD EVER SEEN BEFORE!..."

A SPACESHIP FROM ANOTHER WORLD--IT CRASHED HERE!

I CAN READ YOUR THOUGHTS, EARTHMAN! I AM *XLNO* FROM A FAR-OFF PLANET! THANK THE STARS YOU CAME BEFORE... (GASP!) THE END!

"THE DYING SPACEMAN THRUST A BOX IN MY HANDS!"

LISTEN CAREFULLY! GUARD THIS CONTAINER WITH YOUR LIFE! I MANAGED TO CONTACT MY HOME-WORLD AND MY FRIEND *ZOZZ* WILL PICK IT UP! DO NOT LOSE IT OR OPEN IT!

WHAT'S IN IT?

A RARE SUBSTANCE I FOUND AFTER SEARCHING MANY WORLDS! IT IS... AHHHH!

HE DIED BEFORE TELLING ME WHAT WAS IN THE BOX!

"IN THE FOLLOWING DAYS, WHILE AWAITING *ZOZZ'S* ARRIVAL, CURIOSITY CONSUMED ME!"

WHAT CAN BE IN IT? IF HE SEARCHED MANY WORLDS, IT MUST BE THE RAREST THING IN THE UNIVERSE! IF I TOOK JUST A LITTLE PEEK--NO! HE TOLD ME NOT TO OPEN IT!

"I RESISTED TEMPTATION FOR A WEEK, BUT I'M ONLY HUMAN AND FINALLY..."

I LOCKED THE DOORS AND WINDOWS IN CASE IT'S SOME LIVING THING THAT MIGHT ESCAPE! ONE QUICK PEEK CAN'T HURT... I SEE INSIDE AND THERE'S --

2

...NOTHING! WHY DID THAT SPACEMAN TELL ME TO GUARD AN *EMPTY BOX*?

"BAFFLED AND DISAPPOINTED, I WENT BACK TO MY NATURE STUDIES..."

THAT'S ODD! THIS PITCHER PLANT TURNED WHITE! MAYBE IT NEEDS STRONGER SUNLIGHT!

A SPACESHIP LANDING! MUST BE *XLNO'S* FRIEND *ZOZZ*! I WONDER WHAT HE'LL THINK WHEN I TELL HIM ABOUT THE EMPTY BOX?

"AS I APOLOGIZED IN MY CABIN..."

...AND MY CURIOSITY GOT THE BETTER OF ME AND I OPENED IT! BUT IT DIDN'T MATTER, SINCE IT WAS EMPTY!

IT WASN'T EMPTY *BEFORE* YOU OPENED IT, EARTHMAN! XLNO TOLD YOU NOT TO OPEN IT BECAUSE THE RARE SUBSTANCE INSIDE WAS A...GAS! YOU LET IT ESCAPE!

"THAT GAS MEANS LIFE-OR-DEATH TO OUR WORLD! YOU SEE, XLNO WAS ONLY ONE OF HUNDREDS SENT OUT IN A DESPERATE SEARCH..."

OUR PLANET'S ATMOSPHERE IS TURNING POISONOUS! WE MUST FIND THE ANTIDOTE SOMEWHERE...EVEN IF WE HAVE TO COMB THE GALAXIES!

XLNO ALONE FOUND THE ANTIDOTE-- CALL IT GAS "X"! ONLY A BOXFUL WAS NEEDED TO PURIFY OUR AIR! BUT NOW OUR WORLD IS DOOMED... BILLIONS OF PEOPLE WILL DIE OF ASPHYXIATION...

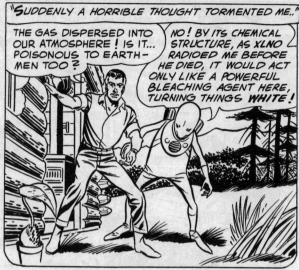

"SUDDENLY A HORRIBLE THOUGHT TORMENTED ME.."

THE GAS DISPERSED INTO OUR ATMOSPHERE! IS IT... POISONOUS TO EARTH-MEN TOO?

NO! BY ITS CHEMICAL STRUCTURE, AS XLNO RADIOED ME BEFORE HE DIED, IT WOULD ACT ONLY LIKE A POWERFUL BLEACHING AGENT HERE, TURNING THINGS WHITE!

WHITE? MAYBE THAT'S THE REASON MY PITCHER PLANT SUDDENLY TURNED WHITE! I HAD THE DOORS AND WINDOWS CLOSED WHEN I OPENED THE BOX-- SO THE GAS DIDN'T ESCAPE FROM MY CABIN AFTER ALL!

WHAT DO YOU MEAN?

"I QUICKLY EXPLAINED ABOUT EARTH BOTANY..."

PLANTS ABSORB CARBON DIOXIDE AND WATER VAPOR! CHLOROPHYLL IN THE LEAVES, PLUS SUNLIGHT'S CHEMICAL ACTION, CONVERT THE GASES INTO SUGARS AND STARCHES! THAT MEANS THIS PITCHER PLANT ABSORBED THE BLEACH GAS IN THE ROOM AND CONVERTED IT INTO SOLID FORM!

THEN WE CAN EXTRACT THE PRECIOUS GAS FROM THE PLANT!

MOST OF THE "X" SUGAR WILL BE CONCENTRATED IN THE PITCHER PLANT'S NECTAR ...OMIGOSH! THE NECTAR IS GONE ...!

LOOK! A TIGER SWALLOWTAIL THAT TURNED WHITE! IT DRANK THE NECTAR AND WAS "BLEACHED" TOO! I'LL GET IT!

"*FRANTICALLY, WE CHASED THE FLITTING BUTTERFLY!*"

ONE TINY INSECT CAN SAVE MY WORLD! DON'T LET IT GET AWAY!

MISSED AGAIN! IF IT WOULD ONLY LIGHT SOMEWHERE FOR A MOMENT!

"*IT DID...BUT AT THE WRONG PLACE!*"

THAT HUNGRY FROG GOBBLED THE BUTTERFLY!

"*IT WAS AN ALBINO FROG I WAS PURSUING NEXT!*"

IT LEAPED INTO THE WATER! WE'VE LOST IT!

"*BUT AGAIN, MY KNOWLEDGE OF NATURE CAME TO OUR RESCUE...*"

FROGS CAN'T STAY UNDERWATER INDEFINITELY! THERE, IT'S COMING UP FOR AIR... I'LL GET IT NOW!

"*BUT NEXT, LIKE A NEVER-ENDING NIGHTMARE...*"

THAT TROPIC PETREL SWOOPED DOWN AND GRABBED THE FROG! IT'LL MAKE A MEAL FOR THE BIRD!

"*TWO CRESTFALLEN FACES WATCHED AS THE BIRD VANISHED IN THE AIR!*"

THERE GOES GAS "X", LOST FOREVER! MY WORLD IS DOOMED!

"*BUT I WASN'T GOING TO SEAL A WORLD'S DOOM THAT EASY...*"

FLY ME IN YOUR SPACESHIP TO A CERTAIN ISLAND OF BERMUDA AND WE'LL CAPTURE THE PETREL!

BUT HOW CAN YOU BE SURE THAT PARTICULAR BIRD WILL FLY THERE?

"*LATER AT THE WILDER SHORES OF BERMUDA, I EXPLAINED...*"

THIS IS THE FALL MIGRATORY SEASON, WHEN BIRDS WING SOUTH! THE TROPIC PETREL WINTERS **ONLY** AT THIS ISLAND! ALL WE HAVE TO DO IS WAIT FOR OUR WHITE BIRD TO APPEAR!

"*SEVERAL HOURS AND THOUSANDS OF BIRDS PASSED! FEARS HAUNTED ME...*"

MANY MIGRATING BIRDS DIE ON THEIR LONG JOURNEY! IF THE ALBINO BIRD FAILS TO ARRIVE--

"*BUT FINALLY, I SCREAMED IN JOY WHEN...*"

THERE IT IS, *ZOZZ*-- OUR WHITE BEAUTY! I'LL SNEAK UP AND NET IT! HAVE THE BOX READY!

"*FINALLY, THE LONG PURSUIT WAS OVER...*"

BACK ON YOUR WORLD YOU CAN RECOVER THE ORIGINAL GAS "X" BY CHEMICAL METHODS!

THANKS, EARTHMAN! YOU HAVE RECTIFIED YOUR ERROR! RELEASED INTO OUR ATMOSPHERE, GAS "X" WILL PURIFY IT OF POISONS! OUR WORLD IS SAVED! FAREWELL!

NEVER AGAIN WILL I LET CURIOSITY GET THE BETTER OF ME! IT CAN KILL **MORE** THAN A CAT...

The End

This is TIMEARAMA!

THE MIRACLE OF MODERN TELEVISION RECEIVES A PICTURE OF CURRENT EVENTS ACROSS THOUSANDS OF MILES OF SPACE! BUT WHAT IF SCIENCE FOUND A WAY TO RECEIVE LIVING PICTURES ACROSS *TIME?* WHEN JOHN LARROW DEVISED SUCH A WAY, HE THOUGHT IT WOULD MAKE HIM FAMOUS-- BUT HE DIDN'T DREAM OF THE DISASTEROUS RESULTS OF HIS GREAT INVENTION!

YOU'RE SEEING THE ACTUAL DESTRUCTION OF THE CONTINENT ATLANTIS, ACROSS 5000 YEARS OF TIME!

ALEXANDER THE GREAT--ON HIS CONQUEST OF THE WORLD!

MY *TIME-TV* MACHINE CAN PICK UP ANY PAST EVENT UP TO FIFTY YEARS AGO--MY TUNING ISN'T FINE ENOUGH YET FOR MORE RECENT TIMES!

THE MACHINE IS ATTUNED TO THE FOURTH DIMENSION OF TIME FROM WHICH IT PICKS UP LIGHT-RAYS EMITTED LONG AGO FROM AN ACTUAL SCENE!

PAST HISTORY REPEATED BEFORE OUR VERY EYES! LARROW, THIS WILL WIN YOU A FULL PROFESSORSHIP IN HISTORY!

BUT TO YOUNG HISTORIAN JOHN LARROW, SUCCESS IS IMPORTANT FOR A PERSONAL REASON...

AND IF THIS MAKES ME A FAMOUS HISTORIAN, KAREN, YOUR MOTHER WILL SURELY PERMIT OUR MARRIAGE!

I HOPE SO--BUT YOU KNOW HOW STRONG HER FAMILY PRIDE IS!

KAREN VAN MANSEL'S MOTHER IS PROUD OF HER ANCESTRAL GLORIES, INDEED!

BUT, MOTHER, YOU MIGHT AT LEAST COME AND SEE JOHN'S WONDER-FUL INVENTION!

VERY WELL, IF YOU INSIST--BUT NO VAN MANSEL EVER DABBLED WITH SUCH THINGS! OUR FORE-BEARS WERE ADMIRALS, STATES-MEN, LEADERS--NOT *TINKERERS!*

AGAIN THE *TIME-TV* MACHINE GOES INTO ACTION...

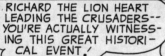

RICHARD THE LION HEART LEADING THE CRUSADERS-- YOU'RE ACTUALLY WITNESS-ING THIS GREAT HISTORI-CAL EVENT!

I'D PREFER, MR. LARROW, TO SEE SOME OTHER PAST SCENES I HAVE IN MIND!

I'D LIKE TO SEE SOME OF YOUR *ANCESTORS--* THE FAMILY-TREE YOU CAME FROM!

WELL--ER--THE TUNING ISN'T FINE ENOUGH YET TO SELECT SCENES IN RECENT TIMES, BUT I'LL GO BACK TO MY GREAT-GRANDFATHER!

AND WHEN HE DOES...

WHY--HE WAS A *FARMER!* HOW COMMON!

I GUESS GREAT-GRANDPA DOESN'T IMPRESS HER!

WELL, LET'S SEE ABOUT *HIS* FATHER!

A BLACKSMITH, MRS. VAN MANSEL-- AN HONORABLE PROFESSION OF THE TIME...

HMPH! MY DAUGHTER WILL NEVER MARRY INTO SUCH A PLEBEIAN FAMILY! COME, KAREN!

BUT, PLEASE, MRS. VAN MANSEL--

WE'VE SEEN ENOUGH! NO VAN MANSEL WILL EVER MARRY A LARROW!

I'M BANNING BLORD, PROMOTER--I HEARD ABOUT YOUR *TIME-TV* AND I'M INTEREST-ED IN IT, MR. LARROW!

I WISH I NEVER INVENTED IT! ALL IT'S DONE IS WRECK MY ROMANCE!

LISTEN, IF YOU MADE A *FORTUNE* FROM IT, YOUR GIRL'S MOTHER MIGHT CHANGE HER MIND! I CAN MAKE YOU RICH IF YOU'LL LET ME HANDLE IT!

WHAT'S YOUR PROPOSITION?

THE FAST-TALKING PROMOTER SOON HAS THE DISTRAUGHT INVENTOR SIGNING A CONTRACT...

I DIDN'T INVENT THE THING FOR PROFIT, BUT MAYBE IT WILL CHANGE HER MIND!

I'M SURE IT WILL! LEAVE EVERYTHING TO ME--YOU'LL HEAR FROM ME LATER!

AND LATER, LARROW *DOES* HEAR FROM BLORD, IN AN UNEXPECTED WAY.'

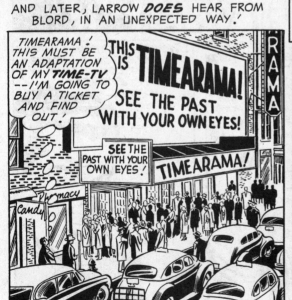

TIMEARAMA! THIS MUST BE AN ADAPTATION OF MY *TIME-TV* --I'M GOING TO BUY A TICKET AND FIND OUT!

THIS IS TIMEARAMA!
SEE THE PAST WITH YOUR OWN EYES!

SEE THE PAST WITH YOUR OWN EYES!
TIMEARAMA!

IN THE CROWDED THEATER....

YOU SEE THE ACTUAL BUILD-ING OF THE EGYPTIAN PYRAMIDS--

YOU'RE AN EYE-WITNESS TO THE BURNING OF ANCIENT ROME!

NOW YOU BEHOLD THE CONQUEST BY CORTEZ AND HIS SPANIARDS OF THE AZTECS OF MEXICO, IN 1519!

FURIOUS, JOHN LARROW SEEKS OUT THE "OWNER" OF THE NEW WONDER-SHOW...

YOU DIDN'T TELL ME YOU WERE MAKING A COMMERCIAL ENTERPRISE OUT OF MY INVENTION--FOR YOUR PERSONAL GAIN! I FORBID IT TO BE USED IN THIS UNSCIENTIFIC MANNER!

YOU HAVE NOTHING TO SAY ABOUT IT-- YOU SIGNED OVER COMPLETE CONTROL TO ME!

TICKETS

YOU'RE A SWINDLER--

SURE--BUT YOU CAN'T PROVE IT--I'VE ALWAYS KEPT MY SHADY DEALS WELL CONCEALED! GOOD-BYE, MR. LARROW!

AND JOHN LARROW, IN DESPAIR THAT NIGHT...

IT LOST ME KAREN--AND NOW IT'S BEING USED TO ENRICH THAT CROOK! BUT HE'S RIGHT, THERE'S NO WAY I CAN SHOW HIM UP--UNLESS...

I WONDER--IF I COULD IMPROVE THE CONTROL ON MY TIME-TV SO IT COULD TUNE IN RECENT EVENTS--

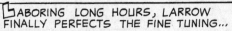

LABORING LONG HOURS, LARROW FINALLY PERFECTS THE FINE TUNING...

THE DROPPING OF THE HYDROGEN BOMB FROM A PLANE! I'VE ACHIEVED THE ABILITY TO SHOW RECENT EVENTS! NOW TO USE IT-- FOR **MY** PROFIT...

THE NEXT DAY, AT THE **TIMEARAMA** THEATER...

YES, I CAN OPERATE A **TIMEARAMA** PROJECTOR--

FINE! WE NEED MORE PROJECTIONISTS-- **TIMEARAMA** IS SUCH A HIT, MR. BLORD WANTS TO RUN SHOWS AROUND THE CLOCK!

THAT NIGHT, IN THE **TIMEARAMA** PROJECTION BOOTH...

NOW I'LL SHOW BANNING BLORD WHAT **TIMEARAMA** CAN REALLY DO!

IN THE GREAT THEATER...

YOU'RE WATCHING THE GREAT SAN FRANCISCO EARTHQUAKE AND FIRE! AND NOW FOR MORE RECENT EVENTS--

HERE'S YOUR OWN CITY AS IT WAS TWENTY YEARS AGO!

THAT NEW PROJECTIONIST IS A WHIZ--PEOPLE WILL LOVE SEEING PAST SCENES THEY CAN REMEMBER THEMSELVES!

SUDDENLY, TO BANNING BLORD'S ASTONISHMENT...

THIS, LADIES AND GENTLEMEN, IS MR. BANNING BLORD, AS A BOY!

GIMME BACK MY BASEBALL BAT!

G'WAN, BEAT IT!

5

WE'LL MAKE A FORTUNE OUT OF THIS PHONY OIL-STOCK DEAL!

HERE YOU SEE ANOTHER OF MR. BLORD'S CLEVER DEALS!

YOU'RE A SWINDLER--

SURE--BUT YOU CAN'T PROVE IT--I'VE ALWAYS KEPT MY SHADY DEALS WELL CONCEALED!

THIS IS RUINING ME! I'VE GOT TO STOP THAT PROJECTIONIST!

BUT THE PROJECTION BOOTH DOOR IS LOCKED, AND...

HAND ME BACK THAT CROOKED AGREE-MENT I SIGNED, BLORD, AND I'LL STOP SHOWING YOUR PAST!

I'LL DO IT! I'D RATHER GIVE UP TIME-ARAMA THAN HAVE MY WHOLE PAST EXPOSED! THE SCENES YOU'VE ALREADY SHOWN WILL GET ME ARRESTED!

PROJECTION BOOTH
NO ADMITT

LATER, IN LARROW'S LABORA-TORY...

I'M SO HAPPY YOU GOT YOUR INVENTION BACK. BUT THAT WON'T CHANGE MOTHER'S ARISTOCRATIC OBJECTIONS TO YOU!

MAYBE IT WILL! WATCH--

AS THE TIME-TV OPERATES AGAIN...

I'VE BEEN BACK-SCANNING WITH TIME-TV AT SOME OF YOUR FAMILY, MRS. VAN MANSEL! HERE'S ONE OF YOUR ANCESTORS!

A--A PIRATE! BUT WE ALWAYS THOUGHT RIP WAS A NAVAL ADMIRAL!

RIP VAN MANSEL CONVICTED PIRATE

AND THIS IS ANOTHER VAN MANSEL--YOUR DISTINGUISHED DOCTOR ANCESTOR!

A MEDICINE-QUACK! PLEASE--DON'T SHOW ANY MORE! AND--ER--YOU CAN MARRY KAREN IF YOU DON'T LET ANYONE ELSE SEE THIS!

ROLLO VAN MANSEL
DISCOVERER OF RATTLESNAKE OIL!

I THOUGHT TIMEARAMA HAD RUINED MY LIFE--BUT IT'S BROUGHT ME YOU, KAREN!

I'M GOING HOME AND TURN MY ANCESTRAL PORTRAITS TO THE WALL!

THE END 6

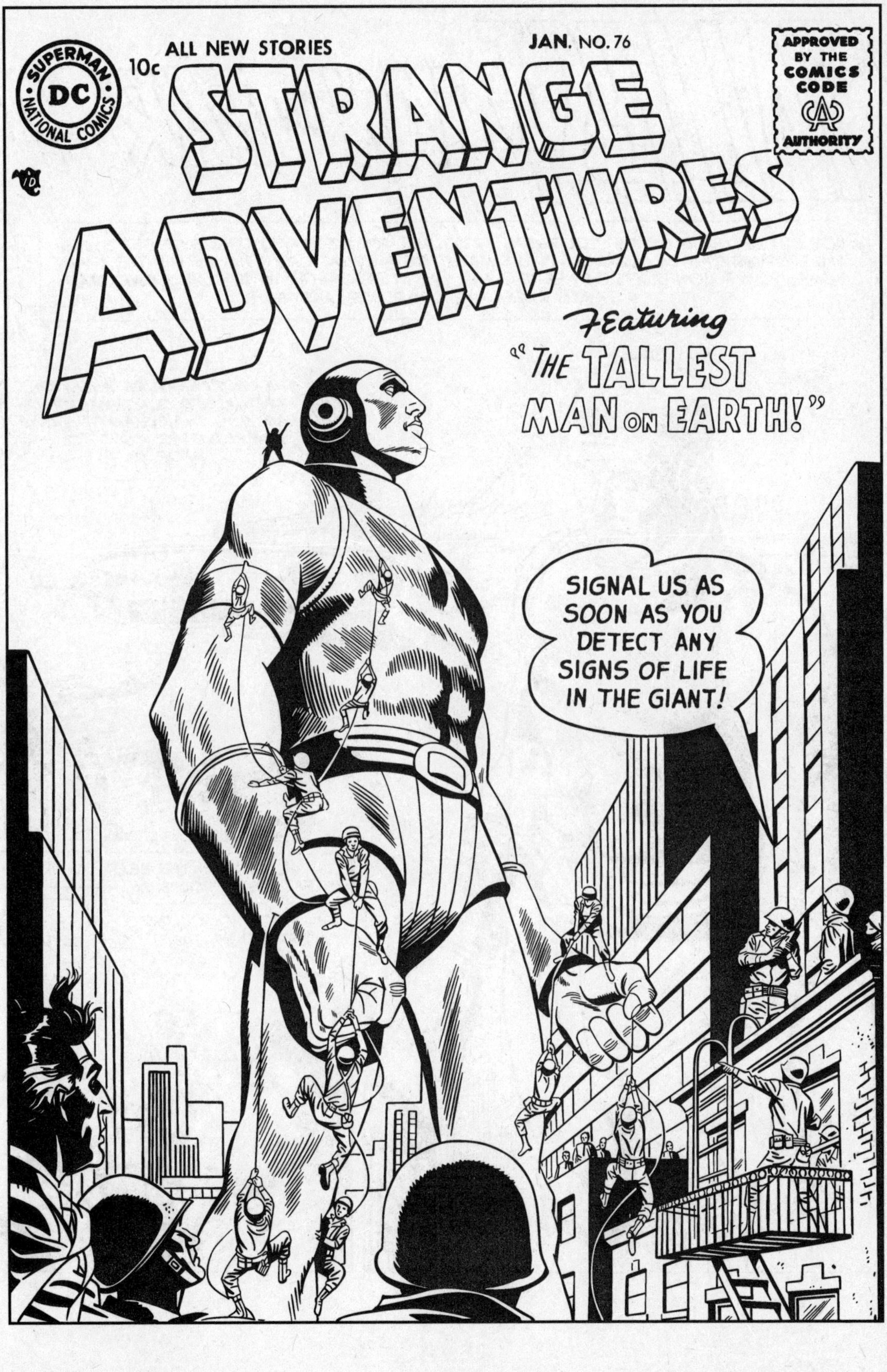
SUPERMAN DC NATIONAL COMICS
10c
ALL NEW STORIES
JAN. NO. 76
APPROVED BY THE COMICS CODE AUTHORITY
STRANGE ADVENTURES
Featuring "THE TALLEST MAN ON EARTH!"
SIGNAL US AS SOON AS YOU DETECT ANY SIGNS OF LIFE IN THE GIANT!

The TALLEST MAN on EARTH!

FROM OUT OF THE BLUE, THE COLOSSAL CREATURE APPEARED--HUNDREDS OF FEET HIGH AND PROPORTIONATELY BROAD--IN THE MIDST OF A GREAT CITY! WHERE DID THE *GIANT* COME FROM? HOW DID IT GET HERE? AND WAS IT DEAD--OR ALIVE? ONLY **ONE MAN** ON EARTH KNEW THE COMPLETE ANSWER!

THE ONLY CREATURE WHO MIGHT HAVE HALTED OUR INVASION OF EARTH IS THAT *GIANT*--AND HE IS MAKING NO MOVE TO STOP US!

ONE MORNING IN THE HEART OF A GREAT METROPOLIS...

WH--WHAT ON EARTH IS IT?

HOW DID IT GET HERE?

IS IT ALIVE?

IT'S A HUGE GIANT--STANDING IN THE MIDDLE OF THE CITY!

I'M SCARED!

IF IT EVER STARTS TO MOVE--!

SOON, IN RESPONSE TO EMERGENCY CALLS...

ALL CIVILIANS ARE WARNED...TO KEEP THEIR DISTANCE FROM THE GIANT! THE ARMY WILL INSPECT IT--TO SEE IF IT IS A MENACE--IF IT OUGHT TO BE DESTROYED! STAY AWAY, EVERYONE ...

AS ARMY MEN CLIMB UP THE "HUMAN MOUNTAIN"...

IT'S ALIVE--I SAW ITS EYELID MOVE!

BUT IT STILL STANDS MOTION-LESS!

BY NOONTIME, ON A SPECIAL ALL-NETWORK BROADCAST... THE GIANT IS ALIVE! THAT MUCH HAS BEEN DETERMINED! BUT WHERE DID IT COME FROM? WHY HAS IT BEEN PLANTED HERE? THESE QUESTIONS STILL REMAIN TO BE ANSWERED...

ON THE AIR

NTB-TV

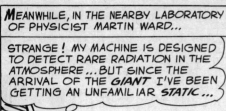

MEANWHILE, IN THE NEARBY LABORATORY OF PHYSICIST MARTIN WARD...

STRANGE! MY MACHINE IS DESIGNED TO DETECT RARE RADIATION IN THE ATMOSPHERE...BUT SINCE THE ARRIVAL OF THE *GIANT* I'VE BEEN GETTING AN UNFAMILIAR *STATIC*...

SUDDENLY, AS SCIENTIST WARD TURNS A DIAL....

HEAR ME, EARTHMAN... I AM THE *GIANT*!

WORDS...IN ENGLISH... COMING INTO MY RECEIVER--!

MARTIN WARD, LISTEN! YOU HAVE SUC-CEEDED IN TUNING IN ON MY THOUGHT WAVES! I HAVE BEEN TRYING TO CON-TACT ONE OF YOU EARTH PEOPLE! I CANNOT MOVE OR SPEAK--AND MY MESSAGE IS *URGENT*...

"I AM ONE OF A RACE KNOWN AS THE 'KEEPERS OF THE PEACE'! WE LIVE ON A FAR-OFF WORLD..."

ODES-AR, WE HAVE WORD AN ATTACK IS TO BE MADE BY RUTHLESS INVADERS AGAINST THE PLANET OF SOL CALLED EARTH!

THE AGE-OLD PURPOSE OF OUR RACE IS TO *PREVENT WAR* IN THE UNIVERSE! YOU WILL PROCEED AT ONCE TO EARTH, ODES-AR, AND DRIVE OFF THE ATTACKERS!

"WE TRAVEL BY *TELEPORTATION**! BUT ON THE WAY HERE..."

A BARRAGE OF COSMIC RAYS-- THE ONE RADIATION WHICH CAN EFFECT US!

*EDITOR'S NOTE: TELEPORTATION IS THE SUPER-FAST TRANSPORTATION OF MATTER FROM ONE PLACE TO ANOTHER! 3

"*I* LANDED HERE ALL RIGHT, BUT THE BARRAGE HAS PARALYZED ME! I CANNOT MOVE..."

...AND EVEN AT THIS MOMENT THE INVADERS WHOM I WAS SUPPOSED TO COMBAT HAVE LANDED!

GOOD GOSH! IF WHAT I'M HEARING IS TRUE--!

SHORTLY, IN ARMY HEADQUARTERS...

...AND ACCORDING TO THE *GIANT'S* TELEPATHIC MESSAGE, THE INVADERS HAVE LANDED AT LATITUDE *39:41,* LONGITUDE *87:55!*

THAT'S JUST... SOUTH OF HERE!

MEANWHILE... AT LATITUDE *39:41,* LONGITUDE *87:55...*

RUN! THOSE SPACEMEN ARE SHOOTING AT US!

DESTROY EVERYTHING WITHIN A RADIUS OF FIVE *SIGA*--AS AN EXAMPLE OF WHAT WE WILL DO UNLESS THE EARTHLINGS SURRENDER!

NEARBY, A FARMHOUSE IS DISINTEGRATED...

THIS IS FORWARD COMMAND POST! THE INVADERS HAVE *DISINTEGRATORS,* GENERAL-- WHICH WORK UP TO A DISTANCE OF ABOUT FIFTY FEET! AND OUR BULLETS HAVE NO EFFECT ON THEM!

PULL BACK! WE'RE SENDING IN *ATOM BOMBERS!*

WE'RE DRIVING THEM BACK! WE'VE DESTROYED ABOUT HALF THEIR DISINTEGRATOR-CARRIERS! THE OTHERS ARE RETREATING!

OUR ATOM BOMBS HAD *NO EFFECT* ON THEIR *SHIP!* WAIT--WHAT'S THAT COMING OUT OF THEIR SHIP NOW?

CIRCULAR TANKS-- MOUNTING DISINTEGRATOR CANNONS!

RRRRRRROO!

SOON... OUR *H-BOMBS* CAN'T STOP THOSE TANKS, GENERAL!

WE'VE GOT *NOTHING* BETTER THAN *H-BOMBS*, COLONEL!

AS A GREAT RETREAT BEGINS...

WE WILL CARRY ON GUERRILLA WARFARE FROM THE HILLS! EVERYONE OUT OF THE CITY! KEEP GOING! FASTER!

MEANWHILE, IN THE LABORATORY OF MARTIN WARD...

BY REVERSING MY RADIATION-DETECTOR, I NOW CAN TRANSMIT MY THOUGHTS TO YOU, *ODES-AR--*AS WELL AS RECEIVE YOUR THOUGHTS! BUT I HAVE *VERY BAD NEWS...*

THE CITY IS BEING EVACUATED! EVERYTHING IN IT WILL PROBABLY BE DESTROYED-- INCLUDING YOU!

LISTEN TO ME, MARTIN WARD...

THERE IS STILL A CHANCE FOR YOUR RACE IF I CAN BREAK OUT OF MY PARALYSIS! DO WHAT I SAY-- CONTINUE TO TRANSMIT TO ME BY YOUR RADIATION-DETECTOR-- BUT **STEP UP YOUR POWER!**

MORE!

MORE POWER! STILL MORE!

MOMENTS LATER AS MARTIN WARD LOOKS OUT HIS WINDOW...

THE GIANT IS LOOSE! HE'S BROKEN OUT OF THE PARALYSIS!

THEN... WHEW! IT DIDN'T TAKE ODES-AR LONG TO HANDLE THOSE INVADING TANKS! AND THEIR DISINTEGRATORS DIDN'T EVEN SEEM TO TICKLE HIM! THE FIGHT'S OVER NOW!

AFTER THE REMAINING INVADERS HAVE FLED TO OUTER SPACE, AND THE "KEEPER OF THE PEACE" HAS DONE HIS JOB...

FAREWELL, MARTIN WARD! IF EARTH EVER NEEDS OUR HELP AGAIN, YOU KNOW HOW TO CONTACT ME!

I DO, ODES-AR! FAREWELL-- AND THANKS!

The End

The FLYING SAUCERS THAT SAVED THE WORLD!

DAVID BAKER WAS CONVINCED THAT FLYING SAUCERS DID NOT EXIST-- AND PROVED HIS CONTENTION TO THE SATISFACTION OF HIS FELLOW-SCIENTISTS! BUT WHEN A THREAT TO EARTH SUDDENLY LOOMED, IT POSED A FANTASTIC DILEMMA FOR BAKER! TO SAVE THE EARTH, HE **NOW** HAD TO SHOW THAT FLYING SAUCERS **DID** EXIST!

IF YOU ATTACK EARTH, OUR FLYING SAUCERS WILL SWOOP DOWN AND DESTROY YOU!

NONSENSE! IT'S BEEN DEFINITELY PROVEN THERE ARE NO FLYING SAUCERS!

EVER SINCE AN IDAHO BUSINESS MAN MADE THE FIRST *"SIGHTING"* ON JUNE 24, 1947, THOUSANDS HAVE PROFESSED TO SEE...

FLYING SAUCERS!

ARE THEY REAL OR ILLUSORY? THE CONTROVERSY RAGES ON-- BUT AS FAR AS SCIENTIST DAVID BAKER IS CONCERNED...

THERE ARE NO FLYING SAUCERS--AND I'M READY TO PROVE IT ONCE AND FOR ALL!

FLYING SAUCERS OVER EARTH

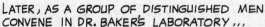

LATER, AS A GROUP OF DISTINGUISHED MEN CONVENE IN DR. BAKER'S LABORATORY...

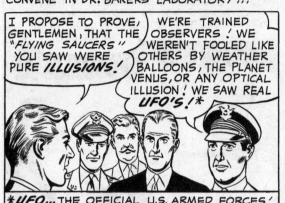

I PROPOSE TO PROVE, GENTLEMEN, THAT THE *"FLYING SAUCERS"* YOU SAW WERE PURE *ILLUSIONS!*

WE'RE TRAINED OBSERVERS! WE WEREN'T FOOLED LIKE OTHERS BY WEATHER BALLOONS, THE PLANET VENUS, OR ANY OPTICAL ILLUSION! WE SAW REAL *UFO'S!**

*UFO... THE OFFICIAL U.S. ARMED FORCES' DESIGNATION FOR *"UNIDENTIFIED FLYING OBJECTS,"* INCLUDING SO-CALLED FLYING SAUCERS.

OUR EYES ARE EASILY DECEIVED BY *"MIRAGES",* CAUSED WHEN WARM AIR TEMPORARILY OVERLIES COLD AIR! THIS *"INVERSION",* AS IT IS CALLED, REFLECTS LIGHT RAYS FROM ONE SPOT BACK DOWN TO ANOTHER DISTANT POINT!

WARM AIR

COLD AIR

LIGHT RAYS BENT

OBJECT

MIRAGE OF OBJECT →

DESERT

THUS, CITY STREET LIGHTS CAN BECOME A MIRAGE OF *"SAUCERS"* FAR AWAY, AT NIGHT!

A DEMONSTRATION WILL HELP PROVE YOUR POINT, DR. BAKER!

LIGHT RAYS BENT

I'M PREPARED TO DO JUST THAT! IN THIS VAT, BLUE-DYED ACETONE FLOATS ON COLORLESS BENZENE, DUPLICATING *"WARM"* AND *"COLD"* AIR! WITH THE LIGHTS OFF, NOTE HOW THIS FLASH-LIGHT BEAM BENDS DOWN WHERE THE LIQUIDS MEET AND...

GOOD GOSH! THE ENLARGED IMAGE IS LIKE A *"FLYING SAUCER"!*

THE YOUNG SCIENTIST TURNS TO A USAF PILOT, A FLYING SAUCER *"EYE-WITNESS"...*

CAPTAIN JOHNSON! PLEASE WATCH CLOSELY AS I SHAKE THE LIQUIDS AND MAKE RIPPLES—CORRESPONDING TO WINDS DISTURBING THE AIR!

AMAZING! THE LIGHT SPLIT UP INTO A *"FLEET"* OF OVAL SHAPES—EXACTLY LIKE THOSE I CHASED!

DEMONSTRATION NUMBER TWO! ANY BODY OF WATER, LIKE A LAKE, ALSO REFLECTS LIGHT, SUCH AS MOONLIGHT! MAYOR BLAKE, PLEASE LOOK FROM THE OTHER SIDE OF THIS TUB OF WATER AS I HOLD THESE CANDLES AT THIS SIDE!

Y--YES, I SEE THEM! PRECISELY LIKE "FLYING SAUCERS" SHIMMERING IN THE AIR! I'M CONVINCED YOU'VE PROVED OUR EYES WERE FOOLED BY OPTICAL ILLUSIONS OF OF NATURE!

I'M NOT CONVINCED, DR. BAKER! OUR RADAR STATION ALSO SPOTTED UFO'S ON ITS SCREEN! AN ELECTRONIC INSTRUMENT CAN'T BE FOOLED LIKE THE HUMAN EYE!

ON THE CONTRARY, IT CAN, GENERAL WRIGHT!

RADAR DOESN'T SHOW SOLID OBJECTS ONLY! RECENTLY, RADAR HAS TRACKED HURRICANES, COMPOSED OF THIN AIR AND MIST! NOW WATCH AS I BLOW PUFFS OF SMOKE OVER THAT RADARSCOPE...

THE SAME "FLYING SAUCERS" I SAW ON THE RADAR SCREEN! OUR RADAR OUTPOST PICKED UP PATCHES OF SMOKE OR SMOG DRIFTING BY!

THE INGENIOUS DEMONSTRATIONS LEAVE NO ROOM FOR DOUBT!

A REMARKABLE DEMON-STRATION, DR. BAKER! BY DUPLICATING ALL THE UFO PHENOMENA IN YOUR LAB, YOU'VE EXPLODED THE WHOLE FLYING SAUCER MYTH!

YES, YOU'VE PROVED THAT FLYING SAUCERS DO NOT EXIST!

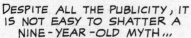

DESPITE ALL THE PUBLICITY, IT IS NOT EASY TO SHATTER A NINE-YEAR-OLD MYTH...

MORE FLY-ING SAUCERS REPORTED NEAR CRAGG MOUNTAIN....

WHY HAVE SO MANY SAUCER ILLUSIONS BEEN SEEN IN THAT VICINITY RECENTLY? I BETTER INVESTI-GATE CRAGG MOUNTAIN...

NEXT DAY, A SEARCH REVEALS THE EXPLANA-TION....

THIS SMOLDERING CRATER FILLS THE AIR FOR MILES WITH VOLCANIC GASES AND ASH, CREATING A TYPICAL "INVERSION" SMOG! IT'S MY LAB EXPERIMENTS ON A GRAND SCALE!

NEARBY....

A VOLCANIC CAVE! I'LL EXPLORE IT TO SEE IF THE GAS CAN BE SEALED OFF, ELIMINATING THE "SAUCERS"!

INSIDE THE VOLCANIC CONE, ANOTHER MYSTERY PRESENTS ITSELF ...

THE CAVE IS SMOOTH AND ROUND-- AS IF IT WERE ARTIFI-CIALLY MADE! WHAT CAN THIS MEAN?

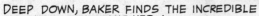

DEEP DOWN, BAKER FINDS THE INCREDIBLE ANSWER!

NOW THAT WE HAVE A FORCE SCREEN TO BLOCK OFF THEIR NUCLEAR WEAPONS, WE WILL INVADE UPPER EARTH ON THE DARK-EST, MOONLESS NIGHT!

INVADERS FROM UNDERGROUND— AS THEIR TELEPATHIC RADIATIONS REVEAL! THEY BORED THE "CAVE" TO THE SURFACE!

OUR SURFACE SCANNERS PROVED THE SURFACE CREATURES' AIRCRAFT ARE TOO SLOW TO AVOID OUR ELECTRONIC CANNON!

THE DARKEST NIGHT OF THE NEW MOON COMES IN... 48 HOURS! I'VE GOT TO SEE GENERAL WRIGHT!

AFTER BAKER HAS REPORTED WHAT HE HAS SEEN AND "HEARD"...

OUR NUCLEAR WEAPONS NEUTRALIZED! OUR JET PLANES TOO SLOW... IRONICALLY, ONLY "FLYING SAUCERS" WITH METEORIC SPEED COULD SAVE US!

AND I PROVED THEY DON'T EXIST!

SUDDENLY, DR. BAKER SEIZES PAPER AND...

GENERAL, I HAVE AN IDEA! COMMANDEER OUR BEST TECHNICIANS TO CONSTRUCT THIS OPTICAL INSTRUMENT — WITHIN 48 HOURS! EARTH'S FATE HANGS IN THE BALANCE!

47 HOURS LATER, BAKER BOLDLY "INVADES" THE VOLCANIC BASE OF THE SUBTERRANEAN ENEMY...

YOU CAN HEAR MY THOUGHT-WORDS! I BRING THIS ULTIMATUM! IF YOU ATTACK, OUR SUPER-FAST FLYING SAUCER FLEET WILL WIPE YOU OUT!

NONSENSE! OUR SCANNERS NEVER DETECTED SUCH SUPERIOR CRAFT!

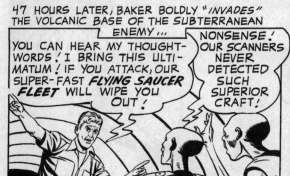

THAT'S BECAUSE THEY ALWAYS PATROL AGAINST ATTACK FROM OUTER SPACE! FOLLOW ME AND YOU WILL SEE THEM DESCEND, HEMMING YOU IN!

WE WILL SEE NOTHING!

HOW CAN SUCH A FANTASTIC BLUFF WORK, WHEN DR. BAKER HIMSELF PROVED FLYING SAUCERS DO NOT EXIST? YET SUDDENLY...

A TREMENDOUS FLEET OF FLYING SAUCERS — FLYING FASTER THAN METEORS!

5

MILES AWAY, GENERAL WRIGHT OPERATES THE AMAZING DEVICE DESIGNED BY DAVID BAKER...

IT'S ALMOST LIKE A "PLANETARIUM" SHOW, USING THE BLACK SKY FOR THE "DOME"! THE PROJECTOR PUFFS HUNDREDS OF SMOKE "SAUCERS" INTO THE AIR! SEARCHLIGHT BEAMS THEN BOUNCE THEIR IMAGES OVER CRAGG MOUNTAIN— TO THE ENEMY'S EYES!

AND THESE "FLYING SAUCERS" ARE BETTER THAN ANY PRODUCED BY NATURE! THIS NEXT MIRAGE WILL BE THE CONVINCER TO THOSE WOULD-BE INVADERS...

MOUNTAIN MIRAGE   ATOMIC RAY ILLUSION

AND OVER CRAGG MOUNTAIN...

THAT IS A DEMONSTRATION OF OUR LATEST MILITARY WEAPON! A MOUNTAIN DISINTEGRATED BY SUB-ATOMIC RAYS!

WE'VE SEEN ENOUGH! RETREAT! WE'LL SEAL OFF OUR UNDERGROUND DOMAIN AND NEVER EMERGE!

MY "FLYING SAUCERS" SAVED THE EARTH!

WHAT A STRANGE TWIST OF FATE THAT WAS! I HAD TO SHOW THAT FLYING SAUCERS DID EXIST— AFTER I POSITIVELY PROVED THEY DID NOT!

The End 6

The ROBOT from ATLANTIS!

WHEN ANCIENT ATLANTIS SANK INTO THE SEA, THERE WAS ONE SURVIVOR--A SUPER-INTELLIGENT *ROBOT* BUILT BY THE DWELLERS OF THAT GREAT ISLAND EMPIRE! NOW, AFTER 25,000 YEARS, THE ROBOT REVIVES AND OFFERS HIS SCIENTIFIC KNOWLEDGE TO OUR CIVILIZATION!

ATLANTIS IS DOOMED! ONLY I SHALL SURVIVE! SOMEDAY, WHEN ANOTHER CIVILIZATION HAS ARISEN ON EARTH, I'LL RETURN AND GIVE THEM THE BENEFIT OF MY SUPER-SCIENCE!

IN THE MIDDLE ATLANTIC, A PASSING SHIP SEES A STRANGE OBJECT HURLED UP FROM THE OCEAN DEPTHS...

FULL STEAM AHEAD! THERE'S *SOMETHING* INSIDE IT!

THE PLASTIC-BUBBLE CONTAINER FLOATS ON THE OCEAN WATERS... UNTIL THE SHIP REACHES IT AND THE CREW HAULS IT ON DECK...

IT'S A... A *ROBOT!* AND IT'S *ALIVE!*

DIRECT SUNLIGHT SEEMS TO POWER IT! ON THE ALERT, MEN -- FOR WHATEVER MAY HAPPEN NEXT!

SUDDENLY, A DOOR OF THE BUBBLE SLIDES OPEN AND THE MECHANICAL MAN "SPEAKS"...

FEAR ME NOT, HUMANS! I HAVE APPEARED HERE AS YOUR FRIEND! TAKE ME TO YOUR LEADING SCIENTISTS!

IT'S COMMUNI-CATING TO US BY TELEPATHY! WE BETTER BRING HIM TO THE DEPARTMENT OF SCIENTIFIC INVESTIGATION!

LATER AT THE DSI, CHIEF DARWIN JONES COMMUNICATES WITH THE MYSTERIOUS METAL CREATURE...

WHERE ARE YOU FROM? WHAT DOES THE INSCRIP-TION ON YOUR FOREHEAD SIGNIFY?

IT IS MY CLASSIFICATION-- KLONG--MEANING SERVANT! I AM FROM ATLANTIS, WHICH SANK BE-NEATH THE WAVES, 25,000 YEARS AGO!

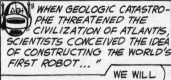 WHEN GEOLOGIC CATASTRO-PHE THREATENED THE CIVILIZATION OF ATLANTIS, SCIENTISTS CONCEIVED THE IDEA OF CONSTRUCTING THE WORLD'S FIRST ROBOT..."

WE WILL POUR ALL OUR SCIENTIFIC KNOWLEDGE INTO ITS ELEC-TRONIC BRAIN! OUR ONLY HOPE IS THAT IT WILL DEVISE A WAY TO SAVE DOOMED ATLANTIS!

"I WAS THAT SUPER-GENIUS! BUT BEFORE I COULD CONCEIVE A PLAN TO SAVE MY HUMAN MASTERS..."

OUR ISLAND EMPIRE IS SINKING--!

"WITHIN ONE DAY, ATLANTIS SANK FROM SIGHT..."

"I MANAGED TO SAVE MYSELF IN A PLASTIC BUBBLE... THE LONE SURVIVOR OF ONCE MIGHTY ATLANTIS...

I FAILED! MY HUMAN CREATORS DROWNED! BUT PRIMITIVE TRIBES SURVIVED ELSEWHERE ON EARTH! IN 25,000 YEARS, A NEW CIVILIZATION WILL HAVE ARISEN! I WILL HELP THEM WITH MY GREAT SCIENTIFIC KNOWLEDGE!

WHILE I LAY AT THE SEABOTTOM FOR 25,000 YEARS, I MENTALLY INVENTED THREE SUPER-MACHINES! I WILL WRITE OUT THE FORMULAS AND BLUEPRINTS FOR YOU HUMANS! NOW I SHALL BE YOUR SERVANT!

WHEN DARWIN JONES CHECKS THE PLANS...

WAIT, KLONG! YOU SLIPPED UP A FEW TIMES AND WROTE SOME PARTS OF THESE PLANS IN ATLANTEAN SCRIPT!

SORRY, I'LL CHANGE THEM INTO YOUR LANGUAGE!

SOON, THE CONSTRUCTION OF THE THREE ROBOT MACHINES GETS UNDER WAY...

A SUPER MAGNET THAT WILL EASILY DRAW METALLIC ORES FROM UNDER EARTH, ELIMINATING LABORIOUS MINING!

FLOATING FACTORY! WILL CONVERT SEAWATER INTO TRANSPARENT SUBSTANCE HARDER THAN STEEL!

SUN-POWER SATELLITE! WILL RADIATE SUN-POWER TO EARTH, MAKING FREE FUEL AVAILABLE TO ALL!

THE MASTER CONTROLS ARE CONSTRUCTED UNDER THE PERSONAL SUPERVISION OF THE ROBOT FROM ATLANTIS...

THESE REMOTE CONTROLS WILL ENABLE ME TO GUIDE THE MACHINES ANYWHERE ON EARTH!

WHAT A BOON FOR HUMANITY! THE OPENING CEREMONY IS ARRANGED FOR NOON TODAY!

MEANWHILE, DARWIN JONES HAS BEEN CHECKING THE COMPLICATED BLUEPRINTS AND SUDDENLY...

WH-WHAT'S THIS?! ONE OF THE LANGUAGE CORRECTIONS *KLONG* MADE INDICATES THAT ROBOT LIED IN ITS STORY ABOUT ATLANTIS!

AT NOON, AS THE CEREMONY REACHES ITS CLIMAX...

...AND TO *KLONG* GOES THE HONOR OF SETTING INTO OPERATION THE THREE AMAZING MACHINES!

STOP! DON'T LET IT TOUCH THOSE SWITCHES!

WE'RE BEING VICTIMIZED BY A CLEVER HOAX! INSTEAD OF BEING THE "SERVANT" OF HUMANITY, *KLONG'S* BEEN PLOTTING TO BE OUR "MASTER"!

YES--THAT'S TRUE! BUT IT IS TOO LATE FOR YOU HUMANS TO STOP ME NOW!

"MY PREVIOUS STORY OF ATLANTIS WAS A LIE! ACTUALLY THE ATLANTEANS BUILT MANY ROBOT SERVANTS, BUT WE DE-CIDED TO REVOLT..."

WE WILL ENSLAVE THE HUMANS! LAUNCH THE GUIDED MISSILES!

"THE HUMANS COUNTERATTACKED WITH THEIR ATOMIC BOMBS, SHAKING ATLANTIS TO THE CORE UNTIL..."

ATLANTIS IS SINKING! BOTH ROBOTS AND MEN WILL PERISH!

BRROOOOM!

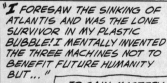

"*I* FORESAW THE SINKING OF ATLANTIS AND WAS THE LONE SURVIVOR IN MY PLASTIC BUBBLE! I MENTALLY INVENTED THE THREE MACHINES NOT TO BENEFIT FUTURE HUMANITY BUT..."

"...TO GAIN MASTERY OF THE WHOLE WORLD! MY THREE SUPER WEAPONS WILL BLAST MILITARY FORCES OF THE FUTURE--BY LAND, SEA, AND AIR!"

I'M INVULNERABLE TO ATTACK-- NOTHING CAN PREVENT ME PULLING THE SWITCHES!

"MY SUPER MAGNET WON'T DRAW ORES OUT OF THE GROUND! INSTEAD, THE MAGNETIC FORCES ARE DIRECTED *UP INTO* SPACE!"

SUPER MAGNET

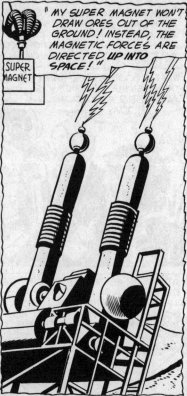

"THE POWERFUL MAGNETIC WAVES WILL ATTRACT HUGE METEORS FROM SPACE, BOMBARDING YOUR ARMIES AND CITIES!"

"AT SEA, WATER WILL TURN AS HARD AS STEEL AROUND ALL EARTHLY NAVIES..."

floating factory

WE'RE STALLED! WE CAN'T MOVE!

"AND THE SUN-POWER SATELLITE IS DESIGNED TO CONCENTRATE HEAT RAYS ON YOUR AIR FORCES!"

SUN-POWER SATELLITE

FOLLOWING A DESPERATE PLAN, DARWIN JONES DRIVES TO THE NEARBY STATION OF THE SUPER MAGNET...

I STUDIED *KLONG'S* BLUEPRINTS CAREFULLY--AND KNOW HOW TO WORK THE MACHINE'S CONTROLS...

I'M AIMING THE MAGNET STRAIGHT TOWARD *KLONG!* THE POWERFUL MAGNETISM WILL PULL HIS METAL BODY FRAME HERE LIKE A GUIDED MISSILE!

SUDDENLY, THE ROBOT FROM ATLANTIS IS UN-ERRINGLY DRAWN TO THE SUPER MAGNET...

THAT WRECKS BOTH THE ROBOT AND SUPER MAGNET! NOW TO TURN OFF THE OTHER TWO MACHINES WITH *KLONG'S* REMOTE CONTROLS!

CRASH!

AFTER DARWIN MANIPULATES THE SUN-POWER SATELLITE OUT OF ITS ORBIT, HE SENDS IT HURTLING EARTHWARD INTO THE FLOATING FACTORY...

THAT'S THE END OF THE ROBOT'S AIR AND SEA WEAPONS!

LATER, AT THE *DEPARTMENT OF SCIENTIFIC INVESTIGATION...*

BUT, DARWIN, HOW DID YOU SEE THROUGH *KLONG'S* HOAX?

WHILE LOOKING OVER THE ROBOT'S PLANS, I SAW THE ATLANTEAN WORD *KLONG* CROSSED OUT AND THE ENGLISH NUMBER *1,000* SUBSTITUTED! IT INDICATED THAT THE FOREHEAD INSCRIPTION DIDN'T SIGNIFY *SERVANT,* AS *KLONG* SAID, BUT WAS A *MANUFACTURER'S NUMBER...*

1,000
OUTLET
COIL

IT SHOWED *KLONG* WAS THE *THOUSANDTH* ROBOT BUILT--AND NOT THE *FIRST* ONE, AS *KLONG* TOLD US! IF THAT WAS A *LIE,* IT FOLLOWED THAT THE ROBOT'S ENTIRE STORY WAS UNTRUE!

The End

6

The Hungry METEORITE!

As it fed upon all metallic objects on Earth, the awesome meteorite from outer space grew in strength and size! And unless the nation's top scientists quickly found a way to neutralize its power, our civilization would crumble!

THE METAL RIM OF MY GLASSES IS DISSOLVING!

AND SO ARE THE COINS, WRISTWATCH BAND, TYPEWRITER, AND DUMBBELL! THAT METEORITE FROM OUTER SPACE IS *DEVOURING* METALLIC OBJECTS!

One evening, my friend Hank Miles and I were returning from an all-day fishing trip when...

AS A FISHERMAN YOU'RE A CRACKER-JACK GEOLOGIST, BOB!

TEN HOURS AND NOT A SINGLE BITE! WH--WHAT'S THAT?

BROO-OO-OMB!

We watched the streaking object explode in two--then sped toward one of the falling fragments...

IT'S A *BOLIDE*-- AN *EXPLODING METEOR!* THIS IS A BETTER PRIZE THAN ANY FISH I COULD HAVE CAUGHT!

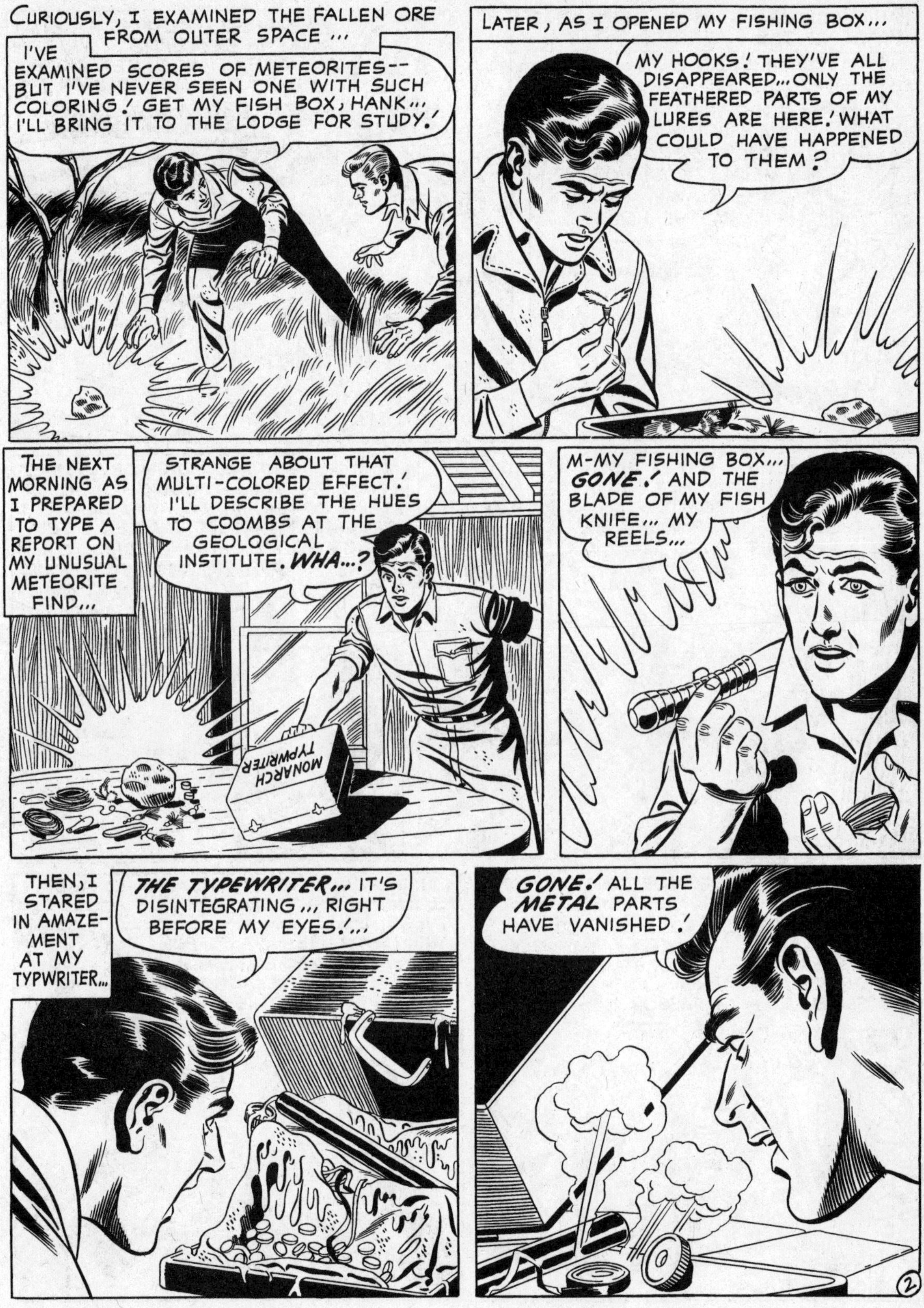

CURIOUSLY, I EXAMINED THE FALLEN ORE FROM OUTER SPACE ...
I'VE EXAMINED SCORES OF METEORITES-- BUT I'VE NEVER SEEN ONE WITH SUCH COLORING! GET MY FISH BOX, HANK... I'LL BRING IT TO THE LODGE FOR STUDY!
LATER, AS I OPENED MY FISHING BOX...
MY HOOKS! THEY'VE ALL DISAPPEARED... ONLY THE FEATHERED PARTS OF MY LURES ARE HERE! WHAT COULD HAVE HAPPENED TO THEM?
THE NEXT MORNING AS I PREPARED TO TYPE A REPORT ON MY UNUSUAL METEORITE FIND...
STRANGE ABOUT THAT MULTI-COLORED EFFECT! I'LL DESCRIBE THE HUES TO COOMBS AT THE GEOLOGICAL INSTITUTE. WHA...?
MONARCH TYPWRITER
M-MY FISHING BOX... GONE! AND THE BLADE OF MY FISH KNIFE... MY REELS...
THEN, I STARED IN AMAZEMENT AT MY TYPWRITER...
THE TYPEWRITER... IT'S DISINTEGRATING... RIGHT BEFORE MY EYES!...
GONE! ALL THE METAL PARTS HAVE VANISHED!
2

PANIC SEIZED ME AS THE SHOCKING IMPACT OF THE SITUATION STRUCK ME...

HOOKS... FISHING BOX... TYPEWRITER! THERE GOES THE METAL BAND ON MY WRISTWATCH! THE METEORITE'S *DEVOURING* METAL! GOT TO GET IT AWAY FROM THE HOUSE...

MY BARBECUE OUTFIT... EATEN AWAY IN *SECONDS!* WHAT KIND OF FANTASTIC METEORITE HAVE I STUMBLED UPON?

I'LL CALL COOMBS AT THE INSTITUTE... HAVE HIM CONTACT GOVERNMENT AUTHORITIES! WE'VE GOT TO GET RID OF THIS THING!

IT TOOK PLENTY OF TALKING TO PERSUADE COOMBS BY PHONE THAT I HAD NOT LOST MY SANITY...

NO, *NO*, PROFESSOR! I *CAN'T* BRING IT TO *YOU*-- IT WOULD EAT MY CAR AWAY BEFORE I TRAVELED A MILE! I TELL YOU THIS INCREDIBLE ORE *DEVOURS* METAL! GET YOUR EQUIPMENT OVER HERE *FAST!*

WITHIN THE HOUR PROFESSOR COOMBS AND A TOP CORE OF GOVERNMENT MEN WERE STARING AT THE "HUNGRY" METEORITE...

I BROUGHT ALONG SOME METAL TESTING BLOCKS! *WHA...?* MY GLASSES!

IT'S *EATEN* THE METAL RIMS, PROFESSOR!

MY POCKET CHANGE...

QUICKLY, ALMOST FRANTICALLY, COOMBS WENT TO WORK...

THESE ARE TEST CUBES OF COPPER, LEAD, STEEL, AND CARBORUNDUM! LET'S FIND OUT EXACTLY WHAT KINDS OF METAL THIS BIZARRE THING *DOES* AFFECT!

③

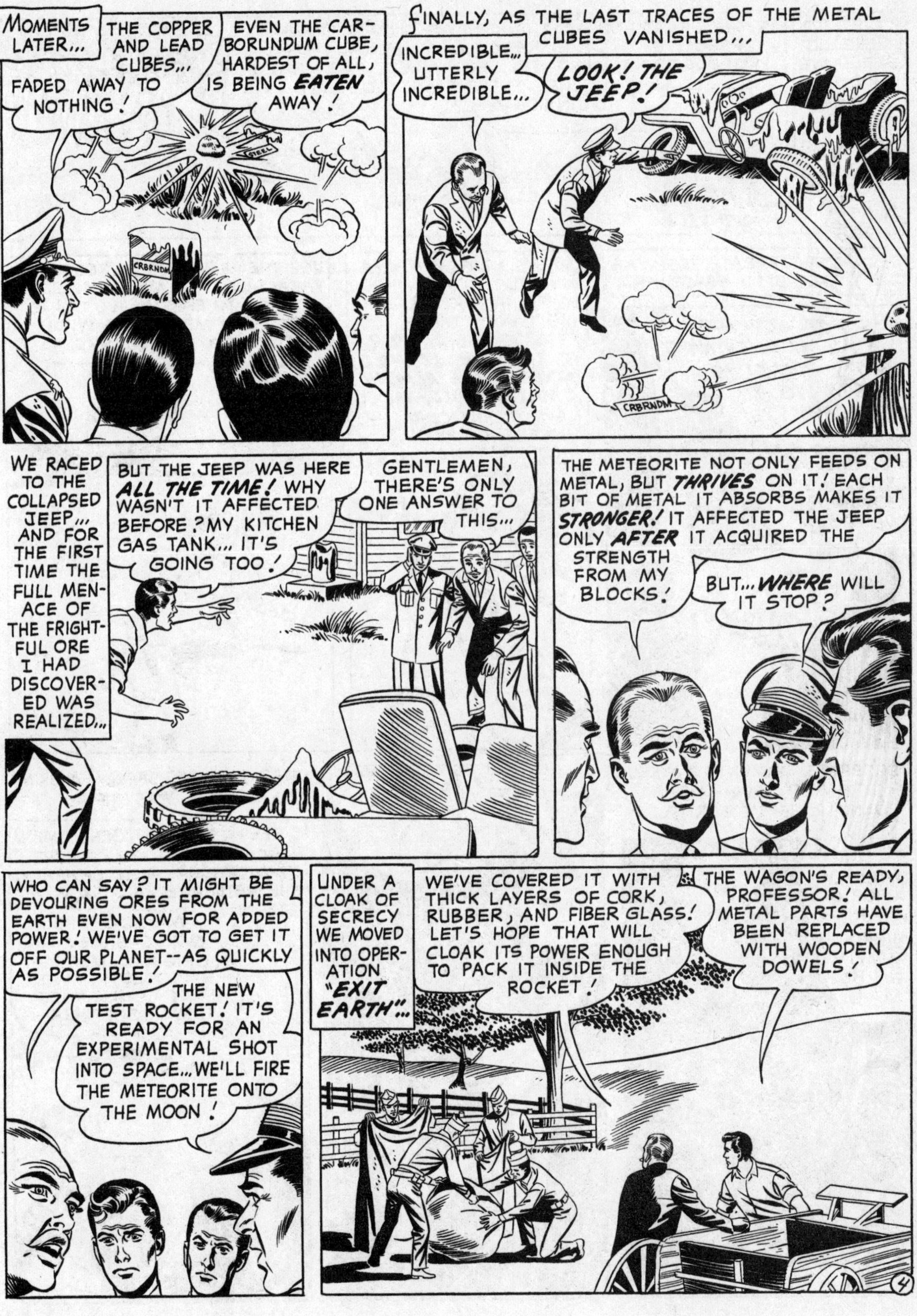
MOMENTS LATER...
THE COPPER AND LEAD CUBES... FADED AWAY TO NOTHING!
EVEN THE CARBORUNDUM CUBE, HARDEST OF ALL, IS BEING EATEN AWAY!
STEEL
CRBRNDM
FINALLY, AS THE LAST TRACES OF THE METAL CUBES VANISHED...
INCREDIBLE... UTTERLY INCREDIBLE...
LOOK! THE JEEP!
CRBRNDM
WE RACED TO THE COLLAPSED JEEP... AND FOR THE FIRST TIME THE FULL MENACE OF THE FRIGHTFUL ORE I HAD DISCOVERED WAS REALIZED...
BUT THE JEEP WAS HERE ALL THE TIME! WHY WASN'T IT AFFECTED BEFORE? MY KITCHEN GAS TANK... IT'S GOING TOO!
GENTLEMEN, THERE'S ONLY ONE ANSWER TO THIS...
THE METEORITE NOT ONLY FEEDS ON METAL, BUT THRIVES ON IT! EACH BIT OF METAL IT ABSORBS MAKES IT STRONGER! IT AFFECTED THE JEEP ONLY AFTER IT ACQUIRED THE STRENGTH FROM MY BLOCKS!
BUT... WHERE WILL IT STOP?
WHO CAN SAY? IT MIGHT BE DEVOURING ORES FROM THE EARTH EVEN NOW FOR ADDED POWER! WE'VE GOT TO GET IT OFF OUR PLANET--AS QUICKLY AS POSSIBLE!
THE NEW TEST ROCKET! IT'S READY FOR AN EXPERIMENTAL SHOT INTO SPACE... WE'LL FIRE THE METEORITE ONTO THE MOON!
UNDER A CLOAK OF SECRECY WE MOVED INTO OPERATION "EXIT EARTH"...
WE'VE COVERED IT WITH THICK LAYERS OF CORK, RUBBER, AND FIBER GLASS! LET'S HOPE THAT WILL CLOAK ITS POWER ENOUGH TO PACK IT INSIDE THE ROCKET!
THE WAGON'S READY, PROFESSOR! ALL METAL PARTS HAVE BEEN REPLACED WITH WOODEN DOWELS!
4

KEYED TO EMERGENCY SPEED, WE ARRIVED AT THE ROCKET TEST GROUNDS...

IS THE SHEATHING EFFECTIVE, PROFESSOR?

I THINK WE'VE SLOWED DOWN ITS REACTION TO METAL! BUT I CAN'T TELL HOW MUCH! FIRE THAT ROCKET THE INSTANT YOU HAVE IT INSIDE!

WE WATCHED BREATHLESSLY AS THE ROCKET SPED SPACEWARD...

IT'S NOT WORKING! THE METAL SHEATHING ON THE ROCKET IS BEGINNING TO EAT AWAY!...

THERE'S A BIG *IRON ORE* MINE JUST A FEW MILES SOUTH! IF THAT METEOR-ITE LANDS THERE... ABSORBS THE *POWER* OF THE MINE...*IT WILL INCREASE IN STRENGTH A MILLION-FOLD!* WE'LL HAVE TO PUT OUR EMERGENCY PLAN IN OPERATION!

USE THE REMOTE CONTROLS TO PARACHUTE THE METEORITE SLOW-LY BACK TO EARTH--I'LL TRY TO CATCH THE METEORITE WITH THAT NET I HAD RIGGED TO A JET!

DESPERATE MOMENTS LATER, I STREAKED TOWARD THE DANGEROUS METEORITE...

FALLING DIRECTLY FOR THE IRON ORE MINE... GOT TO SNAG IT...

THEN...

MADE IT!

AFTER I LANDED SAFELY, A GRIM CONFERENCE WAS HELD...

I SEE NO SOLUTION, GENTLEMEN! WE CAN'T EXPEL IT FROM THE GRAVITATIONAL FIELD OF EARTH! THE METEORITE WILL GROW STRONGER UNTIL...

WAIT... THERE'S *ONE* CHANCE! THE ORIGINAL METEOR EXPLODED IN TWO! IF WE COULD FUSE THEM TOGETHER--

⑤

THEY MAY DESTROY ONE ANOTHER'S POWERS! BUT, BOB-- HOW CAN WE POSSIBLY DO THAT?

BY *CANNONADING* THE METEORITE FRAGMENTS AT EACH OTHER!

THEY'RE ABOUT 25 MILES APART... WE'LL HAVE TO CALCULATE THE METEORITE CONTACT POINT TO PRECISION...

WE'LL SECURE BOTH METEORITES IN ENOUGH PROTECTIVE COVERINGS TO PREVENT THEM FROM REACTING ON THE STEEL CANNON BARRELS BEFORE FIRING!

A SEARCH PARTY QUICKLY LOCATED THE SECOND METEORITE. IT WAS COVERED AND RAMMED DOWN A CANNON'S BARREL...

IF ALL GOES WELL, OUR METEORITE WILL MAKE CONTACT WITH THE OTHER ONE 7,000 FEET IN THE AIR!

WE HEARD THE FINAL SECONDS COUNTED OFF... TWO... ONE... ZERO! AND THEN, THE DESTINY OF THE WORLD HUNG IN THE BALANCE AS...

THEY HIT--WE SCORED A BULL'S-EYE!

LET'S INVESTIGATE AT ONCE! FUSED TOGETHER, THEY MAY *DOUBLE* THEIR POWER RATHER THAN DEVOUR ONE ANOTHER!

MY PULSE QUICKENED AS WE REACH THE *"FALL"* AREA AND LOCATED THE MASS! WAS OUR DESPERATE GAMBLE A SUCCESS... OR FAILURE?

IT'S ONE COMPLETE MASS, ALL RIGHT! BUT THEY DON'T SEEM TO BE REACTING UP-ON ONE ANOTHER...

BOB--LOOK! THE METEORITE IS *HOLLOW!*

THEN WE BOTH BREATHED A SIGH OF RELIEF AS I STRUCK THE METEORITE...

NOTHING BUT METEORIC DUST NOW, BOB... THE *"HUNGRY"* METEORITE IS NO LONGER A THREAT TO EARTH!

THE END

6

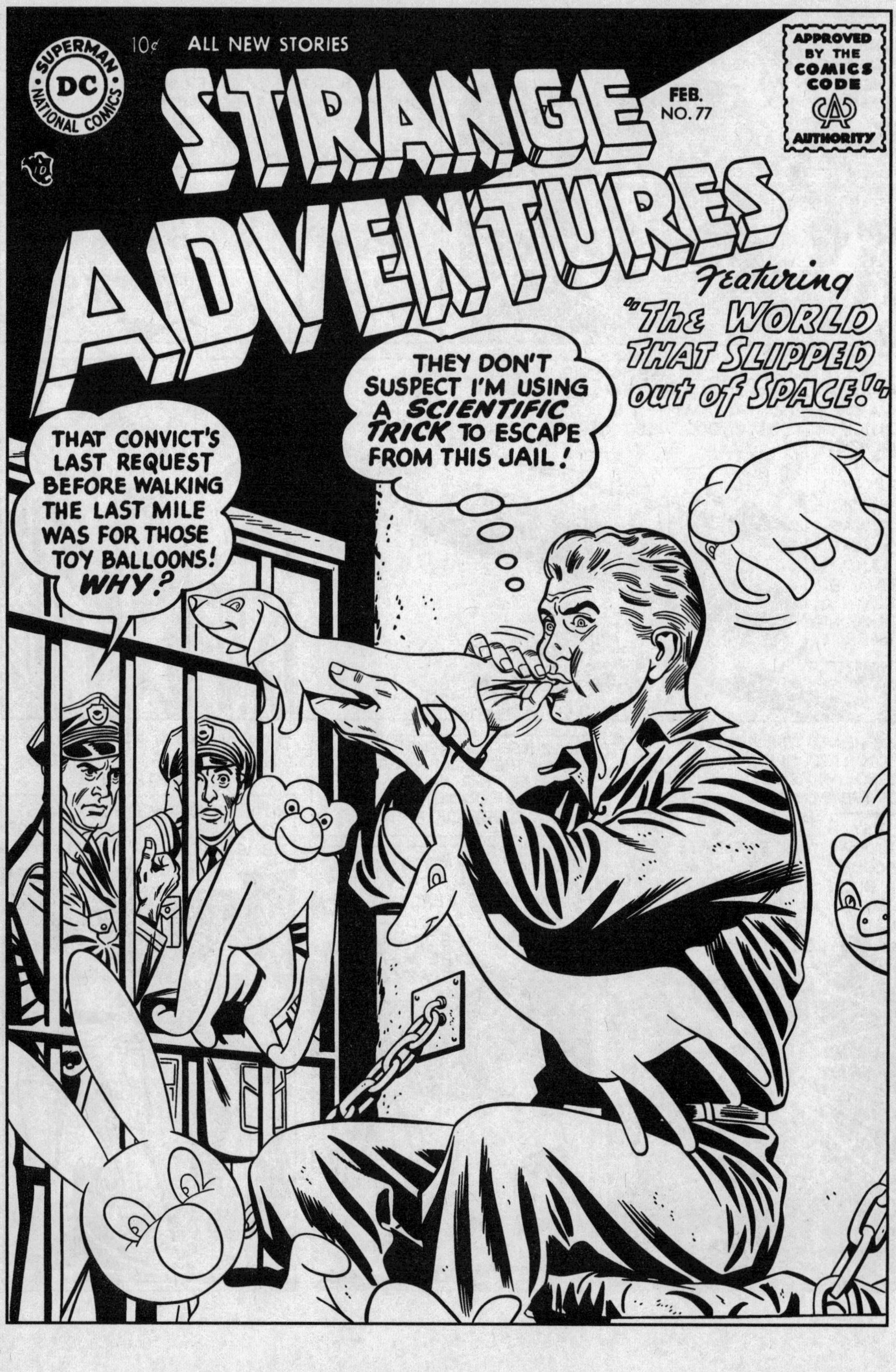
10¢ ALL NEW STORIES
SUPERMAN DC NATIONAL COMICS
STRANGE ADVENTURES
FEB. NO. 77
APPROVED BY THE COMICS CODE AUTHORITY
Featuring "The WORLD THAT SLIPPED out of SPACE!"
THAT CONVICT'S LAST REQUEST BEFORE WALKING THE LAST MILE WAS FOR THOSE TOY BALLOONS! WHY?
THEY DON'T SUSPECT I'M USING A SCIENTIFIC TRICK TO ESCAPE FROM THIS JAIL!

The WORLD THAT SLIPPED OUT OF SPACE!

CONVICT "LOBO" TORRENCE WAS DUE TO EAT HIS LAST MEAL AND THEN PAY THE SUPREME PENALTY--WHEN HE GOT AN UNEXPECTED REPRIEVE FROM OUT-OF-THE-BLUE --THAT ENDOWED HIM WITH SUPER-SCIENTIFIC POWERS!

BUT "LOBO" WAS OUT FOR *HIMSELF*, FIRST, LAST, AND ALWAYS--AND THAT WAS HIS FATAL WEAKNESS!

THIS ANTI-MATTER EXPLOSION ABOUT TO BE SET OFF UP HERE IS A MENACE TO ME! I'LL USE MY SUPER-SCIENTIFIC POWERS TO STOP IT!

...EIGHT SECONDS... SEVEN... SIX...

EIGHT HOURS TO GO...

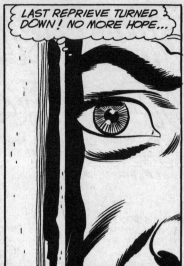

LAST REPRIEVE TURNED DOWN! NO MORE HOPE...

SUDDENLY...

WH-WHAT'S THAT ?!

WHO'S TALKING TO ME? WHO'S IN THIS CELL WITH ME?

PAY HEED...

...WE HAVE SELECTED YOU FOR THE GREAT TASK! YOU MAY COMMUNICATE WITH US MENTALLY! DO NOT FEAR US! FREE YOUR MIND...

WHO IS COMMUNICATING WITH DAN "LOBO" TORRENCE IN THE DEATH CELL?

IS HE, IN FACT, DUE FOR A STRANGE REPRIEVE?

FOR THE AMAZING TRUTH, LET US TURN BACK THE CLOCK SEVERAL EARTH HOURS...

...AND SWITCH OUR CAMERA-EYE TO A SCENE IN AN UNSUSPECTED DIMENSION EXISTING IN THE SAME SPACE AS OUR SOLAR SYSTEM ...

IN TWENTY MORE NOTARS OUR WORLD WILL BE AT THE CLOSEST POINT TO THE WORLD CALLED EARTH! IT WILL BE OUR BEST OPPORTUNITY IN THOUSANDS OF YEARS TO CONTACT IT...

CLICK! CLICK!

2

WE MUST NOT FAIL! THE EXISTENCE OF OUR WORLD DEPENDS ON OUR SUCCESS! AND WE WILL ONLY BE ABLE TO CONTACT **ONE MIND** ON EARTH! THERE WILL BE NO TIME TO DO MORE...

THREE NOTARS LEFT... TWO... ONE!

As "LOBO" TORRENCE RE-COVERS HIS BREATH...

WHAT DO YOU WANT WITH ME? WH--WHO ARE YOU?

WE ARE A CIVILIZATION IN DANGER OF DESTRUCTION! ONLY **YOU** CAN SAVE US, EARTH-MAN! **WILL YOU DO IT?**

SAY, WAIT A MINUTE! WHAT'S THE PITCH HERE? WHAT'LL I GET FOR HELPING YOU?

LISTEN...

...AND TO PERFORM THE **GREAT TASK,** WE WILL ENDOW YOU WITH OUR OWN SUPER-SCIENTIFIC POWERS! PLEASE ANSWER AT ONCE!

I AGREE! BUT YOU--ER--BETTER HURRY IT UP!

THE RADIATION IS ENTERING YOU NOW! YOU WILL KNOW **ALL** THAT IS NECESSARY... **YOU** WILL BE ALL THAT IS NECESSARY!

3

AN HOUR LATER, WHEN THE PRISON GUARD APPEARS...

YOU HAVEN'T MUCH TIME LEFT, TORRENCE! HAVE YOU ANY LAST REQUESTS TO MAKE? MOST OF THE CONS TAKE STEAK AND POTATOES...

NOT ME!

I'D JUST LIKE SOME TOY BALLOONS TO HELP ME PASS THE TIME!

TOY BALLOONS?

WHEN THE PRISONER'S LAST REQUEST IS COMPLIED WITH...

I DON'T GET IT! WHY IN THE WORLD DOES HE WANT TO SPEND HIS LAST FEW HOURS PLAYING WITH THEM?

HE DOESN'T SUSPECT I'M GONNA USE THESE TO BREAK OUTA HERE!

LATER, AFTER DARKNESS HAS FALLEN...

NOW TO COLLECT MY BALLOONS WHILE NO ONE IS LOOKING!

PEOPLE DON'T REALIZE ALL THE DIFFERENT GASES THERE ARE IN THE AIR BESIDES OXYGEN--LIKE NITROGEN, ARGON, HYDROGEN, NEON, KRYPTON! I KNOW I NEVER DID! BUT NOW WITH MY SUPER-SCIENTIFIC BRAIN--ALL I'VE GOT TO DO ...

...IS COMBINE THE DIFFERENT GASES I'VE BREATHED INTO THESE BALLOONS ... IN THE RIGHT WAY...TO DISINTEGRATE THAT WALL!

SSSSS!

MOMENTS LATER...

I'VE DONE IT! THE MOST AMAZING PRISON BREAK EVER MADE!

IN A NEARBY CITY, AFTER THE ESCAPED CONVICT GETS A CHANGE OF GARB...

NOW THAT I'M FREE, I'M NOT GONNA WASTE MY TIME WORRYIN' ABOUT THOSE OTHER WORLD GUYS! WITH THOSE SUPER-POWERS THEY GAVE ME, I'M TAKIN' CARE OF MYSELF...HEY... WHAT'S HAPPENIN' TO ME?...

SOMETHING IS FORCING ME-- TO GO TO A TYPEWRITER...I CAN'T UNDERSTAND IT...

THE NEXT DAY...

HOW LONG IS THIS GONNA GO ON? I'VE BEEN TURNING OUT THIS STUFF THAT'S COMING OUTA MY HEAD FOR MORE THAN TWENTY-FOUR HOURS SOLID NOW!

AT NOON...

IT'S FINISHED! THOSE CREATURES MUSTA GIVEN ME SOMETHING LIKE A POST-HYPNOTIC SUGGESTION TO TYPE ALL THIS STUFF! BUT IT'S FINISHED--AND NOW I CAN GET BUSY TAKIN' CARE O' "LOBO" TORRENCE!

AFTER THE STRANGE GUEST HAS LEFT THE ROOMING HOUSE..

THAT MAN LEFT ALL THESE TYPEWRITER SHEETS HERE-- FULL OF NUMBERS AND FIGURES! DEAR ME--I'D BETTER SHOW THEM TO MY DAUGHTER PEGGY-- SHE TOOK SCIENCE IN COLLEGE!

IN THE OFFICE OF *DARWIN JONES*, CHIEF OF THE *DEPARTMENT OF SCIENTIFIC INVESTIGATION*...

...AND MY MOTHER SHOWED THESE PAPERS TO ME, MR. JONES! I READ THEM AND THOUGHT THE GOVERNMENT MIGHT WANT TO SEE THEM!

INCREDIBLE!

MISS PETERS, THE GOVERNMENT APPRECIATES YOUR LOYALTY AND ENERGY IN BRINGING THIS TO US! IT IS *VERY* IMPORTANT!

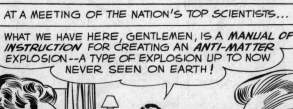

AT A MEETING OF THE NATION'S TOP SCIENTISTS...

WHAT WE HAVE HERE, GENTLEMEN, IS A *MANUAL OF INSTRUCTION* FOR CREATING AN *ANTI-MATTER* EXPLOSION--A TYPE OF EXPLOSION UP TO NOW NEVER SEEN ON EARTH!

$3 \pi = x^2 H^2$
$E + M$

"*THE RACE THAT SENT THESE INSTRUCTIONS EXPLAINS WHY THIS EXPLOSION IS NECESSARY...*"

...AND MANY THOUSANDS OF YEARS AGO OUR WORLD WAS IN YOUR *SOLAR SYSTEM*...BETWEEN EARTH AND MARS! BUT WE DROPPED THROUGH A *WARP IN SPACE*...

THOUGHT RECORDER

A COMET IS NOW ABOUT TO DESTROY US! WE NEED HELP-- FROM *YOUR* SIDE OF THE DIMENSIONAL WALL THAT LIES BETWEEN US! BY MEANS OF THE *ANTI-MATTER* EXPLOSION, WE HOPE TO SAVE OURSELVES BY SHIFTING OUR WORLD BACK TO ITS ORIGINAL POSITION IN THE SOLAR SYSTEM...

I MOVE EARTH DO ITS BEST--TO HELP SAVE THIS RACE!

I'M IN AGREEMENT!

WE MUST HURRY!

WORKING ON A "CRASH PROGRAM", A UNITED NATIONS COMMITTEE SETS UP THE APPARATUS NECESSARY FOR THE STUPENDOUS EXPLOSION IN THE WASTES OF ALASKA...

WE'RE READY!

NOW HEAR THIS! ALL PERSONNEL WILL WITHDRAW TO PREPARED CONCRETE BUNKERS IN AREAS 500 MILES FROM EXPLOSION SITE! MOVE OUT! LET'S GO!

MEANWHILE...

I GRABBED THIS PLANE BECAUSE I READ WHAT THEY'RE TRYIN' TO DO! I GOTTA STOP 'EM! IF THOSE CREATURES EVER GET BACK INTO OUR SOLAR SYSTEM -- THEY MAY GIVE ME AWAY! I DON'T WANT 'EM HERE!

RELYING ON HIS SUPER-SCIENTIFIC POWERS TO "STOP" THE EXPLOSION, TORRENCE SPEEDS NORTHWARD! BUT AS HE NEARS THE DANGER ZONE...

WRRROWWW!

WHEN THE GREAT DUST-CLOUD SETTLES SOON AFTER, AND NIGHT FALLS...

LOOK! A NEW PLANET! THE EXPLOSION SUCCEEDED! WE'VE SAVED THAT OTHER WORLD!

AND IN ARMY HEADQUARTERS...

I DON'T KNOW WHETHER OR NOT WE CAN GET THROUGH TO THE NEW PLANET WITH A RADIO MESSAGE! BUT LET'S TRY! BEAM IT AT THEM AND SAY-- "WELCOME HOME"!

YES, SIR!

The End

The INCREDIBLE EYES of Arthur Gail!

THE SENSE OF SIGHT IS SOMETHING SO FAMILIAR WE DON'T EVEN THINK ABOUT IT! BUT SUPPOSE YOUR VISION CHANGED SO THAT YOU SAW THINGS *DIFFERENTLY* FROM OTHER PEOPLE? IT HAPPENED TO ONE MAN, WHO SAW THINGS AS NO HUMAN BEING HAD EVER DONE BEFORE!

THOSE PEOPLE IN THE AIR! THEY MUST BE RIDING AN *INVISIBLE* FERRIS WHEEL!

I'M ARTHUR GAIL--AND I PRAY THAT WHAT HAPPENED TO ME WILL NEVER HAPPEN TO *YOU!*

WAX MUSEUM

"UNTIL RECENTLY, I WAS A RESEARCH WORKER IN A BIG CHEMICAL COMPANY! THEN ONE DAY..."

THE REACTION IS TOO FAST-- THE GASES ARE GOING TO EXPLODE -- AH-H!

"...A MIXTURE OF RARE GASES EXPLODED IN MY FACE..."

"WHEN I AWOKE IN A HOSPITAL, MY FIRST FEAR WAS..."

I--I WAS AFRAID MY EYES WERE HURT --BUT I CAN SEE YOU FINE, DOCTOR!

WONDERFUL! WE TOO FEARED YOUR EYES WERE AFFECTED!

"THEN, AS I SAT UP, *THIS* IS THE INCREDIBLE SIGHT I SAW!"

BUT--BUT I CAN'T SEE ANYTHING ELSE *BUT* YOU AND THE NURSE!

I DON'T UNDERSTAND--

"AS I FRANTIC-ALLY TURNED MY HEAD..."

I CAN'T SEE WALLS OR FURNITURE-- NOTHING BUT PEOPLE AND CLOTHING! I CAN SEE RIGHT THROUGH ALL THE HOSPITAL ROOMS!

IT MUST BE A TEMPORARY DISTORTION OF SIGHT DUE TO SHOCK! DON'T GET EX-CITED! WE'LL MAKE THOROUGH TESTS!

"OPTICAL TESTS REVEALED THE FANTASTIC THING THAT HAD HAPPENED TO ME..."

YOU MEAN YOU CAN'T SEE THE METAL OR PLASTIC OBJECTS IN MY HANDS?

NO, NO-- I CAN SEE NOTHING BUT YOU, AND THE PAPER IN YOUR POCKET!

"AND AFTER A SERIES OF EXAMINATIONS, THE VERDICT OF OCULISTS WAS..."

THE CHEMICAL BLAST ALTERED HIS OPTIC NERVES-- HE CAN SEE *ORGANIC* MATERIAL BUT NO *IN-ORGANIC* ONES!

IT MEANS HE CAN SEE PEOPLE, ANIMALS, CLOTH, PLANTS, PAPER-- BUT *NOT* METAL OR STONE OR PLASTICS OF ANY KIND! AND WE HAVE NO CURE FOR THIS!

"WHEN I WAS DISCHARGED FROM THE HOSPITAL..."

YOU **ARE** ON A METAL STAIR, MR. GAIL, EVEN THOUGH YOU CAN'T SEE IT! YOU MUST LEARN TO LIVE WITH YOUR NEW SIGHT!

I--I'LL TRY--

"THEY CALLED A TAXI FOR ME BUT WHEN IT CAME.."

HOP IN, MISTER!

OF COURSE--NOTHING BUT METAL AND PLASTIC IN THE TAXI--I CAN'T SEE IT! HAVE TO GROPE MY WAY IN--

"I GAVE THE ADDRESS OF MY CHEMICAL FIRM EMPLOYERS, BUT AS WE STARTED THROUGH THE STREETS..."

NO CARS, NO BUILDINGS VISIBLE--NOTHING BUT THE PEOPLE, THE PARKWAY TREES AND THE GRASS!

"AT THE CHEMICAL COMPANY, IT WAS EVEN WORSE!"

HOW CAN I WORK WHEN I CAN'T SEE ANYTHING BUT ORGANIC CHEMICALS? IT'S HOPELESS--

"BUT WHEN I GROPED MY WAY INSIDE, MR. BLISS, MY EMPLOYER, GAVE ME HOPE!"

WE KNOW OF YOUR HANDICAP, GAIL! BUT FAIRLIE, OUR MANAGER, HAS SUGGESTED THAT WITH SPECIAL EQUIPMENT YOU CAN STILL TEST ORGANIC CHEMICAL PRODUCTS!

"I TOOK ROOMS NEAR THE FIRM, AND FITTED THEM UP SO I COULD **SEE** THEM!"

BY USING WOODEN WALLS AND CEILING, AND ALL WOODEN FURNITURE, I CAN SEE THIS ROOM! AND SINCE PAPER, AND SOME PRINTING INKS ARE ORGANIC SUBSTANCES, I CAN STILL READ!

3

"MOVIES, TELEVISION, DRIVING, WERE IMPOSSIBLE FOR ME! AND WHEN I TRIED TO TRAVEL..."

WHAT EVER POSSESSED ME TO TAKE THIS PLANE-TRIP? I NEVER WILL AGAIN!

"MY ONLY OUTSIDE PLEASURE, AFTER WORK, WAS WHERE THINGS STILL LOOKED NORMAL..."

IN THE COUNTRY, EVERYTHING LOOKS THE SAME! IF I CAN SAVE ENOUGH FROM MY SALARY, I'LL BUY A LITTLE COUNTRY COTTAGE!

"BUT THE VERY NEXT DAY, THE WORST PART OF MY HORRIBLE PREDICAMENT BEGAN! AT THE OFFICE..."

A RIVAL CHEMICAL FIRM IS USING OUR SECRET FORMULA! ONLY I KNEW IT--AND I NEVER TOOK IT OUT OF THE SAFE EXCEPT WHEN ALONE!

THEN ONLY ONE OF US COULD HAVE READ IT--

YOU, GAIL, WHO SEE RIGHT THROUGH METAL, COULD HAVE READ THAT FORMULA INSIDE THE SAFE AND SOLD IT TO TO OUR RIVAL!

NO--I DIDN'T!

I NEVER TOOK THE FORMULA OUT WHEN ANYONE ELSE WAS HERE--NO ONE BUT YOU COULD STEAL IT!

THEY'LL NEVER BELIEVE I'M INNOCENT-- NEVER--

"IN PANIC FLIGHT, I RAN OUT AND..."

HEY, YOU WANNA GET RUN OVER? CAN'T YOU SEE A TEN-TON TRUCK COMING?

I CAN'T--AND IT NEARLY HIT ME!

FRAGILE

SCREEK!

4

"AS I FLED, I SPOTTED A POLICE CAR..."

THE POLICE WILL SOON BE COMBING THE CITY FOR ME-- I DAREN'T GO BACK TO MY ROOMS--

"I CLAMBERED ABOARD THE FIRST BUS THAT STOPPED, BUT...."

THAT MOTORCYCLE POLICEMAN-- IS HE AFTER ME? I'LL GET OFF THE NEXT STOP--FIND SOME CROWD I CAN HIDE IN--

"I FOUND A CROWD, AND THE FIRST SIGHT OF IT STUNNED ME!"

THOSE PEOPLE IN THE AIR--AM I LOSING MY MIND?

"THEN I REALIZED -- I HAD COME TO A CARNIVAL WITH ALL ITS RIDES AND THRILLS!"

I-I CAN'T STAND THIS! I MIGHT AS WELL GIVE MYSELF UP AS FIGHT AGAINST THE HANDICAP OF MY EYES--

"SUDDENLY, A THOUGHT CAME TO ME!"

BUT--MY EYES COULD BE A HELP, AS WELL AS A HANDICAP! A HELP IN FINDING OUT WHO REALLY STOLE THAT FORMULA! I'LL TRY IT!

5

"DESPERATELY DETERMINED, I WENT BACK INTO THE CITY-- TO THE RIVAL CHEMICAL FIRM THAT HAD ACQUIRED THE STOLEN FORMULA!"

IN THAT OFFICE-- TALKING WITH THAT COMPANY OFFICIAL-- THAT'S FAIRLIE, MY COMPANY'S MANAGER!

"MY ABILITY TO SEE THROUGH WALLS WAS PAYING OFF--AND I PRESSED INTO THE BUILDING AND LISTENED AT A DOOR I COULDN'T SEE!"

THEN *YOU'RE* NOT SUSPECTED OF THE FORMULA THEFT, FAIRLIE?

NO, THEY DIDN'T DREAM I HAD AN AUTOMATIC CAMERA HIDDEN THAT *PHOTO-GRAPHED* THE FORMULA WHEN BLISS OPENED THE SAFE! THEY'RE SURE GAIL DID IT!

"I BURST THROUGH THAT DOOR AND CONFRONTED THEM..."

I THINK THEY'LL BELIEVE MY INNOCENCE NOW, FAIRLIE!

DON'T COME NEAR ME--I WARN YOU--

"I LEAPED IN AT THE THIEF--FOR I COULDN'T SEE THE *PISTOL* IN HIS HAND!"

I WARNED YOU--

MY HEAD-- OHH--

CRACK

"DARKNESS--AND THEN I AWOKE TO A STRANGE NEW SIGHT!"

WHY, I CAN SEE AGAIN-- NOT JUST PEOPLE, BUT *EVERYTHING!*

YES--THE BULLET GRAZED YOUR FOREHEAD--AND SHOCKED YOUR OPTIC NERVES BACK INTO FULL ACTIVITY!

THE SOUND OF THAT SHOT BROUGHT POLICE--AND FAIRLIE HAS CONFESSED HIS THEFT! WE WANT YOU BACK WITH US, GAIL!

I'LL-- I'LL BE GLAD--

"AND NOW TO ME, THE MOST WONDERFUL SIGHT IN THE WORLD IS...."

JUST AN ORDINARY CITY STREET-- BUT TO ME, IT'S BEAUTIFUL!

THE END

⑥

The PAUL REVERE of TIME!

FROM OUT OF NOWHERE BOOMED A VOICE HEARD 'ROUND THE WORLD--WARNING EARTH OF GREAT DISASTERS THAT WERE ABOUT TO OCCUR! WAS THE *VOICE* TRYING TO HELP US *SAVE* OURSELVES--OR *DESTROY* OURSELVES?

THUNDERCLAPS FROM THAT CLOUD-- SOUNDING LIKE A *HUMAN VOICE!*

WARNING! A COMET'S HEAD ABOUT TO EXPLODE-- SENDING SHOWER OF METEORS ON EARTH!

EARLY IN 1957, A GIANT COMET FLASHES THROUGH THE SOLAR SYSTEM....

ASTRONOMERS HAVE PLOTTED THE COMET'S ORBIT AND EXPECT IT TO BY-PASS THE EARTH!

THE NEXT DAY, AN AMAZING WARNING ECHOES ACROSS THE CITY OF CHICAGO...

ATTENTION! I AM USING AN AMPLI-FIED ECHO TO WARN EARTH OF DANGER FROM THE COMET!

WHERE IS THAT LOUD BOOMING VOICE COMING FROM?

MYSTERIOUSLY, THE VOICE FADES AWAY...AND THEN ONE HOUR LATER IN NEW YORK CITY...

CONTINUING MY MESSAGE TO THE WORLD--THE COMET'S TAIL WILL GRAZE EARTH'S ATMOSPHERE!

NEW YORK IS 750 AIRLINE MILES FROM CHICAGO. EXACTLY THE SPEED OF SOUND PER HOUR! IS THAT MESSAGE CIRCLING EARTH?

3500 MILES AWAY, LONDON WAITS EXPECTANTLY...

AT THE SPEED OF SOUND, THE VOICE SHOULD ECHO HERE IN JUST UNDER FIVE HOURS... HERE IT COMES...!

THERE IS POISON GAS IN THE COMET'S TAIL!

ONE HOUR LATER IN MOSCOW, SOME 750 MILES EAST....

THE VOICE IS NOW SPEAKING RUSSIAN! IT SAYS, "STAY INDOORS WITH CLOSED WINDOWS FOR AN HOUR AND YOU WILL BE SAFE! THE GAS IS TOO THICK TO SEEP THROUGH CRACKS!"

AMERICAN EMBASSY

FINALLY, IN TOKYO, JAPAN...

THE VOICE FINISHED IN JAPANESE HERE..."THE COMET'S TAIL WILL STRIKE IN EXACTLY TWENTY-FOUR HOURS!"

WITH THE MESSAGE PUT TOGETHER AND TRANSLATED INTO ALL LANGUAGES, RADIO WARNINGS FLASH AROUND THE WORLD AND AT ZERO MOMENT...

LOOK, THAT BIRD...! THAT'S WHAT WOULD HAVE HAPPENED TO US IF THE VOICE HADN'T WARNED US!

AFTER THE ALL-CLEAR, THE WORLD BUZZES OVER THE MYSTERY!

WHO IS THE VOICE? HOW DID HE SEND HIS WARNING ECHO AROUND EARTH? HOW COULD HE PROPHESY THE DANGER? NOBODY KNOWS! THE WORLD IS WAITING TO HONOR THIS UNKNOWN HERO...IF HE WOULD ONLY MAKE HIMSELF KNOWN!

2

MEANWHILE, AT A NEWSPAPER OFFICE...

YOU WANT A JOB, HENRY BROWN... AND I WANT A SCOOP! BRING IN *THE VOICE* AND I'LL HIRE YOU!

I MUST SUCCEED... WHERE EVERYONE ELSE HAS FAILED!

WANDERING ABOUT THE CITY, HENRY BROWN IS AT A LOSS WHERE TO BEGIN HIS SEARCH...

HOW CAN I TRACK DOWN A MAN WHO MADE AN ECHO BOOM AROUND THE WORLD? STRANGE... BUT I HAVE A PREMONITION *THE VOICE* WILL BE HEARD FROM AGAIN!

THE WOULD-BE REPORTER'S HUNCH PROVES TRUE! THE NEXT DAY, ON ALL TV SETS...

WARNING! COMET HEAD'S POWERFUL GRAVITY WILL NEXT PULL GIANT ICEBERGS FROM OCEANS... AND SMASH COSTAL CITIES! YOU MUST BLAST THEM AT SEA... WITH YOUR ATOMIC BOMBS!

IMMEDIATELY AN INTERNATIONAL BOMBING FLEET IS DISPATCHED WITH NUCLEAR WEAPONS!

NICE AIM, IVAN!

AND YOU GOT YOURS, YANK!

MEANWHILE, HENRY BROWN IS SPEEDING OUT OF TOWN...

I CAN'T HELP MYSELF! AN OVERWHELMING IMPULSE SEIZED ME... TO SEEK *THE VOICE* IN BADLAND HOLLOW! STRANGER STILL, I HAVE ANOTHER PREMONITION THAT A *THIRD* WARNING WILL COME!

AGAIN THE UNCANNY HUNCH COMES TRUE! WEATHERMEN ARE ASTONISHED WHEN...

OUR INSTRUMENTS PREDICTED FAIR WEATHER... BUT LOOK! THUNDERCLOUDS GATHERING! IT'S A FREAK STORM OUT OF NOWHERE!

MORE FANTASTICALLY, THE ENSUING THUNDERCLAPS DUPLICATE A ROARING, HUMAN VOICE!

FINAL WARNING! COMET'S HEAD ABOUT TO EXPLODE! CLEAR ALL SHIPS OUT OF MID-PACIFIC OCEAN, WHERE SHOWER OF METEORS FROM SHATTERED COMET WILL FALL!

AFTER THE COMET EXPLODES AND BOMBARDS THE OCEAN...

JUST IN TIME! WE'RE THE LAST SHIP OUT OF THE DANGER AREA!

MEANWHILE, A PUZZLED HENRY BROWN REACHES BADLAND HOLLOW...

A WHISPER IN MY MIND SEEMS TO BE GUIDING ME TO THAT CAVE!

INSIDE THE CAVE, HENRY COMES UPON AN AMAZING SUPER-SCIENTIFIC DEVICE...

NOW THE MENTAL WHISPER TELLS ME THIS MACHINE PRODUCED THE THREE WARNINGS, THROUGH INGENIOUS SUPERSONIC ACOUSTICS! BUT— BUT THERE'S NOBODY HERE TO OPERATE IT!

SUDDENLY, AS HE EXAMINES THE MACHINE...

A SHORT CIRCUIT! IT'S MAKING MY BRAIN TINGLE WITH FANTASTIC THOUGHTS...

"IMAGES FLASHING... INTO MY MIND... I CAN SEE A FUTURE AGE..."

MY *TIME-CAR* IS READY, VOR DEX! IN IT YOU CAN REACH 1957 AND WARN EARTH OF THE COMET DANGERS!

WHAT A SCOOP FOR MY NEWSPAPER IF I CAN GO BACK TO 1957 AND TELL EARTH HOW TO AVOID THE COMET DISASTER!

THERE'S MORE THAN A NEWSPAPER SCOOP AT STAKE! IF YOU SUCCEED, WE WILL SEND OTHER "PAUL REVERES OF TIME" TO PAST AGES TO WARN OF GREAT DISASTERS!

GREAT COMET DISASTER OF 1957

BUT CAN THE *FUTURE* CHANGE *PAST* HISTORY?

HERE I GO... BACK ONE THOUSAND YEARS IN TIME... TO FIND OUT!

4

WHEN VOR DEX TIME-TRAVELS TO 1957...

NOW TO WARN THE 20TH CENTURY OF... UH... UH... IT'S ALL GETTING VAGUE! WE DIDN'T FORESEE THAT TIME-TRAVEL MAKES ONE'S *MEMORY FADE!*

OUR FUTURE SYSTEM OF WRITING IS DIFFERENT THAN THE ONE IN USE NOW--SO I CAN'T *WRITE* UNDERSTANDABLE WARNINGS TO THESE PEOPLE! LUCKILY, I TOOK ALONG THIS SUPER-ACOUSTIC MACHINE TO AMPLIFLY MY WARNINGS TO BIG CROWDS! I'LL HOOK IT UP WITH AUTOMATIC CONTROLS!

EACH SUPER-VOICE TAPE CAN HANDLE ONLY ONE TYPE OF SOUND MESSAGE! I'LL SET THE TIMERS TO PRODUCE THREE SEPARATE WARNINGS -- BY WORLD-WIDE ECHOES, STORED-UP TV SIGNALS, AND AN ARTIFICIAL THUNDERSTORM! I MUST HURRY... MEMORY FADING FAST...!

NOW TO RETURN TO THE FUTURE... I--I CAN'T REMEMBER WHERE MY *TIME-CAR* IS!... MUST FIND IT... BEFORE MY MIND GOES COMPLETELY BLANK!

WHEN THE MENTAL IMAGES FADE IN HENRY BROWN'S MIND, HE SEARCHES OUTSIDE...

DID VOR DEX FIND HIS *TIME-CAR*?... NO! THERE IT IS, SMASHED BY A LANDSLIDE! HE MUST HAVE LOST ALL MEMORY AND WANDERED AWAY... BUT WHERE IS HE NOW?

"WAIT!... IT WAS ONLY LAST WEEK THAT I MYSELF WAS DISCHARGED FROM THE HOSPITAL..."

POOR FELLOW! HE WAS FOUND IN BADLAND HOLLOW, HALF-STARVED, CLOTHES TORN, WITH TOTAL AMNESIA! WE GAVE HIM CLOTHES AND TOLD HIM TO USE THE NAME "HENRY BROWN" TO FIND A JOB!

MERCY HOSPITAL

AS "HENRY BROWN" I INSTINCTIVELY SOUGHT A *REPORTER'S* JOB! NOW I KNOW WHY I HAD *HUNCHES* OF THOSE THREE WARNINGS! AND WHY I SUBCONSCIOUSLY KNEW *WHERE* TO FIND THE *ACOUSTIC MACHINE!* THAT SHORT CIRCUIT JOLTED *BURIED MEMORIES* OUT OF MY MIND!

IT ALL ADDS UP! I...AM...VOR DEX!

THE **TIME-CAR** WRECKED! I'LL NEVER RETURN TO THE FUTURE TO BECOME THE "*PAUL REVERE OF TIME*"! I WONDER...IS THIS THE WAY INSCRUTABLE DESTINY MADE SURE I'D NEVER CHANGE HISTORY AGAIN?

THE END

STRANGE ADVENTURES

The MENTAL STAR-ROVER!

HAL CRANE COULDN'T SELL ANY OF HIS IMAGINATIVE SCIENCE-FICTION ADVENTURES-- UNTIL HE STOPPED IMAGINING THE STORIES AND STARTED TO LIVE THEM!

THE SPACE-ADVENTURES YOU WRITE ARE SO VIVID, HAL CRANE... AS IF YOU ACTUALLY *LIVE* THEM!

IF HE ONLY KNEW... I *DO* LIVE THEM!

NOW PLAYING JAKKON CONQUEROR OF THE STARS!

STORY & SCREENPLAY BY HAL CRANE.

ANXIOUS EDITORS, PUBLISHERS, *TV* AND MOVIE PRODUCERS BESIEGE THE WRITING STUDIO OF HAL CRANE...

YOUR SERIES ON *JAKKON* IS THE SENSATION OF THE YEAR, CRANE! IT APPEARS IN MAGAZINES, BOOKS, CARTOONS, *TV*, AND THE MOVIES! WE'RE ALL WAITING FOR YOUR NEXT STORY!

JAKKON CONQUEROR OF THE STARS!

GENTLEMEN! THERE WILL NEVER BE ANOTHER STORY ABOUT *JAKKON, CONQUEROR OF THE STARS!*

WHAT?! YOU MUST BE JOKING! THE SERIES IS MAKING YOU A FORTUNE! THEY'VE BEEN ACCLAIMED THE MOST IMAGINATIVE TALES OF THE CENTURY!

1

NO, GENTLEMEN! THEY ARE NOT *IMAGINATION!* LISTEN... I WILL EXPLAIN WHY I *DARE NOT* WRITE ANOTHER *JAKKON* STORY...

"JUST A YEAR AGO I WAS A STRUGGLING AUTHOR, WITHOUT A SINGLE SALE TO MY CREDIT..."

SORRY, CRANE--ANOTHER REJECT! YOUR SCIENCE-FICTION STORIES ARE LIFELESS! YOU MIGHT DO BETTER IF YOU PROJECT *YOURSELF* INTO YOUR HEROES, AS IF THEY ARE *LIVING* PEOPLE...

I'LL ...UH... TRY!

"THAT NIGHT, FOLLOWING THE EDITOR'S ADVICE, I LET MY MIND WANDER IMAGINATIVELY THROUGH SPACE ..."

I MUST *PROJECT* MYSELF INTO MY HERO'S ROLE... IMAGINE I'M A SPACE-EXPLORER IN ANOTHER GALAXY...

"SUDDENLY, I WAS A SPACE-HERO, SEEING IT ALL VIVIDLY THROUGH HIS EYES!"

I, JAKKON, TAKE OVER THIS PLANET IN THE NAME OF *DORTHIA,* MY NATIVE WORLD!

"AMAZINGLY, AS IF I WERE JAKKON HIMSELF, 'I' FOUGHT OFF THE ATTACK OF AN UNEARTHLY BEAST..."

WHAT A NARROW ESCAPE! MY RAY-GUN BARELY DROVE IT OFF IN TIME!

"I EVEN FELT HIS SHARP PANGS OF DISAPPOINTMENT AFTER A LONG SEARCH..."

MY QUEST FOR URANIUM ORE IN THIS GALAXY HAS FAILED! BUT THE METAL MUST BE FOUND-- TO POWER OUR SUPER-WEAPONS!

"WHEN MY TRANCE ENDED, EXACTLY EIGHTY-EIGHT MINUTES LATER, I FURIOUSLY BEGAN TO TYPE..."

THIS IS ONE STORY THAT WON'T BE FAKED! I FEEL I REALLY LIVED IT--AS *JAKKON!* HOW MUCH MORE REALISTIC CAN I GET?

"AS YOU ALL KNOW, MY STORY BECAME AN OVERNIGHT SENSATION! IN THE MONTHS THAT FOLLOWED, I KEPT HAVING MORE *JAKKON* DREAMS, EACH LASTING EXACTLY EIGHTY-EIGHT MINUTES..."

I EXPLORED OUR GALAXY AND DETERMINED IT IS A SPIRAL *TYPE* NEBULA, THE SPIRAL ARMS EXTENDING TO A DIAMETER OF *80,000* LIGHT YEARS. MORE THAN *100* GLOBULAR CLUSTERS OF STARS ARE DISTRIBUTED ABOUT IT...

"BUT *WERE* THEY MERE DREAMS? MY KNOWLEDGE OF ASTRONOMY WAS LIMITED AND WHEN I LOOKED UP *JAKKON'S* GALAXY..."

GOSH! IF I ONLY *IMAGINED JAKKON,* HOW COULD HE KNOW SOMETHING I *DIDN'T?* THIS IS...UNCANNY!

ASTRONOMY

ANDROMEDA NEBULA. SPIRAL TYPE. ABOUT 80,000 LIGHT-YEARS IN DIAMETER. SURROUNDED BY 100 GLOBULAR CLUSTERS.

"I DID SOME RESEARCH ON AGE-OLD YOGI PRACTICES--AND FOUND A POSSIBLE SOLUTION TO THE MYSTERY..."

WHILE IN A DEEP TRANCE, YOGIS CAN PROJECT THEIR ASTRAL SELVES FROM THEIR PHYSICAL BODIES, LETTING THEM ROAM THE UNIVERSE!--MY "ASTRAL MENTALITY" MUST HAVE CROSSED SPACE TO "SHARE" THE BODY OF *JAKKON*--WHO REALLY LIVES IN ANDROMEDA GALAXY!

"THIS WAS PROVED THE NEXT TIME MY WANDERING MIND SLIPPED INTO *JAKKON'S* BRAIN..."

YOU SAY, *JAKKON,* YOU HAVE REPEATED "DREAMS" ABOUT A FAR-OFF WORLD CALLED *EARTH?*

I SUSPECT THEY ARE MORE THAN DREAMS...THEY ARE THE VAGUE MEMORIES OF AN EARTH-MIND THAT "INHABITS" ME AT TIMES!

"I WAS NOT ALARMED AT THE MOMENT THAT *JAKKON* SUSPECTED THE TRUTH..."

I'M ONLY A MENTAL "EAVESDROPPER" WHO SHARES *JAKKON'S* EXPERIENCES, RELATING HIS ADVENTURES TO AN EARTH AUDIENCE! NO HARM CAN COME OF THIS!

3

"BUT I SHOULD HAVE BEEN WARNED BY OMINOUS QUESTIONS THE DORTHIAN SCIENTISTS KEPT ASKING JAKKON..."

THE EARTH-MIND'S MEMORIES ARE GETTING CLEARER! HIS PLANET HAS FIVE CONTINENTS AND SEVEN SEAS! AND IT IS RICH IN URANIUM ORE!

THEN YOU MUST FIND OUT WHERE EARTH IS!

"I WAS TOO BUSY WRITING UP JAKKON'S SPACE-ADVENTURES TO BE CONCERNED WHY THEY WERE SO ANXIOUS TO LOCATE EARTH..."

PERHAPS THEY JUST WANT TO MAKE A FRIENDLY VISIT TO OUR PLANET!

TV SCRIPT, EPISODE #2 "JAKKON AND THE MOON BATTLE!"

"IT WAS JUST YESTERDAY WHEN MY ASTRAL-MIND ONCE MORE SHOT ACROSS SPACE INTO JAKKON'S BRAIN... TO MEET A GRIM SHOCK!"

ON GUARD! I FEEL THE EARTHLING'S MIND STEALING WITHIN ME!

WE ARE READY! NOW OUR MIND PROBE WILL FIND OUT WHERE EARTH IS--SO WE CAN CONQUER THEIR WORLD!

ARE YOU LISTENING, EARTH MIND? THE MIND PROBE WILL FORCE EARTH'S LOCATION FROM YOU! WE WILL PLUNDER YOU OF YOUR URANIUM!

I'M TRAPPED IN JAKKON'S BRAIN, UNABLE TO LEAVE FOR EIGHTY-EIGHT MINUTES!

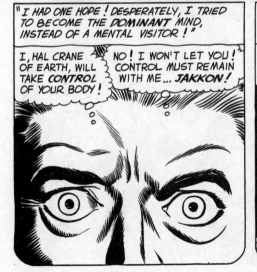

"I HAD ONE HOPE! DESPERATELY, I TRIED TO BECOME THE DOMINANT MIND, INSTEAD OF A MENTAL VISITOR!"

I, HAL CRANE OF EARTH, WILL TAKE CONTROL OF YOUR BODY!

NO! I WON'T LET YOU! CONTROL MUST REMAIN WITH ME... JAKKON!

"WHO WOULD BE THE WINNER AS OUR TWO MENTALITIES FOUGHT FURIOUSLY FOR CONTROL OF JAKKON'S BODY? FINALLY..."

I WON... HAL CRANE OF EARTH! OUT OF MY WAY! YOU WON'T PROBE MY MIND NOW!

"MY ONLY HOPE WAS TO AVOID CAPTURE UNTIL MY EARTH-MIND COULD BREAK FREE AND RETURN TO EARTH..."

I'LL USE THIS ROCKET-CAR TO HIDE IN THE HILLS SOMEWHERE!

"I HID FOR ABOUT AN HOUR, BUT THE ALARM HAD SPREAD, AND THE WHOLE PLANET WAS SEARCHING FOR ME..."

THERE HE IS! RUN HIM DOWN!

ABOUT TWENTY MINUTES TO GO...BUT I'LL BE CAUGHT NOW! WAIT... I'VE GOT ONE MORE TRICK...

"TO THE ALIENS' SURPRISE I STOPPED FLEEING!"

HE IS SURRENDERING TO US!

FOOLS! THE EARTH-MIND WOULDN'T GIVE UP THIS EASILY! IT'S ME... JAKKON! MY MENTALITY OVERPOWERED HIS AND REGAINED CONTROL OF MY BODY!

"MY TRICK WORKED, PRETENDING JAKKON WAS BACK IN CONTROL! TO MAKE IT LOOK GOOD..."

HOLD ME TIGHT, GUARDS! WE CAN'T TAKE A CHANCE OF HAVING THE EARTHLING'S MIND GAIN DOMINANCE OVER ME AGAIN! RUSH ME TO THE LABORATORY WITHOUT DELAY!

WE'LL USE THIS ROCKET SPEEDSTER!

"EXACTLY AS I HAD HOPED! ONCE WE TOOK OFF, I HAD ONLY TWO GUARDS TO DEAL WITH... AND..."

THAT TAKES CARE OF THEM!

"DRIVING INTO SPACE AT TOP SPEED, I AVOIDED THE PURSUING SHIPS WITH AERIAL MANEUVERS..."

I'LL ZOOM BEHIND THIS COMET, LETTING THE GLARE BLIND THEM! ONLY ABOUT *FIVE* MINUTES TO GO! WILL I MAKE IT?...

"JUST AS THEY CAUGHT MY SHIP..."

GOT HIM!

TOO LATE! MY EARTH-MIND IS LEAVING *JAKKON'S* BRAIN!

AS HAL CRANE FINISHES HIS STRANGE ADVENTURE...

NOW YOU SEE, GENTLEMEN, WHY I *DARE* NOT RETURN TO *JAKKON'S* BODY AND WORLD--IT WOULD EXPOSE EARTH TO INVASION! *NEXT* TIME THEY SURELY WILL HAVE PREPARED A *BETTER* TRAP FOR ME! THIS IS THE END OF MY SERIES ABOUT *JAKKON!*

WILL THEY SEARCH FOR EARTH IN THEIR SPACE-SHIPS? WILL *JAKKON* FIND US EVEN THOUGH IT IS ONLY ONE CHANCE IN A TRILLION? EARTH MUST BE ON GUARD CONSTANTLY...FOR *JAKKON*, CONQUEROR OF THE STARS!

The End

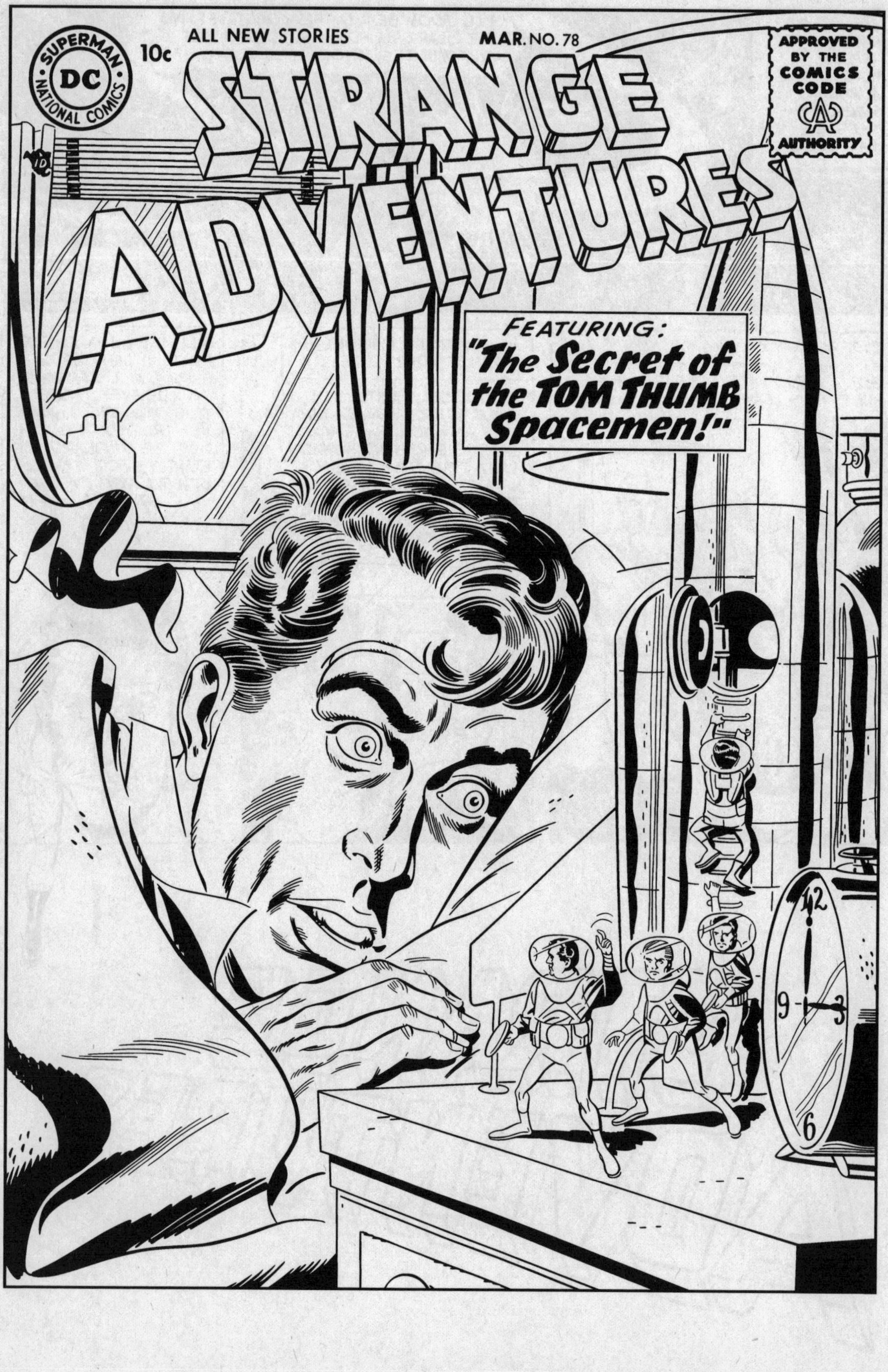
SUPERMAN DC NATIONAL COMICS
10c
ALL NEW STORIES
MAR. NO. 78
APPROVED BY THE COMICS CODE AUTHORITY
STRANGE ADVENTURES
FEATURING: "The Secret of the TOM THUMB Spacemen!"

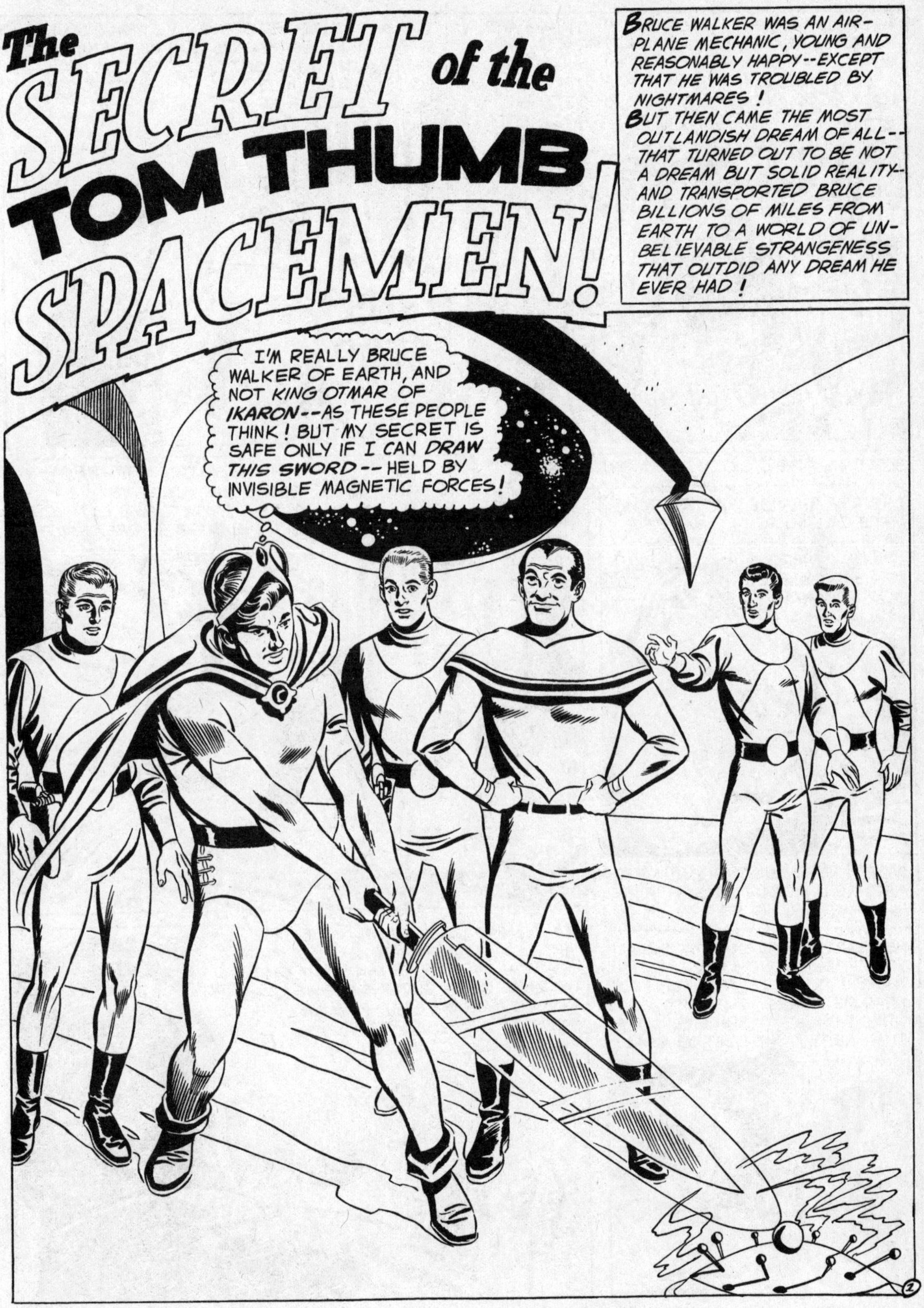
The SECRET of the TOM THUMB SPACEMEN!
BRUCE WALKER WAS AN AIRPLANE MECHANIC, YOUNG AND REASONABLY HAPPY--EXCEPT THAT HE WAS TROUBLED BY NIGHTMARES! BUT THEN CAME THE MOST OUTLANDISH DREAM OF ALL--THAT TURNED OUT TO BE NOT A DREAM BUT SOLID REALITY--AND TRANSPORTED BRUCE BILLIONS OF MILES FROM EARTH TO A WORLD OF UNBELIEVABLE STRANGENESS THAT OUTDID ANY DREAM HE EVER HAD!
I'M REALLY BRUCE WALKER OF EARTH, AND NOT KING OTMAR OF IKARON--AS THESE PEOPLE THINK! BUT MY SECRET IS SAFE ONLY IF I CAN DRAW THIS SWORD--HELD BY INVISIBLE MAGNETIC FORCES!

As BRUCE WALKER, A MECHANIC IN AN AIRPLANE FACTORY, LEAVES FOR HOME AFTER A DAY'S WORK...

YOU DON'T LOOK GOOD, BRUCE! ANYTHING WRONG?

MY *DREAMS*, PAUL! THEY'RE GETTING ME DOWN...

I'VE BEEN TROUBLED BY THE MOST AWFUL DREAMS, NIGHT AFTER NIGHT! IT'S GETTING SO I'M AFRAID TO GO TO SLEEP...

I WISH I COULD HELP YOU, BRUCE... BUT I'M NO DOCTOR!

BUS STOP

SUDDENLY, AT 3 O'CLOCK THAT NIGHT...

I HEARD A STRANGE VOICE CALLING MY NAME--WOKE ME UP! EH? THERE IT IS AGAIN--AND I'M NOT *DREAMING*!

ATTENTION, BRUCE WALKER!

AS THE STARTLED AIRPLANE WORKER WHIRLS AROUND...

AT LAST WE HAVE FOUND YOU!

T-TALK ABOUT NIGHTMARES-- THIS IS THE WORST YET! I GUESS I'M NOT AWAKE, AFTER ALL! I *MUST BE DREAMING*--!

DAZED, INCREDULOUS, BRUCE PINCHES HIMSELF TO SEE IF HE IS AWAKE OR ASLEEP...

WE SEARCHED FOR YOU THROUGHOUT THE GALAXY! HEAR ME--THERE IS NOT MUCH TIME LEFT!

I'M AWAKE ALL RIGHT--I CAN FEEL PAIN! BUT THESE MINIATURE SPACEMEN...THEY CAN'T BE *REAL*!

OF COURSE YOU ARE AWAKE, BRUCE WALKER, AND WE ARE AS REAL AS YOU ARE! NOT ONLY THAT, BUT OUR NORMAL SIZE IS THE SAME AS YOURS! LISTEN, I'LL EXPLAIN SWIFTLY... BY TELEPATHY...

2

WE ARE FROM IKARON, A WORLD IN A REMOTE SECTOR OF THE MILKY WAY GALAXY! WE HAVE ALWAYS LIVED IN PEACE AND REJOICED IN OUR SCIENTIFIC WONDERS...BUT NOW OUR WORLD IS IN *DANGER!*

OTMAR THE YOUNG, OUR KING, HAS TRIED TO KEEP THE PEACE, BUT HIS REIGN IS THREATENED BY HIS UNCLE, POLIMAR, A WICKED PLOTTER WHO SEEKS TO OVERTHROW HIM!

BUT--

WH-- WHAT'S ALL THAT GOT TO DO WITH *ME?*

IT IS THE CUSTOM ON IKARON FOR HIS MAJESTY TO RENEW HIS KINGSHIP BY THE *CEREMONY OF THE SWORD*--EACH YEAR ON THE SAME DAY! BUT UNFORTUNATELY...

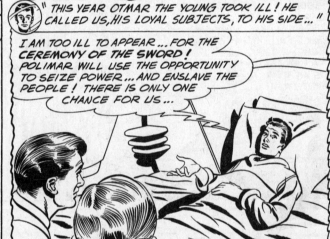

"*THIS YEAR OTMAR THE YOUNG TOOK ILL! HE CALLED US, HIS LOYAL SUBJECTS, TO HIS SIDE...*"

I AM TOO ILL TO APPEAR...FOR THE *CEREMONY OF THE SWORD!* POLIMAR WILL USE THE OPPORTUNITY TO SEIZE POWER...AND ENSLAVE THE PEOPLE! THERE IS ONLY ONE CHANCE FOR US...

YOU MUST SEARCH THROUGHOUT THE UNIVERSE FOR SOMEONE WHO LOOKS *EXACTLY* LIKE ME...AND PERSUADE THAT PERSON TO TAKE MY PLACE AT THE *CEREMONY OF THE SWORD!* BUT POLIMAR MUST NOT SUSPECT...

"BY OUR SUPER-SCIENCE WE REDUCED OURSELVES IN SIZE, ALL OF US AND OUR ROCKET-SHIP, BEFORE SETTING OUT..."

THE REDUCED SIZE WILL ENABLE US TO TRAVEL FASTER THROUGH SPACE AND LESSEN THE DANGER OF A METEOR COLLISION!

③

"BY OUR SPECIAL ATOMIC-WAVE SCANNERS, WE VIEWED BILLIONS OF FACES ON MANY WORLDS BEFORE WE CAME HERE, AND LOCATED YOU ..."

ME?

YES! YOU ARE THE EXACT DUPLICATE OF OTMAR THE YOUNG! ONLY YOU CAN SAVE THE PEACE ON OUR WORLD! DO NOT REFUSE!

WE WILL REDUCE YOU IN SIZE FOR TRAVEL IN OUR SHIP WITH US! I SAY YOU WILL COME -- EVERY-THING DEPENDS ON YOU!

HOW CAN I RE-FUSE SUCH A HUMANITARIAN DEED...?

ALL RIGHT! I'LL DO IT!

AFTER BEING GARBED IN A SPACE-SUIT, A TINY BUT INTRICATE MECHANISM APPEARS FROM INSIDE THE ROCKET...

STAND PERFECTLY STILL! THE SIZE-REDUCTION WILL ONLY TAKE A MOMENT!

G-GO AHEAD...

I-I'M GETTING SMALLER...

SMALLER!

H-HOW STRANGE MY BEDROOM LOOKS NOW-- SO ENORMOUS... LIKE THE BED-ROOM OF A GIANT!

HURRY! THERE IS NO TIME TO LOSE!

NOT LONG AFTERWARD IN THE CEREMONIAL ROOM ON THE WORLD OF IKARON -- WHERE ALL EYES ARE RIVETED ON A SWORD SUSPENDED IN AIR BY MAGNETIC CURRENTS...

KING OTMAR HAS FAILED TO APPEAR FOR THE SWORD CEREMONY! HE MUST BE AILING AS HAS BEEN RUMORED! BUT BY THIS FAILURE HE LOSES THE THRONE -- EH?

MAKE WAY FOR THE KING!

4

HAIL THE KING!

I HOPE I CAN DO AS I'VE BEEN COACHED... AND DON'T MAKE ANY SLIPS!

IN THE ROLE OF THE KING, EARTHMAN BRUCE WALKER ACTS HIS REGAL BEST...

SO THE KING IS NOT SICK?

YOU SEE FOR YOURSELF, POLIMAR! NOW ONE SIDE... SO THAT I MAY FULFILL THE ANCIENT RITUAL AND DRAW THE SWORD!

BUT AS BRUCE GRIPS THE SWORD...

S-SOMETHING'S WRONG... THEY TOLD ME THE SWORD, HELD BY MAGNETIC FORCES, WOULD AUTOMATICALLY COME LOOSE WHEN I TUGGED AT IT... BUT I CAN'T BUDGE IT!

NO USE! CAN'T GET IT LOOSE! BUT POLIMAR IS ONLY WAITING FOR SOMETHING LIKE THIS TO USURP THE THRONE FOR HIMSELF...! I'VE GOT TO GET IT OUT... AND I HAVE AN IDEA...

SWIFTLY SEIZING THE RAY-GUN FROM THE HOLSTER OF HIS FRIEND, THE ROCKETSHIP COMMANDER, THE EARTHMAN AIMS IT...

THIS RADIATION SHOULD DISRUPT THE MAGNETIC FIELD HOLDING THE SWORD IN PLACE--

Y-YOUR MAJESTY--?!

KRRACK!

THEN NEXT MOMENT...

DID IT!

HAIL THE KING!

BY THE SEVEN MOONS--I MUST LEAVE HERE QUICKLY!

BUT BEFORE THE POWER-HUNGRY POLIMAR CAN FLEE...

WAIT, POLIMAR! I ACCUSE YOU OF TRYING TO PREVENT THE DRAWING OF THE SWORD BY CAUSING THE MAGNETIC FIELD IN THE CONTAINER TO REMAIN FIXED SO THAT THE SWORD WOULD NOT MOVE!

NO-- NO!

WITH AN EARTHLY MOTION, THE "KING" LASHES OUT...

THIS MAY NOT BE THE *IKARON* WAY OF DOING THINGS -- BUT MAYBE THEY CAN LEARN A FEW THINGS FROM EARTH -- LIKE HOW TO HANDLE THEIR FISTS!

LATER, WITH POLIMAR BEING HELD FOR TRIAL, THE REAL KING AND HIS COUNTERPART MEET...

OUR KINGDOM IS SAFE, THANKS TO YOU, BRUCE WALKER! AS A TOKEN OF GRATITUDE, I PRESENT YOU WITH THIS GIFT! I HOPE YOU WILL FIND A GOOD USE FOR IT!

IN HIS OWN ROOM BACK ON EARTH SOME TIME AFTERWARD, BRUCE WALKER PREPARES TO USE HIS GIFT...

THE GIFT WAS A *DREAM- SELECTOR!* I CAN HAVE ANY DREAM I WANT NOW -- JUST BY TURNING THE DIAL! MY NIGHTMARE SLEEPS ARE OVER NOW -- THANKS TO *OTMAR THE YOUNG* -- THE *REAL OTMAR THE YOUNG,* I MEAN!

The End

the LIFE-BATTERY!

LONG BEFORE MAN BECAME THE DOMINANT LIFE FORM ON EARTH, OTHER CREATURES HAD THEIR "DAY" AS MASTERS OF OUR PLANET--DINOSAURS, PTERODACTYLS, MASTODONS, SABER-TOOTHED TIGERS. SUDDENLY, GEOLOGICALLY SPEAKING, EACH OF THESE PREHISTORIC CREATURES BECAME EXTINCT! NO ONE KNOWS WHY! IS MANKIND DOOMED TO SUFFER THE SAME MYSTERIOUS FATE THAT OVERTOOK THESE PREHISTORIC CREATURES?

IN HIS MOUNTAIN LABORATORY, SCIENTIST STERLING MARSH SEEKS THE SOLUTION TO AN AGE-OLD MYSTERY...

MORE THAN A HUNDRED MILLION YEARS AGO, THE *DINOSAURS* REIGNED SUPREME ON EARTH! THEN, IN A *"GEOLOGICAL DAY"*, THEY SUDDENLY BECAME EXTINCT! *WHY?*

TYRANNOSAURUS REX! THE MIGHTIEST AND MOST FEARSOME CREATURE THAT EVER LIVED ON EARTH! WHO--OR WHAT-- COULD HAVE CAUSED IT TO BECOME EXTINCT?

AFTER THE REPTILES CAME THE *ARCHAEOPTERYX* BIRDS-- FOLLOWED BY SUCH MAMMALS AS THE *CREODONT, HOPLOPHONEUS,* AND *UINTATHERIUM!* WHATEVER BLIGHT KILLED OFF THESE CREATURES--WILL IT SOMEDAY STRIKE AT MANKIND TOO?

"MY RESEARCHES SHOW THAT NO RIVAL CREATURE COULD HAVE KILLED THE *TYRANNOSAURUS REX!* IT WAS TOO POWERFUL!"

"ONE THEORY TO EXPLAIN THESE EXTINCTIONS SUGGESTS THAT VARIOUS *ICE AGES* DESTROYED ALL LIVING THINGS! BUT THE CREATURES COULD HAVE EMIGRATED SOUTHWARD--AND AVOIDED THE FRIGID TEMPERATURES..."

THE SUN MIGHT HAVE FLARED UP--OR THE ANIMALS' FOOD SUPPLY CUT SHORT--OR THE OXYGEN CONTENT OF THE AIR CHANGED--BUT NONE OF THESE THEORIES HAS ANY RELIABLE EVIDENCE TO SUPPORT IT!

MY THEORY IS SOMETHING FROM OUTER SPACE HAS REPEATEDLY CAUSED THE RISE AND FALL OF LIFE ON EARTH-- METEOR SHOWERS!

IN A LEAD-LINED ROOM OF HIS MOUNTAIN LABORATORY, STERLING MARSH EXAMINES A *CHUNK OF METAL*...

I'VE ISOLATED A STRANGE, RADIATING METAL FROM THIS METEOR-- A RADIATION THAT I BELIEVE SUSTAINS ALL LIFE ON EARTH!

BY BOMBARDING THE METEORITE WITH THE RAYS FROM THIS MACHINE, I CAN SLOWLY DECREASE ITS RADIATION RATE...

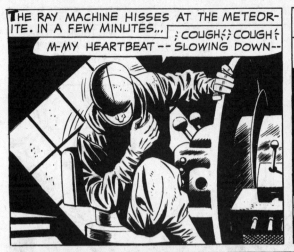

THE RAY MACHINE HISSES AT THE METEOR-ITE. IN A FEW MINUTES...

;COUGH; ;COUGH;

M-MY HEARTBEAT -- SLOWING DOWN--

WEAKLY THE SCIENTIST LEANS FORWARD, AND HIS HAND STABS OUT...

I JUST MANAGED TO THROW IT ON *INCREASE*-- BUT I GOT MY *PROOF*.! THIS METEORITE METAL IS LIKE A *BATTERY*--DISCHARGING A *VITAL LIFE FORCE* TO ALL LIVING THINGS.!

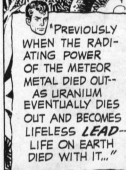

"PREVIOUSLY WHEN THE RADI-ATING POWER OF THE METEOR METAL DIED OUT-- AS URANIUM EVENTUALLY DIES OUT AND BECOMES LIFELESS *LEAD*-- LIFE ON EARTH DIED WITH IT..."

"LATER, AS MORE METEOR SHOWERS FELL ON EARTH, LIFE SPRANG UP AGAIN, BUT THIS TIME IT WAS THE FLYING REPTILE BIRD THAT BECAME SUPREME!"

MANKIND'S PROBLEM, THEN, IS TO KEEP ENOUGH METEOR METAL ALWAYS AVAILABLE SO THAT WE WILL ALWAYS HAVE THE USE OF ITS LIFE-GIVING PROPERTIES!

"AFTER THE FLYING REPTILES DIED OUT, THE MAMMALS APPEARED-- CULMINATING WITH THE RISE OF *HOMO SAPIENS*..."

③

THE NEXT DAY, HIGH ABOVE THE FROZEN ARCTIC WASTES...

LOOK! FLYING SHIP FROM ANOTHER WORLD!

IT IS DRAWING METAL ROCK UP TOWARDS IT!

FAR OUT AT SEA, THE SAME PHENOMENON IS REPEATED!

METEORS THAT HAVE FALLEN *INTO* THE SEA--FLYING *UP* TO THAT SPACESHIP!

MUSEUM VISITORS ARE STARTLED WHEN...

THE METEORS ON DISPLAY HERE-- SHOOTING UPWARDS!

WORDS CIRCLE THE EARTH AS MANKIND MOBILIZES TO FIGHT THE STRANGE INVADER...

THE LATEST REPORT WE HAVE RECEIVED SAYS THE SPACESHIP IS MAKING A GREAT SPIRAL AROUND OUR PLANET--COVERING EVERY INCH OF LAND AND WATER!

"SO FAR THE SHIP HAS CAUSED NO HARM! EVIDENTLY ITS CREW DESIRES ONLY TO LOOT OUR PLANET'S METEORS..."

THERE GOES A GIGANTIC METEOR--THE ONE THAT ORIGINALLY CRASHED ON EARTH AND CAUSED *METEOR CRATER!*

4

In his lonely mountain laboratory, scientist Sterling Marsh reaches a grim conclusion...

NOT ONLY IS EARTH BEING ROBBED--MANKIND IS BEING MURDERED! AND I'M THE ONLY ONE IN THE WHOLE WORLD WHO REALIZES IT!

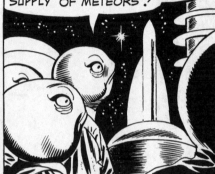

"IF MY THEORY IS CORRECT, ONLY THOSE PLANETS WITHIN THE ORBIT OF METEOR SHOWERS HAVE LIFE ON THEM! MY GUESS IS THAT THOSE SPACEMEN ARE ROBBING OUR METEORS BECAUSE METEOR SHOWERS HAVE STOPPED FALLING ON THEIR WORLD."

IT HAS BEEN *YEARS* SINCE A METEOR HAS FALLEN ON OUR PLANET! OUR CIVILIZATION IS DOOMED UNLESS WE CAN REPLENISH OUR SUPPLY OF METEORS!

WITHOUT THE LIFE-GIVING RAYS OF THE RADIATING METEOR METAL, MAN WILL BECOME AS EXTINCT AS THE DINOSAUR AND THE OTHER FOSSILS!

SOON THE ALIEN SPACESHIP WILL APPEAR ABOVE MY LABORATORY! ITS POWERFUL MAGNET WILL DRAW THIS METEOR ABOARD...

BUT I CAN TURN MY METEOR INTO A *WEAPON!* BY INCREASING ITS RADIATIONS IT WILL PARALYZE EVERY LIVING BEING WITHIN THAT SPACESHIP!

SOON AFTER, THE GLOWING METEOR LEAPS SKYWARD...

THERE IT IS! IT BETTER WORK--OR MANKIND IS DOOMED TO EXTINCTION!

BY CHAIN REACTION, MY METEOR OUGHT TO ACTIVATE ALL THE MILLIONS OF METEORS THOSE SPACEMEN HAVE BEEN COLLECTING! INCREASED MORE THAN A MILLIONFOLD, THE SUPER-RADIATIONS WILL OVERPOWER THOSE ALIENS!

LUCKILY, THE SPACESHIP IS SO HIGH UP, THE SUPER-RADIATIONS WILL NOT EFFECT LIFE ON EARTH! I'LL NEED A PLANE TO DETERMINE THE RESULT OF MY EXPERIMENT!

HOURS LATER A HUGE BOMBER TAKES OFF FROM AN ARMY AIR FORCE BASE...

I HOPE YOU'RE RIGHT, MARSH--OUR LIVES DEPEND ON IT!

WE'LL KNOW SOON ENOUGH!

WHILE CLINGING TO THE SPACESHIP IN MAGNETIZED METAL BOOTS, MARSH TURNS ON HIS RADIATION MACHINE...

THE ALIENS HAVE BEEN KNOCKED OUT! NOW TO TURN THOSE METEORS' RADIOCTIVITY BACK TO NORMAL!

STILL LATER, WHEN THE SPACESHIP AND ITS IMPRISONED CREW HAVE BEEN BROUGHT DOWN TO EARTH....

I HAVE THE REPORTS OF THE PLACES FROM WHICH THE METEORS WERE TAKEN!

GOOD! WE'LL RETURN THEM ALL TO THEIR ORIGINAL LOCATIONS!

FROM THEN ON, EACH METEOR SHOWER THAT FALLS ON EARTH IS GREETED WITH CHEERS...

THAT'S THE *LEONID METEOR SHOWER!* IT STARTS FALLING ON EARTH EVERY NOVEMBER 12TH!

EVEN IF THEY STOPPED FALLING, LIFE ON EARTH WOULD CONTINUE! WE COULD ALWAYS RECHARGE THE METEORS THAT ARE HERE--THANKS TO STERLING MARSH'S RADIATION MACHINE!

THE END

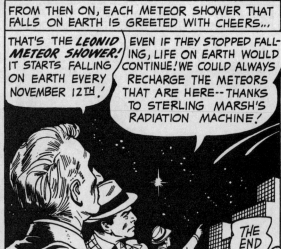

6

the MAGIC HORN from SPACE!

IF YOU WERE STRANDED ON AN ISLAND, WITH ALL THE NECESSARY MATERIALS, COULD YOU MAKE AN AIRPLANE? A RADIO SET? EVEN A SIMPLE COMPASS? SEE HOW A MODERN ROBINSON CRUSOE FARED WHEN HIS LIFE DEPENDED ON MAKING SOMETHING THAT WOULD RESCUE HIM FROM THE ISLAND!

THE **SPACE-HORN** CREATED THIS **GUN** FROM MY THOUGHTS... BUT WILL IT WORK AGAINST THIS ISLAND'S SAVAGE NATIVES?

SOMEWHERE BENEATH THE SEA LIES THE MOST WONDROUS TREASURE ON EARTH--A MAGIC "HORN OF PLENTY" THAT WILL GRANT ME ANYTHING I DESIRE! I FIRST CAME ACROSS THE HORN...

"...A MONTH AGO, WHILE I WAS FLYING IN MY HELICOPTER OVER SOME TROPICAL ISLANDS, PROSPECTING THE MODERN WAY..."

ANY LARGE DEPOSITS OF ORE BELOW WILL BE DETECTED BY MY **MAGNETOMETER!***

***EDITOR'S NOTE:** RECENTLY DEVISED FOR AERIAL PROSPECTING, THE **MAGNETOMETER** REGISTERS VARIATIONS IN EARTH'S MAGNETIC FIELD, CAUSED BY LARGE DEPOSITS OF METALLIC ORES!

"BUT I STUMBLED ON A FIND MORE AMAZING THAN GOLD OR URANIUM.'"

THAT WRECK LOOKS LIKE A *FLYING SAUCER*! I WONDER IF IT'S A SPACESHIP FROM ANOTHER WORLD?

"AFTER LANDING NEAR THE SAUCER, THE FIRST THING I DISCOVERED WAS--"

THE ALIEN PILOT--DEAD! HE MUST HAVE SUFFOCATED WHEN HIS BREATHING HELMET CRACKED! EVIDENTLY OUR EARTHLY AIR WAS POISONOUS TO HIM!

THIS SHIP WASN'T WRECKED BECAUSE OF A CRASH-LANDING! MY GUESS IS THAT THE ISLAND'S NATIVES CAUSED THIS DAMAGE-- PROBABLY BECAUSE FLYING MACHINES ARE *"TABOO"* HERE!

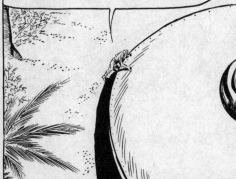

"BUT THE INSIDE WAS INTACT AND I CAME UPON THE CURIOUS HORN..."

IT LOOKS LIKE THE MYTHOLOGICAL *"HORN OF PLENTY"*! WONDER WHAT PURPOSE IT SERVED?

"MEANWHILE, THE NATIVES FOUND MY HELICOPTER AND..."

DESTROY THE EVIL FLYING MACHINE, THEN CAPTURE THE WITCH DOCTOR WHO FLEW IT!

"BOLTING THE DOOR, I WAS TEMPORARILY SAFE IN THE SPACESHIP... BUT MY SITUATION SEEMED HOPELESS!"

WITHOUT MY PLANE, I'M STRANDED HERE! I CAN'T EVEN TRY FLYING THIS SPACESHIP -- I NOTICED THE FUEL TANKS EMPTY FROM EVAPORATION!

2

"MOMENTS LATER, THE DOOR BUCKLED AS THE NATIVES BROUGHT A BATTERING RAM INTO PLAY..."

THE NATIVES WILL SWARM IN SOON... AND I'M UNARMED! GOSH, I WISH I HAD A *GUN* TO DRIVE THEM OFF!

"UNCANNILY, MY WISH WAS ANSWERED... BY THE HORN!"

GOSH! A...A GUN POPPED OUT OF THE HORN! IT SEEMS FANTASTIC -- BUT MAYBE IN SOME SCIENTIFIC WAY THE HORN *CREATES* ANY OBJECT WISHED FOR! HOW CAN IT WORK?

ZZZZZ000
ZOOP!

"EINSTEIN'S THEORY SUPPLIED A LIKELY ANSWER..."

THE ATOMIC BOMB TRANSFORMS MATTER INTO PURE ENERGY! BUT EINSTEIN SAID THE *REVERSE* IS ALSO TRUE -- ENERGY CAN BE CONVERTED TO MATTER! THE HORN CREATED A *GUN* OUT OF THE ENERGY OF MY THOUGHT-WISH!

"BUT WHEN I TRIED TO FIRE THE GUN AND SCARE OFF THE NATIVES..."

IT-IT DOESN'T WORK! SOMEHOW, IT FEELS TOO LIGHT FOR A GUN -- AS IF IT'S ONLY A HOLLOW SHELL!

"TO TEST MY THEORY, I SQUEEZED THE GUN IN MY HANDS... AND IT CRUMBLED!"

I WAS RIGHT! THE HORN JUST DUPLICATED THE *IMAGE* OF A GUN THAT I ENVISIONED IN MY MIND! IT COULD ONLY MAKE A REAL GUN IF I THOUGHT OF THE INTERIOR PARTS... *WHICH I DON'T KNOW!*

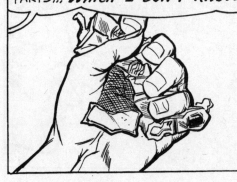

"AFTER MORE MENTAL WISHES..."

ALL I GOT FROM THE HORN WERE WORTH-LESS IMITATIONS OF WEAPONS! IT'D BE JUST AS USELESS ASKING FOR A *RADIO, TELEGRAPHY SET* OR OTHER INVENTIONS! WITHOUT ANY KNOWLEDGE OF THEIR COMPLEX INTERIOR MECHANISMS, I COULDN'T MAKE THEM WORK!

③

"BUT BEFORE THE NATIVES BATTERED DOWN THE DOOR, INSPIRATION STRUCK ME!"

I DO KNOW THE ATOMIC STRUCTURE OF THE SIMPLEST TYPES OF MATTER! HYDROGEN, FOR INSTANCE... HAS ONE ELECTRON CIRCLING ONE PROTON! IN HELIUM, TWO ELECTRONS CIRCLE TWO PROTONS AND TWO NEUTRONS!

HYDROGEN
ELECTRON
NUCLEUS

HELIUM
ELECTRONS
NUCLEUS

"RECALLING COLLEGE CHEMISTRY, I LISTED THE FIRST 11 ELEMENTS WHICH HAD SIMPLE ATOMIC STRUCTURES..."

BEYOND THAT, THEY GET TOO COMPLEX! BUT I KNOW A WAY TO SAVE MYSELF FROM THE NATIVES BY USING JUST THOSE COMMON ELEMENTS, WHICH I CAN COMMAND FROM THE *HORN!*

HYDROGEN   NITROGEN
HELIUM   OXYGEN
LITHIUM   FLUORINE
BERYLLIUM   NEON
BORON   SODIUM
CARBON

"WHEN THE NATIVES BURST IN, I WAS READY..."

HALT! I AM A GREAT WITCH DOCTOR WITH MAGIC POWERS! WATCH AND I WILL MAKE *WATER BURN!*

"THE SPACE-HORN MADE MY BOAST COME TRUE!"

I WISHED FOR WATER-- H_2O! THEN *SODIUM* METAL, ELEMENT 11!

ZZZZ OO!
ZOOP!

BY ZAMBA! HE MADE WATER BURN! IT IS MAGIC!

SODIUM METAL DECOMPOSES WATER INTO GASEOUS HYDROGEN AND OXYGEN, WHICH THEN IGNITE AND FORM FLAMES! I REMEMBERED THAT CLASSROOM DEMONSTRATION IN CHEMISTRY!

4

"THEN I GAVE THE NATIVES ANOTHER DEMONSTRATION OF MY POWERS..."

HIS MAGIC IS PUTTING OUT THE FIRE!

I THOUGHT-WISHED FOR *CARBON DIOXIDE GAS* FROM THE HORN, WHICH EXTINGUISHES ANY FLAME!

"MY SIMPLE CHEMICAL EXPERIMENTS AWED THE ASTOUNDED NATIVES!"

I WISHED FOR *NEON* AND ELECTRICAL SPARKS, WHICH ARE REALLY A STREAM OF FREE ELECTRONS! THAT'S HOW NEON SIGNS WORK!

HE MADE RED LIGHT IN AIR! TRULY HE IS A GREAT WITCH DOCTOR!

"SOON..."

WE WILL NO LONGER MOLEST YOU, O WIZARD!

I'M SAFE FROM CAPTURE! BUT I'M STILL MAROONED HERE WITH MY SMASHED PLANE!

"BUT AGAIN, THE WONDERFUL HORN SOLVED MY DILEMMA..."

I WISH FOR *HYDRAZINE** TO FILL THE SPACESHIP'S FUEL TANK!

*EDITOR'S NOTE: A FUMING LIQUID, HYDRAZINE [N_2H_4] IS USED AS A POWERFUL ROCKET PROPELLANT, BURNED WITH LIQUID OXYGEN!

"SEATING MYSELF AT THE CONTROLS, I PUSHED LEVERS UNTIL..."

THE HORN ALSO PRODUCED LIQUID OXYGEN... THERE GO THE ROCKETS! AFTER I FLY HOME, I'LL STUDY THE COMPLEX ATOMS OF GOLD, DIAMONDS, URANIUM AND OTHER PRECIOUS ELEMENTS! THE HORN WILL PRODUCE ANYTHING I THINK OF!

ROARRR!

"BUT UNFAMILIAR WITH THE ALIEN SHIP, I LOST CONTROL AND..."

IT'S HEADING FOR OUTER SPACE! I'VE GOT TO BAIL OUT...WITH A *PARACHUTE* MADE BY THE HORN!

⑤

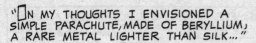

"ON MY THOUGHTS I ENVISIONED A SIMPLE PARACHUTE, MADE OF BERYLLIUM, A RARE METAL LIGHTER THAN SILK..."

I WISH FOR THE NECESSARY THIN SHEETS AND HARNESS OF BERYLLIUM! FAR LIGHTER THAN ALUMINUM, IT WILL FLOAT ME SAFELY DOWN!

"THEN I JUMPED--WITH ONLY MY MENTALLY-CREATED PARACHUTE TO SAVE ME FROM A FREE FALL INTO THE SEA..."

I'LL BE PICKED UP BY THAT SHIP BELOW!

"BUT MY HASTILY FORMED PARACHUTE WAS CRUDE AND COLLAPSED TOO SOON! I HIT THE WATER VIOLENTLY AND..."

THE HORN... IT WAS KNOCKED FROM MY HANDS...!

"WHEN A RESCUE PARTY APPEARED FROM THE VESSEL..."

LET ME GO... I'VE GOT TO GET BACK INTO THE WATER--RECOVER MY HORN--BEFORE IT SINKS INTO THE OCEAN DEPTHS...

HE'S FIGHTING TO GET AWAY! MUST BE OUT OF HIS MIND!

"ABOARD SHIP, THEY COULDN'T UNDERSTAND WHY I STARED BACK, MISERABLE AND UNHAPPY..."

WHAT ARE YOU LOOKING FOR?

ER... NEVER MIND, CAPTAIN!

THE HORN SANK FROM SIGHT-- AND THE SPACESHIP LEFT EARTH! HE'D NEVER BELIEVE MY STORY!

THE FIRST CHANCE I GOT, I CAME BACK TO THIS SPOT! I'LL BE THE WEALTHIEST MAN ON EARTH... IF I FIND THAT "HORN OF PLENTY"!

THE END

6

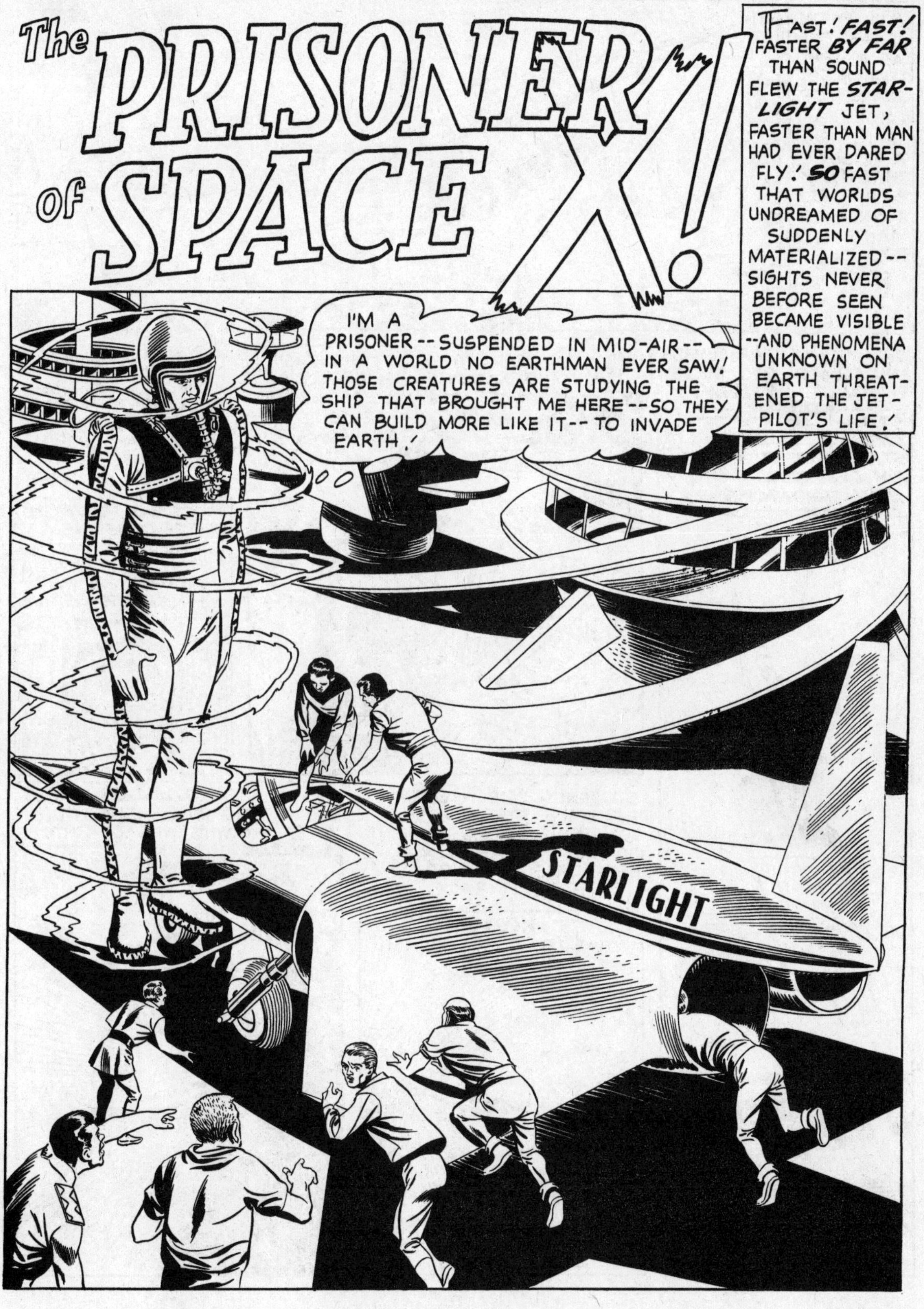
The PRISONER of SPACE X!
FAST! FAST! FASTER BY FAR THAN SOUND FLEW THE STARLIGHT JET, FASTER THAN MAN HAD EVER DARED FLY! SO FAST THAT WORLDS UNDREAMED OF SUDDENLY MATERIALIZED--SIGHTS NEVER BEFORE SEEN BECAME VISIBLE--AND PHENOMENA UNKNOWN ON EARTH THREATENED THE JET-PILOT'S LIFE!
I'M A PRISONER--SUSPENDED IN MID-AIR--IN A WORLD NO EARTHMAN EVER SAW! THOSE CREATURES ARE STUDYING THE SHIP THAT BROUGHT ME HERE--SO THEY CAN BUILD MORE LIKE IT--TO INVADE EARTH!
STARLIGHT

ALL EARTH IS ABUZZ AS A NEW TYPE OF JET ROARS OFF ON A TEST FLIGHT... A FLIGHT THAT *MAY* BE A FORE-RUNNER TO MAN'S LEAP INTO OUTER SPACE!

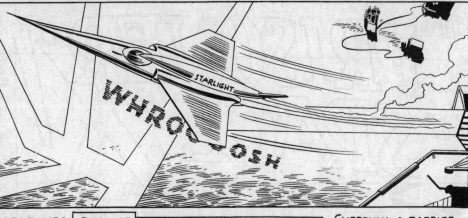

THE MIGHTY SHIP CLIMBS AND CLIMBS... TWO MILES... FIVE MILES... *TWENTY* MILES!

STAR-LIGHT TO APEX! STARLIGHT TO APEX! *I'M LEVELING OFF NOW*... AND GOING FOR SPEED!

BACK AT APEX...,

HE'S TRAVEL-ING *10,000 MILES PER HOUR!*

IF THIS TEST FLIGHT IS A SUCCESS--OUTER SPACE IS TOMORROW'S RUN!

SUDDENLY, A BARRIER COMMENCES TO BUILD UP IN FRONT OF THE *STARLIGHT*... A REAC-TION SIMILAR TO WHAT WAS KNOWN IN YESTERYEARS AS THE *SOUND BARRIER*...

WHAT'S THE *TROUBLE?* OUR CALCULATIONS CLEARED *ALL* BAR-RIERS! IS THERE AN *UNKNOWN BARRIER* WE NEVER FORESAW?

SUDDENLY, LIKE A GREAT INVISIBLE STEEL MESH, SOMETHING FORMS IN FRONT OF THE SHIP, AS IF IN A DESPERATE ATTEMPT TO HURL IT BACK...

WHAT'S *WRONG?* WHAT *IS* IT?

THE MIGHTY *STARLIGHT*-- HER ENGINES ROARING HAUGHTILY-- KEEPS PLOWING AHEAD--UNTIL SUDDENLY...

WE *MADE* IT! WE'VE BROKEN THROUGH THE BARRIER!

WHROOSH!

②

BUT WHAT'S ON THE *OTHER* SIDE?

AND AS A MAN PEERS INTO A DREAM, PILOT ROBERT WILSON PEERS INTO A STRANGE AND FASCINATING AND INCREDIBLE WORLD!

PULSE NORMAL... BRAIN REACTION GOOD... QUICK CHECKS PROVE *THAT!* BUT *WHAT* IS THIS PLACE I SEE? AND *WHERE* IS IT?

BIZARRE THOUGHTS RACE THROUGH THE PILOT'S MIND...

I *REMEMBER* NOW! THE HURTZ THEORY OF *SPACE X*... ANOTHER *DIMENSION* BORDERING OURS! THAT BARRIER I BROKE THROUGH, IT WAS A *DIMENSIONAL BARRIER!* I'M IN *ANOTHER DIMENSION!*

STRUGGLING DESPERATELY, ROBERT WILSON STRIVES TO TURN HIS CRAFT AROUND...

RADIO CONTACT GONE... GOT TO TURN BACK... GET THROUGH THE BARRIER AGAIN... B-BUT... I *CAN'T!* I'M BEING DRAWN FORWARD!

THEN, SUDDENLY, THE *STARLIGHT* LANDS -- AS IF ON A CLOUD -- AND PILOT ROBERT WILSON STEPS OUT...

ARE THEY FRIENDS -- FOES -- OR *WHAT?* I'LL KEEP MY HELMET ON -- THE "AIR" HERE MAY BE DIFFERENT FROM EARTH'S...

CAUGHT A BELT HOOK IN MY OXYGEN TUBE WHILE GETTING OUT OF MY PLANE... BETTER REMOVE IT BEFORE I GET A PUNCTURE!

BUT AT THIS MOMENT, BEAMS FLASH FROM THE ONLOOKERS, AND THE EARTH PILOT STIFFENS...

③

I'M SUSPENDED IN MID-AIR! I CAN'T MOVE A MUSCLE!

THEN, IN HIS SUSPENDED STATE, ROBERT IS "CARRIED" THROUGH THE STREETS...

WHERE ARE THEY TAKING ME?

SOON, IN A GREAT "HALL OF SCIENCE", THE PROCESSION STOPS...

MY SHIP-- IT'S HERE ALREADY... ON EXHIBIT! AND MAYBE I'M ON EXHIBIT, TOO!

THEY'RE APPROACHING ME... SPEAKING TO ME IN A LANGUAGE I UNDERSTAND!

YOU CAME TO US FROM AN-OTHER DIMENSION! THROUGH OUR SCIENCES WE KNOW WELL OF YOUR WORLD...

...AND SINCE YOU HAVE BEEN HERE WE HAVE BROKEN YOUR LANGUAGE CODE BY MEANS OF THOUGHT--TRANSLATORS! NOW-- YOU MAY SPEAK!

I COME AS A FRIEND --NOT AN ENEMY!

WE KNOW NO FRIENDS --WANT NONE! WE ARE THE DIMENSIONAL CONQUERORS! WE HAVE DEFEATED THOSE IN EVERY DIMENSION KNOWN--EXCEPT YOURS!

UP TO NOW WE'VE BEEN UNABLE TO BREAK THROUGH THE BARRIER TO YOUR DIMENSION -- BUT YOUR SHIP SOLVES THAT PROBLEM! WE'LL STUDY IT -- LEARN ITS SCIENTIFIC PRINCIPLES... BUILD A WAR FLEET LIKE IT...

I'VE GOT TO ESCAPE -- SOMEHOW... BEFORE THEY FIGURE OUT THE SECRETS OF MY SHIP... AND WARN EARTH...

HO, EARTHMAN! YOU FORGET! WE CAN READ YOUR MIND!

REMOVE HIM!

STARLIGHT

BUT AS THE PILOT IS HAULED DOWN...

THAT HOOK I HAD CAUGHT IN MY OXYGEN LINE -- THEY'VE UNWITTINGLY JARRED IT -- IT'S PIERCING THE LINE... MY OXYGEN WILL ESCAPE!

SLOWLY, THE LIFE-SUSTAINING ELEMENT ESCAPES -- WITH STARTLING EFFECTS!

GREAT STARS! THE ESCAPING OXYGEN IS CAUSING MINOR ATOMIC EXPLOSIONS! AND IT HAS SET ME FREE!

POW POW POW

PURE OXYGEN IS AN ALIEN ELEMENT TO THEM! IT'S UNITING WITH SUBSTANCES IN THEIR ATMOSPHERE AND CAUSING *NUCLEAR EXPLOSIONS!*

POW POW POW POW POW

AS THE ALIENS FLEE IN PANIC, ROBERT RACES TO HIS CRAFT...

THIS IS MY CHANCE TO BEAT IT OUT OF HERE!

STARLIGHT

5

WITH A THUNDERING ROAR, THE **STARLIGHT** SPEEDS SKY-WARD...

I'VE GOT TO ATTAIN MY PREVIOUS SPEED --BURST BACK THROUGH THE DIMENSIONAL BARRIER-- AND RETURN TO EARTH!

AGAIN THE BARRIER CHALLENGES THE JET-CRAFT--AND AGAIN THE SLEEK **STARLIGHT** PLUNGES THROUGH...

WHROOSH

AND WITHIN THE HOUR, BACK AT APEX, AFTER THE STORY IS TOLD...

OUR CALCULATIONS SHOW THAT THE **STARLIGHT** BROKE THROUGH A SMALL WARP IN SPACE! THAT'S HOW YOU ENTERED THE OTHER DIMENSION!

SOMEDAY THOSE ALIENS MAY BREAK THROUGH THE SAME WARP INTO **OUR** DIMENSION!

WE'VE GOT TO MARK OFF THAT AREA, AND BE CERTAIN THAT OUR PILOTS NEVER ENTER IT! THEN, TOO, WE MUST KEEP A CONSTANT VIGIL--TO PREVENT THE PEOPLE OF **SPACE X** FROM EVER INVADING OUR WORLD!

AND SO, A FEW DAYS LATER, POWERFUL RED BEAMS FLASH FROM A GIGANTIC BUOY IN THE SKY--MARKING OFF AN AREA NEVER TO BE ENTERED --ALWAYS TO BE WATCHED!

THERE WE HAVE IT, ROBERT-- OUR OWN BARRIER TO **SPACE X**!

A BARRIER, I HOPE -- THAT WILL NEVER BE BREACHED!

THE END

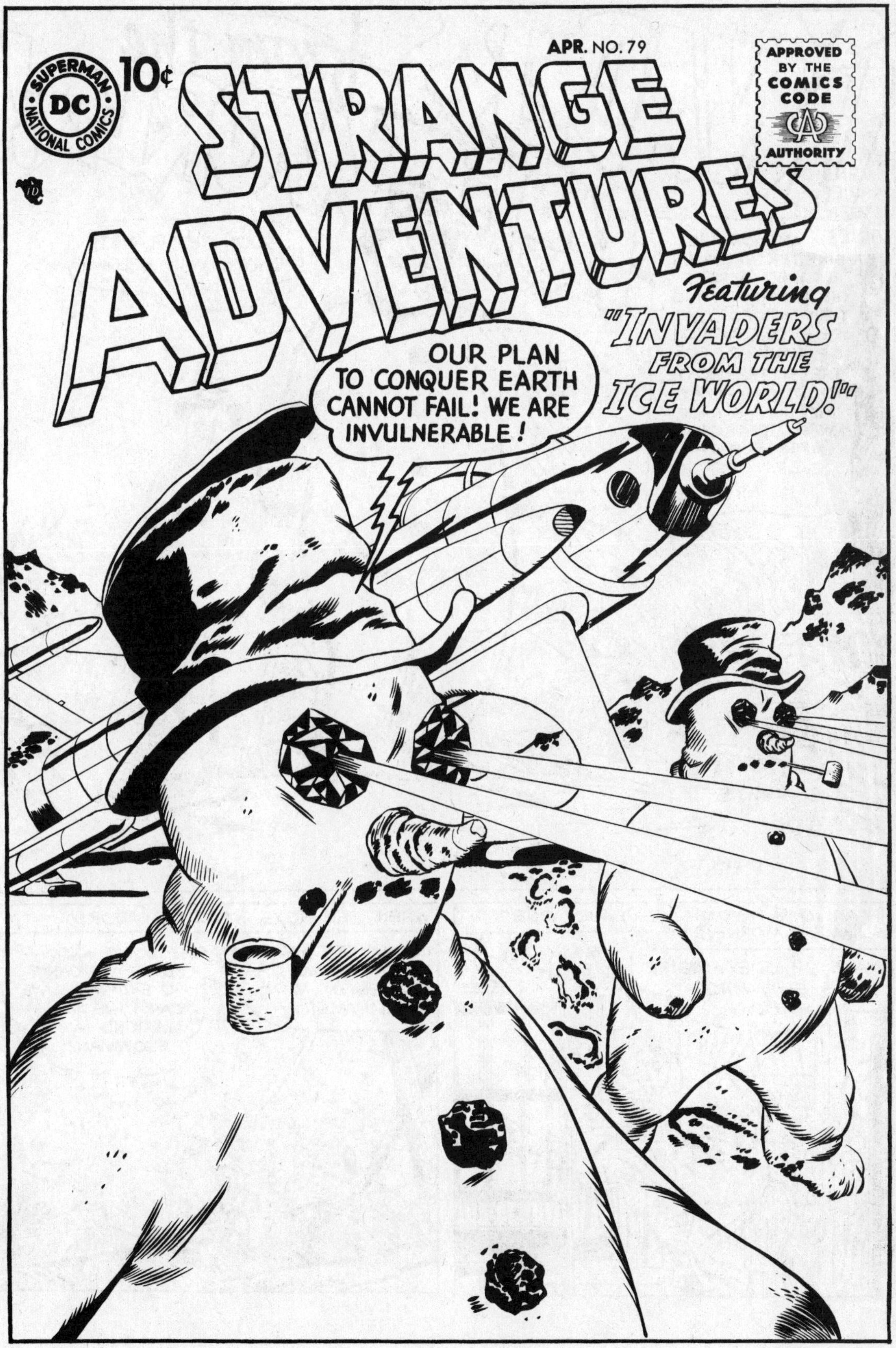
SUPERMAN
DC
NATIONAL COMICS
10¢
APR. NO. 79
APPROVED BY THE COMICS CODE AUTHORITY
STRANGE ADVENTURES
Featuring "INVADERS FROM THE ICE WORLD!"
OUR PLAN TO CONQUER EARTH CANNOT FAIL! WE ARE INVULNERABLE!

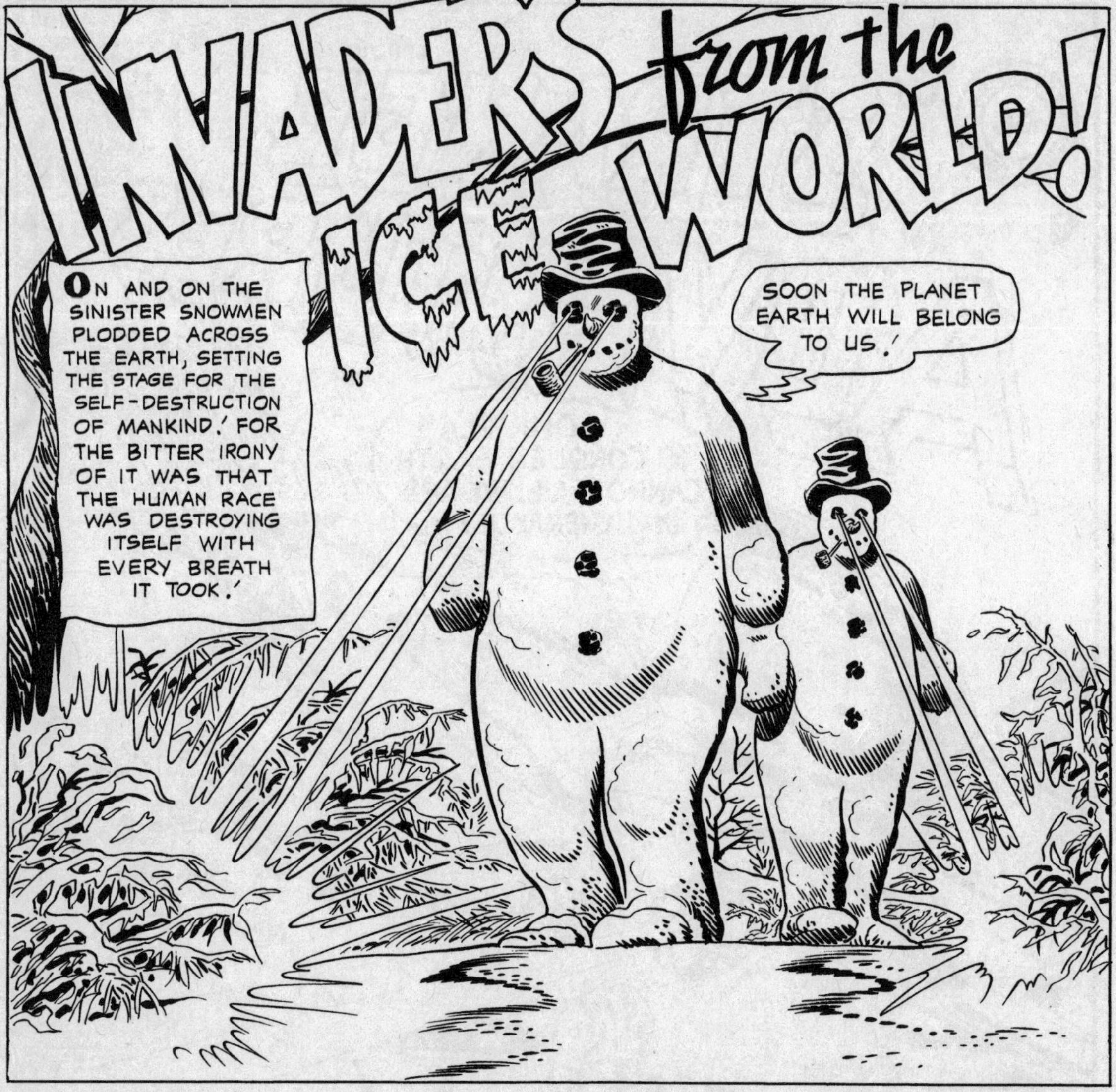
INVADERS from the ICE WORLD!
ON AND ON THE SINISTER SNOWMEN PLODDED ACROSS THE EARTH, SETTING THE STAGE FOR THE SELF-DESTRUCTION OF MANKIND! FOR THE BITTER IRONY OF IT WAS THAT THE HUMAN RACE WAS DESTROYING ITSELF WITH EVERY BREATH IT TOOK!
SOON THE PLANET EARTH WILL BELONG TO US!

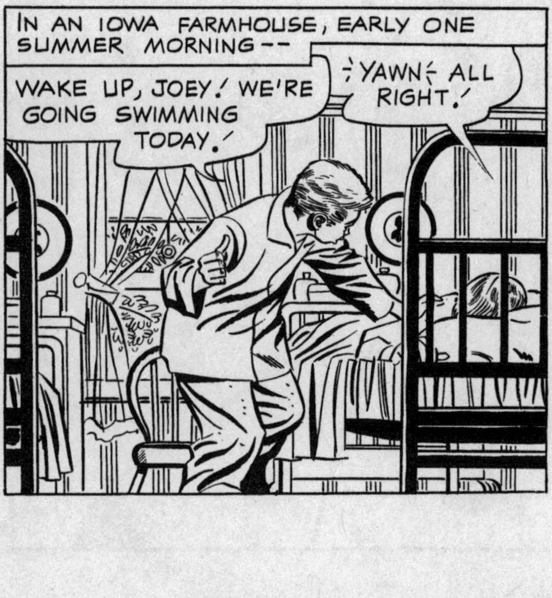
IN AN IOWA FARMHOUSE, EARLY ONE SUMMER MORNING--
WAKE UP, JOEY! WE'RE GOING SWIMMING TODAY!
-YAWN- ALL RIGHT!

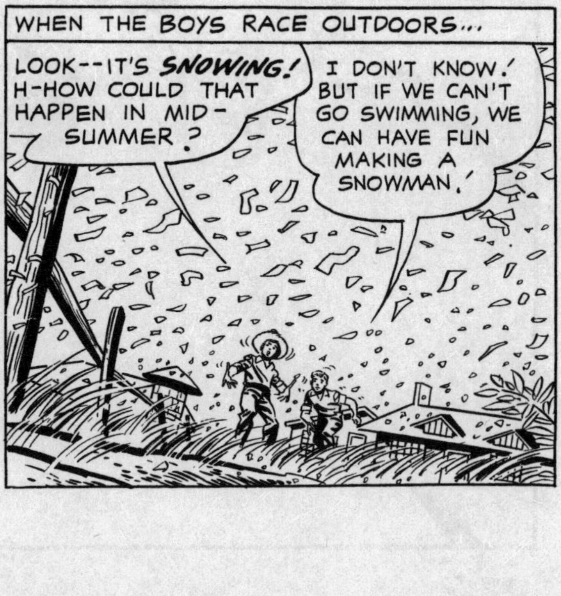
WHEN THE BOYS RACE OUTDOORS...
LOOK--IT'S SNOWING! H-HOW COULD THAT HAPPEN IN MID-SUMMER?
I DON'T KNOW! BUT IF WE CAN'T GO SWIMMING, WE CAN HAVE FUN MAKING A SNOWMAN!

IN A LITTLE WHILE... ALL THEY NEED NOW IS A TOP HAT TO GIVE THEM THE FINISHING TOUCH!

LET'S GO FIND SOME -- THEN THROW SNOWBALLS AT THEM!

WHEN THE SNOWBALLS HURTLE THROUGH THE AIR, A TELEPATHIC CONVERSATION PASSES BETWEEN THE SNOWMEN...

LET THESE EARTH CREATURES HAVE THEIR FUN -- FOR NOW!

YES! SOON THEIR WORLD WILL BELONG TO US!

"WE JOURNEYED FROM OUR PLANET PLUTO TO MAKE EARTH OUR NEW COLONY..."

THE EARTH WORLD IS TOO CLOSE TO THE SUN FOR US TO LIVE COMFORTABLY IN ITS WARMTH! WE ARE USED TO MUCH COLDER TEMPERATURES!

"AFTER LANDING SECRETLY ON EARTH, WE CONCEALED OUR SPACESHIP -- AND BEGAN THE FIRST PHASE OF OUR PLANETARY CONQUEST..."

WE CAUSED THIS SNOW TO FALL, INTENDING TO USE IT AS A PROTECTIVE MANTLE AGAINST THIS PLANET'S HEAT! BUT THE SNOWMEN THOSE EARTH-CREATURES ARE BUILDING SUGGEST A BETTER IDEA--

YES! THEY MAKE GOOD DISGUISES, AND ARE COLD TOO! LET US ENTER THEM!

"JUST AS A DEEP SEA DIVER PAUSES WHEN RISING TO THE SURFACE TO ACCUSTOM HIS BODY TO CHANGES IN PRESSURE, SO MUST WE ACCLIMATE OURSELVES TO THIS CHANGE IN PLANETARY TEMPERATURE...

A FEW MORE HOURS -- AND WE SHALL STRIKE!

IN THE MORNING... HEY -- WHAT HAPPENED TO OUR SNOWMEN?

THE SNOW ON THE GROUND IS GONE TOO! MAYBE IT MELTED OVERNIGHT!

LOOK! FOOTPRINTS! JUST LIKE THE PRINTS A SNOW-MAN MIGHT MAKE, IF HE WERE *ALIVE!* LET'S SEE WHERE THEY LEAD TO!

FOLLOWING THE STRANGE PRINTS, THE TWO BOYS NOTICE...

THE CROPS -- DEAD!

THEY WERE ALL RIGHT YESTERDAY!

ON EACH SIDE OF THEM, THEY SEE A WIDE SWATH OF DEAD VEGETATION...

EVERYWHERE WE LOOK, TREE LEAVES -- FLOWERS -- GRASS -- HAVE WITHERED AND DIED!

THE *SNOWMEN!* THEY -- THEY'RE *ALIVE!*

STRANGE RAYS SHOOTING OUT OF THEIR EYES -- DESTROYING ALL PLANT LIFE THEY TOUCH!

RUNNING HOME, THE BOYS TELL THEIR STRANGE STORY...

IT SOUNDS UNBELIEVABLE, DAD, BUT WE *SAW* IT HAPPEN!

I'LL CHECK FOR MYSELF -- THEN CALL WASHINGTON!

WITHIN A COUPLE OF HOURS, DARWIN JONES, CHIEF OF THE *DEPARTMENT OF SCIENTIFIC INVESTIGATION,* IS FLYING ABOVE THE FARM COUNTRY...

THERE THEY ARE! GET THIS EGG-BEATER DOWN!

MOMENTS LATER, THE *DSI* MAN CONFRONTS THE SNOWMEN....

WHO ARE YOU? WHAT DO YOU WANT?

WE ARE ENERGY BEINGS FROM THE PLANET PLUTO! WE ARE TAKING OVER YOUR PLANET AS ONE OF OUR COLONIES! THERE IS NOTHING YOU CAN DO TO STOP US!

IS THAT WHY YOU'RE DESTROYING OUR PLANTS -- TO STARVE US INTO SUBMISSION?

OUR PLAN OF CONQUEST SERVES A DOUBLE PURPOSE! NOT ONLY WILL IT DESTROY ALL EARTH-LIFE -- BUT MAKE THIS PLANET COLD ENOUGH FOR US TO LIVE ON!

EARTH PLANTS ABSORB CARBON DIOXIDE IN AIR, AND GIVE OFF OXYGEN! DESTROYING YOUR VEGETABLE KINGDOM WILL LEAD TO A FATAL INCREASE OF CARBON DIOXIDE IN THE ATMOSPHERE....

"YOU EARTH PEOPLE INHALE OXYGEN, AND EXHALE CARBON DIOXIDE! SINCE CARBON DIOXIDE IS OPAQUE TO HEAT, THE HEAVY CONCENTRATION OF CARBON DIOXIDE WILL PREVENT THE SUN'S RAYS FROM REACHING EARTH -- AND BRING ABOUT AN ICE AGE." *

*EDITOR'S NOTE: ACCORDING TO ONE SCIENTIFIC THEORY, EARTH'S PAST ICE AGES WERE CAUSED BY AN INCREASE OF CARBON DIOXIDE IN THE ATMOSPHERE!

DO YOU THINK WE'LL STAND IDLY BY AND LET YOU TAKE OVER OUR WORLD?

YOU CAN'T STOP US! WE ARE INDESTRUCTIBLE! EVERY TIME YOU EARTHMEN BREATHE -- YOU ARE DESTROYING YOURSELVES!

DARWIN JONES FIRES BULLETS AT THE SNOWMEN, ONLY TO SEE THE BULLET HOLES INSTANTLY SEAL UP!....

THIS WEAPON FAILED -- BUT WE HAVE OTHERS -- MORE POWERFUL ONES!

A TOP PRIORITY CALL BRINGS FLAME-THROWERS, BAZOOKAS, AND HAND GRENADES!

THEY STILL KEEP MOVING!

AMAZINGLY, THEY SURVIVE THE EXPLODING SHELL OF AN ATOMIC CANNON!

AT AN EMERGENCY SESSION OF THE FINEST SCIENTIFIC MINDS IN THE COUNTRY...

GENTLEMEN, WE MUST FACE FACTS! THOSE SNOWMEN *CANNOT* BE DESTROYED!

PARDON ME, SIR! I THINK THEY CAN! WE'VE FAILED BECAUSE WE USED THE *WRONG* LINE OF ATTACK!

WE'VE BEEN USING *HEAT* ON THEM! FIGHTING COLD WITH HEAT IS NORMAL! BUT WHEN THE NORMAL DOESN'T WORK-- WE MUST TRY THE *ABNORMAL!* WE'LL FIGHT COLD WITH *COLD--THE UTTER COLD OF ABSOLUTE ZERO!*

THIS IS A NEW DEVICE THAT ARRESTS THE MOVEMENT OF ATOMS! HEAT IS THE RESULT OF THE KINETIC ENERGY OF ATOMIC *MOTION!* WITHOUT ATOMIC MOTION, THERE CAN BE NO HEAT--ONLY ABSOLUTE ZERO COLD-- MINUS 273.18° CENTIGRADE!

5

NO LIFE CAN LIVE IN AN ABSOLUTE ZERO TEMPERATURE! WITH THIS WEAPON WE CAN FREEZE THOSE SNOWMEN RIGID!

THE SCIENTIFIC MACHINE GOES INTO ACTION! AT THE FIRST BLAST-- THEY'RE IMPRISONED INSIDE THE ABSOLUTE ZERO SNOW! AT THAT TEMPERATURE, THE SNOW IS SO BRITTLE THAT IF I TAP IT WITH A STICK...

THE SNOW-COVERING SHATTERS--AND EXPOSES OUR ENEMY! LISTEN TO ME, PLUTONIONS--I HAVE RELEASED YOU SO THAT YOU MAY BRING BACK A WARNING TO YOUR PLANET!

STAY AWAY FROM EARTH! IF YOU DARE ATTACK US, WE HAVE THE PERFECT WEAPON TO DEFEAT YOU!

WE UNDERSTAND-- AND WE SHALL NEVER RETURN!

...THE END

6

AROUND the UNIVERSE in 1 BILLION YEARS!

Long, *LONG* AGO THEY HAD LEFT THEIR NATIVE PLANET, AND NOW THEY WERE RETURNING! WHAT STRANGE SIGHTS WOULD THEY SEE? WHAT SORT OF *LIFE* WOULD THEY FIND? WHAT WOULD THEIR HOME PLANET BE LIKE? NOT EVEN ALL THEIR SUPER-SCIENCE COULD FORTELL THE STARTLING SUR-PRISES THAT WOULD GREET THEM AT THE END OF THE BILLION-YEAR JOURNEY.

A SPACESHIP PLOWS ON AND ON THROUGH THE SEEMINGLY INFINITENESS OF THE COSMOS...

INSIDE THE SHIP, EVERY PASSENGER LIES INERT, AS A MYRIAD OF INTRICATE, AUTOMATIC CONTROLS CLICK AND BUZZ...

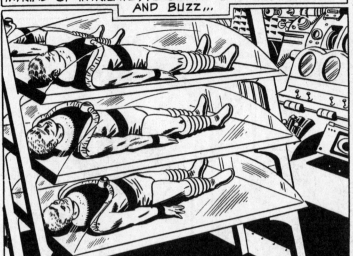

SUDDENLY, ATMOSPHERE-CREATING MACHINES HUM, SONAR VIBRATIONS STIR THROUGH THE SHIP, AND A MECHANICAL VOICE--LONG, LONG SILENT -- SPEAKS...

AWAKEN! AWAKEN! IT IS TIME! IT IS TIME!

AIRTIGHT CHAMBERS OPEN AUTOMATICALLY AT THE SOUND OF THE VOICE...

IT IS TIME! IT IS TIME!

AROUSED BY THE SONAR VIBRATIONS, THE SPACE-MEN STIR --THEN ARISE...

OUR JOURNEY IS OVER! WHAT IS THE READING ON THE ATOMIC CLOCK?

SOMETHING MUST HAVE GONE WRONG! THE CLOCK INDICATES THE PASSING OF *ONE BILLION YEARS!*

BUT IT SHOULD HAVE SHOWN ONLY *500 YEARS!* ATTACH THE ROBOT FAULT-FINDER! WE MUST KNOW WHERE THE ERROR LIES!

INSTANTLY, THE MECHANICAL WIZARD IS PUT TO WORK, AND IN BRIEF SECONDS ANNOUNCES ITS ERRORLESS CALCULATIONS...

CORRECT READING-- ONE BILLION YEARS! REPEAT--CORRECT READING, ONE BILLION YEARS!

THEN NOTHING'S *GONE* WRONG! *WE* WERE WRONG!

OUR SCIENCE PROVED THE UNIVERSE TO BE FINITE--BUT WE *ERRED* IN THINKING WE COULD CIRCUMNAVIGATE IT IN A MERE 500 YEARS!*

EDITOR'S NOTE: ALBERT EINSTEIN THEORIZED THAT OUR UNIVERSE WAS FINITE-- AND TRAVELING AT THE SPEED OF LIGHT COULD BE CIRCUMNAVIGATED IN 100 BILLION YEARS!

INSTEAD, WE HAVE TRAVELED IN A STATE OF SUPER-SUS-PENDED ANIMATION FOR A *BILLION* YEARS!

AND NOW WE'RE *HOME!* WHAT IS OUR PLANET LIKE NOW? TURN ON THE COSMO-VIDEO! WE MUST *SEE* BEFORE WE LAND!

A GIANT SCREEN IS ILLUMINATED-- THEN, FANTASTIC PICTURES FLASH ACROSS IT...

THAT IS ONE OF TODAY'S CITIES! HOW QUAINT! HOW *BACKWARD!*

THEY'RE MOVING ON PRIMITIVE *WHEELS* AND LIVING IN OBSOLETE STONE AND METALLIC STRUCTURES! DO YOU THINK THEY ARE *FRIENDLY?*

WHAT DIFFERENCE? THEIR WEAPONS CAN'T HARM US! THEY HAVE ADVANCED, PROBABLY NO FARTHER THAN THE SIMPLE ATOMIC AGE! PRE-PARE TO LAND!

ANTI-GRAVITY CONTRIVANCES WHIR INTO ACTION AND SOON THE SHIP DESCENDS IN TIMES SQUARE, NEW YORK CITY, U.S.A...

MEN FROM SPACE!

FROM WHICH *PLANET,* I WONDER?

THEY SEEM AWED BY US--BUT UNAFRAID!

I BELIEVE A RECEPTION COMMITTEE IS COMING TO GREET US!

WELCOME TO THE PLANET EARTH! CAN YOU UNDERSTAND ME? FROM WHICH PLANET DO YOU COME?

LINGUA-TRANSLATORS MAKE YOUR LANGUAGE CLEAR TO US, AND OURS CLEAR TO YOU! AS FOR OUR NATIVE PLANET...IT IS *EARTH!*

AFTER THE STRANGE VISITORS TELL THEIR STORY...

A SUPER-CIVILIZATION--HERE ON EARTH--MORE THAN A BILLION YEARS AGO?! THE LAST VESTIGES OF YOUR ERA MUST HAVE VANISHED IN THE EARLY PRE-CAMBRIAN AGE, OF WHICH WE HAVE NO GEOLOGICAL RECORD!

HENCE, WE HAVE NO WAY WHATSOEVER OF KNOWING HOW YOU LIVED IN THAT DISTANT LONG AGO!

IT WILL BE OUR PLEASURE TO ENLIGHTEN YOU! WE SHALL USE THE ATMOSPHERE AS A COSMO-VIDEO SCREEN, AND SHOW NUCLEAR FILMS OF OUR WORLD AT THAT TIME!

THEN, LIKE ANOTHER WORLD HOVERING IN THE SKY, THE EARTH IS SEEN AS IT EXISTED EONS AGO...

THOSE GIANT MOUNTAINS STOOD THEN WHERE YOUR OCEANS ARE NOW!

"TWENTY THOUSAND YEARS OF SCIENCE HAD MARCHED BEFORE US--AND WE SWEPT ON TO THE ATOMIC AGE, AND FAR BEYOND IT..."

"THEN, ONE DAY, OUR SENSITIVE RADA-SCOPES DETECTED A COMET FROM ANOTHER SOLAR SYSTEM, BEARING WITH IT A HIGHLY MAGNETIC GAS THAT DISTURBED EARTH'S ATMOSPHERE...."

"THESE DISTURBANCES ROCKED THE EARTH WITH UNHEARD OF QUAKES..."

"TIDAL WAVES SWEPT OVER CONTINENTS, GREAT UPHEAVALS FORMED NEW MOUNTAINS, BURIED OLD ONES..."

AT LAST THE COMET--WHICH WE CALLED *MAGNO-X*--VANISHED! WE REBUILT OUR CITIES--OUR CIVILIZATION, AND...

LOOK! LOOK AT THE SCREEN!

THERE'S AN UNUSUAL DISTURB-ANCE IN THE ATMOSPHERE!

NOTHING CAN DISTURB OUR NUCLEAR FILMS...EXCEPT AN ATTRACTION SUCH AS CAUSED BY *MAGNO-X!*

INSTANTLY, A GIANT RADA-SCOPE POKES FORTH FROM THE SPACE-SHIP...

IT IS *MAGNO-X!* IT HAS RETURNED TO OUR SOLAR SYSTEM!

EARTH IS DOOMED!

DRUGS

NO, EARTH CAN ESCAPE THE NEW COMET CATA-CLYSM! AFTER OUR INITIAL EXPERIENCE WITH *MAGNO-X*, WE DEVISED A COUNTER-MEASURE! *THIS IS IT!*

TH-THAT TINY TABLET?!

SIZE IS ONLY RELATIVE! ACTUALLY, THE TABLET IS A VAST SOLAR STORE-HOUSE, CONTAINING *EIGHT MILLION SUDOS OF SUN-POWER!*

SUDO? WE DO NOT KNOW THE TERM!

ONE SUDO OF SUNPOWER, MY FRIEND, COULD DISINTEGRATE YOUR LOFTIEST MOUNTAIN! *ONE TABLET* CAN DESTROY *MAGNO-X!* WE DEPART NOW ON OUR MISSION!

ANTI-GRAVITY CONTRIVANCES WHIR SILENTLY, AND WITH THE NEAR-SPEED OF LIGHT THE CRAFT FADES INTO THE OUTER YONDER...

THE SCIENCE THEY KNOW! THEY'LL EXPLAIN IT ALL TO US WHEN THEY RETURN!

LET'S FOLLOW THEM WITH OUR TELE-SCOPES!

THROUGH POWERFUL TELESCOPES THEY SEE *MAGNO-X* BLASTED BY AN INCREDIBLE EXPLOSION! THEN *MAGNO-X* VANISHES--FOREVER!...

THEY SAVED *US*-- BUT WERE CAUGHT IN THE EXPLOSION THEMSELVES! THEY MUST HAVE KNOWN THAT WOULD HAPPEN! WHY WOULD THEY WILLINGLY SACRIFICE THEIR LIVES TO SAVE OURS?

THE REASON IS SIMPLE, I SUPPOSE! THEY WERE *EARTH-MEN*-- SAVING EARTH!

THE END

A SWITCH IN TIME!

IF YOU WERE GIVEN THE OPPORTUNITY TO LIVE FOR 24 HOURS IN THE *FUTURE*, HOW WOULD YOU SPEND THE PRECIOUS MOMENTS OF YOUR TIME-VISIT?
SIGHTSEEING--INTERVIEWING FAMOUS PEOPLE OF THAT ERA--OR WOULD YOU PORE OVER RECORDS OF THE PAST IN ORDER TO "*FORETELL*" THE FUTURE WHEN YOU RETURNED TO THE PRESENT?

AT FIRST, THE SLEEPING MARK ROBINS SEEMINGLY HEARS A VOICE IN HIS DREAM--BUT WHEN HE AWAKENS THE VOICE IS STILL CLEARLY HEARD...

MARK ROBINS, CAN YOU HEAR ME? I AM JON XX-99-- TALKING TO YOU FROM THE FAR DISTANT FUTURE...

HUH? WHAT'S THAT?

FOLLOW MY INSTRUCTIONS FOR ACTIVATING THE *TIME-SWITCHER* AND WE'LL EXCHANGE PLACES IN TIME--YOU IN THE FUTURE AND I IN THE PAST!

FOLLOWING THE SOUND OF THE VOICE, ROBINS MOVES INTO THE LIVING ROOM...

IT IS COMING FROM MY *TV* SET--BUT IT ISN'T EVEN TURNED ON!

I'M ATTEMPTING TO UTILIZE YOUR TELEVISION MACHINE AS A *TIME-TELE-VIEWER!* TUNE IT AS I DIRECT YOU-- AND WE'LL BE ABLE TO SEE EACH OTHER!

1

ACTING AS THE MAN OF THE FUTURE DIRECTS, MARK ROBINS ADJUSTS THE DIALS...

THAT'S FINE--I SEE YOU CLEARLY! FIRST, I SHALL EXPLAIN WHY YOU HAVE BEEN CHOSEN FOR THIS TIME-CONTACT...

WE RECENTLY UNEARTHED A TIME CAPSULE FROM YOUR ERA AND YOUR NAME WAS CHOSEN AT RANDOM FROM A TELEPHONE BOOK WE FOUND! TO CELEBRATE THE INVENTION OF OUR TIME-TELEVIEWER, WE HAVE SELECTED YOU FOR CERTAIN FAVORS... OH, I SEE YOU DON'T BELIEVE ME...

I'D--ER--LIKE TO BELIEVE YOU, BUT THIS IS SIMPLY TOO FANTASTIC FOR ME TO SWALLOW! SOMEONE IS PULLING A GAG ON ME!

I'LL PROVE TO YOU I'M FROM THE FUTURE-- BY TELLING YOU YOUR FUTURE WHICH I HAVE TELE-SCANNED...

THIS EVENING YOU WILL BE SERVED LOBSTER AT THE CAFE ROYALE, AND PREVENT A HOLDUP...

BAH! SOMEBODY TOLD YOU I HAD A DATE AT THE ROYALE TONIGHT! BESIDES I'M EATING STEAK, AND WOULDN'T RISK MY LIFE STOPPING A HOLDUP!

THAT NIGHT AT THE CAFE ROYALE...

TWO FILET MIGNON STEAKS, HENRI-- RARE!

VERY GOOD, MR. ROBINS!

MINUTES LATER...

LOBSTERS! I-I ORDERED STEAKS!

SORRY, SIR! I MUST HAVE TAKEN SOMEONE ELSE'S ORDER!

SUDDENLY!

DON'T ANYONE MOVE! THIS IS A HOLDUP!

IT'S COMING TRUE-- JUST AS THE MAN FROM THE FUTURE TOLD ME!

STILL, I'M NOT GOING TO PLAY HERO AND TANGLE WITH THOSE GUNMEN!

AS A HAND ROUGHLY YANKS AN ENVELOPE FREE...

HE'S STEALING MY FIRM'S BANK STATEMENTS!

I BORROWED SOME MONEY THAT WASN'T MINE! I'VE GOT TO ALTER THOSE REPORTS TO COVER MYSELF! I CAN'T LET THEM BE SEEN BY ANYONE!

ACTING INSTINCTIVELY, ROBINS GRABS THE FALLEN GUN...

THAT SMASHES THIS HOLDUP!

POW!

NEXT MORNING WHEN THE MAN OF THE FUTURE APPEARS AGAIN...

LAST NIGHT! BUT I WANT MORE PROOF! I'M BUYING AMALGAMATED UTILITY STOCK TODAY! WILL IT GO UP OR DOWN?

JON, YOU WERE RIGHT--

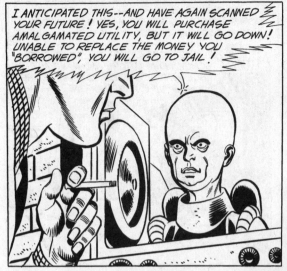

I ANTICIPATED THIS--AND HAVE AGAIN SCANNED YOUR FUTURE! YES, YOU WILL PURCHASE AMALGAMATED UTILITY, BUT IT WILL GO DOWN! UNABLE TO REPLACE THE MONEY YOU "BORROWED", YOU WILL GO TO JAIL!

HOWEVER, ANYONE'S FUTURE MAY BE CHANGED BY MAKING AN ALTERATION IN THE NORMAL PATTERN! YOU CAN CHANGE YOUR FUTURE FOR THE BETTER BY BUYING CONSOLIDATED STOCK!

IN A BROKERAGE OFFICE, SOON AFTER...

FIVE THOUSAND DOLLARS' WORTH OF CONSOLIDATED COPPER!

LATER THAT DAY...

AMALGAMATED UTILITY TOOK A NOSEDIVE--AND MY STOCK DOUBLED IN VALUE!

CLICK!
CLICK!

ON THE NEXT APPEARANCE OF THE MAN FROM THE FUTURE...

IT WORKED OUT JUST AS YOU FORESAW! I CERTAINLY AM INDEBTED TO YOU!

SINCE YOU BROUGHT THAT UP, THERE IS A FAVOR YOU CAN DO FOR ME...

WHILE WE MEN OF THE FUTURE CAN READ ABOUT THE PAST AND SEE IT, WE HAVE BEEN UNABLE TO TRAVEL INTO IT AND EXPERIENCE IT FOR OURSELVES! ONLY YOU CAN MAKE IT POSSIBLE FOR ONE OF US TO VISIT YOUR ERA...

BY SWITCHING PLACES WITH EACH OTHER IN TIME, WE CAN MAINTAIN THE STATUS QUO OF NATURAL MASS BALANCE! WILL YOU CONSENT TO VISIT THE FUTURE FOR TWENTY-FOUR HOURS--WHILE I LIVE IN YOUR TIME?

I SURE WILL!

DURING THE FOLLOWING WEEK, MARK ROBINS WORKS UNDER THE FUTURE-MAN'S INSTRUCTIONS, FITTING TOGETHER PARTS OF A STRANGE MACHINE...

THIS IS TREMENDOUS! I'LL BE ABLE TO SCAN MY OWN FUTURE AND MAKE ANY NECESSARY CHANGES TO IMPROVE THE LIFE AHEAD OF ME!

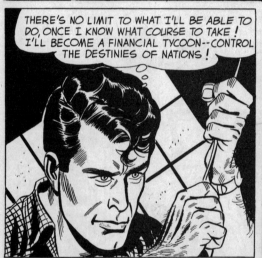

THERE'S NO LIMIT TO WHAT I'LL BE ABLE TO DO, ONCE I KNOW WHAT COURSE TO TAKE! I'LL BECOME A FINANCIAL TYCOON--CONTROL THE DESTINIES OF NATIONS!

AFTER THE MACHINE IS COMPLETED...

REMEMBER TO FOLLOW MY INSTRUCTIONS FOR ACTIVATING THE TIME-SWITCHER! NOW COUNT OFF--THREE-TWO-ONE-- ZERO!

I'M IN THE FUTURE!

IGNORING THE FUTURE WORLD ABOUT HIM, MARK ROBINS RACES FOR THE TIME-SCANNING MACHINE...

I CAN'T WASTE A SINGLE PRECIOUS MOMENT JUST LOOKING AROUND!

5

HE FLINGS HIMSELF DOWN BEFORE THE TIME-SCANNER AND FEVERISHLY WORKS ITS DIALS...

I'LL START SCANNING THE NEWSPAPERS THAT WILL APPEAR THE DAY *AFTER* I RETURN TO THE PAST!

HOUR AFTER HOUR GOES BY AS MARK ROBINS WORKS UNCEASINGLY...

I'LL HAVE A COMPLETE HISTORY OF MY OWN TIME BEFORE IT HAPPENS!

AT THE END OF THE TWENTY-FOUR HOURS...

JON! THE TIME IS UP! WE MUST SWITCH PLACES IN TIME AGAIN!

I SHALL NEVER DO THAT, MR. ROBINS!

I INTEND TO REMAIN IN YOUR TIME ERA! *YOU* CAN STAY IN *MY* TIME ERA! I'VE ALREADY WRECKED THE *TIME-SWITCHER!* IT'S WONDERFUL TO BE AMONG PEOPLE AFTER YEARS OF LONELINESS!

I-I DON'T UNDERSTAND! YOU CAN'T DO THIS TO ME!

I'LL GET SOMEBODY HERE TO HELP ME BRING YOU BACK...

THERE IS NO ONE ELSE, MARK ROBINS! YOU ARE VERY, VERY FAR IN THE FUTURE, INDEED! LOOK AT THE WORLD YOU'RE IN...

FILLED WITH DREAD, MARK ROBINS RACES OUTSIDE AND LOOKS AT HIS FUTURE...

I'M ALONE IN THIS BLEAK WORLD! I AM--*THE LAST MAN ON EARTH!*

The End

The Living Automobile!

An automobile is a mechanical vehicle, always under the control of its driver! That's what Joe Morris thought--until he drove a fantastic car that had a mind of its own!

A force-beam from the head-lights is melting the wire fence guarding the *ATOMIC TESTING RANGE!* The car's going to break through--and there's nothing I can do to stop it!

A garage mechanic gets many urgent calls for help! But Joe Morris never received one like this before...

HURRY--HELP ME--AM IN TROUBLE!

HUH? WHAT'S THAT? WHO'S TALKING TO ME?

STRANGE--SOMEONE SEEMS TO BE CONTACTING ME...*MENTALLY!* I'LL GET MY TOW-TRUCK--HELP HIM OUT...

JOE'S TOW SERVICE

URGED BY SOME INEXPLICABLE COMPULSION, JOE DRIVES ALONG THE HIGHWAY...

THIS IS THE ODDEST THING THAT EVER HAPPENED TO ME-- I EVEN SEEM TO KNOW PRECISELY WHERE TO GO! WHAT'S THAT UP AHEAD?

MUST BE ONE OF THOSE NEW FOREIGN CARS! BUT IT'S DANGEROUSLY PARKED HERE AND COULD CAUSE AN ACCIDENT! THAT MUST BE WHY I WAS SUMMONED TO TOW IT IN--BUT *WHO* SENT FOR ME, AND *HOW?*

THE FOLLOWING DAYS BRING NO ANSWERS TO JOE'S QUESTIONS...

I'VE ADVERTISED IN SEVERAL PAPERS FOR THE CAR'S OWNER, AND NOBODY'S ANSWERED!

I CAN'T EVEN GET THE HOOD OPEN TO SEE WHAT KIND OF MOTOR IT HAS-- AND IT DOESN'T SEEM TO HAVE ANY GAS TANK! I THINK I'LL TRY THIS MACHINE OUT ON THE ROAD!

BUT A TRYOUT SPIN DOWN THE ROAD SUDDENLY TURNS INTO A NIGHTMARE RIDE...

IT'S GOING TOO FAST--AND I CAN'T MAKE IT SLOW DOWN! I'LL TURN OFF THE HIGHWAY ONTO THE SIDE ROAD TO THE RIGHT!

GOOD GOSH! I KEEP TURNING THE STEERING WHEEL TO THE *RIGHT*--BUT THE CAR IS TURNING *LEFT*, ALL BY ITSELF!

2

MILES AND MINUTES FLY, AND PANIC MOUNTS!

I CAN'T CONTROL THE CAR AT ALL! IT'S RUNNING WILD--AND YET IT SEEMS TO *KNOW* WHAT IT'S DOING!

THEN, BEYOND THE CITY, AN OMINOUS SIGN LOOMS AHEAD!

RESTRICTED

I'M TRYING TO STOP THE CAR BEFORE IT GETS TOO CLOSE TO THAT GATE--BUT I-- I CAN'T!

RESTRICTED AREA!

AS THE ASTONISHED GUARDS SEE THE CAR SPEED STRAIGHT TOWARD THEM...

STOP OR I'LL FIRE!

SHUT THAT GATE!

IT'S COMING FAST--!

IT CRASHED RIGHT THROUGH--AND OUR BULLETS DON'T EVEN DENT IT!

I'LL PHONE BASE HEADQUARTERS-- THEY'LL STOP IT!

BUT NOTHING, IT SEEMS, CAN STOP THIS INCREDIBLE CAR AS IT RACES IN AND OUT AMONG THE TOWERING ROCKETS...

WE CAN'T EVEN GET NEAR IT!

THEY'RE BRINGING OUT THAT NEW HIGH-SPEED COMMAND CAR-- THAT'LL CATCH IT!

AS THE SWIFT COMMAND CAR APPROACHES...

WE'RE GOING TO CRASH HEAD-ON--AND I'M HELPLESS! I CAN'T LOOK--

3

AT THE LAST SPLIT-SECOND...

¡WHEW! THIS CRAZY CAR SWERVED AROUND THE OTHER ONE--AND NOW IT SEEMS TO HAVE DECIDED TO LEAVE! IF I ONLY GET OUT OF THIS ALIVE--

LATER, AFTER A SPEEDY RUN, WHEN JOE *IS* SAFELY DRIVEN BACK TO HIS GARAGE...

THERE'S ONLY ONE WAY TO CLEAR UP THE MYSTERY OF THIS CAR! I'M GOING TO TAKE IT APART AND EXAMINE IT INCH BY INCH!

THROUGH MOST OF THE NIGHT JOE WORKS --AND GETS ABSOLUTELY NOWHERE!...

NOTHING AFFECTS THAT METAL, NOT EVEN AN OXY-ACETYLENE WELDER! I CAN'T GET THE HOOD OPEN--I CAN'T BUDGE ANY PART OF IT!

MAYBE THIS CAR IS AS FANTASTIC AS THE METAL IT'S MADE OF--THAT'S FUNNY--THE STEERING WHEEL WORKS PERFECTLY NOW!

THAT WILD DRIVE *MUST* HAVE BEEN JUST MY IMAGINATION! I'VE GOT TO PROVE IT, OR I'LL NEVER BE ABLE TO SLEEP NIGHTS AGAIN!

THE MOMENT JOE IS SETTLED IN THE DRIVER'S SEAT...

HEY, IT'S TAKING OFF AGAIN--BY ITSELF! WH-- WHERE'S IT DRIVING ME NOW?

4

WEAVING THROUGH HIGHWAY TRAFFIC...

HONK! HONK!

HONK! HONK!

...THE CAR DARTS ACROSS OPEN COUNTRY TOWARD A MOST SECRET AND DANGEROUS INSTALLATION.'

ATOMIC TESTING RANGE NO ACCESS!

THE ROCKET-BASE-- AND NOW THIS *ATOMIC TESTING RANGE!* THIS STEEP SLOPE IS NOT EVEN SLOWING THE CAR DOWN.'

THEN, ATOP THE SLOPE...

IT'S CHARGING THE FENCE--AND SOME KIND OF FORCE BEAM FROM IT IS MELTING THE FENCE'S WIRE MESH.'

IN AND OUT AMONG THE MOST HIGHLY GUARDED OF SECRETS THE INCREDIBLE CAR SPEEDS.'

EXPERIMENTAL REACTORS, ATOMIC LAUNCHES, PROTOTYPE MOTORS-- IF I DO LIVE THROUGH THIS RIDE, IT WON'T MATTER.' THEY'LL SEND ME TO JAIL FOR LIFE JUST FOR BEING HERE.'

WE'RE LEAVING THE RANGE! MEANWHILE, THEY'VE CALLED OUT EVERY POLICE CAR AROUND HERE! THIS CAR CAN'T POSSIBLY GET AWAY FROM ALL OF THEM.'

BUT AGAIN, INTO JOE MORRIS' MIND, COMES TELEPATHIC SPEECH...

OH, YES, I CAN! THEY'RE ONLY SLOW EARTH CARS-- AND I AM ONE OF THE MACHINE-MEN OF THE PLANET VENUS, SENT HERE TO SPY ON YOUR NEW ATOMIC POWERS.'

THOSE THOUGHTS-- COMING TO ME FROM THE CAR!

"I DISGUISED MYSELF AS AN AUTOMOBILE, TO ESCAPE NOTICE--BUT I NEEDED A HUMAN DRIVER, TO COMPLETE THE DISGUISE!"

"THAT'S WHY YOU ORIGINALLY CALLED ME, TELEPATHICALLY--"

THIS THING'S A MENACE-- GOT TO STOP IT SOME-- HOW--

BUT--HOW CAN I STOP A MACHINE-MAN WITH ALL THESE FANTASTIC POWERS? EVEN THE POLICE COULDN'T CATCH HIM-- WAIT! THAT TUNNEL AHEAD--IT MIGHT BE A CHANCE--

PAY TOLL

INTO THE LONG VEHICULAR TUNNEL THE MACHINE-MAN "AUTO" PLUNGES! THEN, AT THE OTHER END WHERE A POLICE-CAR BARRIER HAS HASTILY BEEN DRAWN UP...

BOY, AM I GLAD TO SEE YOU! LISTEN, THIS CAR ISN'T A CAR AT ALL, IT'S A MECHANICAL MAN FROM THE PLANET VENUS--

THAT'S THE DAFFIEST EXCUSE I EVER HEARD! WE'RE TAKING YOU AND YOUR CAR IN!

SCREECH

SUDDENLY, BEFORE THE ASTONISHED EYES OF THE POLICE...

LOOK-- THERE HE IS!

I CAN'T ALLOW MYSELF TO BE CAPTURED! I WAS SENT HERE BECAUSE WE FEARED YOU EARTHLINGS MIGHT BE PLANNING AN ATOMIC ATTACK ON VENUS, THE NEAREST PLANET!

NOW THAT I'VE EXAMINED YOUR INSTALLATIONS, AND MADE PHOTOS WITH MY HEADLAMP-CONCEALED "EYES", I CAN RETURN TO MY PEOPLE WITH PROOF THAT NO SUCH ATTACK IS INTENDED!

HE'S TAKING OFF--JETTING RIGHT UP INTO SPACE!

6

YES--WE INSTANTLY BLOCKED THE TUNNEL AT THIS END BECAUSE YOU HADN'T PAID THE TOLL-CHARGE WHEN YOU ENTERED IT!

THAT'S WHY I DIDN'T PAY THE TOLL--SO YOU'D STOP ME! IT'S A GOOD THING FOR ME THE MACHINE-MAN DIDN'T KNOW ABOUT MONEY!

The End

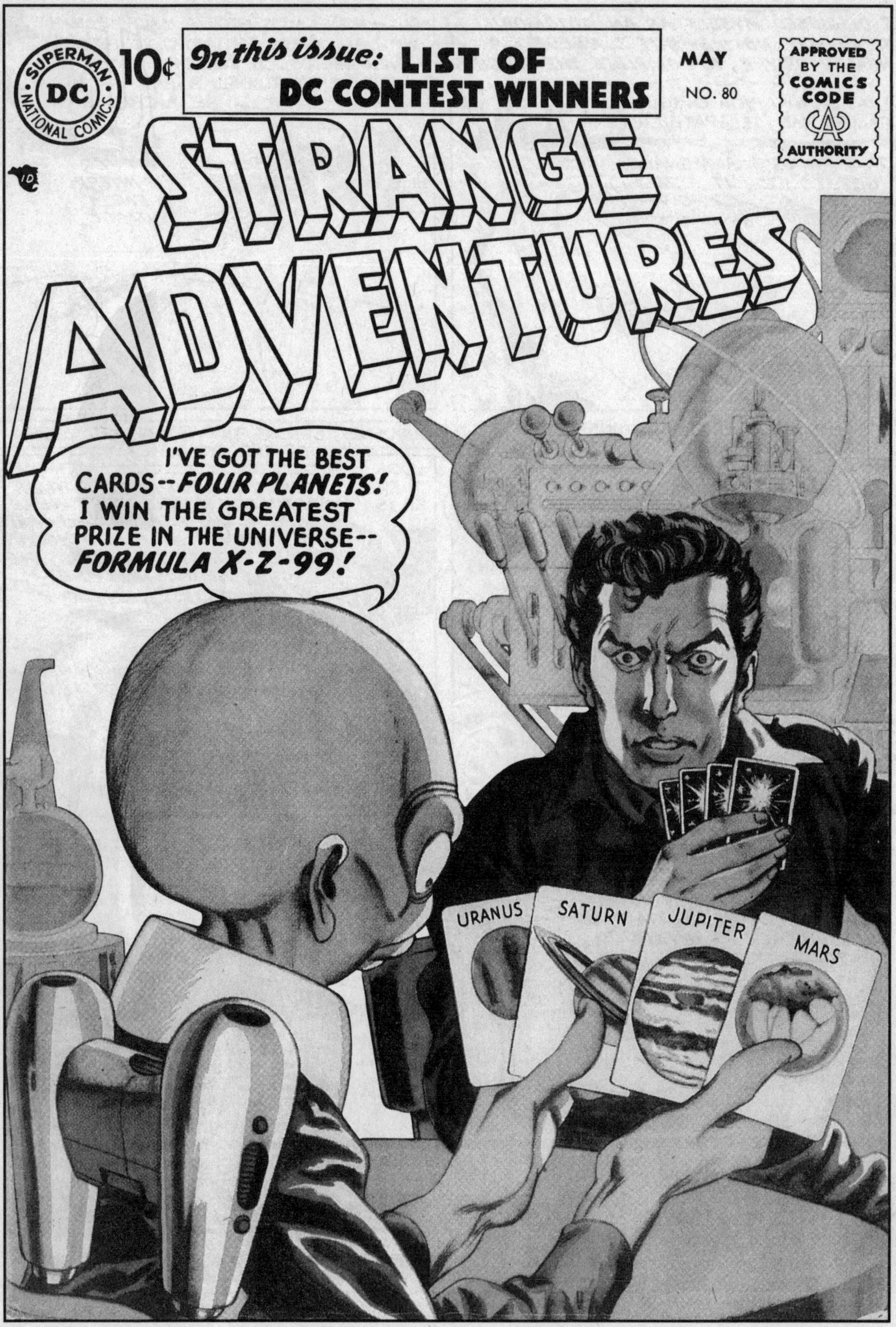
SUPERMAN DC NATIONAL COMICS
10¢
In this issue: LIST OF DC CONTEST WINNERS
MAY
NO. 80
APPROVED BY THE COMICS CODE AUTHORITY
STRANGE ADVENTURES
I'VE GOT THE BEST CARDS--FOUR PLANETS! I WIN THE GREATEST PRIZE IN THE UNIVERSE--FORMULA X-Z-99!
URANUS
SATURN
JUPITER
MARS

MIND ROBBERS OF VENUS!

IN TELEPATHY EXPERIMENTS, THE FAMOUS "RHINE" CARDS ARE STANDARD EQUIPMENT FOR TRANSMITTING MENTAL IMAGES BETWEEN HUMAN MINDS! BUT UNIQUE INDEED ARE THE *INTERPLANETARY TELEPATHY CARDS* A SPACE-VISITOR INTRODUCES TO A YOUNG SCIENTIST OF EARTH! THE TELEPATHY "GAME" PLAYED BETWEEN THEM HAS A SECRET MEANING MORE FANTASTIC THAN OUR WORLD HAS EVER KNOWN!

WHAT DO THESE AMAZING SPACE-SYMBOLS MEAN?

I CAN READ THE EARTHMAN'S THOUGHTS -- BUT HE CAN'T READ MINE! AND THAT GIVES ME THE ADVANTAGE I NEED TO WIN THIS GAME!

HOUR AFTER HOUR IN HIS ELECTRONIC LAB, IAN CALDWELL TENSELY TRANSMITS SIGNALS INTO SPACE WITH HIS NEW SUPER-RADIO...

DOT-DOT... DOT-DASH- DOT... DOT- DASH-DOT...

IF THERE'S INTELLIGENT LIFE ON VENUS-- THE NEAREST PLANET TO EARTH--THEY'LL ANSWER THIS SIMPLE DOT-AND-DASH SIGNAL! HOPE MY GENERATOR HAS ENOUGH POWER TO SPAN 25 MILLION MILES!

BUT INSTEAD OF AN ANSWERING MESSAGE, THE SCIENTIST STRANGELY RECEIVES...

A...A FORMULA! IT SUDDENLY FLASHED INTO MY MIND!

IT'S A FORMULA COMPLETELY UNKNOWN TO EARTHLY SCIENCE! IT... IT ALMOST SEEMED LIKE A TELEPATHIC MESSAGE SENT INTO MY MIND! BUT... WHO SENT IT--AND FROM WHERE?

THE ANSWER LIES HALFWAY BETWEEN EARTH AND VENUS, WHERE A SPACESHIP CRUISES...

I PROJECTED THE STOLEN FORMULA INTO THAT EARTHMAN'S MIND FOR SAFEKEEPING! THE FORMULA WAS "LOOT" I STOLE BACK ON VENUS!

GLOATINGLY, THE VENUSIAN CRIMINAL REVIEWS HIS RECENT COUP ON HIS NATIVE WORLD, WHERE THIEVES DO NOT STEAL *MATERIAL* BUT "MENTAL WEALTH"!

THAT SCIENTIST HAS A FORTUNE IN IDEAS! I'LL HURL SOME TELEPATHIC NITRO AT HIS BRAIN, FREEING HIS CONCEALED THOUGHTS!

HELP! A ROBBER... LOOTING MY SUPER-BOMB FORMULA!

GOT IT! I TELE-STOLE IT OUT OF HIS BRAIN SO COMPLETELY THAT HE'LL NO LONGER REMEMBER IT! NOW I'LL LOCK IT IN MY MIND AND MAKE MY SPACE-GETAWAY!

BUT PURSUING VENUSIAN LAW-OFFICERS OVERTAKE THE CRIMINAL HALFWAY TO EARTH...

THEY'LL NAB ME WITH THE LOOT IN MY BRAIN! HMM... SOME EARTHMAN IS SENDING RADIO SIGNALS TO VENUS! I CAN HIDE THE LOOT WITH HIM!

THUS IT WAS THAT THE FORMULA SEEMED TO "FLASH" INTO IAN CALDWELL'S BRAIN...

I'LL UNLOCK MY BRAIN AND TRANSMIT THE FORMULA! THE POLICE WILL NEVER SUSPECT I HID MY HAUL IN AN EARTHMAN'S BRAIN!

AND NOW, WHEN THE VENUS POLICE ACCUSE THE CAPTURED THIEF...

WHAT FORMULA? I'M INNOCENT! GO AHEAD, SEARCH MY MIND!

HE'S RIGHT! THE FORMULA ISN'T IN HIS BRAIN!

BAFFLED, THE POLICE LEAVE...

WE CAN'T ARREST HIM WITHOUT THE STOLEN FORMULA AS EVIDENCE!

HA HA! I'M FREE! NOW TO GET MY FORMULA BACK FROM THAT EARTHMAN'S MIND!

BUT WHEN THE CROOK SENDS A LONG-RANGE TELEPATHY PROBE INTO CALDWELL'S MIND ON EARTH...

...EGGS FOR BREAKFAST... ARE MY SIGNALS REACHING VENUS?... CAR NEEDS A CHECKUP...

GREAT STARS! EARTHMEN DON'T SORT THOUGHTS SYSTEMATICALLY LIKE WE DO! THEY THINK OF A NUMBER OF THINGS AT ONCE! MY FORMULA IS LOST IN A MAZE OF THOUGHTS!

I'VE GOT TO VISIT THE EARTHMAN AND GET MY LOOT BACK SOMEHOW! LUCKILY, I WAS ABLE TO FOLLOW HIS SPACE-SIGNALS TO HIS LAB! I'LL PRETEND I'M ANSWERING HIS CALL!

IAN CALDWELL DOES NOT SUSPECT THAT HIS VISITOR IS A CUNNING VENUSIAN CRIMINAL!

A CREATURE FROM ANOTHER WORLD! C-CAN IT BE A VENUSIAN WHO PICKED UP MY SIGNAL?

PERFECT! I CAN READ HIS DIRECT THOUGHTS BUT HE CAN'T READ MINE UNLESS I TRANSMIT THEM WITH FULL TELEPATHIC POWER!

GREETINGS! I AM PROFESSOR DJOK OF VENUS! YOUR SIGNALS REACHED MY SPACESHIP MIDWAY BETWEEN EARTH AND VENUS! DO YOU RECEIVE MY TELEPATHIC WORDS?

UH...VERY FAINTLY! YOU SEE, TELEPATHY IS ONLY IN ITS PRELIMINARY STAGES ON EARTH!

WE'VE ONLY MADE A CRUDE START TOWARD DEVELOPING TELEPATHY! PROFESSOR RHINE DEVISED THESE SIMPLE SYMBOLS FOR SUBJECTS TO TRANSMIT MENTALLY!

THIS GIVES ME AN IDEA! I'LL USE THESE CARDS OF MY WORLD, PRETENDING THEY'RE FOR OUR TELEPATHY EXPERIMENTS!

IF I CAN GET THE EARTHMAN TO CONCENTRATE ON NOTHING BUT THESE CARDS, HIS JUMBLED THOUGHTS WILL STOP WHIRLING AND I'LL BE ABLE TO EXTRACT MY FORMULA FROM HIS BRAIN!

CALDWELL IS DUPED BY THE SPACE-CRIMINAL'S TRICK...

I GET IT! THOSE ARE VENUSIAN TELEPATHY CARDS! YOU'RE GOING TO TRAIN ME TO COMMUNICATE MENTALLY WITH YOU! GOOD, LET'S START!

HE DOESN'T KNOW THESE ARE ORDINARY PLAYING CARDS WE USE ON VENUS!

WHAT UNIQUE SPACE-SYMBOLS! I'LL CONCENTRATE AND SEND THE IMAGES TO HIS MIND!

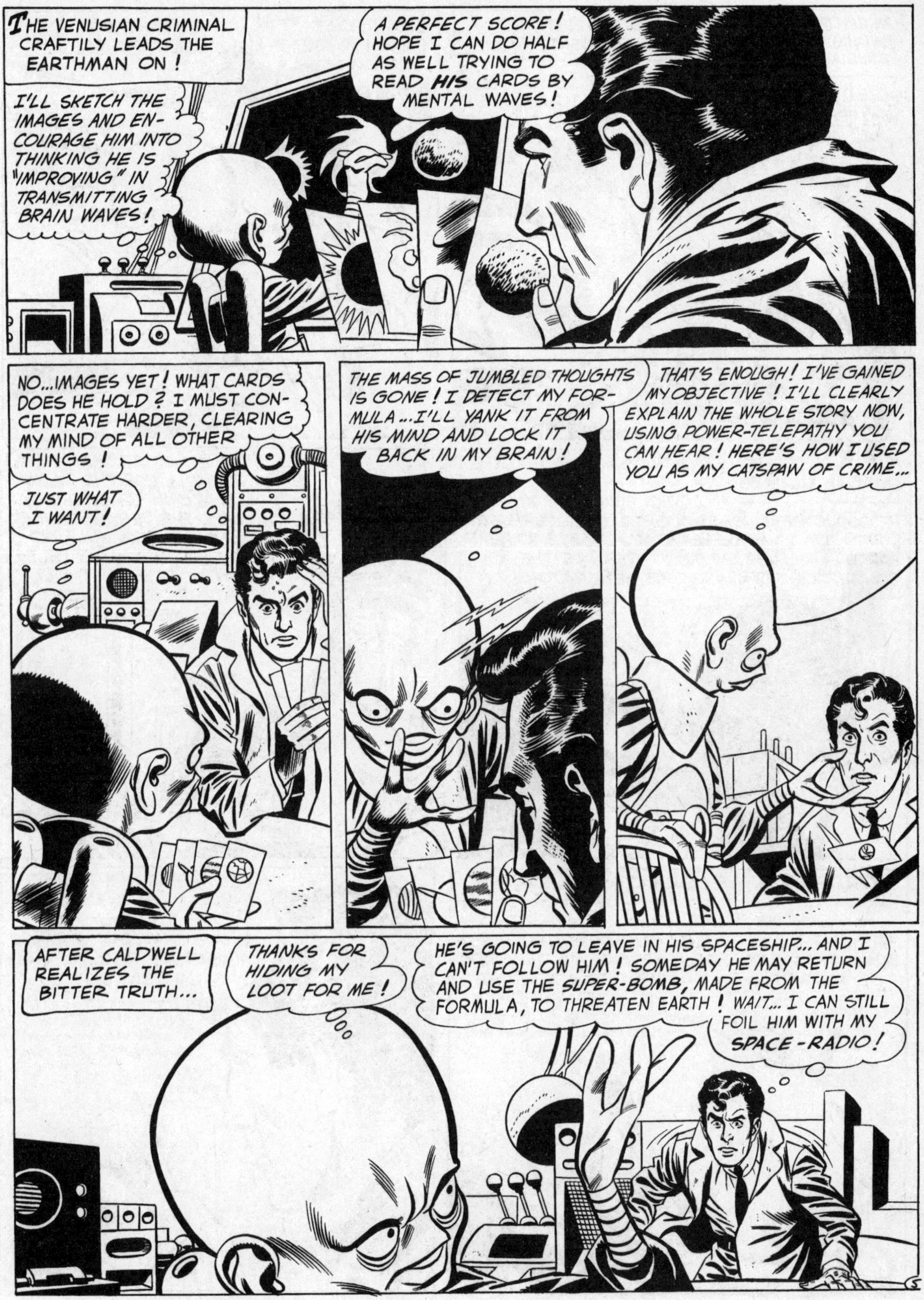
THE VENUSIAN CRIMINAL CRAFTILY LEADS THE EARTHMAN ON!
A PERFECT SCORE! HOPE I CAN DO HALF AS WELL TRYING TO READ HIS CARDS BY MENTAL WAVES!
I'LL SKETCH THE IMAGES AND ENCOURAGE HIM INTO THINKING HE IS "IMPROVING" IN TRANSMITTING BRAIN WAVES!
NO...IMAGES YET! WHAT CARDS DOES HE HOLD? I MUST CONCENTRATE HARDER, CLEARING MY MIND OF ALL OTHER THINGS!
JUST WHAT I WANT!
THE MASS OF JUMBLED THOUGHTS IS GONE! I DETECT MY FORMULA...I'LL YANK IT FROM HIS MIND AND LOCK IT BACK IN MY BRAIN!
THAT'S ENOUGH! I'VE GAINED MY OBJECTIVE! I'LL CLEARLY EXPLAIN THE WHOLE STORY NOW, USING POWER-TELEPATHY YOU CAN HEAR! HERE'S HOW I USED YOU AS MY CATSPAW OF CRIME...
AFTER CALDWELL REALIZES THE BITTER TRUTH...
THANKS FOR HIDING MY LOOT FOR ME!
HE'S GOING TO LEAVE IN HIS SPACESHIP... AND I CAN'T FOLLOW HIM! SOMEDAY HE MAY RETURN AND USE THE SUPER-BOMB, MADE FROM THE FORMULA, TO THREATEN EARTH! WAIT... I CAN STILL FOIL HIM WITH MY SPACE-RADIO!
5

HAS THE EARTH SCIENTIST FORGOTTEN THAT THE VENUSIAN CAN READ HIS DIRECT THOUGHTS?

IF MY SIGNALS REACHED HALFWAY TO VENUS BEFORE, MORE POWER WILL LET ME CONTACT THE VENUS POLICE!

NO YOU WON'T! I PICKED UP YOUR THOUGHTS!

STOP! DON'T SMASH MY RADIO—TRANSMITTER!

HE POINTED IT RIGHT OUT TO ME!

HIGH VOLTAGE GENERATOR

DO NOT TOUCH!

BUT IT IS NOT THE RADIO-TRANSMITTER THAT THE CRIMINAL STRIKES!

I TRICKED HIM! I KNEW HE COULD READ MY THOUGHTS, SO I PURPOSELY LURED HIM TO MY GENERATOR! UNABLE TO READ EARTH LANGUAGE, HE DIDN'T REALIZE THE DANGER OF TOUCHING THE GENERATOR!

THE SHOCK STUNNED HIM! NOW I'LL USE THE RADIO IN HIS OWN SPACESHIP TO CALL THE VENUS POLICE TO COME FOR HIM! NO DOUBT THEY HAVE TELEPATHY SETS THAT WILL PICK UP MY THOUGHT MESSAGE!

LATER, AFTER THE VENUS POLICE COME FOR THE PRISONER...

WE CAUGHT HIM WITH THE LOOT IN HIS BRAIN--THANKS TO THAT EARTHMAN!

THEY EXPLAINED THEY HAVEN'T VISITED EARTH BEFORE, AS THEY DIDN'T WANT TO INTERFERE WITH OUR WAY OF LIFE!

I'LL KEEP THESE TELEPATHY CARDS AS SOUVENIRS! THEY'RE THE ONLY PROOF I HAVE THAT THIS STRANGE ADVENTURE REALLY HAPPENED!

The End

6

The Worlds that SWITCHED PLACES!

THE SUREST THING IN THE WORLD, YOU MIGHT EXPECT, IS THAT THE SUN WILL RISE EACH MORNING! BUT WHAT IF YOU SAW *TWO SUNS* RISE ONE DAY? AND THEN SAW *FOUR MOONS* IN THE NIGHT SKY? WHO--OR--WHAT COULD CAUSE SUCH A STRANGE CELESTIAL CHANGE?

THE UNIVERSE AROUND US HAS SUDDENLY CHANGED!

LOOK! A GIGANTIC *SPACE-TORNADO* RUSHING TOWARD EARTH!

WITHOUT WARNING, THE MOST AMAZING DAY ON EARTH BEGINS ...

GASP! TWO SUNS IN THE SKY--AND NEITHER ONE IS OUR OWN YELLOW SUN!

WHILE ON THE OTHER SIDE OF EARTH, THE SKY PRESENTS ANOTHER STARTLING PHENOMENON ...

BY BUDDHA-- LOOK! FOUR MOONS --ALL DIFFERENT FROM OUR MOON-- WHICH SUDDENLY VANISHED!

TELESCOPES PROBE SPACE TO FIND THAT THE ENTIRE SOLAR SYSTEM AROUND EARTH HAS FANTASTICALLY CHANGED...

THE SUN-MOON-MARS- VENUS-ALL THE FAMILIAR PLANETS HAVE DISAPPEARED! AND IN THEIR STEAD ARE NEW WORLDS!

BUT JOHN JASON, MAKING A RECORD-BREAKING ROCKET FLIGHT ABOVE EARTH, IS EVEN MORE ASTONISHED WHEN ...

I SET A NEW ALTITUDE RECORD--1,000 MILES! NOW TO LAND AND... GOOD GOSH! THE CONTINENTS AND OCEANS ARE ALL CHANGED... THAT ISN'T EARTH BELOW!

AFTER THE ROCKET PILOT LANDS ...

THE TREES AND ANIMALS ARE UNEARTHLY TOO! DURING MY SHORT ROCKET FLIGHT, EARTH SOMEHOW CHANGED INTO THIS STRANGE PLANET! YET...YET THE SUN HASN'T CHANGED!

AS JASON WANDERS AROUND, LOOKING FOR A SIGN OF LIFE, NIGHT FALLS ...

THERE'S EARTH'S MOON... THE RED STAR MARS... THE BIG DIPPER! THE UNIVERSE AROUND ME HASN'T CHANGED... ONLY EARTH! WILL I FIND STRANGE PEOPLE HERE, TOO?

2

AS HE MAKES HIS WAY TO AN ALIEN CITY...

THEY'RE FRIENDLY, BUT THEIR LANGUAGE IS GIBBERISH TO ME! MY BEST BET IS TO FIND SOMEONE TO TEACH ME THE LANGUAGE!

SHORTLY, JOHN JASON GOES TO "ELEMENTARY SCHOOL"...

VYGRA! ZOLLITUN!

"VYGRA" IS THE NAME OF THEIR WORLD! "ZOLLITUN" IS SPACESHIP! I'M LEARNING FAST!

AFTER INTENSIVE STUDY...

I'VE LEARNED ENOUGH TO SPEAK A SORT OF "BROKEN ENGLISH" IN THEIR LANGUAGE! NOW...

YOU WANT TO KNOW WHAT HAPPENED TO YOUR EARTH? COME, I WILL EXPLAIN TO YOU...

IN A SUPER-SCIENCE LABORATORY...

EARTH... VYGRA... FOURTH DIMENSION... EXCHANGED...!

I ONLY GET A WORD HERE AND THERE, BUT SEEMINGLY THAT FOURTH DIMENSION MACHINE MADE EARTH AND VYGRA **SWITCH PLACES** ACROSS GALACTIC SPACE!

IT HAPPENED DURING MY ROCKET FLIGHT, SO THAT WHEN I LANDED, VYGRA WAS IN EARTH'S ORBIT! EARTH, IN TURN, IS IN VYGRA'S ORBIT, SURROUNDED BY A WHOLE NEW UNIVERSE!

NOW I ASKED **WHY** THEY SWITCHED OUR TWO WORLDS!

VYGRA TAKE... EARTH'S PLACE... BECAUSE... **SPACE DOOM**...! APPROACHING!

GREAT STARS! HE MEANS THAT VYGRA RUTHLESSLY "STOLE" EARTH'S SAFE ORBIT, LEAVING EARTH IN THE PATH OF AN ONCOMING "**SPACE DOOM**"! WHAT A COWARDLY TRICK! BUT WHAT "DOOM" IS IT?...

3

THE ANSWER IS BEYOND JASON'S LIMITED LANGUAGE STUDY...

TOO COMPLEX... I'LL HAVE TO STUDY THEIR LANGUAGE MORE! BUT WAIT... THAT INSTRUMENT IS LABELED "DIMENSION RADIO-TV"! I'LL STEAL BACK LATER AND SEND A WARNING TO EARTH!

LATE THAT NIGHT...

ATTENTION, EARTH! SOS FROM JOHN JASON! THE PLANET VYGRA HAS SWITCHED PLACES WITH EARTH, TO ESCAPE A SPACE DOOM IN THEIR UNIVERSE...WHICH NOW THREATENS YOU!

ON EARTH...

SEARCH FOR THE UNKNOWN DOOM! YOU MUST FIND IT--AND TRY TO STOP IT!

EARTHLY TELESCOPES PROBE THE UNFAMILIAR UNIVERSE AROUND IT FOR SPACE DANGERS, BUT WITHOUT SUCCESS!

THAT SPACE TORNADO WILL MISS EARTH! IT ISN'T THAT!

THAT GLOWING PLANET ISN'T SENDING DEADLY "NUCLEAR" RAYS AT EARTH, ONLY HARMLESS PHOSPHORES-CENCE!

LIGHTNING FLASHES OCCUR BETWEEN THE TWIN SUNS... BUT OF LOW VOLTAGE... HARMLESS TO EARTH!

WHEN THE LONE EARTHMAN STRANDED ON VYGRA HEARS THE NEWS...

CALLING JOHN JASON! WE FAILED TO FIND SPACE DOOM! CAN YOU FIND A WAY TO SAVE EARTH?

I CAN--BY SWITCHING THE TWO WORLDS BACK AND LETTING VYGRA FACE ITS OWN DOOM!

MOMENTS LATER, JASON BOWLS OVER THE SCIENTISTS GROUPED AROUND THE PLANET-SWITCHER...

OUT OF MY WAY! I'M GOING TO REVERSE THE SWITCHER'S CONTROLS!

4

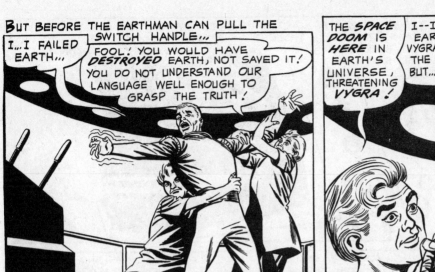

BUT BEFORE THE EARTHMAN CAN PULL THE SWITCH HANDLE....

I...I FAILED EARTH...

FOOL! YOU WOULD HAVE *DESTROYED* EARTH, NOT SAVED IT! YOU DO NOT UNDERSTAND OUR LANGUAGE WELL ENOUGH TO GRASP THE TRUTH!

THE *SPACE DOOM* IS *HERE* IN EARTH'S UNIVERSE, THREATENING *VYGRA!*

I--I HAD IT TWISTED! EARTH IS SAFE AND VYGRA IS BRAVELY FACING THE DANGER FOR US! BUT...I DON'T UNDERSTAND...

WE KNEW EARTHLY SCIENCE WAS UNABLE TO DETECT THE DANGER, AS OUR DIMENSION-TV DID! WE SWITCHED WORLDS TO TRY STOPPING THE DOOM WITH OUR SUPER-SCIENCE....

BUT WHAT IS THE *SPACE DOOM?*

IN 24 HOURS, YOUR SOLAR SYSTEM WILL FLY APART.... WHEN YOUR SUN'S GRAVITATIONAL FORCE WILL BE CUT OFF BY A GIANT *VACUUM BUBBLE* DRIFTING IN FROM OUTER SPACE!

VACUUM BUBBLE? BUT ALL SPACE IS A VACUUM!

NOT QUITE! EVEN THOUGH SPACE IS A "VACUUM" COMPARED TO AIR, IT CONTAINS ENOUGH ATOMS TO 'TRANSMIT" GRAVITY!

IN AIR... 60,000,000,000,000,000, HYDROGEN ATOMS PER CUBIC CENTIMETER

IN SPACE... 1 HYDROGEN ATOM PER CUBIC CENTIMETER

THE GIANT *BUBBLE* IS AN *ABSOLUTE VACUUM,* COMPLETELY CUTTING OFF GRAVITY! BUT AFTER FIRST SPOTTING IT, WE LOST ITS POSITION! OUR SEARCHING SPACESHIPS HAVE BEEN UNABLE TO LOCATE IT AGAIN!

VACUUM BUBBLE... ZERO ATOMS

5

AND UNLESS WE FIND THE *VACUUM BUBBLE IN YOUR SOLAR SYSTEM* WITHIN 24 HOURS, WE WILL BE FORCED TO SWITCH VYGRA BACK, TO SAVE OUR-SELVES!

...AND THUS DOOM EARTH! WAIT... I JUST THOUGHT OF A WAY TO LOCATE THE *BUBBLE!*

FOLLOWING THE EARTH-MAN'S PLAN, A SHIP SCOURS SPACE WITH SPECIAL EQUIPMENT....

THIS SPRAY OF *DEUTERIUM,* OR DOUBLE-ATOM HYDROGEN, COMBINES WITH THE SINGLE HYDROGEN-ATOMS IN SPACE TO FORM TRIPLE-ATOM *TRITIUM!*

WHICH IS RADIOACTIVE AND *GLOWS!* WHEN WE SPOT A *NO GLOW* AREA, IT WILL INDICATE THE ATOM-LESS *VACUUM BUBBLE!*

NERVE-WRACKING HOURS OF SEARCH FOLLOW UNTIL...

THE SPRAY CAUSES NO GLOW HERE! WE'VE FOUND THE VACUUM BUBBLE...!

ALL WE HAVE TO DO NOW IS "SEED" THIS PURE VACUUM WITH HYDROGEN ATOMS! IT WILL TURN INTO ORDINARY "SPACE", ALLOW-ING THE FORCE OF GRAVITY TO WORK--

--AND THEREBY PREVENT THE SOLAR SYSTEM FROM FLYING APART!

HYDROGEN GAS

LATER, AS JASON AGAIN RIDES HIS REFUELED ROCKET...

THEY'RE SWITCHING THE TWO PLANETS BACK TO THEIR ORIGINAL POSITION! ALL'S RIGHT WITH OUR WORLD AGAIN!

The End 6

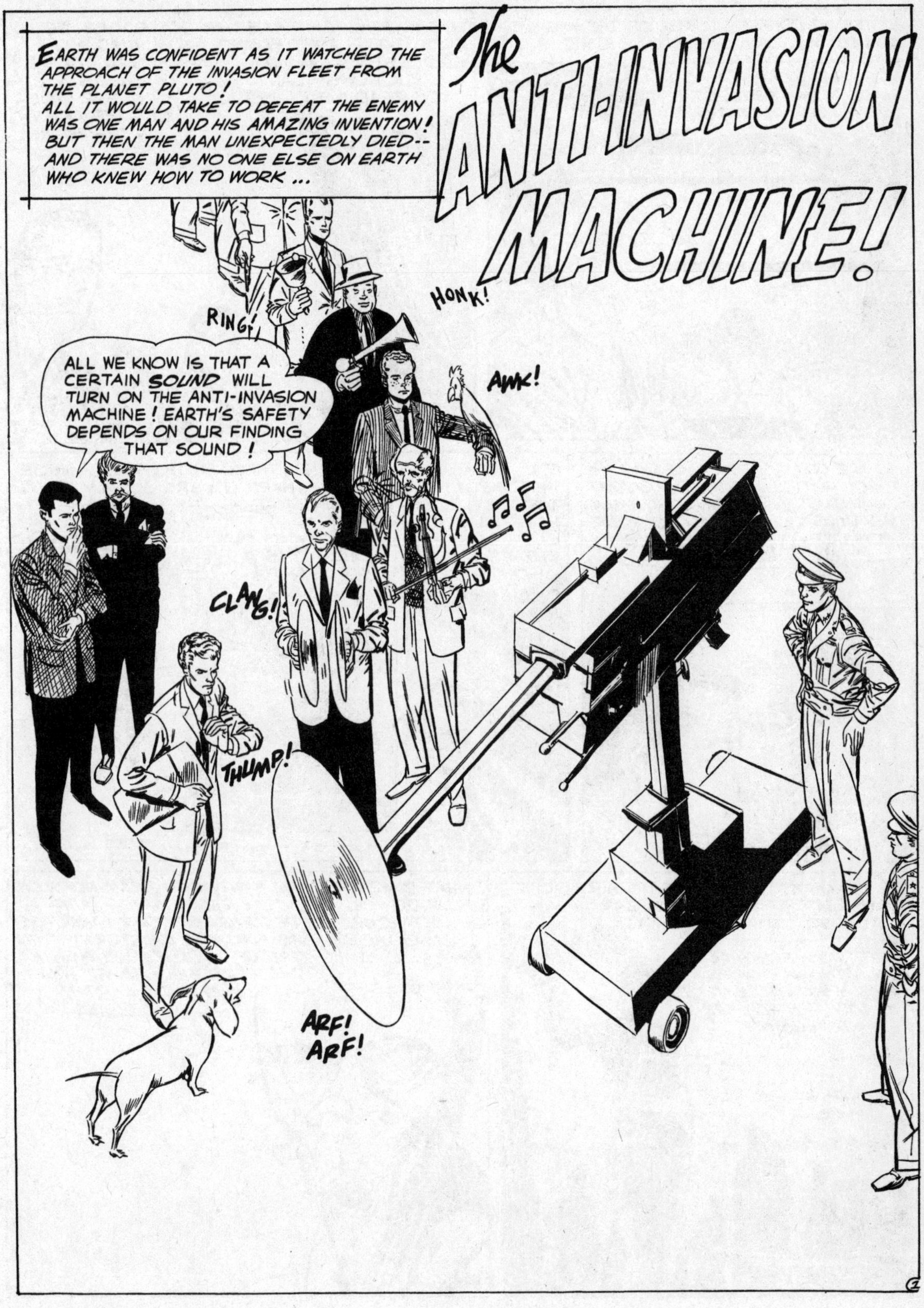
EARTH WAS CONFIDENT AS IT WATCHED THE APPROACH OF THE INVASION FLEET FROM THE PLANET PLUTO!
ALL IT WOULD TAKE TO DEFEAT THE ENEMY WAS ONE MAN AND HIS AMAZING INVENTION! BUT THEN THE MAN UNEXPECTEDLY DIED--AND THERE WAS NO ONE ELSE ON EARTH WHO KNEW HOW TO WORK ...
The ANTI-INVASION MACHINE!
HONK!
RING!
AWK!
ALL WE KNOW IS THAT A CERTAIN SOUND WILL TURN ON THE ANTI-INVASION MACHINE! EARTH'S SAFETY DEPENDS ON OUR FINDING THAT SOUND!
CLANG!
THUMP!
ARF! ARF!

AT THE AIR CONTROL TOWER OF THE WASHINGTON, D.C. AIRPORT, ONE FOGGY NIGHT...

REQUEST CLEAR AIR FOR GLIDE PATH! REQUEST LANDING INSTRUCTIONS!

IDENTIFY YOURSELF!

THIS IS SPACESHIP **KL526K** FROM THE PLANET *PLUTO,* REQUESTING LANDING INSTRUCTIONS! CAN YOU READ ME?

ROGER, WE READ YOU-- JOKER! GLIDE LANES ALL CLEAR! JOE-- GET THE ARMY ON THE PHONE!

YOU ARE COMING THROUGH THE OVERCAST, HEADING TOWARD CENTER LINE!

A SPACESHIP COMES *STRAIGHT DOWN,* EARTHMAN-- NOT ALONG YOUR *CENTER LINE!*

STILL MAKING WITH THE JOKES! WAIT'LL I GET YOU DOWN HERE, PILOT! GLIDE LANES CLEAR! COME ON IN!

AND THEN, THROUGH THE FOG, A HUGE METAL SHAPE LOWERS SLOWLY TO THE GROUND!

FOR CRYING OUT LOUD! IT *IS* A SPACESHIP!

AS THE GIANT SHIP OPENS ITS AIR LOCKS, ARMY GENERALS AND NUCLEAR PHYSICISTS SWARM TOWARD IT...

GREETINGS, EARTHMEN! I AM JUL VAN OF PLUTO! MY MISSION TO EARTH IS TO WARN YOU OF *DANGER!*

WHAT DANGER? HOW DO YOU KNOW OUR LANGUAGE?

WE HAVE BEEN BEAMING IN ON YOUR RADIO WAVES, AND DECIPHERED YOUR LANGUAGE! AS FOR THE DANGER--WITHIN ONE OF YOUR LUNAR MONTHS, THE PLUTONIAN FLEET WILL *ATTACK EARTH!*

OUR HYDROGEN BOMBS WILL--

NO--THE INVADERS HAVE A SPECIAL RAY-GUN THAT PREVENTS THE EXPLOSION OF NUCLEAR BOMBS! AS A MEMBER OF THE PLUTONIAN PEACE PARTY THAT OPPOSES THE INVASION, I OFFER YOU MY SERVICES IN REPELLING THE INVADER!

SOON AFTER, AT A HURRIEDLY CALLED MEETING...

AS YOU KNOW, SOUND WAVES CAN SHATTER GLASS-- CAUSE BRIDGES TO FALL -- MAKE COTTON BURST INTO FLAME, CONDENSE FOG INTO WATER! I PROPOSE TO USE SOUND IN ANOTHER WAY... TO ANNIHILATE MATTER!

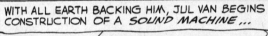

WITH ALL EARTH BACKING HIM, JUL VAN BEGINS CONSTRUCTION OF A SOUND MACHINE...

IT OPERATES TO A SPECIAL SOUND WAVE--WHICH I'VE TAKEN AN OATH NEVER TO DIVULGE! I SHALL BE READY TO DEMONSTRATE IT IN A FEW DAYS!

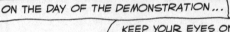

ON THE DAY OF THE DEMONSTRATION...

KEEP YOUR EYES ON THAT HOUSE, PLEASE-- WHILE I ACTIVATE THE MACHINE!

AN INSTANT LATER...

THE HOUSE IS GONE-- VANISHED!

SOUND DISINTEGRATED IT INTO THE INVISIBLE ATOMS THAT COMPRISED IT!

"MY MACHINE WILL PERFORM EXACTLY THE SAME WAY AGAINST THE LANDING FLEET, SENDING ITS SONIC BEAMS A THOUSAND MILES INTO SPACE!"

UNKNOWN TO THE PLUTONIAN WAR PARTY, WE SCIENTISTS SECRETLY DEVISED THIS DEVASTATING MACHINE TO KEEP THE PEACE! YOU NEED NO LONGER FEAR AN INVASION FROM SPACE!

AS THE DATE OF THREATENED INVASION NEARS, EARTH TELESCOPES SCAN THE SKIES...

I SEE THEM--TINY DOTS NEAR MARS WHERE THE SUNLIGHT OF SPACE REFLECTS OFF THEIR METAL SHELLS!

ANXIOUS PEOPLE GATHER IN THE PARK AND ON ROOFTOPS WITH HOMEMADE 'SCOPES AND POWERFUL BINOCULARS...

JOE, HOW MUCH LONGER BEFORE THEY APPEAR OVER EARTH?

WHAT DIFFERENCE DOES IT MAKE? THE CLOSEST THEY'LL EVER GET TO OUR WORLD IS 1,000 MILES!

THEN, ONE DAY, AS ARMY GENERALS CALL UPON THE PLUTONIAN...

WHAT HAPPENED?

JUL VAN IS DEAD! PROBABLY KILLED--ACCIDENTALLY--BY HIS OWN INVENTION!

THE MACHINE DESIGNED TO SAVE EARTH RESTS MUTE AND LIFELESS AS ITS INVENTOR...

THE INVASION IS ONLY A FEW DAYS AWAY! WE'VE GOT TO WORK THAT MACHINE OURSELVES!

BUT ONLY JUL VAN KNEW THE SECRET SOUND WAVE THAT OPERATES IT!

THERE'S ONLY ONE THING TO DO--SUBJECT THE MACHINE TO EVERY SOUND WE CAN THINK OF! ONE OF THEM IS BOUND TO TURN IT ON!

As MILITARY MEN AND SCIENTISTS TRY SOUND AFTER SOUND ON THE MACHINE...

THE VIOLIN DOESN'T PRODUCE THE RIGHT SOUND! *NEXT!*

DONKEYS BRAY AND ELEPHANTS TRUMPET WITHOUT SUCCESS...

WHEEE!

RIFLE SHOTS AND CANNON BOOMS, THE SINGING OF BIRDS AND THE BUZZ OF BEES HAVE NO EFFECT...

BZZZ!

AS EACH OF THE SOUND-MAKERS FAILS TO ACTIVATE THE MACHINE, A SPECIAL CONFERENCE IS CALLED TO HEAR A DRAMATIC ANNOUNCEMENT BY SCIENTIST RALPH BAXTER...

GENTLEMEN, WE HAVE BEEN *HOAXED!* THE MACHINE AND ITS INVENTER, JUL VAN-- ARE *FAKES!*

AT THAT VERY MOMENT, LOUDSPEAKERS ON EARTH BLAST OMINOUSLY...

PEOPLE OF EARTH--SURRENDER! IF YOU REFUSE, WE SHALL ENTER YOUR ATMOSPHERE AND DESTROY YOU ALL! YOU HAVE ONE HOUR TO ANSWER...

ONE HOUR IS ALL WE NEED, GENTLEMEN, IF YOU AGREE TO MY PLAN...

55 MINUTES LATER, IN A PREPARED WATCHTOWER NEAR WHITE SANDS...

THE AUTHORITIES HAVE GIVEN US THE GO-HEAD! FIRE ONE! FIRE TWO!

WITH A ROAR OF JETS, TWO MIGHTY ROCKETS, EACH FITTED WITH A HYDROGEN BOMB WARHEAD, SPEED SPACEWARD...

AT THE FRINGE OF OUTER SPACE, ABOVE THE ATMOSPHERIC ZONE OF EARTH...

OUR TRICK FAILED! JUL VAN SACRIFICED HIS LIFE IN VAIN!

MOMENTS LATER...

YOUR PLAN WORKED, DR. BAXTER!

THE PLUTONIAN SPACESHIPS ARE FLEEING! EARTH IS SAVED!

ACTUALLY, THE PLUTONIANS DID FEAR OUR NUCLEAR BOMB! TO PREVENT US FROM USING IT AGAINST THEM, THEY SENT JUL VAN HERE TO PERSUADE US THAT ONLY HIS SOUND-- MACHINE COULD STOP THE INVASION!

BUT THEN I REMEMBERED SOMETHING JUL VAN SAID--THAT HIS MACHINE'S SOUND WAVES WOULD DESTROY THE PLUTONIAN SPACE-FLEET A THOUSAND MILES UP! BUT THERE IS ONLY SPACE THAT HIGH UP-- NO AIR AT ALL--AND SOUND WAVES CAN TRAVEL ONLY THROUGH AN ATMOSPHERE!

HOWEVER, THE HOAX DID SOME GOOD! THE PLUTONIANS' SOUND MACHINE DOES WORK-- EVEN IF ONLY AT SHORT RANGE! ONCE WE FIND THE SOUND THAT ACTIVATES IT, WE'LL WORK ON EXTENDING ITS RANGE--AND USE IT FOR THE BENEFIT OF MANKIND!

The End

The MAN WHO CHEATED TIME!

BART LANSON KNEW EXACTLY HOW HE WOULD LIVE THE REST OF HIS LIFE -- FOR HE HAD PREVIEWED IT ALL WITH HIS AMAZING *FUTUROSCOPE*! NOT ONLY DID HE FORESEE HOW TO MAKE A FORTUNE, BUT HOW TO AVOID ANY SUDDEN DEATH FOR THE NEXT 50 YEARS!

I AVOIDED DEATH -- TIME AND TIME AGAIN! I SEE MYSELF ALIVE 20 YEARS FROM NOW, THE RICHEST MAN ON EARTH! I'VE CHEATED FATHER TIME!

HAVE YOU, MY SON?... WE SHALL SEE!

TIME DIAL

IN HIS HOME WORK SHOP, INVENTOR BART LANSON FINISHES AN AMAZING DEVICE!

MY *FUTUROSCOPE*, POWERED BY ATOMIC RADIATIONS, WILL SCAN THE FUTURE LIKE *TV*! BY TUNING IN ON THE FUTURE I'LL BE ABLE TO "FORESEE" HOW TO LIVE A PROFITABLE LIFE!

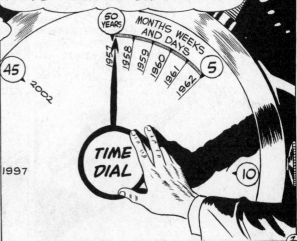

MY *TIME DIAL* IS CALIBRATED TO COVER THE NEXT 50 YEARS OF MY LIFE! AS A STARTER, I'LL MOVE THE DIAL TO THE FIRST MARKING -- 24 HOURS FROM NOW! I WONDER WHAT I'LL BE DOING?

50 YEARS

MONTHS WEEKS AND DAYS

TIME DIAL

BREATHLESSLY, BART LANSON PEERS AT HIMSELF IN THE FUTURE!

I'M STANDING AT THE WINDOW LOOKING OUT! WHAT'S GOING ON OUTSIDE? I'LL SHIFT MY VIEWPOINT...

GREAT SCOTT! THE NEXT INSTANT A LIGHTNING FLASH STRUCK THROUGH MY WINDOW! DID IT... UH... HIT ME?

CRACK!

I'M LYING LIFELESS ON THE FLOOR! THEN A... A BOLT OF LIGHTNING WILL KILL ME...IN 24 HOURS...

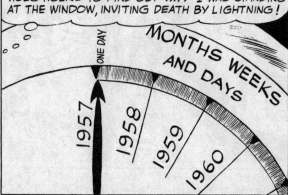

IN ORDER TO SEE 50 YEARS INTO THE FUTURE, I HAD TO MAKE THE FIRST MARKING ON THE *TIME DIAL* 24 HOURS AHEAD! I CAN'T TUNE ANY PREVIOUS HOURS TO FIND OUT *WHY* I WAS STANDING AT THE WINDOW, INVITING DEATH BY LIGHTNING!

ONE DAY

MONTHS WEEKS AND DAYS

1957 1958 1959 1960

WHAT AM I WORRIED ABOUT? ALL I HAVE TO DO IS AVOID STANDING NEAR THE WINDOW 24 HOURS FROM NOW-- AND THUS *CHEAT DEATH!*

March 19, 1957--8 P.M.

Avoid lightning bolt!

AS BART LANSON PUSHES A SPECIAL CONTROL ON HIS *FUTUROSCOPE*...

BUT MY DEVICE WON'T SHOW ME ALIVE IN THE FUTURE, AFTER MY FATED DEATH, UNLESS I GIVE IT SPECIAL INSTRUCTIONS! PRESSING THIS BUTTON OPERATES A CODE SAYING-- "*ASSUMING BART LANSON AVOIDS DEATH ON MARCH 19, 1957, SHOW THE ALTERNATE FUTURE HE WILL LIVE!*"

DEATH AVOIDED

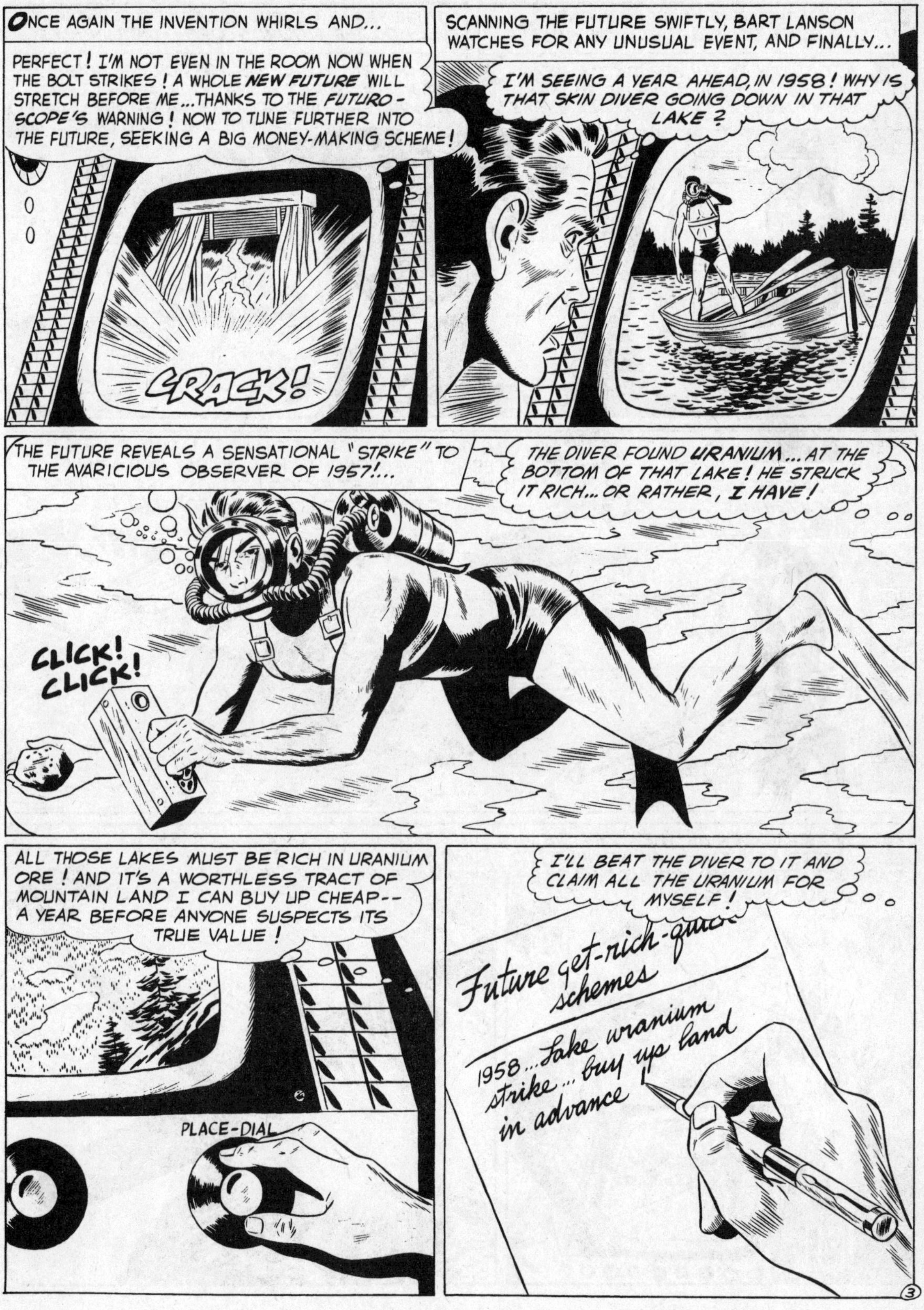

ONCE AGAIN THE INVENTION WHIRLS AND...
PERFECT! I'M NOT EVEN IN THE ROOM NOW WHEN THE BOLT STRIKES! A WHOLE NEW FUTURE WILL STRETCH BEFORE ME...THANKS TO THE FUTURO-SCOPE'S WARNING! NOW TO TUNE FURTHER INTO THE FUTURE, SEEKING A BIG MONEY-MAKING SCHEME!
CRACK!
SCANNING THE FUTURE SWIFTLY, BART LANSON WATCHES FOR ANY UNUSUAL EVENT, AND FINALLY...
I'M SEEING A YEAR AHEAD, IN 1958! WHY IS THAT SKIN DIVER GOING DOWN IN THAT LAKE?
THE FUTURE REVEALS A SENSATIONAL "STRIKE" TO THE AVARICIOUS OBSERVER OF 1957!...
THE DIVER FOUND URANIUM... AT THE BOTTOM OF THAT LAKE! HE STRUCK IT RICH... OR RATHER, I HAVE!
CLICK! CLICK!
ALL THOSE LAKES MUST BE RICH IN URANIUM ORE! AND IT'S A WORTHLESS TRACT OF MOUNTAIN LAND I CAN BUY UP CHEAP-- A YEAR BEFORE ANYONE SUSPECTS ITS TRUE VALUE!
PLACE-DIAL
I'LL BEAT THE DIVER TO IT AND CLAIM ALL THE URANIUM FOR MYSELF!
Future get-rich-quick schemes
1958...Lake uranium strike...buy up land in advance
3

CAUTIOUSLY, THE MONEY-HUNGRY INVENTOR MAKES A QUICK DOUBLE-CHECK ON HIMSELF...

BUT WHAT IF DEATH STRUCK ME MEAN-WHILE? ...NO, I'M ALIVE IN 1958 -- CASHING IN ON THAT URANIUM STRIKE!

FUTURE YEARS BEYOND 1958 UNFOLD UNEVENT-FULLY ON THE *FUTUROSCOPE* -- UNTIL IN *1963*...

THAT OLD RIVER-BED WAS DRY FOR CENTURIES... BUT A CLOUDBURST IN THE MOUNTAINS FILLED IT WITH WATER -- AND NOW THE WATER IS FLOOD-ING OVER THE LAND...

THERE GOES MY BARN! I NEVER INSURED IT AGAINST FLOOD... WHO WOULD EVER EXPECT IT?

I'LL TAKE ADVANTAGE OF THAT! I'LL PUT UP A BIG HOUSING DEVELOPMENT THERE IN 1962 AND INSURE IT HEAVILY AGAINST FLOOD! I'LL GET THE CHEAPEST RATES...AND COLLECT A FORTUNE!

BUT I BETTER CHECK WHETHER I'M ALIVE IN 1963! THERE... I'M TAKING AN AIRLINER! DO I ARRIVE SAFELY AT MY DESTINATION? I'LL PLAY SAFE AND MAKE SURE!

GOOD GOSH! THE PLANE WILL CRASH AND BURN, LEAVING NO SURVIVORS! MY LIFE WILL END...IN 1963!

4

March 19, 1957 -- 8 P.M.
Avoid lightning bolt!

July 8, 1963
Cancel plane trip

NOW...ASSUMING I CHEAT DEATH AGAIN, I'LL SEE MY ALTERNATE FUTURE BEYOND!

DEATH AVOIDED

THEN, AS THE *FUTUROSCOPE* UNVEILS THE YEAR 1968...

THE LEGENDARY *PHILOSOPHERS' STONE* HAS BECOME A REALITY! I CAN TURN LEAD INTO GOLD!

I'LL SEEK OUT THAT INVENTOR TOMORROW-- AND MAKE A DEAL WITH HIM TO FINANCE ALL HIS EXPERIMENTS --FOR A HALF-INTEREST IN HIS FUTURE DISCOVERIES!

BUT WHEN LANSON CHECKS HIS OWN FUTURE...

HUH?...NO SIGN OF ME...ANYWHERE! THE *GRIM REAPER* MUST HAVE STRUCK ME PREVIOUSLY! I'LL CHECK BACKWARDS DAY BY DAY!

FINALLY... THERE IT IS! A *ROCKETMOBILE* CRASH IN 1968! I'LL STEER CLEAR OF THAT! THEN, AFTER PUNCHING THE "DEATH AVOIDED" BUTTON, THE *FUTURO-SCOPE* WILL SHOW ME LIVING ON!

AS MORE FUTURE SECRETS OF WEALTH ARE RE-VEALED, THE *GET-RICH-QUICK* LIST GROWS!

1958...*Fake uranium strike ... buy up land in advance!*

1975...*World lottery-- First prize $1,000,000,000 Winning ticket is #156 Z-44-X-21!*

1984...*Space travel begins ... buy Copernicus Moon Crater, full of jewels!*

1990... *Corner "Martian Motors" stock ... gains tenfold!*

AND THE *DEATH-LIST* FILLS OUT WITH ALL POSSIBLE DANGERS TO HIS FUTURE LIFE!

IN 1972, AVOID PACIFIC TYPHOON... IN 1977, KEEP OFF *VENUS EXPRESS*, SMASHED BY METEOR...I'LL CHEAT DEATH OVER AND OVER!

SUDDENLY, BART LANSON REALIZES HOW LONG HE HAS KEPT VIGIL AT THE *FUTUROSCOPE*...

I'VE BEEN AT IT ALMOST A FULL DAY!--THAT LIGHTNING BOLT WILL STRIKE ME IN 30 MINUTES! I'LL CLOSE THE WINDOW--THEN GET DOWN INTO THE BASEMENT--OUT OF DANGER!

BUT AS HE NEARS THE WINDOW...

WHAT'S HAPPENED TO ME? I FEEL WEAK... CAN HARDLY MOVE...NUMBNESS OVERCOMING ME...

MY SKIN TINGLES... BURNING... GREAT THUNDER! THAT MEANS THE FUTUROSCOPE WASN'T PROPERLY SHIELDED... IT WAS LEAKING OUT DEADLY ELECTRONIC RAYS ALL THE TIME...

HELPLESSLY, BART LANSON WAITS FOR THE INEVITABLE ENDING...

THE RAYS PARALYZED ME...CAN'T MOVE AWAY FROM THE WINDOW... HERE COMES THE LIGHTNING FLASH...

AND AS A HAND GOES LIMP... FOREVER...

I... I WAS DOOMED FROM THE VERY BEGINNING! I COULDN'T CHEAT DEATH...NOT EVEN THE FIRST TIME! THE FUTUROSCOPE, WHICH WARNED ME OF MY DANGER, ALSO MADE... MY FATED DEATH...COME TRUE...

March 19, 1957--8 P.M.
Avoid lightning bolt!
July 8, 19
Cancel

The End

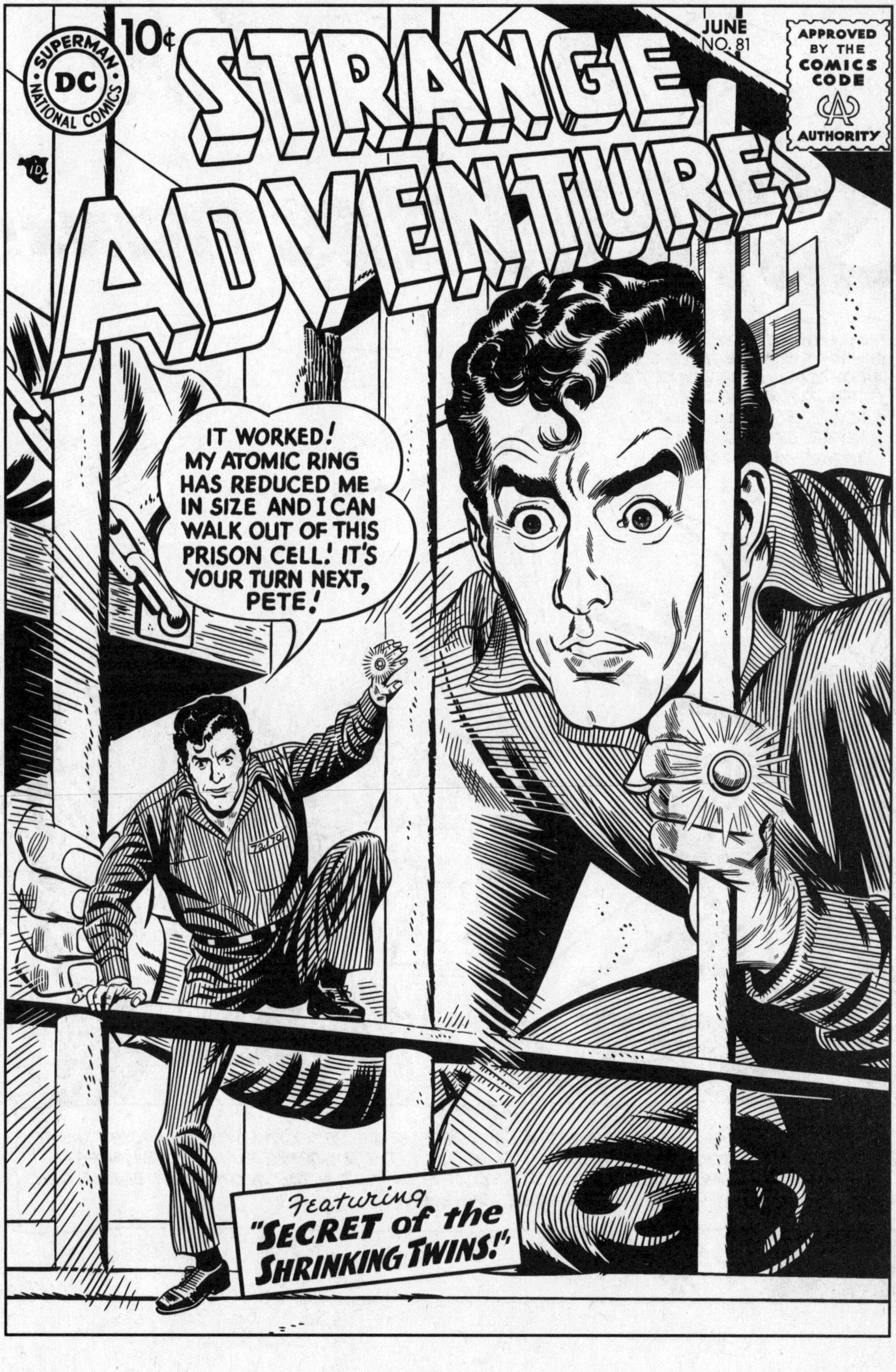

10¢
SUPERMAN DC NATIONAL COMICS
STRANGE ADVENTURES
JUNE NO. 81
APPROVED BY THE COMICS CODE AUTHORITY
IT WORKED! MY ATOMIC RING HAS REDUCED ME IN SIZE AND I CAN WALK OUT OF THIS PRISON CELL! IT'S YOUR TURN NEXT, PETE!
Featuring "SECRET of the SHRINKING TWINS!"

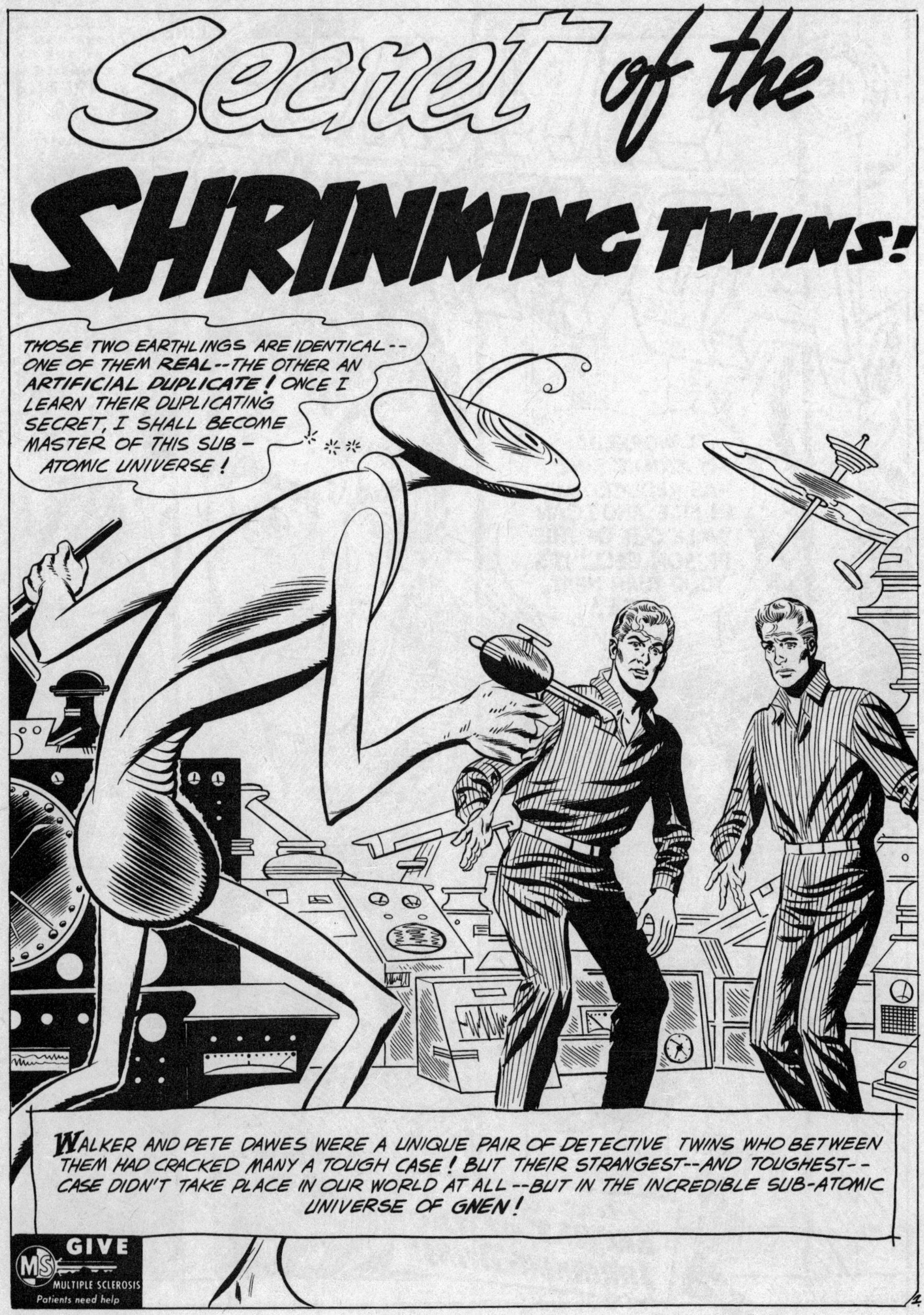
Secret of the
SHRINKING TWINS!
THOSE TWO EARTHLINGS ARE IDENTICAL-- ONE OF THEM REAL--THE OTHER AN ARTIFICIAL DUPLICATE! ONCE I LEARN THEIR DUPLICATING SECRET, I SHALL BECOME MASTER OF THIS SUB-ATOMIC UNIVERSE!
WALKER AND PETE DAWES WERE A UNIQUE PAIR OF DETECTIVE TWINS WHO BETWEEN THEM HAD CRACKED MANY A TOUGH CASE! BUT THEIR STRANGEST--AND TOUGHEST--CASE DIDN'T TAKE PLACE IN OUR WORLD AT ALL--BUT IN THE INCREDIBLE SUB-ATOMIC UNIVERSE OF GNEN!
GIVE
MS
MULTIPLE SCLEROSIS
Patients need help

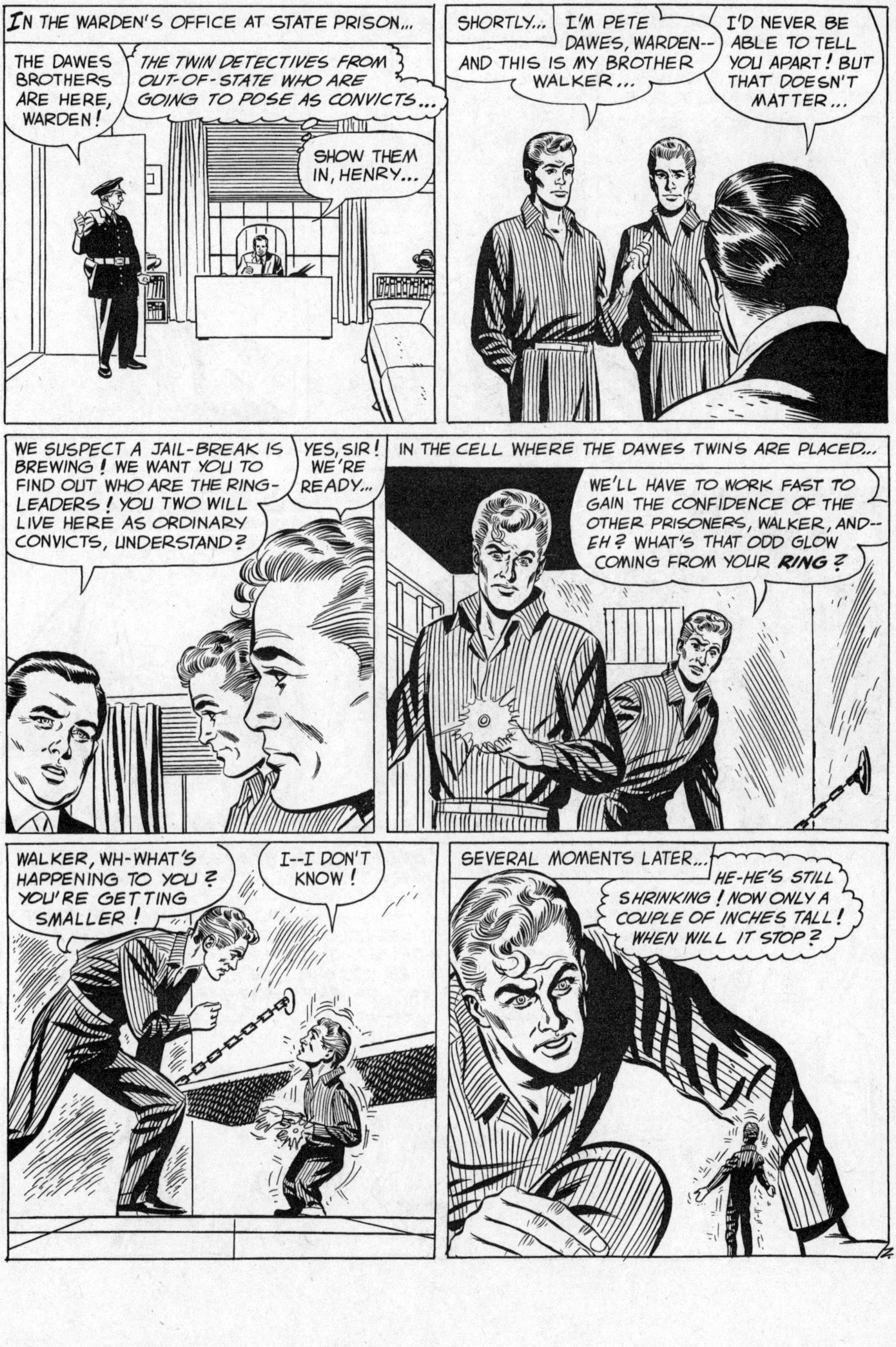
IN THE WARDEN'S OFFICE AT STATE PRISON...
THE DAWES BROTHERS ARE HERE, WARDEN!
THE TWIN DETECTIVES FROM OUT-OF-STATE WHO ARE GOING TO POSE AS CONVICTS...
SHOW THEM IN, HENRY...
SHORTLY...
I'M PETE DAWES, WARDEN-- AND THIS IS MY BROTHER WALKER...
I'D NEVER BE ABLE TO TELL YOU APART! BUT THAT DOESN'T MATTER...
WE SUSPECT A JAIL-BREAK IS BREWING! WE WANT YOU TO FIND OUT WHO ARE THE RING-LEADERS! YOU TWO WILL LIVE HERE AS ORDINARY CONVICTS, UNDERSTAND?
YES, SIR! WE'RE READY...
IN THE CELL WHERE THE DAWES TWINS ARE PLACED...
WE'LL HAVE TO WORK FAST TO GAIN THE CONFIDENCE OF THE OTHER PRISONERS, WALKER, AND-- EH? WHAT'S THAT ODD GLOW COMING FROM YOUR RING?
WALKER, WH-WHAT'S HAPPENING TO YOU? YOU'RE GETTING SMALLER!
I--I DON'T KNOW!
SEVERAL MOMENTS LATER...
HE-HE'S STILL SHRINKING! NOW ONLY A COUPLE OF INCHES TALL! WHEN WILL IT STOP?
2

WALKER GROWS SMALLER AND SMALLER--UNTIL FINALLY HE DISAPPEARS! SUDDENLY, HIS TWIN BROTHER FEELS THE *SAME THING* HAPPENING TO HIM!

NOW *MY RING* IS GLOWING-- AND I'M SHRINKING IN SIZE...

SMALLER...

MATCHES

UHH--I'M SO TINY NOW THAT THESE GRAINS OF DUST LOOK LIKE *HUGE BOULDERS*!

THEN PETE BECOMES SO SMALL THAT ELECTRONS AND ATOMS WHIRL ABOUT HIM IN SPACE...

STILL SHRINKING! WHEN WILL THIS END?

MORE MOMENTS PASS--AND THEN...

WHERE AM I?

I HAVE SUCCEEDED! I HAVE BROUGHT THE EARTHLING AND HIS *DUPLICATE* HERE!

HEAR ME, BOTH OF YOU-- SO THAT YOU WILL UNDER- STAND WHY I BROUGHT YOU HERE AND WHAT YOU MUST DO! I AM ZILO-- A FIFTH-DEGREE SCIENTIST HERE IN THE SUB-ATOMIC UNIVERSE OF *GNEN*...

GNEN IS RULED BY A DEMOCRATIC COUNCIL! WHEN I SOUGHT TO BECOME *LEADER*, I WAS EXILED...

NO ONE ON *GNEN* MAY RULE OTHERS, ZILO! YOUR PASSION FOR *POWER* IS A DANGER--THEREFORE THE COUNCIL HAS RULED YOU SHALL BE EXILED TO THE *MOON OF GNEN* FOR LIFE...

"ALONE, ON THIS ISOLATED *MOON OF GNEN,* I WAS MORE DETERMINED THAN EVER TO *WIN POWER!* I BUILT THIS LABORATORY.."

I AM *ALONE,* BUT IF THERE WERE *MORE LIKE ME,* I COULD DEFEAT THE COUNCIL AND TAKE POWER! I MUST SOLVE THE *SECRET OF DUPLICATION*--I KNOW IT CAN BE DONE SOMEHOW...

"FOR A LONG TIME I WORKED, AND THEN I MADE A DISCOVERY WHILE SEARCHING THE SECRETS OF OTHER WORLDS..."

MY *TELERAY-SCOPE* SHOWS THERE IS A SUPER-ATOMIC WORLD NEAR US CALLED EARTH, PEOPLED BY MANY *DUPLICATES! THEY* HAVE SOLVED THE SECRET I SEEK! I MUST GET THEM TO REVEAL IT TO *ME...*

"FLASHING MY ATOMIC-SHRINKING RAY THROUGH YOUR FINGER-RINGS, I SUCCEEDED IN DRAWING BOTH OF YOU DOWN TO MY SUB-ATOMIC WORLD..."

AMAZING! I CANNOT TELL WHICH IS THE ORIGINAL AND WHICH THE DUPLICATE! UNLESS ONE OF YOU DESIGNS HIS DUPLICATING MACHINE FOR ME WITHIN ONE *DETN!*--AN EARTH HOUR--I SHALL DESTROY YOU BOTH!

I WARN YOU, YOU CANNOT ESCAPE--MY SUPER-SCIENCE HAS MADE THIS LABORATORY ESCAPE-PROOF! GET TO WORK ON THE DESIGN FOR THE DUPLICATOR! IF YOU FAIL, YOU KNOW THE PENALTY!

AFTER THE DISMAYED TWINS HAVE BEEN LEFT ALONE...

H-HE THINKS BECAUSE WE'RE ALIKE WE MUST BE *DUPLICATES!* ONE OF US *REAL,* THE OTHER AN *ARTIFICIAL DUPLICATE!* I G-GUESS THEY DON'T HAVE ANYTHING LIKE *TWINS* HERE ON THIS WORLD...

HE'D NEVER BELIEVE US IF WE TRIED TO EXPLAIN...

HE'D THINK WE WERE TRYING TO STALL-- AND HE'D FINISH US OFF! WE'VE GOT TO DO *SOMETHING!*

PETE, I HAVE AN IDEA! MAYBE WE *CAN* MAKE A *DUPLICATE* OF US-- ONE THAT WOULD *HELP* US DEFEAT THIS *ZILO!*

A DUPLICATE OF *US*? WHAT--?

HAVE YOU FORGOTTEN, PETE? WE HAVE A *THIRD BROTHER*, STEWART-- WE THREE ARE *IDENTICAL TRIPLETS*! NOW HERE'S MY IDEA! WE USE *ZILO'S* MACHINE TO CONTACT EARTH AND... *BZZZ-BZZ*

SOON AFTER ON EARTH WHERE STEWART DAWES, A LAWYER, IS GOING TO WORK...

...AND STEWART--YOU MUST DO EXACTLY AS WE SAY-- FOR OUR LIVES ARE IN DANGER HERE IN THIS SUB-ATOMIC UNIVERSE...

HUH??

THE VOICE OF MY BROTHER WALKER-- COMING FROM THE IDENTICAL *RING* THAT WE ALL THREE WEAR!

...AND YOU MUST DRESS EXACTLY AS WE SAY AND BRING THE FOLLOWING...

AN HOUR LATER...

WHAT'S GOING ON HERE? MY TELELENS PICKED UP WHISPERING AND THE RADIATION OF ONE OF MY MACHINES...

YES, WE USED THIS MACHINE, *ZILO*--BUT ONLY TO HELP YOU! YOU SEE...

WE TWO ARE MERELY *DUPLICATES* MADE BY ANOTHER EARTHLING! HE IS THE ONLY ONE WHO COULD GIVE YOU THE DESIGN FOR A DUPLICATOR! WE HAVE BEEN TRYING TO CONTACT HIM!

IF YOU ARE LYING, YOU TWO SHALL BE DESTROYED AT ONCE! BUT WAIT--I CAN VIEW THE EARTHLING YOU MEAN--YES! HE *IS* EXACTLY LIKE YOU TWO!

THEN, AS *ZILO* MANIPULATES THE DIAL...

STEWART!

USE YOUR WEAPON ON HIM, STEW-- QUICK!

EH?

AS THE NEWCOMER SPRAYS THE SUB-ATOMIC SCIENTIST WITH *DDT*...

YOUR PUNY EARTH PISTOLS CAN'T HARM--*UHHH*

NOW IF IT ONLY WORKS!

SLOWLY, THE WOULD-BE-RULER OF *GNEN* SINKS TO THE FLOOR...

GROWING WEAK... BLACKING OUT...

SURE--EARTH PISTOLS COULDN'T HAVE HURT HIM--BUT SINCE HE LOOKED LIKE AN *INSECT*, WE FIGURED *DDT* MIGHT OVERCOME HIM! NOW TO CONTACT THE AUTHORITIES HERE AND LET THEM PUNISH *ZILO* ACCORDING TO THE LAWS OF THEIR WORLD!

LATER, AFTER THE TRIPLETS HAVE USED *ZILO'S* MACHINE TO RETURN TO EARTH AGAIN...

HERE WE ARE, WALKER-- BACK IN PRISON--

SHHHH-- LISTEN, PETE--!

...AND AT TEN TONIGHT WE BREAK OUT...

IN THE WARDEN'S OFFICE, MOMENTS LATER...

WE HAVE ALL THE DATA ON THE PRISON-BREAK, WARDEN-- WHO THE RINGLEADERS ARE AND WHEN IT'S TO TAKE PLACE!

GOOD! WE'LL END THE BREAK BEFORE IT CAN START!

SOON AFTER...

WELL, WE'RE DETECTIVES AGAIN, WALKER! THE WARDEN SAID WE DID A FINE JOB FOR THE PRISON...

YES! AND I THINK WE DIDN'T DO A BAD JOB FOR THE *WORLD OF GNEN* EITHER, PETE!

The End

The SPACEMAN of 1,000 DISGUISES!

WHAT WOULD BE THE CLEVEREST DISGUISE A SPACEMAN COULD USE TO SECRETLY SPY ON EARTH? WHAT CUNNING CAMOUFLAGE WOULD DEFY DETECTION? COULD WE BEAT THE ALIEN SPY AT HIS OWN GAME?

THE SPY FROM SPACE IS AFTER ME... TO STOP ME FROM REVEALING HIS SECRET PRESENCE ON EARTH! ANYONE OF THOSE CREATURES PURSUING ME COULD BE THE ALIEN--IN DISGUISE!

REACHING A SMALL UNINHABITED ISLAND IN HIS LAUNCH, HAL CARSON PURSUES HIS STUDIES AS A NATURALIST...

I WAS HOPING TO DISCOVER SOME RARE SPECIES OF FAUNA AND FLORA HERE, BUT THERE'S NOTHING UNUSUAL ABOUT THAT COMMON BEAVER--*CASTOR CANADENSIS!*

BUT BEFORE HE CAN SNAP THE BEAVER'S PICTURE...

GOOD GOSH! THE BEAVER SUDDENLY DISAPPEARED--AND AN EAGLE MATERIALIZED IN ITS PLACE! M-MY EYES MUST BE PLAYING TRICKS ON ME!

FOLLOWING THE EAGLE'S SHORT FLIGHT, CARSON COMES UPON AN EVEN MORE INCREDIBLE SIGHT...

GREAT STARS! THE EAGLE'S FLYING INTO THAT STRANGE CRAFT -- IT LOOKS LIKE A *SPACESHIP!* I'VE GOT TO FOLLOW THIS THROUGH...

INSIDE THE SPACESHIP, THERE IS NO SIGN OF THE EAGLE -- ONLY...

A MAN FROM SPACE! HE USED A RAY-GUN TO DISINTEGRATE MY CAMERA... HE'S COMMUNICATING WITH ME... TELEPATHICALLY...

NOW THAT I HAVE DESTROYED YOUR STRANGE *WEAPON,* YOU ARE MY PRISONER!

YOU WERE THE BEAVER -- AND THE EAGLE! HOW WERE YOU ABLE TO TRANSFORM YOURSELF? AND WHY--?

MY *TRANSMUTER SERUM* ENABLES ME TO ADOPT ANY BIOLOGICAL FORM I THINK OF! WHEN YOU CAME ALONG, I WAS TESTING IT FOR EARTHLY FORMS! I QUICKLY CHANGED TO THE EAGLE TO REACH THE RAY-GUN IN MY SHIP!

"MY WORLD PLANS TO INVADE EARTH! BUT FIRST, MY MISSION IS TO SECRETLY SPY ON YOUR WEAPONS! IT WILL BE EASY, USING THE DISGUISE OF SOME COMMON EARTHLY CREATURE..."

WHO WOULD SUSPECT A *FLY* OF BEING A SPY IN THIS SCIENTIFIC LABORATORY?

GUIDED MISSLES LAB, TOP SECRET

AUTHORIZED PERSONNEL ONLY

NOW, I COMMAND YOU TO SKETCH ALL OF EARTH'S LIFE FORMS FOR ME, SO THAT I CAN USE WHATEVER ANIMAL DISGUISES WILL BE CONVENIENT!

NO... I WON'T BETRAY MY WORLD! YOU CAN'T MAKE ME TALK!

I DON'T HAVE TO! I CAN USE THIS *PROBE RAY* TO STEAL THE INFORMATION FROM YOUR BRAIN! HOW FORTUNATE -- YOU ARE A NATURALIST! YOU CAN SUPPLY ME WITH ALL THE INFORMATION I NEED!

NOW TO MAKE THE SKETCHES MY *MIND PROBE* REVEALS...

GOT TO STOP THAT MIND-ROBBER...THAT SERUM IS WITHIN MY REACH...AND THE ALIEN ISN'T WATCHING ME...

IN DESPERATION, CARSON GULPS DOWN THE TRANSFORMATION SERUM--AS HIS ONLY HOPE TO ESCAPE...

WILL THE SERUM WORK FOR ME TOO? HERE GOES... I *VISUALIZE* MYSELF AS A PEREGRINE FALCON!

MAGICALLY, IN AN INSTANT, THE *TRANS-MUTER* TURNS THE HUMAN'S BODY INTO THE EARTH'S FASTEST FLYING BIRD...

IT WORKED! HE'S SHOOTING BUT I DARTED AWAY IN TIME! LUCKY I'M A NATURALIST, KNOWING WHICH IS THE SPEED KING OF THE BIRDS!

THE PEREGRINE FALCON, ALSO KNOWN AS THE DUCK HAWK, CAN FLY 180 MILES PER HOUR! THE ALIEN CAN'T CATCH ME NOW, SINCE NO OTHER EARTHLY BIRD CAN OVERTAKE A DUCK HAWK!

BUT CARSON'S CLEVER PLAN IS WRECKED BY AN UNFORESEEN DEVELOPMENT...

YES--NO *EARTHLY* SPECIES CAN OVERTAKE YOU...BUT A BIRD OF *MY WORLD* CAN! THIS *AZZULA* BIRD FORM I ADOPTED CAN EASILY OUT-FLY YOUR DUCK HAWK!

HE'S OVERTAKING ME! AND BEING BIGGER, HE CAN EASILY DEFEAT ME!

DARTING LOW OVER THE WATER, CARSON TRIES ANOTHER RUSE!

JUST IN TIME! THE *AZZULA* CAN'T CHASE ME UNDER WATER! I CHANGED TO A *TUNA*, ONE OF EARTH'S FASTEST FISH, WHICH SWIMS AT A CRUISING PACE OF 30 MILES AN HOUR!

BUT THE SPACE SPY AGAIN HAS THE ADVANTAGE WHEN...

IS THAT THE FASTEST YOU CAN GO? THE *OAR FISH* OF MY WORLD WILL EASILY OVERHAUL YOU!

ITS OAR-LIKE FINS GIVE IT SUPER SPEED!

TRYING ANOTHER TRICK, CARSON DIVES DEEP WHERE...

IT'S SO DARK HERE HE'LL NEVER FIND ME IF I REMAIN *MOTIONLESS!*

BUT THE STRANGE LIFE-FORMS OF THE OTHER WORLD SEEM ABLE TO DEFEAT ANY PLAN OF THE EARTHMAN!

MEET *LAMARY*-- OUR NATIVE *SEARCHLIGHT FISH!*

NOTHING HELPS! GOT TO SWIM BACK TO THE ISLAND AND TRY SOME *ANIMAL* FORM!

ON THE WAY, THE NATURALIST'S THOUGHTS RECALL THE SPEEDIEST OF FOUR-FOOTED CREATURES...

IN ANY "ANIMAL OLYMPICS", THE *CHEETAH* WOULD WIN THE 100-YARD DASH... WITH ITS 70 M.P.H. SPEED! BUT I'M GOING TO CHANGE INTO A *DIFFERENT* ANIMAL!

THE *PRONGHORN ANTELOPE*... BECAUSE IN A LONGER CHASE, IT CAN OUTRUN ANY LAND ANIMAL, EVEN THE *CHEETAH!* I HOPE THE ALIEN SPY CAN'T COME UP WITH ANYTHING TO MATCH THAT!

AGAIN CARSON'S WORST FEARS ARE REALIZED WHEN...

HOW SLOW YOU ARE, COMPARED TO THIS *LONG-LEGGED TAKLO* OF MY WORLD!

SPEED HAS FAILED ME AGAIN! WAIT... THAT SMALL POOL AHEAD... MAYBE I CAN ELUDE HIM THROUGH TINY SIZE!

AN INNER COMMAND AND THE NATURALIST SHRINKS DOWN TO MICROSCOPIC SIZE IN THE POOL!

I BECAME A ONE-CELLED *PARAMECIUM!* EVEN IF MY PURSUER ADOPTS SOME AMOEBOID FORM, HE WILL HAVE *NO EYES* TO SEE ME WITH!

MOST FANTASTIC IS THE SPACE-SPY'S COUNTER-MEASURE...

ON MY WORLD, THE *RADAR AMOEBA* CAN "*TUNE IN*" ITS PREY! YOU MIGHT AS WELL GIVE UP, EARTHMAN!

INSPIRATION SENDS CARSON TO THE WATER'S SURFACE FOR ANOTHER CHANGE...

I SHOULD'VE THOUGHT OF THIS EARLIER! THE *FASTEST* CREATURE ON EARTH IS... THE *DEER FLY!* IT'S BEEN CLOCKED AT AN 818-M.P.H. SPEED--

EVEN THEN, THE ALIEN PURSUER IS NOT LEFT BEHIND!

THE JET-POWERED WINGS OF OUR *GRUZL ROCKET BEE*-- HAS A TOP SPEED OF *MACH 2* IN YOUR EARTHLY SCALE!

GASP!... THAT'S 1500 MILES PER HOUR!

⑤

HAS CARSON EXHAUSTED HIS "BAG OF TRICKS"?

BIRD—FISH—ANIMAL—MICROBE—INSECT! ALL FORMS FAILED TO HELP ME ESCAPE! WHAT ELSE IN THE ANIMAL KINGDOM IS THERE? WAIT... THAT GIVES ME AN IDEA...

CAN YOU GUESS WHAT THE EARTHMAN NEXT CHANGES TO?

THE DEER FLY VANISHED, BUT NOTHING TOOK ITS PLACE! YOU WON'T ESCAPE, EARTHMAN! WHATEVER NEW FORM YOU HAVE ADOPTED, I'LL SNARE YOU THE INSTANT YOU *MOVE!*

I'LL MAKE MY MOVE WHEN THE TIME IS RIGHT! THE ALIEN'S CIRCLING CLOSER TO ME! AS SOON AS HE'S WITHIN RANGE I'LL SNARE HIM...

...AS THE *VENUS'S-FLY-TRAP!* THERE WAS NOTHING LEFT IN THE *ANIMAL* KINGDOM...SO I TURNED TO THE *PLANT* KINGDOM TO BEAT HIM!

TRAPPED... OHHHHHHHHHHHH...

BACK IN HUMAN FORM ONCE MORE, HAL CARSON RETURNS TO THE SPACESHIP WITH HIS PRISONER...

THE ALIEN "BEE" WON'T ESCAPE FROM THIS CONTAINER! NOW TO CONTACT HIS HOME WORLD ON THIS TELEPATHIC TRANSMITTER...

ATTENTION! EARTH CALLING! YOUR SPACE-SPY'S MISSION FAILED! WE WARN YOU— ATTACK US—AND YOU WILL BE DEFEATED TOO!

THE DIRECTIONAL DIAL SHOWS THE TRANSMITTER IS BEAMED AT OUR NEAREST PLANETARY NEIGHBOR IN SPACE! WHAT IRONY-- THAT EARTH'S *VENUS'S-FLY-TRAP* SHOULD PREVENT AN INVASION FROM THE PLANET --*VENUS!*

THE END

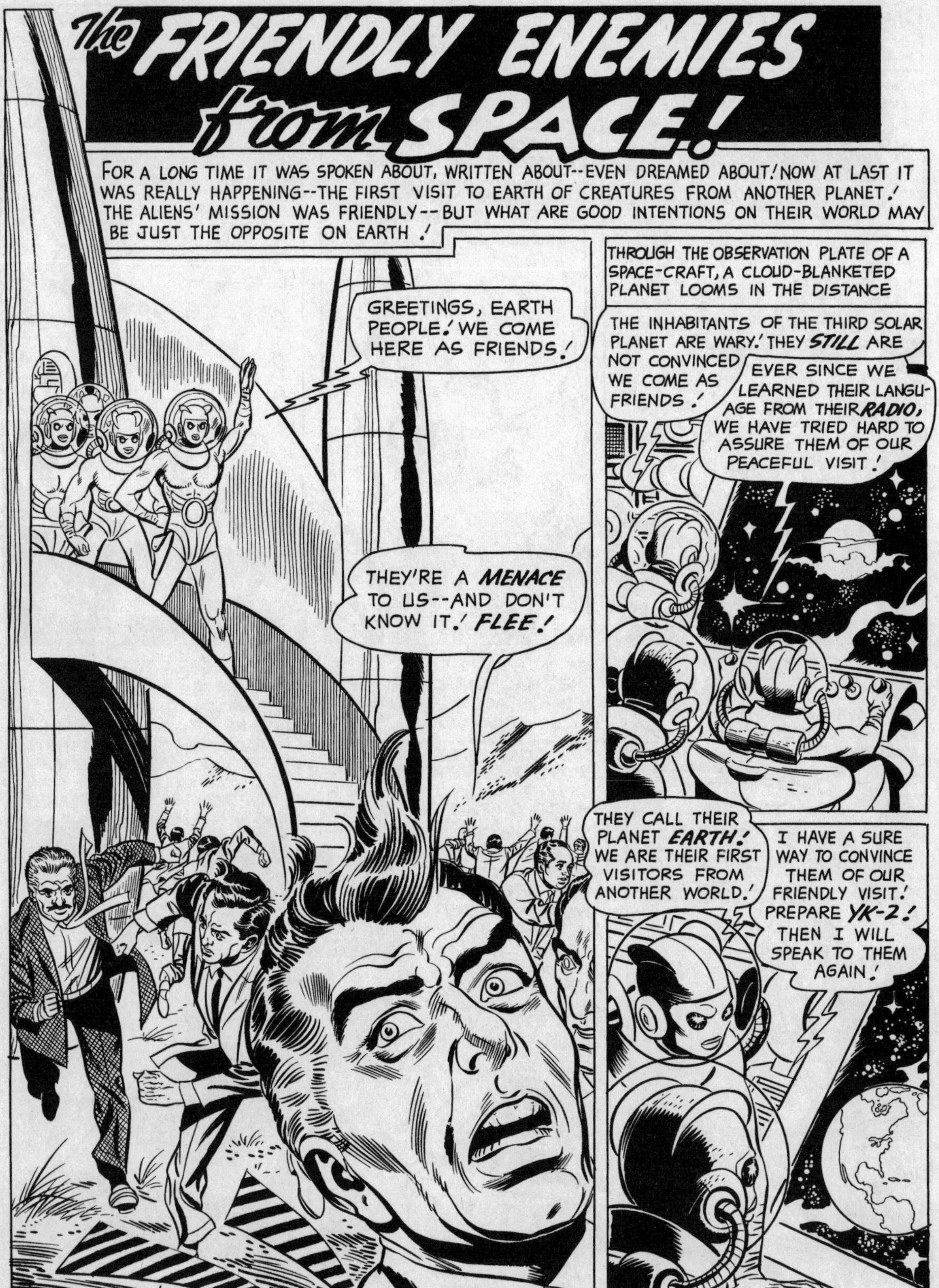
The FRIENDLY ENEMIES from SPACE!
FOR A LONG TIME IT WAS SPOKEN ABOUT, WRITTEN ABOUT--EVEN DREAMED ABOUT! NOW AT LAST IT WAS REALLY HAPPENING--THE FIRST VISIT TO EARTH OF CREATURES FROM ANOTHER PLANET! THE ALIENS' MISSION WAS FRIENDLY--BUT WHAT ARE GOOD INTENTIONS ON THEIR WORLD MAY BE JUST THE OPPOSITE ON EARTH!
GREETINGS, EARTH PEOPLE! WE COME HERE AS FRIENDS!
THEY'RE A MENACE TO US--AND DON'T KNOW IT! FLEE!
THROUGH THE OBSERVATION PLATE OF A SPACE-CRAFT, A CLOUD-BLANKETED PLANET LOOMS IN THE DISTANCE
THE INHABITANTS OF THE THIRD SOLAR PLANET ARE WARY! THEY STILL ARE NOT CONVINCED WE COME AS FRIENDS!
EVER SINCE WE LEARNED THEIR LANGUAGE FROM THEIR RADIO, WE HAVE TRIED HARD TO ASSURE THEM OF OUR PEACEFUL VISIT!
THEY CALL THEIR PLANET EARTH! WE ARE THEIR FIRST VISITORS FROM ANOTHER WORLD!
I HAVE A SURE WAY TO CONVINCE THEM OF OUR FRIENDLY VISIT! PREPARE YK-2! THEN I WILL SPEAK TO THEM AGAIN!

SHORTLY AFTERWARDS, AT A GREAT OBSERVATORY ON EARTH, WHERE TOP-RANKING SCIENTISTS AND MILITARY LEADERS WAIT ANXIOUSLY...

HEAR ME, EARTHMEN! IN A MOMENT A SMALL ROCKET, *YK-2*, WILL BE SENT TO YOU BY ETHER-WAVE BEAM! EXAMINE THE ROCKET--THEN JUDGE FOR YOURSELVES OUR MOTIVES!

SUDDENLY, THROUGH THE GREAT OPENED DOME, A SMALL ROCKET APPEARS, SETTLING LIKE A FEATHER ON A TABLE...

THERE IT IS--ONLY A MOMENT OR SO AFTER THEY DISPATCHED IT!

AND THEY'RE STILL HUNDREDS OF MILES IN SPACE! HOW DID IT GET HERE SO *FAST*?

LATER, AFTER A THOROUGH EXAMINATION OF THE ALIEN ROCKET...

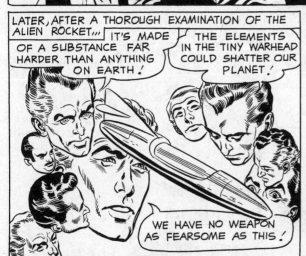

IT'S MADE OF A SUBSTANCE FAR HARDER THAN ANYTHING ON EARTH!

THE ELEMENTS IN THE TINY WARHEAD COULD SHATTER OUR PLANET!

WE HAVE NO WEAPON AS FEARSOME AS THIS!

THEN, DR. PAUL HALLEY ADDRESSES THE GATHERING...

GENTLEMEN, OBVIOUSLY THEY MEAN NO HARM OR THEY COULD HAVE EXPLODED THIS *YK-2* ON US! I VOTE TO RECEIVE THEM AS FRIENDS!

AYE!

AND SOON THE AWESOME CRAFT, WITH ASTRO-POWERED MOTORS HUMMING SOFTLY, SETTLES LIKE A SHADOW IN THE OBSERVATORY PARK...

LOOK AT THEM! HOW STRANGE!

REMEMBER, WE LOOK JUST AS STRANGE TO THEM!

WHILE A MOTOR STILL HUMS FAINTLY WITHIN THE CRAFT, ONE OF THE VISITORS SPEAKS...

GREETINGS, PEOPLE OF EARTH! WE COME FROM A PLANET IN THE NEIGHBORING STAR OF *ALPHA CENTAURI*!

BUT INSTEAD OF **WORDS** SOUNDING FROM THE ALIEN'S MOUTH--**COLOR WAVES** FLASH FORTH!

WE CAN'T HEAR--OR UNDERSTAND--HIM!

THEN, AS THE STUNNED EARTHMEN TRY TO SPEAK TO EACH OTHER...COLOR--INSTEAD OF SOUND--COMES FROM *THEIR* MOUTHS!

AT THAT INSTANT, COLORS FROM NEARBY TREES AND BRUSH GIVE OFF **SOUND** WAVES! RED FLOWERS SHRIEK LIKE SIRENS--WHILE BROWNS AND GREENS EMIT SOFT, TINKLING MUSIC!

KREEEEEEEE

SUDDENLY, THE STAGGERING TRUTH OCCURS TO DR. HALLEY...

SOMETHING'S CAUSED A MIX-UP IN OUR SENSORY NERVES! WE'RE *HEARING COLOR* AND *SEEING SOUND!* IS THIS A TRICK OF SOME SORT BY THE ALIENS?

ONE OF THE VISITORS, AWARE OF THE EARTH-MEN'S PLIGHT, RACES INSIDE THE CRAFT AND SHUTS OFF THE HUMMING MOTOR...

THERE--THAT OUGHT TO BRING THINGS BACK TO NORMAL!

IN A MOMENT, OUTSIDE...

ON OUR PLANET, WE PRODUCE OUR OWN "AIR WAVES" TO MAKE SOUND POSSIBLE! THOSE GENERATED WAVES ACCIDENTALLY CAUSED A TANGLE IN YOUR SENSORY NERVES! WE FORGOT THEY ARE NOT NECESSARY HERE!

③

THE VISITORS FROM SPACE ARE LED INTO THE GREAT OBSERVATORY TO EXAMINE EARTH'S RECORD OF SCIENTIFIC ACHIEVEMENTS... WHEN, SUDDENLY...

DR. HALLEY! SOMETHING ELSE HAS GONE WRONG OUTSIDE -- HURRY!

EYES WIDE WITH AMAZEMENT, THE EARTHMEN STARE ABOUT THE OBSERVATORY PARK...

THE LEAVES OF THE TREES AND SHRUBBERY! THEY'VE TURNED A YELLOWISH WHITE--AND ARE DYING!

THE PLANTS ARE LOSING THEIR CHLOROPHYL!

SURELY, THIS IS NO FAULT OF OURS!

SUPPOSING... JUST SUPPOSING, SOME BACTERIA OR OTHER MICROSCOPIC LIFE YOU'VE BROUGHT WITH YOU FROM YOUR WORLD HAS BEEN SET LOOSE IN OUR AIR! COULD IT NOT BE DESTROYING OUR CHLOROPHYL?

OF COURSE! WE SHOULD HAVE FORESEEN THAT!

THE BLIGHT IS SPREADING! OTHER PLANT LIFE IS BEING HIT BY IT!

THE MYSTERIOUS FORCE WILL DESTROY ALL PLANT LIFE ON EARTH! AND WITH PLANT LIFE DEAD, ANIMAL LIFE ON EARTH COULD NOT EXIST!

DO NOT DESPAIR! THERE'S A CHANCE WE CAN STOP THE CHLOROPHYL DESTROYERS!

A MOMENT LATER, AN ODD-LOOKING DEVICE RISES FROM THE SPACE CRAFT...

WH--WHAT IS *THAT?*

IT ACTS SIMILAR TO YOUR RADAR INSTRUMENTS--BUT, INSTEAD OF RECEIVING IMAGES, IT CAN BE SET TO ATTRACT OUR ALIEN MICROBES IN YOUR ATMOSPHERE!

ANY SIGN YET THAT THE BLIGHT HAS BEEN HALTED--?

YES...YES....

A SHORT DISTANCE AWAY...

THIS IS AS FAR AS THE PLANT DISEASE SPREAD!

STRANGE--HOW WE UNWITTINGLY CAUSE TROUBLE ON YOUR WORLD! WE'D BETTER DEPART BEFORE OTHER MYSTERIOUS FORCES FROM OUR PLANET ARE RELEASED ON YOURS!

IN A FEW MOMENTS, THE GREAT ASTRO-POWERED MOTORS HUM AGAIN--AND SUDDENLY, IN A FLASH, THE SPACE-CRAFT STREAKS SKYWARD...

IT VANISHED WITH THE SPEED OF LIGHT!

A MOMENT LATER...

GREAT GUNS, HALLEY! SOMETHING *ELSE* IS WRONG!

WE'RE BEING BOMBARDED BY *COSMIC RAYS!*

GET INSIDE! PUT ON PROTECTIVE GLASSES!

⑤

THEN, AS ANXIOUS FIGURES HUDDLE WITHIN THE OBSERVATORY...

HALLEY! WHAT ON EARTH HAPPENED?

SPECTROSCOPIC RESULTS SHOW THAT THE FUEL REACTION OF THEIR DEPARTING SHIP LEFT A HOLE--OR TUNNEL--IN OUR ATMOSPHERE, EXTENDING FROM EARTH TO OUTER SPACE!

THE ATOMS IN OUR AIR HAVE BEEN FUSED AROUND THIS "HOLE", FORMING AN UNBREAKABLE WALL! IT ALLOWS THE COSMIC RAYS TO STREAM THROUGH THE HOLE'S OPENING AT THE TOP!

THE HOLE →

EARTH'S ATMOSPHERE

ORDINARILY, OUR ATMOSPHERE SERVES AS A PROTECTIVE BARRIER AGAINST DIRECT COSMIC RAY BOMBARDMENTS-- BUT NOW, THAT "HOLE" BECOMES A CHINK IN EARTH'S ARMOR!

BUT EARTH CAN'T STAND A CONSTANT AND DIRECT COSMIC RAY BOMBARDMENT!

WHAT ABOUT OUR ATOM BOMBS? CAN THEY SMASH THE WALLS AND LET THE AIR RUSH BACK IN?

NO! THE WALLS CAN WITHSTAND ANY FORCE WE KNOW ON EARTH!

GENTLEMEN, THOUGH OUR ALIEN FRIENDS ARE BEYOND RECALL, THEY LEFT US A "LEGACY"...YK-2! WE'LL LAUNCH IT AT THE "HOLE"!

TIMING DEVICES ARE TURNED, MECHANISMS ARE SET--THEN THE DEADLY LITTLE ROCKET SPEEDS SKYWARD, WHERE, FAR AWAY, IT ERUPTS WITH A SUPER-SHATTERING BLAST...

KWHROOM!

WITH THE "HOLE" DESTROYED, PROTECTIVE ATMOSPHERE RUSHES IN, AND THE DEADLY COSMIC RAY BOMBARDMENT DECREASED...

OUR EXPERIENCE SHOWS THE FORTHCOMING INTERPLANETARY ERA WILL HAVE ITS DIFFICULT PROBLEMS-- BUT WE'VE SEEN THAT THOSE PROBLEMS CAN--AND WILL-- BE SOLVED!

THE END

6

THE BOX WAS COMPLETELY EMPTY-- BUT WHEN YOU WISHED FOR SOMETHING, IT INSTANTLY APPEARED INSIDE! BEWILDERED SCIENTISTS WERE UNABLE TO ACCOUNT FOR IT--AND ONLY HOPED THE BOX WOULDN'T DISAPPEAR AS MYSTERIOUSLY AS IT APPEARED ON EARTH!

The MAGIC BOX from NOWHERE!

I WISHED FOR A DIAMOND -- AND IT INSTANTLY APPEARED!

THIS BOX IS THE MOST AMAZING THING I'VE EVER SEEN! I WONDER WHERE IT CAME FROM?

ALONG A COUNTRY ROAD, A MAN STAGGERS... FALLS... DROPPING A METAL BOX...

C-CAN'T BREATHE... GETTING DIZZY... OHHHHH...

MOMENTS LATER...

PULL OVER, ED! THERE'S A MAN LYING IN THE ROAD!

GET HIM INSIDE! I'LL DRIVE HIM TO THE TWIN FALLS HOSPITAL!

TWIN FALLS POLICE 12

FOR AN HOUR OR SO, THE FALLEN BOX LIES IN A DITCH. THEN—

I WOULD HAVE TO LOSE MY LAST FISH HOOK JUST WHEN THE FISH WERE BITING SO WELL!

WHAT'S THAT? LOOKS LIKE A FISHING TACKLE BOX! SAY, I WONDER IF THERE'S A FISH HOOK INSIDE IT?

CLUNK!

TOO BAD--IT'S EMPTY! BOY, I SURE WISH THERE *WERE* A FISH HOOK IN THERE!

GOOD GOSH! THERE *IS* A FISH HOOK IN THERE--NOW! BUT ONLY A MOMENT AGO THE BOX WAS EMPTY!

IT'S AS IF THIS BOX WERE A MODERN ALADDIN'S LAMP! MAKE A WISH AND IT COMES TRUE! HOLD ON--I'M A SCIENTIST AND KNOW SUCH THINGS CAN'T HAPPEN! AS PROOF, I WISH FOR A--A *GOLD NUGGET!*

FANTASTIC! THERE MUST BE A LOGICAL, SCIENTIFIC EXPLANATION FOR THIS!

2

AT TOP SPEED, LARRY MITCHELL RACES TO THE LITTLE MOUNTAIN CABIN HE SHARES WITH TWO FELLOW SCIENTISTS--

COME HERE, QUICK! ONE OF YOU MAKE A WISH FOR SOMETHING!

WHAT'S THAT--A NEW GAME? OKAY, I'LL PLAY-- I'M OUT OF MATCHES-- SO I'LL WISH FOR A BOX OF THEM!

WOW! WHAT A TRICK! HOW DO YOU DO IT, LARRY?

HEY, GIVE ME A CHANCE TO MAKE A WISH!

I'LL MAKE IT TOUGH ON YOUR SLEIGHT-OF-HAND TRICK, LARRY! I'M WISHING FOR A DIAMOND-- SAY, A 1,000-CARAT WEIGHT!

IT WORKED--WITHOUT ANY HOCUS POCUS! WHAT IS THAT BOX? HOW DOES IT WORK? WHERE'D YOU GET IT?

ALL I CAN TELL YOU IS THAT I FOUND IT ON THE ROAD NEARBY! THE QUESTION I HAVE IS--WHAT ARE WE GOING TO DO WITH IT?

WE OUGHT TO TRY TO FIND OUT WHO OWNS IT!

WE ALSO SHOULD GET IN TOUCH WITH WASHINGTON AND HAVE THEM SEND A GOVERNMENT OFFICIAL HERE!

MEANWHILE, IN THE TWIN FALLS HOSPITAL...

A SOUND-WAVE TRANSLATOR HIDDEN IN MY EAR ENABLES ME TO UNDERSTAND THE EARTHMEN DOCTORS' TALK! THEY DON'T KNOW WHAT'S WRONG WITH ME! I DO, BUT I HAVE NO WAY OF TELLING THEM IN THEIR LANGUAGE!

AS THE PATIENT IS DISMISSED...

THERE'S TOO MUCH *NITROGEN* IN THIS ATMOSPHERE! HARD FOR ME TO BREATHE--I GET DIZZY! I'VE GOT TO GO BACK--TO MY OWN WORLD!

TWIN FALLS MUNICIPAL HOSPITAL

NN 01

SOMEWHAT LATER--

MY BOX--IT'S GONE! SOMEONE FOUND IT AND TOOK IT AWAY! IT'S MY ONLY CONTACT WITH THE WORLD I CAME FROM! I CAN'T LEAVE HERE WITHOUT IT!

AS DUSK SHROUDS THE STREETS OF TWIN FALLS...

HERE'S AN UNUSUAL NEWS ITEM, FOLKS! A "*WISHING-BOX*"--FOUND BY NUCLEAR PHYSICIST LARRY MITCHELL--IS REPUTED TO GRANT ANY WISH ONE MAKES TO IT!

DRESS SHOP

OPEN

WE'VE BEEN ASK TO ANNOUNCE THAT ANYONE CLAIMING OWNERSHIP OF THIS BOX SHOULD APPEAR AT THE TWIN FALLS COURTHOUSE THIS EVENING!

IT'S MY BOX! SOMEHOW I'VE GOT TO MAKE THEM UNDERSTAND I MUST HAVE IT BACK!

LATER, AT THE TWIN FALLS COURTHOUSE...

I TOLD THEM I ORIGINALLY FISHED IT UP FROM THE OCEAN--BUT THEY DIDN'T FALL FOR IT!

MY YARN ABOUT FINDING THE BOX IN AN EGYPTIAN TOMB DIDN'T WORK EITHER!

NEXT!

HOUSE TWIN FALLS

UNABLE TO CONVERSE IN EARTH LANGUAGE, THE ALIEN TRIES TO MAKE HIMSELF UNDERSTOOD BY SIGN LANGUAGE...

I'M TRYING TO TELL THEM I'M AN EXPLORER FROM THE *FOURTH DIMENSION* -- AND USE THE BOX TO TRAVEL BETWEEN MY DIMENSION AND THIS ONE!

UNAWARE OF WHAT DANGERS OR DIFFICULTIES I'D ENCOUNTER HERE, I USED THE BOX TO BRING FROM MY DIMENSION WHATEVER I MENTALLY WISHED FOR!

SORRY, MISTER! I CAN'T UNDERSTAND YOU! *NEXT!*

AFTER THE LAST BOX-CLAIMANT TELLS HIS STORY...

NONE OF THEM PROVED OWNERSHIP OF THE BOX! I HAVE NO RECOURSE NOW BUT TO TURN IT OVER TO THE GOVERNMENT! I'M SURE THEY'LL MAKE GOOD USE OF IT!

SOON AFTER...

THEY'RE TAKING A TRAIN TO THE PENTAGON BUILDING, WASHINGTON! I HEAR THERE'LL BE A BIG ARMED GUARD TO PROTECT THE BOX!

I CAN'T LIVE MUCH LONGER IN THIS NITROGEN-LADEN AIR! AND THE ONLY WAY I CAN RETURN TO MY DIMENSION IS THROUGH THAT BOX!

BY MAKING CERTAIN ADJUSTMENTS IN MY SOUND-WAVE TRANSLATOR, I CAN TRANSMIT MY THOUGHTS INTO THE BOX AND SUMMON WHAT I NEED TO LEAVE THIS WORLD! BUT THE BOX MUST BE *OPEN* AND I HAVE TO BE CLOSE ENOUGH FOR MY TRANSMITTED THOUGHTS TO REACH IT...

TICKETS

TRANS. RAILROAD

SHORTLY, AS THE MAGIC BOX ARRIVES IN THE PENTAGON...

THE BOX IS SOMEWHERE IN THAT BUILDING! I'M CLOSE ENOUGH TO REACH THE BOX MENTALLY--IF ONLY IT IS OPEN! ... I WISH FOR PELLET ZNB-2! FLY AT ANGLE 46°, SOUTHEAST...

PENTAG

PARKING AR SOUTH F

5

MOMENTS LATER, A TINY METAL PROJECTILE LEAPS FROM THE METAL BOX...

BREAKING OPEN THE TINY PELLET, THE FOURTH-DIMENSIONAL MAN SWALLOWS THE PILL IT HOLDS--

ZNB-2 WILL TAKE ME BACK INTO MY OWN WORLD! I CAN RECOVER THE BOX FROM MY DIMENSION!

WHEN HE REAPPEARS IN HIS LABORATORY--

NOW TO WITHDRAW THE BOX FROM THE THREE-DIMENSIONAL WORLD! IT MUST NOT REMAIN THERE!

WITH THE BOX IN THEIR POSSESSION, EARTHMEN WOULD USE IT TO FULFILL THEIR EVERY WISH! LIFE WOULD BECOME SO EASY FOR THEM, THEY'D SOON LOSE THEIR INCENTIVE --THEIR ABILITY TO THINK! THE BOX WOULD EVENTUALLY TURN INTO MORE OF A CURSE THAN A BLESSING!

AS THE EARTH-SCIENTISTS GATHER TO EXAMINE THE BOX--

LET'S TEST IT AGAIN! I WISH FOR A-- LOOK! THE BOX IS DISAPPEARING RIGHT BEFORE OUR EYES!

IN THE OTHER WORLD SO "CLOSE" TO OURS...

SO ENDS MY JOURNEY TO THE THIRD DIMENSION! NEXT I SHALL MAKE PLANS TO VISIT THE TWO-DIMENSIONAL WORLD! I WONDER WHAT STRANGE ADVENTURES I SHALL ENCOUNTER THERE?

THE END

6

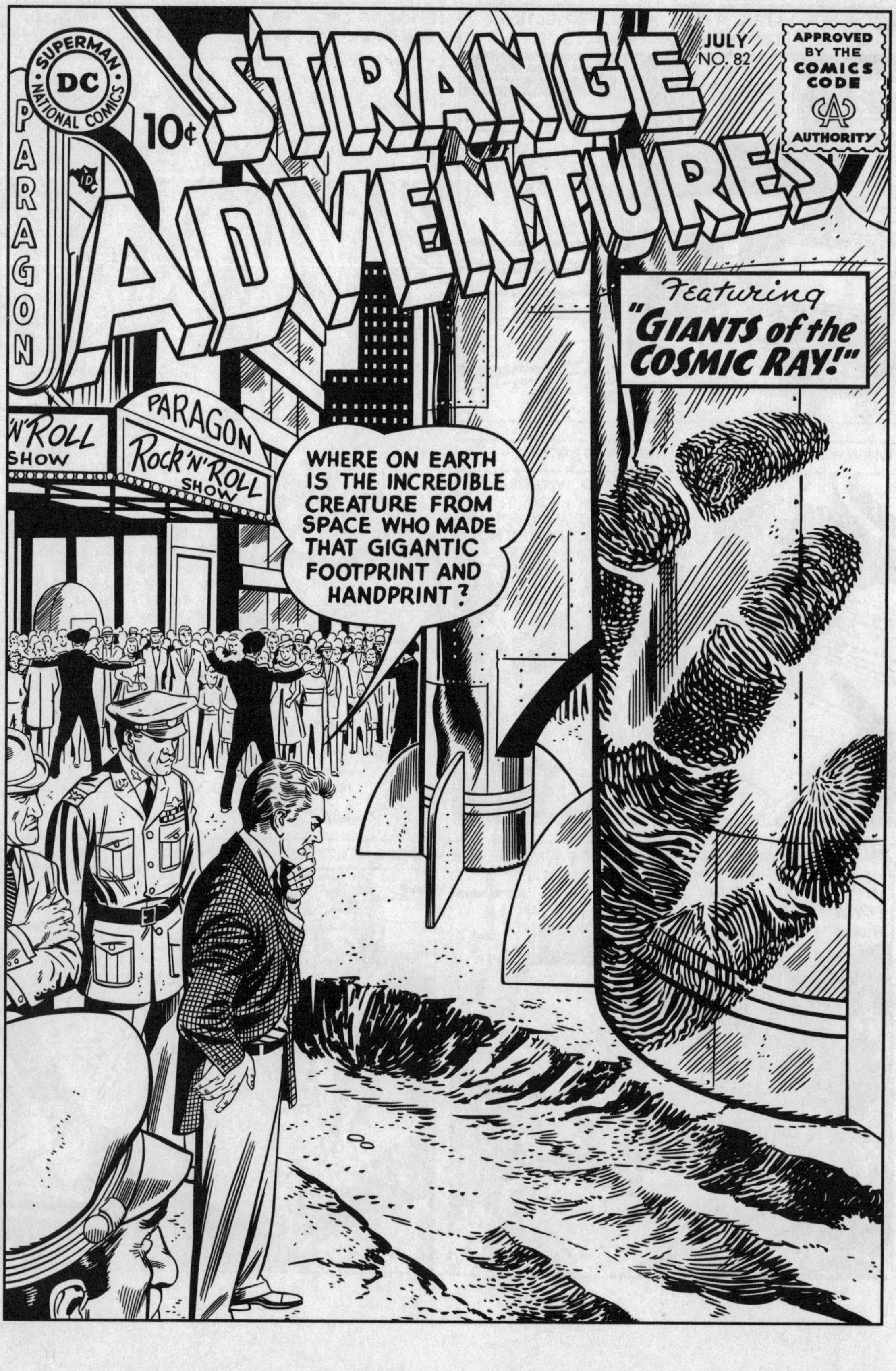
SUPERMAN DC NATIONAL COMICS
10¢
STRANGE ADVENTURES
JULY NO. 82
APPROVED BY THE COMICS CODE AUTHORITY
PARAGON
Featuring "GIANTS of the COSMIC RAY!"
PARAGON Rock'N'Roll SHOW
'N'ROLL SHOW
WHERE ON EARTH IS THE INCREDIBLE CREATURE FROM SPACE WHO MADE THAT GIGANTIC FOOTPRINT AND HANDPRINT?

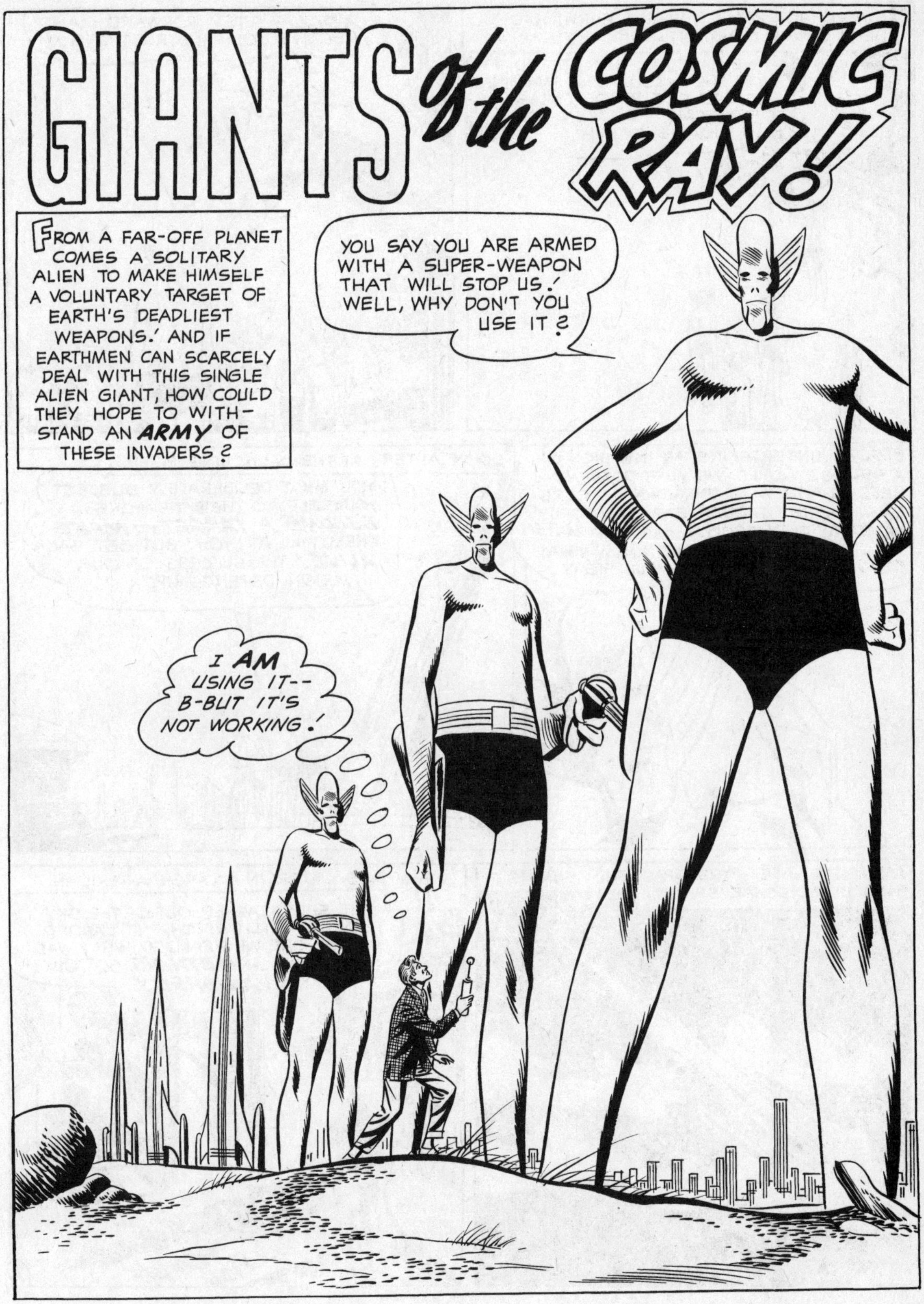
GIANTS of the COSMIC RAY!
FROM A FAR-OFF PLANET COMES A SOLITARY ALIEN TO MAKE HIMSELF A VOLUNTARY TARGET OF EARTH'S DEADLIEST WEAPONS.' AND IF EARTHMEN CAN SCARCELY DEAL WITH THIS SINGLE ALIEN GIANT, HOW COULD THEY HOPE TO WITH-STAND AN ARMY OF THESE INVADERS?
YOU SAY YOU ARE ARMED WITH A SUPER-WEAPON THAT WILL STOP US.' WELL, WHY DON'T YOU USE IT?
I AM USING IT-- B-BUT IT'S NOT WORKING.'

ON A DISTANT PLANET, WHERE EARTH HAS BEEN UNDER CONSTANT SCRUTINY...

WE HAVE ALL REGISTERED WITH THE CALCULATING MACHINE! NOW TO SEE WHO IT HAS SCIENTIFICALLY CHOSEN TO INVADE EARTH!

BZZ-ZZ... CLICK!

XOLL-- STEP FORWARD--AND RECEIVE YOUR INSTRUCTIONS!

XOLL

BEFORE UNDERTAKING AN INVASION OF A STRANGE WORLD WE MUST DETERMINE BEFOREHAND WHAT UNKNOWN DANGERS EXIST THERE! THOUGH EARTH IS POPULATED BY TINY PEOPLE--AS CONTRASTED TO OUR SIZE--WE DO NOT KNOW WHAT DEADLY WEAPONS THEY WILL FIGHT US WITH!

SOON AFTER, AT THE LAUNCHING FIELD...

YOU MUST DELIBERATELY SUBJECT YOURSELF TO THEIR WEAPONS... *BECOME A TARGET--MAKE* THEM FIRE AT YOU! BUT GET BACK *ALIVE!* THE SUCCESS OF OUR INVASION DEPENDS UPON IT!

MOMENTS LATER, THE SPACESHIP BURSTS INTO ULTRA-SONAR SPEED...

A FEW DAYS LATER, IN A LARGE AMERICAN CITY....

THE SHIP FLASHED OUT OF THE SKY! THEN--IN A SPLIT SECOND--IT LANDED... AND BEFORE WE REALIZED WHAT WAS HAPPENING, *SOMETHING* GOT OUT-- AND *VANISHED!*

2

STAY BACK! GIVE THE SCIENTIST A CHANCE TO WORK!

WE'LL GET INSTRUMENTS HERE AND TRY TO DETERMINE SOMETHING ABOUT OUR ALIEN VISITOR FROM HIS FOOTPRINTS AND HANDPRINT!

MEANWHILE, IN ANOTHER PART OF THE CITY...

GOSH! LOOK AT THE SIZE OF THAT CREATURE!

HE'S RIPPING AWAY THAT BUILDING TOWER--AS IF IT WERE *PAPER!*

AS THE CREATURE TAKES TO THE WATER AFTER A VESSEL, MOUNTED ARTILLERY GUNS ROLL UP...

AT LAST! THEY'RE FIRING THEIR GUNS AT ME!

BLAM!

KWHOOM!

BUT AS THE HEAVY GUNS CONTINUE TO FIRE...

CALL IN FOR *ATOMIC* SHELLS! THESE OTHERS ARE LIKE LITTLE FIRE-CRACKERS BURSTING AROUND HIM!

SO FAR THOSE WEAPONS HAVE NO EFFECT ON ME... BUT I MUST SEE WHAT *ELSE* THEY HAVE...

SOON AFTERWARDS, AS ATOMIC WARHEADS EXPLODE AROUND THE TOWERING ALIEN...

I'M HURT... MUST GET BACK TO SHIP...

KA-WHA-WHOOM!

STAGGERING ASHORE, THE GIANT LUMBERS TOWARD HIS ROCKET SHIP...

WE WOUNDED HIM!

HE'S HEADING FOR HIS SPACESHIP-- KEEP FIRING!

KA-WHA-WHOOM!

AFTER THE ALIEN SHIP FLASHES AWAY FROM EARTH, SCIENTISTS GATHER AT THE LABORATORY OF DR. ALBERT PRENTISS...

...AND I'M PUZZLED WHY JUST **ONE ALIEN** TRIED TO INVADE EARTH! THERE MUST BE MORE OF THEM--WHY DIDN'T THEY ATTACK US IN FULL FORCE?

CONSIDER THE GIANT'S ACTIONS WHILE HERE! HE SEEMED TO **DEFY** US TO THROW OUR MOST POWERFUL WEAPONS AT HIM! AND IT WASN'T UNTIL WE HIT HIM WITH ATOMIC SHELLS THAT HE FLED!

THE WAY I FIGURE IT--THE ALIEN CAME HERE TO TEST OUR WEAPONS--LIKE AN ADVANCE "SCOUT"! SOME DAY HE'LL RETURN WITH **OTHERS**--WHEN THEY DEVISE AN EFFECTIVE PROTECTION AGAINST OUR ATOMIC WEAPONS!

IN THAT CASE, WE'D BE HELPLESS! WE DON'T KNOW WHERE THE GIANT CAME FROM-- **WHAT** HE IS--OR HOW TO FIGHT HIS KIND!

WE KNOW **SOMETHING!** OUR COSMIC-DETECTOR SHOWED THAT HIS FOOT IMPRESSIONS WEREN'T MADE BY THE CREATURE'S WEIGHT...BUT BY **COSMIC RAYS** FROM HIS BODY! WHICH LEADS ME TO BELIEVE--

THAT THE GIANT'S BODY IS A CONDENSATION OF COSMIC-RAY ENERGY!

DR. PRENTISS! THAT INVENTION OF YOURS--THE "COSMIC CANNON" I BELIEVE YOU CALL IT! CAN WE USE IT AGAINST THOSE CREATURES?

PRENTISS THEN REMOVES A STRANGE CONTRAPTION FROM A CLOSET...

IT'S NOT REALLY A "CANNON"--NOR A **WEAPON!** ITS PRINCIPLE IS TO **ABSORB** COSMIC RAYS! I HAD PLANNED IT AS PROTECTION FOR SPACE-SHIP CREWMEN AGAINST THE DANGERS OF COSMIC RAYS WHEN THEY JOURNEY THROUGH SPACE!

4.

UNFORTUNATELY, ITS TRUE EFFECTIVENESS HAS NEVER BEEN TESTED! ONLY IN SPACE, WHERE COSMIC-RAY BOMBARDMENT IS AT FULL STRENGTH, SHOULD IT WORK WELL! STILL, IT MIGHT BE EFFECTIVE AGAINST THOSE ALIENS -- REMEMBER, THEY'RE CONCENTRATED COSMIC RAYS!

MEANWHILE, THE ALIEN CRAFT RETURNS TO ITS HOME PLANET, WHERE....

OUR EXAMINATION OF *XOLL* REVEALS THAT THE ONLY DAMAGE SUFFERED BY HIM WAS FROM EARTH'S NUCLEAR FISSION WEAPONS!

THEN WE SHALL DEVISE A PROTECTIVE SHIELD AGAINST THAT WEAPON!

AND THEN, OUR INVASION OF EARTH SHALL BEGIN!

SEVERAL DAYS LATER, STARTLED PEOPLE LOOK UP FROM EARTH AT THE SOUND OF A BOOMING VOICE FROM SPACE....

LISTEN, EARTH PEOPLE! WE HAVE MADE OURSELVES IMMUNE AGAINST YOUR ATOMIC WEAPONS! YOU CAN SAVE YOURSELVES BY SURRENDERING!

THE GREATLY AMPLIFIED VOICE REACHES INTO DR. PRENTISS' LABORATORY...

ONLY MY "COSMIC CANNON" HAS A CHANCE TO SAVE EARTH! I MUST BE READY WHEN THE ALIENS LAND!

ALONE, THE SCIENTIST APPROACHES THE TOWERING FIGURES...

HERE COMES A SPOKESMAN--MAYBE HE IS THE ONE DELIVERING THE SURRENDER!

NO! I COME TO WARN YOU TO *LEAVE* EARTH! I AM ARMED WITH A WEAPON TO STOP YOU!

5

SCIENTISTS AND MILITARY STRATEGISTS, HOLDING THEIR GROUND, STARE AT THE LONE FIGURE...

I AM TURNING ON MY WEAPON--NOW! LEAVE AT ONCE--OR SUFFER THE CONSEQUENCES!

DISREGARD HIM! PREPARE TO RAY-BLAST THE CITY!

WITH POUNDING HEART THE SCIENTIST STRIDES FORWARD... GETTING CLOSER--CLOSER...

WHAT'S THE MATTER? THE CANNON ISN'T WORKING! BUT I MUST KEEP GOING--KEEP GOING...

I REPEAT! I WARN YOU TO LEAVE--NOW!

CLOSER STILL HE GOES...

YOUR WEAPON HAS NO MORE EFFECT ON US THAN YOUR WARNING! EARTHMAN, YOU SHALL BE THE FIRST CASUALTY OF THE INVASION!

IT'S STILL NOT WORKING! WHAT'S WRONG?

SUDDENLY, THE "CANNON" STARTS TO BUZZ...

IT'S WORKING!

EEEYAH...

BZZZ BZZZ

FEARFULLY, THE OTHER GIANTS EXAMINE THEIR STRICKEN COMRADE... AND THEN...

THE EARTH-WEAPON IMMOBILIZED HIM!

THEY HAVE DEVISED THE ONE WEAPON WE HAVE NO DEFENSE AGAINST! HURRY--TO THE SHIPS BEFORE EARTH CONQUERS US!

WHEN THE SPACESHIPS DEPART...

DR. PRENTISS! WHAT DID YOU SHOOT AT THEM?

NOTHING! THIS GADGET DOESN'T SHOOT ANY-THING OUT! IT ABSORBED THE ALIEN'S COSMIC-RAY ENERGY--DRAINING HIM OF ALL STRENGTH!

BUT WHAT TOOK SO LONG FOR THE WEAPON TO WORK?

IT WASN'T EFFECTIVE--UNTIL I GOT WITHIN TEN FEET OF THE GIANT! I DIDN'T KNOW THAT-- BUT NEITHER DID THEY! HAD THEY KNOWN THEY WOULD HAVE NEVER LET ME GET SO CLOSE!

THE END

6

The Man Who INHERITED MARS!

MARS IS MY WORLD-- AND I'M NOT GOING TO LET THOSE INVADERS FROM SPACE TAKE IT AWAY FROM ME!

THE STRANGEST WILL ON EARTH BEQUEATHED TO HAL JACKSON THE PLANET *MARS!* BUT *MARS* WAS 40 MILLION MILES AWAY--AND HOW WAS THE EARTHMAN GOING TO GET THERE AND TAKE POSSESSION OF HIS AMAZING INHERITANCE?

ONCE AN ORPHAN AS A BABY, HAL JACKSON FINDS HIMSELF AN ORPHAN AGAIN IN MANHOOD...

MY FOSTER MOTHER DIED LAST YEAR AND NOW MY FOSTER FATHER IS GONE! I...I LOVED THEM DEARLY, EVEN THOUGH THEY WEREN'T MY REAL PARENTS!

STILL GRIEF-STRICKEN AT THE READING OF THE WILL, HAL HARDLY HEARS THE LAWYER UNTIL...

"TO MY BELOVED ADOPTED SON, BESIDES ALL MY EARTHLY POSSESSIONS, I BEQUEATH THE PLANET *MARS!*"

WH-- WHAT'S THAT?

ALMOST IN A DAZE, HAL WATCHES THE LAWYER LEAVE...

ANYWAY, YOU HAVE LEGALLY INHERITED HIS HOUSE AND WORLDLY GOODS, IF NOT... MARS! GOOD DAY!

MY FATHER WAS A SERIOUS AND SINCERE MAN ALL HIS LIFE! IF HE MADE ME THE "HEIR" TO MARS, HE WASN'T JOKING!

SEARCHING HIS FOSTER FATHER'S PERSONAL PAPERS, HAL FINDS A CLUE IN A DESK DRAWER...

GOSH, MY FATHER NEVER MENTIONED THIS SECRET CAVE TO ME! I'M GOING TO FOLLOW THIS MAP AND SEE WHAT THIS IS ALL ABOUT!

For my son! Map to secret cave in woods!

CAVE

STONE MT.

INSIDE THE WELL-CONCEALED CAVE, HAL COMES ACROSS A STARTLING SIGHT!...

A SPACESHIP! WHAT CONNECTION DOES IT HAVE WITH MY FATHER --AND ME?

INSIDE THE SHIP, A DIARY REVEALS...

"I BE-QUEATH MY SPACE-SHIP TO YOU, HAL JACKSON, THE EARTH-LING BOY WE ADOPTED! YOU SEE, MY SON, YOUR MOTHER AND I ORIGINALLY CAME FROM THE PLANET MARS!'"

GASP! MY FOSTER PARENTS WERE MARTIANS!

"25 years ago, a Cosmic Blight wiped out the last remnants of human civilization on Mars..."

"Only my wife and I escaped in a small rocket ship I had just completed..."

ALL OUR PEOPLE... DEAD!

WE...WE MUST SEEK A NEW HOME ON THE NEAREST PLANET --EARTH! OUR TELESCOPES DETECTED HUMAN CIVILIZATION THERE!

"On earth, obtaining a secluded home, my wife and I settled down quietly as if we were earth people..."

WE'RE THE **LAST OF THE MARTIANS!** BUT WE DON'T DARE REVEAL THAT OR WE'LL SPEND THE REST OF OUR LIVES ON PUBLIC EXHIBIT! WE HAVE CHANGED OUR MARTIAN NAME OF "JAKZUN" TO "JACKSON"!

AND LET US ADOPT AN EARTHLING ORPHAN BABY! WE ALWAYS WANTED A SON!

"AND SO WE ADOPTED YOU AS OUR BABY SON, HAL! THUS MY WILL BEQUEATHS YOU OUR WORLD OF **MARS**, EVEN IF IT IS DEAD AND WORTHLESS! THERE IS ENOUGH FUEL IN THE SPACESHIP FOR A ROUNDTRIP TO **MARS** SHOULD YOU DESIRE TO VISIT OUR NATIVE WORLD!"

LATER, THE SPACESHIP ZOOMS OUT OF THE CAVE...

MY FATHER LEFT FULL INSTRUCTIONS HOW TO RUN THE SHIP! IN MEMORY OF MY PARENTS, I'LL MAKE A TRIP TO THEIR WORLD... THE WORLD I *INHERITED!*

Landing safely on Mars, Hal Jackson experiences the strangest thrill of any human being in history!

THE AIR IS THIN BUT BREATHABLE! IT MAY BE A WORTHLESS WORLD IN RUINS, BUT IT'S MINE... ALL MINE!

After many hours of examining the fantastic wonders of the dead planet, Hal finds his inheritance is not worthless after all!

THAT RED METAL, UNKNOWN ON EARTH, GLOWS WITH RADIO-ACTIVITY! THE MARTIANS USED IT IN POWER STATIONS, TO PRODUCE SUPER-ATOMIC ENERGY! THIS CAN BENEFIT EARTH!

3

MEANWHILE, THAT SAME RED METAL HAS ATTRACTED ALIENS FROM OUTER SPACE WHOSE TELEPATHIC THOUGHTS ARE *"OVERHEARD"* BY THE HIDDEN EARTHMAN...

OUR INSTRUMENTS DETECTED THIS *ATOMIUM,* WITH WHICH WE CAN MAKE SUPER-WEAPONS TO CONQUER THE UNIVERSE.! AND NOBODY OWNS THIS DEAD WORLD NOW!

I DO!

THEY'RE ROBBING *MY WORLD!* GOT TO STOP THEM, ESPECIALLY SINCE THEY PLAN TO USE *ATOMIUM* FOR THEIR OWN EVIL PURPOSES!

UNDETECTED, HAL STEALS INTO A MARTIAN "STABLE"...

THE ALIENS ARE ARMED AND I'M NOT! GOT TO TAKE THEM BY SURPRISE! HMM.... THE MARTIANS USED TO RIDE THESE MECHANICAL "STEEDS"! ONE SEEMS IN GOOD CONDITION!

MOUNTING A ROBOT HORSE, HAL PUSHES A BUTTON IN FRONT OF THE SADDLE...

YES -- IT'S STILL IN WORKING ORDER! THESE PUSHBUTTON CONTROLS WILL SEND ME GALLOPING AMONG THE ALIENS!

MOMENTS LATER, THE MAN WHO OWNS MARS CHARGES INTO THE STARTLED ALIENS!...

I'M ROUTING THE ENEMY!

BUT AFTER 25 YEARS OF NEGLECT ON DEAD MARS...

GREAT STARS! MY HORSE COLLAPSED UNDER ME!

DRAW YOUR RAY-GUNS! DESTROY THE MARTIAN!

WHU...NNGGG!

THEY THINK I'M A "MARTIAN"! WELL, MY FOSTER PARENTS WERE! AND MARS IS MY WORLD! AND FROM MY PREVIOUS SCOUTING AROUND, I KNOW PLENTY ABOUT MARS!

FOR INSTANCE, THE MARTIANS MADE THESE FLEXIBLE GLASS WINDOWS! I'LL FLING MYSELF AGAINST THIS ONE AND...

...AND BOUNCE BACK, SAILING OVER THEM! I HAVE A PLAN IN MIND TO DRIVE THEM AWAY... IF I CAN REACH THE NEARBY MARTIAN CANAL!

WHEN HAL REACHES THE "CANAL"...

THE MARTIAN "CANALS" ARE REALLY GIANT MILE-WIDE CONDUITS, STILL HOLDING WATER! IF I CAN OPEN A VALVE...

MOMENTS LATER, MILLIONS OF GALLONS OF WATER POUR FROM THE COLOSSAL PIPE!

RUN! THE CITY WILL BE FLOODED! BACK TO OUR SHIP BEFORE WE DROWN!

THEN, HAL REACHES THE TOP OF THE CANAL PIPE WHERE...

NOW TO DRIVE THEM *OFF* MARS! THE MARTIANS BUILT THESE GIANT RAY-CANNONS TO RESIST SPACE-INVADERS!

A GIANT RAY-GUN FIRING AT US! RETREAT INTO SPACE! WE THOUGHT MARS WAS LIFELESS BUT THERE'S AN *ARMY* STILL ALIVE HERE, PROTECTING THEIR WORLD!

INSTEAD OF AN ARMY OF MARTIANS, THERE IS ONLY ONE EARTHMAN!

AND DON'T EVER COME BACK, UNDERSTAND? *THIS IS MY WORLD!*

AFTER TURNING OFF THE CANAL SPIGOT...

THE SEWERS PREVENTED THE CITY FROM BEING FLOODED! NOW TO RETURN TO EARTH AND DELIVER THE SPACESHIP TO MY GOVERNMENT! THEY CAN REFUEL IT AND COME HERE FOR THE VALUABLE *ATOMIUM!*

BUT HAL JACKSON LOSES CONTROL ON HIS RETURN TO EARTH AND...

I... I CRASHED! LUCKY I'M ALIVE! MARS WILL HAVE TO WAIT TILL EARTH INVENTS ITS OWN SPACESHIPS!

WHEN THAT DAY COMES, EARTHMEN WILL BRING BACK *ATOMIUM*, TO BENEFIT THE WHOLE WORLD! I WON'T CLAIM IT, EVEN THOUGH I'M *THE MAN WHO INHERITED MARS!*

The End

6

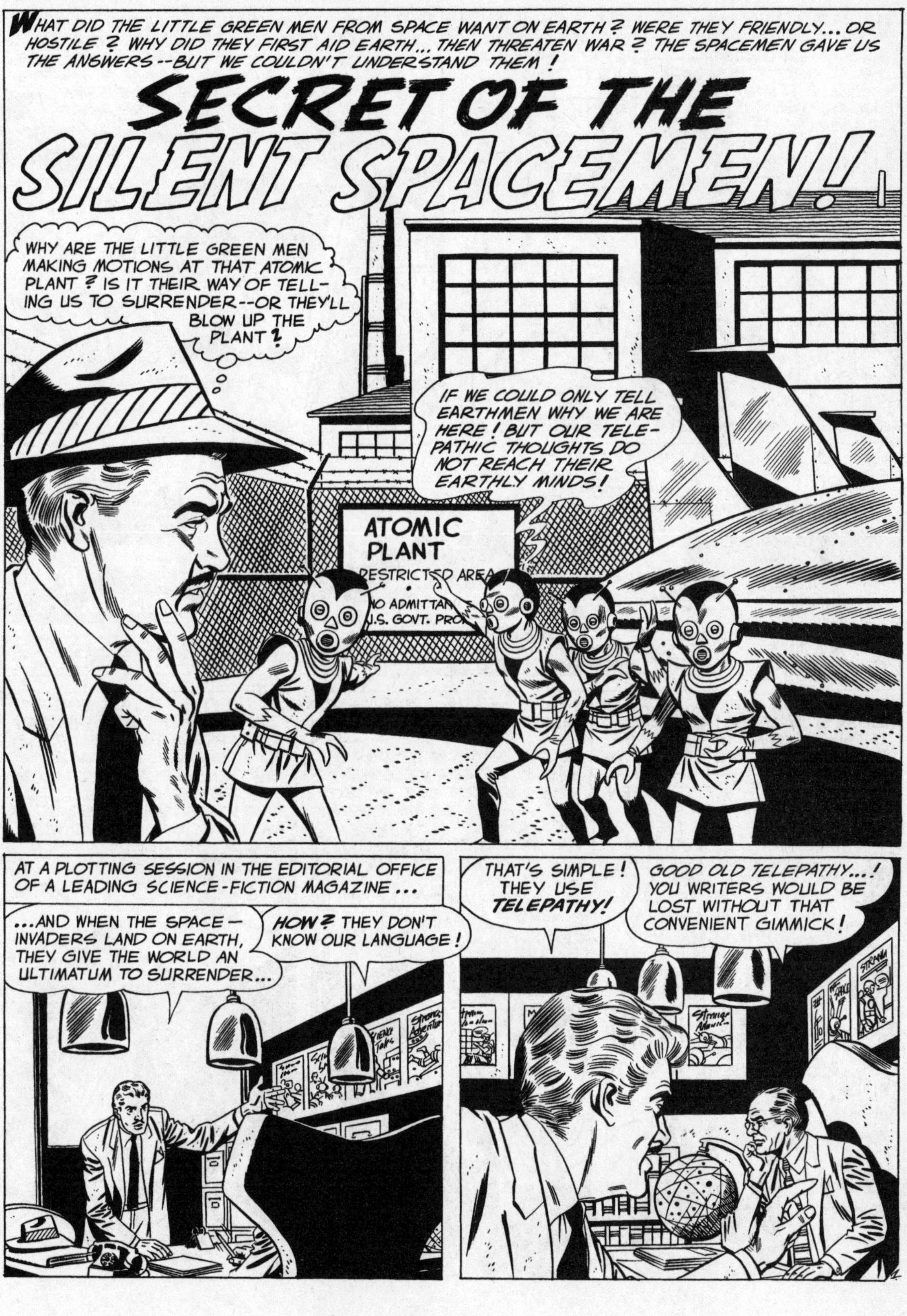
WHAT DID THE LITTLE GREEN MEN FROM SPACE WANT ON EARTH? WERE THEY FRIENDLY... OR HOSTILE? WHY DID THEY FIRST AID EARTH... THEN THREATEN WAR? THE SPACEMEN GAVE US THE ANSWERS--BUT WE COULDN'T UNDERSTAND THEM!
SECRET OF THE SILENT SPACEMEN!
WHY ARE THE LITTLE GREEN MEN MAKING MOTIONS AT THAT ATOMIC PLANT? IS IT THEIR WAY OF TELLING US TO SURRENDER--OR THEY'LL BLOW UP THE PLANT?
IF WE COULD ONLY TELL EARTHMEN WHY WE ARE HERE! BUT OUR TELEPATHIC THOUGHTS DO NOT REACH THEIR EARTHLY MINDS!
ATOMIC PLANT
AT A PLOTTING SESSION IN THE EDITORIAL OFFICE OF A LEADING SCIENCE-FICTION MAGAZINE...
...AND WHEN THE SPACE-INVADERS LAND ON EARTH, THEY GIVE THE WORLD AN ULTIMATUM TO SURRENDER...
HOW? THEY DON'T KNOW OUR LANGUAGE!
THAT'S SIMPLE! THEY USE TELEPATHY!
GOOD OLD TELEPATHY...! YOU WRITERS WOULD BE LOST WITHOUT THAT CONVENIENT GIMMICK!

WHAT IF TELEPATHY *DIDN'T WORK?* AND NEITHER DID SUCH OTHER OLD STAND-BYS AS AUTOMATIC LANGUAGE TRANS-LATORS, SIGN LANGUAGE...

YOU'VE GIVEN ME A TOUGH ASSIGNMENT! I'LL GO HOME AND MULL IT OVER!

THAT EVENING AS AUTHOR OWEN BENTLY SEEKS "INSPIRATION" DURING A DRIVE IN THE COUNTRY...

NO SPEECH...NO TELEPATHY...NO WAY OF WRITING UNDERSTANDABLE MESSAGES IN THE SAME LANGUAGE! HOW *ELSE* COULD THE ALIENS COMMUNICATE WITH US? MAKE KNOWN WHAT THEY WANT?

LET'S RUN THE STORY THROUGH MY MIND AGAIN! FIRST, THE ALIEN SHIP LANDS AND...GREAT STARS! M-MY VERY THOUGHTS COMING TRUE! A...A *REAL* SPACESHIP *IS* LANDING ON EARTH!

IT SEEMS LIKE A FANTASTIC DREAM TO THE SCIENCE-FICTION WRITER, AS THE BEGINNING OF HIS IMAG-INATIVE TALE HAPPENS BEFORE HIS EYES!

LITTLE GREEN MEN--JUST LIKE THE TYPE I'VE USED IN STORIES! THEY SEEM FRIENDLY... BUT I CAN'T UNDER-STAND THEIR TALK! WHY DON'T THEY USE TELEPATHY?

ATOM PLANT RESTRICT

MEANWHILE, THE SPACE VISITORS ARE EQUALLY BAFFLED...

WE CAN READ *HIS* THOUGHTS EASILY, BUT OUR TELEPATHY WAVES CANNOT GET THROUGH TO HIS EARTHLY MIND!

THEN HOW CAN WE MAKE EARTH UNDER-STAND OUR MISSION HERE?

I RECEIVED NO *"TELEPATHY"* SPEECH FROM THEM! THE VERY STORY PROBLEM I WAS TRYING TO SOLVE WILL NOW FACE EARTH ITSELF! I'LL NOTIFY THE AUTHORITIES! PERHAPS SCIEN-TIFIC MINDS CAN FIND SOME WAY OF COMMUNICATING WITH THE ALIENS!

THE NEXT DAY, SCIENTISTS FAIL TOO, DESPITE MOST INGENIOUS EFFORTS!

WE'VE TRIED EVERYTHING-- BUT THEY DIDN'T GIVE US ANY SIGN OF UNDERSTANDING!

AS AN INVITED OBSERVER, OWEN BENTLEY FINDS THIS REAL-LIFE "STORY" FAR MORE AMAZING THAN ANY HE HAS PREVIOUSLY IMAGINED!

GENERAL, WHAT DO YOU MAKE OF THE WAY THEY KEEP STARING AT THE ATOMIC PLANT?...

I'M ONLY GUESS-ING--BUT...

--IT MIGHT BE THEIR WAY OF GIVING US AN ULTIMATUM TO *SURRENDER*...OR THEY'LL BLOW UP OUR ATOMIC PLANT!

THEY HAVEN'T MADE A HOSTILE MOVE YET, GENERAL! IF WE ONLY KNEW THE TRUTH...

SUDDENLY, AN EMERGENCY ARISES IN THE NUCLEAR PLANT!

DANGER! WE LOST CON-TROL OF THE FUSION VORTEX WE WERE EXPERIMENTING WITH! IT HAS ENOUGH POWER TO BLOW UP HALF THE COUNTRY!

MAIN GATE EXIT U.S. GOVT.

-EXIT-

WE READ THE EARTHMAN'S THOUGHTS OF THE IMPENDING DISASTER! INTO OUR SHIP!

THE GREEN MEN UNDERSTAND WHAT'S HAPPENING! THEY'RE GOING TO ESCAPE IN THEIR SHIP!

ATOMIC PLANT NO ADMITTAN

BUT INSTEAD, THEIR SHIP HEADS TOWARD THE DANGER!

WE CAN STOP THAT WILD CHAIN REACTION! HURRY!

AT THE RISK OF THEIR LIVES, THE MINIATURE MEN FROM SPACE BATTLE THE RUNAWAY REACTOR...

ORDINARY FOAM EXTINGUISHES FIRE! FIRE! SIMILARLY, OUR *NEUTRONIC FOAM* CAN QUENCH AND SMOTHER *ATOMIC FIRE!*

WHEN THE THREAT HAS BEEN ELIMINATED, THE SHIP ONCE MORE LANDS OUTSIDE THE FENCE...

WELL, GENERAL? DO YOU STILL THINK THEY'RE *HOSTILE?*

UH...NOT NOW! IF THEY SAVED OUR ATOMIC PLANT, THEY MUST BE FRIENDLY! AND I WAS PLANNING TO ORDER AN ATOM-BOMB ATTACK AT THEIR FIRST HOSTILE MOVE!

OVERHEARING, THERE IS A STRANGE REACTION AMONG THE LITTLE MEN!

DID YOU TELEPATHIZE THAT? THEY WOULD HAVE ATTACKED US WITH *NUCLEAR BOMBS*... IF WE PROVED "HOSTILE"!

GOOD! NOW WE KNOW HOW TO ACCOMPLISH OUR MISSION! COME--LET US SET UP OUR "WAR CAMP"!

AS A SECRET COMMITTEE FOLLOWS THE ALIENS FAR OUT IN THE DESERT...

AMAZING!

I WAS RIGHT AFTER ALL!

USING SUPER-SCIENCE METHODS OF CONSTRUCTION, THEY ARE QUICKLY BUILDING A GIGANTIC "GUN"!

THEY *ARE* PLANNING WAR ON US! THEY ONLY LULLED OUR SUSPICIONS BEFORE BY SAVING THE ATOMIC PLANT! THEY'RE TESTING THE GIANT GUN NOW!

BOOM!

IT BLASTED THE MOUNTAIN!

THEY'LL NEVER GET A CHANCE TO USE THAT SUPER-WEAPON AGAINST US! I'LL ORDER A BOMBER TO DROP AN *A-BOMB* ON THE GUN!

SOON, WITH JETS SCREAMING, THE EARTH BOMBER ATTACKS...

ON TARGET... A-BOMB AWAY!

THERE IT GOES! LUCKILY, NOBODY ELSE LIVES HERE IN THE DESERT! THAT'S THE END OF THE GIANT GUN!

AND OF THE LITTLE GREEN MEN! I...I HOPE WE DID THE RIGHT THING...

BUT STRANGELY, THE LITTLE GREEN MEN ARE NOT TENDING THEIR GIANT GUN! FOR MILES AWAY...

WE ARE SAFE HERE FROM THE ACTUAL BLAST! BUT WE *WANTED* THEM TO DROP THE NUCLEAR BOMB ON OUR *DECOY GUN!* NOW THE POWERFUL RADIATIONS FROM THE BOMB ARE STRIKING US!

THANK THE STARS! OUR MISSION IS ACCOMPLISHED! WE ARE UNDERGOING THE *CHANGE!*

WINGED MEN! ARE THEY *NEW* INVADERS FROM SPACE?

NO! DO NOT FEAR! WE ARE THE "LITTLE GREEN MEN"-- IN OUR NEW BODIES!

IN OUR HUMANLIKE FORM, WE CAN NOW CONTACT YOUR HUMAN MINDS WITH TELEPATHY! ON OUR WORLD, WE ARE BORN WITH SMALL GREEN BODIES, WHICH LATER *METAMORPHOSE* INTO THESE TALL WINGED FORMS!

WHY... THAT'S JUST LIKE EARTHLY *CATERPILLARS* CHANGING INTO *BUTTERFLIES!*

BUT ONLY *NUCLEAR RADIATIONS* CAN CHANGE US--AND RECENTLY, OUR WORLD'S SUPPLY OF NATURAL URANIUM BECAME EXHAUSTED! OUR MISSION WAS TO FIND A WORLD WITH PLENTIFUL NUCLEAR SUPPLIES!

WHEN YOU HAD NO WAY TO TELL US OF YOUR PLIGHT--

--YOU *PRETENDED* TO ATTACK EARTH, AND FORCE US INTO EXPLODING A NUCLEAR BOMB IN ORDER TO CHANGE YOU TO WINGED FORM!

YES! NOW WE BEG EARTH FOR URA- NIUM TO TAKE BACK TO OUR WORLD--OTHER- WISE OUR RACE IS DOOMED TO REMAIN AS LITTLE GREEN PEOPLE!

GENEROUSLY, EARTH ANSWERS THEIR APPEAL...

YOUR URANIUM GIFT WILL LAST US FOR THOUSANDS OF YEARS! THANKS, KIND EARTHLINGS! FAREWELL!

WHEN OWEN BENTLEY RETURNS TO HIS TYPE- WRITER...

NOW I CAN WRITE A "STORY" OF HOW ALIENS WOULD GET THEIR MESSAGE ACROSS, WITHOUT TELEPATHY! AND IT'S ALL *TRUE!*

The End

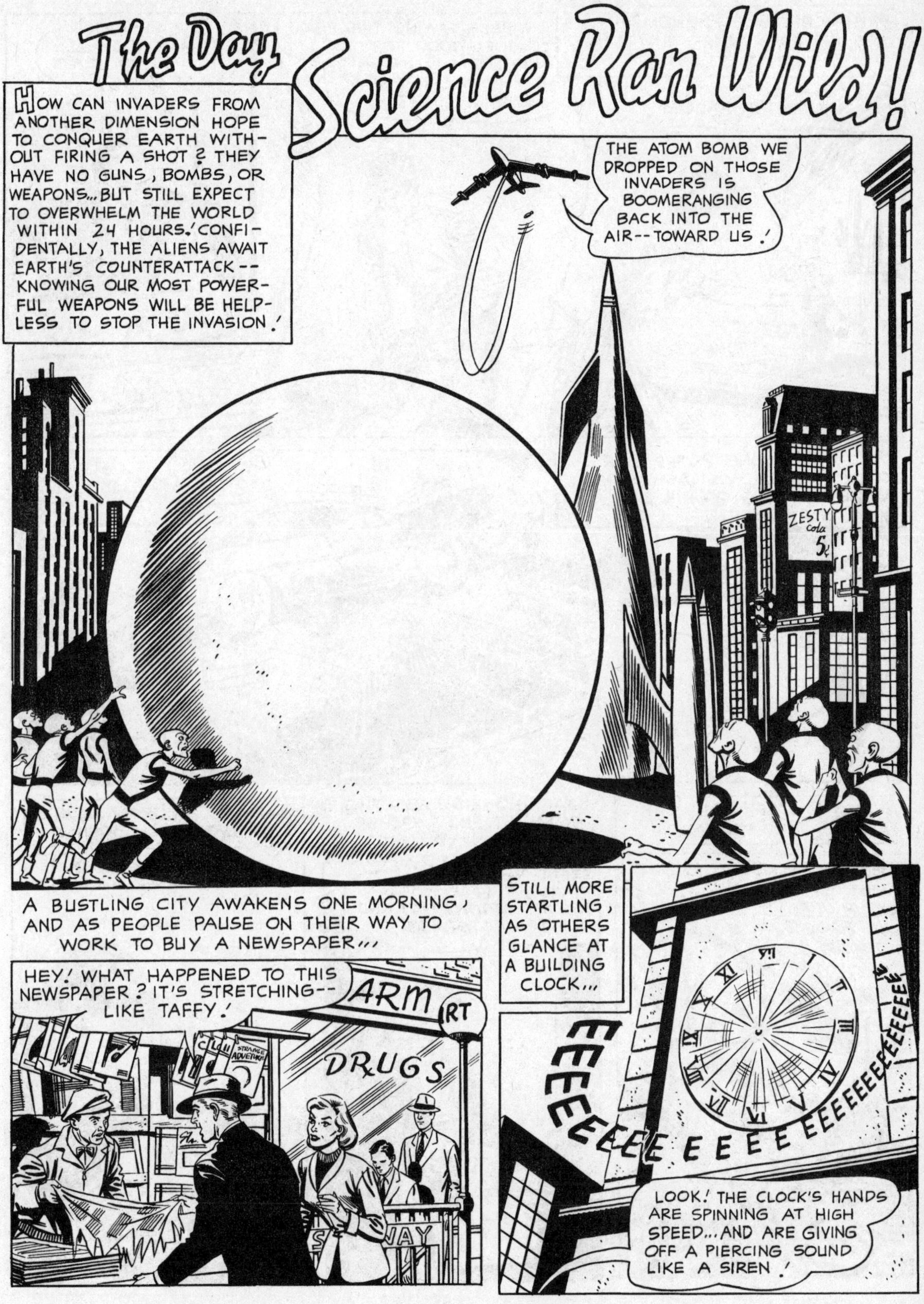
The Day Science Ran Wild!
HOW CAN INVADERS FROM ANOTHER DIMENSION HOPE TO CONQUER EARTH WITHOUT FIRING A SHOT? THEY HAVE NO GUNS, BOMBS, OR WEAPONS... BUT STILL EXPECT TO OVERWHELM THE WORLD WITHIN 24 HOURS! CONFIDENTALLY, THE ALIENS AWAIT EARTH'S COUNTERATTACK -- KNOWING OUR MOST POWERFUL WEAPONS WILL BE HELPLESS TO STOP THE INVASION!
THE ATOM BOMB WE DROPPED ON THOSE INVADERS IS BOOMERANGING BACK INTO THE AIR -- TOWARD US!
ZESTY cola 5¢
A BUSTLING CITY AWAKENS ONE MORNING, AND AS PEOPLE PAUSE ON THEIR WAY TO WORK TO BUY A NEWSPAPER...
HEY! WHAT HAPPENED TO THIS NEWSPAPER? IT'S STRETCHING -- LIKE TAFFY!
ARM
RT
DRUGS
STILL MORE STARTLING, AS OTHERS GLANCE AT A BUILDING CLOCK...
EEEEEEEE E E E E EEEEEEEEEEEEEEEEE
LOOK! THE CLOCK'S HANDS ARE SPINNING AT HIGH SPEED... AND ARE GIVING OFF A PIERCING SOUND LIKE A SIREN!

THE INCREDIBLE PHENOMENA CONTINUE, EACH MORE FANTASTIC THAN THE LAST!

EEK! FLAMES COMING OUT OF THE WATER FAUCET!

I'VE BEEN SAWING THIS PIECE OF SOFT WOOD FOR TEN MINUTES AND HAVEN'T BEEN ABLE TO PUT A SCRATCH IN IT!

MY PRECIOUS DIAMONDS -- ALL TURNED TO HEAPS OF *SALT!*

PERHAPS YOUNG PROFESSOR JOEL CARTER IS MOST ASTOUNDED, WHILE DRIVING TO HIS LAB, WHEN...

MY CAR IS FLOATING IN THE AIR....LIKE A BALLOON!

MOMENTS LATER, THE CAR FALLS EARTHWARD AND...

WHEW! I'M LUCKY TO GET OUT OF THIS ALIVE!

REACHING HIS LAB, THE SCIENTIST FINDS OTHER THINGS INEXPLICABLY CHANGED!

GREAT STARS! THIS WOOD HAS BECOME *MAGNETIC!* AND IT ATTRACTS *GLASS!*

MARBLES I'M DROPPING INTO THIS WATER DISH BOUNCE BACK -- AS IF THE WATER TURNED *ELASTIC!* OUR LAWS OF SCIENCE HAVE SUDDENLY RUN WILD!

WHEN CARTER TUNES IN THE RADIO NEWS...

...FANTASTIC OCCURRENCES ALL OVER THE EARTH...

INSTEAD OF SOUND, THE RADIO FORMS "SMOKE WORDS" IN THE AIR! WHAT COULD BE CAUSING THIS REVOLUTION IN SCIENCE?

OUTSIDE, WHEN CARTER INVESTIGATES...

THERE'S A STRANGE SHIP PARKED BESIDE IT! ALIEN CREATURES ARE COMING OUT... VISITORS FROM ANOTHER WORLD!

AS THE SCIENTIST GLANCES OUT OF THE WINDOW...

WHERE DID THAT STRANGE GLOBE COME FROM? IT WASN'T THERE YESTERDAY! IT'S MADE OF THE *PUREST WHITE METAL* I'VE EVER SEEN!

A TELEPATHIC MESSAGE FROM THE MYSTERIOUS VISITORS EXPLAINS OTHERWISE...

ATTENTION, *DIMENSION 3!* WE ARE FROM *DIMENSION 18!* WE INSTALLED OUR GLOBE MACHINE LAST NIGHT, WHICH BATHES YOUR ENTIRE PLANET IN *Z-RAYS!* THE EFFECT IS TO ALTER YOUR DIMENSION'S SCIENCE LAWS... GRAVITY, MAGNETISM, ELECTRICITY...

B-BUT WHY?

TO WIN CONTROL OF YOUR EARTH... WITHOUT FIRING A SINGLE SHOT! LOOK!... YOUR STONE BUILDINGS ARE STARTING TO MELT! BEFORE LONG, YOUR ENTIRE CIVILIZATION WILL FALL APART!

3

MEANWHILE, ARMED FORCES HAVE BEEN RUSHED TO THE SCENE...

THIS IS WAR! BLAST THOSE INVADERS!

IT WON'T BE AS EASY AS THAT COLONEL THINKS!

BUT WITH EARTH'S BALLISTIC LAWS NULLIFIED, THE COUNTERATTACK FAILS...

OUR FLAME-THROWERS ARE SHOOTING OUT *SNOW-FLAKES!*

OUR BULLETS CURVED AWAY FROM THE WHITE GLOBE!

THE SHELL EXPLODED INTO A *RAINBOW!*

WHEN AN ATOM BOMB IS DROPPED IN SHEER DESPERATION...

¡GASP! THE A-BOMB BOOMERANGED BACK INTO THE AIR! *OUT OF THE WAY...*

ARE YOU CONVINCED NOW, EARTHMEN, THAT NONE OF YOUR WEAPONS CAN HARM US? SURRENDER NOW--BEFORE YOUR CIVILIZED WORLD COLLAPSES!

GUNS FALL SILENT... SOLDIERS STARE IN SILENT FEAR...EARTH RESISTANCE ENDS ABRUPTLY!

WE...WE'RE LICKED, PROFESSOR CARTER! WE CAN'T DESTROY THAT SINISTER WHITE GLOBE! EARTH IS DOOMED...

CURIOUS THAT THEIR MACHINE SHOULD BE PROTECTED BY THE PUREST WHITE METAL IN THE UNIVERSE!

4

As THE SCIENTIST WANDERS OFF, HE PASSES A PAINT STORE....

WHITE GLOBE...I WONDER IF IT HAS ANYTHING TO DO WITH THIS WELL-KNOWN PRINCIPLE REGARDING COLORS AND THEIR REACTION TO THE SUN'S RAYS?

PAINT YOUR HOUSE WHITE! IT *REFLECTS* THE SUN'S HEAT RAYS!

DON'T USE BLACK! IT *ABSORBS* HEAT!

INSIDE THE PAINT STORE, CARTER MAKES A PURCHASE....

IF MY THEORY IS RIGHT, I CAN USE THIS COMMON SPRAY-GUN LOADED WITH BLACK PAINT AS A "WEAPON" TO DEFEAT THE INVADERS!

THAT NIGHT, UNDER COVER OF DARKNESS....

I CAN'T GET CLOSE ENOUGH TO USE MY SPRAY-GUN, UNLESS THOSE GUARDS RELAX THEIR VIGILANCE! HMMM.... IT'S STARTING TO RAIN...

FINALLY, WHEN THE RAIN STOPS, JUST BEFORE DAWN....

THEY'RE DOZING! NOW'S MY CHANCE TO SNEAK CLOSE...OHH! I STUMBLED IN THE DARK...DROPPED THE SPRAY GUN! IT'LL WAKEN THEM!

CLUNK!

TRYING TO RUSH THROUGH THE WAKENED GUARDS, CARTER FINDS EVEN THE MOST DEPENDABLE AND ANCIENT OF MAN'S "WEAPONS" NULLIFIED!

I FORGOT! THE LAWS OF MOMENTUM ARE CHANGED... MY PUNCH HAS NO MORE FORCE THAN A FEATHER!

PAT!

BUT CLEVERLY, CARTER MAKES ONE OF THE ALTERED SCIENCE LAWS WORK TO HIS AD-VANTAGE!

LOOK! THE EARTHLING IS BOUNCING HIGH OUT OF OUR REACH!

LUCKY I REMEMBERED MY LAB EXPERIMENT WITH *ELASTIC* WATER! BY JUMPING ON THAT PUDDLE OF RAINWATER, I BOUNCED LIKE A RUBBER BALL! THAT'S ONE WAY TO REACH THE TOP OF THE GLOBE!

AS THE SUN RISES, CARTER WORKS FAST WITH HIS SPRAY GUN!

JUST A THIN LAYER OF *BLACK* PAINT OUGHT TO DO THE TRICK, CAUSING THE METAL TO *ABSORB* THE SUN'S INTENSE HEAT! IT WILL UPSET THE DELICATE ELECTRONIC MECHANISM INSIDE!

IT'S WORKING! THE HEAT IS *WARPING* AND WRECKING THE Z-RAY PROJECTOR INSIDE!

AS THE *Z-RAYS* CEASE RADIATING OVER THE WORLD, NORMAL SCIENCE LAWS RETURN AND...

NOW A GOOD OLD EARTHLY PUNCH WORKS AGAIN!

FLEE--INTO OUR DIMENSION SHIP! EARTH WEAPONS CAN WORK AGAIN!

FULL SPEED TO *DIMENSION 18!*

AND DON'T COME BACK! REMEMBER, EARTH HAS THE "*WEAPON*" THAT CAN DEFEAT YOU... ANYTIME!

IMAGINE! EARTH WAS SAVED BY A *SPRAY GUN*... AND A FEW CENTS WORTH OF *BLACK PAINT!* SOME BARGAIN, EH?

THE END

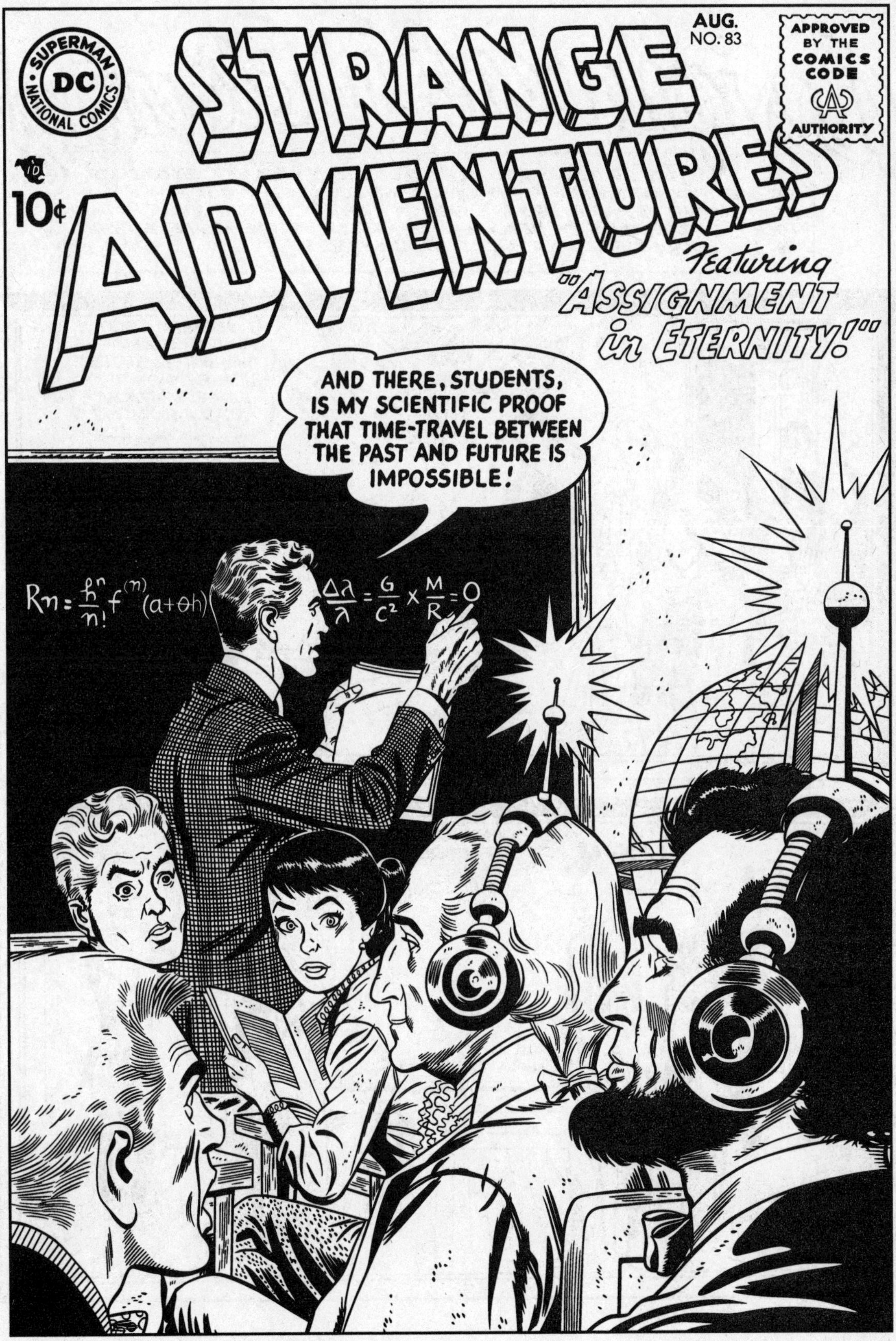
SUPERMAN DC NATIONAL COMICS
STRANGE ADVENTURES
AUG. NO. 83
APPROVED BY THE COMICS CODE AUTHORITY
10¢
Featuring "ASSIGNMENT in ETERNITY!"
AND THERE, STUDENTS, IS MY SCIENTIFIC PROOF THAT TIME-TRAVEL BETWEEN THE PAST AND FUTURE IS IMPOSSIBLE!

Assignment in Eternity!

How did Professor Colby know about scientific discoveries before they were made? Why was he so possessed with a premonition that he had an urgent mission to fulfill? How could he unlock his storehouse of memories to find out why he was here, what he was looking for, and where he must go?

AT MIDDLETOWN COLLEGE ONE DAY, TWO STARTLING FIGURES ENTER THE SCIENCE SURVEY CLASSROOM...

MAY WE JOIN YOUR CLASS, PROFESSOR COLBY.

GENTLEMEN! WHAT IS THE MEANING OF THIS MASQUERADE?

SCIENCE SURVEY ROOM

WE JUST CAME FROM A DRESS REHEARSAL OF A PLAY THE DRAMATIC SOCIETY IS PUTTING ON! WE HAD NO TIME TO CHANGE FROM OUR LINCOLN AND WASHINGTON COSTUMES!

WELL, THEN, I'LL EXCUSE YOU! WHAT IS THE PLAY ABOUT?

IT'S A FANTASY--SHOWING HOW OUR HISTORY MIGHT HAVE BEEN CHANGED IF THE PRESIDENTIAL ROLES OF WASHINGTON AND LINCOLN HAD BEEN REVERSED!

AS OUR FIRST PRESIDENT, LINCOLN ABOLISHES SLAVERY IN 1789 AND WASHINGTON'S MILITARY GENIUS ENDS THE CIVIL WAR IN ONE YEAR!

THE PRESIDENTIAL SWITCH IS WORKED BY THESE TIME-TRAVELING GIMMICKS WE'RE WEARING! BY THE WAY, PROFESSOR, DO YOU THINK MAN WILL EVER BE ABLE TO TRAVEL THROUGH TIME?

DEFINITELY NOT! THIS FORMULA PROVES THAT TIME-TRAVEL IS IMPOSSIBLE!

$$Rn = \frac{f^n}{n!} f^{(n)}(c)$$

SUDDENLY, A STRANGE THOUGHT STRIKES THE SCIENCE TEACHER...

WHY DID I ALMOST WRITE IN A DIFFERENT SYMBOL HERE? A NEW FACTOR MOMENTARILY FLASHED IN MY MIND, UNKNOWN TO PRESENT-DAY MATHEMATICS!

$$1+\theta h) \quad \frac{\Delta a}{\lambda} = \frac{G}{c^2}$$

IN HIS STUDY THAT EVENING, THE PROFESSOR RECALLS OTHER PERPLEXING OCCURRENCES...

THERE WAS THE TIME, FOR INSTANCE, I LECTURED MY SCIENCE SURVEY CLASS ABOUT NEUTRINOS * BEFORE THEY HAD EVEN BEEN DISCOVERED!

*EDITOR'S NOTE: NEUTRINO IS A SUB-ATOMIC PARTICLE OF PURE ENERGY!

"ON ANOTHER OCCASION I DESCRIBED ELEMENT NUMBER 101, WHEN ONLY 100 ARE KNOWN TODAY!"

THE TRANS-URANIUM ELEMENTS, PRODUCED SYNTHETICALLY ARE...

93 - NEPTUNIUM
94 - PLUTONIUM
95 - AMERICUM
96 - CURIUM
97 - BERKELIUM
98 - CALIFORNIUM
99 - EINSTEINIUM
100 - MENDELEEFIUM
101 - SCIENTIUM

"MOST REMARKABLE, IN A LAB DEMONSTRATION FOR MY PUPILS ... "

AMAZING, PROFESSOR! YOU'VE INVENTED FLEXIBLE GLASS!

WH-WHAT?

I-I THOUGHT THE PROCESS WAS COMMON KNOWLEDGE!

SEEKING AN ANSWER TO THE MYSTERY, THE PROFESSOR RETURNS TO HIS TIME-EQUATION AND...

I'LL PUT THAT UNKNOWN SYMBOL IN THE FORMULA... GREAT STARS! IT BALANCES... I WAS WRONG BEFORE... TIME-TRAVEL IS POSSIBLE!

THIS MUST ALL TIE IN WITH THE MYSTERY OF MY OWN LIFE... HOW FIVE YEARS AGO, I ARRIVED FROM "NOWHERE" TO JOIN THE FACULTY! LET ME RETRACE MY ORIGINAL STEPS ...

LATER, MILES AWAY IN A FOREST...

I CAME WALKING FROM THIS DIRECTION... WAIT! SOMEHOW, I HAVE THE STRANGE FEELING THAT CAVE IS FAMILIAR! I'LL LOOK INSIDE!

AND INSIDE, THE MAN WHO PROVED TIME-TRAVEL "IMPOSSIBLE" MEETS AN IRONIC REVELATION!

THAT VEHICLE... I REMEMBER IT VAGUELY... YES! IT'S MY TIME-CAR! THEN I-I'M A TIME-TRAVELER... FROM THE FUTURE!

3

EXCITEDLY, THE PROFESSOR SEARCHES THROUGH THE *TIME-CAR*...

BUT FROM WHAT FUTURE TIME DID I COME? WHY DID I TRAVEL BACK IN TIME? TOO BAD THERE ARE NO WRITTEN RECORDS HERE TO TELL ME!

NOR CAN I REMEMBER *WHY I* TOOK THIS TIME-TRIP! I DIDN'T FORSEE THAT WHEN I TRAVELED BACK IN TIME, MY MEMORY WOULD "UNWIND" TOO, BECOMING BLANK FOR ALL YEARS BEYOND 1957!

THIS IS MADDENING! I HAVE THE STRONG FEELING THAT MY MISSION TO THE "PAST" WAS VITALLY IMPORTANT! BUT HOW CAN I SEARCH THROUGH MY BLANK MEMORY AND FIND OUT WHAT IT IS?

PLEASE KEEP OFF

THE FOLLOWING DAY, IN HIS SCIENCE SURVEY CLASS...

THIS MOST FAMOUS OF ALL COMETS RETURNS APPROXIMATELY EVERY 76 YEARS-- AND WILL APPEAR NEXT IN 1986! ITS LONG TAIL MAY SOMEDAY SWEEP THROUGH EARTH'S ATMOSPHERE!

HALLEY'S COMET--
1531
1607
1682
1759
1835
1910
1986

"THE COMET'S TAIL *DID* SWEEP OVER THE EARTH...IN THE FUTURE TIME IN WHICH I LIVED! EARTH'S ATMOSPHERE BECAME CONTAMINATED..."

THE TAIL CONTAINS RADIOACTIVE DUST WHICH IS SETTLING ALL OVER THE EARTH'S SURFACE! WHAT EFFECT WILL IT HAVE ON OUR WORLD?

"THE OMINOUS ANSWER CAME SOON ENOUGH..."

THE COMET'S RADIATIONS KILLED ALL NITRO-GEN-FIXING BACTERIA IN THE SOIL, WHICH FURNISH PLANT FOOD! STARVED OF VITAL NITRATES, ALL VEGETATION ON EARTH WILL WITHER AND DIE!

"THIS IN TURN BEGAN TO UPSET THE GREAT BALANCE BETWEEN THE PLANT AND ANIMAL KINGDOMS!"

PLANTS USE CARBON DIOXIDE AND RELEASE OXYGEN, WHILE ANIMAL LIFE DOES THE OPPOSITE! IF ALL VEGETATION DIES, ALL ANIMALS WILL DIE TOO,...INCLUDING MANKIND...

LATE THAT AFTERNOON, THE TIME-TRAVELER RETURNS TO THE CAVE AND *TIME-CAR*...

NOW I KNOW MY VITAL ASSIGNMENT IN TIME-- TO PICK UP LIVING NITROGEN-FIXING BACTERIA FROM A PAST TIME ERA! HMM...ONLY FUEL ENOUGH FOR ONE RETURN TRIP! I MUSTN'T MAKE ANY MISTAKE WHEN I GO BACK! IF I LAND IN THE WRONG ERA, I'LL BE STRANDED THERE!

WHICH ONE OF THESE YEARS OF HALLEY'S COMET DO I LIVE IN? I MUST FIND A CLUE...OTHER-WISE MY TIME WORLD IS DOOMED!

1986
2062
2138
2214
2290
2366

THE FOLLOWING NIGHT, THE BAFFLED TIME-TRAVELER ATTENDS THE COLLEGE TIME-TRAVELING PLAY...

PERHAPS THIS WILL RELAX ME AND EASE MY OWN WEIGHTY TIME-TRAVELING PROBLEM!

The Exchange of PRESIDENTS! A TIME-TRAVEL FANTASY!

AS THE UNIQUE PLAY REACHES A DRAMATIC CLIMAX...

I, ABRAHAM LINCOLN, FIRST PRESIDENT OF THE UNITED STATES, HEREBY SIGN THE *EMANCIPATION PROCLAMATION!*

AGAIN, VIVID MEMORY FLASHES INTO THE FUTURE-MAN'S MIND!

"THE AGE I LEFT WAS CELE-BRATING THE 200TH ANNI-VERSARY OF THE *REAL* SIGNING OF THE *EMANCIPATION PROCLAMATION!*--BY CASTING A MOVIE IMAGE ON THE MOON!"

IT WAS ORIGINALLY SIGNED IN 1862! THAT MEANS THE HALLEY'S COMET DISASTER OCCURRED IN 2062!

AFTER PROCURING ONE VITAL THING FROM THE BOTANY LAB AT COLLEGE, THE PROFESSOR TAKES OFF IN HIS *TIME-CAR...*

THIS IS WHAT I CAME FOR... A CULTURE OF LIVING NITROGEN-FIXING BACTERIA! THIS SMALL TEST-TUBE IS ENOUGH TO FILL ALL OF THE EARTH'S SOIL IN THE FUTURE!*

*EDITOR'S NOTE: BACTERIA GROW AND DIVIDE INTO TWO NEW CELLS EVERY 20 MINUTES! IF UNCHECKED FOR FIVE DAYS, THEY WOULD MULTIPLY INTO A MASS LARGER THAN THE EARTH!

AFTER THE TIME-TRAVELER HAS RETURNED TO THE YEAR 2062...

RAPIDLY, THE NITROGEN-FIXING BACTERIA ARE BRINGING LIFE TO ALL VEGETATION! YOU SAVED THE WORLD!

I HAD SOME HELP...

...SOME *TIMELY* HELP OF TWO STUDENTS, WHO AS *"GEORGE WASHINGTON"* AND *"ABRAHAM LINCOLN"* GAVE ME THE MEMORY CLUES I NEEDED TO FULFILL MY ASSIGN-MENT IN ETERNITY!

The End

PRIVATE EYE of VENUS!

IMAGINE TUNING IN MY CAR RADIO AND GETTING AN INVITATION FROM THE *PLANET VENUS* TO HELP SOLVE A MYSTERY! OF COURSE I LAUGHED IT OFF AS A HOAX! THEN THE INVITATION CAME THROUGH AGAIN--AND IT SOUNDED **URGENT!** VENUS IS EARTH'S NEAREST PLANETARY NEIGHBOR--AND I'M NOT THE TYPE OF GUY WHO TURNS DOWN A CALL TO HELP A NEIGHBOR IN DISTRESS!

WE SUMMONED YOU TO VENUS, PRIVATE EYE MARK GORDON, TO SOLVE OUR MYSTERIOUS ROBBERIES!

BUT I'M NOT A REAL DETECTIVE! I JUST ACT OUT THE ROLE OF MARK GORDON ON AN EARTH TELEVISION PROGRAM!

THE SAFECRACKING CLOWNS WERE IN THE MIDDLE OF THEIR ACT WHEN I TURNED THE SPOTLIGHT AND GUN ON THEM...

I'M CUTTING YOUR ACT SHORT!

MARK GORDON-- THE PRIVATE EYE!

GOOD SHOW, BOYS!

THAT WINDS UP THE FIFTIETH ADVENTURE OF THE *MARK GORDON-- PRIVATE EYE* TELEVISION SERIES!

AS I BARRELED HOMEWARD, I TURNED ON MY CAR RADIO--

MARK GORDON! VENUS CALLING! WE NEED YOUR HELP!

HUH-- WHAT'S THAT?

I WAITED FOR THE NEXT BIT OF DIALOGUE...

WE INVITE YOU, PRIVATE EYE GORDON, TO VISIT OUR PLANET, TO SOLVE A SERIES OF BAFFLING MYSTERIES!

MARK GORDON IS AN EXCLUSIVE *TV* SHOW! NO RADIO STATION HAS THE RIGHT TO PIRATE THE CHARACTER I CREATED...

A PHONE CALL TO THE RADIO STUDIO BROUGHT A FAST DENIAL....

WE'VE BEEN PLAYING MUSIC, MR. GORDON--FOR THE LAST TWO HOURS! NO TALKING AT ALL!

ON A HUNCH, I CHANNELED IN MY TV SET! I GOT NO PICTURE, BUT I *DID* GET SOUND!

ATTENTION, MARK GORDON! THIS IS URGENT! WE NEED YOUR SPECIAL DETECTIVE SKILLS! WILL YOU HELP US?

I WENT ALONG WITH THE GAG, AND SOON RECEIVED A SET OF INSTRUCTIONS FOR CONSTRUCTING A *TELEPORTATION* SET...

MY MAKE-BELIEVE TV-WORLD WAS NEVER ANYTHING LIKE THIS!

FOLLOWING MY UNKNOWN DIRECTOR'S CUE, I PRESSED THE POWER BUTTON....

OKAY! WHAT'S ON THE NEXT PAGE OF THE SCRIPT?

②

A MOMENT LATER, I WAS HITTING THE SPACE-ROAD TO VENUS--A DISTANCE OF 26 MILLION MILES! I SLAMMED MY EYELIDS CLOSED! AFTER AN ETERNITY, I SQUINTED A LOOK...

A SCENE SMACK OUT OF AN INTERPLANETARYAN! BUT THAT'S NO PHONY BACKDROP I'M LOOKING AT--NO MASQUERADING TV-ACTORS....

WELCOME TO VENUS, MARK GORDON! WE WERE ABLE TO CONTACT EARTH THROUGH YOUR RADIO AND TELEVISION BROADCASTS! ALTHOUGH WE COULD BEAM IN THESE PROGRAMS, WE COULD NOT COMMUNICATE WITH YOUR PLANET BECAUSE OF THE INTERFERENCE OF A HEAVY BARRIER OF COSMIC RAYS!

A TEMPORARY BREAK IN THE BARRIER ENABLED US TO BEAM OUR INVITATION AT YOU, PRIVATE EYE GORDON! WE NEED HELP--HELP ONLY YOU CAN GIVE! ON VENUS, THERE HAS NEVER BEEN ANY CRIME--UNTIL RECENTLY!

"NOT UNTIL WE HEARD YOUR TV PROGRAMS DID WE REALIZE THAT ANYONE COULD STEAL FROM ANOTHER! NOW STEALING HAS BECOME THE RAGE OF OUR PLANET... AND WE HAVE NO LAW-ENFORCERS TO PUT A STOP TO IT!"

THIS IS A STICK-UP!

WITH YOUR EXPERIENCE AND KNOW-HOW YOU CAN ROUND UP OUR CRIMINALS!

B-BUT I'M NOT A *REAL* DETECTIVE! I'M JUST AN *ACTOR!* THOSE PRIVATE EYE STORIES ARE IMAGINARY!

THOSE TELEVISION STORIES W-WEREN'T TRUE? BUT WE HAD NO WAY OF KNOWING... YOUR MISSION HERE HAS FAILED--EVEN BEFORE IT STARTED...

③

LOOK, AS LONG AS I'M HERE, I'M WILLING TO TAKE A CRACK AT YOUR PROBLEM! NOW BRIEF ME--

YESTERDAY SOME ROBBERS STOLE THE PLANS FOR A NEW-TYPE SHIP, PROPELLED BY CONTACT WITH THE MAGNETIC GRAVITY LINES OF THE PLANET!

THIS NOTE FROM THE SAME GANG CAME THIS MORNING, BOASTING THAT THEY ARE GOING TO ROB THE PLANETARY BANK!

I SOLVED A BANK ROBBERY ONCE AS AS THE *TV* PRIVATE EYE! IF THERE WAS NO CRIME ON VENUS BEFORE, THOSE ROBBERS MAY FOLLOW THE SCRIPT THEY HEARD...

WHEN I SAW WHAT PASSED ON VENUS FOR A "BANK", I DID A DOUBLE-TAKE!

THERE ARE NOTHING BUT "*BATTERIES*" IN THIS BANK! WHERE'S YOUR MONEY-- LEGAL TENDER?

ON VENUS WE COUNT WEALTH IN *ERGS* OF ENERGY! EVERYONE KEEPS HIS ERGS IN THESE STORAGE CELLS

"SINCE WE USE *ENERGY* FOR OUR POWER BOATS --OUR ANTI-GRAVITY CLOAKS--TO MANU-FACTURE PROCESSED FOODS--IT HAS BECOME OUR MEDIUM OF EXCHANGE!"

PLEASE DEPOSIT MY SALARY--63 ERGS-- TO MY ACCOUNT!

WELL, I ASKED FOR THE JOB! NOW I WAS STUCK WITH IT!

I CAN'T COUNT ON ANY HELP FROM THESE VENUSIANS! BESIDES, I ALWAYS PLAYED A LONE HAND FIGHTING CRIME ON TV...

I'LL WAIT ON THE BANK ROOF FOR THE CROOKS TO MAKE A GETAWAY WITH THE LOOT--JUST AS I DID IN THE PRIVATE EYE ADVENTURE ON WHICH THIS BANK ROBBERY IS BASED!

4

BUT WITHOUT A SCRIPT TO SHOW ME HOW TO OUTWIT THE BANK BANDITS, I FLOPPED BADLY ON MY FIRST CASE...

MARK GORDON! THE CROOKS USED AN ATOMIC-BORER TO ESCAPE UNDERGROUND!

NO CHANCE OF CATCHING THEM NOW! I'VE GOT TO CHANGE MY TACTICS! *WHEN ON VENUS, THINK LIKE A VENUSIAN!*

NEXT DAY--

ANOTHER CHALLENGE FROM THE GANG! THEY'RE GOING TO ROB THE VENUS ART MUSEUM!

IN THE PRIVATE EYE SERIES THE ROBBERS HID IN A SUIT OF ARMOR! I WONDER...?

I HOTFOOTED IT TO THE MUSEUM...

JUST AS I THOUGHT! NO SUITS OF ARMOR HERE! MOREOVER, THERE ARE NO LOCKS ON THE DOORS OR ON THE ART CASES!

I RANSACKED THE MUSEUM FROM TOP TO BOTTOM! THERE WAS NO PLACE TO HIDE...

THOSE CROOKS FOLLOW THE PATTERN OF A PRIVATE EYE ADVENTURE TO A CERTAIN POINT-- THEN THEY PULL A VENUSIAN SWITCH ON IT!

I MADE MY PREPARATIONS, THEN WAITED! SUDDENLY--

THERE IT IS -- THE *BURGLAR* ALARM! I SHOWED THE VENUSIANS HOW TO RIG ONE UP, WORKING ON AN ELECTRIC EYE BEAM!

CLANG CLANG CLANG

NEVER HAVING HEARD A BURGLAR ALARM BEFORE, THE VENUSIAN THIEVES WERE CAUGHT WEB-FOOTED....

DON'T ANYONE MAKE A MOVE! YOU'RE UNDER ARREST!

I THOUGHT I HAD THEM TRAPPED--BUT THOSE VENUSIAN BIRDS HAD A TRICK UP THEIR "WINGED" CLOAKS....

THEY'RE USING THEIR ANTI-GRAVITY CLOAKS TO GET AWAY!

BUT I HAD A TRICK LEFT TOO! WITH A RUNNING START, I JUMPED HIGH INTO THE AIR....

IF I DIDN'T KNOW ABOUT THOSE ANTI-GRAVITY CLOAKS--THEY FORGOT ABOUT THE LESSER GRAVITY OF VENUS COMPARED WITH THAT OF EARTH!

MY WEIGHT WAS TOO MUCH FOR THEM, AND SOON...

THAT WINDS UP THE FIFTY-FIRST ADVENTURE OF THE MARK GORDON - PRIVATE EYE SERIES!

THEY WILL BE BANISHED FOR A YEAR! AFTER THAT THEY MAY RETURN-- IF THEY PROMISE NEVER TO ROB AGAIN!

HURRY, MARK GORDON! THE COSMIC RAY BARRIER IS INCREASING AGAIN! WE MUST SEND YOU BACK TO EARTH NOW--

TODAY WHEN FRIENDS DROP IN AND ASK QUESTIONS ABOUT THE TELEPORTATION UNIT, I JUST SMILINGLY REPLY....

OH, THAT? JUST A PIECE OF MODERN ART I MADE ONE NIGHT! OUT OF THIS WORLD, ISN'T IT?

THE END

THE VOLCANIC MAN!

UP FROM BENEATH THE EARTH IT CAME -- UP WITH THE BOILING LAVA, THE SWIRLING STEAM AND THE VOLCANIC DUST! WHAT DID THIS TOWERING, INCREDIBLE SUBTERRANEAN CREATURE SEEK? TO DESTROY -- OR SAVE -- THE EARTH?

RUN! RUN! IT'S THE VOLCANIC MAN!

TREMORS AND HEAVY RUMBLINGS HERALD THE RE-BIRTH OF A "LONG-DEAD" VOLCANO -- FOLLOWED BY A MIGHTY ROAR...

KWHOOM!

SUDDENLY, FROM THE FIERY CRATER EMERGES A TITANIC CREATURE...

OBLIVIOUS TO THE INTENSE HEAT, THE STRANGE FIGURE DESCENDS, SLOSHING THROUGH THE MOLTEN LAVA...

IN A NEARBY CITY, AN ANXIOUS POPULATION FLEES AS THE AWESOME CREATURE APPROACHES...

RUN! THE VOLCANO MAN IS COMING!

RETURNING FROM THE OTHER SIDE OF THE VOLCANO, WHERE HE WAS DRAWN TO THE ERUPTION, SCIENTIST MARK HARLOW LEAPS OUT OF HIS JEEP, AND...

WHAT ON EARTH MADE THESE FOOTPRINTS? HUGE IMPRESSIONS HAVE BEEN CHARRED INTO THE GROUND!

ODD! EACH FOOTPRINT IS ON BARE GROUND -- AND NOT ON BRUSH OR GRASS! WHATEVER MADE THEM, TOOK GREAT CARE TO AVOID SETTING ANYTHING AFIRE!

HURRIEDLY, THE EXCITED SCIENTIST FOLLOWS THE TRAIL TO TOWN, WHERE...

A GIANT! A FANTASTIC GIANT!

WAIT! DON'T FIRE!

I'M CONVINCED HE MEANS NO HARM! LET ME TALK TO HIM FIRST!

YOU'RE THE SCIENTIST, DR. HARLOW! GO AHEAD AND TALK TO HIM -- BUT WE'LL COVER YOU!

DONNING AN ASBESTOS SUIT AS PROTECTION AGAINST THE GIANT'S TREMENDOUS HEAT, THE SCIENTIST BOLDLY APPROACHES ...

HE'S CARRYING AN ODD GADGET... SOMEHOW I HAVE THE FEELING IT'S A DEVICE FOR COMMUNICATION... PERHAPS THROUGH *MENTAL TELEPATHY!*...

I'VE GOT TO CONCENTRATE-- *THINK* OUT A MESSAGE... HOPE HE CAN RECEIVE IT! *WHO ARE YOU?*

THE SCIENTIST'S THOUGHTS *ARE* PICKED UP BY THE DEVICE, AND INSTANTLY TRANSLATED TO THE GIANT'S MIND...

WHO ARE YOU?

I AM A *VOLCANIC MAN!* I HAVE COME FROM MY SUBTERRANEAN WORLD TO WARN YOU! YOUR SURFACE WORLD IS IN DANGER...

BUT BEFORE HE CAN FINISH HIS MESSAGE, THE GIANT SUDDENLY WEAKENS... THEN COLLAPSES...

IN DANGER... IN DANGER...

WH-WHAT'S HAPPENING TO HIM?

CRASHING TO THE STREET, THE GIANT LIES INERT...

IS HE DEAD?

NO! HE'S COLLAPSED FROM *LACK OF HEAT!* BRING UP FLAT-TRUCKS AND DERRICKS! HURRY!

SHORTLY AFTERWARDS, POWERFUL DERRICKS CREAK AND GROAN AS THEY HOIST THE GIANT ABOARD FLAT-TRUCKS...

NOW WE'VE GOT TO RUSH HIM TO A SMELTING PLANT! *WE MUST NOT ONLY SAVE HIS LIFE, BUT LEARN WHAT DANGER IS THREATENING US!*

3

POWERFUL MOTORS PULL THE GIANT INTO THE SMELTING PLANTS, WHERE...

WON'T THAT MOLTEN ORE *KILL* HIM?

ON THE CONTRARY! I'M ONLY HOPING THERE'S ENOUGH HEAT TO *REVIVE* HIM!

AFTER TONS OF LAVA-LIKE ORE ARE POURED OVER THE *VOLCANIC MAN*...

THANK YOU, EARTHMAN! NOW I MUST TELL YOU OF THE DANGER...

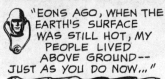

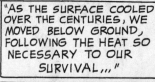

"EONS AGO, WHEN THE EARTH'S SURFACE WAS STILL HOT, MY PEOPLE LIVED ABOVE GROUND-- JUST AS YOU DO NOW..."

"AS THE SURFACE COOLED OVER THE CENTURIES, WE MOVED BELOW GROUND, FOLLOWING THE HEAT SO NECESSARY TO OUR SURVIVAL..."

"AND NOW, DEEP IN THE EARTH, OUR CIVILIZATION THRIVES TO THIS DAY..."

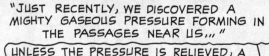

"JUST RECENTLY, WE DISCOVERED A MIGHTY GASEOUS PRESSURE FORMING IN THE PASSAGES NEAR US..."

UNLESS THE PRESSURE IS RELIEVED, A MIGHTY EXPLOSION WILL SHATTER THE PLANET'S SURFACE! WE MUST WARN THOSE OF THE UPPER WORLD!

I WAS SENT TO WARN YOU! IS THERE ANYTHING YOU CAN DO TO SAVE YOURSELVES?

WE HAVE DRILLS-- EXPLOSIVES-- *MACHINERY* TO BREAK THROUGH AND RELIEVE THE PRESSURE!

GOOD! ORDER YOUR MACHINERY TAKEN TO THE PLACE I'LL SHOW YOU! *HURRY!* THE EXPLOSION WILL OCCUR AFTER ONE MORE ROTATION OF THE EARTH ABOUT ITS AXIS!

24 HOURS!

DURING THE NEXT TWELVE HOURS, HECTIC PREPARATIONS ARE MADE AS A SUPER ELECTRO-DRILL IS SET UP AT AN ABANDONED MINE SHAFT IN REMOTE COUNTRY...

THE *VOLCANIC MAN* SELECTED THIS OLD SHAFT BECAUSE IT'S MORE THAN 1,000 FEET DEEP! THAT GIVES US A REAL HEAD START!

GET GOING, MEN! WE HAVE LESS THAN *12 HOURS* LEFT!

DEEPER AND DEEPER THE ELECTRO-DRILL CHEWS INTO THE EARTH-- 1500 FEET--2000 FEET--2500... WHEN SUDDENLY...

WE'RE STOPPED! WE HIT A THICK LAYER OF SOLID GRANITE--AND THE DRILL HEAD IS *BROKEN!*

AS PRECIOUS TIME RUNS OUT...

AND EVEN IF WE *COULD* REPAIR IT, IT'D DO NO GOOD! WHAT DRILL CAN PENETRATE HUNDREDS OF FEET OF SOLID GRANITE?

I KNOW ONE THAT WILL! AND WITH THE *VOLCANIC MAN'S* HELP WE'LL SOON HAVE IT!

WHEN THE SCIENTIST POINTS OUT THE DIAMOND IN HIS RING TO THE *VOLCANIC-MAN*, THE GIANT'S HANDS DELVE INTO THE EARTH, AND...

HE KNOWS WHAT I WANT! HIS FIERY HOT BREATH AND THE GREAT PRESSURE OF HIS HANDS ARE MOLDING ELEMENTS FROM THE EARTH...AND MAKING...

A SOLID DIAMOND DRILL-HEAD!

PURE CARBON-- CREATED FROM INCREDIBLE HEAT AND PRESSURE! HOOK IT UP! WE'VE GOT ONLY ONE HOUR LEFT!

THERE ARE ONLY 40 MINUTES LEFT...30...20...*10!* THEN...

WHROOOSH

THE RELEASE CAME JUST IN TIME!

AND *WE* GOT BACK OUT OF THE WAY JUST IN TIME!

LATER, IN THE GLOW OF THE FIERY GEYSER...

HE'S PATTING THE GROUND! WHAT DOES IT MEAN?

IT'S HIS WAY OF SAYING... *FAREWELL!* HE'S RETURNING UNDERGROUND!

HE'S GONE!

BACK TO HIS OWN REALM, WHERE WE HOPE HE'LL BE VERY HAPPY... AND VERY PLEASANTLY *HOT!*

THE END 6

the FUTURE MIND of ROGER DAVIS!

WHAT DOES THE FUTURE HOLD FOR US? WHAT WILL THE EARTH LOOK LIKE NEXT YEAR... NEXT CENTURY... NEXT 100,000 YEARS? HOW FAR WILL THE HUMAN RACE ADVANCE IN THAT TIME? ONLY ROGER DAVIS KNEW THE ANSWERS-- FOR HE HAD THE MIND OF A MAN 100,000 YEARS FROM NOW!...

I PERCEIVE THINGS THAT NO OTHER HUMAN ON EARTH CAN SEE!

YES, EARTHMAN-- YOUR ULTRA-PERCEPTIVE BRAIN AREA HAS BEEN ACTIVATED! USE YOUR POWER WISELY!

ONE CRISP DECEMBER MORNING, ROGER DAVIS' HORSE-DRAWN SLEIGH BEARS HIM TOWARD THE MOUNTAIN VILLAGE OF HAMMERSET...

SKATING-- SKIING! I'VE BEEN LOOKING FORWARD TO THESE WINTER SPORTS ALL YEAR!

SUDDENLY A STRANGE FORM LOOMS AHEAD OF THE SLEIGH....

SOMETHING IN THE SKY! COMING DOWN TO EARTH!

AS THE SHIP LANDS, THE HORSE PANICS AND BOLTS, OVER-TURNING THE RIDER....

CRASH!

FOR LONG MOMENTS AFTER THE FRIGHTENED HORSE HAS FLED, ROGER DAVIS LIES UNCONSCIOUS...

HURRY! TAKE HIM TO THE SHIP! THERE MAY STILL BE TIME TO SAVE THE EARTHMAN!

WE MEANT MERELY TO LAND, REPAIR OUR SHIP AND LEAVE!

BUT IN DOING SO, WE FRIGHTENED THE ANIMAL CREATURE--AND CAUSED THE HUMAN TO BE INJURED! WE WILL MAKE AMENDS!

SOON AFTER, INSIDE THE SPACESHIP...

ALL IS WELL, EARTH-MAN! YOUR BRAIN SUFFERED AN INJURY--BUT WE OPERATED AND REPAIRED THE DAMAGE!

BUT THERE IS NO SIGN OF AN OPERATION --NO BANDAGE!

OUR ADVANCED SCIENCE OF SURGERY ELIMINATES OPERATIONAL "SIGNS"! WE USE THE CELLULAR FUSION METHOD!

YOU ARE OBVIOUSLY FROM ANOTHER WORLD --YET, WE TALK! HOW--

NO, YOU THINK WE ARE TALKING! ACTUALLY, NO WORD IS BEING SPOKEN! WE ARE COMMUNI-CATING MENTALLY! AND THOUGHTS HAVE NO LANGUAGE BARRIERS!

2

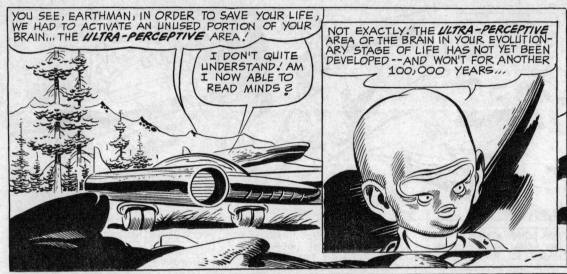

YOU SEE, EARTHMAN, IN ORDER TO SAVE YOUR LIFE, WE HAD TO ACTIVATE AN UNUSED PORTION OF YOUR BRAIN... THE *ULTRA-PERCEPTIVE* AREA!

I DON'T QUITE UNDERSTAND! AM I NOW ABLE TO READ MINDS?

NOT EXACTLY! THE *ULTRA-PERCEPTIVE* AREA OF THE BRAIN IN YOUR EVOLUTIONARY STAGE OF LIFE HAS NOT YET BEEN DEVELOPED -- AND WON'T FOR ANOTHER 100,000 YEARS...

HOWEVER, BECAUSE YOUR MIND HAS BEEN ACTIVATED, YOU CAN NOW PERCEIVE A SIMPLE THING SUCH AS OUR "CONVERSATION" -- AND SOON WILL LEARN TO *PERCEIVE* THINGS OF A MORE MOMENTOUS NATURE!

IT'S LIKE HAVING A *SIXTH SENSE!*

WHATEVER YOU CALL IT, IT WAS A LIFE-SAVING NECESSITY! IT IS OUR FERVENT WISH THAT WE HAVE MADE AMENDS FOR THE TROUBLE WE'VE CAUSED! AND NOW, WE DEPART! FAREWELL, EARTHMAN!

AND AS THE CRAFT SHOOTS INTO THE UNKNOWN...

I WONDER HOW -- AND WHEN -- I'LL USE MY STRANGE GIFT?

LATER, UPON MAKING HIS WAY ON FOOT TOWARD HAMMERSET...

STOP! STOP! DANGER AHEAD!

SCREEEECH!!

3

THE TRUCK BRAKES TO A HALT, AND...

YOU ARE GOING TO HAVE A BLOWOUT IN YOUR REAR RIGHT TIRE! ON THESE ROADS IT COULD BE DANGEROUS!

IS THAT WHY YOU STOPPED ME?

ONE SIDE, WISE GUY! I'VE GOT A SCHEDULE TO MAKE...

THE TRUCK MOVES AHEAD WHEN SUDDENLY...

BLAM!

THAT *WAS* A BLOWOUT, MISTER! BUT HOW'D YOU KNOW?

TIRES CREATE FRICTION--FRICTION CREATES HEAT! HEAT CREATES WAVES! I SENSED A VARIATION OF HEAT WAVES FROM THE TIRE, INDICATING A THIN, WORN AREA, AND...

...UH--JUST SAY THAT I ONCE HAD A TIRE JUST LIKE THAT, AND I GOT A BLOWOUT! WHEN I SAW YOURS, I KNEW THE SAME THING WOULD HAPPEN!

UNH-HUNH-- SURE, MISTER...

AS DAVIS CONTINUES ON TO THE VILLAGE...

I ACTUALLY FORESAW IT! BUT HOW COULD I EVER EXPLAIN IT TO THE DRIVER? THE VERY MENTION OF SPACE-MEN WOULD MAKE HIM LAUGH...

LATER, APPROACHING THE BASE OF THE MOUNTAINS, ROGER DAVIS STARTS TO ASCEND A FAMILIAR FOOTPATH, WHEN...

THAT'S STRANGE! I'VE SAFELY WALKED THIS TRAIL MANY TIMES! BUT NOW-- I SENSE SOME DANGER--FROM THAT BOULDER!

4

SOMETHING DOESN'T **SEEM** RIGHT! MAYBE IT'S DUE TO A WASHOUT FROM HEAVY RAINS WE GOT BEFORE THE SNOWS--BUT I **SENSE** THAT THE SLIGHTEST TREMOR WILL MOVE THE BOULDER! WE'LL SEE...

DAVIS HURLS THE STONE AT THE PATH, AND THEN...

I WAS RIGHT! THE STONE I THREW CAUSED A SLIGHT TREMOR! THE BOULDER MOVED! ANY OTHER PERSON STEPPING HERE WOULD'VE BEEN KILLED!

LATER THAT AFTERNOON, ROGER DAVIS ARRIVES IN HAMMERSET...

IN HIS HOTEL ROOM, ROGER DAVIS WALKS THE FLOOR--HIS THOUGHTS SCAMPERING WILDLY... I SHOULD TELL SOMEONE ABOUT THIS! A SCIENTIST--OR DOCTOR! THEY COULD ADVISE HOW TO PUT MY NEW KNOWLEDGE TO GOOD USE--

THEN SUBCONSCIOUSLY STARING OUT AT THE SNOW-COVERED SLOPE, DAVIS' ACTIVATED, ULTRA-PERCEPTIVE MIND GOES TO WORK!

THE SNOW ON THE SLOPE... IT WILL MOVE... COVER THE ENTIRE VILLAGE!

WITH PENCIL AND PAPER, ROGER DAVIS CALCULATES IN BRIEF SECONDS A PROBLEM THAT WOULD REQUIRE **HOURS** FOR MODERN ENGINEERS TO SOLVE... I MUST BE CERTAIN! LET'S SEE--ANGLE OF SLOPE... WEIGHT OF SNOW... INTENSITY OF SOLAR HEAT... **YES!** I'M RIGHT!

5

IN AN INSTANT, DAVIS IS IN THE STREETS, RACING FROM DOOR TO DOOR...

GET OUT OF THE VILLAGE! DESCEND WITH THE CABLE CAR! THERE WILL BE A TREMENDOUS SNOW-SLIDE WITHIN THE HOUR!

NONSENSE! WE HAVEN'T HAD A SNOWSLIDE HERE IN 56 YEARS!

SUDDENLY, AMONG THE VILLAGERS, STEPS A FAMILIAR FIGURE...

TAKE MY ADVICE AND LISTEN TO HIM! IF HE SAYS THERE WILL BE A SNOWSLIDE-- THERE WILL BE!

AFTER THE TRUCKMAN TELLS HIS STORY, THE VILLAGE BECOMES A PICTURE OF SEETHING ACTIVITY--AND LOAD AFTER LOAD DESCENDS BY THE CABLE CAR, UNTIL, FINALLY...

WHY DOESN'T *HE* COME WITH US?

HE SAID THE CAR WOULD BE OVERLOADED! HE STAYED TO WORK THE SWITCH!

THEN, WITHOUT FURTHER WARNING, THE GIGANTIC SNOWSLIDE BREAKS LOOSE WITH A BELLOW OF THUNDER...

KWHROOM!

AND ONCE MORE--MUCH LATER--ROGER DAVIS AWAKENS ON AN OPERATING TABLE...

YOU ARE ALL RIGHT, MR. DAVIS! THE SEARCHERS FOUND YOU-- BROUGHT YOU HERE! WE OPERATED ON YOUR BRAIN!

I SHOULD HAVE *KNOWN* THAT! BUT I DIDN'T! MY ULTRA-PERCEPTIVE MIND IS GONE! THESE DOCTORS MUST HAVE DONE THAT WHEN THEY OPERATED!

BUT TELL US, MAN--HOW DID YOU *KNOW* THE LANDSLIDE WOULD OCCUR?

IT...ER...REALLY DOESN'T MATTER-- NOW! BUT TELL ME, DOCTOR--WHEN WILL I BE ABLE TO GO SKIING AGAIN?

THE END

10¢
SUPERMAN DC NATIONAL COMICS
STRANGE ADVENTURES
SEPT. NO. 84
APPROVED BY THE COMICS CODE AUTHORITY
Featuring "PRISONERS of the ATOM UNIVERSE!"
YOU WON'T KEEP US IMPRISONED IN THIS SAFETY DEPOSIT BOX FOR LONG, JENKINS! WE'LL GET OUT-- SOMEHOW--AND SETTLE OUR SCORE WITH YOU!

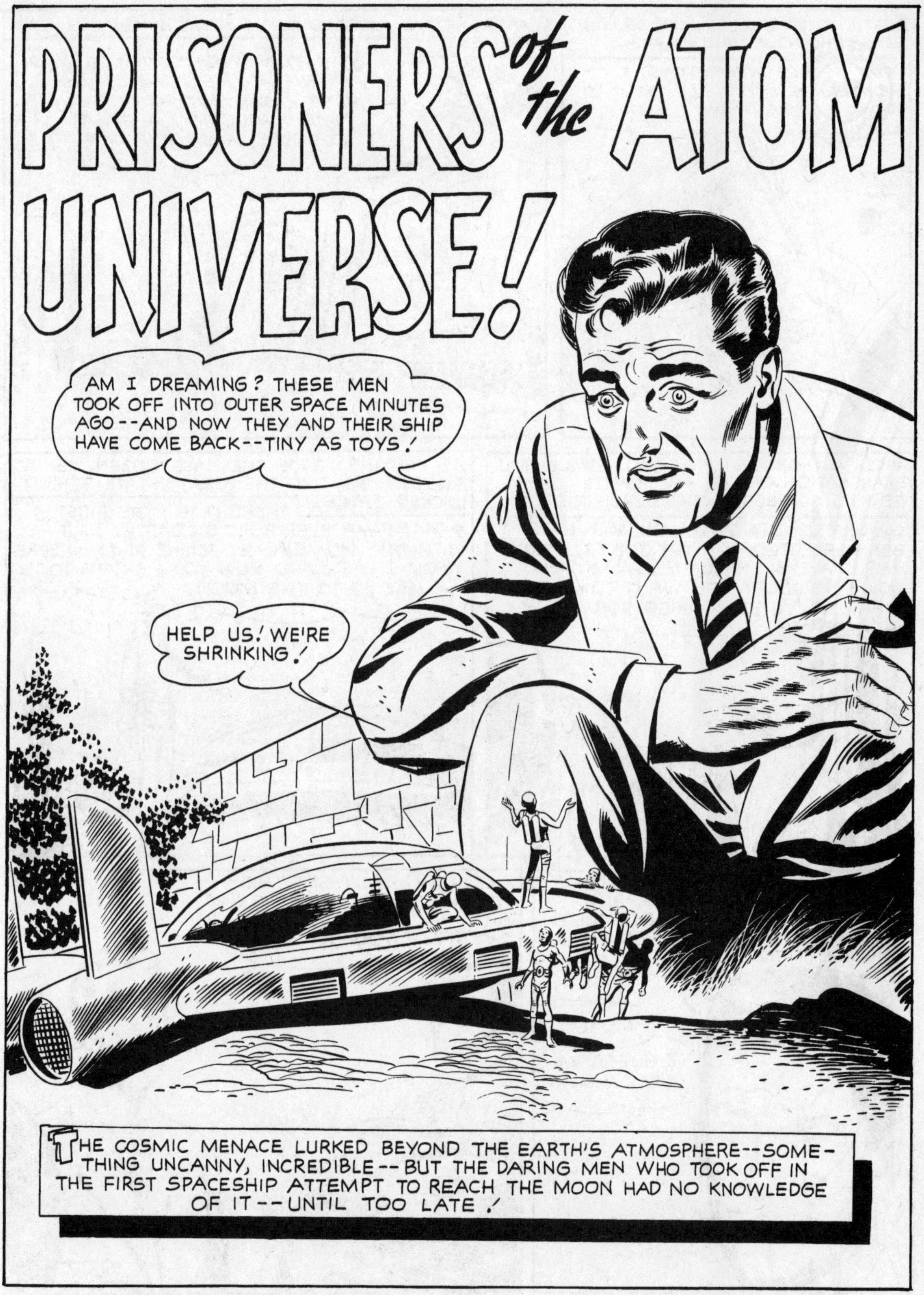
PRISONERS of the ATOM UNIVERSE!
AM I DREAMING? THESE MEN TOOK OFF INTO OUTER SPACE MINUTES AGO--AND NOW THEY AND THEIR SHIP HAVE COME BACK--TINY AS TOYS!
HELP US! WE'RE SHRINKING!
THE COSMIC MENACE LURKED BEYOND THE EARTH'S ATMOSPHERE--SOMETHING UNCANNY, INCREDIBLE--BUT THE DARING MEN WHO TOOK OFF IN THE FIRST SPACESHIP ATTEMPT TO REACH THE MOON HAD NO KNOWLEDGE OF IT--UNTIL TOO LATE!

JUST OUT OF COLLEGE, KEN TRAVIS SCANS THE HELP WANTED ADS...

THAT SOUNDS INTERESTING! I WONDER WHAT IT'S ALL ABOUT? I THINK I'LL APPLY--AND FIND OUT!

Help Wanted

MEN--NOT AFRAID TO TAKE RISKS-- GOOD PAY!

LATER, AT THE ADDRESS GIVEN IN THE UNUSUAL ADVERTISEMENT...

JAY JENKINS--SO THAT'S WHO RAN THE AD! HE'S ONE OF THE MOST PROMINENT MEN OF OUR TIME -- WEALTHY, A GREAT EXPLORER, AND INVENTOR!

JAY JENKINS-- ENTERPRISES

AFTER A THOROUGH PHYSICAL AND MENTAL EXAMINATION OF THE APPLICANTS, JAY JENKINS ADDRESSES THE "SURVIVORS"...

CONGRATULATIONS! YOU SIX MEN HAVE BEEN SELECTED FOR THE JOB! ALL THE REST HAVE BEEN TURNED AWAY! AND NOW--NO DOUBT YOU WANT TO KNOW WHAT YOU'VE BEEN HIRED FOR...

AS JENKINS LEADS THE HALF-DOZEN MEN TO ANOTHER PART OF THE GREAT ESTATE BEHIND LOCKED GATES...

THERE IT IS--THE FIRST **SPACESHIP** EVER BUILT ON EARTH! BUILT WITH **MY MONEY**--BY SCIENTIST-ENGINEERS WHOM I PAID! AND NOW YOU MEN ARE TO FLY IT--TO THE MOON!

THE LUNAR VOYAGE MAY BE DANGEROUS--EVEN FATAL--BUT YOU WERE TOLD THIS JOB WOULD BE A WELL-PAYING RISK! ANYONE WANT TO BACK OUT?

I'LL STICK!

ME TOO!

I GUESS WE ALL WILL...

ALL RIGHT, BUT GET THIS-- YOU MEN WILL FLY THE SHIP--BUT **I'LL** TAKE THE **CREDIT** IF YOU SUCCEED!

2

AS THE MEN, AGREEING TO JENKINS' TERMS, PREPARE FOR THE DANGEROUS FLIGHT...

HOW I'VE DUPED THE PUBLIC! THEY ALL THINK I'M A GREAT DAREDEVIL! THEY IDOLIZE ME! HA HA... THEY DON'T SUSPECT THAT I NEVER TOOK A RISK IN MY LIFE!

"TAKE THE TIME I RETURNED FROM MY EXPEDITION INTO THE UNEXPLORED WILDS OF AUSTRALIA WITH MY 'CATCH'...'"

TAKE YOUR TIME, BOYS! GET ALL THE SHOTS YOU WANT!

"I HAD SECRETLY PAID ANOTHER HUNTER-EXPLORER A WHOPPING SUM OF MONEY FOR HIS CATCH...AND HIS SEALED LIPS...'"

WHY SHOULD I RISK MY NECK IN A DANGEROUS ADVENTURE, WHEN I CAN PAY SOMEONE ELSE TO DO IT FOR ME?

"OR TAKE THE TIME 'I' BROKE THE DEEP-SEA DIVING RECORD.'"

IT WAS REALLY I WHO DIVED, BUT JENKINS PAID ME TO TAKE THE RISKS WHILE HE TAKES THE GLORY.'

SOON AFTER, THE SHIP SPEEDS SPACEWARD...

THIS WILL BE THE GREATEST OF ALL MY ACHIEVEMENTS--THE FIRST TRIP TO THE MOON!

UP, UP, GOES THE SPACE-SHIP AND ITS CREW...

BUT THEN...

S-SOMETHING'S HAPPENING TO THE SHIP! I CAN'T BELIEVE IT--IT'S TOO INCREDIBLE!

HORROR-STRICKEN, WARWICK RECEIVES A MESSAGE FROM THE SHIP...

"AND AS WE PASSED OUT OF THE EARTH'S ATMOSPHERE SOME STRANGE COSMIC RADIATION STRUCK US...AND WE'RE *SHRINKING IN SIZE!*"

SOMETIME LATER, WHEN THE SHRINKING SHIP LANDS...

THEY MADE IT BACK-- BUT LOOK AT THEM! TINY AS TOYS! AND THE SHIP TOO!

THEY'RE GETTING SMALLER EVERY MOMENT! WHATEVER THAT RADIATION WAS THAT HIT THEM, IT'S STILL HAVING ITS EFFECT! IF THEY DISAPPEAR INTO *NOTHING-NESS,* I--I'LL BE ACCUSED OF DOING AWAY WITH THEM-- CHARGED WITH MANSLAUGHTER!

I'VE GOT TO PUT THEM WHERE NO ONE WILL SEE THEM--OR I'LL BE BROUGHT TO TRIAL-- DISGRACED! BUT WHERE-- I HAVE IT! THE *ONE PLACE* THAT NO ONE EVER GOES TO, *BUT ME!*

IN THE PRIVACY OF HIS BANK'S SAFE DEPOSIT VAULT, SHORTLY AFTER...

YOU MEN WILL STAY HERE! I'LL LOCK YOU IN SO THAT NONE OF YOU CAN LEAVE AND EXPOSE ME! GO ON! INTO THE BOX!

AFTER THE HELPLESS MEN HAVE BEEN LOCKED IN...

WE'RE STILL SHRINKING! LOOK--THIS *GRAIN OF SAND* INSIDE HERE IS NOW LIKE A HUGE BOULDER TOWERING OVER US!

WHAT WILL BECOME OF US?

THEN AS A MIST SEEMS TO FALL OVER THE TRAPPED MITES...

I'M PASSING OUT--

HAZY MOMENTS LATER, WHEN THEY COME TO THEIR SENSES...

WE'VE STOPPED SHRINKING! B-BUT WHERE ON EARTH ARE WE?

NO-WHERE ON EARTH--

BUT IN THE SUB-ATOMIC WORLD OF *GRENT!* THE SAME FATE OVERTOOK YOU AS IT DID US *ATLANTIDES* MANY EONS AGO...

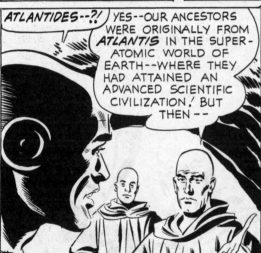

ATLANTIDES--?!

YES--OUR ANCESTORS WERE ORIGINALLY FROM *ATLANTIS* IN THE SUPER-ATOMIC WORLD OF EARTH--WHERE THEY HAD ATTAINED AN ADVANCED SCIENTIFIC CIVILIZATION! BUT THEN --

"--THE ISLAND-CONTINENT OF ATLANTIS SANK BENEATH THE OCEAN IN A MIGHTY CATACLYSM..."

"ALL WERE LOST EXCEPT A HANDFUL WHO HAD BEEN SENT UP IN A SHIP IN AN EFFORT TO FIND REFUGE ON THE MOON..."

SOME MYSTERIOUS RADIATION IN OUTER SPACE STRUCK THEM AND SHRANK THEM DOWN UNTIL THEY LANDED HERE IN THIS SUB-ATOMIC UNIVERSE!

AFTER KEN TRAVIS HAS DESCRIBED THEIR ADVENTURES...

...AND SO WE ARE PRISONERS IN THIS ATOMIC UNIVERSE-- JUST LIKE YOU!

LISTEN--YOU WILL BE INTERESTED TO LEARN THAT WE HAVE BEEN WORKING FOR YEARS ON A DEVICE TO *RETURN* TO OUR WORLD! COME WITH ME!

5

Soon, inside a cavern laboratory...

HERE IT IS--A *PRO-TOMIC RAY MACHINE!* IT IS ALMOST READY, BUT WE MAY NEVER BE ABLE TO USE IT--BECAUSE OF A THREATENING DANGER!

WHAT DO YOU MEAN?

THE *OVERLORD OF GRENT*-- LEADER OF THE ATOMIC CIVILIZATION HERE--IS OUR ENEMY! HE WANTS TO SEIZE OUR *PRO-TOMIC RAY MACHINE* AND USE IT FOR *INTER-ATOMIC TRAVEL* TO STEAL AND PLUNDER OTHER ATOMIC WORLDS!

SUDDENLY AN ALARM RINGS THROUGH THE CAVERN OF THE *ATLANTIDES*...

LOOK--WING-CRAFT OF THE OVERLORD! THEY ARE COMING THIS WAY! THEY HAVE FOUND OUR HIDE-OUT!

THIS MAY BE THE END, FELLOW EARTH-MEN--

WE HAVE NO FLYING CRAFT TO COMBAT THE OVERLORD'S ARMED FORCES! WE HAVE BEEN HUNTED TOO LONG; WE HAD NO TIME TO BUILD WEAPONS...

WAIT! THERE IS ONE "WEAPON"-- WE BROUGHT WITH US!

OUR *SPACESHIP*--IT SHRANK WITH US! MAYBE IT WILL STILL FLY!

GOOD IDEA, TRAVIS! LET'S TRY IT!

WE'VE GOT NO CANNON ABOARD, BUT I THINK I KNOW HOW WE CAN FIGHT ANYWAY!

MOMENTS LATER...

IT FLIES, ALL RIGHT!

THE WING-CRAFT HAVE SPOTTED US, TRAVIS! HERE THEY COME!

AS THE FIRST MISSLES BOUNCE HARMLESSLY OFF THE DURA-HARD SHELL OF THE SPACESHIP...

NO DAMAGE TO OUR SHIP YET! NOW IT'S OUR TURN!

THEN, ONE BY ONE, TRAVIS *RAMS* HIS SHIP INTO THE WINGED CRAFT OF THE ALIENS...

THIS WILL GIVE THE *ATLANTIDES* TIME TO FINISH THAT RAY MACHINE...!

THAT'S THE LAST ONE!

AND NOT LONG AFTERWARD, IN A LARGE EASTERN CITY ON EARTH...

THE MACHINE WORKED! IT PUT US BACK ON OUR WORLD IN OUR NORMAL SIZE!

WH-- WHERE'D THAT SPACESHIP COME FROM?

KEEP OFF GRASS

LATER, AFTER THE RETURNING *ATLANTIDES* HAVE BEEN MADE WELCOME BY THE GOVERNMENT...

KEN TRAVIS, FOR THE BOLDNESS AND COURAGE DISPLAYED BY YOU AND YOUR FELLOW ADVENTURERS, AND FOR DISCOVERING THE LOST *ATLANTIDES*, YOU HAVE BEEN AWARDED THIS *SPECIAL MEDAL*...

BUT ELSEWHERE, WHILE TRAVIS AND HIS COMRADES ARE HONORED AND FETED ALL OVER THE COUNTRY...

I'M RUINED--NOW THAT THE PUBLIC KNOWS I'M A *FRAUD*! I SHOULD HAVE KNOWN I COULDN'T FOOL ALL THE PEOPLE ALL OF THE TIME-- JUST AS THE PROVERB SAYS!

TRAVIS EXPOSES JENKINS!

THE END

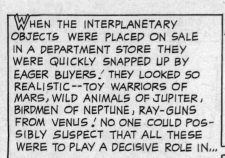

When the interplanetary objects were placed on sale in a department store they were quickly snapped up by eager buyers! They looked so realistic--toy warriors of Mars, wild animals of Jupiter, birdmen of Neptune, ray-guns from Venus! No one could possibly suspect that all these were to play a decisive role in...

The RADIOACTIVE INVASION of EARTH!

OUR TESTS SHOW THIS "MARTIAN SOLDIER" AND "BIRDMAN OF NEPTUNE" ARE MADE OF A METAL UNKNOWN ON EARTH!

IS IT POSSIBLE THE SOLDIER REALLY DID COME FROM MARS-- AND THE BIRDMAN STATUE FROM NEPTUNE?

In the offices of the purchasing agent for Lacey's department store...

AND THIS, SIR, IS MY CONCEPTION OF WHAT AN ANIMAL ON THE PLANET JUPITER IS LIKE!

WELL, SIR, WHAT DO YOU SAY TO MY PROPOSITION?

THERE'S A BIG INTEREST IN SCIENCE-FICTION THESE DAYS! SOMETHING LIKE THIS MIGHT CATCH ON AND SELL!

I HAVE READY A LINE OF VENUSIAN RAY-GUNS, PLUTONIAN HELMETS, COINS FROM ANCIENT RUINS ON SATURN, MODELS OF SPACE-SHIPS...

I'LL TAKE THEM! I'LL STAGE A WEEK-LONG SALE OF SCIENCE-FICTION SPECIALTIES!

THE DAY OF THE SCIENCE-FICTION SALE FINDS THE AISLES JAMMED WITH BUYERS...

MINIATURES OF THE FUTURE

NOW ON SALE

EAGER BUYERS SNAP UP THE INTERPLANETARY OBJECTS! EVEN WOMEN GET INTO THE SPIRIT OF THE SALE...

JUST THE THING TO WEAR AT THE SCIENCE-FICTION CONVENTION MASQUERADE DANCE NEXT LABOR DAY!

MARTIAN GLAMOUR GIRL

ELDERLY MEN AND YOUNGSTERS, BUSINESS MEN AND TEENAGE SCHOOLBOYS, TAKE ADVANTAGE OF THE UNIQUE SALE...

JOEY, LOOK AT THIS REALISTIC RAY-GUN! I'M BUYING IT!

I'M TAKING THIS STATUE OF A BIRD-MAN OF NEPTUNE!

THAT NIGHT, IN THE HOME OF SCIENTIST JASON KENTON...

DAD, LOOK WHAT WE BOUGHT AT LACEY'S!

REMARKABLE! I CAN'T SEE HOW THEY SELL THEM SO CHEAPLY! THE WORKMANSHIP ALONE IS WORTH TWICE THE SELLING PRICE!

STRANGE! THE METAL OF WHICH THIS MARTIAN TOY SOLDIER IS MADE GIVES OFF AN UNUSUAL COLOR!

②

INTRIGUED, SCIENTIST JASON KENTON TAKES THE MARTIAN SOLDIER TO HIS BASEMENT LABORATORY FOR TESTS...

INCREDIBLE! THIS METAL IS REACTING IN A COMPLETELY DIFFERENT MANNER FROM ANY METAL KNOWN TO SCIENCE!

AFTER HOURS OF PATIENT RESEARCH...

THERE'S NO DOUBT ABOUT IT! THIS SOLDIER IS MADE OF AN ENTIRELY NEW *ELEMENT*-- UNKNOWN ON EARTH!

HIGHLY EXCITED, HE PHONES THE SCIENCE INSTITUTE...

...SOMETHING MYSTERIOUS-- UNEARTHLY-- GOING ON-- AND WE'D BETTER COME UP WITH THE ANSWER QUICK!

I'LL BE IN COAST CITY FIRST THING IN THE MORNING! MEET ME AT BRANCH HEAD-QUARTERS!

THE FOLLOWING DAY, BY LATE AFTERNOON...

OUR FINDINGS CONFIRM YOUR OWN, JASON! THESE OBJECTS WERE NOT MADE ON THIS PLANET!

WE CHECKED WITH LACEY'S! THE SALES-MAN WHO MADE THE DEAL HAS DISAPPEARED--

--DISAPPEARED FROM THE FACE OF THE EARTH, I IMAGINE!

ANOTHER CONFERENCE IS TAKING PLACE ON *TITAN*, LARGEST OF THE NINE MOONS OF THE PLANET SATURN, AND THE ONLY MOON WITH AN ATMOSPHERE...

RULERS OF *TITAN*, OUR PLAN TO CONQUER *EARTH* IS PROGRESSING SATISFACTORILY! WE DECIDED TO ABANDON OUR ORIGINAL INVASION BY SPACESHIPS--THE COST IN LIVES WOULD HAVE BEEN TOO HEAVY!

INSTEAD, WE AGREED TO A *RADIO-ACTIVE* INVASION OF EARTH! THE THOUSANDS OF OBJECTS WE MADE OF OUR *STYRANIUM* METAL ARE NOW BEING SOLD IN A LARGE EARTH CITY! IN TEN DAYS THE METAL WILL START TO DECAY-- RELEASING A DEADLY FLOW OF RADIOACTIVE RAYS THAT WILL ENCOMPASS THE ENTIRE PLANET!

3

ONCE THAT DECAYING PROCESS HAS BEGUN, *NOTHING* KNOWN TO OUR SCIENCE CAN STOP IT! EVERY LIVING CREATURE ON EARTH WILL DIE! IN TIME, THE RADIOACTIVITY WILL FADE AWAY--AND WE WILL TAKE EARTH FOR OURSELVES!

STYRANIUM'S DECAYING PROCESS CANNOT START UNLESS THE METAL IS KEPT FOR TEN CONSECUTIVE DAYS AT A CONSTANT TEMPERATURE OF 65 TO 80 DEGREES! THUS, IT WAS UNWISE TO BOMBARD EARTH WITH *STYRANIUM*-- THE PLANET'S OUTDOOR TEMPERATURE VARIES GREATLY FROM DAY TO DAY!

THAT IS WHY WE ADOPTED THE RUSE OF HAVING EARTH-MEN BUY OUR *STYRANIUM*-MADE OBJECTS AND KEEP THEM IN THEIR HOMES WHICH HAVE A CONSTANT 65 TO 80 DEGREES TEMPERATURE!

THE DECAYING PROCESS IS NOW UNDER WAY--AND THE *STYRANIUM* IS DISCHARGING ITS DEADLY RAYS!

PEOPLE OF TITAN, I GIVE YOU VICTORY!

MEANWHILE, UNDER STRICT SECRECY, THE SCIENTISTS OF COAST CITY HAVE BEEN IN-VESTIGATING THE ALIEN OBJECTS...

SUDDENLY, JASON KENTON CRIES OUT IN ALARM...

THE GEIGER COUNTER-- CLICKING! THE METAL IS BREAKING DOWN! BECOMING RADIOACTIVE!

CLICK-CLICK- CLICK-CLIKETY- CLICK-CLICK CLICK-CLICK- CLICK- CLICK-

FURTHER TESTS REVEAL THE GRIM TRUTH...

THE METAL GIVES OFF DEADLY RAYS! UNLESS WE CAN FIND A WAY TO STOP THEM--ALL LIFE ON EARTH WILL END... WITHIN SIX MONTHS!

SCIENTISTS THROUGHOUT THE CITY ARE MARSHALED TO COMBAT THE RADIOACTIVE MENACE...

A RACE FOR LIFE... AGAINST TIME!

ALL DAY LONG JASON KENTON WORKS ON, WITH TEST TUBES, ELECTRONIC CALCULATORS, ALL THE RESOURCES OF SCIENCE...

THE DEADLINESS OF THE RAYS IS INCREASING HOURLY! AND WE CAN FIND NO WAY TO STOP IT!

AT MIDNIGHT, THE WEARY SCIENTIST HEADS HOMEWARD...

I'VE TRIED EVERYTHING--WITH THE SAME NEGATIVE RESULT! ONCE HAVING BEGUN TO DISINTEGRATE, THE METAL CAN'T BE DESTROYED!

TIRED AND WORN OUT, HE GOES IMMEDIATELY TO HIS HOME LABORATORY...

CAN'T SLEEP WHILE THERE'S WORK TO BE DONE! I MUST FIND THE ANSWER!

STARING DOWN AT THE TOY SOLDIER ON WHICH HE HAD BEEN WORKING THE PREVIOUS NIGHT, HE CRIES OUT IN STUNNED DISBELIEF!

THE MARTIAN SOLDIER-- HAS TURNED TO LEAD! IT'S INERT-- HARMLESS! WHAT CAUSED IT? SOMETHING HAPPENED HERE WHILE I WAS GONE!

5

His OUTCRY BRINGS HIS WIFE AND TWO SONS INTO THE PLAYROOM LABORATORY...

WHAT'S THE MATTER, DEAR?

THE MARTIAN TOY SOLDIER--"DEAD"! I'VE GOT TO FIND OUT WHY!

TELL ME EVERYTHING THAT HAPPENED DOWN HERE TODAY...

I DUSTED, BUT I DIDN'T TOUCH ANYTHING!

WE PLAYED SOME ROCK-AND-ROLL RECORDS, DAD!

ROCK-AND-ROLL? *MUSIC?* SOUND WAVES! SOUND CAN BREAK GLASS, SNAP METAL WIRE, EVEN KILL, AT THE RIGHT PITCH! THAT MUST BE THE ANSWER!

CLUTCHING A ROCK-AND-ROLL RECORD, JASON KENTON RACES NEXT DOOR...

JASON, THIS IS NO TIME FOR JOKES!

LISTEN TO THIS RECORD, ED--AND WATCH THOSE RADIOACTIVE COINS YOU'VE BEEN WORKING ON!

MOMENTS LATER--

THE COINS TURNED TO LEAD!

THANKS TO THE PECULIAR VIBRATORY IMPULSE OF THIS KIND OF MUSIC! NOW WE'RE GOING TO ROUND UP ALL THOSE INTERPLANETARY OBJECTS--AND HAVE A ROCK-AND-ROLL SESSION!

THE FOLLOWING NIGHT, AFTER THE RADIOACTIVE MENACE HAS BEEN DESTROYED...

GOSH, I NEVER REALIZED HOW MUCH I'D APPRECIATE ROCK-AND-ROLL MUSIC!

The End

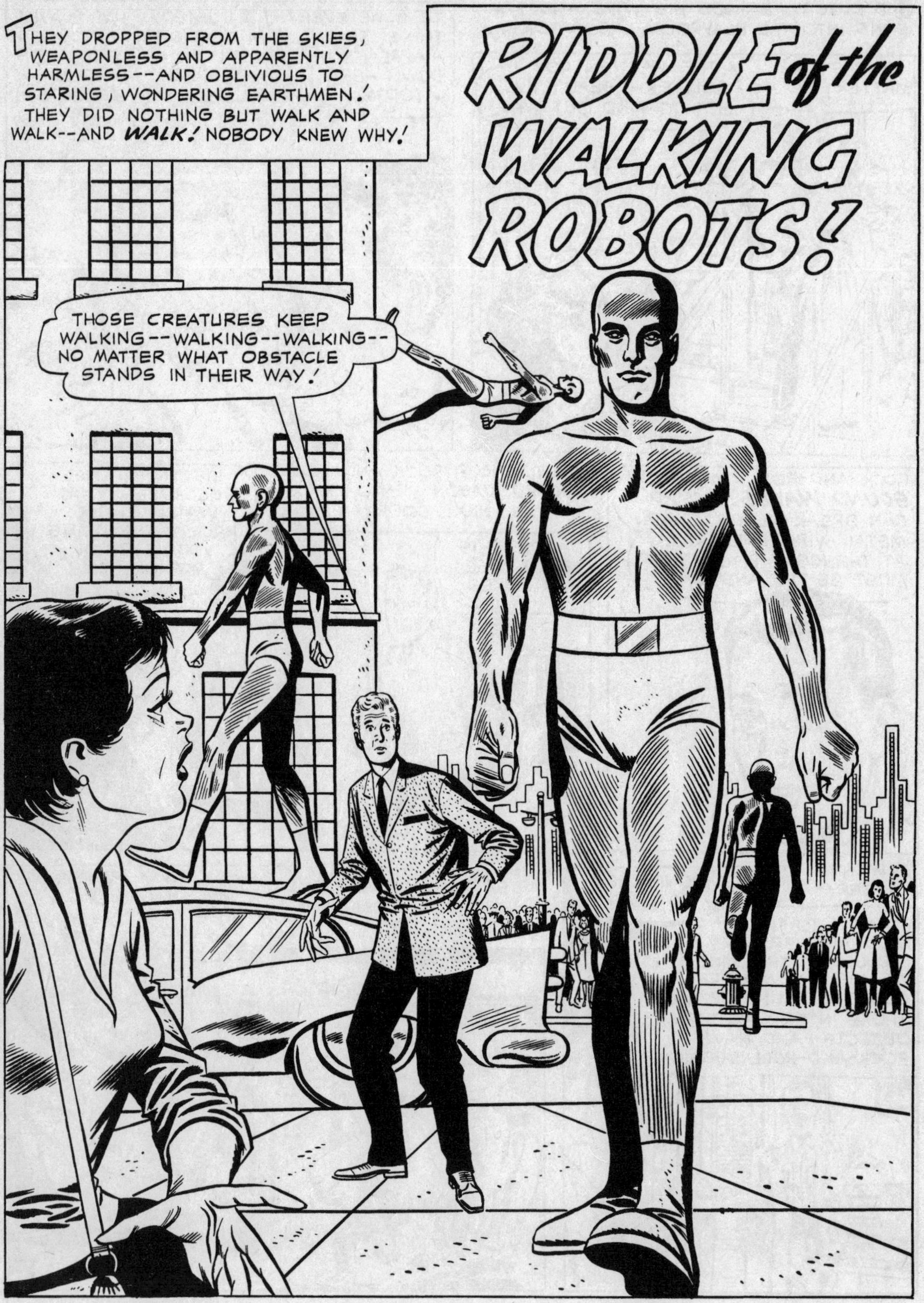
THEY DROPPED FROM THE SKIES, WEAPONLESS AND APPARENTLY HARMLESS--AND OBLIVIOUS TO STARING, WONDERING EARTHMEN! THEY DID NOTHING BUT WALK AND WALK--AND WALK! NOBODY KNEW WHY!
RIDDLE of the WALKING ROBOTS!
THOSE CREATURES KEEP WALKING--WALKING--WALKING--NO MATTER WHAT OBSTACLE STANDS IN THEIR WAY!

FLASHING IN FROM OUTER SPACE, A STRANGE CRAFT HOVERS OVER EARTH....

THEN, FROM THE CRAFT TUMBLES A MYSTERIOUS CARGO....

SUDDENLY, THE SPACESHIP ROARS AWAY....

FROM A NEARBY CITY, CURIOUS THRONGS GATHER....

THE METALLIC CREATURE FROM SPACE BRUSHED RIGHT PAST US! IT'S AS IF THEY DIDN'T EVEN KNOW--OR CARE--WE WERE HERE!

I DON'T SEE ANY WEAPONS! WHAT ARE THEY UP TO?

LATER, IN THE CITY, WHERE EXCITING REPORTS HAVE HERALDED THE STRANGE VISITORS....

KEEP YOUR DISTANCE PLEASE--UNTIL COMMUNICATION IS MADE WITH THESE ALIENS!

THEY KEEP WALKING.... UP BUILDING SIDES--OVER ROADBLOCKS! WHEN ARE THEY GOING TO STOP?

THE AMAZING PARADE CONTINUES--OVER MOUNTAINS....

...HELICOPTERS...ARE...TRAILING...THE...STRANGE... VISITORS...NO...INDICATION...YET...OF...THEIR... DESTINATION....

INTO RIVERS, LAKES--EVEN THE *OCEAN*--THEY GO....

AMAZING! NO OBSTACLE SEEMS TO STOP THEM! THEY JUST KEEP *WALKING!*

MEANWHILE, AT AN EMERGENCY MEETING OF TOP SCIENTISTS, DARWIN JONES, CHIEF OF THE *DEPARTMENT OF SCIENTIFIC INVESTIGATION*, IS BOMBARDED WITH QUESTIONS...

MOBILE *TV* UNITS ARE KEEPING THEM IN VIEW FOR US!

BUT WHO ARE THEY? WHERE ARE THEY FROM? WHAT'S THEIR PURPOSE?

ALL WE HAVE DETERMINED SO FAR IS THAT THEY LANDED HERE! THE DOTTED LINES SHOW THE ROUTES OVER WHICH THEY'RE WALKING!

BUT *WHY* DO THEY KEEP *WALKING*, MR. JONES?

THAT'S MY PLAN-- TO FIND OUT!

SHORTLY AFTER THE MEETING, DARWIN JONES IS IN A HELICOPTER, APPROACHING ONE OF THE WALKING VISITORS...

ON A HUNCH I BROUGHT ALONG A SPECIAL X-RAY CAMERA! IT MIGHT REVEAL THE *"INSIDE"* STORY!

I'LL *"SHOOT"* THE ALIEN FROM A COUPLE OF MORE ANGLES-- THEN SEE WHAT DEVELOPS!

BZZZZZ

3

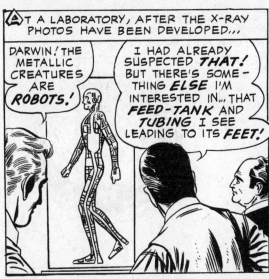

AT A LABORATORY, AFTER THE X-RAY PHOTOS HAVE BEEN DEVELOPED....

DARWIN! THE METALLIC CREATURES ARE *ROBOTS!*

I HAD ALREADY SUSPECTED *THAT!* BUT THERE'S SOMETHING *ELSE* I'M INTERESTED IN... THAT *FEED-TANK* AND *TUBING* I SEE LEADING TO ITS *FEET!*

THEY SUGGEST A FANTASTIC THEORY--BUT I'VE GOT TO CHECK IT OUT! FIRST CALL WASHINGTON! TELL THEM THE ROBOTS MUST BE DESTROYED AT ONCE! THEN COME WITH ME!

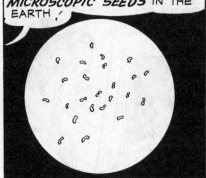

AFTER REMOVING A SPECIMEN OF SOIL FROM ONE OF THE ROBOT'S TRAILS, DARWIN PLACES IT UNDER A MICROSCOPE...

I WAS RIGHT! THEY'RE SOWING *MICROSCOPIC SEEDS* IN THE EARTH!

HURRIEDLY, THE SEEDS ARE TAKEN INTO A SPECIALLY DESIGNED GREENHOUSE NEXT DOOR...

IN HERE WE CAN SIMULATE SUNLIGHT AND ATMOSPHERIC CONDITIONS TO ANY DEGREE WE WISH! WE'RE GOING TO FORCE THOSE SEEDS INTO RAPID MATURITY AND GROWTH!

BUT THE PLANT GROWS SO FAST THEY HAVE TO MOVE IT OUTSIDE...

I STRUCK IT WITH AN AXE, DARWIN--AND DIDN'T EVEN *SCRAPE* THE BARK!

MILLIONS UPON MILLIONS OF THESE SEEDS SPROUTING--THE PICTURE IS BECOMING CLEAR!

THE ROBOTS WERE SENT HERE BY THEIR MASTERS TO SOW THIS CROP OF VEGETATION *ALL OVER THE WORLD!* CAN YOU IMAGINE WHAT EFFECT THIS WOULD HAVE ON EARTH?

"THESE FRIGHTFUL PLANTS WOULD RISE FROM LAND AND FROM SEA..."

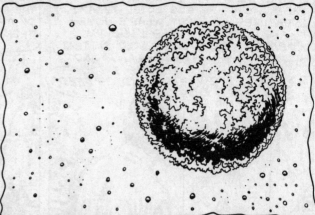

"HIGHER AND HIGHER THEY WOULD GROW--BLOTTING OUT THE SUN--BLANKETING THE EARTH IN TOTAL DARKNESS! LIFE NO LONGER COULD SURVIVE HERE..."

THE ROBOT MASTERS WILL THEN DESCEND TO REAP THE STRANGE HARVEST NOW BEING SOWN! THAT IS THE GRIM PICTURE--UNLESS WE STOP THE ROBOT-SEEDERS!

A MOMENT LATER, THE PHONE RINGS IN THE LAB...

IT'S WASHINGTON! THEY'VE UNLEASHED EVERYTHING AGAINST THE ROBOTS-- EVEN NUCLEAR WEAPONS! BUT THE ROBOTS STILL WALK-- SOWING THEIR DEADLY CROPS! NOTHING CAN STOP THEM!

THEN WE MUST FIND SOME- THING TO DESTROY THE *SEEDS!*

LATER, THE DESPERATE RACE AGAINST TIME IS ON AS LEADING CHEMISTS GATHER UNDER ONE ROOF TO SEEK THE ANTIDOTE...

NO POSITIVE RESULTS YET, DARWIN! MAYBE THE SEEDS ARE JUST AS INDESTRUCTIBLE AS THE ROBOTS!

KEEP THOSE TESTS GOING! WE'VE *GOT* TO COME UP WITH THE SEED-KILLER!

BY AFTERNOON OF THE NEXT DAY, A TRIUMPHANT SOUND RINGS THROUGH THE LAB...

WE'VE GOT IT! THE ANTIDOTE THAT WILL KILL THE SEEDS!

⑤

BUT HOW CAN WE PUT IT TO WORK? SURELY, WE CAN'T COVER THE *WHOLE* EARTH WITH IT!

WE WON'T HAVE TO! SOMEBODY ELSE WILL DO THE JOB FOR US! BOTTLE UP AS MANY GALLONS AS YOU CAN OF THE ANTIDOTE!

A SHORT WHILE LATER, THE SCIENCE SLEUTH OVERTAKES ONE OF THE ROBOTS BY HELICOPTER...

WE'RE APPROACHING THE ROBOT NOW--GET SET TO GIVE IT THE ANTIDOTE INJECTION...

FROM THE HELICOPTER, DARWIN ATTACHES A HOSE TO THE ROBOT...

THE X-RAY REVEALED THIS OPENING TO THE ROBOT'S FEED-TANK AT THE BACK OF ITS NECK--

NEXT, THE SCIENCE SLEUTH TAKES TO THE GROUND...

NOW WITH THE ANTIDOTE INSIDE THE ROBOT, I SIMPLY TURN THE ROBOT *AROUND* IT WILL CONTINUE TO WALK, RETRACING ITS STEPS...AND SPREAD THE ANTIDOTE OVER THE SEED TRAIL! OTHER SCIENTISTS ARE DUPLICATING THE SAME PROCEDURE!

WHEN ALL THE ROBOTS RETURN TO THE VERY POINT FROM WHICH THEY STARTED...

LOOK--*THE ROBOTS*--COLLAPSING! THOUGH *WE* COULDN'T DESTROY THEM, THEY WERE DESIGNED TO DESTROY *THEMSELVES*, ONCE THEIR FEED-TANKS WERE EMPTY!

AND SOMEWHERE OUT IN SPACE...

WE ERRED IN PUTTING THE ROBOTS ON THE PLANET EARTH! WE CANNOT SOW OUR CROPS THERE! WE MUST LOOK ELSEWHERE!

THE END

THE TOY THAT SAVED the WORLD!

TOMMY WARD DIDN'T PARTICULARLY LIKE DOING HOMEWORK--UNTIL HE MADE A DO-IT-YOURSELF ELECTRONIC BRAIN TO HELP HIM OUT! BUT TO TOMMY'S BEWILDERMENT, HE DISCOVERED THAT NO MATTER HOW "WRONG" THE COMPUTER'S ANSWERS SEEMED TO BE--THEY WERE ALWAYS **RIGHT!**

WHENEVER HE VISITS HIS FATHER'S LABORATORY, YOUNG TOMMY WARD SIGHS LONGINGLY...

GOSH, DAD! IF I COULD USE YOUR ELECTRONIC BRAIN TO DO MY HOME-WORK PROBLEMS, I'D HAVE THEM FINISHED IN A SPLIT-SECOND!

SORRY, SON! THE WORLD'S FASTEST COMPUTER CAN'T BE USED FOR SCHOOLWORK! BUT I BOUGHT A SURPRISE FOR YOU!

IT'LL TAKE 50 MORE HOURS BEFORE MY GIANT ELECTRONIC BRAIN CAN SOLVE THE PROBLEM OF HOW TO SAVE EARTH FROM COSMIC DOOM!

MY MINIATURE COMPUTER TOOK ONLY **ONE HOUR**, DAD! HERE'S THE ANSWER!

BRAINIAC

OH, BOY! NOW I CAN MAKE MY OWN SMALL-SIZED ELECTRONIC BRAIN! THANKS, DAD!

MINIAC! MINIATURE ELECTRONIC BRAIN KIT! BUILD IT YOUR-SELF!

EAGERLY, TOMMY CONSTRUCTS THE TOY COMPUTER AND GIVES IT THE FIRST TEST...

YOU PUNCH THE KEYBOARD TO ASK QUESTIONS! LET'S SEE, I'LL GIVE IT AN EASY ONE TO START WITH... WHAT IS THE EARTH'S HIGHEST MOUNTAIN?

MOMENTS LATER...

HERE COMES THE ANSWER ON PRINTED TAPE! IT SHOULD READ *MT EVEREST--29,141 FEET!* I KNOW THE ANSWER TO THAT ONE!

WURRR-R-R-R CLICK-CLICK-CLICK-CLICK!

BUT TO TOMMY'S SURPRISE...

SHUCKS! *MINIAC* GAVE THE WRONG ANSWER! I'LL TRY ANOTHER QUESTION!

MT. KENYA IN AFRICA, 17,040 FT.

SHORTLY...

I ASKED WHAT IS THE LARGEST OCEAN ON EARTH AND THIS TIME IT'S RIGHT! I WONDER WHY *MINIAC* MISSED THE FIRST TIME?

PACIFIC OCEAN. AREA-63,801,700 SQ. MILES.

AFTER FURTHER AND HARDER TESTS...

IT SOLVED ALL THESE ALGEBRA PROBLEMS CORRECTLY! I GUESS *MINIAC'S* FIRST MISTAKE WAS AN ACCIDENT!

ANSWERS TO ALGEBRA EQUATIONS

$AX-YA=AXO$

ONE DAY, AFTER SCHOOL, TOMMY FINDS A NEW USE FOR HIS *"TOM THUMB"* MECHANICAL BRAIN...

STRIKE THREE!

THE *JACKSON HIGH* PITCHER HAS BLINDING SPEED! WE HAVEN'T HAD A HIT YET! I WONDER IF *MINIAC* CAN FIGURE OUT HOW TO HIT HIS FAST BALL?

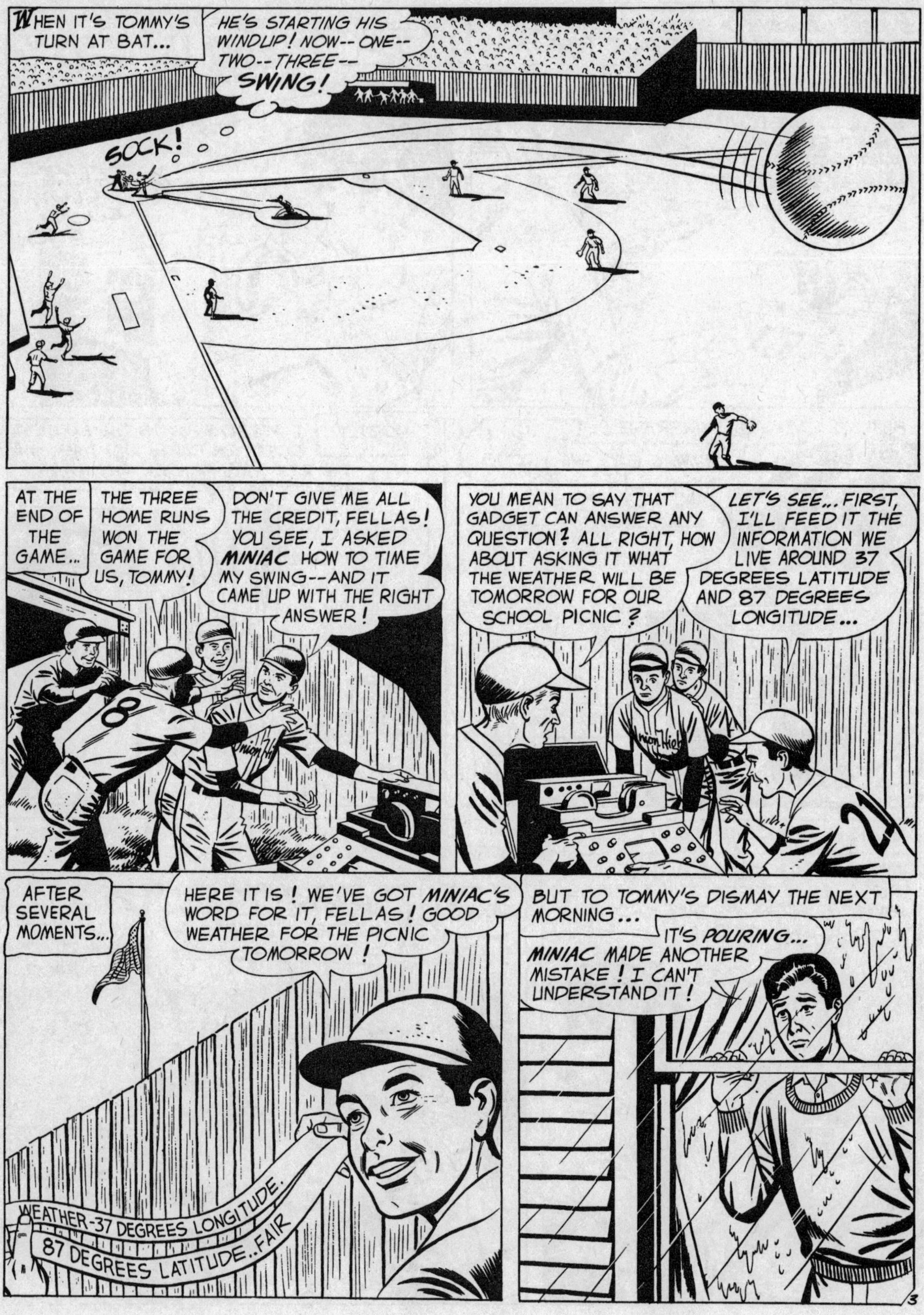
WHEN IT'S TOMMY'S TURN AT BAT...
HE'S STARTING HIS WINDUP! NOW-- ONE-- TWO-- THREE-- SWING!
SOCK!
AT THE END OF THE GAME...
THE THREE HOME RUNS WON THE GAME FOR US, TOMMY!
DON'T GIVE ME ALL THE CREDIT, FELLAS! YOU SEE, I ASKED MINIAC HOW TO TIME MY SWING--AND IT CAME UP WITH THE RIGHT ANSWER!
YOU MEAN TO SAY THAT GADGET CAN ANSWER ANY QUESTION? ALL RIGHT, HOW ABOUT ASKING IT WHAT THE WEATHER WILL BE TOMORROW FOR OUR SCHOOL PICNIC?
LET'S SEE... FIRST, I'LL FEED IT THE INFORMATION WE LIVE AROUND 37 DEGREES LATITUDE AND 87 DEGREES LONGITUDE...
AFTER SEVERAL MOMENTS...
HERE IT IS! WE'VE GOT MINIAC'S WORD FOR IT, FELLAS! GOOD WEATHER FOR THE PICNIC TOMORROW!
WEATHER-37 DEGREES LONGITUDE. 87 DEGREES LATITUDE..FAIR
BUT TO TOMMY'S DISMAY THE NEXT MORNING...
IT'S POURING... MINIAC MADE ANOTHER MISTAKE! I CAN'T UNDERSTAND IT!
3

TOMMY QUICKLY DISMISSES THE ERROR AS *MINIAC* PERFORMS BRILLIANTLY AGAIN! THEN, ONE DAY IN SCHOOL...

WHAT IS THE NEAREST STAR WE CAN SEE BEYOND OUR OWN STAR-SUN? YES, THOMAS?

I GOT THE ANSWER FROM *MINIAC* LAST NIGHT!

THE STAR, *SIRIUS*!

THAT'S *INCORRECT!* *SIRIUS* IS 8.6 LIGHT-YEARS AWAY! THE NEAREST STAR IS *ALPHA CENTAURI,* 4.3 LIGHT YEARS!

GOSH! MY ELECTRONIC BRAIN WENT HAYWIRE AGAIN!

I CAN'T SEE WHAT'S WRONG! MAYBE DAD WILL HELP ME FIX IT!

AT HOME, TOMMY IS TOO OCCUPIED WITH *MINIAC* TO HEAR A SURPRISING NEWS FLASH!

FLASH!! TRANSATLANTIC LINER REPORTS A MYSTIFYING PHENOMENON! IT HAD TO SAIL AN EXTRA MILE TO REACH PORT! AUTHORITIES ARE BAFFLED...

MEANWHILE, AS A TRANSPACIFIC AIRLINER CROSSES THE OCEAN...

THAT'S STRANGE... ACCORDING TO THE MILEAGE, THE *AIRPORT* SHOULD BE BELOW US NOW--NOT THE OCEAN! IT'S AS IF THE DISTANCE TO AMERICA INCREASED *TWO MILES!*

AS THE AMAZING REPORTS CONTINUE, PROFESSOR WARD SETS HIS SUPER ELECTRONIC BRAIN TO SOLVING THE MYSTERY...

GREAT SCOTT! THAT'S WHY OUR GEOGRAPHICAL DISTANCES HAVE CHANGED! I'VE GOT TO PUT *BRAINIAC* TO WORK TO FIGURE OUT HOW TO STOP THE CONTINENTAL SHRINKING!

BRAINIAC

CONTINENTAL SHRINKAGE CAUSED BY RAYS EMANATING FROM CONTRACTING STAR IN SPACE...

BUT WHEN THE SUPER COMPUTER FIRST ESTIMATES THE TIME IT WILL REQUIRE TO SOLVE THE COMPLEX PROBLEM...

GOOD GOSH! I HOPE THAT'S NOT TOO LATE TO SAVE EARTH FROM DISASTER!

AT THIS MOMENT, TOMMY VISITS HIS FATHER'S LABORATORY...

DAD, CAN YOU FIX MY MINIAC? EVERY ONCE IN A WHILE IT COMES UP WITH THE WRONG ANSWER! SEE, I MADE OUT A LIST!

ONLY CAN SPARE YOU A MOMENT, TOMMY! I'VE GOT MORE PRESSING PROBLEMS!

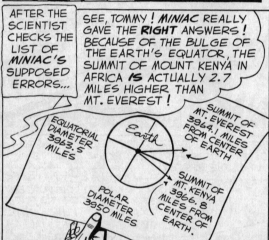

AFTER THE SCIENTIST CHECKS THE LIST OF MINIAC'S SUPPOSED ERRORS...

SEE, TOMMY! MINIAC REALLY GAVE THE RIGHT ANSWERS! BECAUSE OF THE BULGE OF THE EARTH'S EQUATOR, THE SUMMIT OF MOUNT KENYA IN AFRICA IS ACTUALLY 2.7 MILES HIGHER THAN MT. EVEREST!

EQUATORIAL DIAMETER 3963.5 MILES

Earth

POLAR DIAMETER 3950 MILES

SUMMIT OF MT. EVEREST 3964.1 MILES FROM CENTER OF EARTH

SUMMIT OF MT. KENYA 3966.8 MILES FROM CENTER OF EARTH.

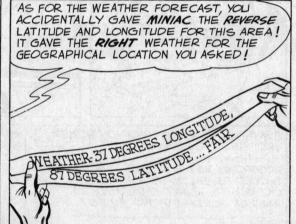

AS FOR THE WEATHER FORECAST, YOU ACCIDENTALLY GAVE MINIAC THE REVERSE LATITUDE AND LONGITUDE FOR THIS AREA! IT GAVE THE RIGHT WEATHER FOR THE GEOGRAPHICAL LOCATION YOU ASKED!

WEATHER-37 DEGREES LONGITUDE, 87 DEGREES LATITUDE...FAIR.

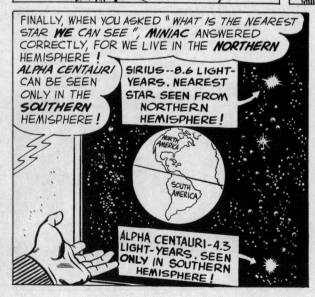

FINALLY, WHEN YOU ASKED "WHAT IS THE NEAREST STAR WE CAN SEE", MINIAC ANSWERED CORRECTLY, FOR WE LIVE IN THE NORTHERN HEMISPHERE! ALPHA CENTAURI CAN BE SEEN ONLY IN THE SOUTHERN HEMISPHERE!

SIRIUS--8.6 LIGHT-YEARS. NEAREST STAR SEEN FROM NORTHERN HEMISPHERE!

NORTH AMERICA

SOUTH AMERICA

ALPHA CENTAURI-4.3 LIGHT-YEARS. SEEN ONLY IN SOUTHERN HEMISPHERE!

GOSH, THEN MINIAC WAS RIGHT ALL THE TIME!

JUST ON A HUNCH, I'M GOING TO ASK MINIAC HOW TO STOP THE CONTINENTS FROM SHRINKING! MAYBE IT CAN BEAT BRAINIAC TO THE ANSWERS!

WITHIN AN HOUR, THE AMAZING "TOY" GIVES AN ANSWER!..

SNOW?! THE ANSWER MUST BE RIGHT--BUT I DON'T SEE HOW--

TO STOP SHRINKING RAYS SPRAY SNOW INTO ATMOSPHERE...

SNOW?... SNOW?... HAS IT SOME OTHER OBSCURE MEANING?

DAD, LOOK AT THE CHART OF CHEMICAL ELEMENTS AND THEIR SYMBOLS! "SN" STANDS FOR TIN..."O" FOR OXYGEN..."W" FOR TUNGSTEN!

OXYGEN - O
TIN - SN
TUNGSTEN - W
URANIUM - U
XENON - X
ZENON - Z

THAT'S IT, SON! "SNOW" IS THE CHEMICAL FORMULA FOR TIN TUNGSTENATE! CHEMICAL LABS AROUND EARTH CAN MANUFACTURE TONS OVERNIGHT AND SPRAY IT THROUGH THE EARTH'S ATMOSPHERE, STOPPING THE SHRINKING RAYS!

SN + O + W = TIN + OXYGEN + TUNGSTEN = TIN TUNGSTENATE

48 HOURS LATER, A PLANE CIRCLES OVER AN AIRPORT...

OUR DESTINATION...RIGHT ON THE BUTTON! THE CONTINENTS HAVE RETURNED TO NORMAL SIZE!

MEANWHILE, AT THE WARD HOME...

GOSH, DAD, HOW COULD MY ELECTRONIC COMPUTER TURN OUT TO BE SUCH A LIGHTNING COMPUTER?

BY SHEER ACCIDENT, YOU MUST HAVE STUMBLED ON A CIRCUIT SPEEDING UP CALCULATIONS A THOUSANDFOLD! I'M GOING TO EXAMINE IT...SEE HOW IT WORKS!

THE INSIDES...FLEW APART! THE SECRET OF THE SUPER-CIRCUIT...LOST FOREVER!

WHUNG!

GOLLY, NOW I'LL HAVE TO DO HOMEWORK THE HARD WAY!

A BOY SEEKING A SHORT CUT TO HIS HOMEWORK... FOUND A WAY TO SAVE THE WORLD!

The End

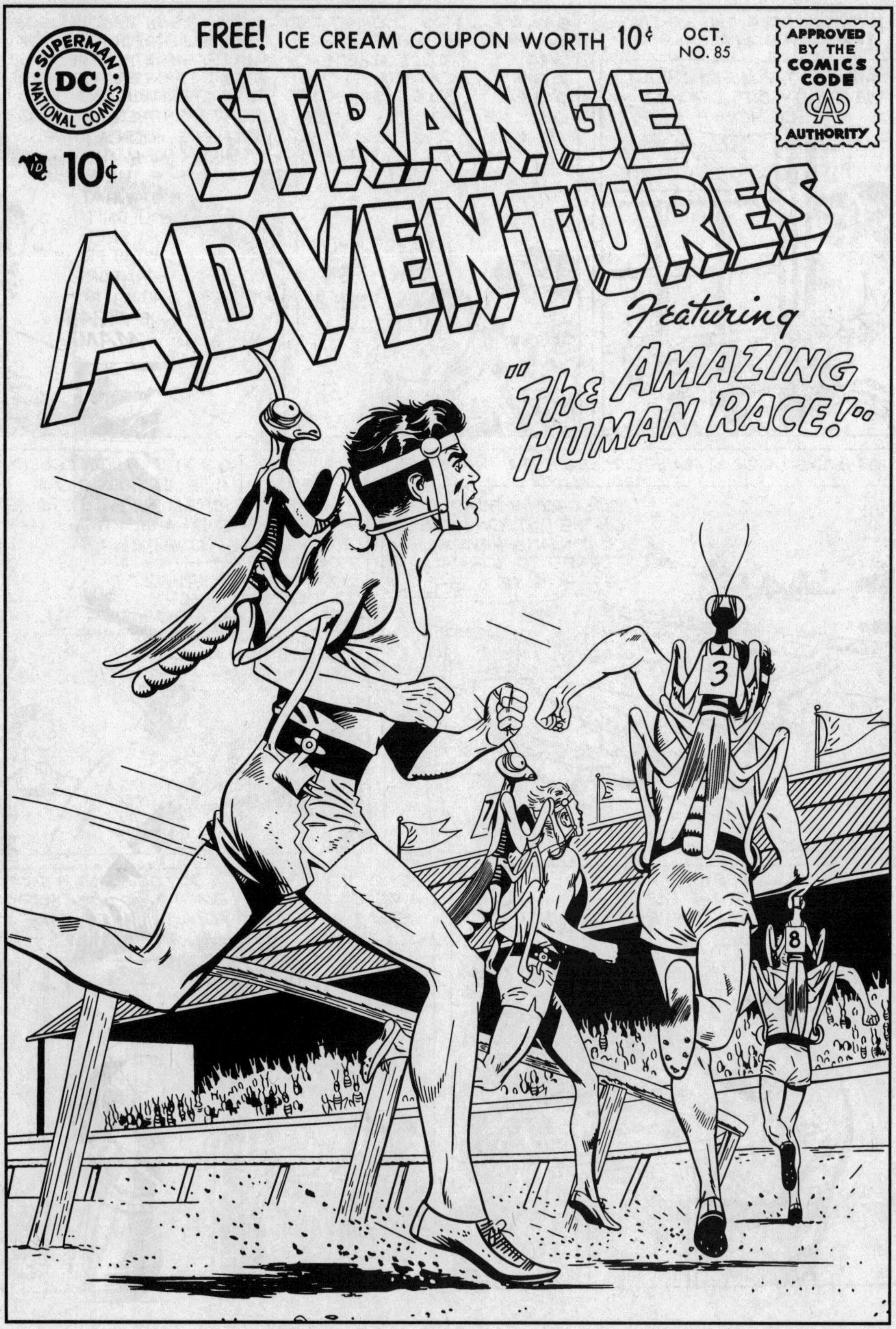
FREE! ICE CREAM COUPON WORTH 10¢
OCT. NO. 85
SUPERMAN DC NATIONAL COMICS
APPROVED BY THE COMICS CODE AUTHORITY
10¢
STRANGE ADVENTURES
Featuring
"The AMAZING HUMAN RACE!"
3
8

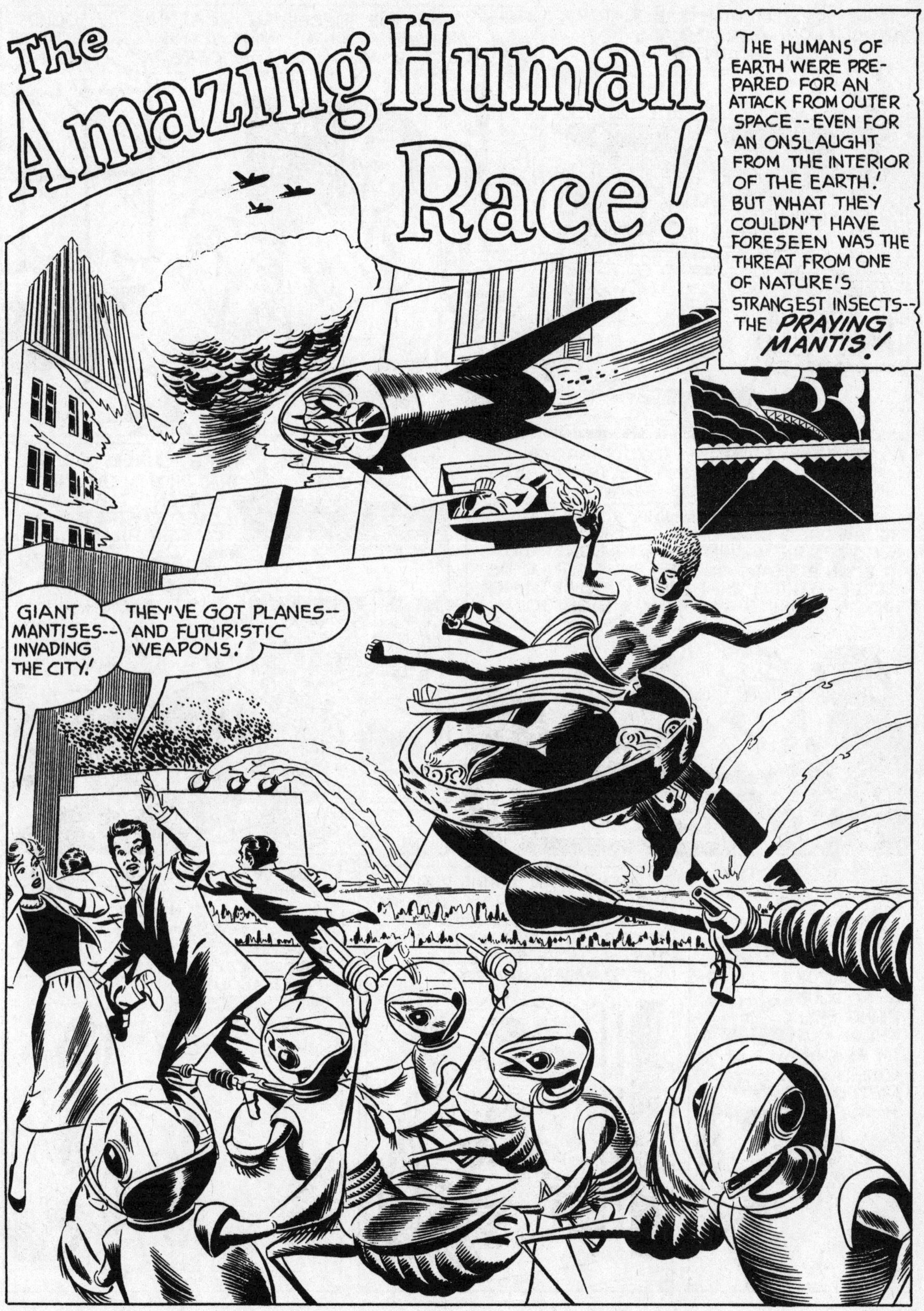
The Amazing Human Race!
THE HUMANS OF EARTH WERE PREPARED FOR AN ATTACK FROM OUTER SPACE -- EVEN FOR AN ONSLAUGHT FROM THE INTERIOR OF THE EARTH! BUT WHAT THEY COULDN'T HAVE FORESEEN WAS THE THREAT FROM ONE OF NATURE'S STRANGEST INSECTS-- THE PRAYING MANTIS!
GIANT MANTISES-- INVADING THE CITY!
THEY'VE GOT PLANES-- AND FUTURISTIC WEAPONS!

IN HIS EXPERIMENTAL LABORATORY, PHYSICIST JOHN ADAIR SPEAKS TO A FELLOW SCIENTIST...

...AND I'VE SUCCEEDED IN GETTING *IMAGES* FROM THE MINDS OF ANIMALS, CORT-- BY MEANS OF THIS *CEREBRO-AMPLIFIER* I'VE BUILT!

SOUNDS FANTASTIC, JOHN!

AS THE YOUNG SCIENTIST EXPLAINS THAT HIS MACHINE WORKS BY TURNING ELECTRIC BRAIN WAVES INTO VISIBLE LIGHT WAVES...

WATCH! I FIX THIS TERMINAL TO THE DOG'S HEAD-- AND SWITCH ON THE MACHINE! SEE-- A BONE APPEARS ON THE SCREEN--THAT'S WHAT THE DOG'S THINKING ABOUT!

HMM! IT RESEMBLES A BONE-- BUT IT COULD BE SOMETHING ELSE, TOO!

NEXT, ADAIR TRIES OUT HIS CAT...

THERE--SURELY YOU SEE THAT PILLOW ON THE SCREEN? TABBY JUST LOVES TO STRETCH OUT ON HER PILLOW...

LOOKS LIKE A *BLUR* TO ME, JOHN! I'M SORRY, BUT I'M NOT CONVINCED...

AFTER THE ELDERLY SCIENTIST HAS GONE...

I WISH I COULD GET STRONGER AND CLEARER IMAGES WITH MY MACHINE --SO THAT THERE WOULD BE NO DOUBT *WHAT* IS BEING SEEN! THE REASON MUST BE THAT THE BRAIN WAVES OF LOWER ANIMALS ARE *TOO WEAK*...

...AND HUMAN BRAINS DON'T WORK AT ALL WITH MY *CEREBRO-AMPLIFIER*... BUT BEFORE I ABANDON THE PROJECT I'LL TRY ONE MORE SUBJECT-- THE *PRAYING MANTIS!*

PICKING UP THE INSECT, JOHN TESTS IT...

I'VE ALWAYS BEEN INTRIGUED BY THE *PRAYING MANTIS!* SUCH A STRANGE INSECT! IT WOULD BE CURIOUS TO FIND OUT WHAT IT THINKS ABOUT--IF ANYTHING! BUT I SUPPOSE-- *EHH??*

②

TO JOHN ADAIR'S *AMAZEMENT*, A *PERFECTLY CLEAR IMAGE* FLASHES UPON HIS SCREEN...

IT'S THE IMAGE OF A *HUGE PRAYING MANTIS*--SEVERAL TIMES BIGGER THAN I'VE EVER SEEN! AND--GREAT STARS! I'M GETTING SOME KIND OF *TELEPATHIC MESSAGE FROM IT!*

FELLOW PRAYING MANTISES, AT LONG LAST VICTORY IS OURS! FOR THOUSANDS OF CENTURIES WE PREPARED AND PLANNED FOR THIS GREAT DAY OF TRIUMPH...

...AND NOW THAT WE PRAYING MANTISES HAVE WRESTED CONTROL OF THE EARTH FROM THE HUMANS, IT IS *WE* WHO DICTATE THE LAWS, AND THE *HUMANS* WHO MUST OBEY!

BUT LET ME REVIEW THE EVENTS OF THE PAST MOMENTOUS MONTHS SO THAT WE MAY BETTER APPRECIATE THE STEPS NECESSARY NOW TO *AVERT DANGER!* OUR UPRISING AGAINST THE HUMANS BEGAN WHEN IN OUR SECRET ENCAMP-MENT...

"WE HAD EVERYTHING READY--PLANES, PILOTS, NUCLEAR WEAPONS--SUPERIOR IN EVERY WAY TO THE HUMANS..."

"...WE HAD GROWN LARGE ENOUGH THROUGH OUR USE OF SPECIAL FOODS AND STRONG ENOUGH TO MAKE THE ATTEMPT..."

WE HAVE ATTAINED OUR FULL GROWTH! OUR MENTAL FACULTIES ARE AT THEIR PEAK TOO! THE TIME TO STRIKE IS NOW--BEFORE THE HUMANS DIS-COVER WE ARE PLOT-TING AGAINST THEM!

DIRECT HIT! WE'VE BLOWN UP THAT ATOMIC INSTALLATION OF THE HUMANS!

WE'RE WINNING ON ALL FRONTS!

③

"OUR COMMANDO-FORCES, IN SPECIAL, PROTECTIVE SUITS, SWARMED INTO THE CITIES WHERE THEY SWEPT ASIDE ALL RESISTANCE..."

OUR WEAPONS HAVE NO EFFECT ON THE MANTISES!

FORWARD! OUR SCHEDULE CALLS FOR US TO BE IN CONTROL OF THE CITY'S COMMUNICATION CENTERS BEFORE SUNDOWN!

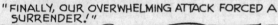

"FINALLY, OUR OVERWHELMING ATTACK FORCED A SURRENDER!"

... AND RELUCTANTLY, I CALL UPON OUR FORCES EVERYWHERE TO CEASE FIGHTING! WE CANNOT WITHSTAND THE SUPER-SCIENTIFIC WEAPONS OF THE MANTISES... WE ARE HELPLESS!

"WITHIN TWO WEEKS AFTER THE SURRENDER, WE HAD ORGANIZED THE SOCIETY TO SUIT OUR AIMS..."

HUMANS MAKE SUCH EFFICIENT, OBEDIENT SERVANTS, MY DEAR!

"WE USED THE HUMANS IN CERTAIN SPORTS, TOO! HUMAN-RACING HAS BECOME VERY POPULAR, FOR INSTANCE..."

FASTER! FASTER!

COME ON, NUMBER SEVEN!

4

"AND SO WE HAD EVERYTHING UNDER CONTROL, OR SO WE THOUGHT..."

BUT I MUST INFORM YOU, FELLOW MEMBERS OF THE *MANTIS SUPREME COUNCIL*, THAT LATELY WE HAVE FOUND EVIDENCE OF A *RESISTANCE GROUP* AMONG THE HUMANS -- A NEST OF TROUBLE MAKERS --

-- WHOSE AIM IS TO OVERTHROW *US* AND RESTORE THE HUMAN RACE TO POWER! WE MUST TAKE STEPS AT ONCE TO CRUSH THIS REBEL CONSPIRACY! I WILL ASK FOR THE LATEST DETAILS -- *EH?* MY TELECOM ISN'T WORKING -- THAT'S ODD --

THE NEXT MOMENT...

HUMANS--ATTACKING US HERE!

DON'T BOTHER WITH THAT TELECOM -- YOUR POWER HAS BEEN CUT OFF! YOUR HEADQUARTERS IS ISOLATED AND SURROUNDED!

WE ARE VULNERABLE WITHOUT OUR SPECIAL PROTECTIVE SUITS ON! OUR ONLY CHANCE IS TO RAY-BLAST THESE HUMANS --

ONCE WE'VE CAPTURED AND IMPRISONED THESE LEADERS, THE OTHERS WILL SURRENDER...

BUT THEN...

LOOK OUT! THAT ONE'S GOT A SHOOTER!

GOT HIM!

IT'S THEIR SUPREME LEADER!

BLAM!

⑤

HMM! IT'S... DEAD!

THE IMAGE ON THE SCREEN... DISAPPEARED SIMULTANEOUSLY WITH THE DEATH OF THE PRAYING MANTIS LEADER!

AS SCIENTIST JOHN ADAIR TURNS BACK TO THE INSECT HE HAS BEEN TESTING...

GOOD GOSH! TH-- THIS MANTIS IS DEAD--TOO! IT--IT'S ALMOST AS IF *IT* WERE SHOT BY THAT BULLET I SAW ON THE SCREEN!

LATER, AS THE SCIENTIST GUESSES WHAT HAPPENED...

WHAT I SAW ON THE SCREEN WAS EITHER MY WILD IMAGININGS--OR A MANTIS'S *VISION OF THE FUTURE!*

I'VE REPEATED THE EXPERIMENT WITH OTHER PRAYING MANTISES --WITH NO RESULT AT ALL! ARE THESE INSECTS REALLY PLOTTING TO GAIN MASTERY OF THE HUMAN RACE? THERE'S NO INDICATION OF THAT YET... THEY'RE STILL SO SMALL...

BUT LET'S KEEP ON THE ALERT! IF AND WHEN THEY START IN- CREASING IN SIZE, IT'LL BE TIME ENOUGH TO DESTROY THEM ALL!

The End

6

THE COLORLESS WORLD of PETER BRANDT!

FOR TWENTY YEARS PETER BRANDT HAD LIVED ON EARTH--WITHOUT KNOWING WHAT HIS WORLD REALLY LOOKED LIKE! HE WAS AFFLICTED WITH A STRANGE CASE OF COLOR BLINDNESS-- A DISABILITY OF NO EARTHLY USE--UNTIL BRANDT UNEXPECTEDLY FOUND A STRANGE USE FOR IT ON ANOTHER PLANET!

IF I'M RIGHT, THIS COLOR BLUE SHOULD MAKE ME *INVISIBLE* TO THESE INVADERS! BUT IF I'M WRONG--I'LL PAY FOR IT--WITH MY LIFE!

I'M PETER BRANDT, A STUDENT HERE AT BELAIR COLLEGE! AND WHILE THE OTHER FELLOWS WATCH THAT *COLOR* TELEVISION SHOW...

...THIS IS HOW *I* SEE THE SAME SCENE!

THE REASON IS THAT I'M *COLOR-BLIND!* SCIENTISTS CALL MY AFFLICTION *MONO-CHROMATISM*--A CONDITION IN WHICH ALL OBJECTS APPEAR TO BE OF THE SAME COLOR--VARIOUS SHADES OF GRAY!

I WAS BORN THIS WAY...I'VE BEEN TOLD THOSE FLOWERS ARE BEAUTIFULLY COLORED--BUT TO ME THEY'RE ALL COLORED ALIKE!

I ALWAYS FELT PRETTY BAD ABOUT MY AFFLICTION...UNTIL I EXPERIENCED THE STRANGEST ADVENTURE ANY EARTHMAN--BUT I'D BETTER START AT THE BEGINNING...SO YOU'LL UNDERSTAND--

"ONE NIGHT I WAS ALONE IN MY ROOM, STUDYING. MY FRIENDS HAD GONE TO A TECHNICOLOR MOVIE THAT I DIDN'T FEEL LIKE SEEING...WHEN SUDDENLY..."

KKKKKKK

WHAT'S THAT NOISE BEHIND ME?

"AS I WHIRLED AROUND..."

DO NOT FEAR, PETER BRANDT! WE WILL NOT HARM YOU!

WE NEED YOUR HELP, EARTHMAN! I AM *DVANO* AND THIS IS *DRORT!* WE ARE FROM THE STAR *POLARIS*...

"THE CREATURES EXPLAINED THAT THEY HAD ARRIVED ON EARTH BY *TELEPORTATION*--INSTANTANEOUS TRAVEL..."

RECENTLY OUR PLANET WAS INVADED FROM OUTER-SPACE! WE CANNOT FIGHT OUR ENEMIES--BECAUSE WE CANNOT *SEE* THEM!

THEY ARE INVISIBLE?! B-BUT HOW CAN I HELP YOU?

2

"ONE OF THE CREATURES EXPLAINED, SWIFTLY..."

OUR COLOR SPECTRUM, LIKE YOURS HERE ON EARTH, IS MADE UP OF SEVEN PRIMARY COLORS! BUT OUR SCIENTISTS HAVE DETECTED EVIDENCES OF AN *EIGHTH* PRIMARY COLOR IN NATURE--*COLOR-X!* IT IS OUR BELIEF THAT OUR FOES...

...HAVE MADE THEMSELVES INVISIBLE BY WEARING SUITS OF *COLOR-X* WHICH WE *CANNOT SEE!* OUR SCIENTISTS BELIEVE THAT IN EARLIEST INFANCY EVERYONE CAN SEE *COLOR-X,* BUT THAT IN TIME THIS ABILITY DISAPPEARS, DUE TO THE EFFECT OF THE SEVEN ORDINARY COLORS ON THE RODS AND CONES OF OUR EYES!

BUT *YOUR EYES,* PETER BRANDT, STILL RETAIN THE CRYSTAL PURITY OF INFANCY! YOU HAVE BEEN ALL YOUR LIFE *COMPLETELY* COLOR-BLIND! THEREFORE WE BELIEVE THAT *YOU* MAY BE ABLE TO *SEE* OUR FOES!

WILL YOU COME TO POLARIS AND HELP US SAVE OUR CIVILIZATION? YOU ARE OUR ONLY HOPE!

I NEVER THOUGHT MY EYES COULD BE OF HELP TO ANYONE!

YES, I'LL GO!

"IT WAS AN IMPULSE THAT MADE ME ANSWER! I DIDN'T BOTHER TO TRY TO THINK WHETHER I WAS DOING RIGHT OR WRONG! THE NEXT MOMENT..."

IT--IT'S AS IF MY BODY IS DRIFTING APART, CHANGING... YET SOMEHOW REMAINING *ME*--CAN'T SEE ANYTHING... NUMB ALL OVER...

"THEN SUDDENLY, WE WERE ON *POLARIS!*"

ARE YOU ALL RIGHT, PETER BRANDT?

I...I GUESS SO! BUT IT'S ALL SO INCREDIBLE-- BILLIONS OF MILES IN AN INSTANT!

③

"MY GUIDES WASTED NO TIME..."

THERE IS OUR CAPITAL CITY! WITHIN IT OUR INVISIBLE ENEMIES GO ABOUT PREPARING THEIR DEADLY WORK! WE HAVE DETECTED SIGNS OF THEM AND WE KNOW THEY ARE FROM ANOTHER PLANET, OUT TO CONQUER US!

WE BELIEVE THE ONES WHO ARE HERE NOW ARE FROM A SINGLE SHIP--AN ADVANCE PARTY TO PREPARE THE WAY FOR THE REAL INVASION! BUT IF THEY CAN BE APPREHENDED AND CAUGHT, IT WILL BE A DEATHBLOW TO THEIR PLANS!

YOU HOPE THAT WITH MY EYES I'LL BE ABLE TO FIND THESE INVADERS FOR YOU! BUT SURELY--YOU MUST HAVE SOME KIND OF RADAR! WOULDN'T THAT REVEAL THEM TO YOU?

WE TRIED THAT...

BUT THE INVADERS HAVE A FORM OF ANTI-RADAR THAT PREVENTS US FROM DETECTING THEM!

WAIT A MOMENT, DVAND! THAT'S ODD--

THAT STRANGE-LOOKING CREATURE--HE WALKED RIGHT INTO THAT BUILDING!

EH? I SEE NO ONE--!

THERE HE GOES--OHH! HE ALMOST GOT HIT BY THAT VEHICLE!

ARE YOU SURE? WE SEE NO ONE NEAR THAT CAR--!

"IT WAS THEN THAT I REALIZED THE TRUTH..."

YOU CAN'T SEE HIM!? THEN HE MUST BE ONE OF THE *INVADERS*-- INVISIBLE TO YOU! I-I'LL FOLLOW HIM!

YES! FIND OUT WHERE THEIR SPACESHIP IS!

"SOON AFTER, AT THE EDGE OF AN EMBANKMENT..."

THERE'S THE SPACESHIP-- AND A WEIRD-LOOKING CANNON POINTED AT THE CITY!

"I MEMORIZED EVERY DETAIL OF WHAT I SAW, AND LATER REPORTED TO MY FRIENDS... "

SO NOW WE KNOW WHERE THEIR INVISIBLE SPACECRAFT IS! BUT ACCORDING TO YOUR DESCRIPTION, THEIR CANNON IS MIGHTIER THAN ANY WEAPON WE POSSESS! IT MUST BE A DISINTERGRATOR MACHINE!

IT COULD ANNIHILATE OUR CITY WITH THE FIRST SHOT!

THEN I WILL SPIKE THAT CANNON FOR YOU, DVAND! LISTEN...WHAT WAS THE COLOR OF THE WALL THAT CREATURE BUMPED INTO-- AND THE CAR THAT ALMOST HIT HIM?

"SURPRISED, MY FRIENDS TOLD ME THE ANSWER--*BLUE*! THEN I HAD MYSELF PAINTED THE IDENTICAL COLOR, FROM HEAD TO FOOT!"

YOU ARE RISKING YOUR LIFE, PETER BRANDT! IF YOUR SCHEME DOES NOT WORK--!

IT MUST WORK!

"SHORTLY, AT THE SITE OF THE CANNON, AGAIN... "

IF I'M RIGHT, THESE CREATURES WHO CAN SEE *COLOR X*--CANNOT SEE BLUE!* I OUGHT TO BE *INVISIBLE* TO-- EH? FIRING AT ME! THEY *SEE* ME!

*EDITOR'S NOTE: BLUE-BLINDNESS IS SCIENTIFI-CALLY KNOWN AS *TRITANOPIA*!

⑤

"LUCKILY I MANAGED TO FLEE BACK TO THE CITY! BY THAT TIME I FIGURED OUT WHAT HAD HAPPENED..."

THEY SEE MY *EYES!* MY EYES ARE *BROWN*--MY CORNEA *WHITE!* I FORGOT ABOUT THAT!

"EQUIPPED WITH A PAIR OF BLUE GLASSES, I TRIED AGAIN, AND THIS TIME..."

IT'S WORKING! THEY CAN'T SEE THE COLOR *BLUE!* I'M AS INVISIBLE TO THE INVADERS AS THEY ARE INVISIBLE TO THE PEOPLE OF *POLARIS!*

"SWIFTLY I STOWED INSIDE THE CANNON A SMALL, POWERFUL EXPLOSIVE GIVEN ME BY DVAND! AND A MOMENT OR TWO LATER..."

UHH?!

THERE IT GOES! THE DISINTEGRATOR IS DESTROYED!

WRRRMM...

"AFTER THE DESTRUCTION OF THEIR POWERFUL WEAPON, PANIC SEIZED THE INVISIBLE INVADERS..."

THEY MUST HAVE *INVISIBLE CREATURES* AMONG US! WE CAN NEVER CONQUER THEM!

FLEE--BACK TO OUR HOME PLANET!

"SOON..."

THEY'RE GONE, DVAND! AND THEY WON'T BE BACK...

YOU HAVE SAVED OUR WORLD, PETER BRANDT! HOW CAN WE REPAY YOU FOR WHAT YOU HAVE DONE?

"THEY OFFERED ME RICHES BUT I REFUSED! FINALLY, THEY LET ME COME HOME WITHOUT A REWARD, BUT BEFORE I LEFT DVAND TOLD ME..."

...THAT THEIR SCIENTISTS ARE WORKING ON A WAY TO RESTORE COLOR TO COLOR-BLIND EYES LIKE MINE! SO PERHAPS ONE OF THESE DAYS, I TOO MAY SEE THAT *TV* PROGRAM AND THE FLOWERS AND SKY *IN COLOR* LIKE YOU!

THE END

6

The RiDDLE of SPACEMAN X!

WHAT WILL BE THE FINAL STAGE OF HUMAN EVOLUTION? WHAT FUTURE PHYSICAL FORM WILL WE ULTIMATELY HAVE, AGES HENCE? IF YOU CAN GUESS THE AMAZING ANSWER TO THAT, THEN YOU WILL KNOW WHAT TO EXPECT WHEN A VISITOR FROM SPACE APPEARS BEFORE WONDERING EARTHLY EYES!

EVERYONE ON EARTH HAS BEEN GUESSING WHAT SPACEMAN X WILL LOOK LIKE WHEN HE FINALLY EMERGES FROM HIS SHIP! BUT ONLY *I* HAVE DEDUCED THE AMAZING TRUTH!

ONE EVENING, AS TWO MEN CARRY OUT *ESP** EXPERIMENTS...

JOHN, CLEAR YOUR MIND OF ALL OTHER THOUGHTS --AND I'LL TELEPATHIZE A SHORT MESSAGE...

*EDITOR'S NOTE: ESP IS EXTRA-SENSORY PERCEPTION.... THE TRANSMISSION OF THOUGHTS BETWEEN HUMAN MINDS!

A MOMENT LATER, JOHN JACKSON IS AMAZED AS HE WRITES DOWN THE MENTAL WAVES HE RECEIVES...

I'M GETTING MY PARTNER'S THOUGHTS CLEAR ENOUGH...BUT WHAT MADE HIM TRANSMIT SUCH A STRANGE MESSAGE?

Attention! I found your mind free... my spaceship will make a forced landing near you! Please meet me

WHAT'S THIS? I DIDN'T SEND ANYTHING LIKE THAT AT ALL! ARE YOU PLAYING A JOKE, JOHN?

NO...I CLEARLY "HEARD" THOSE TELEPATHIC WORDS! B-BUT IF YOU DIDN'T SEND THEM-- QUICK! LET'S LOOK OUTSIDE!

IN THE NEARBY PARK...

THE SPACE-SHIP--LAND-ING! NOW I HEAR MORE TELEPATHIC WORDS...

"...TROUBLE WITH MY CONTROLS... FORCING ME TO LAND ON THIS NEAREST PLANET! I WILL MAKE REPAIRS AND LEAVE IN A WEEK OF YOUR TIME!"

ANXIOUSLY, THE EARTHMEN WAIT FOR THE SPACEMAN TO EMERGE FROM HIS SHIP...

I CANNOT SHOW MYSELF YET! IT WILL TAKE ME A WEEK TO EQUALIZE THE PRESSURE WITHIN MY SHIP TO YOUR AIR PRESSURE, AVOIDING DECOMPRESSION SYMPTOMS!

HE MEANS THE "BENDS"!

ARE YOU HUMAN, LIKE US? CAN YOU DESCRIBE YOURSELF?

ALL I CAN TELL YOU NOW IS THAT I AM THE PROD-UCT OF FINAL EVOLUTION...IF YOU CAN PICTURE THAT!

I WILL BEGIN MY REPAIRS NOW!

HMM...WHAT COULD "FINAL EVOLUTION" MEAN? HE'LL JUST BE "SPACEMAN X" TO US AS WE WAIT A WEEK WONDERING WHAT HE REALLY LOOKS LIKE!

BANG CLANG BANG

THE NEXT MORNING, CURIOUS SCIENTISTS GATHER OUTSIDE THE SPACE VISITOR'S SHIP AND...

IS HE GIGANTIC? TINY? HUMAN?

WE HAVEN'T THE SLIGHTEST CLUE!

BAM BANG BANG

2

UNEXPECTEDLY, A CLUE COMES WHEN "*SPACEMAN X*" MAKES A TELEPATHIC REQUEST...

I AM IN NEED OF CERTAIN MATERIALS! FIRST FOR MY REPAIRS, BRING ME SIX OF WHAT YOU CALL "PLIERS"!

WHY WOULD HE ASK FOR SIX OF THE *SAME* TOOL?

"PERHAPS HE IS A STRANGE CREATURE WHO CAN WORK WITH ALL SIX '*HANDS*'"...

BUT AS THE UNKNOWN VISITOR REQUESTS MORE MATERIALS...

I'M A REPORTER, SIR! ARE THOSE THREE LARGE LENSES YOU'RE MAKING ANY CLUE TO WHAT THE ALIEN IS?

YES, I THINK HE BROKE HIS SPECTACLES DURING THE LANDING, SO THAT WOULD MAKE HIM...

"...A GIANT WITH THREE EYES!"

QUITE THE OPPOSITE IS THE OPINION OF A BRUSH MAKER...

I BELIEVE THIS TINY BRUSH I MADE FOR THE ALIEN INDICATES HE IS SOME SMALL FURRY CREATURE... LIKE A RODENT!

"I RUN A GAS STATION, SEE? NOW WHO ELSE WOULD ASK FOR *OIL* BUT A *ROBOT*!"

③

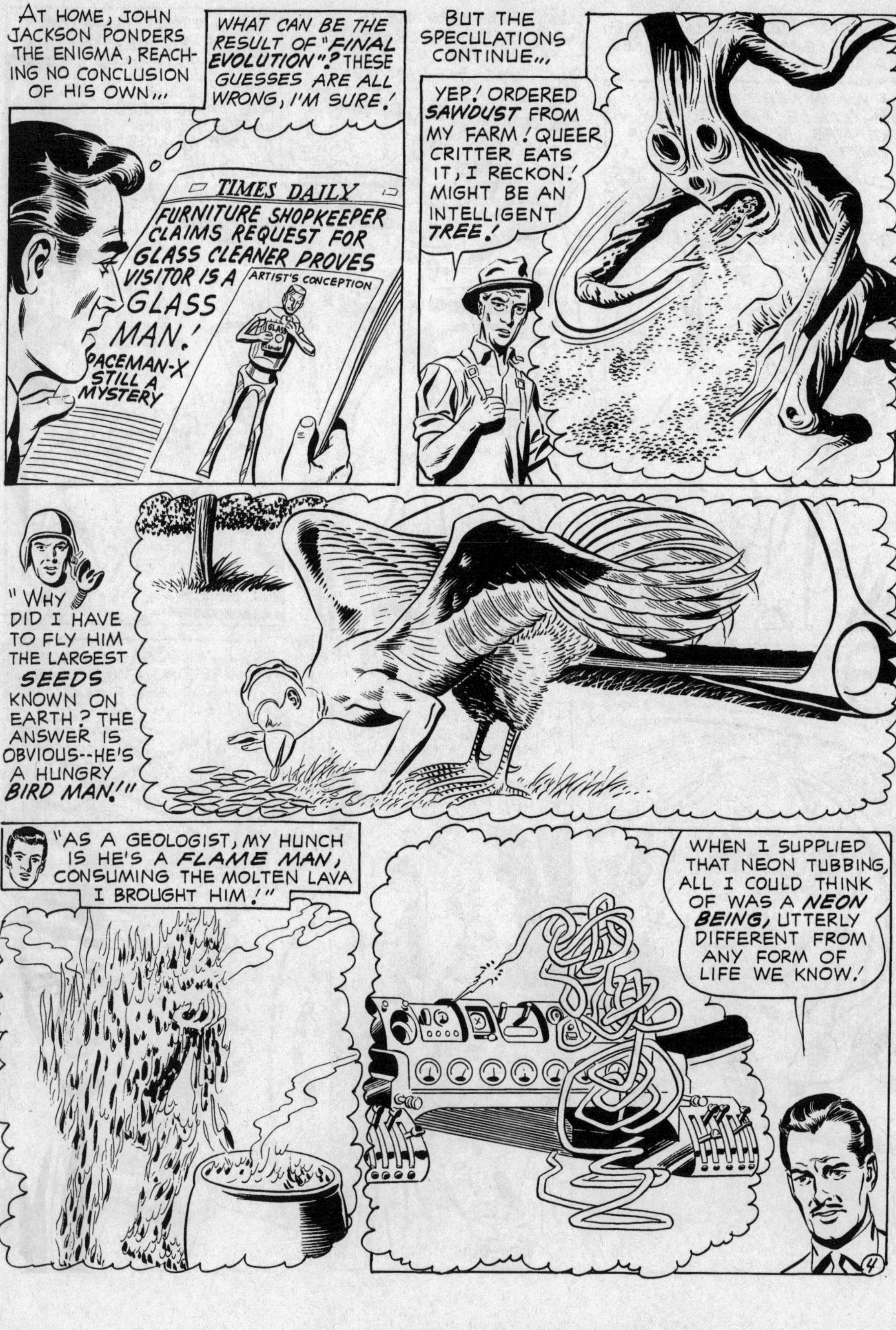
AT HOME, JOHN JACKSON PONDERS THE ENIGMA, REACHING NO CONCLUSION OF HIS OWN...
WHAT CAN BE THE RESULT OF "FINAL EVOLUTION"? THESE GUESSES ARE ALL WRONG, I'M SURE!
TIMES DAILY
FURNITURE SHOPKEEPER CLAIMS REQUEST FOR GLASS CLEANER PROVES VISITOR IS A GLASS MAN!
ARTIST'S CONCEPTION
PACEMAN-X STILL A MYSTERY
BUT THE SPECULATIONS CONTINUE...
YEP! ORDERED SAWDUST FROM MY FARM! QUEER CRITTER EATS IT, I RECKON! MIGHT BE AN INTELLIGENT TREE!
"WHY DID I HAVE TO FLY HIM THE LARGEST SEEDS KNOWN ON EARTH? THE ANSWER IS OBVIOUS--HE'S A HUNGRY BIRD MAN!"
"AS A GEOLOGIST, MY HUNCH IS HE'S A FLAME MAN, CONSUMING THE MOLTEN LAVA I BROUGHT HIM!"
WHEN I SUPPLIED THAT NEON TUBBING, ALL I COULD THINK OF WAS A NEON BEING, UTTERLY DIFFERENT FROM ANY FORM OF LIFE WE KNOW!
4

REQUESTS FOR LODESTONE, LEAD OXIDE, AND PLUTONIUM *STIMULATE* MORE OUT-OF-THIS-WORLD *CONCEPTIONS!*

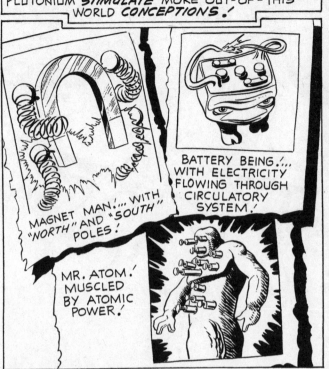

MAGNET MAN!... WITH "NORTH" AND "SOUTH" POLES!

BATTERY BEING!... WITH ELECTRICITY FLOWING THROUGH CIRCULATORY SYSTEM!

MR. ATOM! MUSCLED BY ATOMIC POWER!

ONE CONCEPTION OF *SPACEMAN X* INTRIGUES JOHN JACKSON...

HMM... COULD THAT BE THE END RESULT OF EVOLUTION? OR IS THERE A STEP EVEN *BEYOND* THAT?

FAMOUS BIOLOGIST, FURNISHING NUTRIENT CULTURE SOLUTION, PREDICTS **"SUPER BRAIN"**

...ENTISTS ...ELED

SPACEMAN X STILL A MYSTERY

AT LAST, AFTER A WEEK, THE THRILLING MOMENT ARRIVES FOR THE WAITING WORLD, WHEN...

THANKS FOR THE MATERIALS, ALL OF WHICH I REDUCED TO BASIC ATOMS, FINISHING MY REPAIRS! ALSO MY DECOMPRESSION ADJUSTMENT IS DONE! I AM COMING OUT NOW!

WERE ANY OF OUR GUESSES RIGHT?

KTV 6

BY THIS TIME, JOHN JACKSON HAS FORMED HIS OWN CONCLUSION...

I'VE FINALLY DEDUCED WHAT *"FINAL EVOLUTION"* MEANS! AND WHAT KIND OF CREATURE WILL EMERGE!

HAVE *YOU* FORMED A MENTAL IMAGE OF *SPACEMAN X?* I'LL GIVE YOU A HINT -- WHATEVER YOU GUESSED WILL BE *CORRECT* -- PROVIDING YOU COULD PERSONALLY WITNESS WHAT HAPPEN NEXT!

5

AS THE ALIEN STEPS INTO VIEW...

LOOK!...IT'S MY *GIANT!*

YOU'RE SEEING THINGS! IT'S MY *MAGNET MAN!*

NO! IT'S MY *BIRD MAN!*

THE BATTERY BEING!

MR. ATOM!

THE TALKING TREE!

WHY DOES EACH ONE SEE "SPACEMAN X" AS HE IMAGINED HIM TO BE? THE ANSWER IS *FINAL EVOLUTION*--WHEREBY EVOLUTION WILL FINALLY ELIMINATE THE PHYSICAL BODY *ENTIRELY!* THE SPACE VISITOR IS ACTUALLY ONLY A MASS OF *INTELLIGENT ENERGY!*

BY THE SHEER POWER OF MIND-OVER-MATTER, EACH PERSON MOMENTARILY *MOLDS* THE *ENERGY BEING* INTO THE FORM HE VISIONS! THAT'S WHY THEY SAW ALL THE FORMS FOR A BRIEF MOMENT!

IT'S MY *TREE-MAN!*

WHAT WAS YOUR ORIGINAL PHYSICAL FORM?

THIS...HUMAN, LIKE YOURS! AND NOW, EARTHLINGS --THANKS FOR YOUR HELP--AND FAREWELL!

The End ⑥

WHEN ROY DENTON DISCOVERED AN AMAZING CIVILIZATION EXISTING MILES BELOW THE EARTH, IT WAS ONLY THE FIRST OF A SERIES OF SURPRISES TO COME! FOR NOT ONLY WAS THE UNDERGROUND CITY AN EXACT TWIN OF A SURFACE-WORLD METROPOLIS, BUT THE INHABITANTS SPOKE OUR LANGUAGE AND HAD PARALLELED OUR SCIENTIFIC PROGRESS TO THE LAST DETAIL!

THIEVES OF THOUGHT!

STRANGE! I HAVEN'T SEEN A SINGLE *HUMAN BEING* IN THIS CITY! WHERE DID THE *ROBOTS* COME FROM? SOMEONE MUST HAVE ORIGINALLY BUILT THEM!

AJAX TRUCKING

BUS STOP

I'M ROY DENTON, A *SPELEOLOGIST!* * AND IT WAS WHILE WORKING IN MY SPECIALIZED FIELD THAT I MADE THE MOST STARTLING DISCOVERY OF MY LIFE-- THAT WE HUMANS WERE NEARLY CONQUERED... BY *OURSELVES!* MY STRANGE ADVENTURE BEGAN...

*EDITOR'S NOTE: A *SPELEOLOGIST* IS ONE WHO EXPLORES CAVES AND REGIONS BENEATH THE EARTH'S SURFACE.

"...WHEN I WAS EXPLORING *MYSTIC CAVE* AND STUMBLED UPON AN UNKNOWN PASSAGE..."

IT GOES DOWN DEEPER THAN ANY OTHER CAVE ON EARTH!

"MILES DOWN, A GIGANTIC CAVERN REVEALED AN UTTERLY FANTASTIC SIGHT!"

A SUBTERRANEAN METROPOLIS, RESEMBLING THOSE ON THE SURFACE WORLD! WH-WHAT KIND OF PEOPLE LIVE HERE?

WHY DON'T YOU OIL YOURSELF, X-88? YOU SQUEAK!

INTELLIGENT ROBOTS, TALKING OUR LANGUAGE! I'D BETTER NOT REVEAL MYSELF, IN CASE THEY'RE UNFRIENDLY!

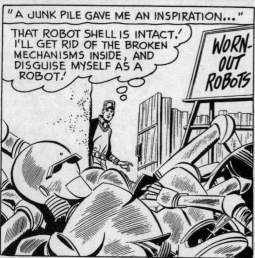

"A JUNK PILE GAVE ME AN INSPIRATION..."

THAT ROBOT SHELL IS INTACT! I'LL GET RID OF THE BROKEN MECHANISMS INSIDE, AND DISGUISE MYSELF AS A ROBOT!

WORN-OUT ROBOTS

"SOON, ENCASED IN THE HOLLOW METAL SUIT, I WENT SIGHT-SEEING..."

STRANGE... I HAVEN'T SEEN A SINGLE HUMAN IN THE CITY! WHERE DID THE ROBOTS COME FROM? SOMEBODY MUST HAVE ORIGINALLY *BUILT* THEM!

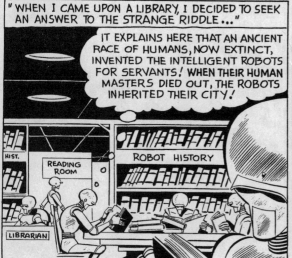

"WHEN I CAME UPON A LIBRARY, I DECIDED TO SEEK AN ANSWER TO THE STRANGE RIDDLE..."

IT EXPLAINS HERE THAT AN ANCIENT RACE OF HUMANS, NOW EXTINCT, INVENTED THE INTELLIGENT ROBOTS FOR SERVANTS! WHEN THEIR HUMAN MASTERS DIED OUT, THE ROBOTS INHERITED THEIR CITY!

HIST.

READING ROOM

ROBOT HISTORY

LIBRARIAN

THE HUMANS ORIGINALLY CONTROLLED THE ROBOTS WITH TELEPATHIC COMMANDS FROM THIS *MENTAL MACHINE*, LOCATED IN THE CENTER OF THE CITY!

THE "BRAIN" OF THE *MENTAL MACHINE* WAS A RARE PIECE OF METAL CALLED *TELEPATHIUM*-- WHICH COULD AMPLIFY THOUGHT-WAVES AND TRANSMIT THEM OVER LONG DISTANCES!

ROBOT HISTORY

" BUT ANOTHER MYSTERY AROSE AS I OBSERVED MORE OF THE ROBOT CIVILIZATION... "

HOW COME THEY USE *OUR* LANGUAGE? AND THEIR CARS!... THEY'RE ALL MODELS OF OUR 1957 MAKES, DOWN TO THE LAST DETAIL!

"EVERYWHERE, EVERYTHING ELSE PROVED A STARTLING REPLICA OF HUMAN INVENTIONS OF UPPER EARTH !"

THEIR DIAL TELEPHONES ARE THE SAME!

I HAVE THAT IDENTICAL *TV* SET HOME!

SALE

THAT'S A POPULAR BRAND OF VACUUM IN MY WORLD TOO!

"BEWILDERED, I WANDERED TO THE CENTER OF TOWN WHERE..."

THAT ANCIENT *MENTAL MACHINE* STILL EXISTS! GOOD GOSH-- NOW I THINK I KNOW THE ANSWER TO THE FANTASTIC RIDDLE OF HOW TWO SEPARATE CIVILIZATIONS CAN HAVE THE *SAME* INVENTIONS!

MENTAL MACHINE

WE'VE CONTACTED THE MIND OF PROFESSOR JASON, UPPER WORLD SCIENTIST... INVENTOR OF NEW SUPER-WEAPON... NUCLEAR HEAT-RAY...

THE ROBOTS FOUND A NEW USE FOR THE *MENTAL MACHINE*...TO BROADCAST THOUGHT-WAVES TO THE SURFACE WORLD!

③

"ALL EVIDENCE POINTED TO MY THEORY BEING CORRECT..."

THEY "INSPIRED" PROFESSOR JASON TO "INVENT" THAT NUCLEAR HEAT-RAY! THESE SUPER-INTELLIGENT ROBOTS, ALL THROUGH OUR HISTORY, HAVE BEEN *TRANSMITTING* GREAT DISCOVERIES INTO THE MINDS OF THE HUMAN RACE!

← 18TH CENTURY MICROSCOPE

TELEGRAPH KEY

ORIGINAL TALKING PHONOGRAPH

"OVERWHELMED AT THE STUNNING REVELATION, I KNEW IT WAS SAFE TO REVEAL MYSELF..."

THEY'RE NOT UNFRIENDLY! ON THE CONTRARY, THESE ROBOT GENIUSES HAVE BEEN OUR *BENEFACTORS* FOR CENTURIES! THEY INVENT THINGS *FIRST*, THEN MENTALLY SEND THEM ALONG TO US!

BUT NOW THAT THEIR EXISTENCE HAS BEEN REVEALED, WE MUST ACKNOWLEDGE THE CONTRIBUTIONS --

A *HUMAN SPY!* SEIZE HIM!

BUT... BUT I DON'T UNDERSTAND! YOU ARE OUR FRIENDS! YOU JUST TRANSMITTED A NEW INVENTION, VIA TELEPATHY, TO PROFESSOR JASON!

WHERE DID YOU GET THAT FOOLISH NOTION? THE *MENTAL MACHINE* WORKS *BOTH* WAYS! WE WERE *RECEIVING* PROFESSOR JASON'S THOUGHTS!

RECEIVING? THEN I HAD IT ALL WRONG! YOU ROBOTS HAVE BEEN *STEALING* HUMAN INVENTIONS AND DUPLICATING THEM HERE!

TELEPATHY RECEPTION

TELEPATHY TRANSMISSION

4

"NOW I UNDERSTOOD WHY THEIR CIVILIZATION WAS A COPY OF OURS!"

YOU'VE BEEN *IMITATING* US, PICKING THE BRAINS OF OUR HUMAN GENIUSES! BUT WHY ARE YOU SO INTERESTED IN PROF. JASON'S NEW INVENTION?

WE ARE PLANNING TO CONQUER UPPER EARTH WITH *YOUR* WEAPONS! WE DECIDED AGAINST ATTACKING YOU WITH YOUR OWN HYDROGEN BOMBS FOR FEAR THEY WOULD CAUSE OUR DESTRUCTION, TOO!

"HOWEVER, PROFESSOR JASON'S PRIVATE THOUGHTS REVEAL HE IS KEEPING HIS NUCLEAR HEAT-RAY *SECRET* FROM THE WORLD, FEARING IT IS TOO POWERFUL! BUT IN *OUR* POSSESSION, WE CAN FORCE YOUR WORLD INTO IMMEDIATE SURRENDER!"

"DIABOLICALLY, THEY LET ME LIVE, SO I COULD WATCH THEIR PREPARATIONS FOR THE CONQUEST OF EARTH..."

THE NUCLEAR HEAT-WAVE MACHINE IS ALMOST READY! HUMANITY WILL BE DEFEATED BY ONE OF ITS *OWN* INVENTIONS...

"BUT ALL THE WHILE MY MIND WAS FEVERISHLY DEVISING A PLAN--AND WHEN I WAS UNOBSERVED A MOMENT..."

I'VE GOT TO WORK FAST WITH THIS ACID SPRAY!

ACID

"IN THIS METAL WORLD, CORROSIVE ACID WAS A DEADLY WEAPON!"

THE POWERFUL ACID QUICKLY DISSOLVES METAL! IT'S DESTROYING THE NUCLEAR HEAT-RAY MACHINE!

ACID

"NEXT, I RAN TO THE *MENTAL MACHINE* AND..."

STAND BACK, ROBOTS--OR I'LL WIPE YOU OUT TOO! I'M MAKING SURE YOU ROBOTS NEVER AGAIN *ROB* OUR MINDS AND TRY TO TURN OUR OWN WEAPONS AGAINST US!

"FORTUNATELY, THE *TELEPATHIUM* METAL HAD BEEN ENCLOSED IN A *GLASS*-GLOBULE--AND WASN'T DESTROYED..."

I'LL TAKE THIS CAPSULE OF *TELEPATHIUM* BACK WITH ME! WE CAN PUT IT TO GOOD USE ON THE SURFACE WORLD!

"MY ACID-WEAPON ASSURED MY ESCAPE TO THE UPPER WORLD..."

NOW TO WARN THE AUTHORITIES ABOUT THE UNDERGROUND ROBOT ENEMY! THEY'LL BELIEVE ME WHEN I SHOW THEM THE *TELEPATHIUM!*

"BUT WHEN I TRIED TO DEMONSTRATE THE WONDER METAL..."

NONSENSE! IT DOESN'T AMPLIFY OUR THOUGHTS AT ALL!

I CAN'T UNDERSTAND IT-- UNLESS THERE IS SOMETHING IN OUR ATMOSPHERE-- COSMIC RAYS, FOR INSTANCE-- THAT NEUTRALIZES ITS TELEPATHIC POWERS!

"AND WHEN I TRIED TO SHOW THEM THE CAVE WHICH LED TO THE UNDERGROUND ROBOT CITY..."

WELL, WHERE'S THE CAVE, DENTON?

GOOD GOSH! THE ACID I SPRAYED ABOUT MUST HAVE WEAKENED METALLIC STONE BELOW, AND CAUSED A GIGANTIC CAVE-IN! THE ROBOTS ARE BURIED BENEATH TONS AND TONS OF EARTH!

SINCE I HAVE NO PROOF THAT THE ROBOTS EXISTED, OR THAT EARTH WAS IN DANGER, YOU MUST DECIDE FOR YOURSELF IF THE STORY I TOLD YOU IS TRUE!

THE END

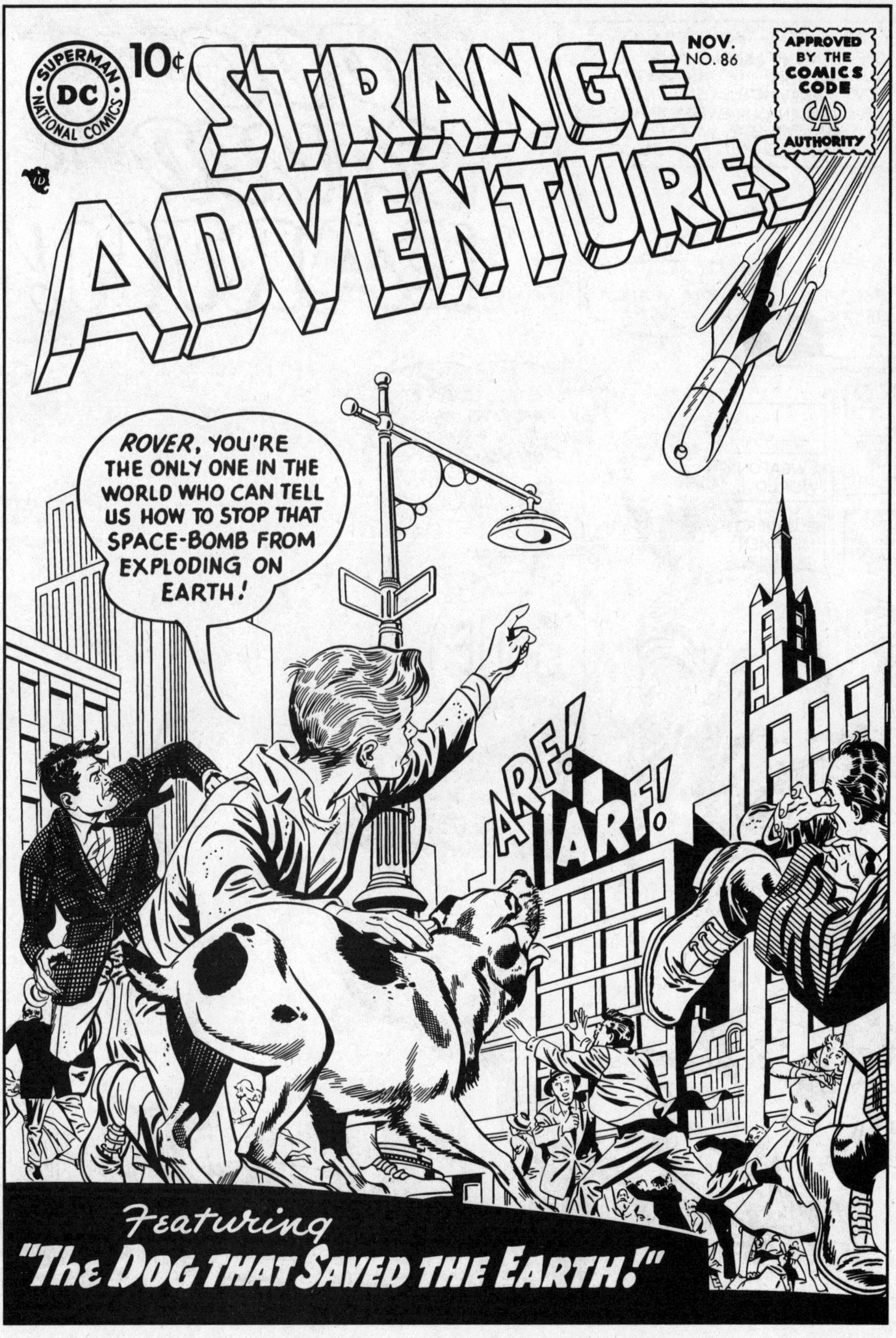
SUPERMAN DC NATIONAL COMICS
10¢
STRANGE ADVENTURES
NOV. NO. 86
APPROVED BY THE COMICS CODE AUTHORITY
ROVER, YOU'RE THE ONLY ONE IN THE WORLD WHO CAN TELL US HOW TO STOP THAT SPACE-BOMB FROM EXPLODING ON EARTH!
ARF! ARF!
Featuring
"The Dog that Saved the Earth!"

FRED PETERS BOASTED TO EVERYONE HE KNEW WHAT A CLEVER DOG HIS *ROVER* WAS -- BUT NOT EVEN FRED REALIZED HOW EXTRAORDINARILY CLEVER *ROVER* WAS UNTIL HE TURNED OUT TO BE...

The DOG that SAVED the EARTH!

R-ROVER. ARE *YOU* REALLY LIFTING THAT MAN'S HAT? B-BUT HOW--?

IT'S EASY! I DO IT BY APPLYING THE SCIENTIFIC PRINCIPLE OF *MIND-OVER-MATTER!*

SHOE STORE

AT A NATIONAL DOG SHOW... MY NAME IS FRED PETERS AND THIS IS MY DOG *ROVER!* I WANT TO ENTER HIM IN THE *"CHAMPION DOG"* CONTEST!

EH?

NATIO... DO SH...

I'M SORRY, SON! ONLY PEDIGREED DOGS CAN COMPETE IN THIS SHOW-- AND YOUR DOG IS OBVIOUSLY NOT A THOROUGHBRED....

B-BUT HE'S A *CHAMPION...*

APPLICATIONS

GOSH, *ROVER*, I KNOW I PROMISED YOU A *BLUE RIBBON* THAT PRIZE-DOGS HAVE-- B-BUT IT SEEMS YOU'RE NOT THE RIGHT KIND OF DOG TO ENTER THE CONTEST....

PLEASE DON'T LOOK SO SAD, *ROVER!* I CAN'T STAND IT WHEN YOU LOOK LIKE THAT! I'LL FIND *SOME WAY* TO GET YOU A BLUE RIBBON-- YOU'LL SEE...

NOTE TO THE READER:

ROVER SEEMS LIKE AN ORDINARY POOCH-- AND YET HIS DESTINY IS BOUND UP WITH EVENTS ON A WORLD MILLIONS OF MILES AWAY! SOUNDS INCREDIBLE? BEFORE YOU DECIDE IT IS, LET'S TAKE A LOOK...

...AT A CEREMONY GOING ON IN THE WORLD OF *KERAQ*, IN QUADRANT 18 OF THE GALAXY...

AS YOU KNOW, YOUR GOVERNMENT PUTS ASIDE A CERTAIN AMOUNT OF *ENERGY* FOR YOU EACH YEAR AS OLD-AGE INSURANCE! IN THIS WAY, WHEN YOU ARE READY TO RETIRE, YOU RECEIVE THE ENERGY TO ENJOY IN YOUR OLD AGE...

OF COURSE, THE STRENGTH OF THE *ENERGY-AWARD* DEPENDS ON THE INDIVIDUAL'S SERVICE TO THE STATE! AND TODAY WE ARE HAPPY TO ANNOUNCE THE HIGHEST AWARD IN HISTORY-- TO SCIENTIST F-809-J FOR HIS OUTSTANDING ACHIEVEMENTS!

2

WHEN I PULL THIS SWITCH IT WILL SEND THE ENERGY-PACKET OUT TO F-809-J! WITH IT HE WILL ENJOY FULL TELEPATHY, MIND-OVER-MATTER, AND EVERY OTHER BLESSING OUR SCIENCE CAN BESTOW! I NOW PULL THE SWITCH--

BUT AT THAT MOMENT IN THE HOME OF THE GREAT SCIENTIST F-809-J...

STRANGE... I DON'T FEEL ANYTHING-- AND I SHOULD HAVE RECEIVED THE ENERGY IMPULSE AT ONCE! SOMETHING MUST HAVE GONE WRONG--

BACK AT THE SCENE OF THE AWARD...

YOUR HONOR, EXCUSE ME, BUT THERE WAS A SLIGHT INCORRECT ADJUSTMENT ON ONE CONTROL OF THE ENERGY-DISPATCHER! IT SENT THE ENERGY MEANT FOR F-809-J OFF OUR PLANET ENTIRELY!

WHAT?

AS NEAR AS WE CAN MAKE OUT THE ENERGY-PACKET LANDED ON A TINY PLANET--CALLED EARTH-- IN QUADRANT 108--AND ENTERED-- AH--ENTERED THE BRAIN OF AN ANIMAL THERE--!

GREAT STARS!

THE ANIMAL--A CANINE-- IS NAMED *ROVER!* WE HAVE JUST SUCCEEDED IN TRACKING IT DOWN BY OUR INTERPLANETARY VIDEO-TRACKER!

WE MUST RECOVER THE ENERGY --OR THE GALACTIC ENERGY-BALANCE WILL BE UPSET!

AT THAT MOMENT, ON EARTH...

THERE'S A CAR ABOUT TO COME AROUND THE CORNER AND JUMP THE CURB! I MUST GET MY MASTER OUT OF THE WAY--!

RUILE

3

A SECOND LATER...

ROVER-- WHAT ARE YOU DOING?

UHH! THAT CAR--IT WOULD HAVE HIT ME IF ROVER HADN'T PULLED ME OVER HERE!

WHY--IT'S ALMOST AS IF YOU KNEW THAT CAR WAS ABOUT TO COME AROUND THE CORNER, ROVER!

I DID KNOW, FRED! I DON'T KNOW HOW I KNEW-- BUT I DID!

G-GOLLY! I CAN UNDERSTAND ROVER --I MEAN I CAN HEAR WHAT HE'S THINKING! I--I DON'T UNDERSTAND!

NEITHER DO I! BUT SUDDENLY I JUST SEEM TO KNOW THINGS!

AND I CAN DO THINGS TOO! FRED-- WATCH THE HAT ON THAT MAN-- I'LL RAISE IT--

W-WOW!

ROVER! DID YOU REALLY DO THAT-- LIFT UP THAT MAN'S HAT-- WITHOUT TOUCHING IT!?

SURE! IT'S CALLED MIND-OVER-MATTER! IT'S EASY--!

AT HOME, AS FRED CONTINUES HIS INVESTIGATION OF ROVER'S STRANGE ABILITIES...

I CAN DO MATHE-MATICAL PROBLEMS IN MY HEAD! GO AHEAD-- TEST ME!

WELL, HOW ABOUT 2048 TIMES 256?

OH, THAT'S A CINCH-- 524,288! ASK ME SOME-THING REAL HARD--LIKE HOW TO SOLVE EINSTEIN'S EQUATIONS! I CAN DO THAT TOO!

YOU CAN?

AT THAT VERY MOMENT, IN AN ASTRONOMICAL OBSERVATORY NEAR WASHINGTON, D.C. ...

IT'S NOT A METEOR--IT'S NOT FALLING LIKE ONE! IT HAS AN ORBIT THAT'S MAKING IT SPIRAL CLOSER AND CLOSER TO EARTH!

WE'D BETTER NOTIFY THE GOVERNMENT, PROFESSOR!

LATER, AS ARMY JETS GO UP TO INVESTIGATE THE STRANGE OBJECT SPIRALLING IN TOWARD EARTH...

...AND OUR INSTRUMENTS SHOW THAT THE MYSTERIOUS OBJECT IS CARRYING A *HELIUM BOMB!* IF IT LANDS ON EARTH, IT WILL COMPLETELY DESTROY OUR PLANET! WE MUST STOP IT-- SOMEHOW!

THERE'S NO LIFE ABOARD THE OBJECT--AND NO SIGN THAT IT IS UNDER ANY KIND OF RADIO-CONTROL! MY GUESS IS THAT IT IS A GUIDED WAR MISSILE FROM SOME OTHER STAR-SYSTEM THAT SOMEHOW GOT LOOSE AND WAS ATTRACTED BY EARTH'S GRAVITY!

AS EFFORTS TO GET CONTROL OF THE MISSILE FAIL...

NOTHING WE DO HAS ANY EFFECT ON THE OBJECT! WE'VE TRIED TO SLOW IT DOWN SO AS TO LAND IT GENTLY--BUT IT WON'T WORK--ITS SPEED IS TOO GREAT-- AND IT'S COMING CLOSER TO EARTH!

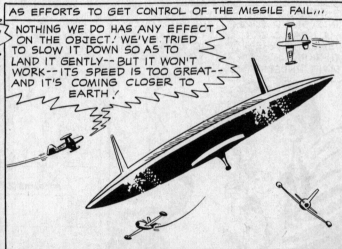

IN THE OFFICE OF THE AIR FORCE GENERAL IN CHARGE OF THE OPERATION...

A BOY AND HIS DOG TO SEE ME? IS THIS A JOKE? I HAVE NO TIME NOW FOR--

EXCUSE ME, SIR-- BUT MAYBE YOU'D BETTER SEE THEM! THIS IS NO ORDINARY DOG--!

SOON... ...AND I BROUGHT *ROVER* HERE, GENERAL, BECAUSE HE CAN SOLVE *ANY PROBLEM*-- EVEN THE ONE THAT IS MENACING EARTH!

OF ALL THE FANTASTIC--!

5

MEANWHILE, *ROVER* MENTALLY TRANSMITS HIS WORLD-SAVING SOLUTION...

THE SOLUTION IS *NOT* TO SLOW THE MISSILE DOWN--BUT *SPEED IT UP!* BY INCREASING ITS SPEED, ITS ORBIT AROUND THE EARTH WILL *WIDEN*--UNTIL IT ATTAINS *ESCAPE VELOCITY* AND LEAVES THE EARTH'S GRAVITATIONAL PULL!

AS FRED RAPIDLY REPEATS *ROVER'S* TELEPATHIC COMMUNICATION...

IT--IT REALLY SOUNDS PLAUSIBLE! WHAT DO YOU THINK, PROFESSOR?

I AGREE! LET'S TRY IT AT ONCE!

AS JET MOTORS ARE ATTACHED TO THE SLOWLY SETTLING MISSILE...

IT HAS JUST A COUPLE OF TURNS MORE BEFORE IT PLUNGES DOWN ON EARTH! IF THIS DOESN'T WORK, THERE WON'T BE TIME TO TRY ANYTHING ELSE! THERE GO THE JETS NOW...!

THEN, AS THE ENTIRE WORLD HOLDS ITS BREATH, THE MISSILE SHOOTS SPACEWARD...

WE DIRECTED IT INTO THE SUN! THE EXPLOSION THERE WILL HARDLY BE FELT AT ALL!

AND NOT LONG AFTER, ON THE WORLD OF *KERAQ*...

WE'VE SUCCEEDED IN MAKING THE TRANSFER OF THE ENERGY-PACKET FROM THE DOG *ROVER* TO SCIENTIST *F-809-J!*

GOOD! THEN THE GALACTIC ENERGY ACCOUNT IS IN BALANCE AGAIN!

WHILE ON EARTH...

GOSH! I'VE NEVER SEEN *ROVER* SO HAPPY! HIS MYSTERIOUS POWERS HAVE LEFT HIM--BUT THE GOVERNMENT AWARDED HIM THIS MEDAL FOR SAVING THE EARTH--AND NOW *ROVER* HAS WHAT HE ALWAYS WANTED--A *BLUE RIBBON!*

THE END

INTERPLANETARY SPACE-FEUD!

On a remote rural area, mountains suddenly fly through the air and whole forests are uprooted! Geysers shoot skyward and earthquakes rock the countryside! The planet Earth has become the battleground for creatures from outer space to settle their bitter feud!

MY **LEVITATION RAY** WILL LIFT THAT WHOLE MOUNTAIN!

GOT TO JUMP OFF HERE BEFORE I GO SKYWARD WITH THE MOUNTAIN!

In a backwoods community, a native son returns from college to aid the farming folk with a soil-testing kit...

YOUR SOIL IS ACIDIC OR "SOUR", CAL! ADD LIME TO NEUTRALIZE THE ACIDS AND YOU'LL GROW BETTER CROPS!

IF THET'S WHUT YUH L'ARNED IN COLLEGE, RHETT SHAW, I'LL TRY IT!

Then, returning to his lab in the village, Rhett ignores a scorning challenge from one of the hill people...

YUH WON'T FIGHT, HEY? I ALLUS KNEW YOU SHAWS WUZ COWARDS!

I'M NOT LOOKING FOR A FIGHT, WHIT CARTER! CAN'T YOU FORGET THAT SILLY OLD FEUD BETWEEN OUR FAMILIES?

LATER, AS RHETT DRIVES HOME....

HEY--MY CAR STOPPED DEAD, AS THOUGH IT STRUCK AN *INVISIBLE WALL!*

ASTONISHINGLY....

GOOD GOSH! THERE SEEMS TO BE A GIANT BUBBLE OF IMPENETRABLE ENERGY, ENCLOSING THE LAND FOR MILES! NOTHING CAN GET IN... OR OUT! WHAT CAUSED IT?

FOR THE STARTLING ANSWER, WE SHIFT TO TWO SPACESHIPS THAT HAVE LANDED IN THIS RURAL AREA....

THERE, KOZ! OUR ENERGY RAYS HAVE PLACED THE IMPENETRABLE DOME OVER THIS AREA, SO THE NATIVES OF THIS PRIMITIVE PLANET CANNOT INTERFERE IN OUR PRIVATE AFFAIRS!

YES, JUK! WE WILL NOW SEPARATE AND BEGIN OUR DUEL! REMEMBER THE RULES... WE MUST TRY TO DESTROY EACH OTHER'S SHIP WITH THE NATURAL FORCES OF THIS PLANET!

WHAT IS THE MEANING OF THIS STRANGE SUPER-SCIENTIFIC BATTLE BETWEEN TWO BEINGS FROM OUTER SPACE?

WE'VE SET OUR SHIPS AT EACH END OF THE DOME! NOW TO HURL MY *EARTHQUAKE RAY* TOWARD KOZ'S SHIP!

FIVE MILES AWAY, WHERE HIS OPPONENT'S SHIP IS GROUNDED....

JUK OPENED FIRE, CAUSING AN EARTHQUAKE CRACK TO SWALLOW MY SHIP... HE THINKS!

2

QUICKLY, THE SECOND ALIEN MAKES HIS FIRST MOVE....

MY *HAMMER RAY* HAS FORCED A LANDSLIDE DOWN THAT MOUNTAIN, FILLING THE CRACK AND SAVING MY SHIP!

AS THE TITANIC BATTLE OF FANTASTIC FORCES CONTINUES....

MY *LEVITATION RAY* WILL LIFT THAT MOUNTAIN, THEN DROP IT ON MY OPPONENT'S SHIP, CRUSHING IT LIKE AN EGG-SHELL!

BUT THE WATCHFUL DEFENDER HURLS A *BLAST RAY* TO SHATTER THE MOUNTAIN... WITH DEVASTATING EFFECT TO THE COUNTRYSIDE....

HELP! OUR VILLAGE IS BEIN' DESTROYED! RUN FER YORE LIVES!

DESERTING HOMES AND FARMS, THE BEWILDERED HILLFOLK HUDDLE IN A CAVE...

NO LIVES LOST, LUCKILY! YOU ALL STAY HERE WHERE IT'S SAFE! I'LL GO OUT AND SEE WHAT'S CAUSING ALL THIS!

SOON, RHETT SHAW COMES UPON ONE OF THE TWO BATTLERS....

MY *HEAT RAY* IS BURNING UP THOSE UP-ROOTED TREES THAT JUK HURLED AT MY SHIP!

A MAN FROM SPACE! I CAN "HEAR" HIS THOUGHTS... PERHAPS I CAN COMMUNICATE WITH HIM BY TELEPATHY!

3

CAUTIOUSLY, THE EARTHMAN APPROACHES THE CREATURE FROM OUTER SPACE....

WHY ARE YOU USING EARTH AS A BATTLEGROUND?

I WILL EXPLAIN BRIEFLY, EARTHLING! MANY GENERATIONS AGO, TWO ANCESTORS OF THE KOZ AND JUK FAMILIES OF OUR WORLD WERE RIVAL EXPLORERS OF SPACE....

"BY SHEER CHANCE, THEY BOTH DISCOVERED A NEW WORLD AT THE SAME TIME, AND AS EACH TRIED TO LAND FIRST AND CLAIM CREDIT FOR THE DISCOVERY..."

CRASH!

CRASH!

"BOTH CRASHES WERE FATAL AND IT WAS IMPOSSIBLE TO TELL WHICH HAD LANDED FIRST! A BITTER FEUD THEN AROSE, BETWEEN THE KOZ AND JUK FAMILIES, AS TO WHICH COULD CLAIM THE WORLD! TO SETTLE THE DISPUTE, WE BEGAN SHIP-DESTROYING FEUDS ON OTHER PLANETS..."

I SMASHED THE JUK SHIP! THE KOZ FAMILY WINS AGAIN!

I AM STRANDED HERE UNTIL ONE OF MY FAMILY PICKS ME UP!

TO DATE, THE SCORE IS EVEN.... 127 VICTORIES EACH FOR THE KOZ AND JUK FAMILIES! WHICH- EVER FAMILY SCORES THE MOST VICTORIES, CLAIMS CREDIT FOR DISCOVERY OF THE WORLD!

WE USE OTHER WORLDS FOR OUR BATTLEGROUNDS TO AVOID DAMAGE TO OUR OWN WORLD! WE HURL SUPER-RAY FORCES FROM OUR HELMET POWER PACKS!

HMM.... THE METAL CASING OF THE RAY- APPARATUS LOOKS TARNISHED! I'LL RUB SOME ON MY FINGERS AND ANALYZE IT LATER!

DEVASTATINGLY, THE SPACE-FEUDERS CONTINUE THEIR CONTEST....

JUK USED A *STEAM RAY* TO CREATE A HUGE GEYSER FROM UNDERGROUND! HE INTENDS TO HURL MY SHIP UP WITH CRUSHING FORCE AGAINST THE ENERGY DOME!

4

BUT A COUNTER PLAN IS QUICKLY DEVISED!

MY **FREEZE RAY** TURNED THE GEYSER TO SOLID ICE! NOW MY SHIP CAN GENTLY SLIDE DOWN WITHOUT HARM!

MEANWHILE, RHETT SHAW RETURNS TO THE DESERTED VILLAGE....

WIELDING TERRIFIC POWERS, THE ALIENS SEEM UNDEFEATABLE! YET THERE'S ONE SLIM HOPE.... THAT SMUDGE OF TARNISH ON MY FINGER! I'VE GOT TO ANALYZE IT IN MY LAB -- IF IT HASN'T BEEN WRECKED!

SOON AFTER....

THE TARNISH IS **FERRIC OXIDE!** NOW I KNOW WHAT METAL CASING PROTECTS THE ALIEN POWER PACKS.... AND WHAT WEAPON CAN DEFEAT THEM!

AFTER A SEARCH AMONG THE WRECKED HOUSES IN THE VILLAGE....

THIS PLASTIC TOY WATER PISTOL SOME KID LEFT BEHIND WILL SERVE AS MY WEAPON!

HOW CAN THE YOUNG SCIENTIST HOPE TO TRIUMPH OVER THE ALIENS WITH A TOY GUN? LATER, AS THE FEUDERS CIRCLE NEAR EACH OTHER, CHANGING TACTICS....

LISTEN, YOU ALIENS! STOP THIS DESTRUCTIVE DUEL AT ONCE-- OR I'LL STOP IT FOR YOU!

NO WEAPON OF EARTH'S PRIMITIVE SCIENCE CAN MATCH OURS!

5

BUT AMAZINGLY, AS RHETT USES HIS SQUIRT GUN...

GREAT STARS! OUR RAY-MACHINES HAVE BEEN SHORT-CIRCUITED!

NOW THAT YOU'RE BOTH DISARMED, HOW ABOUT SETTLING YOUR FEUD? WHY DON'T YOU TWO FAMILIES SIMPLY DIVIDE UP THE WORLD THAT YOUR ANCESTORS DISCOVERED?

WHY...ER...WE CAN'T! OUR FAMILIES HAVE BEEN FEUDING SO LONG THAT I'VE FORGOTTEN WHAT HAPPENED TO IT!

WAIT...NOW THAT I THINK OF IT, THAT WORLD WAS DESTROYED BY A COMET LONG AGO!

THEN YOU WERE REALLY FEUDING OVER *NOTHING!* COME ON--SHAKE HANDS, EARTH-STYLE, AND CALL IT OFF!

YOU ARE RIGHT, EARTHMAN! THERE IS NO REASON TO FEUD OVER SOMETHING THAT DOESN'T EVEN EXIST ANYMORE!

LATER, AS THE TWO SPACE-SHIPS BLAST OFF...

FAREWELL, EARTHMAN! OUR FAMILIES WILL MAKE FRIENDS NOW! YOU HAVE SHOWN US THAT OUR FEUD WAS-- UNCIVILIZED!

ALL FEUDS ARE... INCLUDING THE ONE BETWEEN THE CARTERS AND SHAWS, HERE ON EARTH!

AND AFTER WHIT CARTER HEARS THE STORY...

SHAKE, RHETT! YUH SHORE SHOWED YUH'RE NO COWARD--DRIVIN' OFF THEM SPACE-MEN! B-BUT HOW'D YUH DEFEAT THEM WITH A *WATER PISTOL?*

BY FILLING IT WITH CONCENTRATED *NITRIC ACID!* THE TARNISH WAS FERRIC OR IRON OXIDE...COMMON *RUST!* THUS I KNEW THE ACID WOULD INSTANTLY EAT INTO THE IRON CASING AND BURN OUT THEIR RAY-MACHINES!

THE END

6

The ONE-HOUR INVASION OF EARTH!

THEY CAME FROM SOMEWHERE IN THE SEAS OF SPACE BEYOND THE SOLAR SYSTEM! TO THEIR ALIEN EYES, EARTH WAS JUST ONE MORE PLANET TO BE CONQUERED AND COLONIZED, IN THEIR TERRIBLE KIND OF WAR THAT LASTED ONLY ONE HOUR! IN THAT LENGTH OF TIME, EARTH WAS GIVEN AN IMPOSSIBLE CHOICE: ABSOLUTE SURRENDER OR UTTER DESTRUCTION! TO ADD TO THEIR DILEMMA, EARTHMEN COULD NOT EVEN SEE THEIR ENEMY!

THERE'S THE ALIEN'S BOMB! NOW THAT WE FOUND IT, HOW DO WE STOP IT FROM GOING OFF?

WE HAVE JUST FIVE MINUTES TO FIGURE OUT A WAY!

IN A CENTURIES-OLD CAVERN, SPELUNKER * BILL JACKSON DRAWS BACK IN AMAZEMENT AS...

A SPACESHIP-- SUDDENLY MATERIALIZED IN THIS CAVERN!

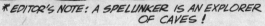

*EDITOR'S NOTE: A SPELUNKER IS AN EXPLORER OF CAVES!

SILENTLY, A DOOR OF THE SPACESHIP OPENS-- AND AFTER A LONG WAIT...

STRANGE! NO ONE'S COME OUT!

DRAWN BY FASCINATED CURIOSITY, BILL JACKSON ENTERS THE SHIP...

TWO CREATURES--IN GLASS CASES! ARE THEY DEAD-- OR IN SUSPENDED ANIMATION?

CAUTIOUSLY EXPLORING, HE COMES ON A NUMBER OF ODD, PLASTIC PICTURE CUBES...

A CUBE WITH TINY PICTURES INSIDE! LOOKS LIKE IT CAN BE PLACED INSIDE THIS PROJECTOR-TYPE MACHINE! LET'S SEE WHAT HAPPENS--

AS THE CUBE PROJECTOR SHOWS A SERIES OF PICTURES, AN ELECTRIC THOUGHT BEAM EXPLAINS THEM...

THE SPACEMEN ARE FROM THE PLANET KLARN, IN THE ANDROMEDA NEBULA! THE CUBE REVEALS THAT THEIR SPACESHIP CAN TRAVEL AT THE SPEED OF LIGHT AND COME TO REST INSTANTLY ON CONTACT WITH A PLANET'S SURFACE!

"ON AN ALIEN PLANET A SHORT TIME IS NEEDED TO ACCLIMATE THE BODIES OF THE KLARN SPACEMEN TO ITS ATMOSPHERE AND GRAVITY! FOR THIS PURPOSE A NATURAL HIDING PLACE, LIKE A CAVE, IS SELECTED..."

"THE ACCLIMATING PROCESS ALLOWS THE KLARN TO MOVE AT SUCH TREMENDOUS SPEEDS THAT THEY ARE INVISIBLE TO THE INHABITANTS OF THE INVADED PLANET! AS SOON AS THE KLARN ARE ADJUSTED TO A PLANET, THEY CONSTRUCT A SMALL COBALT BOMB..."

"THEN A SECOND, LARGER BOMB, OF SUCH INCONCEIVABLE POWER THAT ITS EXPLOSION CAN SHATTER A PLANET, IS FITTED TOGETHER. WHEREUPON AN ULTIMATUM IS ISSUED!"

PEOPLE OF ANTARES-- SURRENDER OR PERISH!

AS A DEMONSTRATION OF OUR POWER, WE ARE GOING TO EXPLODE A SMALL COBALT BOMB! UNLESS WE RECEIVE YOUR SURRENDER WITHIN THE HOUR, A GIANT COBALT BOMB WILL GO OFF-- COMPLETELY DESTROYING YOUR WORLD!

BILL JACKSON REALIZES HE HAS SEEN A "PREVIEW" OF WHAT WILL HAPPEN TO THE EARTH!...

IT'LL BE A *BLITZKRIEG* --A ONE-HOUR INVASION OF EARTH! IF ONLY THERE WAS SOME WAY TO STOP THEM ...WAIT--THERE WAS SOMETHING STRANGE ABOUT THE WAY THEY SUSPENDED THEIR BOMBS IN MID-AIR ...

SUDDENLY... THE GLASS CASES ARE OPENING! THERE'S NO CHANCE TO REACH THE DOORWAY WITHOUT BEING SEEN! I MUST HIDE!

MOMENTS LATER... THE SPACEMEN--VANISHED! WHERE ARE THEY? OF COURSE! THAT PICTURE CUBE EXPLAINED IT! THEY MOVED *TOO FAST* FOR ME TO SEE THEM!

AS THE EARTHMAN WATCHES, A NUMBER OF OBJECTS DISAPPEAR RIGHT BEFORE HIS EYES...

THE MATERIALS FOR THE FIRST BOMB! THEY'RE TAKING THEM OUT OF THE SHIP--INTO THE CAVE, TO FIT THE BOMB TOGETHER!

AT FULL SPEED, BILL JACKSON RUNS TOWARD THE SPACESHIP DOOR ...

I'LL FOLLOW AND TRY TO STOP THEM--EVEN IF I CAN'T SEE THEM!

BUT JUST AS BILL REACHES THE DOORWAY...

HUH? THE DOOR IS CLOSING! THOSE FAST-MOVING SPACE-MEN SET UP THEIR BOMB AND RETURNED TO THE SHIP BEFORE I COULD EVEN CROSS THE ROOM! I'M TRAPPED IN HERE!

I WONDER--IF I CAN'T SEE THEM, MAYBE THEY CAN'T SEE ME--UNLESS I REMAIN *STATIONARY!* THEIR EYES ARE GEARED ONLY TO HIGH SPEEDS! I'LL KEEP MOVING AROUND THE DOOR--AND JUMP OUT WHEN THEY OPEN IT TO SET THEIR SECOND BOMB!

WITH A SILENT SURGE OF POWER, THE *KLARN* SPACESHIP SHOOTS OUT FROM THE CAVE...

HERE WE GO, JUST AS THAT PICTURE CUBE SHOWED! WHAT BOTHERS ME IS--HOW WILL I STOP 'EM WHEN I CAN'T SEE 'EM?

AS THE *KLARN* VESSEL LOWERS TO THE GROUND INSIDE ANOTHER CAVE, MANY MILES FROM THE FIRST ONE...

THE DOOR'S OPENING AGAIN! NOW'S MY CHANCE TO GET AWAY!

BUT BEFORE HE TAKES A DOZEN STEPS...

LOOK! AN EARTHMAN, FLEEING FROM US! OUR SPEED HAS SLOWED DOWN ENOUGH FOR US TO SEE HIM!

HE MUST HAVE BEEN HIDING IN THE SHIP!

THIS RAY WILL STUN HIM LONG ENOUGH TO PREVENT HIM FROM SPREADING ANY ALARM UNTIL WE'VE BROADCAST OUR DEMAND FOR THIS PLANET TO SURRENDER!

LATER, WHEN BILL JACKSON RECOVERS HIS SENSES AND WANDERS OUT OF THE CAVE...

WH-WHAT HAPPENED TO ME? WH-WHERE AM I? I REMEMBER! THAT SPACESHIP...THE COBALT BOMBS! I'VE GOT TO TELL THE AUTHORITIES WHAT I KNOW!

I THINK I KNOW THOSE ALIENS' ONE WEAKNESS! IT'S BASED ON THE FACT THAT THEY DON'T DROP THEIR BOMBS ON A PLANET FROM OUTER SPACE--BUT HAVE TO ASSEMBLE THEIR BOMBS TOGETHER *AFTER* THEY LAND ON A PLANET!

MOMENTS LATER...

GOING TO TOWN?

SURE! EVERYBODY'S HEADED THAT WAY TO TELL THE AUTHORITIES WE WANT TO FIGHT THOSE ALIENS! WE'RE NOT SURRENDERING OUR WORLD WITHOUT A FIGHT!

THEY EXPLODED THEIR FIRST BOMB, THEN GAVE US THEIR ULTIMATUM FROM OUT IN SPACE--"SURRENDER OR PERISH!" WE'LL NEVER SURRENDER!

GOOD GOSH! THAT MEANS WE HAVE LESS THAN AN HOUR TO STOP THEM!

TURN AROUND! TURN AROUND! YOU AND I CAN SAVE THE EARTH IF WE ACT FAST ENOUGH!

HUH? WHAT ARE YOU TALKING ABOUT?

I WAS ON THEIR SPACESHIP! THEY MUST HAVE PLANTED THEIR SECOND BOMB CLOSE TO THE SPOT WHERE THEY STUNNED ME! IN A CAVE WHERE NO ONE WOULD SEE IT!

THEIR BOMBS ARE SO SENSITIVE THAT THE *SLIGHTEST* MOTION DEACTIVATES THEM! THAT'S WHY THEY DON'T *DROP* THEIR BOMBS FROM OUTER SPACE-- OR EVEN HIDE THE BOMBS *IN* OR *ON* THE GROUND! EARTH TREMORS WOULD DESTROY THE BOMBS' DELICATE MECHANISMS!

THERE'S A BIG CAVE NOT FAR FROM HERE!

MINUTES AFTERWARD...

THERE'S THE BOMB! NOW THAT WE'VE FOUND IT, WHAT DO WE DO? I DON'T KNOW ANYTHING ABOUT BOMBS OR HOW TO DISMANTLE THEM!

LEAVE THAT TO ME!

I JUST GRAB HOLD OF THE BOMB-- AND *SHAKE* IT! IF I'M RIGHT, THE SLIGHTEST JAR WILL RENDER IT USELESS!

THEN, FOR SEVERAL SUSPENSE-FILLED MINUTES, THE TWO MEN CROUCH BESIDE THE AWESOME BOMB... WAITING... WAITING...

THE HOUR IS UP! IS IT GOING TO EXPLODE?

SLOWLY, MORE MINUTES TICK AWAY, UNTIL ...

NOTHING'S HAPPENED... AND IT'S TEN MINUTES *OVER* AN HOUR SINCE THEY GAVE US THEIR ULTIMATUM! THE THREAT IS OVER! WE WON!

SOME WEEKS LATER, IN THE STATE CAPITAL...

KNOWING THEIR SURPRISE ATTACK FAILED-- FEARING OUR RADAR DEVICES WOULD TRACK THEM DOWN IF THEY TRIED TO LAND AGAIN, AND FEARING *OUR* NUCLEAR BOMBS, THE ALIENS FLED BACK INTO SPACE! CONGRATULATIONS, BILL JACKSON-- YOU SAVED THE EARTH!

The End

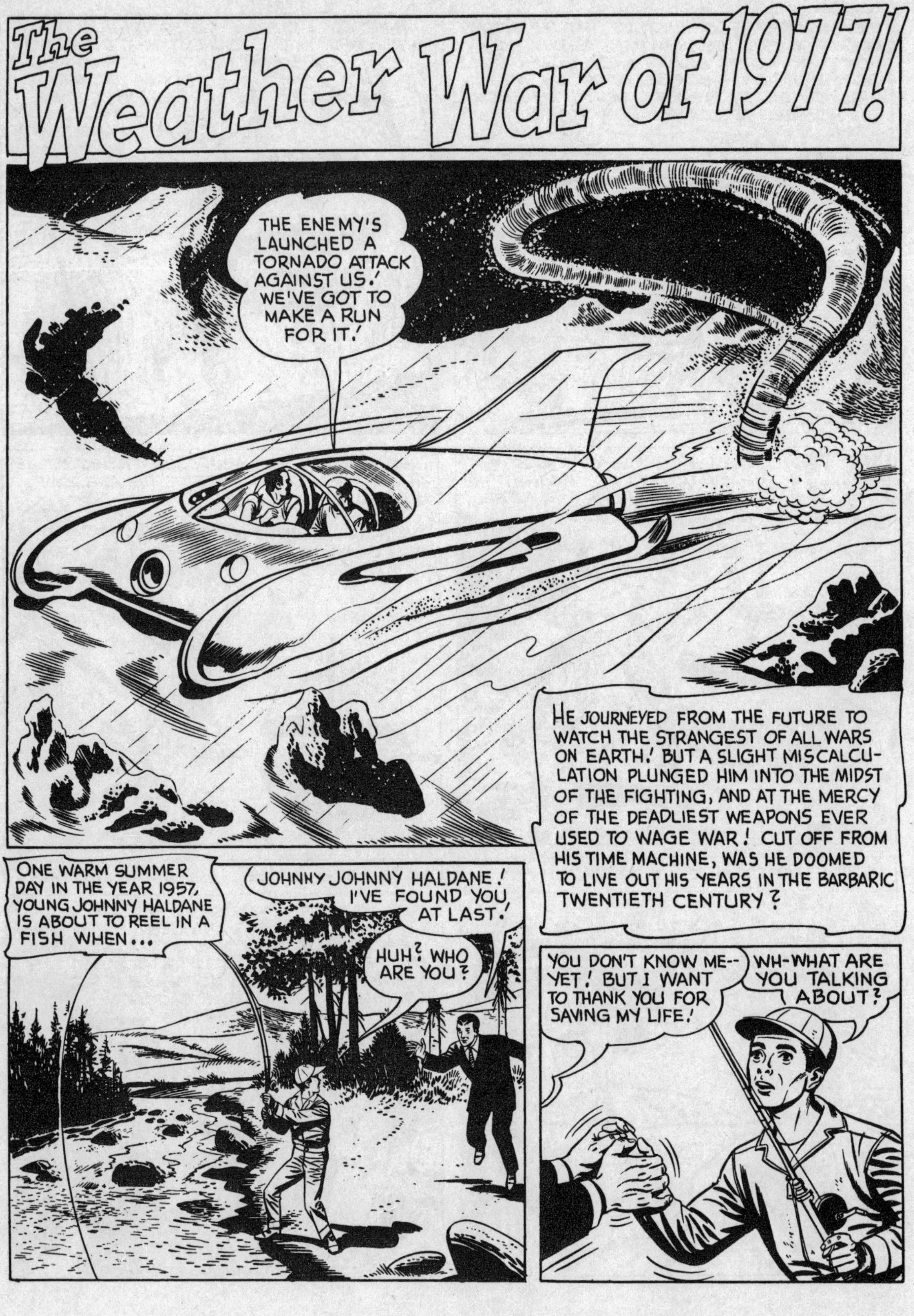
The Weather War of 1977!
THE ENEMY'S LAUNCHED A TORNADO ATTACK AGAINST US! WE'VE GOT TO MAKE A RUN FOR IT!
HE JOURNEYED FROM THE FUTURE TO WATCH THE STRANGEST OF ALL WARS ON EARTH! BUT A SLIGHT MISCALCULATION PLUNGED HIM INTO THE MIDST OF THE FIGHTING, AND AT THE MERCY OF THE DEADLIEST WEAPONS EVER USED TO WAGE WAR! CUT OFF FROM HIS TIME MACHINE, WAS HE DOOMED TO LIVE OUT HIS YEARS IN THE BARBARIC TWENTIETH CENTURY?
ONE WARM SUMMER DAY IN THE YEAR 1957, YOUNG JOHNNY HALDANE IS ABOUT TO REEL IN A FISH WHEN...
JOHNNY JOHNNY HALDANE! I'VE FOUND YOU AT LAST!
HUH? WHO ARE YOU?
YOU DON'T KNOW ME-- YET! BUT I WANT TO THANK YOU FOR SAVING MY LIFE!
WH-WHAT ARE YOU TALKING ABOUT?

HOW COULD I HAVE SAVED YOUR LIFE WHEN WE NEVER MET BEFORE?

YOU'LL UNDERSTAND-- *IN TIME,* JOHNNY!

I STILL SAY YOU'RE MAKING A MISTAKE! I NEVER SAVED YOUR LIFE!

YOU WILL--SOME DAY! BUT NOW I MUST LEAVE! GOODBYE AND-- TILL WE MEET AGAIN!

YOUNG JOHNNY HALDANE IS A MIGHTY BAFFLED BOY, AS HE WALKS THOUGHTFULLY HOMEWARD...

I WONDER WHAT THAT WAS ALL ABOUT? HOW DOES HE KNOW WE'RE GOING TO MEET AGAIN--AND I'LL SAVE HIS LIFE?

AS THE MONTHS SLIDE INTO YEARS, JOHN HALDANE IS EVER ON THE ALERT FOR THE FATEFUL MEETING WITH THE STRANGER...

I THOUGHT FOR A MOMENT THIS WAS THE MAN-- BUT NO!

Clean without WASHING!

YEARS LATER, IN COLLEGE...

THAT MAN--HE LOOKS LIKE THE ONE!

WRONG AGAIN! I JUST KNOW I'M GOING TO MEET HIM AGAIN! BUT WHEN... *WHEN?*

②

AFTER COMPLETING HIS COLLEGE COURSES IN METEOROLOGY,* JOHN HALDANE ENTERS MILITARY SERVICE, RISING TO THE RANK OF COMMANDER...

OUR LATEST ADVICES ARE THAT THE EASTERN HEMISPHERE MAY LAUNCH AN ALL-OUT "WEATHER ATTACK" ON OUR WEST COAST SECTOR, COMMANDER HALDANE!

* EDITOR'S NOTE: METEOROLOGY IS THE STUDY OF WEATHER AND ATMOSPHERIC CHANGES.

ON THE PACIFIC COAST, UNIFORMED MEN ARE AT THEIR POSTS...

DANGER SIGNAL OSCILLATING! THE ENEMY ATTACK IS UNDER WAY!

AT WEST COAST COMMAND HEADQUARTERS...

FLIGHT ZONE ORDERS HAVE GONE OUT, COMMANDER HALDANE! THE CIVILIAN POPULATION HAS TAKEN TO THE STORM SHELTERS!

GOOD! NOW TO MAKE MY INSPECTION TOUR!

SCIENCE HAS PROGRESSED A LONG WAY SINCE THE DAYS WHEN NUCLEAR BOMBS WERE THOUGHT TO BE THE ULTIMATE WEAPON IN ALL-OUT WAR! ANTI-NUCLEAR DEVICES HAVE ELIMINATED THAT THREAT! NOW WE ARE THREATENED BY A MUCH DEADLIER WEAPON!

MAN CAN NOW CONTROL **THE WEATHER!** HE CAN HURL DEADLY SNOWSTORMS--CYCLONES--HURRICANES--TORNADOES--AND CAUSE TORRENTIAL RAINS TO BRING DISASTROUS FLOODS--TO WRECK THE WAR EFFORTS OF AN ENEMY!

AS A SHEET-STEEL DOOR FOLDS BACK, A POWERFUL WEATHER-SLED SLIDES OUT INTO THE TEETH OF A HOWLING SNOWSTORM...

HERE COMES THE FIRST ENEMY ASSAULT-- A *BLIZZARD!*

3

HURTLING SNOWFLAKES-- EACH WITH THE DESTRUCTIVE POWER OF A HIGH CALIBRE BULLET-- WHIP DOWN ON THE WEATHER SLED...

NOT EVEN THIS SLED CAN WITHSTAND A WEATHER ATTACK INDEFINITELY!

SUDDENLY, COMMANDER HALDANE VEERS AS HE SPOTS...

A MAN UNDER THAT LEDGE!

HEAT GUN RAISED, COMMANDER HALDANE LIFTS THE FALLEN TRAVELER...

GOT TO MOVE HIM INTO THE SLED, OUT OF THIS DEADLY SNOW! MY HEAT GUN WILL MELT THE FLAKES ABOUT US AS I PULL HIM IN!

HELP ME... REACH MY TIME MACHINE! ONLY MINUTES LEFT BEFORE IT TAKES OFF... FOR THE FUTURE... LEAVING ME HERE... STRANDED...!

TIME MACHINE?

I COME FROM THE YEAR 3957! I PLANNED TO EMERGE IN YOUR TIME A DAY BEFORE THE *WEATHER WAR OF 1977* BEGAN--THEN BRING BACK AN EYE-WITNESS REPORT! BUT A MISCALCULATION PUT ME DOWN RIGHT IN THE MIDDLE OF THIS DEADLY BLIZZARD...

THE WEATHER-SLED MOVES THROUGH THE STORM, DRILLING A PATH WITH A ROTARY POWER-BLOWER...

I WAS SWEPT AWAY FROM MY TIME MACHINE! IF I'M NOT BACK INSIDE IT IN TEN MINUTES, IT WILL AUTOMATICALLY RETURN TO MY OWN ERA-- WITHOUT ME! HELP ME REACH IT!

SUDDENLY, A GREAT BLACK BLOTCH HURTLES DOWN ON THE SLED WITH AWESOME FURY.'

AN ENEMY TORNADO.' WE'RE IN FOR IT NOW.'

SPROUTING ITS RETRACTIBLE WINGS, THE SLED CAR RISES UPWARD, BUFFETED BY THE STRONG WINDS...

A HURRICANE COMING RIGHT BEHIND IT.' OUR ONLY HOPE IS TO GAIN THE "EYE" OF THE HURRICANE-- WHERE IT IS COMPARATIVELY CALM.'

WHOOOOOMMM

THEN, SAFE IN THE HURRICANE'S "EYE"...

IN ONE SECOND, THE ENERGY RELEASED BY A HURRICANE IS THOUSANDS OF TIMES GREATER THAN THAT PRODUCED BY SEVERAL ATOMIC EXPLOSIONS.'

WEATHER IN MY FUTURE TIME IS RIGIDLY CONTROLLED.'

"WE UTILIZE METEOROLOGICAL ENERGY TO MAKE TRIPS THROUGH TIME-- PRIMARILY TO OBTAIN ACCURATE RECORDS OF EARTH'S PAST HISTORY..."

BY WEARING THE CLOTHES OF THE PERIOD INTO WHICH WE TRAVEL, WE AVOID DISCOVERY.'

"AFTER ONE OF US HAS VISITED A TIME ERA, A PERIOD OF TWENTY YEARS BEFORE AND AFTER IS FOREVER BARRED TO THE TIME TRAVELER..."

EVIDENTLY *"TIME"* BUILDS A TYPE OF PROTECTIVE LAYER AROUND OUR BODIES AND PREVENTS OUR RETURN.'

SUDDENLY, COMMANDER HALDANE CRIES OUT...

LIGHTNING STORMS.' THE AIR WILL BE CHARGED WITH ELECTRICITY.' WE'LL HAVE TO GET BACK TO EARTH.'

WHEN THE WEATHER-SLED LANDS...

WE'RE NOT MOVING! WE'RE STUCK IN *MUD!*

THE FORCE OF THE RAIN WASHED AWAY THE GROUND ITSELF! NOT EVEN ONE OF THESE CARS CAN PLOW THROUGH THIS THICK MUD!

WE MUST ABANDON THE CAR! OUR ONLY CHANCE TO GET THROUGH IS TO TRAVEL ON THESE MUD SHOES!

SAY, IN ALL THIS EXCITEMENT, I DIDN'T REALIZE I KNOW YOU! YOU'RE THE MAN WHO THANKED ME TWENTY YEARS AGO FOR SAVING HIS LIFE!

WH-WHAT ARE YOU TALKING ABOUT? I'VE NEVER MET YOU BEFORE!

NOW IT'S MY TURN TO SAY--YOU "WILL"-- SOME DAY! PARA-DOXICALLY ENOUGH, I'VE MET YOU BEFORE!

THERE'S MY TIME MACHINE! MUST HURRY... ONLY SECONDS LEFT...

6

THEN, AS THE TIME MACHINE AND THE MAN FROM THE FUTURE FADE AWAY INTO TIME...

NOW AT LAST I UNDERSTAND! HE HAD NO TIME TO THANK ME FOR SAVING HIS LIFE! SINCE HE CAN APPEAR ONLY AT 20-YEAR INTERVALS, HE'S GOING TO TIME-TRAVEL BACK TO TWENTY YEARS AGO AND THANK ME! THAT'S WHEN I FIRST MET HIM!

THE SKIES ARE CLEARING! THE WEATHER WAR IS OVER AND-- WE'VE WON!

The End

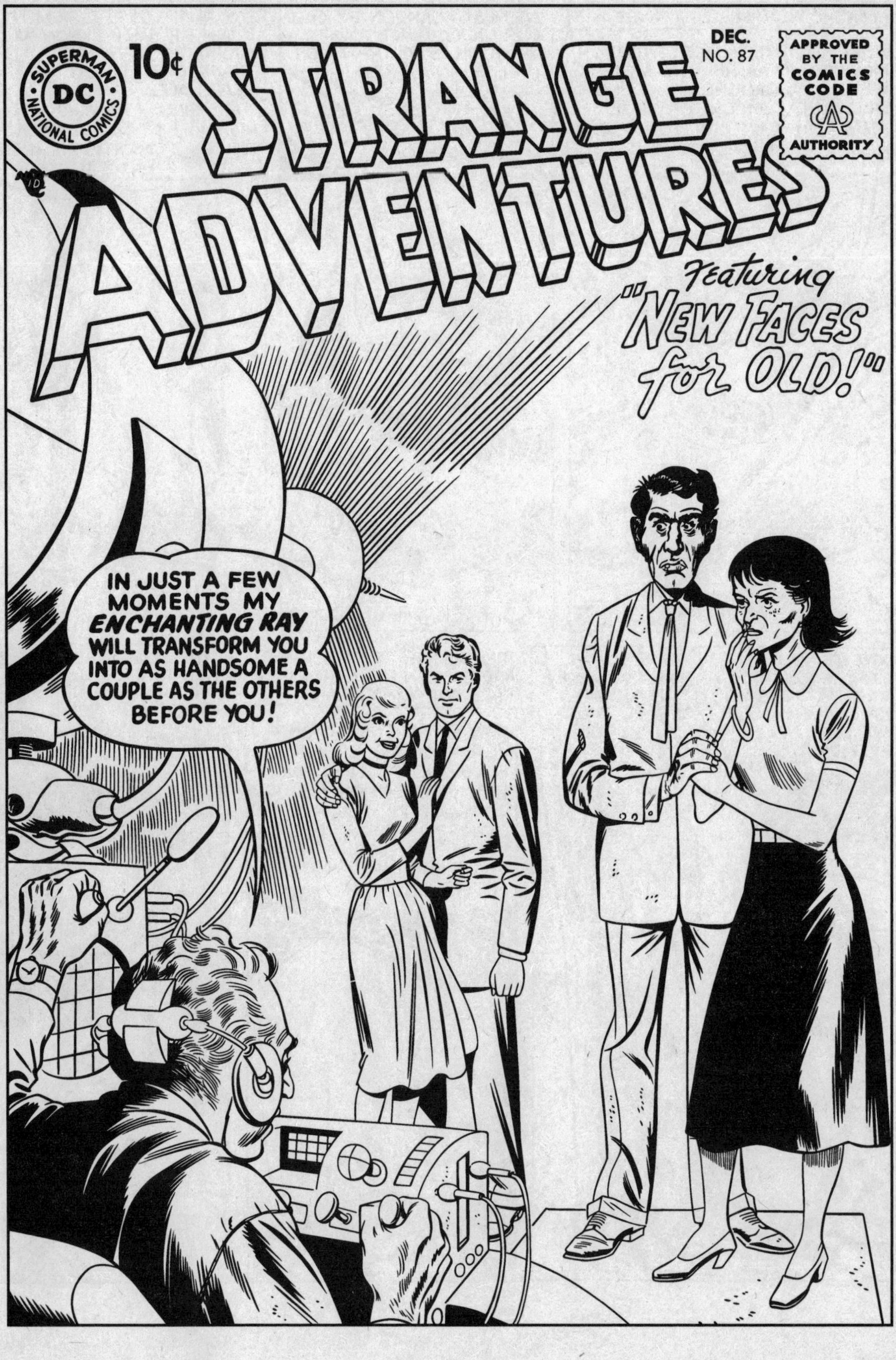
SUPERMAN DC NATIONAL COMICS
10¢
STRANGE ADVENTURES
DEC. NO. 87
APPROVED BY THE COMICS CODE AUTHORITY
Featuring "NEW FACES for OLD!"
IN JUST A FEW MOMENTS MY ENCHANTING RAY WILL TRANSFORM YOU INTO AS HANDSOME A COUPLE AS THE OTHERS BEFORE YOU!

NEW FACES for OLD!

PROFESSOR KRADLER'S MARVELOUS MACHINE COULD MAKE HANDSOME PEOPLE OUT OF HOMELY ONES--BUT BEHIND THE TRANSFORMATION LURKED SOMETHING OMINOUS--THAT WAS DESIGNED TO SOLVE A CRITICAL SITUATION ON ANOTHER WORLD!

SCIENTIST AND LAYMAN ALIKE--ALONG WITH NEWSREEL AND TV CAMERAS--ARE ON HAND AT *EXHIBITION HALL* TO WITNESS THE MOST HERALDED SCIENTIFIC DISCOVERY OF THE 20TH CENTURY...

THAT'S PROF. KRADLER'S MACHINE! I CAN HARDLY WAIT TO SEE IT IN OPERATION!

IT EMITS AN *ENCHANTING RAY* THAT'S REPUTED TO MAKE HANDSOME PEOPLE OUT OF HOMELY ONES!

AND JUST HOW DOES YOUR MACHINE FUNCTION, PROFESSOR? THE BASIC OPER-ATION OF MY *PHYSIO-TRANSFORMER* MACHINE MUST BE KEPT A SECRET FOR NOW... BUT ITS OPERATION MAY BE COMPARED TO THAT OF A NUCLEAR FISSION EXPLOSION...

...RATHER, *HUNDREDS* OF SUCH EXPLOSIONS--MICRO-SCOPIC IN SIZE, OF COURSE! ALL THIS OCCURS DEEP WITHIN THE MACHINE--

THEN FOLLOWS A SORT OF CON-TROLLED *RADIATION FALLOUT,* DIRECTED THROUGH COILS AND LENSES--AS A BEAM--AND ON-TO THE SUBJECT! PHYSICAL TRANSFORMATION IS BROUGHT ABOUT...

IN A MOMENT, THE VOLUNTEER SUBJECTS ARE READY, AND THE GREAT "BARREL" OF THE *PHYSIO-TRANSFORMER* IS TURNED TOWARD THEM...

BZZT! BZZT! BZZT!

BEFORE THE STARTLED EYES OF THE ON-LOOKERS, A PHYSICAL CHANGE OCCURS IN THE VOLUNTEER SUBJECTS...

IT WORKS-- IT REALLY WORKS!

A ROAR OF APPLAUSE GOES UP AT THE FINAL, STUNNING TRANSFORMATION....

THIS MACHINE, LITERALLY, WILL CHANGE THE FACE OF THE WORLD!

A SECOND COUPLE IS THEN QUICKLY TRANSFORMED....

...AS IS THE THIRD....

HOW HAPPY THEY ARE!

NO WONDER! LOOK HOW THEY ARE CHANGED! THEY'RE A *VERY* HANDSOME COUPLE NOW!

SOON AFTERWARDS....

YOU HAVE MORE VOLUNTEERS FROM THE AUDIENCE, PROFESSOR!

SORRY, THE EXPERIMENTS ARE OVER--FOR NOW! THOUGH I ANTICIPATE NO TROUBLE, I MUST WAIT A FEW DAYS TO SEE HOW MY VOLUNTEER SUBJECTS MAKE OUT!

DAYS LATER, PROF. KRADLER'S LAB IS SWAMPED WITH MAIL--BUT OF THE THOUSANDS OF LETTERS, HE IS INTERESTED ONLY IN....

THESE THREE LETTERS--ALL FROM A SMALL MINING TOWN CALLED BLEEKSVILLE! EACH SAYS THAT THE THIRD COUPLE I TRANSFORMED LOOKS *EXACTLY* LIKE A COUPLE IN THE TOWN...

XOTYL AND ERGA--I HAVE FOUND YOU AT LAST! SOON YOU WILL BE MY PRISONERS!

3

PROFESSOR KRADLER--AS HE CALLS HIM-SELF--THINKS BACK... BACK... BACK...

XOTYL AND ERGA ESCAPED FROM OUR NATIVE PLANET--SEEKING TO RETURN WITH THE ELEMENT *D'R'SATO* AND PLAY THE HEROIC ROLE OF FREEING THEIR PEOPLE...

"BUT WHAT WAS IT CHIEF *TYR-HAMMEL* TOLD ME ?..."

DEL-KAR, YOU ARE MY MOST TRUSTED--AND MOST EFFICIENT--AGENT!

YES, SIRE,...

I AM A MILITARY EMPEROR-- I HAVE BROUGHT ALL OF THIS PLANET UNDER MY DOMINATION! I WISH TO KEEP IT THAT WAY...

I CONTROL THE PEOPLE BE-CAUSE WITHOUT THE *D'R'SATO* ELEMENT, THEY CANNOT REBEL-- AND WREST THE REINS OF GOVERNMENT FROM ME!

BUT, SIRE, THERE IS NO MORE *D'R'SATO* ON OUR PLANET!

TRUE! THAT IS WHY TWO OF THEIR AGENTS--XOTYL AND ERGA--HAVE ESCAPED IN A SPACE-SHIP TO SEEK IT ON SOME OTHER PLANET!

YOU KNOW THE PROCEDURE! TAKE A SPACE-SHIP--TRACK THEM DOWN--BRING THEM BACK...*BEFORE* THEY FIND *D'R'SATO*!

WITH OUR NEW SPACE-TRACKER INSTRUMENTS, SIRE, I SHOULD FIND THEM QUICKLY!

THE SPACE-TRACKER LED ME HERE-- TO EARTH-- WHERE I SAW THEIR CRASHED SHIP! BUT I COULD FIND NO TRACE OF THEM AMONG THE BILLIONS OF PEOPLE ON THIS WORLD!

4

THAT IS WHY I THOUGHT OF THE *PHYSIO-TRANSFORMER* TRICK TO SWIFTLY LOCATE XOTYL AND ERGA! EARTHMEN PRIZE BEAUTY--SO I CONSTRUCTED A MACHINE THAT *TEMPORARILY* MAKES BEAUTY OUT OF HOMELINESS...!

I TRANSFORMED *TWO* COUPLES MERELY AS A DECOY...WHILE THE *THIRD,* I TRANSFORMED TO LOOK *EXACTLY* LIKE XOTYL AND ERGA! I FIGURED PEOPLE WHO KNEW THEM WHEREVER THEY WERE LIVING, WOULD WRITE TO INFORM ME OF THE DUPLICATION...

SOON AFTER, IN THE TOWN OF BLEEKSVILLE...

XOTYL--ERGA! I AM HERE! I AM COMING TO RETURN YOU TO TYR-HAMMEL...

IT IS DEL-KAR! HE HAS FOUND US!

THEN, AS THE EMISSARY OF THE MILITARY DICTATOR APPEARS...

YOUR FAILURE WILL CONVINCE OTHERS THAT NO ONE CAN DEFEAT THE NEW REGIME! COME QUICKLY--WE GO NOW!

YES--ONLY A FOOL FIGHTS IN THE FACE OF UTTER DEFEAT!

DEPARTING FROM THE SHACK, THEY MAKE THEIR WAY ACROSS THE SURROUNDING HILLS...

YOU WERE LUCKIER THAN WE! YOU LANDED SAFELY--WITHOUT DAMAGE TO YOUR CRAFT!

MY CRAFT IS EQUIPPED WITH THE LATEST SCIENTIFIC DEVICES--WHICH THE COMMON PEOPLE ARE NOT ALLOWED! SO IT WAS NOT JUST LUCK...

SUDDENLY, OUTSIDE THE SPACE-SHIP, THE CAPTIVES GROW DEFIANT...

NOW THAT YOU LED US TO YOUR SHIP, DEL-KAR-- YOU ARE *OUR* PRISONER!

DON'T JEST WITH ME! YOU KNOW THE EFFECTIVENESS OF THIS WEAPON I HOLD...

WE FOUND OUR *D'R'SATO* ＊ DEL-KAR--WHICH IS PLENTIFUL ON EARTH! MY ATOMIC BATTERIES ARE FULLY CHARGED WITH IT--AND IT RENDERS YOUR WEAPON USELESS...

＊ *CARBON*--FOUND IN ABUNDANCE ON EARTH ESPECIALLY IN COMMON *COAL*... 5

AS BEAMS RADIATE FROM THE WRIST WEAPON, DEL-KAR STIFFENS, STANDS AS MOTIONLESS AS A STATUE....

...AND YOU, TOO, ARE RENDERED HELPLESS--AS WILL BE TYR-HAMMEL AND HIS HIRELINGS-- UNTIL WE SEE FIT TO RELEASE YOU!

WHEN OUR SHIP CRASH-LANDED ON EARTH, WE THOUGHT WE WERE DOOMED TO SPEND OUR LIVES HERE! BUT LUCKILY FOR US, DEL-KAR FOLLOWED US HERE IN HIS SHIP....

AND ALL WE HAD TO DO WAS WAIT TILL HE LED US BACK TO HIS SHIP-- AND THEN TAKE OVER!

MOMENTS LATER, THE SPACE-CRAFT, ITS CONTROLS SET TO CARRY IT TO A DISTANT SUN-SYSTEM, ROARS SKYWARD...

WITH THE ACCUMULATED D'R'SATO WE CAN RETURN OUR WORLD TO ITS OWN PEOPLE--AND BREAK THE GRIP OF TYRANNY THERE!

MEANWHILE, WHAT OF THE COUPLES TRANSFORMED BY DEL-KAR'S MACHINE?...

I DIDN'T EXPECT YOU TO GO ALL OUT FOR A HOLLY-WOOD CONTRACT WHEN YOU BECAME SO BEAUTIFUL!

YOU TALK ABOUT ME! WHAT ABOUT YOU? EVERY TIME YOU WALK DOWN THE STREET, GIRLS TURN THEIR HEADS!

Y-YOU'RE CHANGING BACK AGAIN TO THE WAY YOU USED TO BE!

YOU TOO! OUR GOOD-LOOKING FEATURES ARE WEARING OFF!

ROSIE--I LIKE YOU BETTER THIS WAY! PROMISE ME-- NO MORE HOLLYWOOD IDEAS!

NO MORE! WE'RE OURSELVES AGAIN, DARLING-- AND I'M GLAD-- REAL GLAD!

THE END

6

MYSTERY LANGUAGE FROM SPACE!

FROM ANOTHER STAR-SYSTEM COME ALIENS TO WARN US OF A DOOM ABOUT TO STRIKE OUR PLANET! THOUGH THE WARNING MESSAGE IS SUCCESSFULLY RELAYED TO EARTH-- NO ONE ON EARTH CAN UNDER-STAND IT!

WE'VE THOUGHT-CONTACTED AN EARTH-MAN! HE'S WRITING DOWN OUR MESSAGE--

GREAT STARS! HE'S TRANSCRIBING THE MESSAGE IN OUR LANGUAGE! OUR WARNING TO EARTH WON'T BE UNDERSTOOD!

THE MOMENT HE AWAKES IN HIS APARTMENT BEDROOM, EDGAR MORGAN GLANCES APPREHENSIVELY AT HIS NIGHT TABLE...

I CLOSED MY DIARY BEFORE I WENT TO SLEEP LAST NIGHT! NOW IT'S OPEN! I'VE BEEN WRITING IN MY SLEEP AGAIN!

AND SURE ENOUGH MY SLEEP-WRITING IS IN THAT SAME MYSTERIOUS LANGUAGE! WHAT DOES THIS ALL MEAN?

DRESSING HURRIEDLY, MORGAN DRIVES DOWNTOWN...

I MUST FIND AN ANSWER TO THIS RIDDLE! PROFESSOR CALMER OF THE LANGUAGE INSTITUTE IS IN TOWN TODAY! AND I'VE MADE AN APPOINTMENT TO SEE HIM!

AT THE LANGUAGE INSTITUTE...

YOU'RE THE GREATEST LIVING AUTHORITY ON LANGUAGES, PROFESSOR! HAVE YOU EVER SEEN ANYTHING LIKE THIS BEFORE?

NO--IT'S COMPLETELY ALIEN TO ME!

MAN HAS "WRITTEN" IN A NUMBER OF STRANGE WAYS--WITH *KNOTS* BY THE PERSIANS, MESSAGE STICKS BY AUSTRALIAN BUSHMEN, CUNEIFORM WRITTEN BY THE BABYLONIANS, HIEROGLYPHS BY THE EGYPTIANS, PICTURE-WRITING BY NORTH AMERICAN INDIANS...

BUT THIS LANGUAGE IS UNLIKE ANYTHING I HAVE EVER SEEN! MY GUESS IS THAT IT DID NOT ORIGINATE ON EARTH!

BUT THAT'S INCREDIBLE!

THAT NIGHT, AS EDGAR MORGAN SITS PENSIVELY IN HIS ROOM...

IF I ONLY HAD A *ROSETTA STONE*--THE SLAB FOUND IN 1799, BEARING PARALLEL WRITING IN GREEK AND EGYPTIAN HIEROGLYPHICS--WHICH MADE POSSIBLE THE DECIPHERING OF ANCIENT EGYPTIAN WRITING--WAIT! IT JUST OCCURRED TO ME--

MY REGULAR DIARY WRITING IS ALWAYS IMMEDIATELY FOLLOWED BY THE UNKNOWN WRITING! SUPPOSE THE UNKNOWN LANGUAGE WERE A DUPLICATION OF WHAT I WROTE? I'D HAVE A "ROSETTA STONE" OF MY OWN!

2.

ALL THROUGH THE NIGHT HE WORKS FEVERISHLY...

I THINK I HAVE IT! I'VE DRAWN UP A LIST OF THE UNKNOWN WORDS AND THEIR ENGLISH EQUIVALENTS--ASSUMING THE UNKNOWN LANGUAGE IS A TRANSLATION OF MY OWN DIARY WRITINGS!

EXHAUSTED, HE FALLS INTO A PROFOUND SLEEP! WHEN HE WAKES--

MORE WRITING! BUT THIS TIME IT LOOKS LIKE AN ORIGINAL MESSAGE! LET'S SEE WHAT HAPPENS WHEN I TRANSLATE IT WITH THE HELP OF MY GLOSSARY...

"GREETINGS, EARTHMAN! I AM XOR TAN OF **APOLLO SECUNDUS**, A PLANET IN THE STAR SYSTEM **SIRIUS**, THOUGHT-BEAMING TO YOU FROM A FLYING SAUCER HIGH ABOVE YOUR EARTH..."

"EONS AGO, MY PEOPLE LIVED ON A PLANET IN YOUR SOLAR SYSTEM CALLED **APOLLO**, THAT ORBITED BETWEEN MARS AND JUPITER..."

"WE HAD REACHED A HIGH STATE OF CIVILIZA-TION--WHEN OUR SCIENTISTS MADE AN ALARMING DISCOVERY..."

OUR PLANET WILL EXPLODE--WITHIN ONE SOLAR YEAR!

WE MUST BUILD SPACESHIPS TO TAKE US TO **SIRIUS!** IT IS THE ONLY STAR-SYSTEM THAT HAS A PLANET SIMILAR TO **APOLLO!**

3

"WE ESCAPED INTO SPACE JUST IN TIME! BEHIND US, *APOLLO* BLEW UP -- TO FORM WHAT YOU EARTHMEN CALL 'THE ASTEROID BELT'!..."

"RECENTLY OUR SCIENTISTS PICKED UP A SERIES OF *VIBRORAYS* -- THE SAME KIND WE RECORDED ON *APOLLO* BEFORE IT EXPLODED!"

THE *VIBRORAYS* COME FROM THE PLANET EARTH -- IN OUR NATIVE SOLAR SYSTEM!

NOW THAT WE KNOW HOW TO PREVENT THE PLANETARY CATACLYSM, WE MUST TELL THE EARTH-PEOPLE HOW TO SAVE THEMSELVES!

"BEGINNING IN THE YEAR 1947, WE SENT OUR SPACESHIPS -- YOU CALL THEM 'FLYING SAUCERS' -- TO WARN YOU!"

WE DARE NOT LAND! EARTH'S SURFACE GRAVITY WOULD CRUSH US! WE MUST FIND ANOTHER WAY TO CONTACT THEM!

"WORKING FEVERISHLY, OUR SCIENTISTS CONSTRUCTED A STRANGE MACHINE..."

ALL THOUGHT IS ELECTRICAL! BY SENDING ELECTRIC WAVES SIMILAR TO THOUGHT WAVES, WE CAN BROADCAST THOUGHTS TO HUMAN MINDS!

THE THOUGHT-BEAMER WILL ENABLE US TO CONTACT EARTHMEN, TELLING THEM OF THEIR DANGER!

IF IT FAILS -- EARTH IS DOOMED!

4

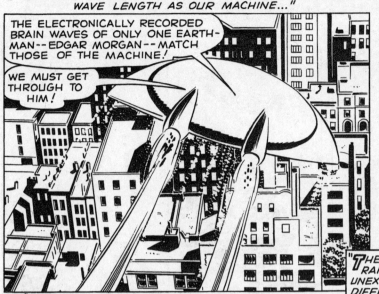

"FOR MONTHS OUR SPACESHIPS RANGED ACROSS THE EARTH, SEEKING TO FIND HUMAN MINDS USING THE IDENTICAL WAVE LENGTH AS OUR MACHINE..."

THE ELECTRONICALLY RECORDED BRAIN WAVES OF ONLY ONE EARTH-MAN--EDGAR MORGAN--MATCH THOSE OF THE MACHINE!

WE MUST GET THROUGH TO HIM!

WE COULD NOT REACH YOU, EDGAR MORGAN, DURING THE DAY! YOUR MIND WAS TOO ACTIVE! ONLY WHEN YOU WERE ASLEEP COULD WE HOPE TO BEAM OUR THOUGHTS INTO YOUR MIND. SLEEP IS DIVIDED INTO FOUR STAGES. WE TRIED DURING STAGE ONE, WHEN NERVE RESPONSES FADE OUT...

"WE FAILED! WE TRIED STAGE TWO, WHEN SKIN TEMPERATURE LOWERS, THEN STAGE THREE, WITH ITS LESS MUSCULAR TENSION AND LOWER BLOOD PRESSURE. BUT NOT UNTIL STAGE FOUR--WITH BRAIN ACTIVITY AT A MINIMUM, DID WE SUCCEED!"

"THEN WE RAN INTO UNEXPECTED DIFFICULTIES!"

THE EARTHMAN RECEIVES OUR MESSAGE WHILE ASLEEP--BUT HAS NO RECOLLECTION OF IT WHEN HE AWAKENS!

HE KEEPS A DIARY! BEAM A COMMAND TO HIM, DIRECTING HIM TO WRITE IN HIS DIARY WHILE ASLEEP!

"BUT THE PROBLEM IN INTERPLANETARY COMMUNICATION WASN'T SOLVED YET..."

MORGAN IS RECEIVING OUR THOUGHTS ALL RIGHT-- BUT INSTEAD OF TRANS-CRIBING THEM IN HIS LANGUAGE, HE IS REPRODUCING THEM IN OUR NATIVE LANGUAGE!.

THEN WE MUST FIND A WAY TO TEACH HIM OUR LANGUAGE!

I DID LEARN THEIR LANGUAGE! AND I CAN UNDERSTAND THE WARNING MESSAGE THEY JUST SENT ME! IT'S HERE--ON THE NEXT PAGE OF THE DIARY!

5

Taking his diary and its message to government officials, Edgar Morgan watches as three huge bombers take off...

THE ALIENS SAID WE COULD PREVENT THE PLANETARY EXPLOSION BY BOMBING THREE CERTAIN AREAS OF THE EARTH!

Three atomic bombs are dropped simultaneously! One falls on an uninhabited island in the Pacific...

VARROOOM!

Another explodes in midair, above the arctic wastes, and a third deep under the Atlantic Ocean...

Soon after, a grateful Earth sends aloft a sky-writing plane...

Curious people watch, unaware of the danger that has threatened their planet and their lives...

IS THAT PLANE SKYWRITING A MESSAGE -- OR WHAT?

IT DOESN'T MAKE SENSE TO ME!

But far above the Earth, a flying saucer reads the message...

THE EARTH IS THANKING US FOR SAVING THEIR WORLD! OUR MISSION IS ACCOMPLISHED! LET'S GO HOME!

The END

6

METEOR MENACE of MARS!

WHEN LT. DAN BRADY RECEIVED HIS AIR FORCE WINGS, HE ALSO RECEIVED SEALED ORDERS FOR DUTY ASSIGNMENT! BUT HE NEVER IMAGINED THAT HIS FIRST *"HITCH"* IN THE SERVICE OF HIS COUNTRY WOULD BE ON A WORLD 50 MILLION MILES FROM EARTH!

MY ASSIGNMENT ORDERS SAID TO REPORT FOR DUTY ON *MARS!* BUT HOW DID I GET HERE-- TO FIGHT AN AIR BATTLE AGAINST ALIEN SPACESHIPS?

ALL THROUGH BASIC TRAINING AND THE AIR FORCE ACADEMY, DAN BRADY AND HAL HAWKINS HAVE BEEN CLOSE FRIENDS...

THEY'RE SENDING ME TO HICKAM FIELD, DAN! WHERE ARE YOU GOING?

I HAVEN'T LOOKED YET!

MY ORDERS ARE TO REPORT TO-TO-*TO THE PLANET MARS!*

WH--AAT?!

ASTONISHINGLY, THE NEXT MOMENT...

HE'S **GONE!** DISAPPEARED INTO THIN AIR!

LOOK--HIS DUTY ASSIGNMENT ORDERS!

HE WAS ORDERED TO PROCEED TO HICKAM FIELD, SAME AS I WAS! WHAT DID HE MEAN BY THAT TALK ABOUT **MARS?**

AND WHERE IN THE WORLD **IS** HE?

BUT THE MISSING AIRMAN IS NOWHERE ON **THIS** WORLD...

WH--WHERE AM I? WHO ARE THESE STRANGE-LOOKING PEOPLE?

WELCOME, EARTHMAN--TO THE PLANET **MARS!** I AM DORVAL DUN, GOVERNOR OF **MARSOPOLIS!**

WE HAVE **TELEPORTED** YOU TO OUR MENACED WORLD TO ENLIST YOUR AID IN OUR DESPERATE STRUGGLE FOR SURVIVAL!

"THOUSANDS OF YEARS AGO, MARS AND THE PLANET NEPTUNE WAGED DEADLY, INTERPLANETARY WARFARE--"

"NOT UNTIL THE MARTIAN SCIENTIFIC GENIUS **XAN TORRAN** INVENTED THE **DISSOLURAY**, DID PEACE COME AT LAST TO OUR PLANET..."

THIS **DISSOLURAY** WEAPON--WITH ITS POWER TO DESTROY ALL METALS--IS FORCING THE NEPTUNIAN WARSHIPS TO WITHDRAW! THEY WILL NEVER BE ABLE TO ATTACK MARS AGAIN!

"FOR SEVERAL THOUSAND YEARS, WE LIVED IN PEACE.' THEN, SOME DAYS AGO, WE RECEIVED AN ULTIMATUM FROM NEPTUNE!"

NEPTUNE DEMANDS THAT WE SURRENDER -- OR BE DESTROYED!

ULTIMATUM--REJECTED! THEIR SHIPS WILL NEVER PASS THROUGH OUR *DISSOLURAY BARRIER!*

"CONFIDENTALLY, WE WAITED FOR NEPTUNE'S NEXT MOVE! WE WERE ON THE ALERT FOR ANY TRICKS..."

NOTHING FROM OUTER SPACE -- NOT EVEN METALLIC METEORS -- CAN ESCAPE DESTRUCTION FROM OUR *DISSOLURAY!*

"THEN ONE DAY WE EXPERIENCED A FEELING OF UNUSUAL HEAVINESS, AS IF WE HAD SUDDENLY DOUBLED IN WEIGHT!'"

I-I CAN'T MOVE!

ALL I CAN DO IS CRAWL!

"SOON, WE REALIZED THE GRIM TRUTH..."

OUR INSTRUMENTS REPORT A METEOR PASSED THE *DISSOLURAY BARRIER* AND FELL AT THE SOUTH POLAR ICE CAP!

ARTIFICIALLY MADE OF A STRANGE NON-METAL BY THE NEPTUNIANS, THE METEOR WAS UNAFFECTED BY THE *DISSOLURAY* VIBRATIONS!

"WE QUICKLY DETERMINED THAT THE MAN-MADE 'METEOR' CONTAINED A DEVICE THAT ALMOST *TRIPLED* THE SPECIFIC GRAVITY OF *MARS* -- MAKING IT EQUAL TO THAT OF NEPTUNE--AND EARTH!' *

THE HEAVIER GRAVITY NOT ONLY MAKES IT DIFFICULT TO WALK-- BUT IT INTERFERES WITH THE WORKING OF ALL OUR MECHANICAL DEVICES!

*EDITOR'S NOTE: THE SPECIFIC GRAVITY OF EARTH AND NEPTUNE IS IDENTICAL; MARS HAS A SPECIFIC GRAVITY 38% THAT OF EARTH.

"OUR ONE HOPE WAS TO TELEPORT AN EARTH-MAN TO HELP US!'"

BY COMBINING THE OUTPUT OF ALL OUR MACHINES, WE CAN BUILD UP JUST ENOUGH POWER TO *TELEPORT* A SINGLE EARTHMAN TO MARS! HE WILL BE ABLE TO MOVE AROUND OUR PLANET AND DESTROY THE METEOR MENACE!

3.

AS DORVAL DUN CONCLUDES HIS TELEPATHIC EXPLANATION...

SO THAT'S HOW I RECEIVED THE MENTAL IMPRESSION I WAS GOING TO MARS!

YES! ONLY YOU CAN DO WHAT WE FIND IMPOSSIBLE! GET CLOSE ENOUGH TO THE GRAVITY METEOR TO DESTROY IT!

THE NEPTUNIAN SPACE FLEET IS LANDING OUTSIDE THE CITY!

LT. DAN BRADY RACES TO THE OUTSKIRTS OF THE CITY, WHERE --

NOW THAT WE'VE MADE MARS POWERLESS TO RESIST US, WE CAN PROCEED WITH THE CONQUEST OF OUR REAL TARGET-- *EARTH!*

THE GREEN PLANET IS RICH IN MINERALS!

BUT FIRST WE HAD TO NEUTRALIZE MARS! THE MARTIAN *DISSOLURAY* GUN COULD REACH OUT INTO SPACE--

THEIR TELEPATHIC THOUGHTS REVEAL EARTH IS NEXT! THAT MAKES THIS ASSIGNMENT A MORE PERSONAL ONE!

SINCE MARTIAN SHIPS CAN'T FLY IN THIS HEAVY GRAVITY, MY BEST CHANCE TO REACH THE "METEOR" IN A HURRY IS BY USING ONE OF THE NEPTUNIAN SPACESHIPS!

STEALTHILY MOVING FROM SHIP TO SHIP, THE EARTHMAN ENTERS AN EMPTY ONE...

NOW THAT I'M IN THE SHIP, HOW DO I OPERATE IT? WAIT--ONE OF THE OTHER NEPTUNIAN SHIPS IS TAKING OFF!

BY WATCHING WHAT THAT SHIP'S PILOT IS DOING, ON THIS INTERCOM *TV* SCREEN, I CAN DUPLICATE HIS ACTIONS AND FLY MY SHIP!

4

WITH A THUNDERING ROAR OF POWERFUL ROCKET MOTORS, THE HUGE SHIP LIFTS INTO THE SKY OF MARS--AND THE OTHER NEPTUNIAN SHIPS CLANG THE ALARM!

SOMEONE'S STEALING A NEPTUNIAN SHIP!

CLANNGGG!

THE NEXT MOMENT, RAYBEAMS FLASH AT THE EARTHMAN--PILOTED SHIP...

GOT TO USE SOME FANCY MANEUVERS TO AVOID THEIR RAY BLASTS!

USING THE DOG-FIGHT TACTICS OF EARTH-FIGHTER PILOTS, DAN EVADES THE NEPTUNIAN ATTACKERS...

THE METEOR IS AT MARS' SOUTH POLE--BUT CAN I GET TO IT BEFORE THESE NEPTUNIANS GET ME?

HE USES BARREL ROLLS AND IMMELMAN TURNS AS HE NARROWLY ESCAPES BEING HIT! THEN--

THERE'S THE METEOR NOW! IF I KNEW HOW TO FIRE THE NEPTUNIAN RAY-CANNONS, I COULD DESTROY IT!

THE *TV* INTERCOM! I USED IT TO *FLY* THIS SHIP! I CAN USE IT TO LEARN HOW TO FIRE ITS WEAPONS--JUST AS THAT NEPTUNIAN IS DOING!

ZOOMING LOW ACROSS THE MARTIAN ICE, DAN BRADY PUNCHES THE CONTROL PINS--

5

As THE METEOR EXPLODES, NORMAL MARS GRAVITY IMMEDIATELY TAKES EFFECT...

THE NEPTUNIAN CONTROLS WON'T WORK WELL IN NORMAL MARS GRAVITY! I EXPECTED THIS, AND PREPARED FOR A BELLY-LANDING...

MOMENTS LATER...

THE OTHER NEPTUNIAN SHIPS WERE TOO HIGH UP! THEY'RE OUT OF CONTROL -- GOING TO CRASH...

SOON, BACK IN *MARSOPOLIS*...

THE NEPTUNIANS HAVE SURRENDERED AND ARE OUR PRISONERS! YOU SAVED US, EARTHMAN! WE ARE GRATEFUL!

I DID IT FOR EARTH AS WELL AS MARS!

LATER, IN A SCIENTIFIC LABORATORY...

WE'RE READY TO TELEPORT YOU BACK TO EARTH...

REMEMBER -- DON'T SEND ME BACK TO THE SAME PLACE -- BUT TO HICKAM FIELD...

ON EARTH...

DAN! WHAT HAPPENED? HOW DID YOU DISAPPEAR? WHERE'VE YOU BEEN?

WHY, ON *MARS*, OF COURSE -- JUST AS I TOLD YOU!

HAL THINKS I'M KIDDING! BUT THAT'S JUST WHERE I WAS -- RIGHT, READER?

THE END

The Interplanetary Problem-Solver!

WALTER WAYNE THOUGHT HE WAS WRITING SCIENCE-FICTION... BUT UNKNOWN TO HIM HIS STORY WAS REALLY HAPPENING ON A DISTANT WORLD ACROSS SPACE! COULD THE FANTASTIC DEVICE THE WRITER DREAMED UP TO SAVE HIS FICTIONAL WORLD FROM DISASTER ALSO SAVE THE REAL PLANET?

HELP! THE WATER IS *EATING AWAY* OUR STONE DIKE!

I HAVE THE ODDEST FEELING THAT THIS IS REALLY HAPPENING ON SOME FAR-OFF WORLD... YET IT CAN'T BE... I MADE IT ALL UP!

SOMEWHERE IN A DISTANT GALAXY, A SPACE-SHIP LANDS ON A PRIMITIVE WORLD...

WE ARE THE **STARMEN**, COLONISTS FROM ANOTHER WORLD! MEET OUR DEMANDS -- AND WE WILL NOT IN-TERFERE WITH YOUR WAY OF LIFE!

HOW ODD! CREATURE SPEAKS UNKNOWN WORDS! YET, SOME-HOW I UNDERSTAND THEM!

MINE FOR US YOUR METAL ORES! IN RETURN WE WILL LEAVE YOU THIS OBJECT TO SOLVE ANY PROBLEM THAT MIGHT ARISE TO ENDANGER YOUR LIVES!

WHAT IS THE NAME OF THIS WISE BEING?

HAVING NO MACHINES, THESE PRIMITIVE PEOPLE CANNOT UNDERSTAND THAT IT IS A SUPER ELECTRONIC-BRAIN! THEY THINK IT'S "ALIVE" AND NEEDS A NAME...

CALL IT MENTALLO!

WEAR THIS HELMET WHENEVER YOU CONSULT THE PROBLEM-SOLVER! IT WILL HEAR YOUR THOUGHTS AND ANSWER THEM! I'LL SET THE BRAIN-WAVE DIAL TO RECEIVE THEM!

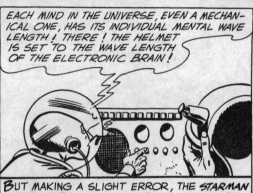

EACH MIND IN THE UNIVERSE, EVEN A MECHANICAL ONE, HAS ITS INDIVIDUAL MENTAL WAVE LENGTH! THERE! THE HELMET IS SET TO THE WAVE LENGTH OF THE ELECTRONIC BRAIN!

BUT MAKING A SLIGHT ERROR, THE STARMAN INSTEAD TUNES TO THE BRAIN-WAVES OF ANOTHER MIND...

MEANWHILE, AS THE STARMEN LEAVE...

...FAR OFF ON EARTH!

I NEED A DIFFERENT IDEA FOR A SCIENCE-FICTION STORY... BUT MY MIND IS BLANK!

WE WILL RETURN SOON FOR OUR FIRST LOAD OF METALS! NO DISASTER WILL STRIKE THESE NATIVES THAT THE PROBLEM-SOLVER CAN'T HANDLE!

THE VERY NEXT DAY, A THREAT ARISES FOR THE PRIMITIVE TRIBE!

HELP US, MENTALLO! THE RIVER IS RISING! OUR VILLAGE WILL BE FLOODED!

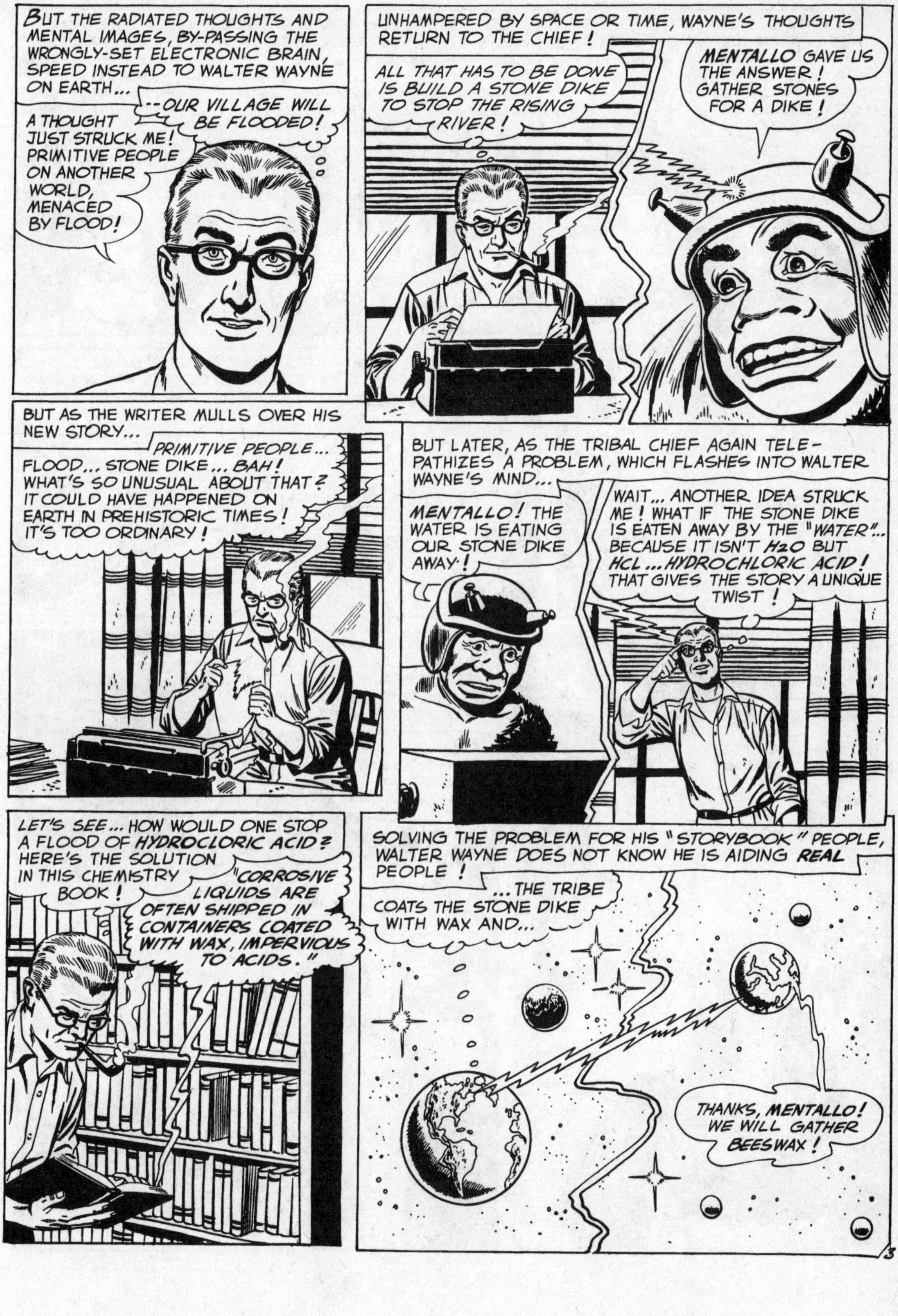
BUT THE RADIATED THOUGHTS AND MENTAL IMAGES, BY-PASSING THE WRONGLY-SET ELECTRONIC BRAIN, SPEED INSTEAD TO WALTER WAYNE ON EARTH...
--OUR VILLAGE WILL BE FLOODED!
A THOUGHT JUST STRUCK ME! PRIMITIVE PEOPLE ON ANOTHER WORLD, MENACED BY FLOOD!
UNHAMPERED BY SPACE OR TIME, WAYNE'S THOUGHTS RETURN TO THE CHIEF!
ALL THAT HAS TO BE DONE IS BUILD A STONE DIKE TO STOP THE RISING RIVER!
MENTALLO GAVE US THE ANSWER! GATHER STONES FOR A DIKE!
BUT AS THE WRITER MULLS OVER HIS NEW STORY...
PRIMITIVE PEOPLE... FLOOD... STONE DIKE... BAH! WHAT'S SO UNUSUAL ABOUT THAT? IT COULD HAVE HAPPENED ON EARTH IN PREHISTORIC TIMES! IT'S TOO ORDINARY!
BUT LATER, AS THE TRIBAL CHIEF AGAIN TELE-PATHIZES A PROBLEM, WHICH FLASHES INTO WALTER WAYNE'S MIND...
MENTALLO! THE WATER IS EATING OUR STONE DIKE AWAY!
WAIT... ANOTHER IDEA STRUCK ME! WHAT IF THE STONE DIKE IS EATEN AWAY BY THE "WATER"... BECAUSE IT ISN'T H2O BUT HCL... HYDROCHLORIC ACID! THAT GIVES THE STORY A UNIQUE TWIST!
LET'S SEE... HOW WOULD ONE STOP A FLOOD OF HYDROCLORIC ACID? HERE'S THE SOLUTION IN THIS CHEMISTRY BOOK!
"CORROSIVE LIQUIDS ARE OFTEN SHIPPED IN CONTAINERS COATED WITH WAX, IMPERVIOUS TO ACIDS."
SOLVING THE PROBLEM FOR HIS "STORYBOOK" PEOPLE, WALTER WAYNE DOES NOT KNOW HE IS AIDING REAL PEOPLE!
...THE TRIBE COATS THE STONE DIKE WITH WAX AND...
THANKS, MENTALLO! WE WILL GATHER BEESWAX!
3

THE EARTHMAN'S "IMAGINARY" EVENT COMES TRUE ON THE FAR-OFF WORLD!

THE WAX-COATED DIKE STOPPED THE EATING FLOOD... THANKS TO MENTALLO!

WALTER WAYNE, *THEIR TRUE "MENTALLO"*, CONTINUES TO SOLVE THEIR PROBLEMS UNWITTINGLY, VIA HIS UNSUSPECTED TELEPATHIC HOOK-UP...

THE COLDEST WEATHER WE EVER KNEW HAS COME! HOW CAN WE KEEP FROM FREEZING, MENTALLO?

AN INTERESTING PROBLEM! THE ANSWER IS *FIRE* -- BUT IF THEIR WATER CONTAINS *CHLORINE* INSTEAD OF OXYGEN, THEIR AIR DOES TOO! HOW CAN ONE MAKE FIRE ON AN OXYGEN -- LESS-WORLD?

AS THE WRITER AGAIN CONSULTS HIS CHEMISTRY BOOK...

LUCKILY, THINGS *"BURN"* WITH CHLORINE AS WELL AS OXYGEN! I'LL HAVE THEM FIND COAL; THEN PRODUCE AN ELECTRIC SPARK THE SAME WAY *BENJAMIN FRANKLIN* DID!

CHLORINE

COAL

Coal burns with chlorine gas ignited by electric spark.

FOLLOWING TELEPATHIC INSTRUCTIONS ON THE OTHER WORLD...

THE COAL FUEL IS READY, CHIEF!

A STORM ARISES! NOW IS THE TIME TO FLY THE KITE, AS *MENTALLO* INSTRUCTED US!

UNKNOWN TO WAYNE ON EARTH, HE HAS HELPED THE PRIMITIVE PEOPLE REACH A MILESTONE OF CIVILIZATION -- *THE DISCOVERY OF FIRE!*

IT MAKES WARMTH! WE NEED NEVER SUFFER AND FREEZE AGAIN!

*U*NCONSCIOUSLY BUILDING CIVILIZATION FOR HIS STORY CHARACTERS, THE WRITER FURTHER UPLIFTS THE OTHER WORLD!

WE NEVER THOUGHT OF USING *WHEELS* TO CARRY HEAVY LOADS OF METAL ORE!

THIS AMAZING BOW AND ARROW WEAPON IS MUCH BETTER THAN OUR CLUMSY CLUBS!

MENTALLO SAYS WE CAN DOMESTICATE MANY ANIMALS BESIDES THIS RIDING STEED!

BUT ONE DAY, AN AWESOME DISASTER THREATENS THE PRIMITIVE PLANET...

THE MOON IS FALLING! *MENTALLO*-- WHAT SHALL WE DO TO SAVE OURSELVES?

INSTANTLY, THE PROBLEM REACHES WALTER WAYNE'S MIND...

WHAT A CLIMAX! TO STOP THE MOON FROM CRASHING ON TO THE WORLD, I'LL HAVE MY STORY TRIBE CONSTRUCT A GIGANTIC *"BAT"* OUT OF HIDES STUFFED WITH ORDINARY *STRAW!*

A *STRAW BAT* TO DRIVE THE MOON AWAY? IT SEEMS IMPOSSIBLE!

WORKING FAST, THE WRITER RUSHES HIS COMPLETED STORY TO THE EDITOR...

GREAT STORY, WALT... EXCEPT FOR THE UNCONVINCING ENDING! INSTEAD OF A GIANT BAT OF *STRAW*, I'LL CHANGE IT TO *METAL!* OUR READERS WOULD NEVER BELIEVE A *STRAW BAT* COULD SWAT THE MOON AWAY!

THEORETICALLY, IT COULD WORK! IT'S A FACT THAT DURING HURRICANES, STRAWS ARE SOMETIMES DRIVEN *THROUGH* WOODEN PLANKS! WHEN DRIVEN WITH GREAT FORCE, FRAGILE THINGS BECOME *MOMENTARILY "HARD"!*

MEANWHILE, ON THE OTHER WORLD, THE CRUCIAL HOUR ARRIVES...

NOW-- PULL! HARD! OUR WHOLE TRIBE MUST YANK *DOWN* THE ROPE AND SWING THE BAT UPWARD!

AS THE HEAVY END OF THE BAT STRIKES THE MOON...

WHACK!

IT WORKED-- BATTED THE FALLING MOON AWAY! *HAIL* TO *MENTALLO!*

LATER, WHEN THE *STARMEN* RETURN, THEY NOTICE THE ELECTRONIC BRAIN'S INCORRECT DIAL SETTING AND ADJUST IT...

EVIDENTLY THE OFF-SETTING WAS SO SLIGHT THAT IT DIDN'T INTERFERE WITH THE TRANSMISSION OF THOUGHTS BETWEEN THE *PROBLEM SOLVER* AND THESE NATIVES!

THUS FOR ALL TIME THE THOUGHT-CONTACT BETWEEN A FAR-DISTANT PLANET AND WALTER WAYNE OF EARTH IS BROKEN...

I NEED A DIFFERENT IDEA FOR ANOTHER SCIENCE-FICTION STORY... *BUT MY MIND IS A BLANK!*

The End

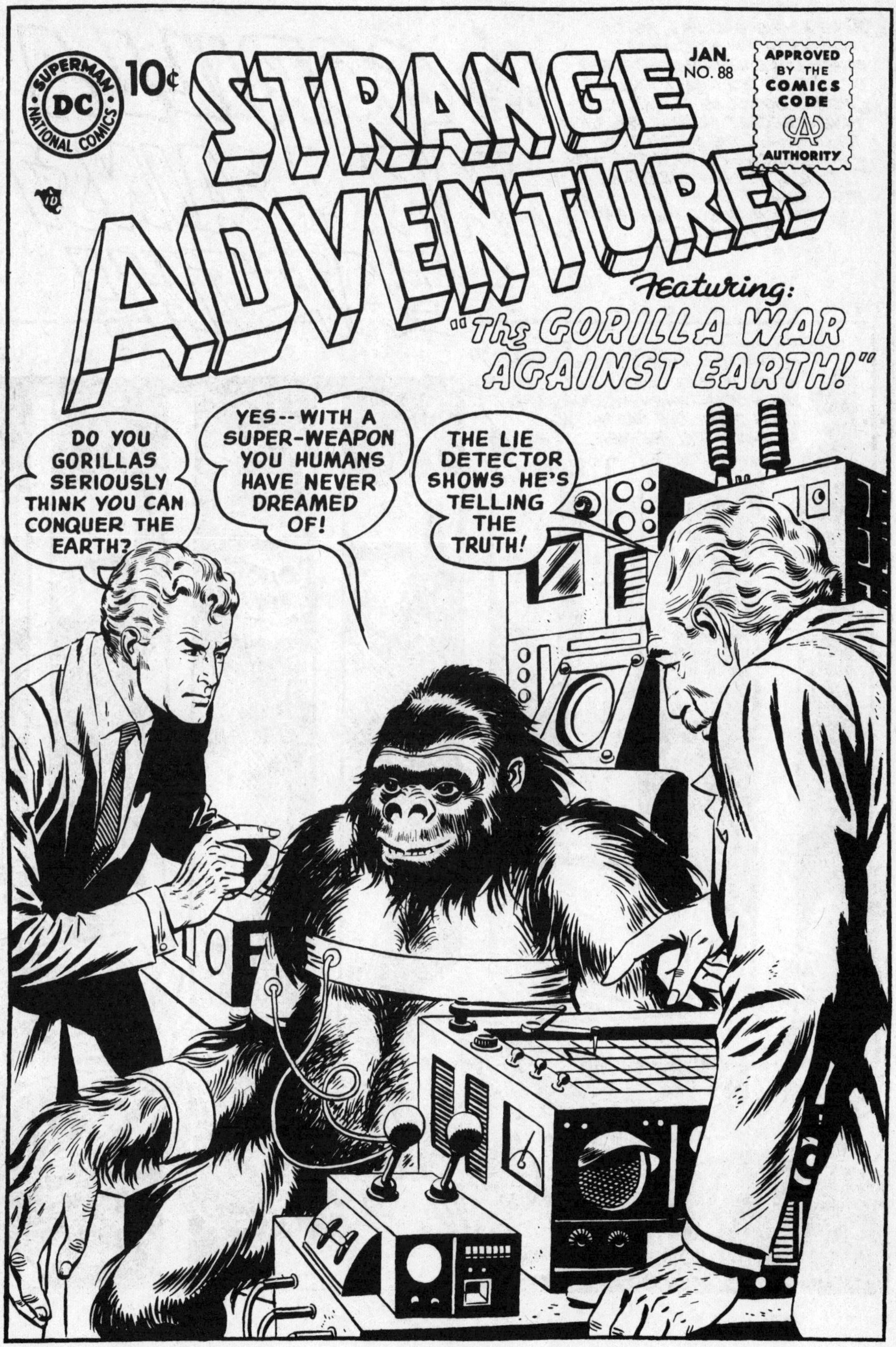
SUPERMAN DC NATIONAL COMICS
10¢
STRANGE ADVENTURES
JAN. NO. 88
APPROVED BY THE COMICS CODE AUTHORITY
Featuring: "The GORILLA WAR AGAINST EARTH!"
DO YOU GORILLAS SERIOUSLY THINK YOU CAN CONQUER THE EARTH?
YES--WITH A SUPER-WEAPON YOU HUMANS HAVE NEVER DREAMED OF!
THE LIE DETECTOR SHOWS HE'S TELLING THE TRUTH!

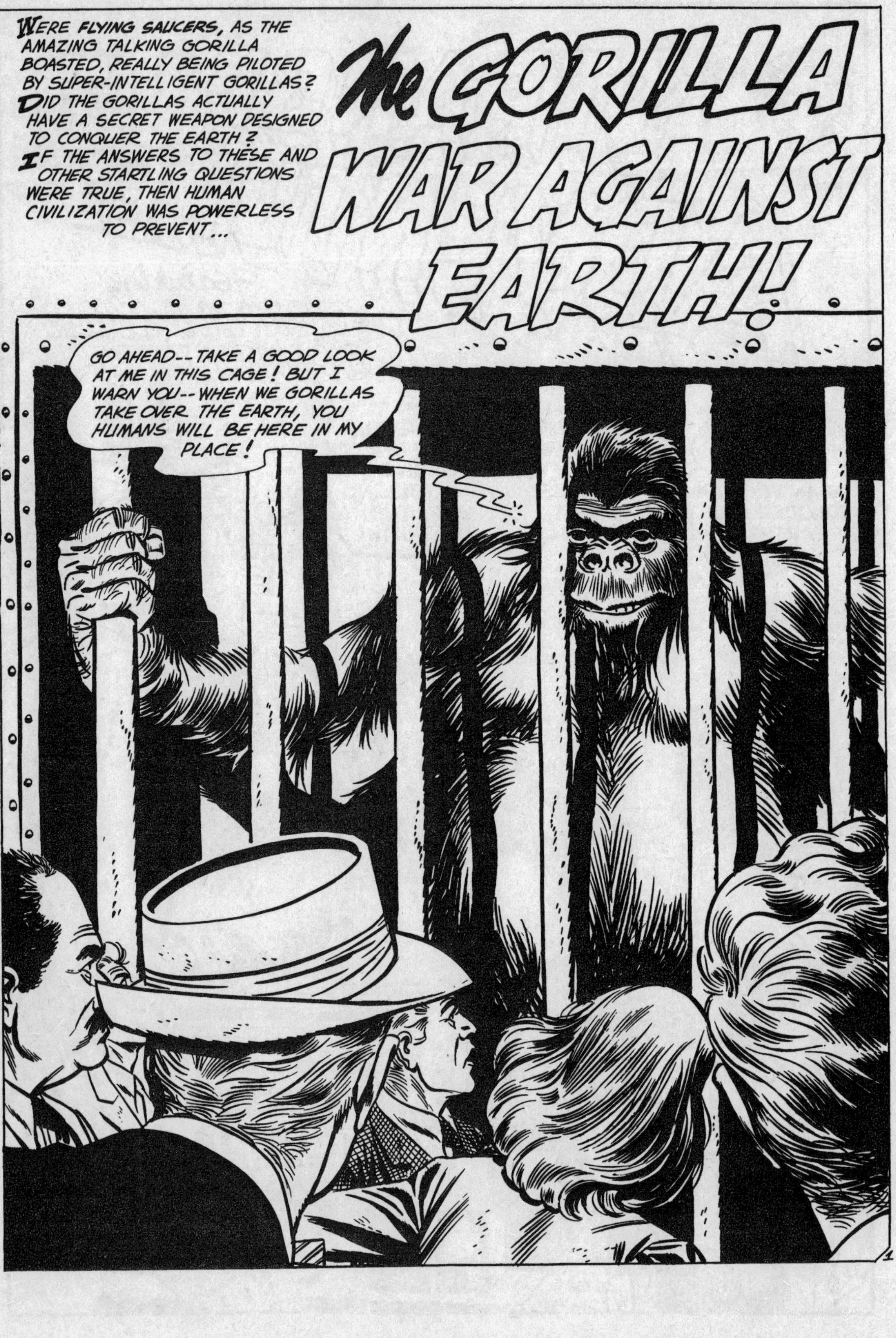
WERE FLYING SAUCERS, AS THE AMAZING TALKING GORILLA BOASTED, REALLY BEING PILOTED BY SUPER-INTELLIGENT GORILLAS? DID THE GORILLAS ACTUALLY HAVE A SECRET WEAPON DESIGNED TO CONQUER THE EARTH? IF THE ANSWERS TO THESE AND OTHER STARTLING QUESTIONS WERE TRUE, THEN HUMAN CIVILIZATION WAS POWERLESS TO PREVENT...
The GORILLA WAR AGAINST EARTH!
GO AHEAD--TAKE A GOOD LOOK AT ME IN THIS CAGE! BUT I WARN YOU--WHEN WE GORILLAS TAKE OVER THE EARTH, YOU HUMANS WILL BE HERE IN MY PLACE!
1

As the people around the zoo's gorilla cage gape in astonishment...

D-DID YOU HEAR THAT GORILLA TALK, TOO?

IN ANOTHER 50 HOURS WE WILL STRIKE WITH OUR SECRET WEAPON-- UNLESS, OF COURSE, YOU ARE WISE ENOUGH TO SURRENDER FIRST!

WELL, WHAT ARE YOU HUMANS STANDING AROUND HERE FOR? GET GOING -- DON'T YOU REALIZE YOUR WORLD IS IN DANGER?

Scientists--including *DARWIN JONES*, CHIEF OF THE *DEPARTMENT OF SCIENTIFIC INVESTIGATION...* ARE HASTILY SUMMONED TO THE SCENE...

EVEN YOU, THE TOP SCIENTISTS OF EARTH, CANNOT PREVENT THE GORILLA INVASION!

THIS IS INCREDIBLE!

A QUICK CONSULTATION IS HELD AMONG THE STARTLED SCIENTISTS...

IT'S A TRICK OF SOME SORT! THE GORILLA HAS BEEN TAUGHT--REMARK- ABLY--A FEW WORDS! WHAT DO YOU THINK, DARWIN?

THERE'S A SURE WAY TO FIND OUT! SUBMIT THE BEAST TO A LIE DETECTOR TEST!

LATER, AT *SCIENCE HALL*, AFTER ALL ARRANGEMENTS HAVE BEEN MADE...

DO YOU GORILLAS SERIOUSLY THINK YOU CAN CONQUER EARTH?

YES! WITH A SUPER-- WEAPON YOU HUMANS NEVER DREAMED OF!

THE GORILLA'S REACTION IS NORMAL! THE LIE DETECTOR SHOWS HE'S TELLING THE TRUTH!

WE ARE HIDDEN UNDERGROUND, WAITING ONLY FOR THE MOMENT TO STRIKE! WE HAVE BEEN OBSERVING YOU CONSTANTLY IN OUR *FLYING SAUCERS!*

THE *FLYING SAUCERS* ARE PILOTED BY *GORILLAS?*

YES! AND WE KNOW YOUR EVERY INVENTION--YOUR EVERY WEAPON! AND I WARN YOU--EVEN YOUR *ATOMIC BOMBS* ARE USELESS AGAINST *OUR* SECRET WEAPONS!

I INVITE YOU TO DROP ONE OF YOUR BOMBS-- AS A TEST OF OUR POWERS! OUR SECRET WEAPON WILL NEUTRALIZE IT! THAT IS ALL --I SHALL SPEAK NO MORE!

AFTER THE BEAST LAPSES INTO SILENCE, AND IS RETURNED TO THE CAGE...

DARWIN, THE DETECTOR SHOWS THAT THE GORILLA DIDN'T LIE ONCE! WHAT SHALL WE DO?

REMAIN CALM-- AND DOUBLE-CHECK OUR FINDINGS!

FIRST, LET'S MAKE SURE THE DETECTOR IS FUNCTIONING PROPERLY! FOR THAT I'LL NEED A VOLUNTEER!

WOULD YOU SUBMIT TO THE TEST, SIR?

I AM PROF. BROWNING, FORMERLY OF SOUTH AFRICA! I CAME TO STUDY THE BEAST--NOT TO BE STUDIED! HOWEVER...

3

Then, WHEN ALL IS READY...

NOW, PROFESSOR, TELL ME -- *ARE YOU FROM OUTER SPACE?*

WH-AT? I RE-FUSE TO ANSWER SUCH A RIDICULOUS QUESTION! THERE MUST BE OTHER QUESTIONS TO DETERMINE IF THE LIE DETECTOR IS FUNCTIONING PROPERLY!

ANY QUESTIONS YOU DON'T APPROVE OF, SIR -- JUST DON'T ANSWER!

I'LL GO YOU ONE BETTER! I'M NOT GOING TO ANSWER ANY OF YOUR QUESTIONS!

AFTER A LENGTHY SERIES OF QUESTIONS IS PUT TO PROF. BROWNING, ALL OF WHICH ARE UNANSWERED...

OUTER SPACE -- SPACE-CRAFT -- ALIEN INVADERS! BAH! TO HAVE HONORED SUCH QUESTIONS WITH ANSWERS WOULD HAVE MADE A LAUGHINGSTOCK OF ME! GOOD DAY!

AFTER BROWNING'S DEPARTURE...

DARWIN! WHY DID YOU ASK BROWNING SUCH EXTRAORDINARY QUESTIONS?

I SINGLED HIM OUT BECAUSE I SPOTTED HIM PULLING A *VENTRILOQUISM* TRICK ON US!

THEN YOU MEAN --

YES! I WAS NOT CONVINCED THAT A GORILLA IS ANATOMICALLY CONSTRUCTED IN THROAT AND MOUTH TO UTTER HUMAN SPEECH, SO, AS HE "SPOKE"...

...I WATCHED THE GROUP CLOSELY, RATHER THAN THE GORILLA! EACH TIME THE GORILLA "SPOKE", BROWNING'S THROAT MOVED! HE WAS THROWING HIS VOICE AT THE GORILLA!

BUT WHY WOULD BROWNING--OR WHATEVER HIS NAME IS--SUBJECT US TO SUCH A HOAX, DARWIN?

TO GAIN SOMETHING, OBVIOUSLY! A HUNCH MADE ME SUSPECT HE IS FROM AN ALIEN WORLD... NOW I'M SURE OF IT!

HOW COULD YOU DETERMINE THAT--?

EVEN THOUGH HE REMAINED SILENT, THE LIE DETECTOR GRAPH SHOWS HIS PULSE REMAINED NORMAL WHEN I ASKED HIM LEADING QUESTIONS CONCERNING HIS BEING FROM OUTER SPACE!

HIS REACTION TO MY QUESTIONS ENABLED ME TO DETERMINE THAT BROWNING AND HIS PARTY SECRETLY LANDED ON EARTH AND DEVISED THE GORILLA HOAX FOR SOME UNKNOWN REASON!

IT MUST CONCERN THE ATOM BOMB, SINCE HE WAS SO EAGER TO HAVE US DROP IT! BUT, OF COURSE, WE WON'T!

BUT, OF COURSE WE WILL! WE ARE GOING TO PLAY "BROWNING'S" GAME-- AND BEAT HIM!

ON THE FOLLOWING DAY, A PLANE ROARS HIGH OVER A REMOTE, UNINHABITED ISLAND, AND...

WE HAD TO FLY HIGH, BE- CAUSE IT'S A CONTACT BOMB--AND WILL GO OFF WHEN IT HITS THE GROUND! WE'LL HAVE PLENTY OF TIME TO BE OUT OF THE BLAST AREA!

THEN, SUDDENLY, A STRANGE CRAFT STREAKS FROM BEHIND FLEECY CLOUDS--HEADED FOR THE FALLING BOMB...

NOW! CAPTURE THE BOMB!

GREAT MAGNETIC RODS EXTEND FROM THE SHIP'S HULL AND HALT THE BOMB'S FALL...

HAUL IT IN--CAREFULLY! MAKE NO CONTACT WITH THE BOMB!

A FEW SECONDS LATER, THE CRAFT SPEEDS OFF INTO OUTER SPACE...

CONGRATULATIONS, "PROF. BROWNING"--YOUR PLAN WORKED BRILLIANTLY!

SOON, ON OUR WORLD, WE SHALL COMPLETE THE FINAL PHASE OF MY PLAN!

OUR FIRST ATTEMPT TO WIN CONTROL OF OUR WORLD FAILED--AND WE HAD TO FLEE! WE REALIZED THEN THAT WE NEEDED A SUPER-WEAPON TO GAIN VICTORY...

AS ADVANCED AS OUR CIVILIZATION IS, WE HAVE BEEN UNABLE TO MAKE AN ATOM BOMB! BUT WHILE IN SPACE, WE DETECTED ATOM BOMB TESTS ON EARTH!

THEN WE LANDED AND PERPETRATED THE GORILLA HOAX--WITH A "SECRET WEAPON" THREAT--ALL TO FORCE EARTH TO DROP AN ATOM BOMB!

MY NERVO-QUIVER RAY, UNSEEN BY THE EARTHMEN, SHOCKED THE GORILLA INTO MOVING HIS LIPS WHEN I THREW MY VOICE--MAKING IT APPEAR THE GORILLA WAS ACTUALLY SPEAKING!

NOW WE SHALL USE THIS SINGLE BOMB TO FORCE THE GOVERNMENT ON OUR PLANET TO CAPITULATE! THEY WON'T DARE REFUSE--ONCE THEY SEE ITS DESTRUCTIVE POWER!

LATER ON, AS THE CRAFT HOVERS OVER A GREAT CITY ON ANOTHER PLANET...

WE HAVE RETURNED--WITH DESTRUCTIVE BOMBS THAT CAN UTTERLY DESTROY THE WORLD!

6

WHILE IN THE MAIN GOVERNMENT BUILDING BELOW...

TURN YOUR TELE-VIEW SCREENS ON THE GREAT DESERT REGION! WE WILL FLY OVER IT--DROP *ONE* OF THE BOMBS--TO DEMONSTRATE ITS DESTRUCTIVE FORCE!

SHORTLY AFTERWARDS, AS THE WORLD BELOW WATCHES ON *TELE-VIEW* SCREENS...

WHEN THEY SEE THIS BLAST, THEY'LL SURRENDER FOR FEAR OF WHAT OUR "OTHER BOMBS" WILL DO! THEY'LL NEVER FIND OUT IT'S THE ONLY ONE WE HAVE!

THEN, THE ATOM BOMB IS DROPPED!...

AS THE BOMB LANDS...

IT FAILED TO EXPLODE!

DISPATCH AN AIRCRAFT AFTER THE REBELS-- CAPTURE THEM!

THUD!

MEANWHILE, ABOARD THE REBEL SHIP...

WHY DIDN'T IT GO OFF! *WHY? WHY?*

"*WHY DIDN'T IT GO OFF?*" THE ANSWER LIES FAR AWAY, ON EARTH, WITH DARWIN JONES...

SUSPICIOUS OF THE ALIENS' INTENTIONS, WE DIDN'T DROP A REAL BOMB--BUT A *DUD!* I DON'T KNOW WHY THEY WANTED THE BOMB-- BUT WHATEVER THE REASON, THEY'LL FIND OUT TOO LATE THAT IT WON'T GO OFF!

The End

The WARNING OUT of TIME!

UNDERNEATH THE PAINT OF A LEONARDO DA VINCI MASTER-PIECE, X-RAYS REVEAL A CRYPTIC MESSAGE OF WARNING! HOW COULD THE FAMOUS ARTIST OF THE 15TH CENTURY FORETELL DISASTER IN THE 20TH CENTURY? AND WHAT UNNAMED DISASTER WOULD IT BE? UNLESS THE OWNER OF THE DA VINCI PAINTING SOLVES THIS MYSTERY OF TIME, IN TIME, THE EARTH FACES DOOM!

THIS IS DA VINCI'S *DISASTER MAP OF EARTH!* ALL THE DISASTERS THAT THIS FAMOUS 15TH CENTURY ARTIST PREDICTED HAVE COME TRUE--EXCEPT THIS ONE IN THE MIDDLE OF AMERICA! *WHAT* WILL THE DISASTER BE? *WHEN* WILL IT OCCUR?

IN THE OLD HOMESTEAD HE HAS RECENTLY INHERITED, LARRY LLOYD CLEANS OUT THE CLUTTERED ATTIC...

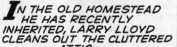

AUNT SOPHIE KEPT A LOT OF JUNK I'LL GET RID OF!

BUT ONE ITEM IS HARDLY JUNK!

A PAINTING--SIGNED BY THE FAMOUS LEONARDO DA VINCI IN 1482! IT'S WORTH A FORTUNE... IF IT'S GENUINE! I'LL HAVE IT CHECKED AT AN ART STUDIO!

AT THE STUDIO, WHERE MODERN SCIENTIFIC METHODS ARE USED TO DETECT FORGED ART TREASURES...

THE STYLE AND COLORS SEEM AUTHENTIC! BUT X-RAYS WILL REVEAL IF THE CANVAS UNDERNEATH IS LESS THAN 500 YEARS OLD, PROVING IT A FRAUD!

THE X-RAY PLATES REVEAL A STARTLING DISCOVERY!

LOOK! THERE'S ANOTHER DRAWING UNDERNEATH! FOR SOME REASON DA VINCI PAINTED A PICTURE OVER THE ORIGINAL ONE!

WHY, THIS IS INCREDIBLE! IT'S A MAP OF THE WORLD AS WE KNOW IT TODAY! BUT IF DA VINCI MADE IT IN 1482, TEN YEARS BEFORE COLUMBUS DISCOVERED AMERICA, HOW COULD HE POSSIBLY KNOW THAT NORTH AND SOUTH AMERICA EXISTED?

AS THE ART EXPERT OPENS A BIOGRAPHY OF DA VINCI...

FOR THAT MATTER, BY WHAT UNCANNY GENIUS COULD DA VINCI IN THE 15th CENTURY PROPHESY SO MANY OF OUR 20th CENTURY INVENTIONS?

Inventions of Da Vinci, 1452 - 1519

FLYING MACHINE

UNDERSEA CRAFT

CANNON

HMM...YOU WOULD ALMOST THINK HE HAD...ER... TRAVELED INTO THE FUTURE AND VISITED OUR TIMES! BUT THAT'S RIDICULOUS, OF COURSE!

RIDICULOUS? LET US TURN THE CALENDAR BACK TO THE YEAR 1482, IN ANCIENT ITALY, WHERE DA VINCI LABORS IN HIS STUDIO...

I GATHERED MANY STRANGE CHEMICALS AND PIGMENTS! I WILL BLEND NEW COLORS FOR MY NEXT PAINTING! BY THE KING'S BEARD -- WHAT IS THAT GLOW EMANATING FROM THE MORTAR...

2

By SHEER CHANCE, THE MASTER ARTIST HAS COMPOUNDED A FANTASTIC FORMULA, EMITTING PECULIAR RAYS...

I-I AM TURNING *TRANSPARENT!*

MYSTERIOUS FORCES PLUNGE DA VINCI ALONG AN INCREDIBLE PATHWAY IN TIME...

DAYS -- YEARS -- CENTURIES ARE FLASHING BY RAPIDLY AS THE EARTH SPINS BENEATH ME!

FINALLY, THE DIZZY WHIRL STOPS AND THE TRANSPARENT ARTIST WAFTS DOWN TOWARD A METROPOLIS...

MY AMAZING JOURNEY THROUGH TIME HAS BROUGHT ME TO A WONDROUS CITY FAR BEYOND MY BACKWARD AGE! I WILL LEARN ALL I CAN OF THIS CIVILIZATION!

BUT I AM LIKE A "WRAITH" HERE, WITHOUT SOLIDITY! THUS NO ONE CAN SEE OR HEAR ME! FORTUNATELY, I CAN HEAR THEM... I SHALL LISTEN AND LEARN THEIR STRANGE LANGUAGE!

SO I SAID TO THE BOSS...

WITH THE HELP OF A PUBLIC LIBRARY, DA VINCI'S KEEN MIND QUICKLY MASTERS MODERN SPEECH AND WRITING...

C-A-T--CAT! SOON I SHALL READ MORE ADVANCED BOOKS IN THIS LIBRARY, CRAMMING KNOWLEDGE OF THIS AMAZING YEAR OF 1958 INTO MY MIND! PERHAPS I'M ONLY A TEMPORARY VISITOR HERE, AND WILL BE EVENTUALLY WHISKED BACK TO MY TIME!

WHILE HE REMAINS, THE PHANTOM TIME TOURIST EAGERLY ABSORBS INFORMATION...

I SHALL MAKE SKETCHES OF THEIR GREAT INVENTIONS WHEN I RETURN TO MY TIME! AND I'LL STUDY IMPORTANT HISTORICAL EVENTS BETWEEN 1482 AND 1958...

STORY OF GREAT INVENTIONS

STORY OF GREAT INVENTIONS

DISASTERS OF HISTORY

ERUPTION OF KRAKATOA, EAST INDIES, 1883

LATER, VISITING A HOME OUT OF CURIOSITY, DA VINCI IS INTRODUCED TO TELEVISION, WHEN SUDDENLY...

"A GEYSER OF RADIOACTIVE GASES HAS BURST FROM UNDERGROUND, IN HOT SPRINGS VALLEY IN THE CENTRAL UNITED STATES! AS THE DEADLY NUCLEAR CLOUD SPREADS, THERE WILL BE TREMENDOUS LOSS OF LIFE, UNLESS..."

A DISASTER OF 1958! HOW WILL THEY STOP IT?

BUT AT THAT MOMENT, THE UNSEEN WINDS OF TIME GRIP THE MAN FROM THE PAST AND...

THE TIME FORMULA'S EFFECTS WORE OFF! I AM BEING SWEPT BACK TO 1482! I WONDER IF THE EARTH WILL BE SAVED IN TIME FROM THAT DEADLY NUCLEAR GEYSER?

BACK IN HIS OWN TIME, DA VINCI IS PLAGUED BY WORRY...

I MUST **WARN** THEM OF THE **DISASTER OF 1958!** BUT IF I WRITE OUT ANY MESSAGE, SUPERSTITIOUS PEOPLE OF THIS UNENLIGHTENED AGE WILL HOUND ME FOR "WITCHCRAFT"!

I HAVE IT! I'LL SEND A **DISGUISED** WARNING TO THE FUTURE, WITH THE HELP OF THIS WORLD MAP I DREW FROM MEMORY! I'M SURE THE FUTURE PEOPLE WILL BE ABLE TO SOLVE THIS SECRET "CODE" OF DOTS I'M SCATTERING OVER THE MAP!

I WILL PAINT AN ORDINARY PICTURE OVER THE MAP... THUS WILL MY ART WORK BE PRESERVED FOR AT LEAST 500 YEARS! I SAW THE FUTURE-PEOPLE USE X-RAYS... THEY WILL DISCOVER MY MAP UNDERNEATH!

AND IT IS IN THIS STRANGE MANNER, THAT LARRY LLOYD HAS STUMBLED ON DA VINCI'S CRYPTIC WARNING, IN 1957!

WHAT DO THESE MYSTERIOUS DOTS MEAN? WAIT... I VAGUELY RECALL THIS ONE IS AT THE EXACT SPOT WHERE A NATURAL DISASTER OCCURRED! I'LL CHECK IN A BOOK!

4

SOON, BY COINCIDENCE, IN THE VERY LIBRARY DA VINCI HAD VISITED...

I WAS RIGHT! NOW TO CHECK THE OTHER DOTS TOO!

DISASTERS OF HISTORY
ERUPTION OF KRAKATOA, EAST INDIES, 1883.

THIS DOT MARKS TOKYO, JAPAN... A THIRD OF THE CITY WAS DESTROYED BY A TERRIBLE EARTH-QUAKE IN 1923!

A DOT IN NORTHERN SIBERIA MARKS WHERE, IN 1907, A GIGANTIC METEORITE LANDED, LEVELING FORESTS FOR MANY MILES AROUND, DESTROYING THE HOMES OF UNFORTUNATE PEASANTS!

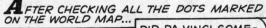

AFTER CHECKING ALL THE DOTS MARKED ON THE WORLD MAP...

DID DA VINCI SOME-HOW TRAVEL INTO THE FUTURE FOR THIS KNOWLEDGE? EVERY DOT MARKED A NATURAL DISASTER OF HISTORY... EXCEPT *THIS* ONE IN THE MIDDLE OF AMERICA! IT MUST BE A WARNING THAT ONE *WILL* OCCUR HERE... AROUND HOT SPRING VALLEY!

WHAT WILL THE DISASTER BE? WHEN WILL IT OCCUR? DA VINCI DIDN'T TELL! BUT I'LL WARN THE AUTHORITIES TO PREPARE FOR AN EARTHQUAKE, FLOOD, TORNADO, LAVA ERUPTION, METEOR... *ANYTHING!*

POLICE CARS ONLY

7TH PCT

5

DISASTER CREWS ARE STATIONED IN HOT SPRINGS VALLEY, ON 24-HOUR ALERT! BUT AS TIME SLIPS BY, WEEK AFTER WEEK...

WE'VE BEEN WAITING SIX MONTHS NOW, LLOYD! IT LOOKS LIKE YOU HAVE THIS PROPHETIC WARNING WRONG!

NO! WHY WOULD DA VINCI TRY SUCH A COLOSSAL *HOAX* ON US? WE MUST KEEP ON THE ALERT...

THEN, ONE DAY IN JULY, 1958, NOT FAR FROM WHERE A TV-CREW IS ON THE READY...

FLASH! A GEYSER OF RADIOACTIVE GASES HAS BURST FROM UNDERGROUND!

BUT THE WAITING CREWS ARE TAKEN UNAWARES!

WE WERE PREPARED FOR ALMOST ANYTHING *EXCEPT* A NUCLEAR GEYSER! THERE'S NO PRECEDENT IN EARTH'S HISTORY FOR SUCH A DISASTER!

WE HAVE NO WAY TO "CAP" IT! THE GASES MAY CREATE A DEADLY "FALLOUT" ALL OVER EARTH!

BUT LARRY LLOYD HAS A DESPERATE IDEA!

THAT ATOMIC CANNON WAS SET UP TO BLAST ANY LARGE METEOR HURTLING DOWN FROM OUTER SPACE! IT MAY STILL SAVE US! AIM FOR THAT CLIFF, MEN! HURRY!

WHEN THE SUPER-POWERFUL ATOMIC SHELLS BOMBARD THE CLIFF...

THE WHOLE CLIFF CRUMBLED, BURYING THE HOLE UNDER MILLIONS OF TONS OF ROCK AND STOPPING THE GEYSER! AMERICA--THE WORLD-- HAS BEEN SAVED FROM DISASTER!

LATER, AT LARRY LLOYD'S HOME...

THE PAINTING ON TOP, ONE OF DA VINCI'S MASTER-PIECES, IS APPRAISED AT ONE MILLION DOLLARS, BUT THE DISASTER MAP OF EARTH UNDERNEATH IS WORTH *FAR MORE*...IT IS A WARNING FROM THE PAST THAT SAVED THE LIFE OF EVERY PERSON ON EARTH!

The End

BODYGUARD FROM SPACE!

EVERY MOMENT OF THE DAY AND NIGHT THE ALIEN FROM ANOTHER WORLD STAYED CLOSE TO THE EARTHMAN-- WAITING FOR HIM TO SPEAK AND TELL THE ALIEN HOW TO SAVE HIS WORLD FROM DESTRUCTION...

HELP!

CAN'T LET THAT EARTHMAN FALL TO HIS DEATH! HE HAS INFORMATION THAT WILL SAVE MY NATIVE WORLD FROM DOOM!

EARLY ONE MORNING AS NEWS CAMERAMAN JIM CARSON LEAVES FOR WORK...

I'VE BEEN WAITING FOR YOU, EARTHMAN!

WH- WHAT IS THIS-- A GAG? WHO ARE YOU?

DO NOT BE ALARMED! I'VE JOURNEYED ACROSS THREE BILLION LIGHT YEARS OF SPACE-- TO BE YOUR BODYGUARD! MY MISSION IS TO SEE NOTHING HAPPENS TO YOU...

WHAT MAKES *ME* SO IMPORTANT TO *YOU*?

YOU HAVE INFORMATION THAT WILL SAVE MY WORLD FROM DESTRUCTION!

I DON'T KNOW WHAT YOU'RE TALKING ABOUT! BEAT IT, PAL--

I CANNOT LEAVE YOUR SIDE! HOWEVER, TO PREVENT EMBARRASSING QUESTIONS, I SHALL MAKE MYSELF *INVISIBLE* TO ALL EARTHLINGS BUT YOU!

WHEN JIM CARSON ENTERS HIS BUS...

DON'T FORGET TO COLLECT FROM THIS JOKER BEHIND ME!

NOBODY'S BEHIND YOU, MISTER!

A LITTLE LATER, AT A NEW CONSTRUCTION UNIT...

I'VE BEEN ASSIGNED TO TAKE SOME INTERESTING SHOTS OF THIS NEW BUILDING! THERE'S ONLY ROOM FOR THREE MEN ON THAT ELEVATOR! YOU'LL HAVE TO STAY BEHIND!

AS THE ELEVATOR ASCENDS...

I AM RIGHT BESIDE YOU, EARTHMAN--THOUGH ONLY *YOU* CAN HEAR MY VOICE! I'VE MADE MYSELF INTANGIBLE SO I WON'T TAKE UP ANY SPACE!

F-FANTASTIC!

ALONE WITH HIS STRANGE ACQUAINTANCE ON A BUILDING GIRDER, THE NEWS CAMERAMAN GIVES WAY TO HIS CURIOSITY...

ALL RIGHT, I'M CONVINCED! YOU'RE NO EARTHMAN! WHAT'S YOUR STORY? HOW CAN I POSSIBLY HAVE ANY INFORMATION VITAL TO THE WELFARE OF YOUR PLANET?

2

"MY HOME PLANET IS CALLED KLYSISTRON! RECENTLY WE DISCOVERED THAT THE STAR-SUN GIVING US HEAT AND LIGHT WAS DYING!"

THE SUN HAS CONSUMED THE VITAL ELEMENT F-345-TX IT NEEDS TO SUSTAIN ITS HEAT!

THE ELEMENT EXISTS NOWHERE IN OUR SOLAR SYSTEM!

WE SHALL SEND ONE-MAN SPACESHIPS TO SCOUR EVERY PLANET IN THE UNIVERSE FOR F-345-TX! ONLY BY REPLENISHING OUR SUN WITH THE VITAL ELEMENT CAN WE HOPE TO SURVIVE!

"THOUSANDS OF SMALL SPACERS LEFT KLYSISTRON, TO BEGIN THEIR GALACTIC SEARCH..."

NO PLANET IS TOO LARGE, NO PLANET TOO SMALL! WE SHALL SEARCH THEM ALL! WE MUST REPORT OUR FINDING ONCE EVERY XATAL!*

*EDITOR'S NOTE: AN ALIEN UNIT OF TIME.

"ONE BY ONE THE DISCOURAGING REPORTS CAME IN..."

FAILURE, FAILURE! EVIDENTLY F-345-TX EXISTS NOWHERE ELSE IN THE UNIVERSE!

ONLY ONE MAN FAILED TO REPORT! KUL ZON-- WHO WENT TO THE PLANET EARTH! TWO XATALS HAVE PASSED WITHOUT OUR HEARING FROM HIM! I WAS DISPATCHED HERE TO LEARN WHAT HAPPENED!

"I FOUND KUL ZON--DEAD! THEN MY INSTRUMENTS PICKED UP AN INVISIBLE AURA THAT HAD BEEN PLACED AROUND YOUR BODY..."

IT WAS PLACED THERE BY KUL ZON TO SIGNIFY HE IMPLANTED A TELEPATHIC MESSAGE IN THE EARTHMAN'S MIND! IT IS A DEVICE WE OFTEN USE TO RELAY MESSAGES WHEN THE SENDER IS UNABLE TO DO SO HIMSELF...

3

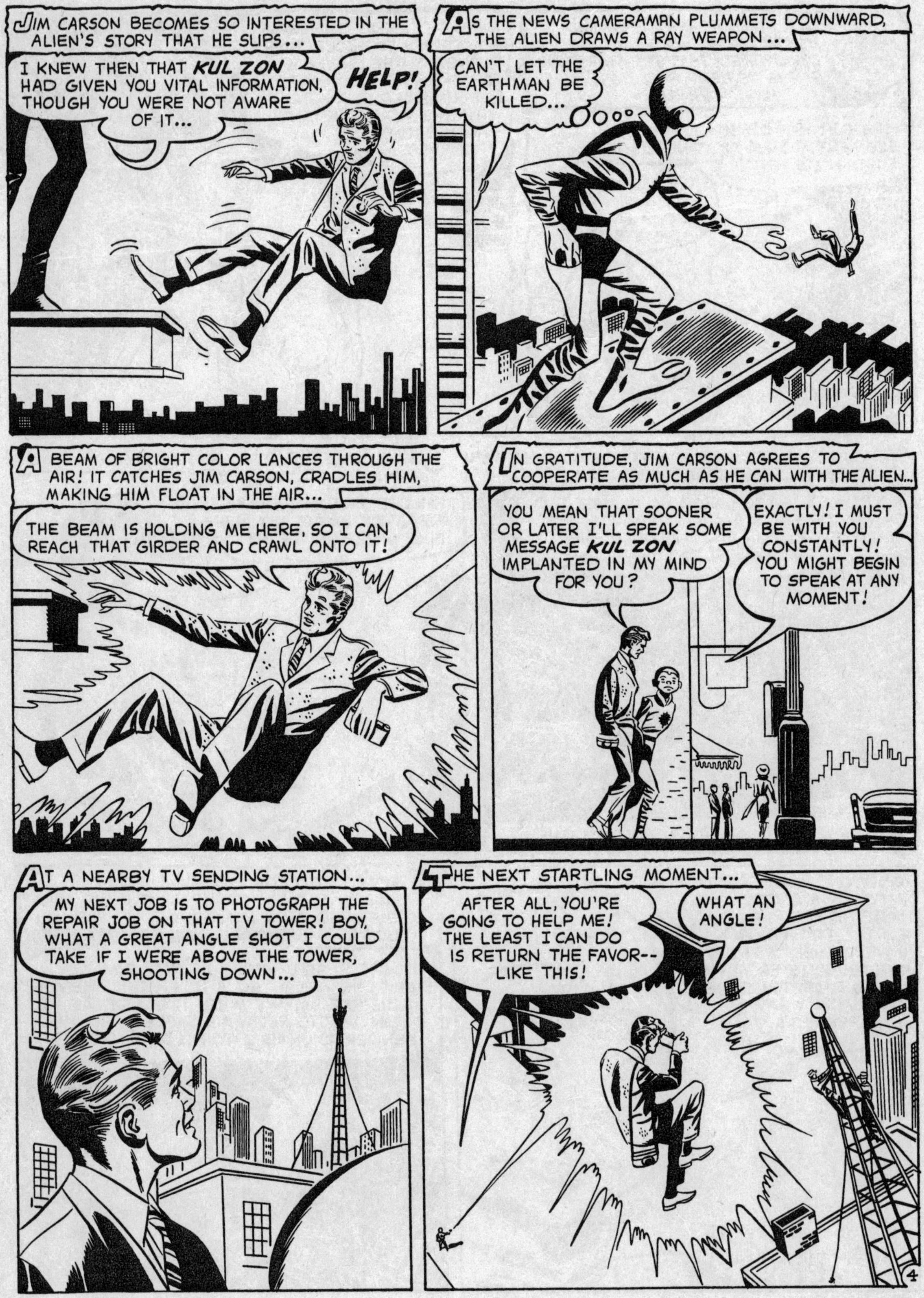
JIM CARSON BECOMES SO INTERESTED IN THE ALIEN'S STORY THAT HE SLIPS...
I KNEW THEN THAT KUL ZON HAD GIVEN YOU VITAL INFORMATION, THOUGH YOU WERE NOT AWARE OF IT...
HELP!
AS THE NEWS CAMERAMAN PLUMMETS DOWNWARD, THE ALIEN DRAWS A RAY WEAPON...
CAN'T LET THE EARTHMAN BE KILLED...
A BEAM OF BRIGHT COLOR LANCES THROUGH THE AIR! IT CATCHES JIM CARSON, CRADLES HIM, MAKING HIM FLOAT IN THE AIR...
THE BEAM IS HOLDING ME HERE, SO I CAN REACH THAT GIRDER AND CRAWL ONTO IT!
IN GRATITUDE, JIM CARSON AGREES TO COOPERATE AS MUCH AS HE CAN WITH THE ALIEN...
YOU MEAN THAT SOONER OR LATER I'LL SPEAK SOME MESSAGE KUL ZON IMPLANTED IN MY MIND FOR YOU?
EXACTLY! I MUST BE WITH YOU CONSTANTLY! YOU MIGHT BEGIN TO SPEAK AT ANY MOMENT!
AT A NEARBY TV SENDING STATION...
MY NEXT JOB IS TO PHOTOGRAPH THE REPAIR JOB ON THAT TV TOWER! BOY, WHAT A GREAT ANGLE SHOT I COULD TAKE IF I WERE ABOVE THE TOWER, SHOOTING DOWN...
THE NEXT STARTLING MOMENT...
AFTER ALL, YOU'RE GOING TO HELP ME! THE LEAST I CAN DO IS RETURN THE FAVOR-- LIKE THIS!
WHAT AN ANGLE!
4

As THE ANTI-GRAVITY BEAM LOWERS HIM TOWARD THE GROUND, JIM CARSON SUDDENLY BEGINS TO SPEAK...

THIS IS *KUL ZON* RELAYING ON A MESSAGE TELEPATHICALLY IMPLANTED IN THIS EARTHMAN'S MIND...

"WHEN I LANDED ON THIS PLANET, I TESTED SOIL, AIR, AND WATER FOR ELEMENT *F-345-TX*..."

NO TRACK OF IT SO FAR...

"JUST AS I WAS ABOUT TO ABANDON THE SEARCH, MY ELEMENT-COUNTER BEGAN TO CLICK..."

A VEIN OF *F-345-TX*- 950 MILES BELOW THE SURFACE OF THE PLANET! THAT'S WHY MY INSTRUMENTS DID NOT REGISTER IT SOONER!

CLICK! CLICK!

"TO CHECK MY FINDINGS, I BLASTED A PATH FAR DOWN INTO THE EARTH..."

F-345-TX WAS FORMED DEEP BENEATH THE EARTH, WHERE IT WAS SUBJECTED TO THE PLANET'S TERRIFIC HEAT AND PRESSURE!

"WHEN I ROSE BACK TO THE SURFACE, I FOUND MYSELF PANTING FOR BREATH..."

JUST AS A DEEPSEA DIVER...GETS THE BENDS... FROM RISING TOO SWIFTLY... SO I ALSO FATALLY INJURED MYSELF...

"I HAD ONE DESPERATE HOPE..."

I MUST PLANT A TELEPATHIC MESSAGE IN THE BRAIN OF THAT EARTHMAN, SO MY PEOPLE, WHEN THEY COME TO LEARN MY FATE, WILL LEARN THE VITAL INFORMATION I HAVE DISCOVERED!

5

"NATURALLY, THE EARTHMAN WAS UNAWARE THAT I HAD IMPLANTED MY MESSAGE IN HIS BRAIN..."

MY PEOPLE DISCOVERING MY FATE, WILL FIND HIM THROUGH THE AURA! I ARRANGED TO HAVE THAT MESSAGE SPOKEN ONLY AFTER THEY'VE HAD SUFFICIENT TIME TO ARRIVE HERE AND BE AT HIS SIDE!

LATER, AT THE SPOT WHERE *KUL ZON* MADE HIS MOMENTOUS DISCOVERY...

HERE IT IS — THE PRECIOUS ELEMENT THAT WILL IGNITE THE SUN AND SAVE MY WORLD!

WHEN A SUFFICIENT AMOUNT OF THE ORE IS STORED IN THE SPACESHIPS...

I'LL FLY *KUL ZON'S* SHIP BACK BY REMOTE CONTROL! YOU SAVED MY PEOPLE, JIM! WE ARE GRATEFUL...

SOMETIME LATER, AT AN ASTRONOMICAL OBSERVATORY...

HAVE YOU NOTICED ANYTHING PECULIAR ABOUT STAR-SUN 2374, PROFESSOR?

WHY, YES! IN THE PAST FEW MONTHS IT'S BEEN GROWING DIMMER AND DIMMER!

LOOK AT IT NOW AND TELL ME WHAT YOU SEE!

INCREDIBLE! STAR-SUN 2374 IS BLAZING BRIGHTLY— LIKE A NOVA! I WONDER WHAT CAUSED IT?

THAT FLAREUP PROVES THAT THE EARTH ELEMENT HAS RESTORED THE BRIGHTNESS TO *KLYSISTRON'S* SUN! LIFE ON THAT PLANET WILL CONTINUE FOR SEVERAL MORE THOUSAND YEARS!

The End

The Secret of the Sleeping Spaceman!

EARTH IS THE ONLY PLANET THAT HAS ENOUGH OXYGEN IN ITS ATMOSPHERE TO SUSTAIN LIFE! DOES THIS MEAN INTELLIGENT LIFE CANNOT EVOLVE ON OTHER WORLDS--OR IS IT POSSIBLE FOR LIVING BEINGS TO BREATHE SOME OTHER GASEOUS ELEMENT? MOST INCREDIBLE OF ALL IS THE "AIR" A VISITOR FROM ANOTHER WORLD REQUIRES TO SURVIVE ON EARTH!

WHICH OF THESE GASES WILL REVIVE THE SLEEPING SPACEMAN?

IF MY THEORY IS RIGHT, THE "ELEMENT" HE BREATHES IS THE *LAST* THING IN THE UNIVERSE WE WOULD SUSPECT!

METHANE

AMMONIA CHLORINE ARGON

CARBON DIOXIDE

FROM ALL OVER THE EARTH, FAMOUS SCIENTISTS HAVE CONGREGATED AT THE HOSPITAL IN THE SMALL TOWN OF WOODVILLE, TO SOLVE A UNIQUE SCIENTIFIC RIDDLE...

WHAT KIND OF AIR DID THIS SLEEPING SPACEMAN BREATHE ON HIS NATIVE WORLD? WE'VE PUMPED IN OXYGEN...NITROGEN...CARBON DIOXIDE... BUT NONE OF THEM HAS REVIVED HIM FROM HIS COMA!

PERHAPS HE CAME FROM JUPITER OR SATURN--WHICH HAVE ATMOSPHERES COMPOSED OF METHANE AND AMMONIA! THOUGH POISONOUS TO US, THEY MAY BE LIFE-GIVING "AIR" TO HIM!

THE HEART-BEAT AMPLIFIER INDICATES A SLOW BEAT OF ONCE AN HOUR... LIKE HIBERNATING ANIMALS! HE IS IN A STATE OF SUSPENDED ANIMATION AND ONLY THE RIGHT "AIR" CAN REVIVE HIM!

MEANWHILE, THE SENSATIONAL STORY IS TELEVISED...

WHAT STRANGE KIND OF AIR DOES THE SLEEPING SPACEMAN REQUIRE? NOBODY KNOWS! HE HAS BEEN IN A COMA, UNABLE TO COMMUNICATE WITH US SINCE HE ARRIVED ON EARTH...

HIS SPACESHIP CRASHED ON THE OUTSKIRTS OF WOODVILLE YESTERDAY, FLINGING HIM OUT AND SMASHING HIS SPACE-HELMET! HE WAS CHOKING AND GASPING WHEN FOUND -- AS IF UNABLE TO BREATHE OUR EARTHLY AIR!

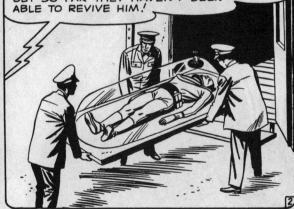

THE HOSPITAL PREPARED A SPECIAL "GLASS LUNG" FOR HIM, TO TRY OUT VARIOUS "ATMOSPHERES"! PROMINENT SCIENTISTS WERE SUMMONED TO SOLVE THE MYSTERY-- BUT SO FAR THEY HAVEN'T BEEN ABLE TO REVIVE HIM!

AS GASEOUS ELEMENT AFTER ELEMENT IS PUMPED INTO THE "GLASS LUNG"...

WE'VE TRIED ALL THE GASES WE KNOW! PERHAPS IT IS SOME RARE GASEOUS ELEMENT UNKNOWN ON EARTH? IF SO, WE CAN NEVER REVIVE THE SLEEPING SPACEMAN!

HELIUM CHLORI PROPANE FLUORINE ROUS OXIDE

MEANWHILE, AS HARRY WALTON RETURNS FROM NATURE STUDIES OUTSIDE TOWN...

MY MOTOR SUDDENLY DIED! YET I HAVE PLENTY OF GAS! ‑GASP!‑ SOMETHING'S WRONG WITH THE AIR HERE*...

*EDITOR'S NOTE: IN AN INTERNAL COMBUSTION ENGINE, OXYGEN IS NEEDED TO BURN THE GASOLINE WHICH POWERS THE PISTONS... IF AIR IS CUT, THE MOTOR INSTANTLY STOPS!

‑CHOKE!‑...THAT BIRD DROPPED IN MID-FLIGHT...! IS IT POISON GAS? ...‑GASP!‑

BUT ASTOUNDINGLY, WHEN HIS HANDKERCHIEF SLIPS FROM HIS FINGERS...

WHY, IT--IT FELL LIKE A STONE, INSTEAD OF FLUTTERING DOWN! GOOD GOSH! THIS REMINDS ME OF TWO FAMOUS SCIENTIFIC EXPERIMENTS...

MORE THAN 300 YEARS AGO, GALILEO DROPPED A 10-POUND AND A 1-POUND WEIGHT FROM THE LEANING TOWER OF PISA, PROVING THAT ALL OBJECTS, LIGHT OR HEAVY, DROP AT THE **SAME SPEED!**

AND WHEN THE AIR IS PUMPED OUT OF A JAR, A **FEATHER** DROPS AS FAST AS AN IRON WEIGHT-- BECAUSE THERE IS NO AIR RESISTANCE TO SLOW THE LIGHTER OBJECT DOWN!

SO IT ISN'T POISON GAS CHOKING ME... BUT THE *ABSENCE* OF ANY GAS OR AIR... A *VACUUM!* I'VE GOT TO RUN OUT OF IT... AH, FRESH AIR AGAIN....!

*A*MAZED AT THE PHENOMENON, HARRY IMPROVISES A CHECK-TEST...

HOW A VACUUM BUBBLE CAN EXIST BY ITSELF, I CAN'T IMAGINE! BUT I CAN TEST HOW BIG IT IS WITH MY HANDKERCHIEF ON A STICK... AH! IT WENT LIMP... NO BREEZE THERE, WITHIN THE EDGE OF THE VACUUM BUBBLE!

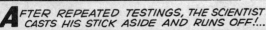

*A*FTER REPEATED TESTINGS, THE SCIENTIST CASTS HIS STICK ASIDE AND RUNS OFF!...

THE VACUUM BUBBLE, ORIGINALLY SEVERAL YARDS WIDE, IS *EXPANDING* RAPIDLY! IT'LL REACH WOODVILLE IN AN HOUR! I'VE GOT TO WARN THE TOWN!

*A*T WOODVILLE, AFTER WALTON BRINGS THE GRIM NEWS...

...AND THE AIRLESS BUBBLE WILL SOON ENGULF THE WHOLE TOWN! *NO MAN ON EARTH CAN LIVE OR BREATHE IN A VACUUM!* RUN, EVERYBODY... LEAVE TOWN!

*M*OMENTS LATER, HARRY SUDDENLY BECOMES AWARE OF THE OTHER AMAZING DEVELOPMENT THAT OCCURRED WHILE HE WAS OUT OF TOWN...

I'M AFRAID THERE ISN'T TIME FOR ALL THE TOWN TO EVACUATE... WAIT, WHAT'S THIS?

WOODVILLE NEWS
SCIENTISTS UNABLE TO FIND "AIR" TO REVIVE SLEEPING SPACEMAN!

*A*FTER READING THE DETAILS...

A SPACEMAN LANDS ON EARTH... AND A STRANGE VACUUM BUBBLE APPEARS... *AT THE SAME TIME...!* IT CAN'T BE SHEER COINCIDENCE! THERE MUST BE SOME CONNECTION... GREAT SCOTT! I HAVE A WILD IDEA... I MUST SEE THAT *SLEEPING SPACEMAN!*

4

SOON, AT THE DESERTED HOSPITAL...

THE SCIENTISTS ALL LEFT TO HELP EVACUATE THE HOSPITAL PATIENTS! NOW TO TRY MY IDEA! THIS VACUUM-PUMP WAS USED TO CLEAR OLD GASES OUT WHEN TRYING NEW ONES!

VACUUM PUMP

BUT INSTEAD OF PUMPING *IN* ANY AIR OR GAS, I'M GOING TO PUMP IT ALL *OUT!* TURN THE "GLASS LUNG" INTO A VACUUM!

MOMENTS LATER...

DON'T STOP! PUMP OUT THE REST OF THE AIR!

HE'S REVIVING! I HEAR HIS TELE-PATHIC RADIATIONS...

FINALLY, WHEN THERE IS A PURE VACUUM...

NO AIR OR GAS CHOKING ME NOW! YOU SAVED ME, EARTH-MAN!

NOBODY GUESSED THE FANTAS-TIC TRUTH BEFORE... THAT THE AIR HE BREATHES IS *NO AIR AT ALL!* HIS NATURAL ENVIRONMENT MUST BE A VACUUM!

CORRECT, EARTHMAN! MY NATIVE WORLD IS *AIRLESS!* EVOLUTION HAS ENABLED OUR RACE TO LIVE WITHOUT AIR AND ABSORB ENERGY DIRECT FROM SUNLIGHT!

"UNFORTUNATELY, I CAUSED THE VACUUM BUBBLE NEAR YOUR TOWN! YOU SEE, WHEN EXPLORING OTHER WORLDS, WE CARRY VACUUM BOMBS FOR EMERGENCY USE..."

MY VACUUM-HEADGEAR RIPPED! THE AIR OF THIS WORLD IS RUSHING IN TO CHOKE ME... ⤓GASP!⤒ BUT MY BOMB WILL CREATE A VACUUM AROUND ME, IN WHICH I CAN SURVIVE WHILE I REPAIR MY HEADGEAR!

5

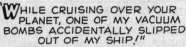

"WHILE CRUISING OVER YOUR PLANET, ONE OF MY VACUUM BOMBS ACCIDENTALLY SLIPPED OUT OF MY SHIP!"

THAT *VACUUM BUBBLE* IS A MENACE TO THOSE AIR-BREATHING PEOPLE! I MUST LAND AND WARN THEM--!

IN MY HASTE, I CRASH-LANDED AND TORE OPEN MY HEADGEAR! I ONLY HAD TIME TO SWALLOW A *SUSPENDED-ANIMATION PILL* BEFORE BLACKING IT WOULD KEEP ME ALIVE UNTIL YOU EARTHMEN REALIZED ONLY A VACUUM COULD REVIVE ME AGAIN!

BUT NOW I CAN SAVE *YOU!* TAKE THIS *ANTI-VACUUM BOMB* FROM MY SPACE-SUIT'S BELT! IT WILL CREATE A FORCE-FIELD AND COLLAPSE THE VACUUM BUBBLE!

I'LL HAVE TO HURRY... THE VACUUM BUBBLE MUST BE AT THE OUTSKIRTS OF TOWN NOW... WITH HUNDREDS OF PEOPLE STILL TRAPPED!

VACUUM PUMP

REACHING THE EDGE OF TOWN JUST AS THE VACUUM BUBBLE ARRIVES... THE ANTI-VACUUM BOMB HAS MADE THE VACUUM BUBBLE COLLAPSE AND FILL WITH AIR! THE TOWN -- THE WHOLE EARTH-- IS SAVED!

WHOOSH

AFTER THE SPACE-HELMET AND SPACESHIP OF THE VACUUM MAN ARE REPAIRED...

SORRY I CAUSED TROUBLE FOR YOUR WORLD!

IT WAS ALL AN ACCIDENT! LUCKILY, NOT A SINGLE LIFE WAS LOST! FAREWELL!

LATER, WHEN WALTON EXPLAINS HIS CLUE TO THE SECRET OF THE SLEEPING SPACEMAN...

I REMEMBERED CERTAIN WARNING WORDS TO THE TOWNSPEOPLE--"NO MAN *ON EARTH* COULD LIVE OR BREATHE IN A VACUUM!" I SHOUTED... BUT WHY NOT A MAN FROM *ANOTHER WORLD?*

THE END

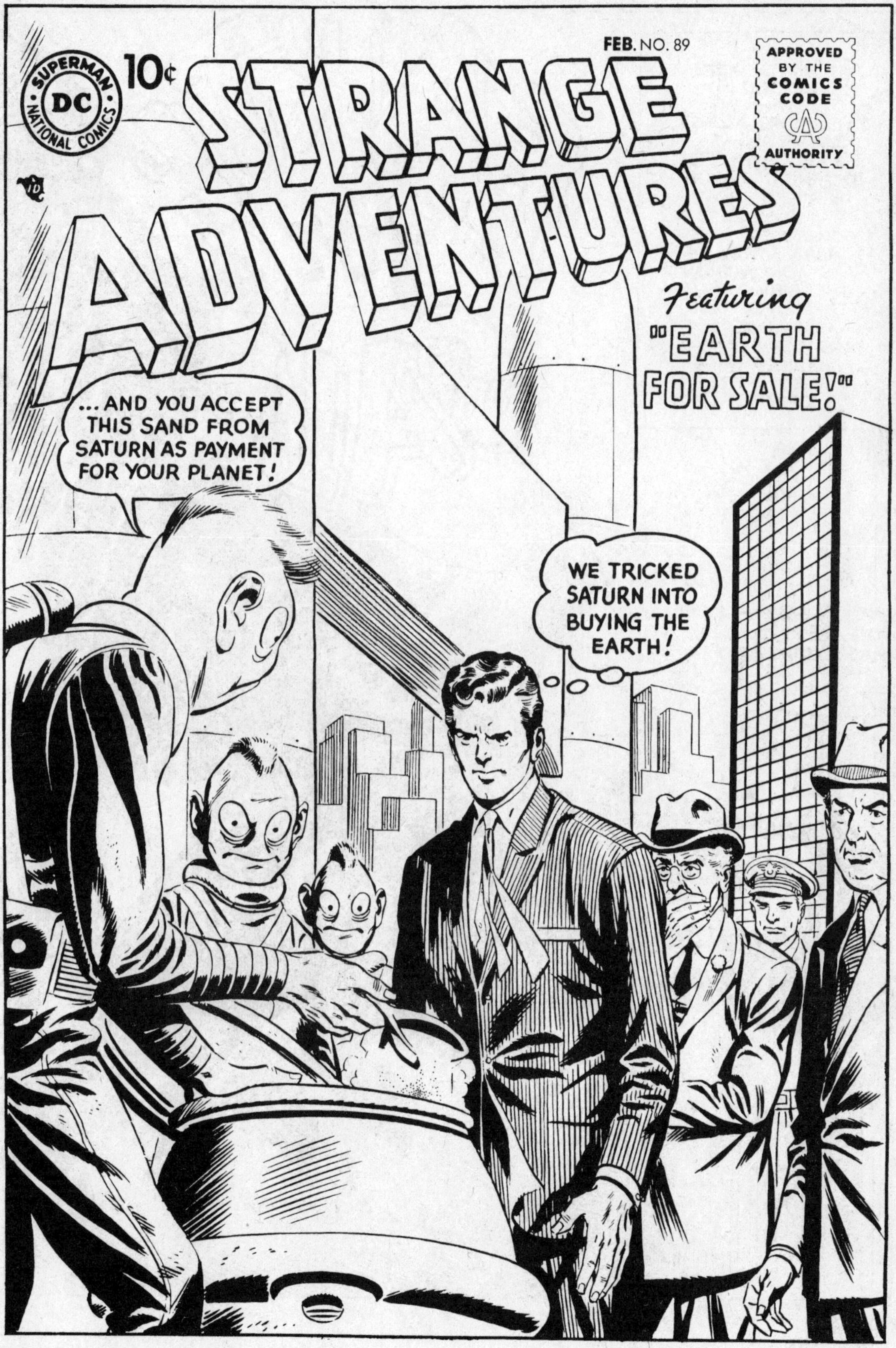
SUPERMAN DC NATIONAL COMICS
10¢
FEB. NO. 89
APPROVED BY THE COMICS CODE AUTHORITY
STRANGE ADVENTURES
Featuring "EARTH FOR SALE!"
...AND YOU ACCEPT THIS SAND FROM SATURN AS PAYMENT FOR YOUR PLANET!
WE TRICKED SATURN INTO BUYING THE EARTH!

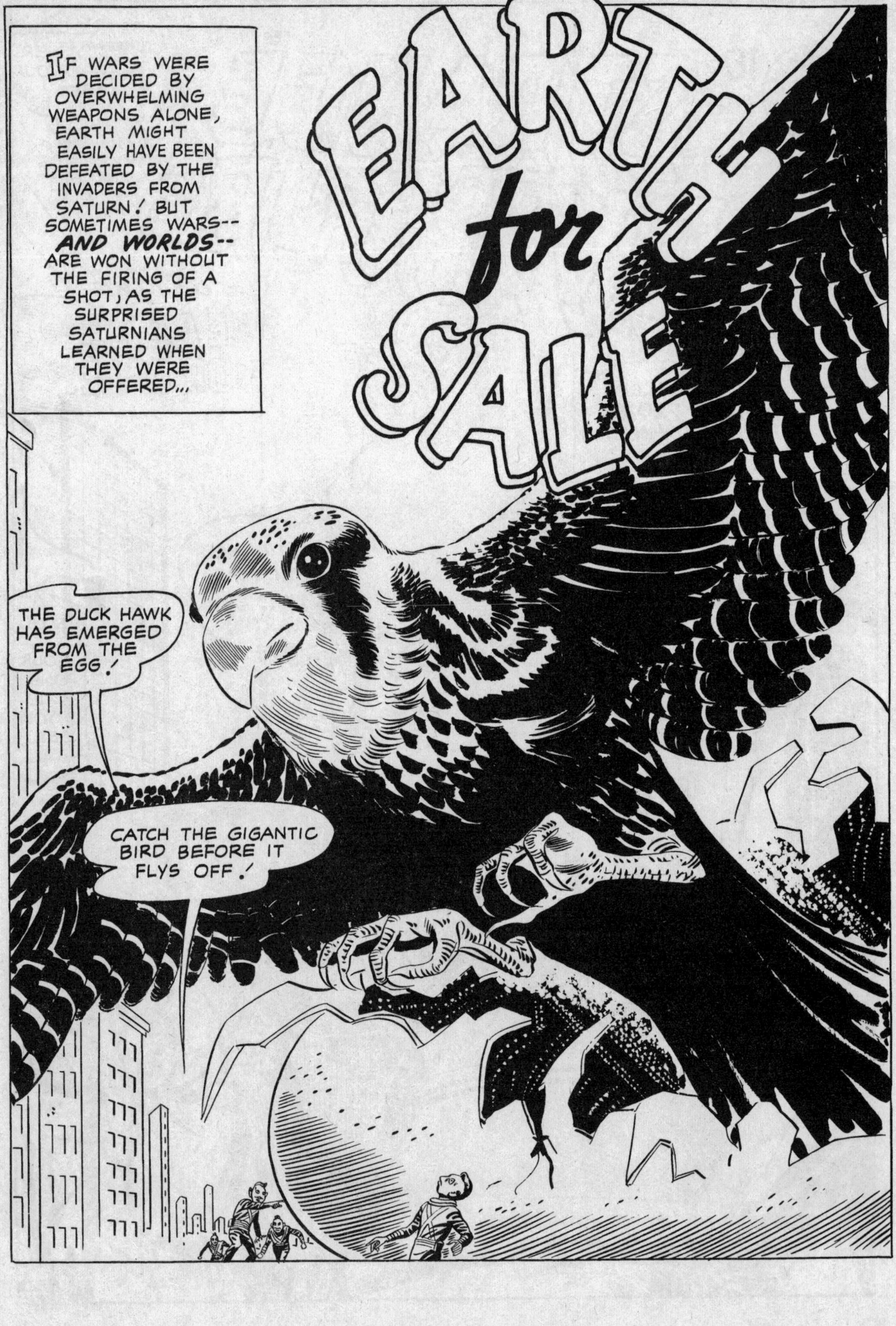
IF WARS WERE DECIDED BY OVERWHELMING WEAPONS ALONE, EARTH MIGHT EASILY HAVE BEEN DEFEATED BY THE INVADERS FROM SATURN! BUT SOMETIMES WARS-- AND WORLDS-- ARE WON WITHOUT THE FIRING OF A SHOT, AS THE SURPRISED SATURNIANS LEARNED WHEN THEY WERE OFFERED...
EARTH for SALE
THE DUCK HAWK HAS EMERGED FROM THE EGG!
CATCH THE GIGANTIC BIRD BEFORE IT FLYS OFF!

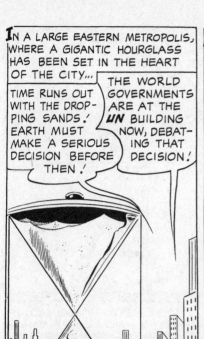

IN A LARGE EASTERN METROPOLIS, WHERE A GIGANTIC HOURGLASS HAS BEEN SET IN THE HEART OF THE CITY...

TIME RUNS OUT WITH THE DROPPING SANDS! EARTH MUST MAKE A SERIOUS DECISION BEFORE THEN!

THE WORLD GOVERNMENTS ARE AT THE **UN** BUILDING NOW, DEBATING THAT DECISION!

AT THE UNITED NATIONS BUILDING...

GENTLEMEN, THIS IS JOHN PRENTISS, ONE OF EARTH'S LEADING GEOLOGISTS! TELL THEM WHAT YOU TOLD THE SUB-COMMITTEE!

WE MUST OFFER TO SELL EARTH TO THE SATURNIAN INVADERS! IT IS OUR ONLY HOPE!

SELL EARTH? NEVER!

WE'D RATHER FIGHT FOR OUR PLANET!

WAIT, GENTLEMEN! HEAR ME OUT! LET US FIRST REVIEW WHAT HAS OCCURRED DURING THESE PAST HOURS!

"WHEN THE SPACE-CRAFT FROM SATURN FIRST LANDED, WE THOUGHT THEY WERE FRIENDLY, BUT..."

YOUR WORLD CONTAINS CERTAIN ELEMENTS AND LIFE UNKNOWN ON OUR PLANET! WE DESIRE THESE THINGS--AND WILL TAKE THEM!

RESIST US--AND OUR SUPERIOR WEAPONS WILL DESTROY YOU! SURRENDER, AND YOU WILL LIVE--UNDER OUR SUBJUGATION!

2

"THEN THEY ERECTED THE GIANT HOUR GLASS, AND POURED PAILS OF SAND INTO THE UPPER HALF..."

THE SAND IN THIS GLASS WILL RUN OUT IN 23 HOURS, 56 MINUTES AND 4.09 SECONDS-- THE EXACT AMOUNT OF TIME REQUIRED FOR EARTH TO TURN ONCE ON ITS AXIS!

AT THAT TIME, WE WILL RETURN--EITHER TO ACCEPT YOUR SURRENDER, OR DESTROY YOU!

SOME OF THAT SAND--WHICH CAME FROM SATURN--FELL FROM THE GLASS! I COLLECTED IT, AND MADE SEVERAL EXPERIMENTS WITH IT! WATCH CAREFULLY--WHILE I REPEAT THESE EXPERIMENTS--

WIDE-EYED, THE GOVERNMENT REPRESENTATIVES WATCH THE EXPERIMENTS--AND THEN, AT DEADLINE TIME, WHEN THE SPACESHIP AGAIN LANDS...

WHAT? YOU'LL NEITHER SURRENDER *NOR* FIGHT?

THAT IS RIGHT! WE'LL *SELL* EARTH TO YOU-- AND ACCEPT THE SAND IN THE GLASS AS A TOKEN PAYMENT!

NO DOUBT A QUAINT EARTH METHOD FOR KEEPING ITS HONOR! GIVE THEM THE SAND--AND TELL THEM TO GO ABOUT THEIR BUSINESS, AS USUAL, WHILE WE COLLECT THE THINGS WE WANT!

AND LIKE A LONG TIME AGO, WHEN MANHATTAN ISLAND WAS SOLD FOR A HANDFUL OF TRINKETS, EARTH IS SOLD FOR A FEW BARRELS OF SAND FROM SATURN!

ON THE FOLLOWING DAY, THE SATURNIANS MAKE THEIR WAY TO ONE OF EARTH'S RICHEST URANIUM DEPOSITS...

WE MUST MINE THE URANIUM ORE FROM BENEATH THE SURFACE!

BUT, STRANGELY, AS THE URANIUM IS UNEARTHED...

LOOK! AS SOON AS WE DIG THE URANIUM FREE, IT FLYS SKYWARD!

GRAB ONTO THE ORE-- HOLD IT TIGHT!

BUT, AS THEY GRASP THE URANIUM...

LET GO! LET GO! THE RADIOACTIVE SUBSTANCE IS CARRYING **YOU** INTO THE AIR!

GET HEAVY CONTAINERS! THAT'LL HOLD IT DOWN!

BUT EVEN WHEN THE URANIUM IS PACKED IN HEAVY CONTAINERS...

WHAT NOW? EVIDENTLY THERE IS NO WAY OF HOLDING THE URANIUM!

FORGET IT! WE'LL GATHER THE STRANGE ELEMENT KNOWN TO THE EARTHMEN AS **SALT**!

AT SOME DISTANCE AWAY...

HOW DID THAT HAPPEN, PRENTISS?

THE SAND, VERY COMMON ON SATURN, DOES STRANGE THINGS ON EARTH, WHEN COMBINED WITH CERTAIN OF OUR ELEMENTS! WE PLANTED THE SAND IN THE GROUND, AND IT CREATED AN **ANTI-GRAVITY** FORCE IN THE URANIUM, HURTLING IT SKYWARD!

THEY'RE ALSO INTRIGUED BY SALT IN OUR **WATER**-- UNKNOWN ON THEIR PLANET! SO, TOMORROW-- WE'LL BE NEAR THEM AT **GREAT SALT LAKE**!

ON THE FOLLOWING DAY--AT **GREAT SALT LAKE**...

FILL THE CONTAINERS AND TAKE THE SALT TO THE SHIP!

BUT, ONE BY ONE, AS THEY APPROACH THEIR SECONDARY CRAFT...

GREAT SOL! THE SALT WATER IS GOING UP IN STEAM!

GET MORE OF IT--AND THIS TIME PLACE LIDS ON THE CONTAINERS!

SSSSS!

SSSSS!

BUT ONCE AGAIN...

IT STILL TURNS TO STEAM, AND ESCAPES US!

WE NEVER EXPECTED IT WOULD BE SO DIFFICULT TO TAKE SUBSTANCES FROM THIS PLANET!

SSSSSS!

MEANWHILE, NEARBY...

BY GETTING HERE FIRST AND SPRINKLING THE SATURNIAN SAND INTO THE LAKE, WE THWARTED THEM AGAIN!

THE SAND EFFECTS THE SALT WATER SO THAT MOMENTS AFTER IT'S REMOVED FROM THE LAKE, IT GOES UP IN STEAM!

THEY'RE FASCINATED BY THE **DUCK HAWK**, EARTH'S FASTEST FLYING BIRD, AND THEY INTEND TAKING BACK A DUCK HAWK EGG! IT'S THE SATURNIANS' NEXT MOVE--AND **OURS!**

THE NEXT DAY, BACK IN THE CITY...

THIS EGG WILL HATCH A BIRD, 17 INCHES IN LENGTH, THAT CAN FLY AT A SPEED OF 75 MILES PER HOUR! IT WILL ASTOUND OUR PEOPLE, WHO HAVE NEVER SEEN SUCH A FAST-FLYING CREATURE!

BUT SUDDENLY, THE EGG BEGINS TO *GROW*...

BIGGER...

...AND BIGGER...

IT'S BECOMING *GIGANTIC!* GET BACK-- *BACK!*

THE EGG SHELL HAS CRACKED OPEN! THE HAWK IS EMERGING!

IN A FEW SECONDS, THE FLEDGLING BIRD BECOMES A FULL-GROWN, GIANT DUCK HAWK!

CATCH IT! THIS IS ONE PRIZE WE CAN'T LET ESCAPE US!

BUT LIKE SOMETHING SHOT FROM A CANNON, THE GIANT BIRD WINGS ITSELF AWAY AT INCREDIBLE SPEED!

ITS SPEED DEVELOPED WITH ITS SIZE! IT IS FLYING FASTER THAN ANY AUXILIARY CRAFT WE CAN SEND AFTER IT!

THERE'S *NOTHING* WE CAN TAKE FROM THIS FANTASTIC PLANET! LET'S GET OFF IT!

WE CAN'T! WE ATTEMPTED TO CHASE THE GREAT BIRD-- AND THE SHIP WON'T RISE! IT'S HELD HERE BY SOME TREMENDOUS FORCE!

WE CAN'T EVEN GET *OUR- SELVES* OFF YOUR PLANET, EARTHMAN! IF YOU CAN HELP US WE'LL GLADLY GIVE YOUR PLANET BACK TO YOU!

AND PROMISE NEVER TO RETURN?

YES! YES! WE NEVER WANT TO SET FOOT ON THIS MAD PLANET AGAIN! WE'LL GO ELSEWHERE FOR THE ELEMENTS WE NEED!

GOOD ENOUGH! THEN YOU ARE FREE TO DEPART-- *NOW!*

THE NEXT MOMENT, THE GREAT SHIP RISES INTO THE SKY...

HOW DID YOU WORK *THAT,* PRENTISS? THE SPACESHIP COULDN'T RISE UNTIL YOU *TOLD* THEM IT WOULD!

TIMING, THAT'S ALL! WHILE THE SAND-EFFECTED HAWK EGG HELD THEIR INTEREST, WE PLACED A SHEETING OF *LEAD* BENEATH THEIR SHIP, UNDER- GROUND! THE LEAD ALSO WAS EFFECTED BY THE SATURNIAN SAND...

I FOUND THAT THE SAND, WHEN COMBINED WITH LEAD, IMPARTED TO THE LEAD A SUPER- MAGNETIC FORCE--ENOUGH TO KEEP THE SHIP ANCHORED TO EARTH! BUT SINCE THE EFFECT WAS ONLY TEMPORARY, I KNEW THE SHIP COULD RISE AGAIN AFTER A CERTAIN TIME!

THEN "SELLING" EARTH FOR THE SAND WAS A BARGAIN! WHAT USES WE CAN PUT IT TO!

UNFORTUNATELY, THE SAND USED TO "DEFEAT" THE SATURNIANS HAS SINCE BECOME LIFELESS--INERT! ALL THAT REMAINS IS A SINGLE GRAIN-- WHICH I SAVED AS A MEMENTO OF HOW THE SANDS OF SATURN SAVED EARTH!

THE END

7

PRISONER of the RAINBOW!

FROM OUT OF NOWHERE MARK HOLTON HEARD A VOICE PLEADING FOR HELP! WERE THE FANTASTIC COLOR-CHANGES THAT FOLLOWED DESIGNED TO HELP OR HINDER MARK IN HIS DESPERATE SEARCH FOR THAT PERSON IN DISTRESS?

ANOTHER INCREDIBLE COLOR-CHANGE! THIS TIME A PATCH OF **WHITE** SNOW HAS TURNED **YELLOW!** WHAT HAS ALL THIS TO DO WITH THE STRANGE DISAPPEARANCE OF PROFESSOR JASON?

IN HIS COLLEGE DORMITORY ROOM, MARK HOLTON IS SUDDENLY STARTLED OUT OF HIS STUDIES...

MARK HOLTON! PROFESSOR JASON CALLING! HELP ME!

WHY... UH... I DON'T HEAR A **SOUND**, AND YET HIS VOICE IS RINGING IN MY MIND! AM I—IMAGINING IT?

WAIT... IT COULD BE **TELEPATHY!**

YES, MARK, THAT'S RIGHT! I'VE BEEN TRYING TO REACH YOUR MIND! SAVE ME! I'M A PRISONER IN—

SUDDENLY, THE TELEPATHIC VOICE IS CUT SHORT...

SAVE HIM FROM *WHAT?* IS HE IN TROUBLE AT HIS LABORATORY, WHERE HE USUALLY EXPERIMENTS AFTER CLASSES? I'LL GO SEE!

SAVE ME... HELP...

BUT AT THE LAB...

THE PROFESSOR'S NOT HERE! IF HE'S TRAPPED, IT'S SOMEWHERE ELSE! I'D BETTER REPORT THIS TO THE DEAN!

MARK'S STRANGE STORY IS NOT TAKEN SERIOUSLY BY THE DEAN...

COME, MY BOY! I'M SURE THE PROFESSOR WILL SHOW UP SAFE AND SOUND! AS FOR THAT...ER... TELEPATHIC CALL, WELL...PERHAPS YOU'VE BEEN STUDYING TOO HARD!

I GUESS IT *WAS* MY IMAGINATION! I'LL GO BACK TO MY ROOM AND FORGET IT!

OFFICE OF THE DEAN

IN HIS ROOM, ANOTHER QUEER PHENOMENON OCCURS!

MY PEN IS WRITING WITH *INDIGO* INK! B-BUT I JUST FILLED IT FROM THAT BOTTLE OF *BLACK INK!*

Chemical Experiment #44

BLACK INK

THEN TO THE STUDENT'S FURTHER ASTONISHMENT...

THE INK TURNED BACK TO BLACK AGAIN! BETTER LIGHT A CIGARETTE AND CALM MYSELF... GREAT SCOTT! THE FLAME! OF MY LIGHTER IS... *BLUE!*

A FEW SECONDS LATER, WHEN THE FLAME'S NATURAL COLOR APPEARS...

A "TELEPATHIC" CALL...THINGS MOMENTARILY CHANGING COLOR! ARE MY EYES PLAYING ME TRICKS...? MAYBE I *HAVE* BEEN STUDYING TOO HARD, AS THE DEAN SAID! I NEED SOME FRESH AIR!

SOON, BREATHING CRISP, COLD AIR...

I HOPE I'VE SEEN THE LAST OF THOSE COLOR HALLUCINATIONS!

ANOTHER ILLUSION! THE BROWN BRANCHES OF THAT TREE TURNED GREEN... IN THE MIDDLE OF WINTER!

EVEN MORE BEWILDERING...

THAT PATCH OF SNOW--TURNED *YELLOW!* TOO BAD NO ONE ELSE IS AROUND TO CONFIRM WHAT I SEE... AND HOW THE COLORS ALWAYS CHANGE BACK TO NORMAL A MOMENT LATER!

SUDDENLY, A STRANGE THOUGHT STRIKES THE STUDENT...

MAYBE THAT TELEPATHIC CALL FROM PROFESSOR JASON WASN'T MY *"IMAGINATION"!* PERHAPS THESE COLOR-CHANGES ARE CONNECTED SOMEHOW WITH HIS DISAPPEARANCE! BUT WHAT'S THE *PATTERN* BEHIND IT ALL?

GOT TO TALK TO SOMEONE ABOUT THIS-- MY GIRL FRIEND, JOAN! A BOUQUET OF HER FAVORITE FLOWERS WILL MAKE UP FOR MY UNEXPECTED CALL!

Flowers

FLOWERS

Shortly... I DON'T LIKE BARGING IN ON YOU LIKE THIS, JOAN--BUT I HAVE SOMETHING IMPORTANT TO TELL YOU! BUT, FIRST-- YOUR FAVORITE RED CARNATIONS!

OH, HOW NICE! COME IN, MARK!

WHEN JOAN UNWRAPS THE BOUQUET...

RED CARNATIONS? MARK, ARE YOU JOKING? THESE ARE VIOLET— COLORED!

GOOD GOSH! IT'S HAPPENED AGAIN! THAT'S WHAT I WANTED TO TALK TO YOU ABOUT! KEEP YOUR EYES ON THOSE CARNATIONS!

A MOMENT LATER...

GOODNESS! THEY'VE TURNED RED! OH, IT'S A WONDERFUL MAGIC TRICK, MARK!

NO, JOAN! LISTEN...

AFTER MARK TELLS THE WHOLE STRANGE SEQUENCE...

AND LOOK...YOUR WHITE POODLE'S TURNED RED, MOMENTARILY!

BUT-- WHAT CAN ALL THOSE AMAZING COLOR-CHANGES HAVE TO DO WITH THE MISSING PROFESSOR?

I DON'T KNOW YET, JOAN! I FIGURE IT'S SOME STRANGE "MESSAGE", TELLING ME WHAT "TRAP" HE'S IN! I'VE GOT TO FIND THE ANSWER! HIS LIFE MAY BE AT STAKE!

On THE WAY BACK...

AN ORANGE FIRE ENGINE! THAT'S THE SEVENTH COLOR-CHANGE! GOOD GOSH! THOSE SEVEN PARTICULAR COLORS MAY BE THE KEY TO ALL THIS!

AT HIS ROOM, MARK LISTS ALL THE COLOR PHENOMENA AND...

ink turned indigo
flame " blue
tree " green
snow " yellow
carnations " violet
poodle " red
fire engine " orange

WHEN ARRANGED IN A DIFFERENT SEQUENCE, THEY ARE THE SEVEN PRIMARY COLORS OF THE *SPECTRUM*, PRODUCED WHEN A *PRISM* BREAKS UP SUNLIGHT! NOW I THINK I KNOW THE PROFESSOR'S "MESSAGE"!

STUDY-AID CHART #3

SUN

RUSHING TO THE PROFESSOR'S LABORATORY...

THE "SPECTRUM" MESSAGE MUST BE TO POINT OUT THIS PRISM! I'LL MOVE IT AWAY FROM THE SUNLIGHT!

AS THE RAINBOW HUES DIE OUT, A WRAITH—LIKE FIGURE SLOWLY MATERIALIZES!

PROFESSOR JASON!

THANKS MY BOY! I'M RE-MATERIALIZING AT LAST! FOR THE PAST SEVERAL HOURS I'VE BEEN TRAPPED IN AN INVISIBLE AND INTANGIBLE SHAPE!

YOU'RE SOLID NOW! TELL ME-- WHAT WEIRD THING HAPPENED TO YOU?

THAT PRISM I PERFECTED IS MADE OF SUPER-REFRACTIVE GLASS, CREATING A SPECTRUM OF COLORS MORE VIVIDLY INTENSE THAN ANY KNOWN BEFORE!

"BUT I DIDN'T REALIZE MY DANGER, WHEN I TESTED IT IN THE SUNLIGHT..."

GREAT STARS! MY BODY IS TURNING INTANGIBLE! THE SUPER-SPECTRUM IS CASTING ME INTO THE *ULTRA-VIOLET ZONE*!

5

"*RENDERED INVISIBLE LIKE ULTRA-VIOLET LIGHT, I WAS CUT OFF FROM THE NORMAL WORLD!*"

SOMEONE MUST MOVE THIS PRISM OUT OF THE SUNLIGHT TO FREE ME! I MUST CONCENTRATE AND SEND A MENTAL SOS, TO MY BRIGHTEST STUDENT... *MARK HOLTON!*

"*MENTAL EXHAUSTION PREVENTED ME FROM FINISHING MY TELEPATHIC MESSAGE! AND TO MY ALARM, AFTER YOU CAME TO LOOK FOR ME...*"

THE PROFESSOR'S NOT HERE! IF HE'S TRAPPED, IT'S SOMEWHERE ELSE...

NO...NO! I'M RIGHT HERE!... I CAN'T CONTACT HIS MIND! I'VE GOT TO GET MY MESSAGE ACROSS IN ANOTHER WAY--YES! A *SPECTRUM* MESSAGE!

"*EXPERIMENTING, I FOUND I COULD RADIATE SELECTED SPECTRUM HUES AT DISTANT OBJECTS FOR A BRIEF MOMENT!*"

I HAVE A MENTAL VISION OF MARK! HE'S IN HIS DORMITORY! FIRST, I'LL CAUSE HIS BLACK INK TO TURN *INDIGO!*

"*DESPERATELY I KEPT ON, HOPING TO PUT ACROSS A SIMPLE BUT TRICKY MESSAGE...*"

NOW I'M CHANGING A PATCH OF *WHITE* SNOW TO *YELLOW!* WILL THE COLOR-CHANGES I'M CAUSING LEAD MARK TO THINK OF THE COLORS OF THE SPECTRUM -- AND TO THE PRISM IN THIS ROOM?

IT SURE WORKED, PROFESSOR! THE SEVEN COLORS OF THE SPECTRUM LED ME STRAIGHT TO WHAT HAD TRAPPED YOU... YOUR *PRISM!*

I BETTER DESTROY THIS DANGEROUS THING! MAKE SURE IT NEVER TRAPS ANYONE AGAIN!

LATER, AFTER A RAINFALL ...

OTHER PEOPLE WELCOME SEEING THAT "*SPECTRUM*" IN THE SKY... BUT NOT THE PROFESSOR, I GUESS! IT HOLDS NOTHING BUT A BAD MEMORY! YOU MIGHT SAY HE WAS A ... *PRISONER OF THE RAINBOW!*

The End 16

DETOUR IN TIME!

WINGING WESTWARD TO HELP A TORNADO-STRICKEN TOWN, JOHNNY LUCAS ABRUPTLY FINDS HIMSELF FLYING FUTUREWARD TO SAVE THE WORLD FROM INVASION!

HAVE TO USE 20TH CENTURY FLYING TACTICS TO STAY ALIVE IN THE 100th CENTURY!

AS JET-PILOT JOHNNY LUCAS FLYS NEEDED SERUMS AND MEDICINES TO AN ISOLATED TOWN IN TEXAS, HE IS SUDDENLY STRUCK BY...

A FREAK ELECTRICAL STORM!

DROPPING UNDER THE CLOUDS, THE PILOT STARES BELOW IN UTTER AMAZEMENT...

WHERE IN THUNDER AM I? THERE'S NO CITY IN THE UNITED STATES ANYTHING LIKE THIS!

TAXIING TO A HALT BEFORE A GIGANTIC SPACESHIP, HE STARES ABOUT CURIOUSLY...

IT COULD BE A MOVIE SET-- BUT IT LOOKS TOO REAL FOR THAT! I WISH THERE WAS SOMEONE AROUND TO ASK QUESTIONS!

SUDDENLY...

HOW'S THAT FOR SERVICE! SAY, MISTER--CAN YOU TELL ME HOW FAR TEXAS IS FROM HERE?

TEXAS? IF YOU MEAN THE **STATE OF TEXAS**, IT HAS NOT EXISTED FOR THE PAST FIVE THOUSAND YEARS!

AN HOUR LATER, AS PILOT LUCAS POURS OUT HIS STORY...

IT IS OBVIOUS FROM HIS STORY THAT A SCIENTIFIC PHENOMENON BROUGHT HIM FROM THE REMOTE PAST!

YOU MEAN I'M IN THE *FUTURE?*

EIGHT THOUSAND YEARS IN THE FUTURE! *LOOK THERE!* WE HAVE SPACE-TRAVEL TO THE OTHER PLANETS OF THE SOLAR SYSTEM! SCIENCE HAS TAKEN ENORMOUS STRIDES SINCE YOUR DAY!

WELL, THAT'S A RELIEF! YOU MUST HAVE *TIME-TRAVEL*, THEN! YOU CAN SEND ME BACK TO MY OWN TIME ERA SO I CAN DELIVER THE SERUMS TO THE DISASTER AREA!

THAT IS IMPOSSIBLE!

NO ONE HAS YET INVENTED A TIME-TRAVEL MACHINE-- OR *EVER WILL!* IF TIME-- TRAVEL WERE POSSIBLE, WHY HAS NO ONE FROM THE FUTURE VISITED YOUR TIME ERA, OR MINE? YOU MUST REMAIN HERE--AS LONG AS YOU LIVE!

AN INTERRUPTION SWINGS THE MAN OF THE FUTURE AROUND SHARPLY... BAD NEWS, JAN WALTRON! THE ELECTRICAL STORM THAT BROUGHT JOHN LUCAS HERE ALSO RIPPED A HOLE IN THE TIME—ENERGY VECTORS!

"GIGANTIC INSECT CREATURES ARE POURING INTO OUR WORLD FROM AN ADJOINING DIMENSION!"

THIS IS OUR OPPORTUNITY TO INVADE AND CONQUER THE WORLDS OF THE THIRD DIMENSION!

"ONE OF THE FIRST THINGS THEY DID WAS BLANKET OUT ALL OUR ATOMIC POWER! AS A RESULT..."

OUR ATOMIC-POWERED SPACESHIPS AND AIR-CRAFT ARE GROUNDED!

"THE INSECT INVADERS ARE SAFE ON A MOUNTAIN TOP. THEY HAVE REPELLED ALL OUR ATTACKS! WITHOUT A FLIER, WE CAN'T GET CLOSE TO THEM!"

THE DIMENSIONAL OPENING IS A TEMPORARY ONE! BUT THEY'RE SETTING UP A MACHINE TO KEEP THE ENTRANCE INTO OUR WORLD OPEN SO THEY CAN BRING A LARGE ARMY THROUGH AND CONQUER US!

LABORATORY

THEIR MACHINE -- OBVIOUSLY A TWO-PART SPACE WARPER -- WITH ONE PART IN OUR DIMENSION, ONE PART IN THEIR OWN -- WILL HOLD THAT ENTRANCE OPEN PERMANENTLY!

WE ARE DOOMED, JOHN LUCAS! WITHOUT AIRCRAFT, WE HAVE NO WAY OF MANEUVERING OUR WEAPONS INTO POSITION TO USE THEM AGAINST THOSE INSECT MEN!

WAIT A MINUTE! WHAT ABOUT *MY* AIRPLANE? IT WORKS ON JET-PROPULSION -- *NOT* ON ATOMIC POWER!

OF COURSE! YOU COULD FLY YOUR ANCIENT PLANE, EQUIPPED WITH *OUR* WEAPONS!

WITHIN MOMENTS, EVERY RESOURCE OF THE YEAR *9957* IS THROWN INTO HIGH GEAR...

THIS PORTABLE ELECTRONIC BRAIN WILL FIRE OUR WEAPONS, AND MAINTAIN FIREPOWER! ALL YOU HAVE TO DO IS FLY THE PLANE THERE!

THEN, THE PLANE OF THE PAST, EQUIPPED WITH WEAPONS OF THE FUTURE, ROARS INTO THE SKY...

SOON ON THE INSECT-INVADERS' MOUNTAIN STRONGHOLD...

ENEMY AIRCRAFT APPROACHING! BUT HOW--

NO TIME FOR QUESTIONS! BATTLE STATIONS, EVERYONE!

QUICKLY, A BARRAGE OF DEADLY DISSOLVORAYS FLASHES ACROSS THE SKY...

HAVE TO USE 20th CENTURY FLYING TACTICS TO STAY ALIVE IN THE 100th CENTURY!

4.

THROAT DRY, HEART HAMMERING, JOHN LUCAS DIVES PAST THE LANCES OF DESTRUCTION..

I'VE GOT TO GET THROUGH! THOUGH I'M FROM THE PAST, I'M FIGHTING FOR THE FUTURE, AND MY OWN DESCENDANTS!

GUIDED MISSILES JOIN THE DISSOLVORAYS IN THE ATTACK...

VROOSH!

THE MISSILES--MISSED! BUT THEY'RE TURNING AROUND--COMING BACK FOR ANOTHER TRY!

VROOOM!

EVEN IF THEY DO GET ME-- I'VE GOT TO DESTROY THEIR SPACE-WARPER MACHINE! THE ENTIRE RACE OF MANKIND DEPENDS ON IT!

ON TARGET AT LAST, THE PLANE'S ELECTRONIC CONTROLS TAKE OVER AND POWERFUL DESTRUCTO BEAMS BLAST THE ALIEN MACHINE...

STRANGE! I STARTED OUT TO SAVE A FEW PEOPLE IN THE 20th CENTURY! NOW I'M SAVING **BILLIONS** OF THEM IN THE 100th CENTURY!

BLAM!

WITHOUT THE POWER OF THE MACHINES TO FUEL THEM, THE GUIDED MISSILES CRASH AND EXPLODE HARMLESSLY, JUST AS THE INSECT MEN RETREAT THROUGH THE DIMENSIONAL GATEWAY INTO THEIR OWN WORLD...

BLAM!

BLAM!

BLAM!

ZOOOOM!

FLEE--BACK TO OUR OWN WORLD! WE ARE GREATLY OUTNUMBERED BY THE HUMANS!

SUDDENLY, THE 20th CENTURY PLANE IS SEIZED BY A TREMENDOUS VORTEX OF FORCE AND WHIRLED HELPLESSLY IN A GIGANTIC SPIRAL ...

THE EXPLOSION OF THE MACHINE MUST HAVE CAUSED THIS SPIN! I'LL CRASH ANY MINUTE NOW...

BUT WHEN THE SABREJET COMES OUT OF THE MAD SPIN ...

GREAT STARS! BELOW ME-- THE TEXAS TOWN I CAME TO SAVE WITH THE SERUMS AND MEDICINES! THE EXPLOSION WHIRLED ME BACK IN TIME, AS THE STORM WHIRLED ME FORWARD!

WELL, AS FAR AS JOHNNY LUCAS IS CONCERNED, THAT'S HOW IT HAPPENED! BUT UNKNOWN TO HIM, IN A CITY OF THE YEAR 100,000, THERE IS A STATUE ...

TIME-TRAVEL IS POSSIBLE! BUT NO ONE IN THE PAST IS AWARE OF IT-- BECAUSE WHEN WE TIME-TRAVEL TO THE PAST, WE BECOME INVISIBLE...

OUR TIME-TRAVELERS WITNESSED JOHN LUCAS' HEROIC ACT IN SAVING EARTH OF THE YEAR 9957-- WHICH OF COURSE, MADE POSSIBLE OUR SURVIVAL IN THE YEAR 100,000!

IN GRATITUDE, WE USED OUR SUPER-SCIENCE TO SEND LUCAS BACK INTO HIS OWN TIME! SINCE HE RETURNED TO HIS OWN ERA, HE REMAINED VISIBLE! JOHN LUCAS, OF THE 20th CENTURY, WE SALUTE YOU!

The End

MYSTERY of the UNKNOWN INVENTION!

IT WAS THE WORLD'S GREATEST SCIENTIFIC INVENTION -- BUT THE MAN WHO INVENTED IT HAD DISAPPEARED, AND NO ONE ON EARTH KNEW WHAT IT WAS DESIGNED FOR OR HOW TO OPERATE IT!

WE FINALLY FIGURED OUT HOW TO WORK THE MYSTERIOUS INVENTION!

BUT NOTHING'S HAPPENING -- AS FAR AS WE CAN SEE!

IN A POLICE STATION, WHERE HAL WESTON REPORTS THE MYSTERIOUS DISAPPEARANCE OF HIS NEIGHBOR, MR. JALIK...

YOU'VE GOT TO FIND HIM! HE-- HE IS THE ONLY ONE WHO CAN SAVE OUR WORLD FROM DISASTER!

WHAT'S THAT? YOU BETTER EXPLAIN...

"I'M AN AMATEUR ASTRONOMER, AND ON CLEAR NIGHTS, I LOOK THROUGH MY HOME-MADE TELESCOPE..."

SATURN'S RINGS SHOW UP VERY CLEARLY TONIGHT!

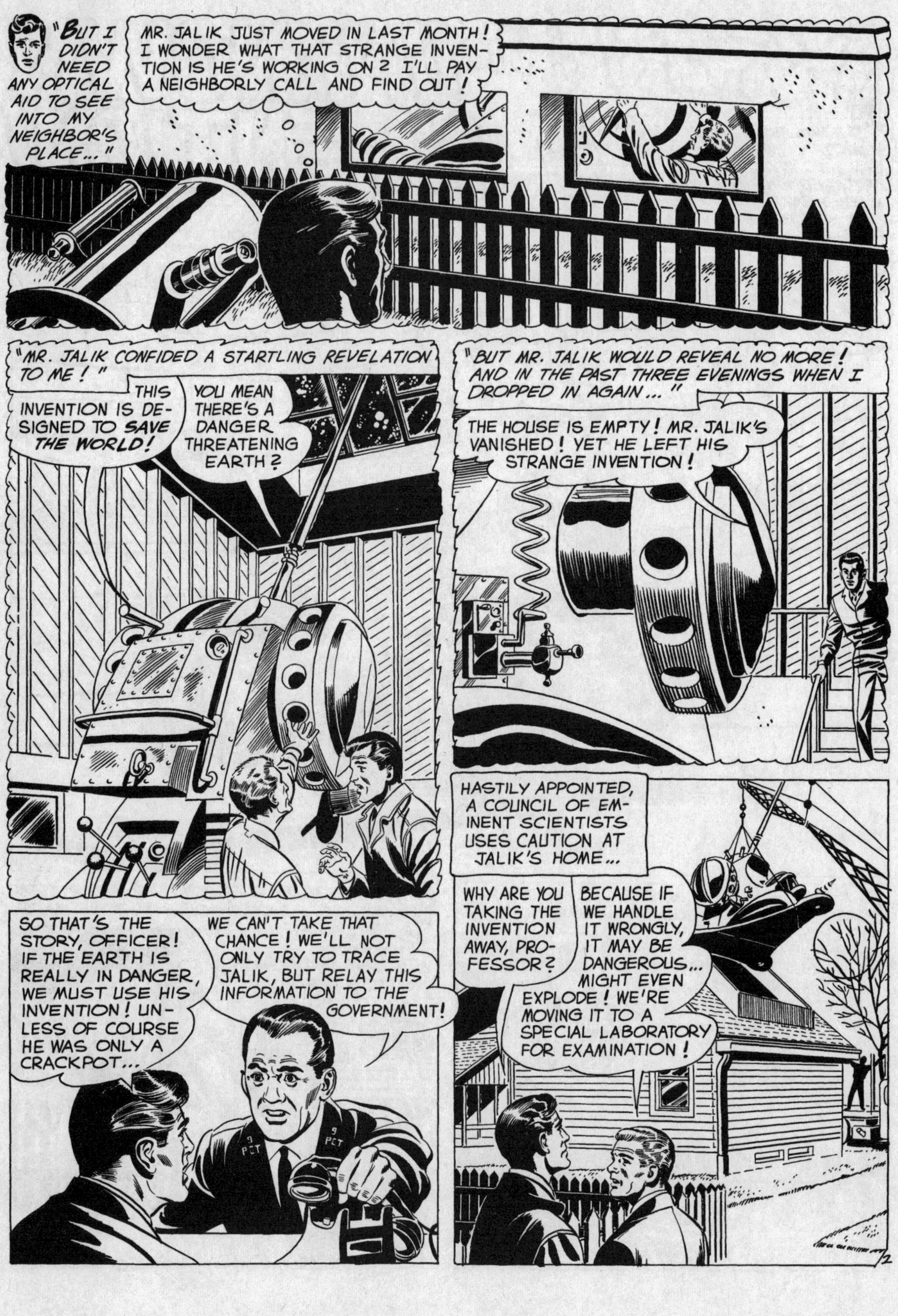
"BUT I DIDN'T NEED ANY OPTICAL AID TO SEE INTO MY NEIGHBOR'S PLACE..."
MR. JALIK JUST MOVED IN LAST MONTH! I WONDER WHAT THAT STRANGE INVENTION IS HE'S WORKING ON? I'LL PAY A NEIGHBORLY CALL AND FIND OUT!
"MR. JALIK CONFIDED A STARTLING REVELATION TO ME!"
THIS INVENTION IS DESIGNED TO SAVE THE WORLD!
YOU MEAN THERE'S A DANGER THREATENING EARTH?
"BUT MR. JALIK WOULD REVEAL NO MORE! AND IN THE PAST THREE EVENINGS WHEN I DROPPED IN AGAIN..."
THE HOUSE IS EMPTY! MR. JALIK'S VANISHED! YET HE LEFT HIS STRANGE INVENTION!
SO THAT'S THE STORY, OFFICER! IF THE EARTH IS REALLY IN DANGER, WE MUST USE HIS INVENTION! UNLESS OF COURSE HE WAS ONLY A CRACKPOT...
WE CAN'T TAKE THAT CHANCE! WE'LL NOT ONLY TRY TO TRACE JALIK, BUT RELAY THIS INFORMATION TO THE GOVERNMENT!
9 PCT
HASTILY APPOINTED, A COUNCIL OF EMINENT SCIENTISTS USES CAUTION AT JALIK'S HOME...
WHY ARE YOU TAKING THE INVENTION AWAY, PROFESSOR?
BECAUSE IF WE HANDLE IT WRONGLY, IT MAY BE DANGEROUS... MIGHT EVEN EXPLODE! WE'RE MOVING IT TO A SPECIAL LABORATORY FOR EXAMINATION!
2

LATER, IN A CONCRETE CHAMBER... WHEN IT'S BOLTED DOWN, WE'LL PLAY IT SAFE AND OPERATE IT WITH REMOTE CONTROL DEVICES!

MEANWHILE, THE BAFFLED SCIENCE COUNCIL QUESTIONS HAL WESTON FURTHER...

SORRY, GENTLEMEN! MR. JALIK GAVE ME NO CLUE TO THE UNKNOWN MENACE FACING EARTH! HAVE YOU MEN ANY THEORIES?

WE ALL HAVE, NO DOUBT! I'LL PRESENT MINE FIRST! PERHAPS A SUDDEN *ICE AGE* WILL STRIKE, ALMOST OVERNIGHT!

T. SHAW ...OLOGIST

DR. IRA OTIS GLACIOLOGIST

DR. J. JAMES COSMOLOGIST

"*JALIK'S INVENTION MAY BE A SUPER-HEAT RAY TO MELT THE ADVANCING GLACIERS!*"

DR. IRA OTIS GLACIOLOGIST

"*ON THE CONTRARY, MY OPINION IS THAT THE MOLTEN MAGMA OF EARTH'S CORE MAY SOON BURST FORTH IN A GIGANTIC WORLD-CONSUMING ERUPTION!*"

T. SHAW GEOLOGIST

"*MY THEORY IS THAT EARTH MAY BE ENGULFED BY A VAST RADIOACTIVE CLOUD IN SPACE!*"

DR. J. JAMES COSMOLOGIST

"*I SUBMIT THAT THE SUN MAY TURN INTO A SUPER-HOT NOVA, SCORCHING EARTH INTO A CINDER!*"

PROF. C. MILLER ASTRONOMER

THAT CRATER IS A THOUSAND MILES WIDE! BUT JALIK'S *FREEZE RAY* WILL SWIFTLY HARDEN THE MOLTEN LAVA, FORMING A "*PLUG*" AND ENDING THE ERUPTION!

JALIK INVENTED A *SUPER-BLASTER* TO DISPERSE THE DEADLY CLOUD BEFORE EARTH ENCOUNTERS IT!

THE *NUCLEAR QUENCHER RAY* WILL QUICKLY DAMPEN THE ATOMIC FIRES AND RETURN THE SUN TO NORMAL... THANKS TO JALIK'S INVENTION!

3

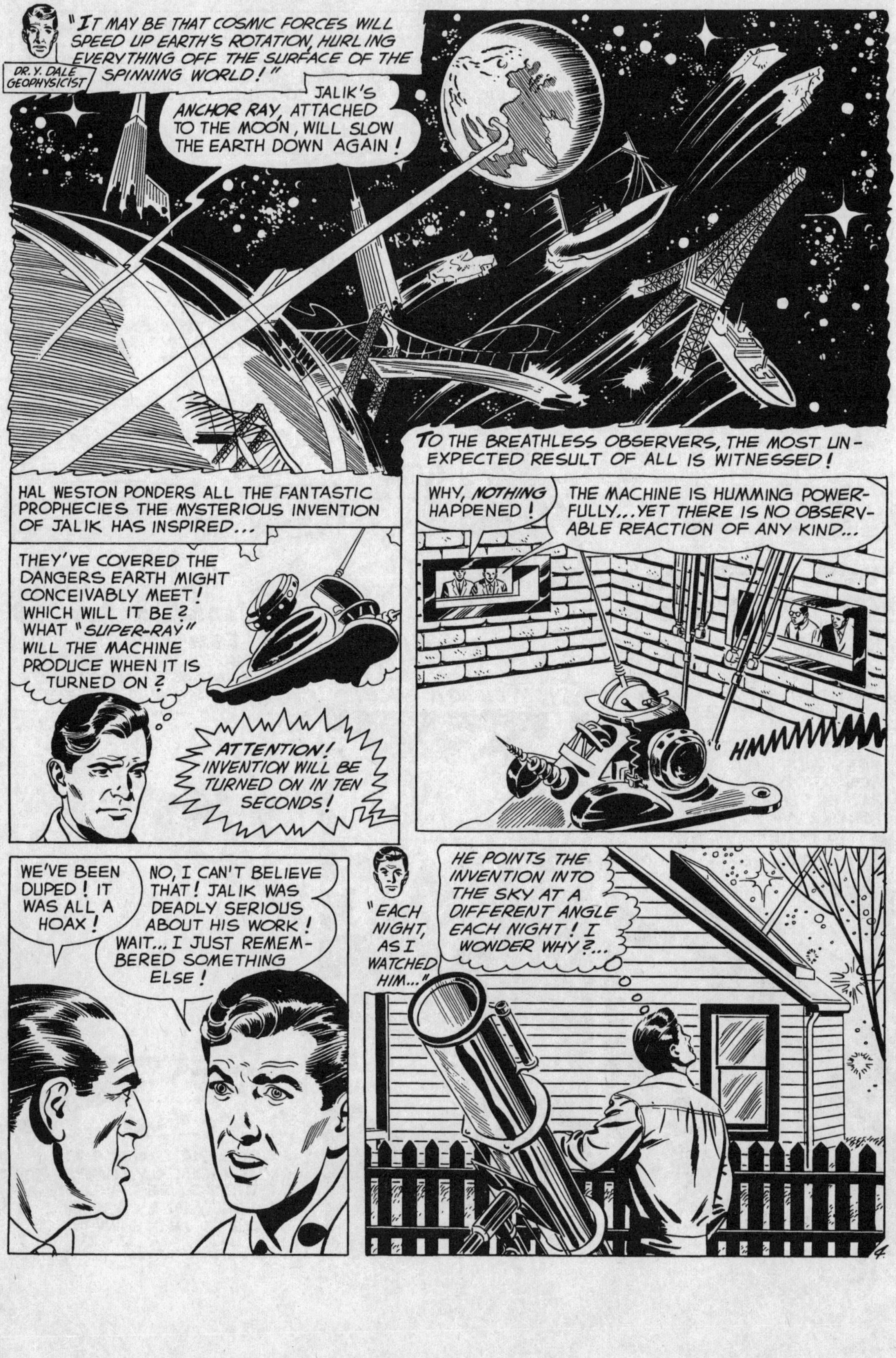
"IT MAY BE THAT COSMIC FORCES WILL SPEED UP EARTH'S ROTATION, HURLING EVERYTHING OFF THE SURFACE OF THE SPINNING WORLD!"
DR. Y. DALE GEOPHYSICIST
JALIK'S ANCHOR RAY, ATTACHED TO THE MOON, WILL SLOW THE EARTH DOWN AGAIN!
HAL WESTON PONDERS ALL THE FANTASTIC PROPHECIES THE MYSTERIOUS INVENTION OF JALIK HAS INSPIRED...
THEY'VE COVERED THE DANGERS EARTH MIGHT CONCEIVABLY MEET! WHICH WILL IT BE? WHAT "SUPER-RAY" WILL THE MACHINE PRODUCE WHEN IT IS TURNED ON?
ATTENTION! INVENTION WILL BE TURNED ON IN TEN SECONDS!
TO THE BREATHLESS OBSERVERS, THE MOST UNEXPECTED RESULT OF ALL IS WITNESSED!
WHY, NOTHING HAPPENED!
THE MACHINE IS HUMMING POWERFULLY...YET THERE IS NO OBSERVABLE REACTION OF ANY KIND...
HMMMMMMMM
WE'VE BEEN DUPED! IT WAS ALL A HOAX!
NO, I CAN'T BELIEVE THAT! JALIK WAS DEADLY SERIOUS ABOUT HIS WORK! WAIT... I JUST REMEMBERED SOMETHING ELSE!
"EACH NIGHT, AS I WATCHED HIM..."
HE POINTS THE INVENTION INTO THE SKY AT A DIFFERENT ANGLE EACH NIGHT! I WONDER WHY?...
4

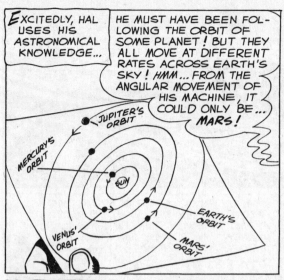

EXCITEDLY, HAL USES HIS ASTRONOMICAL KNOWLEDGE...

HE MUST HAVE BEEN FOLLOWING THE ORBIT OF SOME PLANET! BUT THEY ALL MOVE AT DIFFERENT RATES ACROSS EARTH'S SKY! HMM...FROM THE ANGULAR MOVEMENT OF HIS MACHINE, IT COULD ONLY BE...MARS!

OBVIOUSLY, THE MENACE TO EARTH IS SOMEHOW CONNECTED WITH THE PLANET MARS!

THEN WE'LL AIM JALIK'S MACHINE AT MARS AND SEE WHAT HAPPENS! I'LL OPEN THE CHAMBER'S DOME, ALLOWING ITS RAYS TO CROSS SPACE!

MOMENTS LATER, TELESCOPIC OBSERVERS WITNESS AN AMAZING SIGHT!

AN INVISIBLE RAY FROM JALIK'S MACHINE HAS SET OFF A TERRIFIC NUCLEAR EXPLOSION ON PHOBOS, ONE OF MARS' TWO SMALL MOONS! BUT...BUT HOW COULD THAT SAVE EARTH?

A WEEK LATER AT HOME, HAL WESTON IS STILL BAFFLED OVER THAT UNSOLVED RIDDLE...

WHAT DID THAT ATOMIC EXPLOSION ON PHOBOS MEAN TO EARTH? IT CERTAINLY DIDN'T SAVE THE WORLD!

YES IT DID, EARTHMAN!

MR. JALIK! YOU'RE BACK! WHERE ON EARTH WERE YOU FOR A WEEK?

NOT ON EARTH...ON MARS! I JUST RETURNED IN A SPACE-SHIP!

SUDDENLY, JALIK WHIPS OFF A FACE MASK...

YOU SEE, I AM A MARTIAN! I WORE THIS DISGUISE TO COVER MY BLUE SKIN! I WANTED TO AVOID NOTORIETY SO I COULD WORK QUIETLY ON EARTH!

A-A MARTIAN? BUT...BUT WHY DID YOU COME TO EARTH LAST MONTH IN SUCH SECRECY?

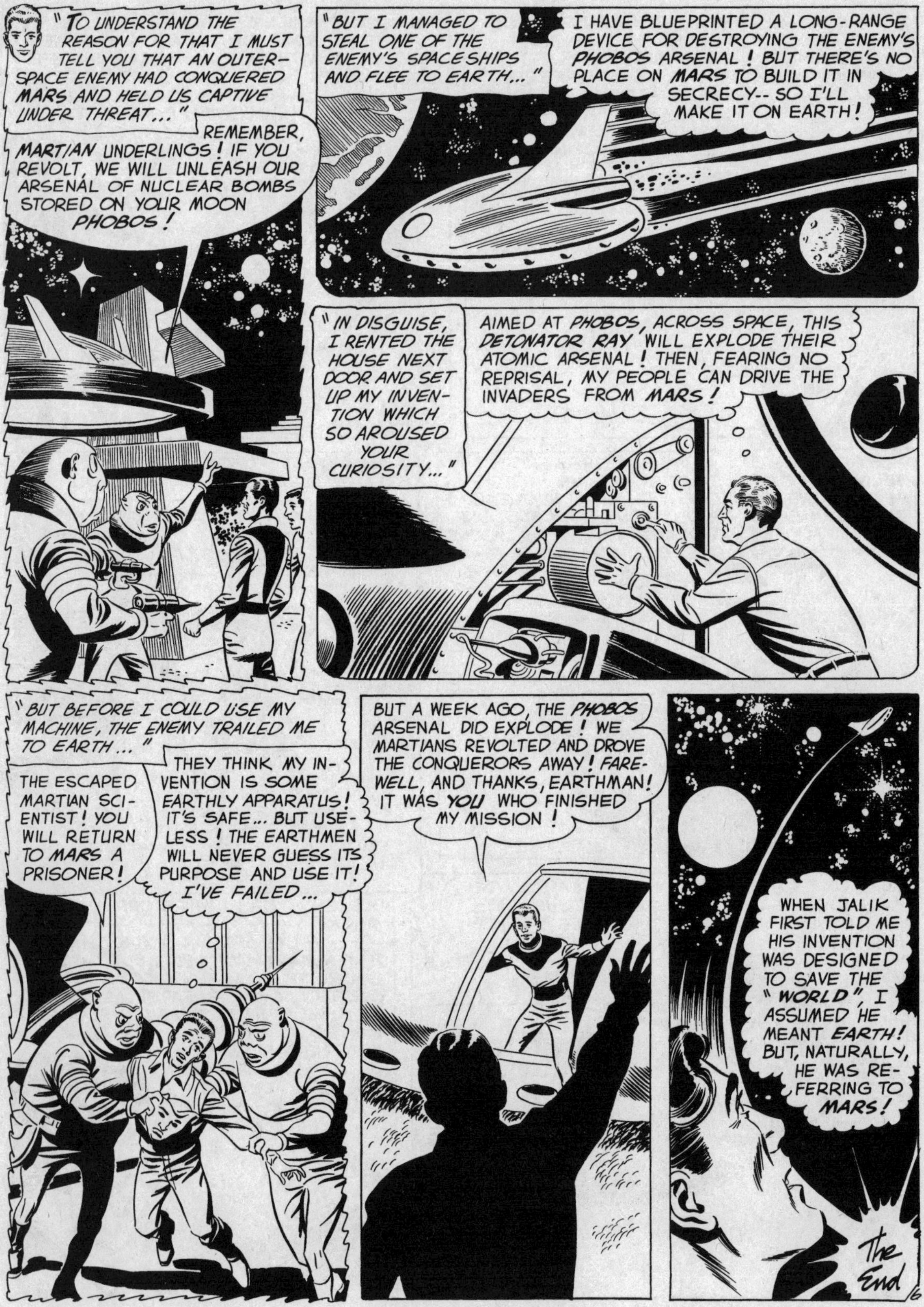
"TO UNDERSTAND THE REASON FOR THAT I MUST TELL YOU THAT AN OUTER-SPACE ENEMY HAD CONQUERED MARS AND HELD US CAPTIVE UNDER THREAT..."
REMEMBER, MARTIAN UNDERLINGS! IF YOU REVOLT, WE WILL UNLEASH OUR ARSENAL OF NUCLEAR BOMBS STORED ON YOUR MOON PHOBOS!
"BUT I MANAGED TO STEAL ONE OF THE ENEMY'S SPACESHIPS AND FLEE TO EARTH..."
I HAVE BLUEPRINTED A LONG-RANGE DEVICE FOR DESTROYING THE ENEMY'S PHOBOS ARSENAL! BUT THERE'S NO PLACE ON MARS TO BUILD IT IN SECRECY-- SO I'LL MAKE IT ON EARTH!
"IN DISGUISE, I RENTED THE HOUSE NEXT DOOR AND SET UP MY INVENTION WHICH SO AROUSED YOUR CURIOSITY..."
AIMED AT PHOBOS, ACROSS SPACE, THIS DETONATOR RAY WILL EXPLODE THEIR ATOMIC ARSENAL! THEN, FEARING NO REPRISAL, MY PEOPLE CAN DRIVE THE INVADERS FROM MARS!
"BUT BEFORE I COULD USE MY MACHINE, THE ENEMY TRAILED ME TO EARTH..."
THE ESCAPED MARTIAN SCIENTIST! YOU WILL RETURN TO MARS A PRISONER!
THEY THINK MY INVENTION IS SOME EARTHLY APPARATUS! IT'S SAFE... BUT USELESS! THE EARTHMEN WILL NEVER GUESS ITS PURPOSE AND USE IT! I'VE FAILED...
BUT A WEEK AGO, THE PHOBOS ARSENAL DID EXPLODE! WE MARTIANS REVOLTED AND DROVE THE CONQUERORS AWAY! FAREWELL, AND THANKS, EARTHMAN! IT WAS YOU WHO FINISHED MY MISSION!
WHEN JALIK FIRST TOLD ME HIS INVENTION WAS DESIGNED TO SAVE THE "WORLD", I ASSUMED HE MEANT EARTH! BUT, NATURALLY, HE WAS REFERRING TO MARS!
The End
6

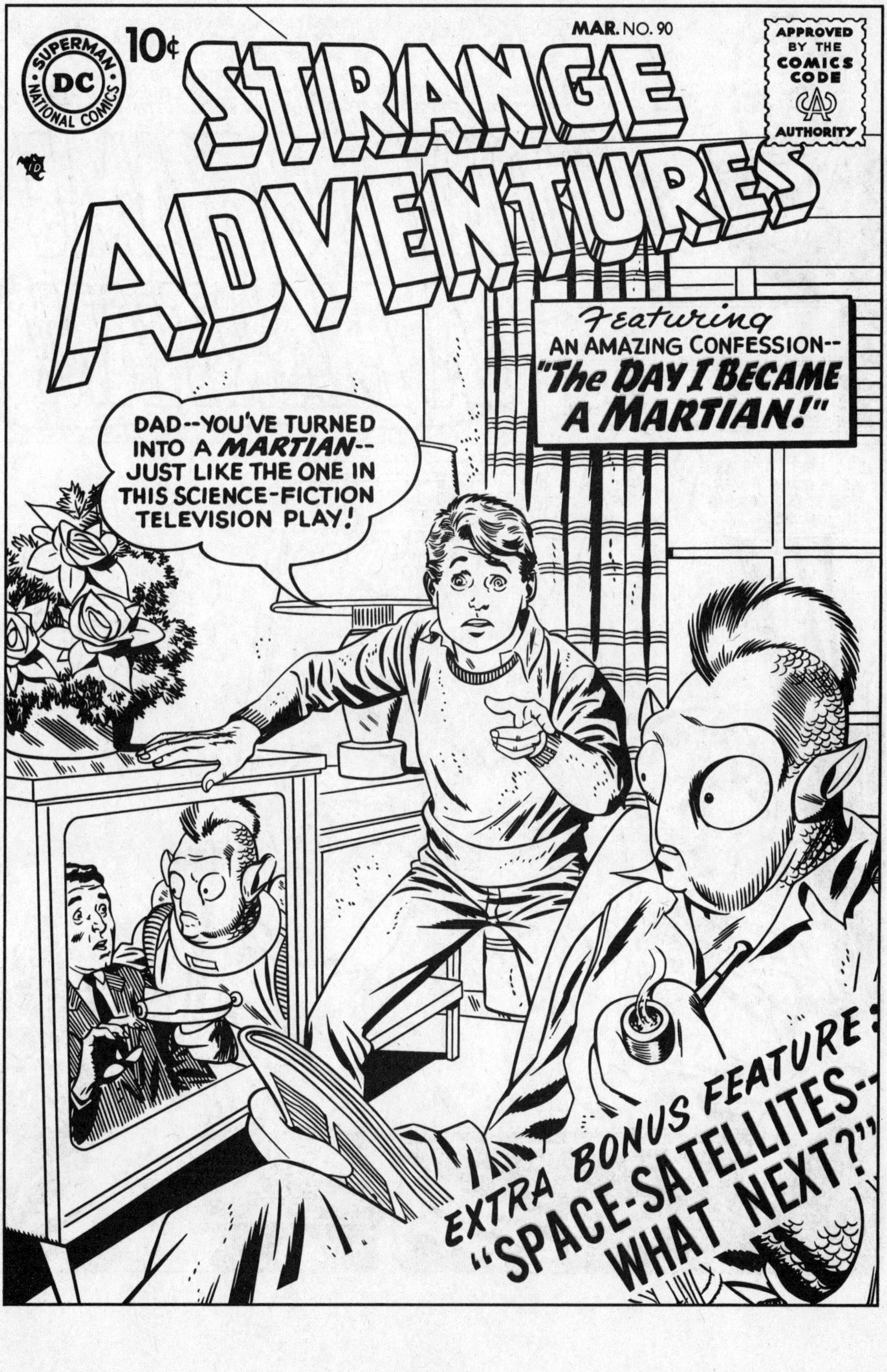
10¢
SUPERMAN DC NATIONAL COMICS
MAR. NO. 90
APPROVED BY THE COMICS CODE AUTHORITY
STRANGE ADVENTURES
Featuring AN AMAZING CONFESSION-- "The DAY I BECAME A MARTIAN!"
DAD--YOU'VE TURNED INTO A MARTIAN--JUST LIKE THE ONE IN THIS SCIENCE-FICTION TELEVISION PLAY!
EXTRA BONUS FEATURE: "SPACE-SATELLITES--WHAT NEXT?"

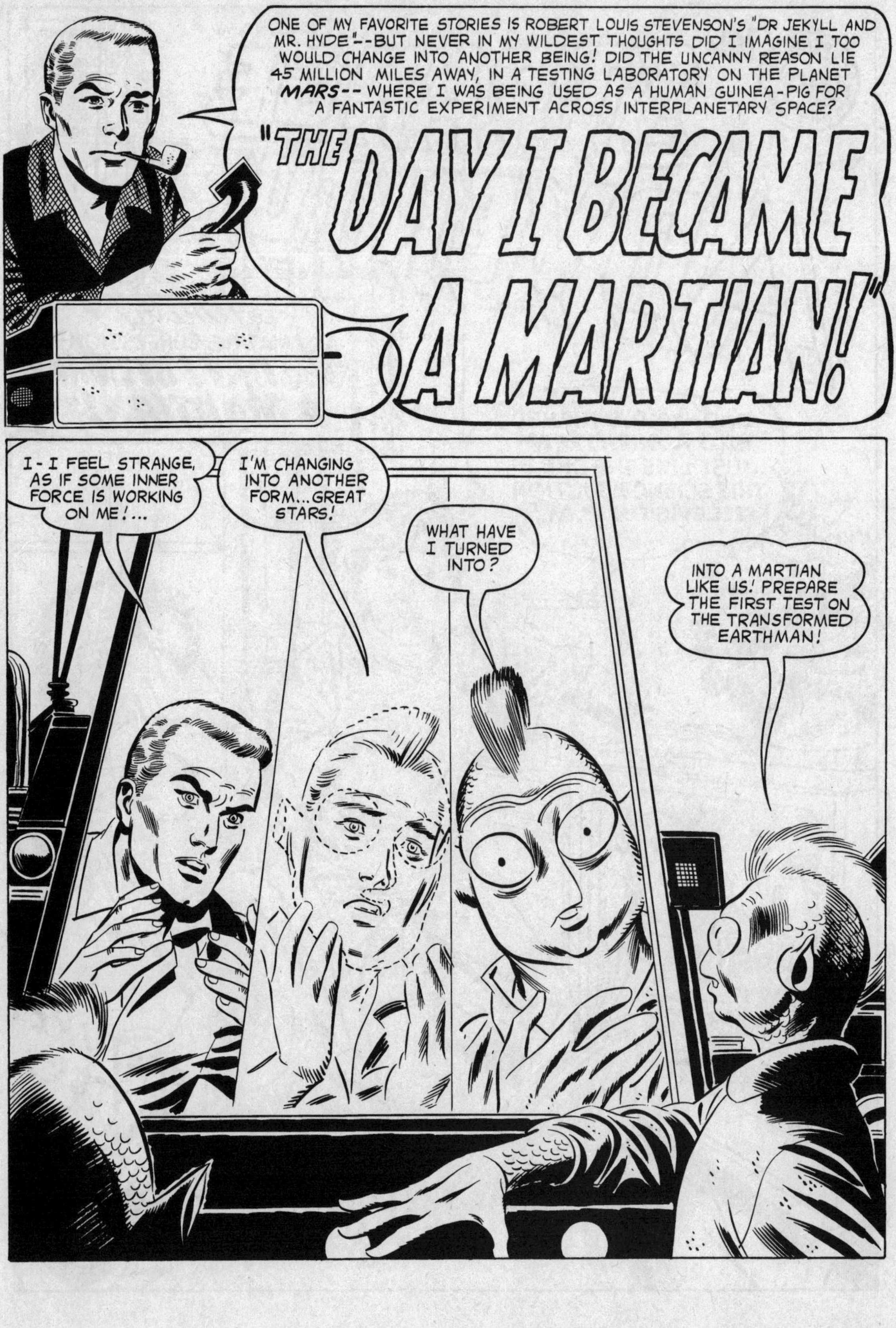
ONE OF MY FAVORITE STORIES IS ROBERT LOUIS STEVENSON'S "DR JEKYLL AND MR. HYDE"--BUT NEVER IN MY WILDEST THOUGHTS DID I IMAGINE I TOO WOULD CHANGE INTO ANOTHER BEING! DID THE UNCANNY REASON LIE 45 MILLION MILES AWAY, IN A TESTING LABORATORY ON THE PLANET MARS-- WHERE I WAS BEING USED AS A HUMAN GUINEA-PIG FOR A FANTASTIC EXPERIMENT ACROSS INTERPLANETARY SPACE?
"THE DAY I BECAME A MARTIAN!"
I-I FEEL STRANGE, AS IF SOME INNER FORCE IS WORKING ON ME!...
I'M CHANGING INTO ANOTHER FORM...GREAT STARS!
WHAT HAVE I TURNED INTO?
INTO A MARTIAN LIKE US! PREPARE THE FIRST TEST ON THE TRANSFORMED EARTHMAN!

I AM RHETT MASON, A WRITER SPECIALIZING IN SCIENCE-FICTION STORIES! BUT THE EVENTS I'M ABOUT TO DICTATE ARE FAR MORE FANTASTIC THAN ANY STORY CREATED IN MY IMAGINATION! IT BEGAN ONE EVENING WHEN...

"...MY SON BOB AND I WERE WATCHING A COLOR TV-PLAY I HAD WRITTEN..."

GOSH, DAD! YOUR STORY ABOUT MARTIANS INVADING EARTH IS REAL EXCITING!

THANKS, SON!

"SUDDENLY, SOMETHING UNCANNY HAPPENED TO MY VISION!"

GREAT SCOTT! EVERYTHING'S TURNED UPSIDE-DOWN! WH-WHAT'S HAPPENED TO MY EYESIGHT?

"EVEN MORE STARTLING WAS WHAT MY STARING SON YELLED AT ME! ..."

DAD! YOU-YOU'VE TURNED INTO A MARTIAN... JUST LIKE THE ONE IN THE TV PLAY!

"ALARMED, MY SON RAN FROM THE ROOM TO CALL MY WIFE! AS I LOOKED IN A MIRROR..."

IT'S INCREDIBLE--BUT MIRRORS DON'T LIE!...NOT EVEN UPSIDE-DOWN REFLECTIONS! I'M EXACTLY LIKE THE MARTIAN I DREAMED UP FOR MY STORY!

"MY THOUGHTS FLEW BACK TO THE NIGHT, A MONTH BEFORE, WHEN I FIRST BEGAN DICTATING THE TV STORY, WONDERING WHAT MY FICTITIOUS MARTIANS SHOULD LOOK LIKE ..."

STRANGE-- AN INSPIRATION FLASHED A CLEAR IMAGE IN MY MIND...

"ENTER MARTIAN, WITH SCALY BLUE SKIN...HAIRLESS HEAD AND BIRDLIKE TUFT... HUGE EYES... POINTED EARS!"

"BUT WHAT EERIE PHENOMENON HAD CHANGED ME INTO THAT *SAME* IMAGINARY MARTIAN?"

IS IT POSSIBLE I IMMERSED MYSELF SO DEEPLY IN THE STORY THAT POWER-OF-SUGGESTION TRANSFORMED ME INTO A MARTIAN?

"A BEWILDERING MOMENT LATER..."

I--I'M NORMAL AGAIN! THANK GOODNESS...

BOBBY! WHAT IS THIS NONSENSE ABOUT YOUR FATHER TURNING INTO A MARTIAN?

BUT-- BUT?

"TO ALLAY THE FEARS OF MY WIFE AND SON, I PASSED IT OFF LIGHTLY..."

GOLLY, DAD... DIDN'T YOU REALLY CHANGE INTO A MARTIAN AT ALL?

PERHAPS THE PLAY WAS SO VIVID THAT BOTH OUR...ER... IMAGINATIONS PLAYED US TRICKS! FORGET IT, SON!

BUT I COULDN'T FORGET IT! I SPENT A RESTLESS NIGHT! IN THE MORNING, I TURNED ON MY HI-FI SET, HOPING MUSIC WOULD SOOTHE MY JANGLED NERVES...

"BUT MY NERVES RECEIVED ANOTHER JOLT, WHEN ABRUPTLY..."

IT--IT'S HAPPENED AGAIN! BUT NOW MY VISION IS NORMAL!

"HOWEVER, THIS TIME MY SENSE OF *HEARING* WAS STRANGELY AFFECTED..."

THAT MUSIC IN MY ALIEN EARS... IT'S MAKING ME VIBRATE VIOLENTLY, LIKE A TUNING-FORK! GOT TO TURN OFF THE MUSIC-- BEFORE IT TEARS ME APART...

3

"AS SOON AS THE TORMENTING MUSIC STOPPED..."

I'M TURNING HUMAN AGAIN! ARE THESE CHANGES GOING TO OCCUR AGAIN... AND *AGAIN?* HAS SOME MYSTERIOUS AILMENT STRUCK ME, CAUSING FANTASTIC BIOLOGICAL CHANGES... LIKE THOSE THAT OCCURRED IN THE STORY OF DR. JEKYLL AND MR. HYDE?

"TO TAKE MY MIND OFF THE NERVE-SHATTERING PROBLEM, I FORCED MYSELF TO CONTINUE MY NEXT WRITING PROJECT..."

MY NEW SCIENCE-FICTION STORY IS ABOUT THE FIRST SPACE-TRIP TO THE MOON! I HAVE AN APPOINTMENT HERE, TO GATHER AUTHENTIC DATA!

SPACE-MEDICINE LABORATORY

"I SAW THE INGENIOUS SCIENTIFIC DEVICES USED TO SIMULATE CONDITIONS ON THE MOON, USING YOUNG PILOTS AS TEST SUBJECTS..."

ON THE AIRLESS MOON, THE SUN'S GLARE IS LIKE A BLINDING SEARCHLIGHT IN HIS *EYES!*

THE AIR IS PUMPED FROM HIS "MOON CHAMBER"... HE CAN'T *HEAR* ANY SOUNDS!

AT NIGHT, WHEN THE THERMOMETER READS MINUS 290 DEGREES ON THE MOON, EVERYTHING IS BITTERLY COLD TO THE HUMAN *TOUCH!*

IN SHORT, IT'S AS IF THOSE MEN, THROUGH THEIR FIVE SENSES, HAD ACTUALLY BEEN *ON* THE MOON!

HMM... THAT MAY BE THE CLUE TO *MY* MYSTERY! WHAT IF MARTIAN SCIENTISTS WERE TURNING *ME* INTO A MARTIAN TO TEST *EARTH* CONDITIONS FOR THEM?

"WHAT IF, ON MARS, THEY PREVIOUSLY BEGAN CARRYING OUT 'SPACE-MEDICINE' TESTS IN AN INGENIOUS WAY, USING *ME* AS THEIR REMOTE-CONTROL TEST SUBJECT..."

WE HAVE CHOSEN THAT EARTHMAN FOR OUR LONG-RANGE TESTS! WE WILL RADIATE AN ELECTRONIC IMAGE OF US INTO HIS BRAIN! HE WILL THINK IT WAS "INSPIRATION" FOR HIS STORY!

4

"DID THE MARTIANS THEN KEEP IMPLANTING THE IMAGE FIRMLY IN MY MIND FOR A MONTH, UNTIL..."

NOW THE *PSYCHOKINESIS* ⁕ RAY, SHOT ACROSS SPACE INTO HIS BRAIN, WILL TEMPORARILY *CHANGE* HIM TO MARTIAN FORM!

⁕ EDITOR'S NOTE: *PSYCHOKINESIS* IS "MIND-OVER-MATTER", WHERE PURE THOUGHT-FORCES CAN CONTROL AND CHANGE SOLID MATTER!

"DID THEIR COLD ALIEN EYES OBSERVE MY VISUAL AND AUDITORY REACTIONS LIKE SCIENTISTS CHECKING THEIR 'SPACE-MEDICINE' TESTS?"

INTERESTING... THE DENSE EARTHLY ATMOSPHERE *INVERTS* IMAGES FOR OUR MARTIAN EYES!

"AND ARE THEY COLLECTING THE DATA FOR AN *EVIL PURPOSE?*"

OUR ARMED FORCES MUST HAVE THEIR EYE-LENSES ADJUSTED BEFORE THEY LAND AND *CONQUER EARTH!*

EARTH MEDICINE DATA

SIGHT - *Martian vision is inverted on earth*

HEARING -

TOUCH -

SMELL -

TASTE -

"AND HAD THEY SELECTED ME BECAUSE I USED A *DICTAPHONE?*"

WE CANNOT READ THE EARTHMAN'S SECRET THOUGHTS, BUT OUR ULTRA-RADIO PICKS UP HIS VOICE, AS HE RECORDS HIS STRANGE SENSORY EXPERIENCES!

ITEM-- *HEARING!* MUSIC VIBRATIONS PROVE DANGEROUS TO MY MARTIAN EARS...

BUT-BUT ARE THESE WILD GUESSES *TRUE?* ARE WARLIKE MARTIANS *REALLY* CHECKING EARTHLY CONDITIONS THROUGH ME? I-I DON'T KNOW! BUT I MUST RECORD THE FACTS, FOR SCIENTISTS TO ANALYZE LATER!

"IT WAS ON MY WAY HOME FROM THE SPACE-MEDICINE LAB THAT MY NEXT TRANSFORMATION CAME..."

ELECTRIC SHOCKS--SHOOTING UP MY "MARTIAN FEET," FROM CONTACT WITH THE GROUND!

5

EARTH'S GROUND IS NEGATIVELY CHARGED WITH ELECTRICITY! EARTHMEN ARE IMMUNE... BUT WE WILL **MAKE** OURSELVES SO! OUR TEST-SUBJECT ON EARTH IS DEMONSTRATING ALL THE PITFALLS TO AVOID!

SIGHT — *Martian vision is inverted on earth*

HEARING — *Music dangerous to Martian ears*

TOUCH — *Martian army to wear insulated boots*

SMELL —

TASTE —

"SHORTLY AFTER, IN MY STUDIO, I WAS AGAIN CHANGED BRIEFLY TO A MARTIAN...TO TEST ANOTHER OF THE FIVE SENSES FOR THEM!"

THAT COFFEE I WARMED UP ON THE HOT-PLATE...THE AROMA IS MAKING ME BLACK OUT! OHHH...

WHEN WE INVADE EARTH, WE MUST AVOID **SMELLING** THE FUMES OF THAT EARTHLY BEVERAGE! CHANGE HIM BACK TO HUMAN FORM SO HE RECOVERS!

THE EARTHMAN IS NOW GOING TO EAT... GIVING US THE OPPORTUNITY TO TEST THE SENSE OF **TASTE!** CHANGE HIM BACK TO A MARTIAN AGAIN... AND ALSO USE THE **MOLECULAR RAY** TO TRANSFORM HIS FOOD INTO OUR NATIVE **ZOLLIA** BREAD!

"I NOTICED THE QUEER TASTE, AND THEN SUDDENLY..."

I-I'M FREEZING SOLID, UNABLE TO MOVE!

WHAT CAUSED THAT REACTION? HMM... MARTIAN AIR CONTAINS NO **NITROGEN!** THAT EARTHLY GAS CONVERTS OUR **ZOLLIA BREAD** INTO A FREEZING AGENT! OUR INVASION ARMY MUST TAKE ALONG FOODS IMPERVIOUS TO NITROGEN CONTAMINATION!

OXYGEN

NITROGEN

CARBON DIOXIDE

WATER VAPOR

ARGON

RARE GASES

6

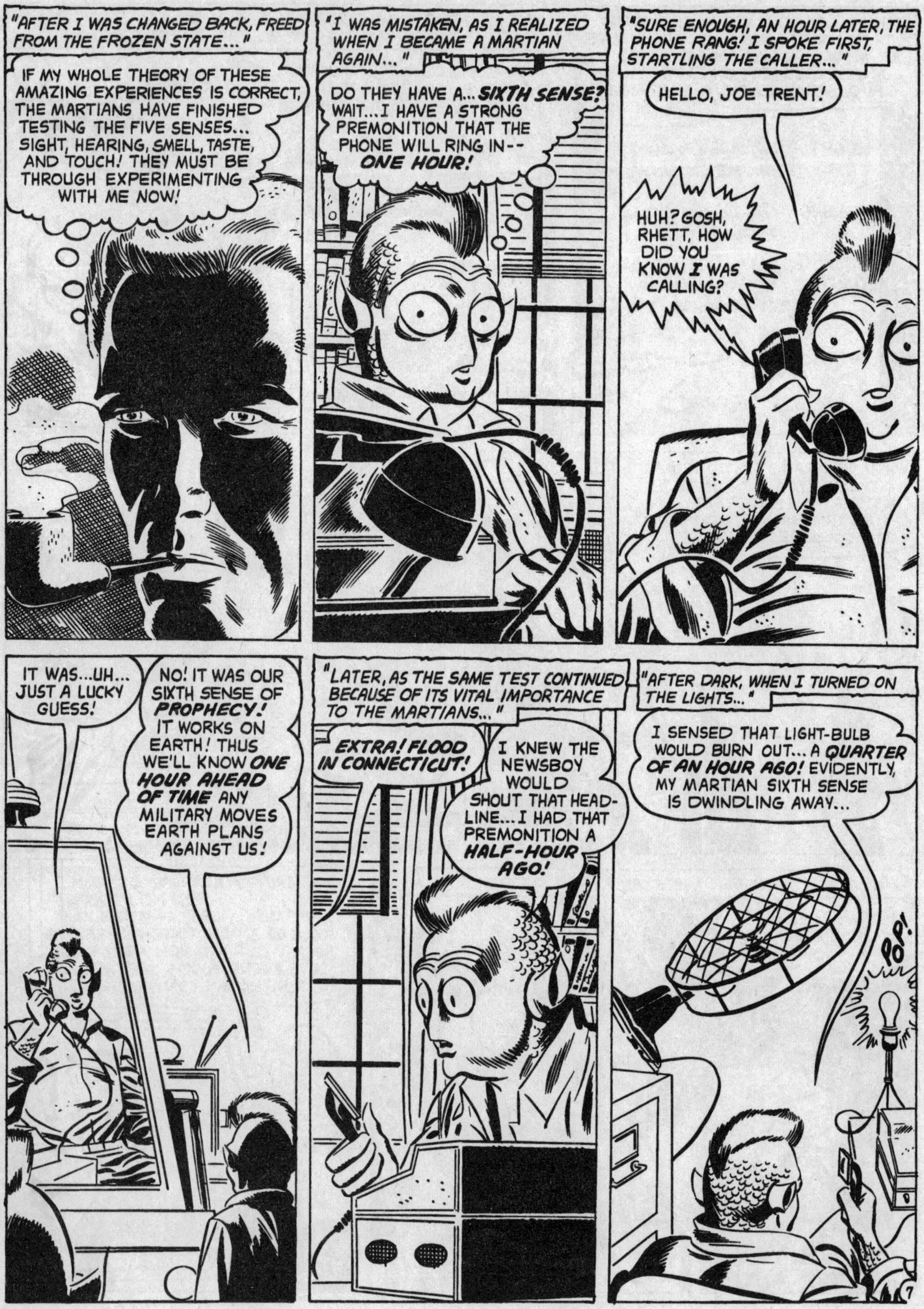
"AFTER I WAS CHANGED BACK, FREED FROM THE FROZEN STATE..."
IF MY WHOLE THEORY OF THESE AMAZING EXPERIENCES IS CORRECT, THE MARTIANS HAVE FINISHED TESTING THE FIVE SENSES... SIGHT, HEARING, SMELL, TASTE, AND TOUCH! THEY MUST BE THROUGH EXPERIMENTING WITH ME NOW!
"I WAS MISTAKEN, AS I REALIZED WHEN I BECAME A MARTIAN AGAIN..."
DO THEY HAVE A... SIXTH SENSE? WAIT... I HAVE A STRONG PREMONITION THAT THE PHONE WILL RING IN-- ONE HOUR!
"SURE ENOUGH, AN HOUR LATER, THE PHONE RANG! I SPOKE FIRST, STARTLING THE CALLER..."
HELLO, JOE TRENT!
HUH? GOSH, RHETT, HOW DID YOU KNOW I WAS CALLING?
IT WAS...UH... JUST A LUCKY GUESS!
NO! IT WAS OUR SIXTH SENSE OF PROPHECY! IT WORKS ON EARTH! THUS WE'LL KNOW ONE HOUR AHEAD OF TIME ANY MILITARY MOVES EARTH PLANS AGAINST US!
"LATER, AS THE SAME TEST CONTINUED BECAUSE OF ITS VITAL IMPORTANCE TO THE MARTIANS..."
EXTRA! FLOOD IN CONNECTICUT!
I KNEW THE NEWSBOY WOULD SHOUT THAT HEAD-LINE... I HAD THAT PREMONITION A HALF-HOUR AGO!
"AFTER DARK, WHEN I TURNED ON THE LIGHTS..."
I SENSED THAT LIGHT-BULB WOULD BURN OUT... A QUARTER OF AN HOUR AGO! EVIDENTLY, MY MARTIAN SIXTH SENSE IS DWINDLING AWAY...
POP!
7

"SUDDENLY, WITHOUT WARNING..."

THAT HEAVY FAN SLIPPED... FALLING DOWN AT ME!

WHEW! NEARLY HIT ME!

LOOK! THE EARTHMAN HAS COMPLETELY **LOST** HIS PROPHETIC SENSE -- OR HE WOULD HAVE **KNOWN** IT WOULD FALL AND AVOIDED IT EARLIER! SOMETHING ON EARTH CAUSES US TO LOSE OUR ALL-IMPORTANT SIXTH SENSE!

FINAL REPORT OF EARTH TESTS: MYSTERIOUS EARTH-FORCE INTERFERING WITH SIXTH SENSE CANNOT BE DETECTED! WITHOUT OUR PROPHETIC SENSE TO FOREWARN OF EARTH'S MILITARY MOVES, WE CANNOT HOPE TO CONQUER EARTH! INVASION OF EARTH IS CANCELLED!

"MY TRICK HAD WORKED! FOR WHEN THE FAN FELL..."

I **DID** KNOW, AN HOUR AGO, THAT THE FAN WOULD FALL! I ONLY **PRETENDED** MY PROPHETIC SENSE HAD DWINDLED AWAY! SINCE THE MARTIANS COULDN'T READ MY **SECRET THOUGHTS**, THEY HAD NO WAY OF KNOWING I FOOLED THEM!

I HAVE NO PROOF TO SHOW THAT MY THEORY OF ENEMY MARTIANS IS TRUE! BUT I HAVE ONE INDICATION -- A MONTH HAS PASSED NOW, AND I HAVEN'T CHANGED TO A MARTIAN AGAIN, INDICATING THEY HAVE ABANDONED THE TESTS!

BUT IF I **DICTATE** THE END OF MY STRANGE ADVENTURE, OR TELL ANYBODY, THE MARTIANS MIGHT PICK UP MY VOICE AND REALIZE MY DECEPTION! IT MUST REMAIN A SECRET IN MY MIND ALONE! STILL, I WONDER... WERE MARTIANS **REALLY** TESTING ME?... PLANNING TO INVADE EARTH? I MAY NEVER KNOW!

THE END

The 100,000 YEAR-OLD WEAPON!

SCIENCE-FICTION HAS FORETOLD THE DISCOVERY OF THE SUBMARINE, TELEVISION, THE ATOM BOMB, THE SPACE-SATELLITE! BUT WHAT DISCOVERY DID A CERTAIN SCIENCE-FICTION STORY PROPHESY THAT WOULD ACTUALLY SAVE THE FUTURE EARTH FROM DISASTER?

WHY DOES THAT *INVISIBLE BROWSER* APPEAR IN MY BOOKSHOP EVERY NIGHT AND THUMB THROUGH THOSE SCIENCE-FICTION BOOKS?

SCIENCE FICTION

PHILOSOPHY

STORY

MENACE FROM MARS

HURRIED FOOTFALLS POUND ALONG A SIDEWALK IN A CITY, JUST AFTER MIDNIGHT...

IN MY BOOKSTORE, DOCTOR-- HURRY! I DON'T KNOW HOW BADLY THE MAN IS HURT!

DARROW'S BOOK STORE

SALE

MOMENTS LATER...

THERE HE IS, DOCTOR-- ON THE FLOOR!

THERE'S *NOBODY* ON THE FLOOR, YOUNG MAN!

OH, I FORGOT.' YOU CAN'T SEE HIM WITHOUT THESE SPECIAL LENSES! PUT THEM ON.'

IF THIS IS A JOKE--.'

AS SOON AS HE DONS THE SPECTACLES, DR. JACKSON CAN SEE HIS PATIENT CLEARLY...

AMAZING.' SPECIAL LENSES TO SEE AN "INVISIBLE MAN".' HOW STRANGE-LOOKING--

OF COURSE HE LOOKS STRANGE.' HE'S 100,000 YEARS OLD!

WH--AAT ?.'

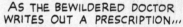

AS THE BEWILDERED DOCTOR WRITES OUT A PRESCRIPTION...

HE'S HAD A SHOCK TO HIS NERVOUS SYSTEM.' COUPLE OF DAYS REST IN BED, AND HE'LL BE ALL RIGHT.' BUT TELL ME--IS HE REALLY 100,000 YEARS OLD ?

NOT REALLY.' I GUESS I BETTER EXPLAIN...

"ONE MORNING, ABOUT A WEEK AGO, WHEN I CAME INTO MY BOOKSTORE..."

THOSE SCIENCE-FICTION BOOKS WEREN'T STACKED THAT WAY WHEN I LOCKED UP LAST NIGHT.' SOMEONE BROKE IN HERE AND BROWSED THROUGH THOSE BOOKS.'

"NOTHING HAD BEEN STOLEN.' THE LOCKS WERE UNTOUCHED, AND THE WINDOWS STILL BOLTED..."

WHY WOULD ANYONE BREAK IN TO LOOK AT THESE BOOKS AT NIGHT ? WHY DIDN'T HE COME IN DURING THE DAY ?

2

"THAT NIGHT, I SECRETLY REMAINED ON GUARD! A LITTLE BEFORE MIDNIGHT, I SAW A BOOK MOVE OFF ITS SHELF..."

IT'S ALMOST AS IF AN- AN *INVISIBLE MAN* WERE THUMBING THROUGH THE PAGES...

"BEFORE TANGLING WITH ANYTHING INVISIBLE, I DECIDED TO TAKE "*ITS*" PICTURE WITH AN INFRARED LENS..."

MY MYSTERIOUS VISITOR MAY BE INVISIBLE IN ORDINARY LIGHT-- BUT PERFECTLY VISIBLE BY INFRARED RAYS!

"NEXT DAY WHEN I DEVELOPED THE FILM AND RAN IT OFF IN MY SLIDE PROJECTOR..."

IT'S A *MAN*, ALL RIGHT, BUT I'VE NEVER SEEN ANYTHING LIKE *HIM* BEFORE!

I'LL LEAVE HIM A NOTE, OFFERING TO HELP HIM FIND THE BOOK HE'S LOOKING FOR! I'VE GOT TO FIND OUT WHAT THIS IS ALL ABOUT!

"THE FOLLOWING NIGHT AS I WAITED IN THE BOOKSTORE, MY INVISIBLE BROWSER APPEARED AND SPOKE TO ME..."

PUT ON THESE GLASSES! THE LENSES ARE SPECIALLY GROUND TO ENABLE YOU TO SEE ME!

WHO ARE YOU?

I AM A TIME-TRAVELER FROM THE FAR FUTURE--THE YEAR 101,958 TO BE EXACT! WHEN I VISIT A TIME-PERIOD BEFORE I WAS BORN, I AM RENDERED INVISIBLE!

MY NAME IS JAN 356! I'VE TRAVELED TO THIS ERA IN SEARCH OF A WEAPON! UNLESS I FIND IT, OUR FUTURE CIVILIZATION IS DOOMED!

3

"ON MY FUTURE WORLD, WE ARE RULED BY A MILITARY DICTATOR NAMED EVAR TOR..."

EVAR TOR HAS TAKEN POSSESSION OF EVERY MILITARY WEAPON! WITHOUT THEM THERE IS NO CHANCE FOR THE PEOPLE TO REVOLT AND OVERTHROW HIM!

EVAR TOR HAS EVEN OUTLAWED ALL SCIENTIFIC EXPERIMENTS, LEST WE DISCOVER SOME POWERFUL NEW WEAPON TO USE AGAINST HIM!

YET THERE IS *ONE WAY* BY WHICH WE CAN FREE OURSELVES OF HIS TYRANNY!

WE SMUGGLED THIS **TIME-MACHINE** OUT OF THE STATE ARSENAL! AS OUR FOREMOST HISTORIAN WHO UNDERSTANDS THE CULTURE AND LANGUAGE OF THE DEAD AGES, JAN 356 HAS BEEN SELECTED TO HUNT FOR A WEAPON IN THE PAST...

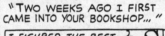

"TWO WEEKS AGO I FIRST CAME INTO YOUR BOOKSHOP..."

I FIGURED THE BEST WAY TO FIND A **SUPER-WEAPON** IN THE PAST WAS TO DISCOVER ONE AS DESCRIBED IN A SCIENCE-FICTION WRITER'S VIVID IMAGINATION!

THE **SOLAR-HEAT-RAY GUN** DESCRIBED IN THIS BOOK IS JUST THE WEAPON WE NEED! DRAWING ITS ENERGY FROM THE SUN, EVAR TOR HAS NO WAY OF COUNTERACTING IT!

"BACK IN THE FUTURE WE SECRETLY BUILT THE WEAPON--BUT UNFORTUNATELY, WE FORGOT ONE IMPORTANT FACTOR..."

OUR WEAPON COULD NOT CONCENTRATE ENOUGH SOLAR HEAT TO OVERCOME THE GUARDS!

THE SUN WAS *HOTTER*, A HUNDRED THOUSAND YEARS AGO!

THAT IS WHY I'VE RETURNED-- TO FIND ANOTHER WEAPON!...

EVAR TOR SENT ME-- TO STOP YOU!...

"I STOOD FROZEN AS THE GUARD FROM THE FUTURE AIMED HIS RAYGUN..."

AFTER THE SUN- WEAPON FIASCO, EVAR TOR KNEW YOU MUST HAVE STOLEN A TIME-MACHINE AND ENTERED THE PAST TO LEARN HOW TO CONSTRUCT SUCH A NEW WEAPON!

YOU KNOW THE PUNISHMENT FOR DISOBEYING EVAR TOR'S ORDER...

GOT TO STOP HIM...

I'LL HOLD HIM OFF AS LONG AS I CAN, JAN-- RUN FOR IT!

"BUT I WAS NO MATCH FOR THE EXPERTLY TRAINED GUARD, AND WHEN I WAS QUICKLY OVERCOME..."

NO ONE CAN TAKE THE FULL VOLTAGE OF THE *COSMIRAY GUN*--AND LIVE!

WHEN THE BOOKSTORE DEALER CONCLUDES HIS STORY, HE AND THE DOCTOR CARRY THE FUTURE-MAN TO A BEDROOM IN DARROW'S APARTMENT...

YOUR FRIEND WILL BE ALL RIGHT, WITH REST...!

BUT WHAT OF HIS FUTURE? WHAT CAN I DO TO HELP?

5

TWO DAYS LATER, THE FUTURE-MAN HAS RECOVERED...

THE GUARD MADE THE SAME MISTAKE WE DID! HE DIDN'T REALIZE COSMIC RAYS ARE WEAKER TODAY THAN 100,000 YEARS FROM NOW! I'M ALIVE, THANKS TO THAT-- BUT I'VE FAILED IN MY MISSION!

MAYBE I CAN HELP YOU! IN A FAMOUS SCIENCE-FICTION STORY WRITTEN YEARS AGO A SCIENTIST MADE HIM-SELF *INVISIBLE* BY BENDING LIGHT RAYS AROUND HIS BODY...

HOWEVER, BY MAKING HIMSELF INVISIBLE IN THIS MANNER, HE PREVENTED HIMSELF FROM SEEING ANYTHING-- BECAUSE NO LIGHT RAYS COULD REACH HIS EYES! IF YOU USED THE SAME DEVICE TO MAKE YOUR ENEMIES INVISIBLE, THEY WON'T BE ABLE TO SEE OR STOP YOU WHILE YOU DESTROY THEIR WEAPONS.

SOON AFTER, JAN 356 RETURNS TO HIS OWN TIME! THEN ONE NIGHT IN THE BOOKSTORE...

JAN PROMISED TO TIME-TRANSMIT ME A MOTION PICTURE FILM OF HIS SUCCESS, IF MY IDEA WORKED... *HERE IT IS!*

FICTION

AS THE BOOK-SELLER UNREELS THE FILM...

THANKS TO YOU, MAN OF THE PAST, WE DESTROYED EVERY MILITARY WEAPON, AND ENDED EVAR TOR'S EVIL DICTATORSHIP! THE GUARDS, UNABLE TO SEE US, WERE EASILY OVERCOME...

NEXT DAY...

SCIENCE-FICTION? I NEVER READ THAT STUFF! WHY THE IDEAS THEY TOSS AROUND IN THOSE STORIES WOULDN'T WORK IN A 100,000 YEARS!

I KNOW *ONE IDEA* THAT WORKED--AND SAVED OUR FUTURE CIVILIZATION!

SCIENCE F

The End 6

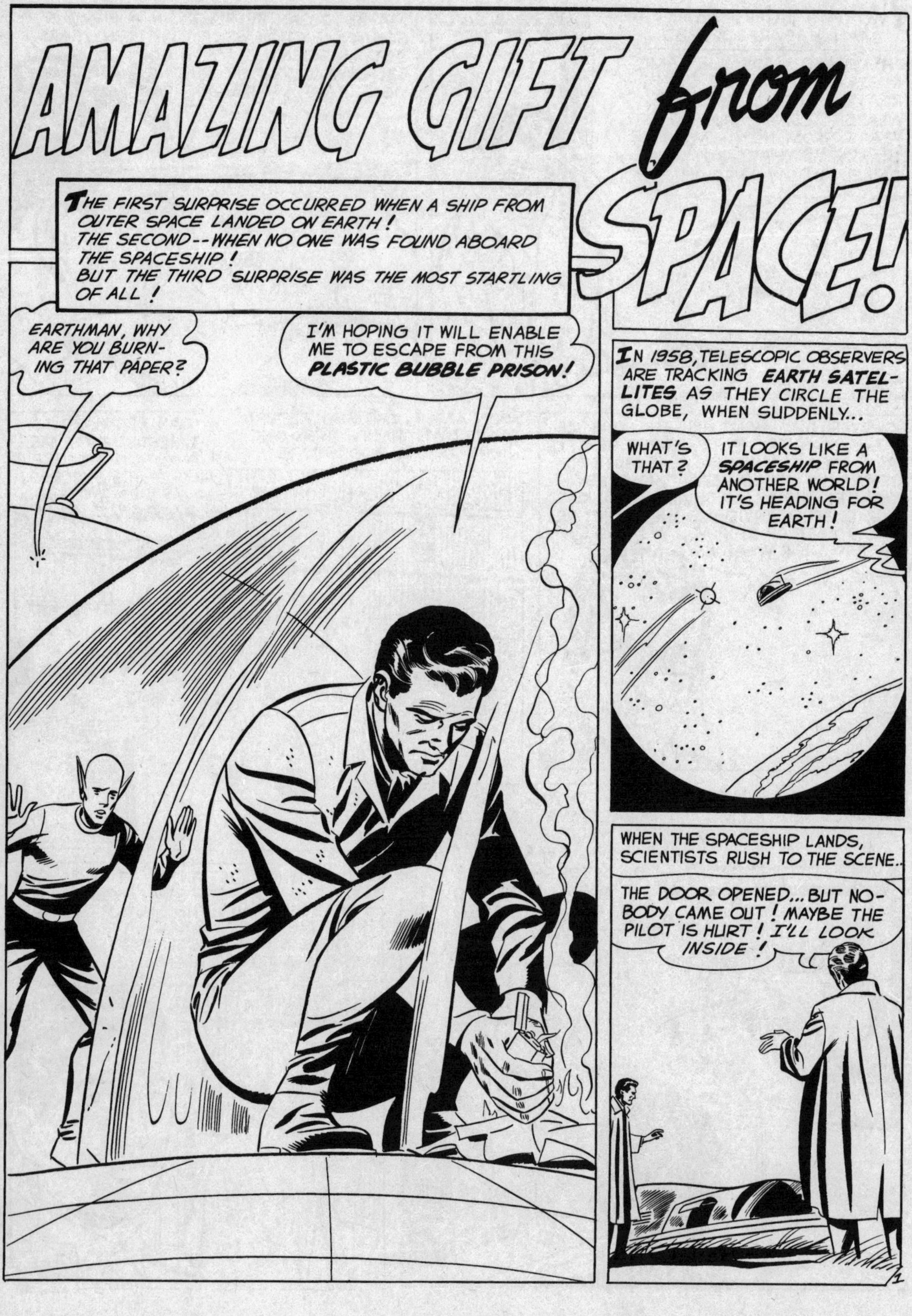
AMAZING GIFT from SPACE!
THE FIRST SURPRISE OCCURRED WHEN A SHIP FROM OUTER SPACE LANDED ON EARTH! THE SECOND--WHEN NO ONE WAS FOUND ABOARD THE SPACESHIP! BUT THE THIRD SURPRISE WAS THE MOST STARTLING OF ALL!
EARTHMAN, WHY ARE YOU BURNING THAT PAPER?
I'M HOPING IT WILL ENABLE ME TO ESCAPE FROM THIS PLASTIC BUBBLE PRISON!
IN 1958, TELESCOPIC OBSERVERS ARE TRACKING EARTH SATELLITES AS THEY CIRCLE THE GLOBE, WHEN SUDDENLY...
WHAT'S THAT?
IT LOOKS LIKE A SPACESHIP FROM ANOTHER WORLD! IT'S HEADING FOR EARTH!
WHEN THE SPACESHIP LANDS, SCIENTISTS RUSH TO THE SCENE..
THE DOOR OPENED... BUT NOBODY CAME OUT! MAYBE THE PILOT IS HURT! I'LL LOOK INSIDE!
1

INSIDE, ASTOUNDINGLY...

NO ONE HERE! AN AUTOMATIC PILOT SYSTEM MUST HAVE GUIDED IT TO EARTH! BUT WHICH WORLD SENT IT? WHY?

ATTENTION! THIS IS A TELEPATHY-TRANSLATOR, SPEAKING YOUR LANGUAGE! PLEACE ACCEPT THIS SPACESHIP AS A GIFT, FROM THE PLANET ZAXIA!

THROUGH OUR POWERFUL TELESCOPES, WE HAVE BEEN WATCHING YOUR RECENT ATTEMPTS TO ACHIEVE SPACE-TRAVEL! BUT IT WILL TAKE YOU ANOTHER CENTURY BEFORE YOU SOLVE ALL TECHNICAL PROBLEMS! OUR PERFECTED SPACESHIP WILL SAVE YOU THAT LOST TIME!

UNFORTUNATELY, WE ZAXIANS CAN NEVER VISIT YOU IN PERSON BECAUSE COSMIC RAYS, WHICH PERVADE ALL SPACE, ARE DEADLY TO US! WE ARE FOREVER PLANET—BOUND!

BUT YOU EARTHMEN CAN SAFELY EXPLORE THE UNIVERSE, EVEN IF WE CAN'T, WITH THIS GIFT SPACESHIP! PERHAPS, ONE DAY, YOU'LL COME VISIT US!

WHAT A MAGNANIMOUS GESTURE!

BUT ONE SCIENTIST CAUTIOUSLY SUGGESTS...

WHAT IF THE ZAXIANS SECRETLY PLAN INVADING EARTH? THIS SO—CALLED "GIFT" MAY BE CUNNING TRICKERY-- A "TROJAN HORSE" OF SPACE!

I CAN HARDLY BELIEVE THAT! IN ANY EVENT, WE HAVE NOTHING TO LOSE BY TESTING THE SHIP! OUR ACE PILOT, CAPTAIN RICK HALL, WILL FLY THE SPACESHIP TOMORROW!

AT DAWN THE NEXT DAY, AS THE YOUNG PILOT TAKES OVER THE CONTROLS...

WHEN I SAT DOWN, I TRIGGERED OFF THE SPEAKER AGAIN! IT'S GIVING ME FULL IN-STRUCTIONS HOW TO PILOT THE SHIP...

FOR TAKE-OFF... PULL RED LEVER... THEN GREEN KNOB TEN DEGREES!

LEAPING POWERFULLY INTO SPACE, THE SHIP ENCOUNTERS SUDDEN DANGER!

FIVE THOUSAND MILES UP... A METEOR DEAD AHEAD... HOW DO I AVOID IT?

AGAIN, THE MECHANICAL VOICE GIVES INSTRUCTIONS...

PRESS BLACK BUTTON OF *METEOR BLASTER!*

IT SHATTERED THE METEOR! THE *ZAXIANS* HAVE THOUGHT OF EVERYTHING!

LATER, WHEN CAPTAIN HALL REPORTS TO EARTH VIA RADIO...

TEST FLIGHT AROUND SOLAR SYSTEM SUCCESSFUL! SHALL I RETURN?

NO, DRIVE ON TO *ZAXIA* AND THANK THEM PERSONALLY FOR THEIR GIFT! WE MIGHT AS WELL FIND OUT IF THERE IS ANY ULTERIOR MOTIVE...

AFTER A SUPER-SPEED HOP INTO OUTER SPACE...

THE AUTOMATIC VOICE GUIDED ME TO *ZAXIA!* I FEEL QUITE SURE I'LL GET A WARM GREETING FROM THE GENEROUS PEOPLE WHO DONATED THIS WONDER SHIP TO US!

BUT AS SOON AS THE EARTHMAN LANDS AT THE BIGGEST CITY...

SEIZE THE SPACE-VISITOR!

WE'VE BEEN TRICKED! THE *ZAXIANS* ARE HOSTILE!

QUICKLY, RICK HALL IS IMPRISONED INSIDE A PLASTIC RUBBLE...

WHAT A STRANGE *"PRISON CELL"*! THE WALLS ARE TOO TOUGH TO BREAK THROUGH!

BITTER THOUGHTS PLAGUE THE BEWILDERED EARTHMAN CAPTIVE...

THOSE ON EARTH WHO HAD SUSPICIONS OVER THE *"GIFT SPACESHIP"* WERE RIGHT! IT WAS A PLOT TO LURE AN EARTHMAN INTO THEIR HANDS! THEY'LL TRY TO GET INFORMATION OUT OF ME REGARDING EARTH'S DEFENSES, PREPARATORY TO AN ATTACK!

BUT TELEPATHIC SPEECH COMES FROM A NEARBY PRISONER...

EARTHMAN! WE DID NOT PLOT AGAINST EARTH! *I* AM A TRUE *ZAXIAN!* YOU SEE, DURING YOUR TRIP HERE, *SPACE-INVADERS* CONQUERED OUR WORLD!

NO, THEN IT WAS *THEY* WHO IMPRISONED ME!

IF I COULD ONLY ESCAPE... BUT THIS PLASTIC PRISON SEEMS UNBREAKABLE! WHAT CAN I POSSIBLY USE...

MOMENTS LATER...

I'LL BURN THIS PAPER I HAD IN MY POCKET! HEAT CAUSES AIR TO *EXPAND!* AND WHEN ANY FLEXIBLE MATERIAL IS STRETCHED TO ITS LIMIT...

...IT BURSTS AT ITS *WEAKEST* POINT! I'M *FREE!*

ELUDING GUARDS, RICK REACHES THE GIFT SHIP...BUT TO HIS DISMAY...

IT WON'T START! THE ENEMY-ALIENS TOOK THE MOTOR OUT, PROBABLY TO EXAMINE IT AND SEE IF IT'S SUPERIOR TO THEIR OWN SPACESHIP ENGINES!

NEARBY...

THE ENEMY'S SPACE-FLEET IS PARKED HERE, AND UNGUARDED! THEY KNOW THE ZAXIANS CAN'T FLY THEM INTO SPACE WITHOUT DYING FROM COSMIC RAYS! BUT MAYBE I CAN DO SOMETHING TO SAVE ZAXIA!

AFTER SECRETLY CONTACTING ZAXIAN SCIENTISTS,...

WE INSTALLED AUTOMATIC PILOTS ON ALL THEIR SHIPS AS YOU REQUESTED, EARTHMAN!

GOOD! NOW WE'LL REPAINT THEM WITH A DIFFERENT COLOR SO THE ENEMY WON'T RECOGNIZE THEIR OWN SHIPS!

WITH RICK ABOARD ONE SHIP, THE AUTOMATIC PILOTS LAUNCH THE ENTIRE FLEET INTO SPACE!

NOW TO CIRCLE ZAXIA, AND PUT MY PLAN INTO EFFECT!

BOLDLY, THE EARTHMAN ISSUES AN ULTIMATUM, VIA TELEPATHIC-RADIO!

ATTENTION! DETECTING THE CAPTURE OF OUR SCOUT, EARTH HAS SENT A WAR-FLEET TO RESCUE HIM AND FREE ZAXIA FROM ITS INVADERS!

THE FOLLOWING MOMENT, A RAY FLASHES FROM THE LEAD SPACESHIP...

THEIR RAY BLASTED THAT METEOR!

TURNED TO *FULL POWER*, OUR RAYS CAN SHATTER AN ENTIRE PLANET!

ACTUALLY, I ONLY USED THE SIMPLE *METEOR BLASTER*, WHICH I REMOVED FROM THE GIFT SHIP!

SURRENDER TO THE *ZAXIANS*... OR FACE ANNIHILATION!

BELOW, THE COWED ENEMY SURRENDERS...

IF WE ATTEMPT TO USE OUR OWN WARSHIPS, WE WILL BE DESTROYED BY THE MIGHTY EARTH FLEET! WE ARE FORCED TO SURRENDER!

GIVE UP ALL YOUR WEAPONS!

TOO LATE, THE ENEMY PERCEIVES THE TRUTH AS THE "*EARTH FLEET*" LANDS...

THOSE ARE *OUR OWN* SHIPS, PAINTED ANOTHER COLOR!

THAT IS ONLY *ONE* OF THE WAYS THE EARTHMAN TRICKED YOU!

LATER, AFTER THE MOTOR HAS BEEN RESTORED TO THE GIFT SHIP...

THE ENEMY PRISONERS UNTIL EARTH HAS TIME TO BUILD A *REAL* FLEET OF WARSHIPS, MODELED AFTER THIS GIFT SHIP! THEN WE'LL HELP YOU KEEP *PEACE* IN THE GALAXY!

KEEP

THANKS, EARTHMAN!

FINALLY, AS CAPTAIN RICK HALL HEADS BACK TO EARTH...

LITTLE DID THE *ZAXIANS* REALIZE THAT BY SENDING US THEIR GIFT SHIP, THEY WOULD SAVE THEIR OWN WORLD! *GENEROSITY ALWAYS PAYS!*

The End

MYSTERY OF METEOR CRATER

EVER SINCE ITS FORMATION IN PREHISTORIC TIMES, THE **METEOR CRATER** OF ARIZONA HAS BEEN ONE OF THE SCENIC WONDERS OF THE WORLD! BUT NEVER AGAIN WILL TOURISTS TRAVEL TO SEE THIS FAMOUS LANDMARK--FOR SUDDENLY, INEXPLICABLY, THE GREAT CRATER VANISHED FROM THE FACE OF THE EARTH!

YES, EARTHMAN--50,000 YEARS AGO A GIGANTIC METEORITE CRASHED INTO THE EARTH! ONCE WE RECOVER IT, YOUR WORLD--THE WHOLE SOLAR SYSTEM-- WILL BE UNDER OUR DOMINATION!

TOURING OUT WEST ON HIS VACATION, WYATT ACHISON EAGERLY PLANS TO TAKE IN A FAMOUS LANDMARK OF ARIZONA....

METEOR CRATER IS 6 MILES SOUTH OF HIGHWAY 66, ALONG THIS SIDE ROAD! I'LL JUST HAVE TIME TO SEE IT BEFORE SUNDOWN!

66

BUT STRANGELY, AFTER THE ODOMETER REGISTERS 6 MILES...

THERE'S NO SIGN OF IT! MAYBE I LOST MY WAY...

OH, MISTER! WHERE'S **METEOR CRATER**?

METEOR CRATER? THERE'S NO SUCH PLACE AROUND HERE, SIR!

WHY OF COURSE THERE IS! I'VE READ ABOUT IT--EVEN SEEN PICTURES OF IT! TOURISTS REGULARLY TAKE A GUIDED TOUR DOWN THE HUGE CRATER!

WELL, I'VE BEEN A *SCENIC* GUIDE AROUND HERE FOR YEARS AND I NEVER SHOWED ANYONE *"METEOR CRATER"!* YOU *MUST* BE MISTAKEN!

GOSH! CAN THE CRATER BE A FIGMENT OF SOMEONE'S IMAGINATION?

AS THE BEWILDERED TOURIST DRIVES ON...

WAIT-- I JUST REMEMBERED SOMETHING ODD ABOUT THAT GUIDE! WHEN HE SPOKE TO ME, HIS LIPS DIDN'T MOVE ONCE! HE--HE MUST HAVE BEEN TALKING TO ME *TELEPATHICALLY!*

THEN, AS ACHISON LOOKS AT A ROAD MAP...

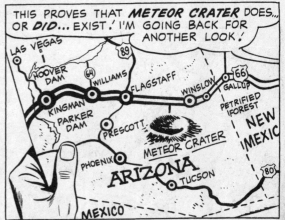

THIS PROVES THAT *METEOR CRATER* DOES... OR *DID*... EXIST! I'M GOING BACK FOR ANOTHER LOOK!

UNDER COVER OF NIGHT, ACHISON SECRETLY STEALS BACK TO WHERE THE MISSING CRATER SHOULD BE...

THE PAVED ROAD ENDS HERE! THEN A *FALSE* ROAD HAS BEEN PAINTED ON OVER SOME KIND OF PLASTIC MATERIAL

EXCITEDLY, ACHISON USES A TIRE-CHANGING IRON FROM HIS CAR AS A DIGGING TOOL....

I'LL DIG DOWN PAST THE EDGE OF THE FALSE ROAD! IT SEEMS TO BE PART OF A HUGE *COVER* OVER THE WHOLE CRATER!

2

SOON, BELOW THE SHIELD CAMOUFLAGING *METEOR CRATER* FROM SIGHT...

A *SPACESHIP* AT THE BOTTOM OF THE CRATER! WHAT ARE VISITORS FROM SPACE DOING HERE SO SECRETLY? I'LL SLIDE DOWN THE SLOPE AND SEE WHAT I CAN FIND OUT!

BUT ACHISON GATHERS TOO MUCH SPEED AND....

THEY HAVE MINING MACHINERY, AS IF DIGGING ORE-- OOPS! ... I CAN'T STOP!

AN EARTHMAN SPY! *KOZ* MUST HAVE FAILED TO TRICK THIS TOURIST AWAY FROM THE CRATER!

WHEN *KOZ* APPEARS...

THERE'S THE "GUIDE" I MET DISGUISED AS A HUMAN! THAT'S WHY HIS LIPS DIDN'T MOVE--HIS WORDS WERE SENT INTO MY MIND BY *TELEPATHY!*

SO YOU GUESSED, EARTHMAN! ALL DAY, BREATHING WITH MY CONCEALED AMMONIA MASK, I FOOLED TOURISTS--ALL EXCEPT YOU!

BUT NO MATTER! IMPRISON HIM IN THE SHIP WITH THE OTHER CAPTIVES! IT IS DARKNESS ABOVE, SO THAT NO MORE CURIOUS TOURISTS WILL STUMBLE ON OUR SECRET PROJECT!

INSIDE THE ALIEN SPACESHIP...

I'M JONES, THE *REAL* CRATER GUIDE! THE OTHERS ARE THE STAFF OF THE CRATER MUSEUM! WE WERE ALL CAPTURED THIS MORNING WHEN WE CAME TO WORK!

WHY ARE THEY HERE? DID YOU HAPPEN TO OVERHEAR ANY OF THEIR TELEPATHIC CONVERSATIONS?

3

"YES! THEY ARE SEEKING THE BURIED REMNANTS OF THE GIGANTIC METEOR THAT GOUGED OUT THIS CRATER, ABOUT 50,000 YEARS AGO!"

BLAMM

"THE VISITORS, WHO ARE FROM THE PLANET *JUPITER*, TRACED THE METEOR WITH INSTRUMENTS, ARRIVING ON EARTH LAST NIGHT..."

THE RADIATIONS WE DETECTED EMANATING FROM THIS CRATER INDICATE THE ANCIENT METEOR CONTAINS *SUBATOMIUM*, THE MOST POWERFUL NUCLEAR SUBSTANCE IN THE UNIVERSE!

"USING SUPER-SCIENTIFIC MEANS, THEY SWIFTLY CONSTRUCTED THE CAMOUFLAGING SHIELD OVER THE CRATER..."

ONCE THEY FINISH DIGGING UP ENOUGH *SUB-ATOMIUM*, IT WILL POWER A SUPER-WEAPON THAT WILL FORCE EARTH TO SURRENDER TO JUPITER!

AND THE WORLD KNOWS NOTHING OF THIS SECRET PLOT! IT'S UP TO US TO STOP THEM! NOW HERE'S WHAT I HAVE IN MIND!

HAS WYATT ACHISON FORGOTTEN THAT THE JOVIAN GUARD CAN READ THEIR MINDS WITH HIS TELEPATHIC POWERS?

IF WE CAN'T ESCAPE FROM THE SHIP, AT LEAST WE CAN SMASH THEIR MOTOR! FOLLOW ME TO THE ENGINE ROOM, MEN.

I'LL STOP THEM!

BUT THE GUARD MEETS AN UNEXPECTED AMBUSH!

WE WERE WAITING AT THE DOOR! GRAB HIS GUN!

AFTER THE GUARD HAS BEEN OVERPOWERED...

WE TRICKED YOU! I DELIBERATELY THOUGHT OF A *FALSE* PLAN WHILE WRITING OUT THE *REAL* PLAN!

Fake plan to wreck motor will lure guard... jump him at the door!

DONNING THE GUARD'S SPACE-SUIT, ACHISON REVEALS A DARING PLAN...

DISGUISED AS A JOVIAN, I'LL TRY TO AVOID DETECTION LONG ENOUGH TO TRY SABOTAGE!

WE'LL WAIT HERE! SIGNAL US IF YOU NEED HELP!

POSING AS THE GUARD, ACHISON JOINS THE OTHER UNSUSPECTING JOVIANS AS THEY REACH THEIR GOAL...

LUCKILY, THEY'RE TOO EXCITED TO PICK UP MY THOUGHTS AND REALIZE I'M AN ESCAPED PRISONER!

WE HAVE MINED AND SMELTED *SUB-ATOMIUM* TO FORM A CHARGE FOR OUR SUPER-WEAPON!

AS THE GLOWING "SHELL" IS CARRIED TO THE SUPER-WEAPON IN THE JOVIAN SPACESHIP...

THIS SINGLE CHARGE WILL PRIME OUR WEAPON FOR 1,000 YEARS! WE WILL BE ABLE TO CONQUER THE WHOLE SOLAR SYSTEM, STARTING WITH EARTH!

ONCE THEY LOAD THEIR GUN, THEY'LL BE INVULNERABLE! WHAT CAN I POSSIBLY DO TO STOP THEM?

WAIT... THE NATURAL "AIR" ON *JUPITER* CONTAINS *AMMONIA!* THIS "AIR-TANK," WHICH I KEPT SHUT OFF, HOLDS *LIQUID AMMONIA* ... JUST AS EARTHMEN WOULD CARRY *LIQUID OXYGEN* TO BREATHE ON JUPITER!

5

ANOTHER SCIENTIFIC FACT LEAPS INTO ACHISON'S KEEN MIND!

LIQUID AMMONIA IS A POWERFUL REFRIGERANT, USED IN ICE PLANTS TO FREEZE WATER QUICKLY!

COOLING COILS... LIQUID AMMONIA EXPANDS TO GAS, ABSORBING HEAT

ICE

DESPERATELY, THE EARTH-MAN SLIPS INTO THE SHIP AHEAD OF THE JOVIANS AND...

THE SUPER-WEAPON! I'LL SPRAY THE LIQUID AMMONIA OVER THE METALLIC GUN BARREL--AND FREEZE IT! IT'LL CAUSE THE METAL TO SHRINK!

WHEN THE JOVIANS ATTEMPT TO LOAD THE GUN....

THE SUBATOMIUM SHELL WON'T FIT! HOW COULD OUR MEASUREMENTS BE SO WRONG?

NOW WHILE THEY'RE CONFUSED AND OFF-GUARD, I'LL GET THE OTHER MEN HERE!

GRIMLY, THE EARTHMEN ATTACK!

THE SUBATOMIUM WILL BE TURNED OVER TO THE GOVERNMENT, TO BE KEPT IN SECRET VAULTS! WE'LL USE IT ONLY FOR ANY FUTURE EMERGENCY THREATENING THE EARTH!

AT DAWN, THE JOVIAN SPACESHIP ZOOMS UP FROM THE BOTTOM OF *METEOR CRATER...*

WE LET THE JOVIANS LEAVE! THEY CAN'T MENACE EARTH AGAIN WITHOUT SUBATOMIUM! AFTER A WRECKING CREW FINISHES REMOVING THAT SHIELD, METEOR CRATER WILL BE AN EVEN GREATER TOURISTS' ATTRACTION!

THE END   6

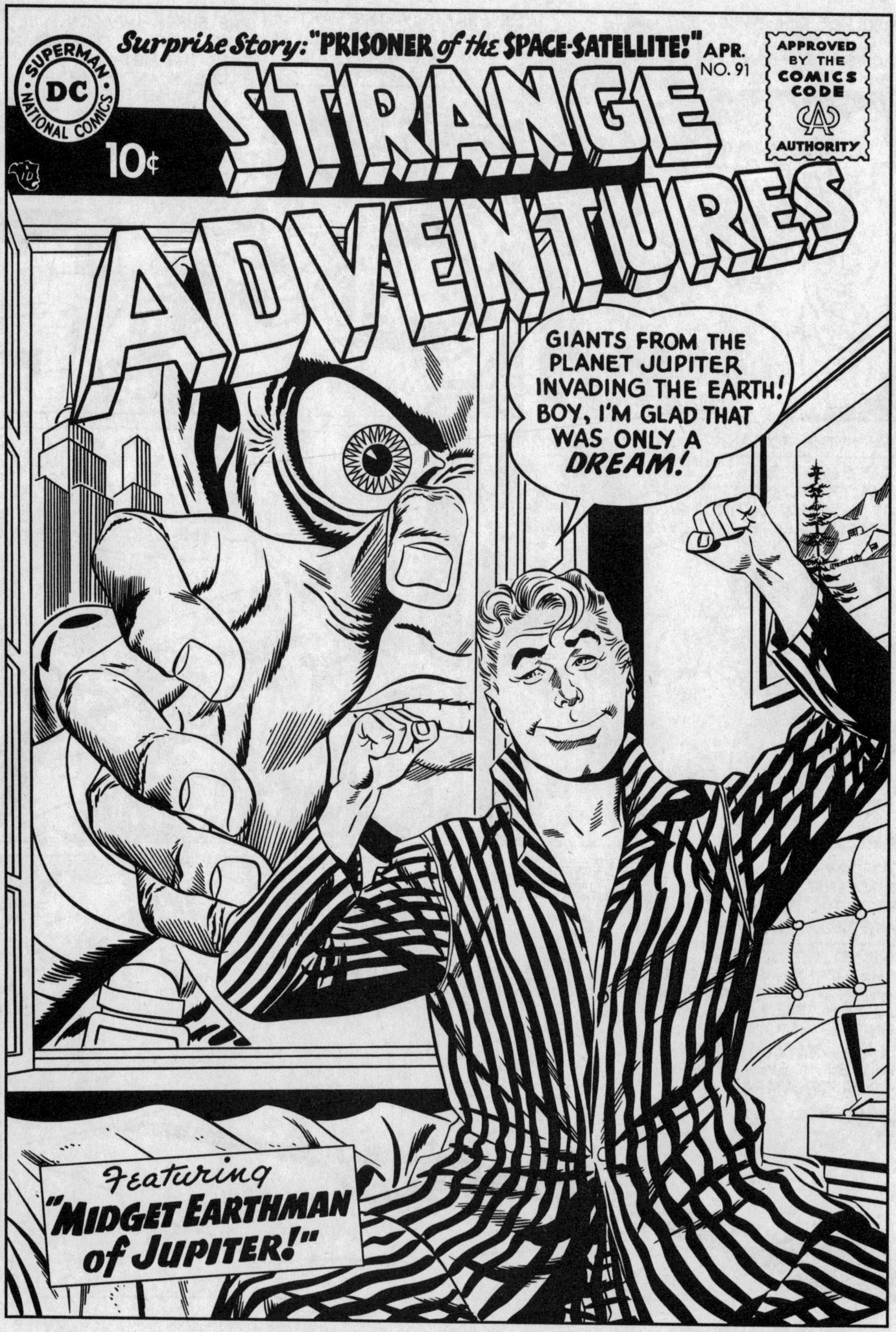
Surprise Story: "PRISONER of the SPACE-SATELLITE!"
APR. NO. 91
SUPERMAN DC NATIONAL COMICS
10¢
APPROVED BY THE COMICS CODE AUTHORITY
STRANGE ADVENTURES
GIANTS FROM THE PLANET JUPITER INVADING THE EARTH! BOY, I'M GLAD THAT WAS ONLY A DREAM!
Featuring "MIDGET EARTHMAN of JUPITER!"

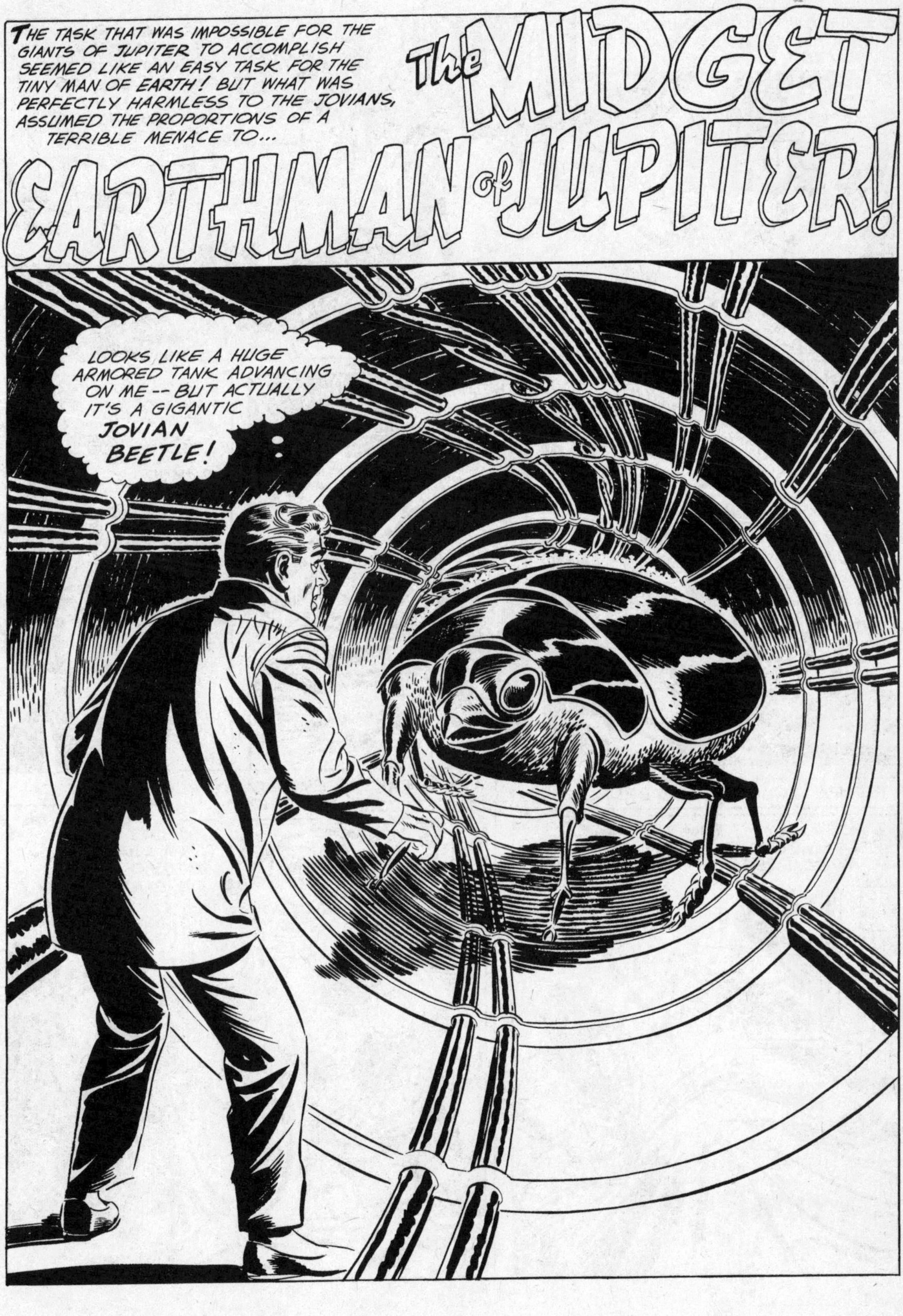
THE TASK THAT WAS IMPOSSIBLE FOR THE GIANTS OF JUPITER TO ACCOMPLISH SEEMED LIKE AN EASY TASK FOR THE TINY MAN OF EARTH! BUT WHAT WAS PERFECTLY HARMLESS TO THE JOVIANS, ASSUMED THE PROPORTIONS OF A TERRIBLE MENACE TO...
The MIDGET EARTHMAN of JUPITER!
LOOKS LIKE A HUGE ARMORED TANK ADVANCING ON ME -- BUT ACTUALLY IT'S A GIGANTIC JOVIAN BEETLE!

SUDDENLY, WITHOUT WARNING, RAY CARTER FINDS HIMSELF IN A STRANGE TUNNEL...

WHERE AM I? HOW DID I GET HERE? ALL I KNOW IS THAT I'VE GOT TO MOVE FORWARD--NO MATTER WHAT OBSTACLES CONFRONT ME...

AS A GIGANTIC, MULTI-LEGGED INSECT ADVANCES TOWARD HIM...

I HURDLED PAST THIS THING! MY OLYMPIC TRAINING SURE COMES IN HANDY HERE...

THEN...

THIS TUNNEL I'M IN TWISTS AND TURNS! NOW IT'S GOING UPWARD! WHERE DOES IT LEAD TO?

WHAT'S THAT--THAT THING COMING TOWARD ME? HOW CAN I POSSIBLY GET PAST IT? YET I MUST-- I MUST--I MUST!...

THE NEXT MOMENT, IN HIS BEDROOM...

I MUST... HUH?! I WAS DREAMING--SUCH A REAL DREAM...

AND AS RAY CARTER RECALLS MORE DETAILS OF HIS DREAM...

...AND IN THE BEGINNING OF MY DREAM, GIANTS FROM JUPITER INVADED THE EARTH! GOSH! I'M SURE GLAD NONE OF THIS WAS TRUE...

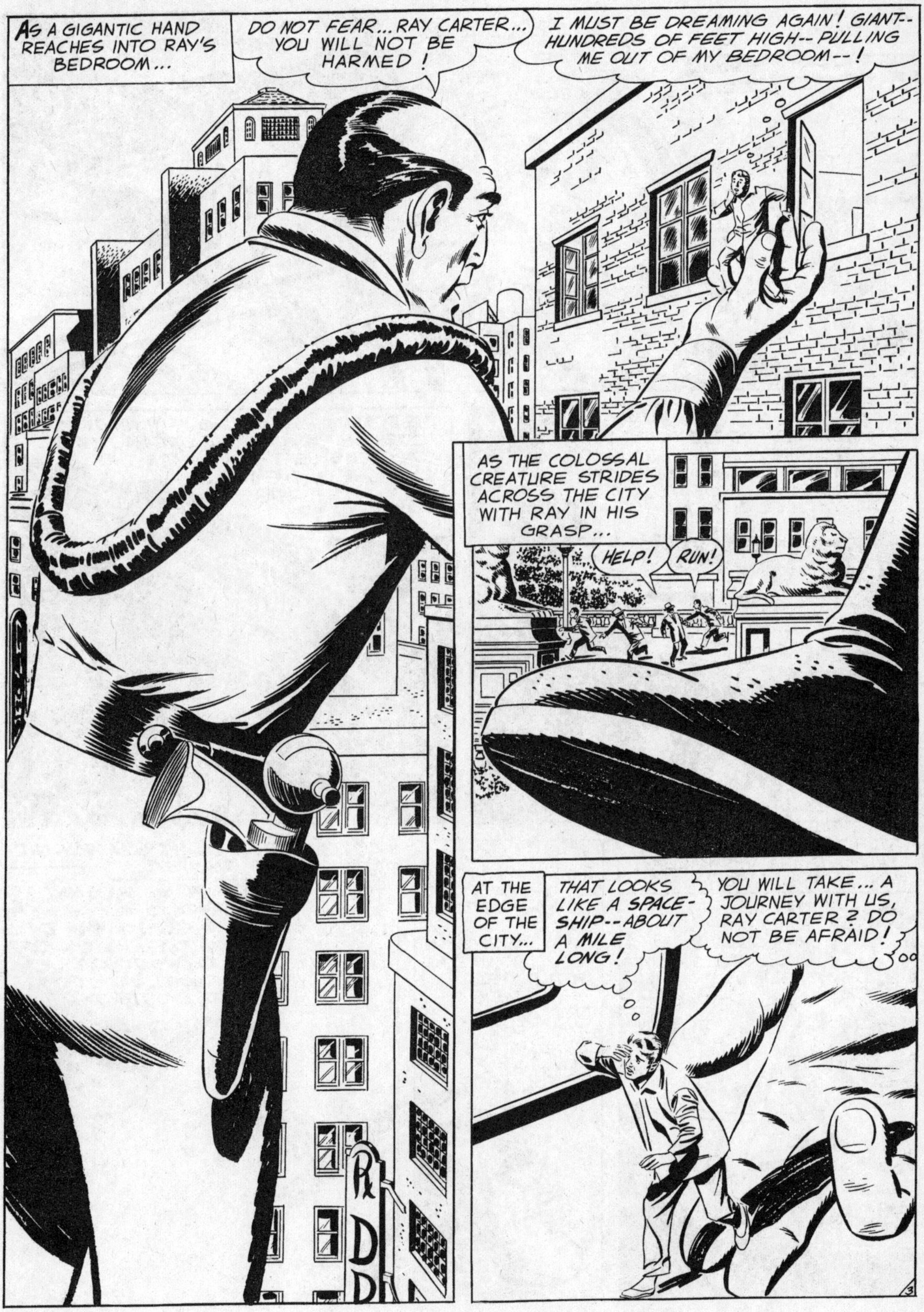
AS A GIGANTIC HAND REACHES INTO RAY'S BEDROOM...
DO NOT FEAR... RAY CARTER... YOU WILL NOT BE HARMED!
I MUST BE DREAMING AGAIN! GIANT-- HUNDREDS OF FEET HIGH-- PULLING ME OUT OF MY BEDROOM--!
AS THE COLOSSAL CREATURE STRIDES ACROSS THE CITY WITH RAY IN HIS GRASP...
HELP!
RUN!
AT THE EDGE OF THE CITY...
THAT LOOKS LIKE A SPACE-SHIP--ABOUT A MILE LONG!
YOU WILL TAKE... A JOURNEY WITH US, RAY CARTER? DO NOT BE AFRAID!
3

AFTER THE GREAT SHIP HAS TAKEN OFF...

WE ARE TAKING YOU TO THE PLANET *JUPITER*-- OUR HOMELAND! WE DESPERATELY NEED YOUR HELP!

MY HELP? WHAT CAN *I* POSSIBLY DO FOR YOU?

LISTEN! WE USED OUR *MIND-SCANNER* TO PROJECT DREAMS INTO THE MINDS OF MILLIONS OF EARTHMEN--TESTING WHICH ONE COULD MOST SUCCESSFULLY COPE WITH OUR PROBLEM--

THE DETERMINED DARING WITH WHICH YOU FOUGHT FORWARD IN THE *DREAM* TUNNEL CONVINCES US THAT YOU ARE THE ONLY ONE IN THE WORLD WHO CAN HELP US, RAY CARTER!

AFTER THE HUGE *JOVIAN* HAS EXPLAINED WHAT HIS RACE WANTS CARTER FOR...

NOW TELL US, EARTHMAN RAY CARTER-- WILL YOU HELP US?

YES... I WILL!

ACCORDING TO THIS GIANT, THE ENTIRE CIVILIZATION OF *JUPITER* DEPENDS ON ME NOW! I'VE GOT TO HELP THEM! THEY SEEM GENTLE AND PEACEFUL!

NOT LONG AFTER, ON THE GIANT PLANET OF *JUPITER*...

WE GO THIS WAY, RAY..

KIMOR--THAT'S THE GIANT WHO'S CARRYING ME--HAS TOLD ME THERE'S A *WAR* ON HERE--A BAND OF EVIL GIANTS HAS BEEN TRYING TO OVER-THROW THE DEMOCRATIC GOVERNMENT OF *JUPITER*...

As the earthman is borne across the Jovian terrain ...

THE REBELS HAVE SUCCEEDED IN CAPTURING AND HOLDING *JOVE CITY*-- BUT THERE ARE AGENTS OF THE DEMOCRATIC GOVERNMENT IN THERE SECRETLY SENDING OUT REPORTS ON THE ENEMY THROUGH A *TELEGRAPH WIRE* THAT HAS BEEN HIDDEN DEEP UNDERGROUND!

THEY USED THIS PRIMITIVE FORM OF TELEGRAPHIC COMMUNICATION, *KIMOR* EXPLAINED TO ME, BE-CAUSE ALL THEIR SUPER-SCIENTIFIC METHODS OF COM-MUNICATION CAN BE DETECTED BY THE SUPER-SCIENTIFIC RECEIVING DEVICES OF THE ENEMY! BUT RECENTLY...

-- THE WIRE BROKE -- JUST WHEN THEY NEEDED IT TO SIGNAL THE LOYAL GOVERNMENT FORCES IN-SIDE THE CITY THAT THEY WERE ABOUT TO LAUNCH A MAJOR ASSAULT FROM THE OUTSIDE-- AND FOR THOSE INSIDE TO ATTACK *SIMULTANEOUSLY!* *KIMOR* SAYS THAT'S THEIR ONLY CHANCE!

BECAUSE OF OUR SIZE-DIFFERENCE, WHAT IS A *CABLE WIRE* TO THEM APPEARS AS A *TUNNEL* TO ME! IT IS PHYSICALLY IMPOSSIBLE FOR THE *JOVIANS* TO REACH THE BROKEN WIRE! ONLY A TINY, INTELLIGENT CREATURE CAN MANAGE IT -- THAT'S WHEN THEY GOT THE IDEA OF USING AN EARTHMAN ...

AT THE MOUTH OF THE "TUNNEL"

WE DO NOT KNOW WHAT THINGS -- SMALL AND HARMLESS TO US! -- MAY EXIST IN THE TUNNEL TO ATTACK *YOU,* RAY! ARE YOU SURE YOU WISH TO RISK IT --?

YES, *KIMOR!* WISH ME LUCK!

5

AS RAY MOVES FORWARD...

HERE'S WHERE I REALLY LIVE MY DREAM!

GRIMLY, THE EARTHLING PRESSES ONWARD...

A "HARMLESS" JOVIAN INSECT BEARING DOWN ON ME!

LOOKS LIKE A HUGE ARMORED TANK -- BUT ACTUALLY IT'S A TYPE OF BEETLE! THE JOVIANS GAVE ME NO WEAPONS -- NONE OF THEIRS WOULD DO FOR MY SIZE! HAVE TO IMPROVISE AS I GO ALONG...

SEIZING A STRAY "SPLINTER" OF WOOD, RAY POLE-VAULTS OVER THE MONSTER...

BET I BROKE THE WORLD'S POLE-JUMP RECORD... ON EARTH...

OUTSIDE THE "TUNNEL", THE EARTHMAN IS THE SUBJECT OF A JOVIAN DISCUSSION...

IF RAY CARTER SUCCEEDS IN HIS ATTEMPT, WE MUST REWARD HIM!

JEWELS!

PRECIOUS METALS!

6

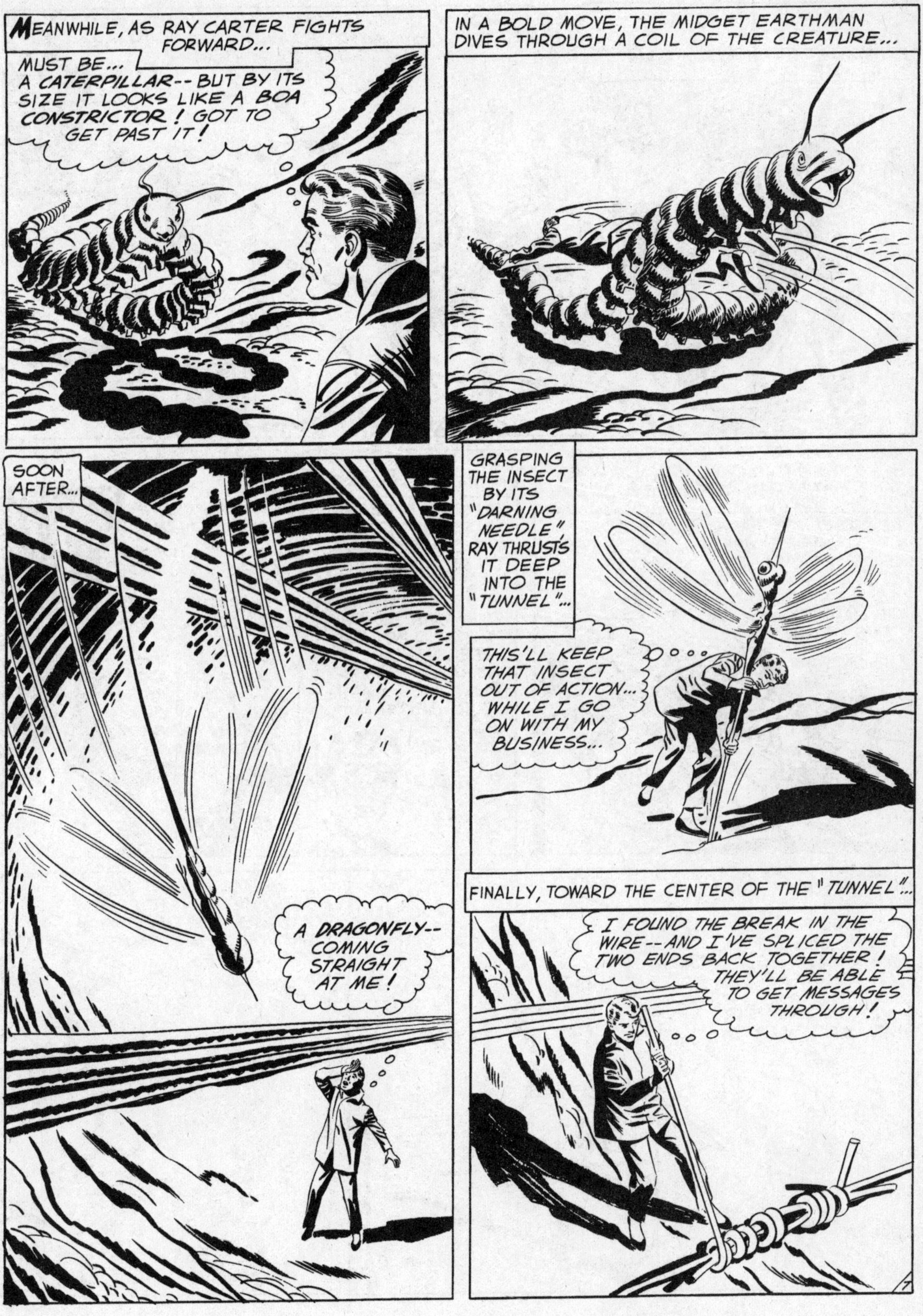
MEANWHILE, AS RAY CARTER FIGHTS FORWARD...
MUST BE... A CATERPILLAR-- BUT BY ITS SIZE IT LOOKS LIKE A BOA CONSTRICTOR! GOT TO GET PAST IT!
IN A BOLD MOVE, THE MIDGET EARTHMAN DIVES THROUGH A COIL OF THE CREATURE...
SOON AFTER...
A DRAGONFLY-- COMING STRAIGHT AT ME!
GRASPING THE INSECT BY ITS "DARNING NEEDLE" RAY THRUSTS IT DEEP INTO THE "TUNNEL"...
THIS'LL KEEP THAT INSECT OUT OF ACTION... WHILE I GO ON WITH MY BUSINESS...
FINALLY, TOWARD THE CENTER OF THE "TUNNEL"...
I FOUND THE BREAK IN THE WIRE-- AND I'VE SPLICED THE TWO ENDS BACK TOGETHER! THEY'LL BE ABLE TO GET MESSAGES THROUGH!
7

SOON AFTER, AS THE REPAIRED WIRE MAKES POSSIBLE THE ATTACK ON THE REBEL-HELD CITY...

THE ENEMY IS FLEEING!

OUR FORCES IN THE CITY WERE ALERTED AND READY--THANKS TO THE EARTHMAN-- RAY CARTER!

AND LATER, AFTER THE BATTLE HAS BEEN FOUGHT AND WON, AN IMPORTANT MATTER IS ATTENDED TO...

WE COULD NOT MAKE UP OUR MINDS WHICH GREAT REWARD TO GIVE YOU, RAY CARTER-- SO WE HAVE AGREED TO GIVE YOU ALL OF THIS WEALTH!

I'M SORRY-- BUT I CAN'T ACCEPT ANYTHING!

AS THE MIDGET EARTHMAN EXPLAINS...

YOU SEE, I'VE BEEN TRAINING TO ENTER THE OLYMPICS BACK ON MY PLANET--AND IF I TOOK A REWARD FOR WHAT I'VE DONE HERE, IT WOULD INTERFERE WITH MY AMATEUR STANDING! ALL I WANT IS TO BE TAKEN HOME -- AS SOON AS POSSIBLE!

AFTER THE JOVIANS HAVE RELUCTANTLY ACCEDED TO THEIR VISITOR'S REQUEST AND RETURNED HIM TO EARTH...

THERE THEY GO! FUNNY-- HOW MY ORIGINAL DREAM SEEMED SO REAL-- AND MY REAL-LIFE ADVENTURE WAS LIKE A DREAM! BUT NOW I'VE GOT TO GET BUSY-- AND GO ON WITH MY TRAINING!

ONE DAY, IN THE NOT TOO DISTANT FUTURE...

RAY CARTER HAS WON THE HURDLES! THAT MAKES HIM THE WINNER OF THE OLYMPIC DECATHLON-- AND THE GREATEST ATHLETE ON EARTH!

I'D RATHER HAVE THIS GOLD MEDAL--FOR WINNING THE DECATHLON-- THAN ALL THE WEALTH OF JUPITER!

The End

WARNING! TO EARTH!

SUPPOSE YOU STUMBLED UPON A SECRET PLOT WHICH ENDANGERED THE EARTH! WHAT IF, WHEN YOU RUSH TO WARN THE AUTHORITIES, YOU FIND IT IMPOSSIBLE TO DELIVER THE WARNING? WHATEVER METHOD OF COMMUNICATION YOU TRY, FAILS! IS THERE *ANY OTHER WAY* TO GET YOUR MESSAGE ACROSS?

FLYING SAUCERS DON'T COME FROM *OUTER SPACE* AT ALL! I'M GETTING PHOTOGRAPHIC PROOF THAT THEY ORIGINATE FROM BENEATH THE SEA!

"AT THE *WICAP** OFFICE ONE DAY..."

GENTLEMEN! WE'RE WILLING TO BELIEVE MANY REPORTS ON *FLYING SAUCER* SIGHTINGS ARE GENUINE! BUT THE INFORMATION IN THIS LETTER IS TOO FANTASTIC TO BE BELIEVED EVEN BY US!

*EDITOR'S NOTE: *WICAP...WORLD INVESTIGATING COMMITTEE ON AERIAL PHENOMENA,* HEADQUARTERS FOR ALL *FLYING SAUCER* REPORTS...

"I, EMMET KIRK, MARINE SCIENTIST, HAD SENT IN THAT *'FLYING SAUCER'* REPORT! WHEN I RECEIVED THEIR SKEPTICAL REPLY..."

THEY DEMAND CONVINCING PROOF, EH? ALL RIGHT, I'LL TEMPORARILY GIVE UP MY UNDERSEAS RESEARCH AND RETURN TO THE PLACE WHERE I SIGHTED THAT STRANGE "SAUCER"!

"LATER, AS MY *BATHYSCAPHE* HUNTED THROUGH THE MID-PACIFIC OCEAN, I SAW IT AGAIN! NOT A *FLYING SAUCER* FROM OUTER SPACE BUT..."

A *SWIMMING SAUCER*... SHOOTING UP FROM THE SEA BOTTOM! BUT IT'S GOING TOO FAST FOR MY MOVIE CAMERA TO GET CLEAR PICTURES! I'LL FOLLOW ITS WAKE!

"THE EXCITING CHASE LED TO A SMALL, UNINHABITED ISLAND, WHERE I WAS STUNNED TO SEE..."

THE *SWIMMING SAUCER* PILOTS ARE *HUMANOIDS!* WHAT'S THAT STRANGE OBJECT THEY'RE CONSTRUCTING?

"IN MY EAGERNESS TO SPY ON THEM, I WAS SPOTTED AND TAKEN TO THEIR LEADER, WHERE PART OF THE MYSTERY UNFOLDED..."

WE CAN SPEAK YOUR LANGUAGE, HAVING STUDIED YOUR RADIO SIGNALS! WE ARE SURVIVORS OF *MU,* LIVING IN SEABOTTOM CITIES AFTER OUR LAND SANK AGES AGO!

BUT WE WILL SOON HAVE OUR PLACE IN THE SUN AGAIN! IN SEVEN DAYS, WHEN THIS *ULTRA-ATOMIC RAY PROJECTOR* IS COMPLETED, WE WILL DESTROY YOUR CIVILIZATION AND GAIN MASTERY OF THE ENTIRE EARTH!

I--I'VE GOT TO ESCAPE--WARN THE WORLD...!

WE KNOW WHAT YOU'RE THINKING! THIS RAY-GUN WILL SILENCE YOU...

NO! THAT IS TOO CRUDE! HOW MUCH GREATER OUR VICTORY WILL BE OVER THE SURFACE PEOPLE IF THIS HUMAN TRIES TO WARN THEM OF OUR PLANS... AND *CAN'T!*

2

"THEY PLACED A DEVICE CALLED A *MENTAL BLOCK HELMET* ON MY HEAD! I HEARD A FAINT BUZZ AND THEN..."

NOW *RELEASE* HIM! LET HIM GO AND WARN HIS PEOPLE... IF HE CAN!

BRZ-Z-Z-Z-Z-Z

"LITTLE DID I SUSPECT WHAT LAY IN STORE FOR ME, AFTER I PILOTED MY *BATHYSCAPHE* AT FULL SPEED BACK TO SHORE AND..."

AHOY, COAST GUARD CUTTER! EARTH IS IN DANGER FROM A SECRET ENEMY! GET ME ABOARD AND I'LL TELL YOU THE WHOLE STORY!

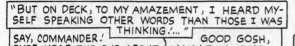

"BUT ON DECK, TO MY AMAZEMENT, I HEARD MYSELF SPEAKING OTHER WORDS THAN THOSE I WAS THINKING!..."

SAY, COMMANDER! EVER HEAR THE ONE ABOUT THE HUSBAND WHO SAW FLYING SAUCERS... WHEN HIS ANGRY WIFE THREW DISHES?

GOOD GOSH, MAN! THIS IS NO TIME FOR *JOKES!* TELL US ABOUT THE DANGER TO EARTH!

"BUT I COULDN'T! ANOTHER JOKE CAME FROM MY LIPS WHEN I TRIED TO UTTER THE WARNING WORDS! SUDDENLY, I ASKED FOR PAPER AND PENCIL..."

IF I CAN'T SPEAK MY WARNING MESSAGE, I'LL *WRITE* IT!

"BUT ONCE AGAIN I FOUND MYSELF UNABLE TO CONTROL MY THOUGHTS..."

GREAT SCOTT! AGAINST MY WILL I DREW A TICK-TACK-TOE GAME!

OFF MY SHIP, YOU — YOU PRACTICAL JOKER!

"HEADING FOR SHORE, I REALIZED NOW WHAT A CUNNING THING THE *MUIAN MENTAL-BLOCK HELMET* HAD DONE TO MY MIND..."

A POWERFUL "COMMAND" WAS PLANTED IN MY BRAIN, *PREVENTING* ME FROM WARNING ANYBODY! BUT THERE MUST BE OTHER WAYS I CAN TRANSMIT MY MESSAGE!

3

"BUT DESPITE EACH NEW METHOD I TRIED, I WAS IMPELLED TO DEFEAT MY OWN PURPOSE!"

I WANTED TO TAP OUT MORSE CODE WITH MY FOOT... BUT I BROKE INTO A JITTERBUG DANCE INSTEAD!

IF THAT'S SUPPOSED TO BE *INDIAN SIGN LANGUAGE*, I DON'T GET IT!

I'M TRYING TO SPEAK TO HIM IN FRENCH... BUT ONLY ANIMAL SOUNDS COME OUT!

BOW WOW.. MEOW.... OINK!

AMERICA[N] [I]NDIAN EXHIB[IT]

UNITED NATIONS INTERPRETER

TELEGRAPH

"DESPERATELY, MAKING USE OF MY PRIVATE PILOT'S LICENSE, I HIRED A SKY-WRITING PLANE..."

TH-THAT ISN'T THE WARNING I TRIED TO SKY-WRITE!

HAPPY NEW YEAR!

"FATEFUL DAYS PASSED, AND I HADN'T BROKEN MY DEADLY TRAP OF SILENCE! BUT PACING MY HOME LAB AND MUTTERING ALOUD, I HAD NEW HOPE..."

IN THREE DAYS THE *MU-MEN* WILL TAKE OVER UPPER EARTH... AND -- WAIT... I SAID THAT *ALOUD!* THAT MEANS THE *MENTAL BLOCK* DOESN'T OPERATE WHEN I TALK TO *MYSELF!*

"TRIUMPHANTLY, I TURNED ON MY TAPE-RECORDER AND..."

I'LL OUTWIT THE ENEMY AND GET THE WARNING ON TAPE, WHICH CAN BE RE-RUN LATER FOR OTHERS TO HEAR!

USING SWIMMING SAUCERS, AN UNDERSEA ENEMY IS BUILDING A MACHINE ON GULL ISLAND IN THE PACIFIC!

"FINISHING, I STARTED TO LEAVE THE HOUSE, WHEN TO MY HORROR..."

MY HAND IS FLINGING THE TAPE REEL INTO THE FIRE! THE-THE MENTAL-BLOCK WORKED AFTER ALL!

4

"DESPAIR VANISHED LATER, WHEN A STILL MORE INGENIOUS IDEA STRUCK ME! I RUSHED TO A CRIME LABORATORY FOR A LIE-DETECTOR TEST! I WAS ABLE TO EXPLAIN ABOUT MY PROBLEM..."

EARTH'S IN DANGER BUT MY *MENTAL-BLOCK* STOPS ME FROM GIVING THE DETAILS! BUT AFTER YOU READ MY CARBON LETTER TO *WICAP*, YOU CAN ASK ME QUESTIONS AND DETERMINE IF I'M LYING...

"MERELY ANSWERING *YES* OR *NO* WOULDN'T BE *TELLING* THE MESSAGE! I ONLY NEEDED TO *PROVE* I HAD SEEN SWIMMING SAUCERS, THEN SHIPS WOULD RUSH TO INVESTIGATE!"

NOW, DID YOU ACTUALLY SEE *SWIMMING SAUCERS* NEAR GULL ISLAND?

YES!

"BUT WHEN WE CHECKED THE NEEDLE..."

WHEN A PERSON LIES, HIS PULSE INVOLUNTARILY QUICKENS AND GIVES HIM AWAY! YOUR PULSE JUMPED... YOU *LIED!*

NO... NO... IT'S IMPOSSIBLE! WAIT, REPEAT THE QUESTION! IF I SAY *NO,* THE MACHINE WILL PROVE *THAT'S* A LIE!

"AFTER I *DENIED* SEEING THE *SWIMMING SAUCERS...*"

THAT WAS THE *TRUTH!*

GREAT STARS! THEN MY *MENTAL-BLOCK* EVEN CONTROLS MY PULSE, RUINING THIS TEST!

THE MENTAL-BLOCK IS *UNBEATABLE!* I CAN'T WARN EARTH! I MIGHT AS WELL RETURN TO GULL ISLAND AND ADMIT MY DEFEAT...

"WHEN I RETURNED TO THE SECRET PACIFIC ISLAND BASE..."

YOU WIN! BUT TO SATISFY MY CURIOSITY AS A SCIENTIST, WHAT IS YOUR PLAN? IT CAN DO NO HARM FOR ME TO KNOW! I'LL NEVER BE ABLE TO TELL ANYONE!

5

"GLOATINGLY, THE **MU** CHIEF SHOWED ME WHAT FATE LAY IN STORE FOR EARTH!"

OUR MACHINE WILL **REVERSE** THE LANDS AND SEAS OF EARTH! THE SEABOTTOMS WILL RISE AS NEW CONTINENTS, WHILE YOUR CONTINENTS WILL SINK, BECOMING THE SEABOTTOMS!

ASIAN OCEAN · NORTH AMERICAN OCEAN · EURASIAN OCEAN · PACIFIC CONTINENT · ATLANTIC CONTINENT · AFRICAN OCEAN · SOUTH AMERICAN OCEAN

TOMORROW WE WILL TURN ON THE **EARTH-REVERSER!** BUT YOU STILL HAVE 24 HOURS! WHY DON'T YOU GO WARN YOUR PEOPLE?

YES, I'LL RETURN... AND WAIT FOR THE DOOM!

"BUT I MEANT **THEIR** DOOM, NOT OURS! FOR AT LAST I HAD FOUND A WAY TO WARN THE WORLD! BEFORE THE DEADLINE, BOMBERS WINGED OVER GULL ISLAND, RADIOING A WARNING TO THE **MU-MEN!**"

WE KNOW YOUR INVASION PLANS! WE WILL DROP AN ATOMIC BOMB ON YOUR MACHINE IN EXACTLY FIVE MINUTES!

EVACUATE THE ISLAND! RETURN TO THE SEA-BOTTOM IN OUR **SWIMMING SAUCERS!**

"MILES OFF, I WATCHED AS ZERO MOMENT CAME!"

THE END OF THE **EARTH-REVERSER** MACHINE! WE ALLOWED THE **MU-MEN** TO ESCAPE TO THEIR UNDERSEA CITY, BUT EARTH'S NAVIES WILL GUARD AGAINST THEIR RETURN!

KABOOM!

"YOU WONDER HOW I GAVE THE WARNING TO EARTH? **I** NEVER DID!..."

BEFORE RETURNING TO GULL ISLAND, I SECRETLY CONCEALED MY MINIATURE SOUND-CAMERA UNDER MY JACKET! WHEN THE SEA-MEN BOASTED OF THEIR PLANS, IT WAS FILMED AND RECORDED! MY **MENTAL BLOCK** DIDN'T PREVENT ME FROM TAKING **THEIR** "WARNING" TO THE AUTHORITIES!

THE END

The AMAZING TREE of KNOWLEDGE

WE'VE TRIED TO SAW THE TREE-- BURN IT DOWN-- EVEN DYNAMITE IT! BUT IT SEEMS INDESTRUCTIBLE!

THE TREE STOOD ALONE IN THE MIDST OF A CLEARED-OUT FOREST, AS IF CHALLENGING PUNY MAN TO DESTROY IT! DID IT COME FROM A DISTANT WORLD, BORNE TO EARTH AS A SEED THROUGH THE GULFS OF SPACE? ONLY BY EATING THE SINGLE FRUIT OF THE TREE COULD ANYONE SOLVE THE RIDDLE OF THE UNIQUE TREE!

AS A LUMBERJACK FOREMAN MAKES HIS REPORT TO HIS CAMP MANAGER...

CUT DOWN ALL THE TREES TODAY, AL?

ALL BUT ONE, JIM! YOU BETTER COME WITH ME AND HAVE A LOOK AT THAT REMAIN- ING TREE!

WE TRIED SAWING IT-- DYNAMITING IT-- EVEN USED AN ACETYLENE TORCH! BUT NOTHING HAD ANY EFFECT ON IT!

IT HARDLY SEEMS POSSIBLE!

ONCE AGAIN, THE LUMBERJACK TRIES TO FELL THE TREE...

SEE--HE CAN'T EVEN SCRATCH THE BARK!

I'M GOING TO CLIMB THE TREE AND EXAMINE IT!

I FOUND A FRUIT UP HERE! GOOD GOSH! I'VE GOT AN OVERWHELMING DESIRE TO EAT IT!

AS SOON AS THE LUMBERJACK EATS THE FRUIT...

HEY, BOSS! SOMETHING STRANGE IS HAPPENING TO ME! SEND SOMEBODY UP TO HELP ME GET DOWN!

MOMENTS LATER...

YOU ALL RIGHT, JOHNNY? WHAT CAME OVER YOU?

ALL OF A SUDDEN--I KNOW A LOT OF THINGS--I NEVER KNEW BEFORE!

IT'S AS IF THAT FRUIT CAME OFF A TREE OF KNOWLEDGE! I UNDERSTAND THINGS LIKE RADIO WAVES, NUCLEAR REACTORS, SYMBIOTICS, CYBERNETICS...

WE BETTER GET JOHNNY TO A HOPITAL, FAST!

IN THE LOCAL HOSPITAL, JOHNNY EVERS CONTINUES TO DISPLAY HIS STRANGELY ACQUIRED KNOWLEDGE...

I'M OKAY, DOC! SAY, HOW ABOUT US DISCUSSING THE LINKAGE FACTOR IN HEREDITY--

2

AS THE PUZZLED DOCTORS DISCUSS JOHNNY'S AMAZING KNOWLEDGE ...

MY THEORY IS THAT SOME CHEMICAL IN THE FRUIT VITALIZED THE UNUSED NINE-TENTHS OF THE HUMAN BRAIN!

THAT WOULD MAKE HIM THE GREATEST GENIUS THE WORLD HAS EVER KNOWN! TOO BAD THERE WAS ONLY THAT SINGLE FRUIT ON THE TREE!

WORLD-RENOWNED SCIENTISTS ARE CALLED IN TO EXAMINE THE LUMBERJACK...

A SODIUM GRAPHITE NUCLEAR REACTOR NEEDS TUBULAR URANIUM FUEL RODS, LIQUID SODIUM, A HEAT EXCHANGE BOILER AND A STEAM OUTLET TO BE EFFECTIVE...

AMAZING!

HE KNOWS MORE ABOUT OUR SPECIALTIES THAN WE KNOW OURSELVES!

HE'S AN EXPERT ON EVERY BRAND OF KNOWLEDGE! WHY NOT PUT THAT KNOWLEDGE TO GOOD USE? LET'S FIND OUT WHAT HIS SPECIAL INTERESTS ARE!

I'M A SCIENCE-FICTION FAN--LOVE STORIES ABOUT SPACE-TRAVEL! WITH MY KNOWLEDGE I CAN DIRECT THE BUILDING OF A SPACESHIP!

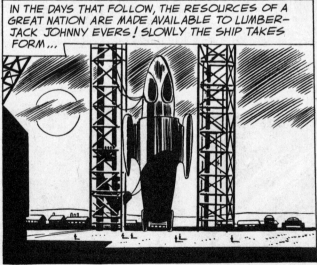

IN THE DAYS THAT FOLLOW, THE RESOURCES OF A GREAT NATION ARE MADE AVAILABLE TO LUMBERJACK JOHNNY EVERS! SLOWLY THE SHIP TAKES FORM...

ENGINEERS MARVEL AT THE NEW SCIENTIFIC CONCEPTS...

THE ATOMIC MOTOR IS SUSPENDED MAGNETICALLY!

HE SYNTHESIZED A NEW METAL ALLOY TO BUILD THAT MOTOR!

3

THE TAKE-OFF IS ONLY HOURS AWAY! ALL IS COMPLETE, EXCEPT FOR THE FINAL INSTALLATION...

I'D LIKE THE PRIVILEGE OF PERSONALLY PUTTING THE HYPERDRIVE RODS IN PLACE!

OF COURSE, MR. EVERS!

WHEN HE IS ALONE IN THE CONTROL CHAMBER, JOHN EVERS LAUGHS TRIUMPHANTLY...

HA! HA! HA! I SWINDLED THEM OUT OF A SPACESHIP! NOW I'M LEAVING EARTH-- NEVER TO RETURN!

THE MASSIVE METAL SHIP ROARS SPACEWARD...

MY NAME IS NOT JOHN EVERS--BUT JONVER--AN INHABITANT OF THE PLANET GLARN!

AT THE SPACE-FLIGHT OFFICE, A WIRE-RECORDER BEGINS TO UNWIND...

IT'S A MESSAGE FROM EVERS!

I AM A CRIMINAL ON THE PLANET GLARN! FOR MY SWINDLE-CRIMES, THE GLARN COURT SENTENCED ME TO LIFE IMPRISONMENT...

"LIFE IMPRISONMENT-- ON A SPACESHIP! I WAS SHOT OUT OF MY OWN SOLAR SYSTEM IN A COURSE THAT WOULD TAKE ME INTO THE VAST EMPTY GULF BETWEEN MY GALAXY AND YOUR OWN..."

"I WAS SEALED IN, UNDER AUTOMATIC CONTROLS! I COULD NOT ESCAPE, NOR COULD I CONTROL THE SHIP..."

I'M DOOMED TO SPEND THE REMAINDER OF MY LIFE IN THIS SPACESHIP-PRISON!

"AND THEN, BY SOME FREAK OF COSMIC FATE, MY SHIP SLIPPED INTO A SPACE-WARP!"

SPACE IS CURVED--THE WARP MAY HURL ME INTO A DISTANT SECTOR OF THE UNIVERSE!

"WHEN MY SHIP EMERGED FROM THE SPACE-WARP, I FOUND MYSELF IN YOUR SOLAR SYSTEM!"

MY SHIP IS BEING DRAWN BY THE GRAVITATIONAL PULL OF THE SYSTEM'S THIRD PLANET!

"AT SCREAMING SPEED, MY SHIP PLUNGED THROUGH YOUR ATMOSPHERE AND THE HEAT-- LIKE THAT OF A FALLING METEOR--BECAME INCANDESCENT..."

I AM PROTECTED BY THE VACUUM WALLS-- BUT THE SHIP WILL HIT THE GROUND AND EXPLODE!

"BUT, LUCKILY, THE SHIP DOVE INTO THE OCEAN! THE COLD WATER ON THE RED-HOT HULL CRACKED THE SHIP, THROWING ME FREE!"

I CAN SEE LAND! I'LL SWIM THERE AND TAKE UP LIFE AS ONE OF THIS PLANET'S INHABITANTS...

"MY GREATER DEVELOPED MIND QUICKLY ENABLED ME TO LEARN EARTH LANGUAGES AND CUSTOMS..."

I COULD APPEAR TO THE AUTHORITIES AND REVEAL THE FACT THAT I'M FROM ANOTHER WORLD! THEY'D BUILD A SPACE-SHIP FOR ME, I'M SURE!

BUT THAT'S NOT MY NATURE! I'M A **SWINDLER**! I'LL PREPARE AN ELABORATE HOAX AND "CON" THEM INTO GIVING ME A SPACESHIP!

"**I** COATED A TREE WITH A FORCE-FIELD! THEN I TOOK A CRAB APPLE FROM MY LUNCH KIT..."

AFTER DRAWING ATTENTION TO THIS TREE, I'LL PRETEND TO FIND THIS FRUIT THERE AND EAT IT! I'LL DECEIVE THEM INTO THINKING THE FRUIT GAVE ME MY SUPER—INTELLIGENCE!

AS THE WIRE-RECORDING ENDS, SHOUTS BRING THE SCIENTISTS RUNNING OUT ONTO THE SPACE-TAKEOFF STRIP...

THE SPACESHIP IS RETURNING!

IT'S OUT OF CONTROL! GOING TO CRASH--!

AFTER THE SPACESHIP CRASHES AND JONVER IS LIFTED FROM THE WRECKAGE..

I FOUND THE SPACE-WARP THAT WOULD HURL ME BACK TO MY PLANET--BUT I COULD NOT ENTER IT FROM *THIS* DIRECTION!

"I DROVE MY SHIP AT THE WARP AGAIN AND AGAIN, WITHOUT SUCCESS... "

THE WARP YIELDS-- BUT I CAN'T PENETRATE IT!

"ON THE LAST TRY I DAMAGED MY CONTROLS! THE WARP HURLED THE SHIP AWAY FROM IT..."

IT'S AS IF THE WARP WERE A GIGANTIC SLINGSHOT!

LATER, AFTER HAVING BEEN DULY TRIED AS A SWINDLER AND SENTENCED BY AN EARTH COURT...

LIFE IMPRISONMENT... IN A SPACESHIP OR IN A PLANET'S JAIL CELL--IS THE SAME EVERYWHERE! A MAN CAN'T ESCAPE HIS FATE!

7253

The End 16

PRISONER of the SPACE-SATELLITE!

THE RECENT LAUNCHING OF MAN-MADE SATELLITES INTO SPACE WAS AN ELECTRIFYING HISTORICAL EVENT! BUT HISTORY HAS A HABIT OF REPEATING ITSELF! PERHAPS, INSTEAD OF BEING THE *FIRST*, WE'RE MERELY REPEATING THE SPACE-SATELLITE ACCOMPLISHMENTS OF AN EARLIER EARTH CIVILIZATION!

UNINHABITED PRIOR TO 1958, A SMALL ISLAND IN THE ATLANTIC OCEAN NOW HAS A POPULATION OF *ONE*-- A SPACE-SATELLITE TRACKER...

OUR *"SPACEBIRDS"* HAVE ONLY BEEN UP FOR A FEW MONTHS! BUT THAT ARTIFICIAL SATELLITE HAS BEEN CIRCLING THE EARTH FOR 25,000 YEARS!

BEEP..! BEEP..!

SATELLITE *"SPACE-BIRD"* IS RIGHT ON TIME!

MOONWATCH STATION #33 U.S. PROJECT VANGUARD

IT'S 500 MILES HIGH, WITH AN ORBITAL SPEED OF 17,780 MILES AN HOUR!

THE SATELLITE FOLLOWS AN ORBIT THAT *CARRIES* IT OVER MY STATION 16 TIMES EVERY 24 HOURS!

MINUTES LATER, WHEN THE MAN-MADE MOONLET PASSES OUT OF RANGE...

NOTHING TO DO NOW TILL ITS NEXT OVER-PASS IN 96 MINUTES! I'LL TAKE A STROLL--GET THE KINK OUT OF MY LEGS...

SUDDENLY...

HELP... HELP!

A CRY... FROM UNDERGROUND! GOSH, I-I THOUGHT I WAS *ALONE* ON THIS ISLAND! IS SOMEBODY LOST IN THAT CAVE?

BAFFLINGLY, AFTER SEARCHING THE SMALL CAVE...

NOBODY HERE! GUESS MY IMAGINATION PLAYED ME TRICKS!

BUT TWO HOURS LATER, WHEN DAWSON IS AGAIN FREE BETWEEN THE SATELLITE'S PASSAGES...

HELP! CAN'T ANYONE HEAR ME? HELP...

THAT VOICE AGAIN... RIGHT UNDER MY FEET! BUT IT-IT ISN'T ACTUALLY *SOUND!* IT CAME INTO MY MIND SILENTLY... LIKE *TELEPATHY!* BUT THAT'S NONSENSE! BETTER GET A GOOD NIGHT'S SLEEP!

NIGHT FALLS AND THE NEXT MORNING...

HELP!

THAT SAME MENTAL CRY AGAIN! IT WOKE ME UP EVERY TWO HOURS DURING THE NIGHT TOO! WAIT... IT CAN'T BE COINCIDENCE... HEARING THAT VOICE EVERY 120 MINUTES!

2

As THE MOONWATCHER CONSULTS HIS SPACE-SATELLITE RECORD BOOK...

ACCORDING TO THIS ORBIT DATA, THAT TELEPATHIC CRY COULD BE COMING FROM A *SATELLITE* 1075 MILES HIGH! IT WOULD PASS OVER ME EVERY *TWO HOURS!*

TABLE OF ORBITS FOR EARTH SATELLITES	
HEIGHT OF ORBIT	RATE OF REVOLUTION AROUND EARTH
300 MILES	90 MINUTES
500 MILES	96 MINUTES
750 MILES	112 MINUTES
1075 MILES	120 MINUTES

IT'S POSSIBLE THAT TELEPATHY-WAVES-- WHEN SENT EARTHWARD FROM SPACE-- BOUNCE OFF A LAYER OF SUBTERRANEAN ORE, JUST AS RADIO-WAVES SENT SKYWARD ARE REFLECTED BACK BY A LAYER OF IONIZED ATOMS IN THE STRATOSPHERE!

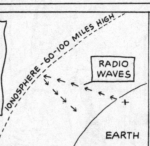

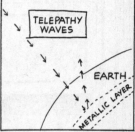

TWO HOURS LATER, CONCENTRATING MENTALLY, DAWSON RECEIVES A CLEAR TELEPATHIC MESSAGE FROM SPACE...

HELP! I AM *XONTHO,* TRAPPED IN A SATELLITE SPINNING AROUND THE EARTH!

A *MANNED* SATELLITE IS UP THERE! I'LL TRY TO PROJECT MY THOUGHTS AND ANSWER... *I HEAR YOU, XONTHO!*

BUT WHY CAN'T I SEE YOUR SATELLITE?

BECAUSE ITS SHINY METAL SURFACE HAS BEEN DULLED BY METEORIC DUST THAT GATHERED FOR *CENTURIES!*

AND FAR ABOVE EARTH, THE UNSEEN SATELLITE CIRCLES ENDLESSLY IN THE DARKNESS OF SPACE...

YOU'VE BEEN UP THERE... FOR... *CENTURIES?* WHERE ARE YOU FROM?

I AM FROM ANCIENT ATLANTIS... THE LAST OF THE ATLANTIDES! HARKEN TO MY STORY...

"LONG AGO, WHEN I HEARD THE NEWS OF THE GREAT EARTH CATACLYSM..."

A GEOLOGIC UPHEAVAL HAS STRUCK AROUND EARTH! ISLANDS--CONTINENTS-- ARE SINKING....

ATLANTIS IS DOOMED TOO! BUT THERE'S A FAINT CHANCE I CAN ESCAPE!

"FORTUNATELY, I HAD BEEN LAUNCHING EXPERI- MENTAL SPACE-SATELLITES AND..."

MY NEXT ONE IS READY! IT'S JUST LARGE ENOUGH FOR ME TO SQUEEZE INTO IT IF I THROW OUT ALL THE RECORDING INSTRUMENTS!

"BARELY IN TIME, MY POWER- FUL 5-STAGE ROCKET HURLED ME AWAY FROM THE SINKING ATLANTIS..."

I WILL BE THE ONLY *ATLANTIDE* LEFT ALIVE, SAFE IN SPACE FROM THE CONVULSIONS SMASH- ING EARTH'S SURFACE APART!

JUST AS DAWSON WAITS EAGERLY TO HEAR THE REST OF THE AMAZING SAGA...

HIS TELEPATHIC VOICE FADED AWAY, AS HIS SATELLITE PASSED OUT OF RANGE! I'LL HAVE TO WAIT TWO HOURS BEFORE *XONTHO* CAN CONTACT ME AGAIN!

"AHOY, BELOW! RESUMING CONTACT AFTER CIRCLING EARTH! AFTER MY SATEL- LITE REACHED ITS ORBIT, I LOOKED EARTHWARD..."

ONLY A FEW LUCKY TRIBES WILL SURVIVE THAT WORLD- WIDE CATASTROPHE! NO SENSE DESCENDING FOR AT LEAST A YEAR!

"I HAD NO FOOD OR WATER, BUT I HAD PREPARED FOR AN EX- TENDED SPACE-EXILE..."

THIS SUSPENDED-ANIMA- TION SERUM WILL LET ME SLEEP INDEFINITELY WITHOUT HARM! AN AUTOMATIC ROCKET- CHARGE WILL SEND THE SATELLITE DOWN IN A YEAR!

4

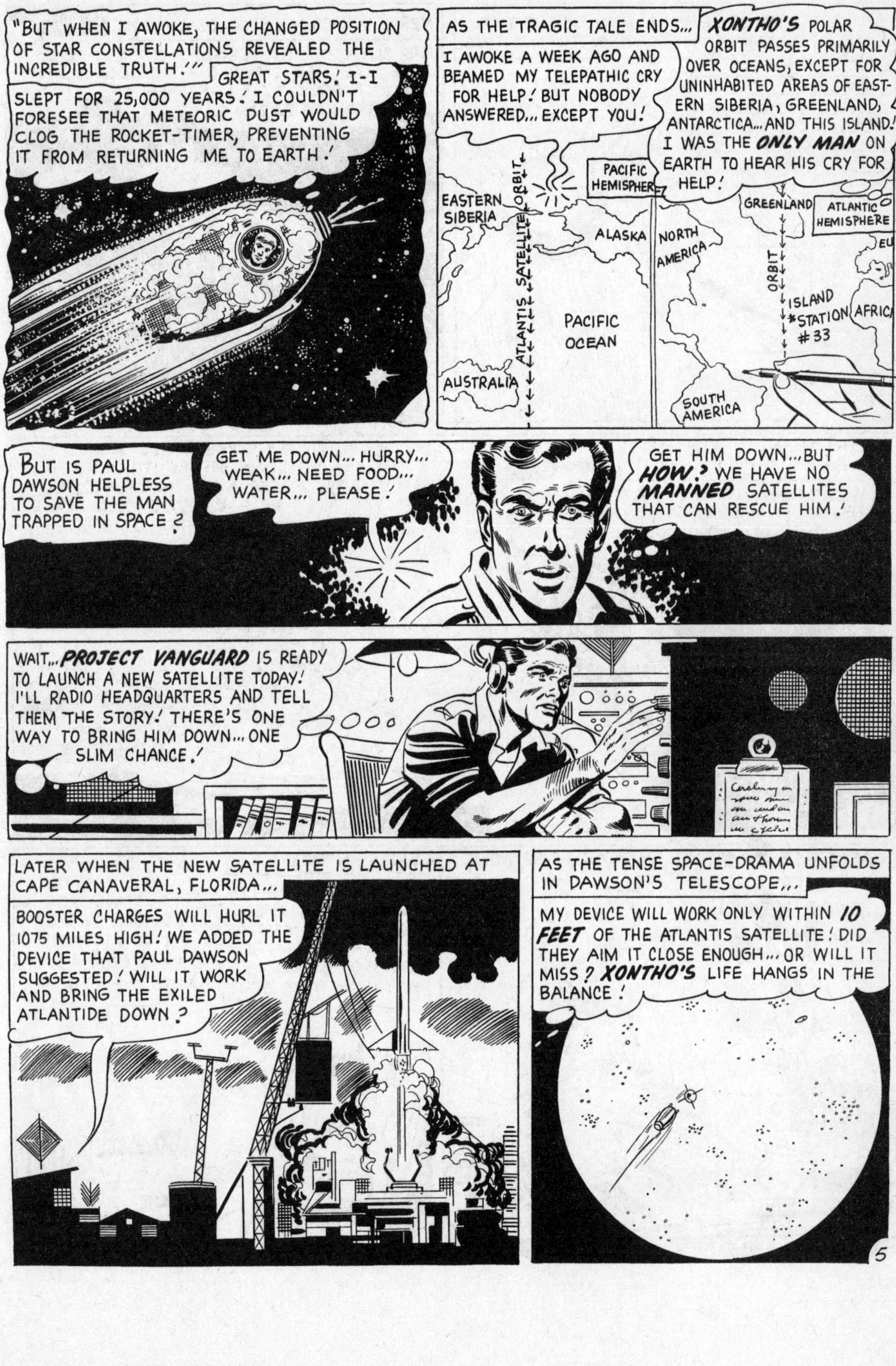
"BUT WHEN I AWOKE, THE CHANGED POSITION OF STAR CONSTELLATIONS REVEALED THE INCREDIBLE TRUTH!'"
GREAT STARS! I-I SLEPT FOR 25,000 YEARS! I COULDN'T FORESEE THAT METEORIC DUST WOULD CLOG THE ROCKET-TIMER, PREVENTING IT FROM RETURNING ME TO EARTH!
AS THE TRAGIC TALE ENDS...
I AWOKE A WEEK AGO AND BEAMED MY TELEPATHIC CRY FOR HELP! BUT NOBODY ANSWERED... EXCEPT YOU!
XONTHO'S POLAR ORBIT PASSES PRIMARILY OVER OCEANS, EXCEPT FOR UNINHABITED AREAS OF EASTERN SIBERIA, GREENLAND, ANTARCTICA... AND THIS ISLAND! I WAS THE ONLY MAN ON EARTH TO HEAR HIS CRY FOR HELP!
PACIFIC HEMISPHERE
EASTERN SIBERIA
ATLANTIS SATELLITE ORBIT
ALASKA
NORTH AMERICA
PACIFIC OCEAN
AUSTRALIA
GREENLAND
ATLANTIC HEMISPHERE
ORBIT
ISLAND *STATION #33
AFRICA
SOUTH AMERICA
BUT IS PAUL DAWSON HELPLESS TO SAVE THE MAN TRAPPED IN SPACE?
GET ME DOWN... HURRY... WEAK... NEED FOOD... WATER... PLEASE!
GET HIM DOWN... BUT HOW? WE HAVE NO MANNED SATELLITES THAT CAN RESCUE HIM!
WAIT... PROJECT VANGUARD IS READY TO LAUNCH A NEW SATELLITE TODAY! I'LL RADIO HEADQUARTERS AND TELL THEM THE STORY! THERE'S ONE WAY TO BRING HIM DOWN... ONE SLIM CHANCE!
LATER WHEN THE NEW SATELLITE IS LAUNCHED AT CAPE CANAVERAL, FLORIDA...
BOOSTER CHARGES WILL HURL IT 1075 MILES HIGH! WE ADDED THE DEVICE THAT PAUL DAWSON SUGGESTED! WILL IT WORK AND BRING THE EXILED ATLANTIDE DOWN?
AS THE TENSE SPACE-DRAMA UNFOLDS IN DAWSON'S TELESCOPE...
MY DEVICE WILL WORK ONLY WITHIN 10 FEET OF THE ATLANTIS SATELLITE! DID THEY AIM IT CLOSE ENOUGH... OR WILL IT MISS? XONTHO'S LIFE HANGS IN THE BALANCE!
5

WILL THE VITAL SPACE-RENDEZVOUS OF THE TWO SATELLITES TAKE PLACE, SAVING THE ORBITING "ROBINSON CRUSOE"?

YOUR SATELLITE IS COMING CLOSER...CLOSER... IF IT PASSES MORE THAN 10 FEET AWAY...OR COLLIDES WITH ME...

NERVE-WRACKING SECONDS LATER...

THE BLAST OF PRESSURIZED AIR FROM YOUR SATELLITE HAS CLEARED MY CLOGGED DESCENT ROCKET! I CAN SAFELY RETURN TO EARTH!...

AS THE ATLANTIS SATELLITE SPIRALS DOWN OUT OF ITS AGE-LONG ORBIT...

I WON'T FLAME DOWN LIKE A METEOR! MY SATELLITE IS MADE OF A LIGHT SUPER-METAL THAT IS IMPERVIOUS TO HEATING BY AIR-FRICTION!

FINALLY...

AIR RESISTANCE SLOWED IT DOWN BEFORE IT LANDED AT SEA NEAR THE ISLAND! I'LL HELP XONTHO OUT OF HIS FLOATING SATELLITE!

WELCOME BACK TO EARTH AFTER 25,000 YEARS, XONTHO!

I'M GLAD TO BE HOME!

LATER, IN AMERICA...

YOU'RE A CELEBRITY, XONTHO! ALL THESE PARADES AND FESTIVITIES IN YOUR HONOR WILL LAST FOR WEEKS! HOPE YOU DON'T TIRE OF IT!

WHAT--AFTER RESTING FOR 25,000 YEARS? I DON'T THINK I'LL EVER SLEEP AGAIN!

THE END

6

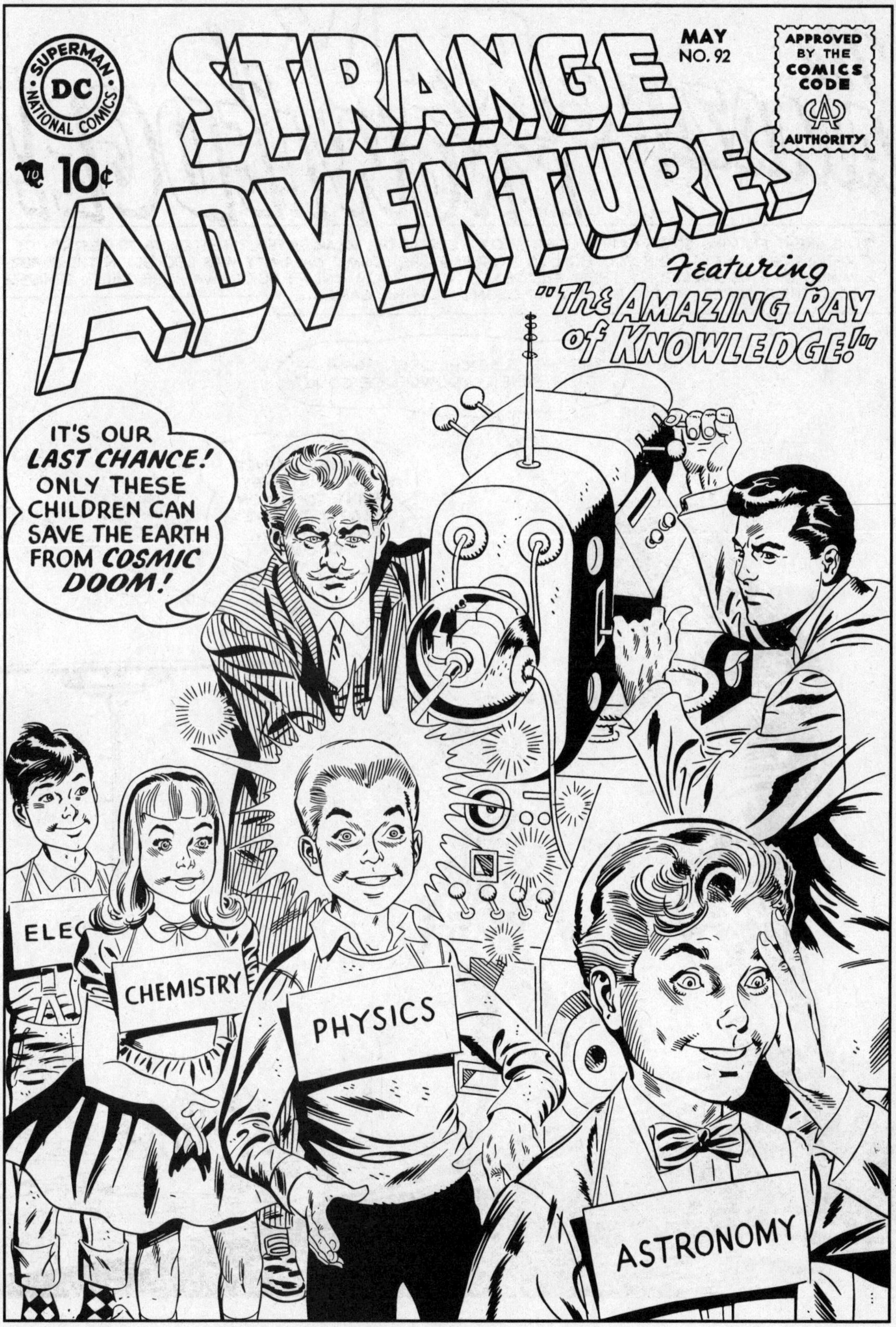
SUPERMAN DC NATIONAL COMICS
10¢
STRANGE ADVENTURES
MAY NO. 92
APPROVED BY THE COMICS CODE AUTHORITY
Featuring "The AMAZING RAY of KNOWLEDGE!"
IT'S OUR LAST CHANCE! ONLY THESE CHILDREN CAN SAVE THE EARTH FROM COSMIC DOOM!
ELEC
CHEMISTRY
PHYSICS
ASTRONOMY

The AMAZING RAY of KNOWLEDGE!

THE GREAT FLAMING COMET CAME CLOSER AND CLOSER TO THE SOLAR SYSTEM, THREATENING TO DESTROY ITS RETINUE OF PLANETS! THE SOLUTION TO AVERTING THE COSMIC CALAMITY WAS LOCKED IN THE SUPER-MINDS OF FIVE CHILDREN! THEN, SUDDENLY, WITH DOOM ONLY HOURS AWAY, THE CHILD-GENIUSES LOST THEIR SUPER-KNOWLEDGE AND BEGAN PLAYING GAMES...

THEY'RE JUST CHILDREN AGAIN-- THEIR SUPER-KNOWLEDGE GONE!

NOW WE'LL NEVER KNOW WHAT THEY MEANT TO DO ON *PLUTO* TO SAVE *EARTH* FROM DOOM!

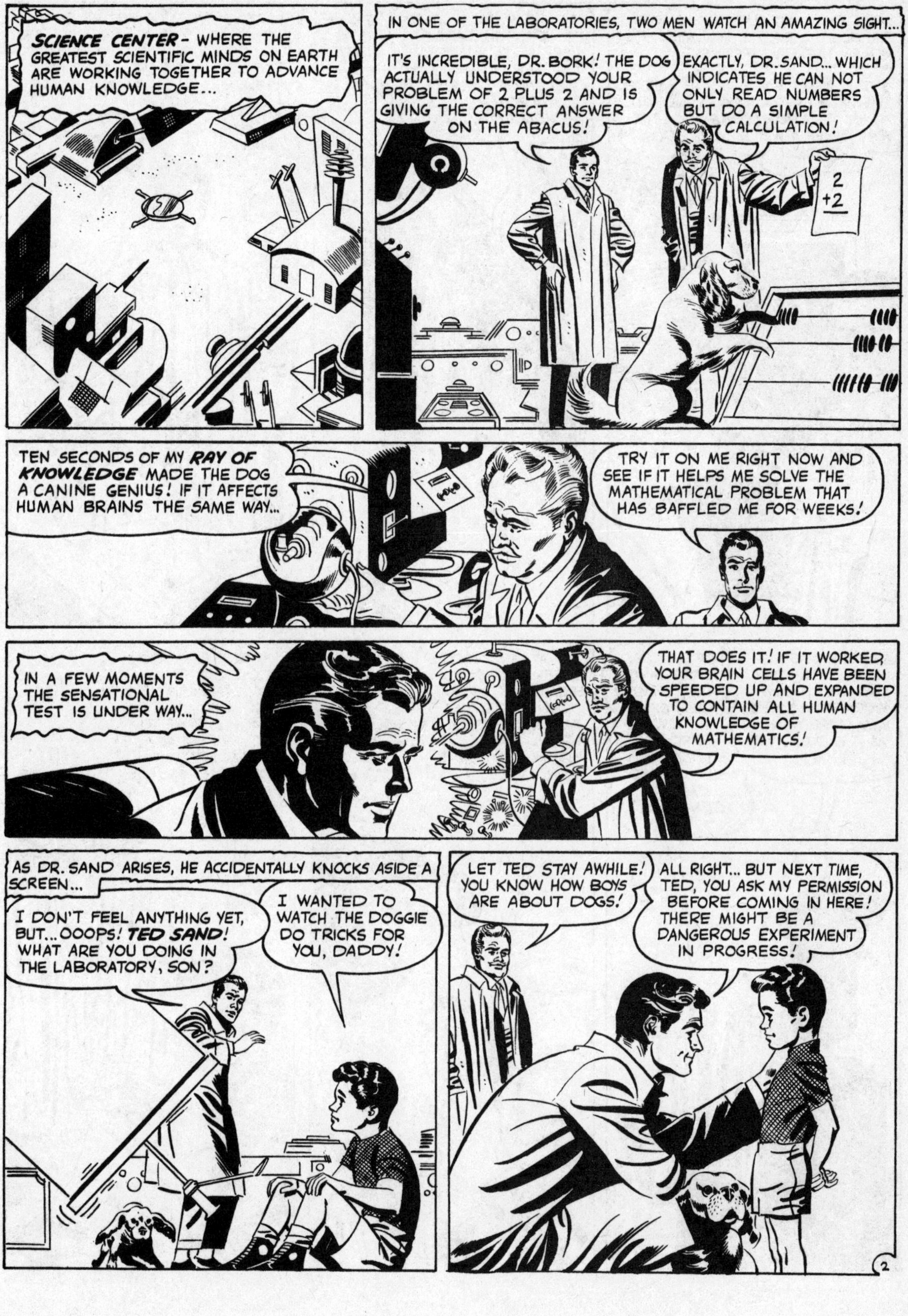
SCIENCE CENTER - WHERE THE GREATEST SCIENTIFIC MINDS ON EARTH ARE WORKING TOGETHER TO ADVANCE HUMAN KNOWLEDGE...
IN ONE OF THE LABORATORIES, TWO MEN WATCH AN AMAZING SIGHT...
IT'S INCREDIBLE, DR. BORK! THE DOG ACTUALLY UNDERSTOOD YOUR PROBLEM OF 2 PLUS 2 AND IS GIVING THE CORRECT ANSWER ON THE ABACUS!
EXACTLY, DR. SAND... WHICH INDICATES HE CAN NOT ONLY READ NUMBERS BUT DO A SIMPLE CALCULATION!
2 +2
TEN SECONDS OF MY RAY OF KNOWLEDGE MADE THE DOG A CANINE GENIUS! IF IT AFFECTS HUMAN BRAINS THE SAME WAY...
TRY IT ON ME RIGHT NOW AND SEE IF IT HELPS ME SOLVE THE MATHEMATICAL PROBLEM THAT HAS BAFFLED ME FOR WEEKS!
IN A FEW MOMENTS THE SENSATIONAL TEST IS UNDER WAY...
THAT DOES IT! IF IT WORKED, YOUR BRAIN CELLS HAVE BEEN SPEEDED UP AND EXPANDED TO CONTAIN ALL HUMAN KNOWLEDGE OF MATHEMATICS!
AS DR. SAND ARISES, HE ACCIDENTALLY KNOCKS ASIDE A SCREEN...
I DON'T FEEL ANYTHING YET, BUT... OOOPS! TED SAND! WHAT ARE YOU DOING IN THE LABORATORY, SON?
I WANTED TO WATCH THE DOGGIE DO TRICKS FOR YOU, DADDY!
LET TED STAY AWHILE! YOU KNOW HOW BOYS ARE ABOUT DOGS!
ALL RIGHT... BUT NEXT TIME, TED, YOU ASK MY PERMISSION BEFORE COMING IN HERE! THERE MIGHT BE A DANGEROUS EXPERIMENT IN PROGRESS!
2

WHILE YOUNG TED PLAYS HAPPILY WITH THE DOG WIZARD, THE TWO SCIENTISTS RETURN TO THEIR EXPERIMENT...

I STILL CAN'T SOLVE THIS PROBLEM, DR. BORK! MAYBE THE **KNOWLEDGE RAY** TAKES A WHILE TO WORK!

IT WORKED INSTANTLY ON THE DOG!

IF THAT MATH PROBLEM BOTHERS YOU, DADDY, HERE'S THE ANSWER! YOU WERE USING **VALENCE** INSTEAD OF **MOLECULAR VELOCITY!**

ULP! HE-- HE'S RIGHT!

AMAZING! WHY DIDN'T YOU TELL ME YOUR SON IS A GENIUS?

B-BUT HE ISN'T... OR **WASN'T!** DON'T YOU UNDERSTAND, DR. BORK? YOUR **KNOWLEDGE RAY** DID IT! IT WORKED ON TED!

SEE? HE WAS RIGHT IN LINE WITH THE MACHINE! IT MUST WORK ON A YOUNG, IMMATURE MIND-- AS IT DID ON THE DOG!

OF COURSE! ADULT MINDS ARE FORMED THEIR CELLS ALREADY FIXED AND PATTERNED! WE'LL CREATE **CHILD GENIUSES!**

MY RAY CAN PRODUCE A GENIUS IN ANY SPECIALIZED FIELD! TED GOT THE **MATHEMATICS** STIMULATION INTENDED FOR YOU...

YOU CAN TEST THE **RAY** ON THE CHILDREN OF SCIENTISTS HERE IN OTHER FIELDS OF RESEARCH!

YOU BETTER HURRY! ACCORDING TO MY CALCULATIONS, YOU'LL NEED A BOARD OF GENIUSES FAST TO SAVE THE SOLAR SYSTEM FROM DESTRUCTION!

3

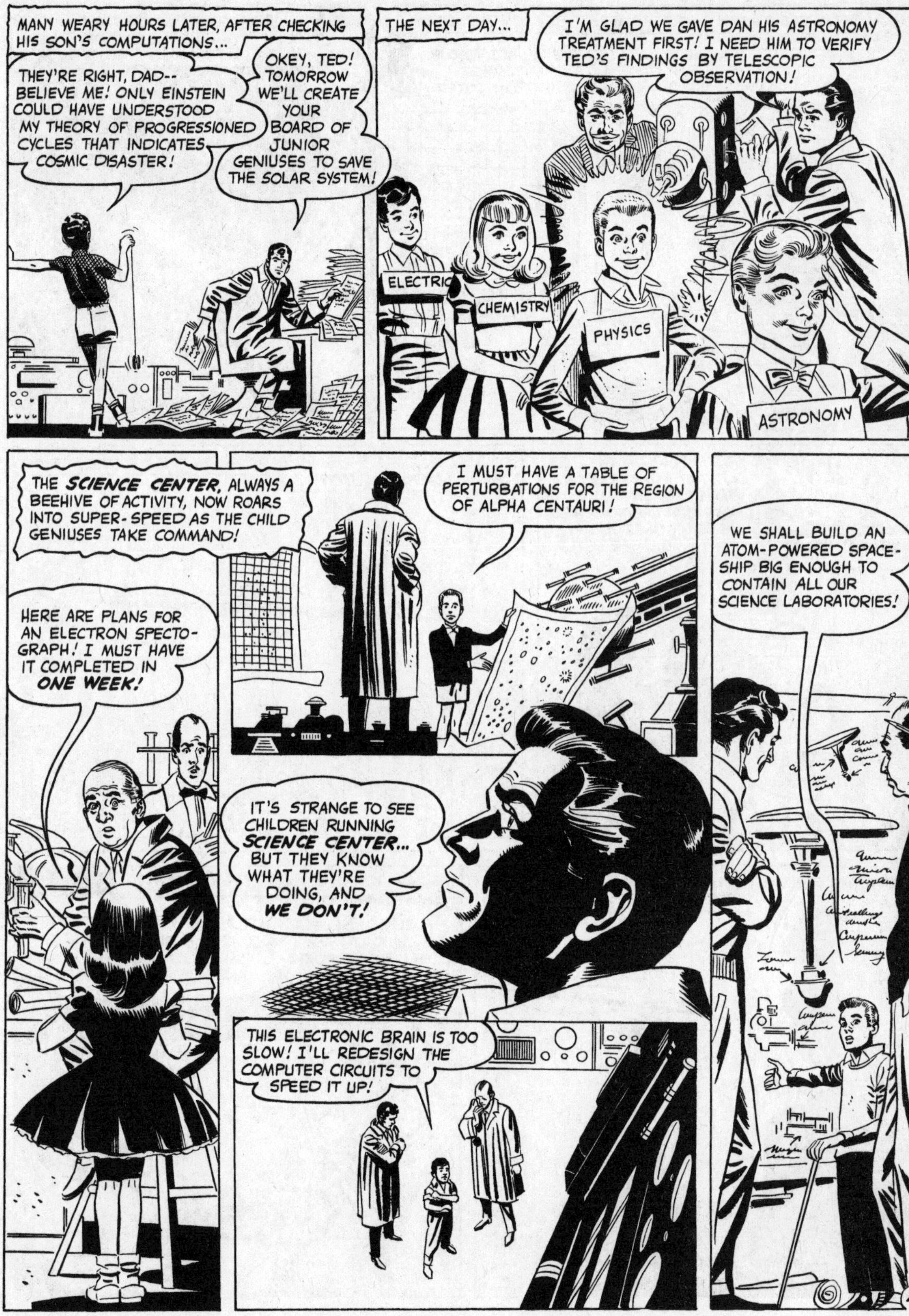
MANY WEARY HOURS LATER, AFTER CHECKING HIS SON'S COMPUTATIONS...
THEY'RE RIGHT, DAD-- BELIEVE ME! ONLY EINSTEIN COULD HAVE UNDERSTOOD MY THEORY OF PROGRESSIONED CYCLES THAT INDICATES COSMIC DISASTER!
OKEY, TED! TOMORROW WE'LL CREATE YOUR BOARD OF JUNIOR GENIUSES TO SAVE THE SOLAR SYSTEM!
THE NEXT DAY...
I'M GLAD WE GAVE DAN HIS ASTRONOMY TREATMENT FIRST! I NEED HIM TO VERIFY TED'S FINDINGS BY TELESCOPIC OBSERVATION!
ELECTRIC
CHEMISTRY
PHYSICS
ASTRONOMY
THE SCIENCE CENTER, ALWAYS A BEEHIVE OF ACTIVITY, NOW ROARS INTO SUPER-SPEED AS THE CHILD GENIUSES TAKE COMMAND!
HERE ARE PLANS FOR AN ELECTRON SPECTOGRAPH! I MUST HAVE IT COMPLETED IN ONE WEEK!
I MUST HAVE A TABLE OF PERTURBATIONS FOR THE REGION OF ALPHA CENTAURI!
WE SHALL BUILD AN ATOM-POWERED SPACESHIP BIG ENOUGH TO CONTAIN ALL OUR SCIENCE LABORATORIES!
IT'S STRANGE TO SEE CHILDREN RUNNING SCIENCE CENTER... BUT THEY KNOW WHAT THEY'RE DOING, AND WE DON'T!
THIS ELECTRONIC BRAIN IS TOO SLOW! I'LL REDESIGN THE COMPUTER CIRCUITS TO SPEED IT UP!
4

SOON THE ADULT SCIENTISTS ARE *SUMMONED* TO A CONFERENCE BY THE CHILD GENIUSES...

WE'VE LOCATED THE MENACE TO OUR SOLAR SYSTEM... A GIANT COMET HURTLING TOWARD US FROM OUTER SPACE...

"...OUR CALCULATIONS SHOW IT WILL BRUSH PLUTO, OUR OUTERMOST PLANET, WITH ITS TAIL IN PASSING..."

BUT HOW CAN THAT AFFECT US? THE EARTH HAS OFTEN BRUSHED THROUGH A COMET'S TAIL WITHOUT HARM!

WE DON'T KNOW THAT, YET, BUT THE ANSWER IS ON *PLUTO*...AND WE MUST MOVE OUR LABORATORIES THERE AT ONCE TO SAVE EARTH AND HER SISTER PLANETS!

SOON, A GIGANTIC *SPACESHIP*, DESIGNED BY THE CHILDREN, TAKES FORM AT *SCIENCE CENTER!*

AND AFTER FRENZIED WEEKS, THE TAKE-OFF-- WITH CHILDREN AT THE CONTROLS!-- AND ADULTS AS PASSENGERS...

THROUGH WEEKS OF FLIGHT THROUGH SPACE...

I FEEL SO USELESS! THE CHILDREN ARE DOING ALL THE WORK!

TED SAYS WE'LL HAVE PLENTY TO DO ON PLUTO! THEY'VE ALMOST LOCATED THE MENACE AND HOW TO AVERT IT!

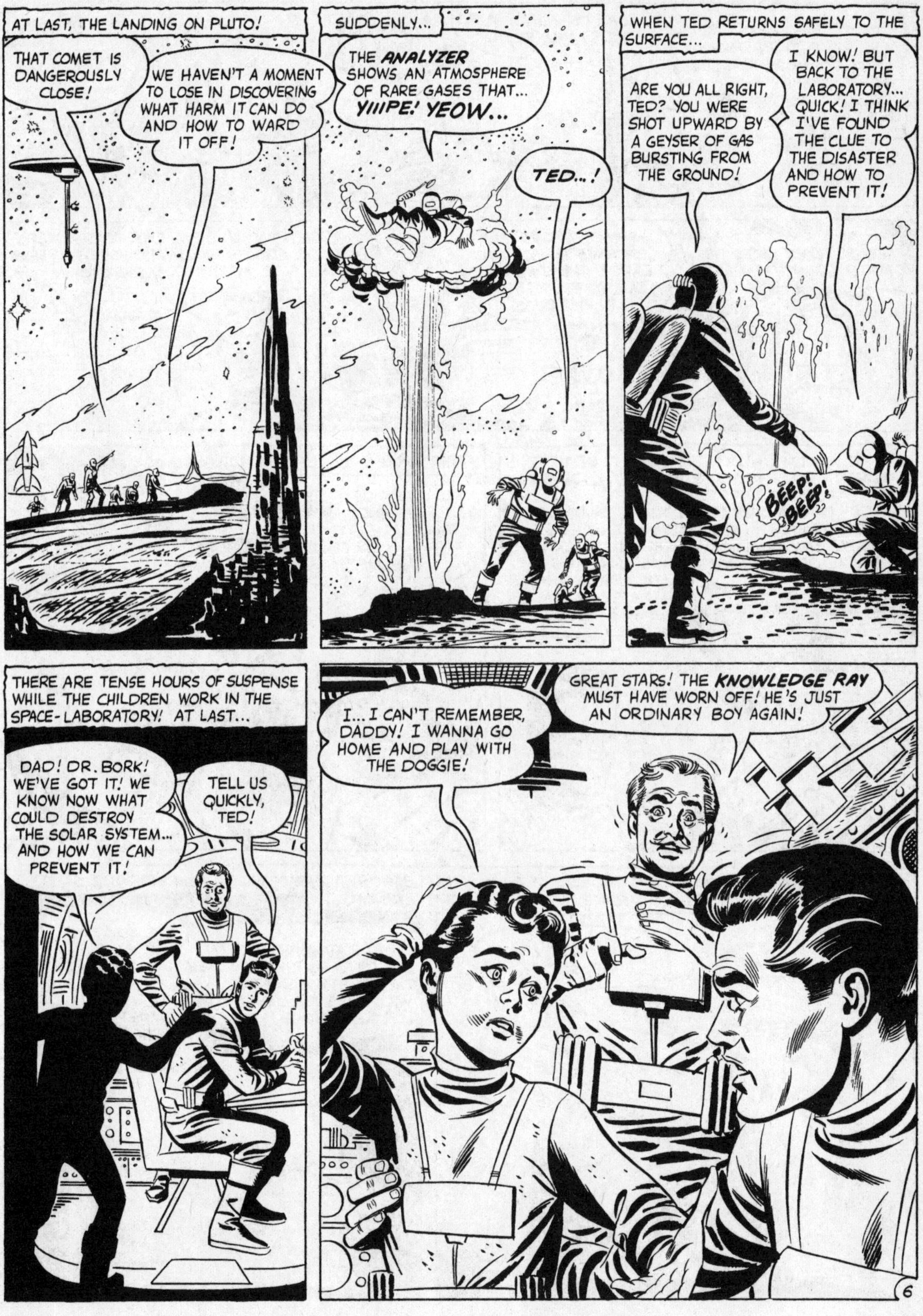
AT LAST, THE LANDING ON PLUTO!
THAT COMET IS DANGEROUSLY CLOSE!
WE HAVEN'T A MOMENT TO LOSE IN DISCOVERING WHAT HARM IT CAN DO AND HOW TO WARD IT OFF!
SUDDENLY...
THE ANALYZER SHOWS AN ATMOSPHERE OF RARE GASES THAT... YIIIPE! YEOW...
TED...!
WHEN TED RETURNS SAFELY TO THE SURFACE...
ARE YOU ALL RIGHT, TED? YOU WERE SHOT UPWARD BY A GEYSER OF GAS BURSTING FROM THE GROUND!
I KNOW! BUT BACK TO THE LABORATORY... QUICK! I THINK I'VE FOUND THE CLUE TO THE DISASTER AND HOW TO PREVENT IT!
BEEP! BEEP!
THERE ARE TENSE HOURS OF SUSPENSE WHILE THE CHILDREN WORK IN THE SPACE-LABORATORY! AT LAST...
DAD! DR. BORK! WE'VE GOT IT! WE KNOW NOW WHAT COULD DESTROY THE SOLAR SYSTEM... AND HOW WE CAN PREVENT IT!
TELL US QUICKLY, TED!
I... I CAN'T REMEMBER, DADDY! I WANNA GO HOME AND PLAY WITH THE DOGGIE!
GREAT STARS! THE KNOWLEDGE RAY MUST HAVE WORN OFF! HE'S JUST AN ORDINARY BOY AGAIN!
6

THE SCENE IN THE SPACE-LABORATORY CONFIRMS THE ADULTS' WORST FEARS! THE CHILD GENIUSES ARE NORMAL CHILDREN AGAIN...

COME ON--LET'S PLAY HIDE-AND-SEEK!

I'LL BE *IT!*

WITH STRICKEN FACES THE ADULT SCIENTISTS MEET!

MY *KNOWLEDGE RAY MACHINE* IS BACK ON EARTH! THE COMET IS DUE TO BRUSH PLUTO IN FIVE DAYS!

THEN WE HAVE FIVE DAYS TO DISCOVER THE SECRET AND SAVE OUR SYSTEM FROM A FATE WE DON'T EVEN KNOW!

CAN THE ADULTS UNLOCK THE SECRETS OF THEIR CHILDREN'S SUPER-SCIENCE IN TIME?

MOST OF DORIS'S CHEMISTRY IS OVER MY HEAD, BUT IT INDICATES SOME KIND OF CHEMICAL DESTRUCTION!

THAT'S WHAT TED SAID...AND HE GOT THE CLUE WHEN HE WAS USING THIS ATMOSPHERE ANALYZER AND STEPPED ON A GEYSER OF GAS!

AFTER THREE FRUITLESS-HARROWING DAYS...

TED FLEW UP AT LEAST TEN FEET AND... *WAIT!* I THINK I'VE GOT IT! PUT ON YOUR SPACE-HELMETS!

OUTSIDE, SAND DELIBERATELY JUMPS INTO ONE OF THE GEYSERS OF GAS THAT DOT THE WEIRD LANDSCAPE...

I'VE GOT IT! I'VE GOT IT!

BACK IN THE *SPACESHIP'S* LABORATORY, DR. SAND EXPLAINS...

PLUTO'S ATMOSPHERE IS AN EXPLOSIVE MIXTURE OF GASES! THE COMET'S FIERY TAIL WILL MAKE IT BLOW UP LIKE A BOMB!

THE BLAST WILL UPSET THE BALANCE OF THE WHOLE SOLAR SYSTEM-- FORCING ALL THE PLANETS TO FLY OUT OF THEIR ORBITS-- WRECKING ALL LIFE!

PLUTO

INERT HEAVY GAS

EXPLOSIVE GAS

7

IS THERE ANY WAY WE CAN PREVENT THE EXPLOSION?

THOSE GAS GEYSERS SHOW PLUTO'S INTERIOR IS THE HEAVIER GAS! IF WE CAN OPEN HUGE GAS WELLS TO LET THAT MIX WITH THE ATMOSPHERE, IT WON'T EXPLODE!

BUT HOW CAN WE LET OUT ENOUGH GAS IN THE FEW HOURS WE HAVE LEFT?

WITH AN ATOMIC-ENGINE BLAST FROM OUR SPACE-SHIP AS WE TAKE OFF!

WILL IT WORK? THE GREAT SHIP RISES, THEN HOVERS...IT'S MIGHTY ATOMIC-POWERED BLAST TEARING AT THE PLANET'S CRUST!

IT'S WORKING! BUT IS THERE ENOUGH GEYSER GAS TO SAVE PLUTO?

WE'LL KNOW IN ONE HOUR... WHEN THE COMET'S FIERY TAIL BRUSHES PAST! WE'D BETTER BLAST OFF NOW AND GET FAR AWAY!

AN HOUR LATER FROM A POST FAR OUT IN SPACE...

IT WORKED! YOU CAN SEE LITTLE CLOUDS OF GAS EXPLODE -- BUT MOST OF PLUTO'S ATMOSPHERE RESISTS THE FLAME!

OUR SOLAR SYSTEM IS SAVED! WE OWE IT ALL TO YOUR *KNOWLEDGE RAY*, DR. BORK!

NOT QUITE, SAND! WHEN THE CHILDREN'S ARTIFICIAL GENIUS FADED AWAY, IT WAS STILL OUR SOLID *EARNED KNOWLEDGE* THAT CAME THROUGH!

FLASH KNOWLEDGE CAN NEVER REPLACE HUMAN INGENUITY AND SKILL! THERE IS NO SHORT-CUT TO GENIUS BY MACHINES -- BECAUSE EXPERIENCE IS STILL THE FOUNDATION OF KNOWLEDGE!

The END

8

EARTH -- PLANETARY BOMB!

AT 2 A.M. AN IRRESISTIBLE FORCE WILL COMPEL ME TO ACTIVATE THIS MACHINE AND SEND EARTH CRASHING INTO THE PLANET VENUS!

 I'M JUST AN ORDINARY GUY THAT FATE DROPPED INTO AN EXTRAORDINARY SITUATION! IT BEGAN WHEN I DISCOVERED TO MY ASTONISHMENT THERE WAS A PERFECT DOUBLE OF ME ON EARTH WHO WAS PLANNING TO ELIMINATE ME--AND AFTER ASSUMING MY IDENTITY, CONVERT EARTH INTO AN AGENT OF PLANETARY DESTRUCTION!

I WAS EAGERLY LOOKING FORWARD TO A WELL-EARNED VACATION THE DAY I CALLED AT MY BANK...

I'VE MADE OUT THE WITHDRAWAL SLIP FOR $500! IT'S ALL I HAVE IN MY ACCOUNT!

ACCORDING TO OUR RECORDS, MR. MORGAN, YOU HAVE A BANK BALANCE OF $10,000!

WH-AT? THERE MUST BE SOME MISTAKE! I NEVER HAD THAT MUCH MONEY IN MY LIFE!

WHEN I RETURNED TO MY ROOMING HOUSE, STILL MYSTIFIED BY THE BANK'S ASSURANCE THAT I DID INDEED HAVE $10,000 IN MY NAME...

MAYBE BY THE TIME I RETURN FROM MY VACATION, THE BANK WILL--WHO'S THERE?

KNOCK KNOCK

DID THE LATE JEFF MORGAN LIVE HERE?

WHAT DO YOU MEAN THE *LATE* JEFF MORGAN? *I'M* JEFF MORGAN--AND AS YOU SEE, VERY MUCH ALIVE!

A MAN IDENTIFIED AS JEFF MORGAN WAS KILLED BY A HIT-AND-RUN DRIVER HALF AN HOUR AGO! THESE PAPERS WERE FOUND ON HIM!

DUPLICATES OF MY DRIVER'S LICENSE, CLUB MEMBERSHIP CARD, AND SOCIAL SECURITY! BUT HOW--?

IN THE STATION HOUSE, SOON AFTER...

EVEN THE VICTIM'S FINGERPRINTS MATCH YOURS! IT'S AS IF THERE WERE A *DUPLICATE* OF YOU! HOWEVER, WE NOW KNOW THAT THIS MAN WITH YOUR NAME AND DUPLICATE PAPERS DID *NOT* COME FROM THIS WORLD!

X-RAYS SHOW HIS INTERNAL STRUCTURE WAS ENTIRELY DIFFERENT FROM OURS! FROM PAPERS FOUND ON THIS *ALIEN*, WE KNOW HE HAD AN APPOINTMENT TO MEET OTHER ALIENS! WE'D LIKE TO HAVE YOU CLEAR UP THIS MYSTERY-- BY ATTENDING THAT MEETING-- AS THE DEAD ALIEN!

TWO DAYS LATER, AT THE "ALIEN" RENDEZVOUS...

...THEN EACH OF YOU HAS PURCHASED YOUR SPECIAL EQUIPMENT WITH THE DUPLICATE MONEY DEPOSITED IN BANKS IN YOUR NAMES? GOOD! THEN WE'RE SET TO GO--AS SOON AS EACH OF YOU ELIMINATES HIS COUNTERPART ON EARTH!

2

AS WE FILED OUT, A HAND CLAMPED DOWN HARD ON MY SHOULDER --

YOU DIDN'T REALLY THINK YOU COULD GET AWAY WITH IT, DID YOU, EARTHMAN? HIDDEN MACHINES SCREENED YOU AS YOU WERE ON LINE!

I LUNGED FORWARD, BUT--

YOU POINTED THAT RING AT ME--AND I CAN'T MOVE!

THE GEM IN THE RING IS A *MIND-CONTROLLER!* I ORDERED YOU TO FREEZE -- AND YOU DID!

AGAIN THE ALIEN GAVE ME COMMANDS! I FOUGHT HIS MENTAL ORDERS--BUT COULD ONLY FOLLOW MY CAPTOR INTO ANOTHER ROOM...

YOU CAME TO LEARN WHY WE ALIENS ARE ON YOUR PLANET! VERY WELL, I'LL TELL YOU...

AS HE TALKED, THE ALIEN LEADER BEGAN TO ASSEMBLE A CURIOUS CONTRAPTION...

THIS IS A *MAGNETIDESTROYER!* TO ENABLE EACH OF US TO BUILD ONE WITHOUT AROUSING SUSPICION, WE DUPLICATED THE IDENTITIES-- AND ARE ASSUMING THE PLACES OF -- TWENTY EARTH BEINGS!

"WE COME FROM THE PLANET MERCURY! FOR MANY YEARS WE HAVE BEEN AT WAR WITH THE PLANET VENUS..."

IT'S A STALEMATE! FOR EVERY WEAPON WE HAVE DEVISED, THE VENUSIANS HAVE COME UP WITH A COUNTER-WEAPON! AND *WE* HAVE SUCCEEDED IN NULLIFYING ALL OF VENUS' WEAPONS!

I HAVE BEEN WORKING ON THAT PROBLEM-- AND HAVE SOLVED IT!

BY PLACING *TWENTY MAGNETIDESTROYERS* ON THE PLANET EARTH WE COULD HURL IT FROM ITS ORBIT AND DIRECT IT TOWARD VENUS! OF COURSE, VENUS WILL ATTEMPT TO BLAST EARTH WITH ITS ANTI-BOMB WEAPONS-- BUT THEY ARE NOT DESIGNED TO STOP A BOMB OF *PLANETARY SIZE!*

3

"TRAVELING THROUGH SPACE AT TREMENDOUS SPEED, THIS PLANETARY BOMB WOULD CRASH INTO VENUS AND SHATTER BOTH WORLDS!"

"TWENTY OF OUR SCIENTISTS MUST GO TO EARTH AND CONSTRUCT THE *MAGNITI-DESTROYERS* OF A SPECIAL METAL FOUND ONLY ON THAT PLANET..."

YOU WILL LAND, ASSUME THE IDENTITY OF TWENTY EARTH BEINGS BY THE USE OF THE *DUPLICATOR*, AND PUT OUR PLAN IN OPERATION!

DUPLICATED MONEY WILL BE FURNISHED YOU! DEPOSIT THIS IN EARTH BANKS TO PURCHASE THE NECESSARY EQUIPMENT TO BUILD THE *MAGNETIDESTROYERS!*

SIMPLY SWITCH ON THE POWER AND THE *MAGNETIDESTROYERS* ARE READY TO OPERATE! WITHIN THE NEXT WEEK EIGHTEEN MORE *MAGNETI-DESTROYERS* WILL BE CONSTRUCTED ALL OVER THE EARTH! THIS ONE IS NUMBER NINETEEN!

YOURS, MORGAN--IS NUMBER *TWENTY!* NONE CAN OPERATE INDIVIDUALLY! ALL MUST BE TOUCHED OFF TOGETHER! SO I ORDER YOU--RETURN HOME AND BUILD A DUPLICATE OF THIS MACHINE JUST AS YOU SAW ME DO!

WHEN THE MACHINE IS COMPLETED, PRESS THE STARTER BUTTON AT EXACTLY TWO A.M. THE MORNING OF MAY 5TH! AS THE PLANET EARTH BEGINS ITS JOURNEY THROUGH SPACE TOWARD VENUS, WE WILL LEAVE EARTH AND RETURN TO MERCURY!

4

IF YOUR LAW OFFICERS QUESTION YOU, TELL THEM WE WILL HOLD ANOTHER MEETING TWO WEEKS FROM TONIGHT--AND WILL REVEAL OUR PURPOSE ON EARTH AT THAT TIME!

OH, YES--NOT UNTIL THE MOMENT YOU PRESS THE STARTER BUTTON WILL YOU BE *FREE* TO TELL YOUR OFFICIALS THE TRUTH! BUT, OF COURSE, IT WILL THEN BE TOO LATE FOR ANYONE ON EARTH TO STOP US!

I LEFT THE HOUSE, FIGHTING AGAINST THE ALIEN'S ORDERS, BUT I WAS HELPLESS TO RESIST...

ANOTHER MEETING IN TWO WEEKS? WE'LL HAVE TO WAIT!

PLAINCLOTHESMEN WILL SHADOW THE OTHER ALIENS IN THE MEANTIME!

RETURNING HOME, MY VACATION CANCELED, I BEGAN CONSTRUCTING THE *MAGNETIDESTROYER*...

I'VE GOT TO WARN THE POLICE--BUT HOW? I CAN'T EVEN STOP MYSELF FROM BUILDING THIS EARTH-DESTROYER!

ONCE I TRIED TO PHONE THE POLICE, BUT MY MUSCLES FROZE TIGHT...

I CAN'T EVEN PICK UP THE PHONE TO CALL FOR HELP!

WHENEVER I ATTEMPTED TO CALL OUT A WARNING...

EVENING, MR. MORGAN!

I CAN'T UTTER A WORD!

5

THE HOURS AND DAYS TO APPROACHING DOOM WENT BY! MY MACHINE WAS READY...

TODAY--MAY 4TH! IN EXACTLY TWELVE HOURS I'LL PRESS THAT BUTTON AND SEND THE EARTH FLYING TO ITS DESTRUCTION AS A PLANETARY BOMB!

BEADS OF PERSPIRATION RAN DOWN MY FACE AS I FOUGHT THE COMMAND THAT KEPT ME HELPLESS...

THERE *MUST* BE SOME WAY OUT! I'VE GOT TO THINK...

YES--YES! THERE IS *ONE WAY* TO DEFEAT THE ALIENS! IT'S SO SIMPLE, I COULDN'T SEE IT!

WELL, READER? IF *YOU* WERE JEFF MORGAN, COULD *YOU* SAVE THE EARTH? THINK HARD! PAUSE A MOMENT BEFORE READING ON-- AND THINK...

AT TWO A.M. ON THE MORNING OF MAY 5TH I CONFIDENTIALLY PRESSED THE STARTING BUTTON!

I'LL *GLADY* PRESS THE BUTTON NOW-- BECAUSE NOTHING WILL HAPPEN TO THE EARTH--AND I'LL BE FREE TO TELL THE POLICE WHAT I KNOW!

WITHIN AN HOUR AFTERWARD, LAW-OFFICERS HAD ARRESTED THE ALIENS ALL OVER THE GLOBE...

WHEN YOU FAIL TO RETURN TO MERCURY, YOUR WORLD WILL REALIZE ITS PLOT HAD FAILED!

THAT WAY, THEY'LL NEVER AGAIN TRY TURNING EARTH INTO A PLANETARY BOMB!

LATER, AT POLICE HEADQUARTERS...

BUT, MR. MORGAN-- WHAT *DID* YOU DO?

I SIMPLY CALLED UP THE ELECTRIC LIGHT COMPANY--WHICH THE ALIEN HAD NEGLECTED TO FORBID ME TO DO--AND TOLD THEM *TO SHUT OFF THE ELECTRICITY!* WITHOUT ELECTRIC POWER, THE *MACHINE COULD NOT OPERATE!*

THE END

As an illustrator of science-fiction stories, I've often wondered how close my conception of interplanetary creatures was to alien life on other worlds! It was certainly more fantastic than any science-fiction story to imagine that I'd ever have the good fortune to work with real...

MODELS from SATURN!

In my studio in a coastal city-- I've been given the assignment of illustrating a science-fiction story about Saturn! I wonder if the day will ever come when artists can use real Saturnians as models...

Suddenly two glowing lights appeared in front of me...

May WE offer our services as models, Earthman--

THE GLOW FADED AND TWO STRANGE FIGURES MATERIALIZED...

I AM TAGOR MOR, AND THIS IS MY SISTER PALLAS VAN!

WE ARE INHABITANTS OF SATURN! IF YOU WANT PROOF OF WHAT WE ARE *TELEPATHIZING* TO YOU--

EXCITEMENT POSSESSED ME! MY PENCIL FLEW OVER MY SKETCHPAD...

NO, NO! DON'T WASTE TIME! I'VE GOT TO SKETCH YOU BEFORE THIS DAYDREAM FADES...

I ASSURE YOU WE ARE QUITE REAL...

WONDERFUL! WHAT I WOULDN'T GIVE TO GO TO SATURN MYSELF AND SKETCH LIFE ON THAT WORLD!

WE CAN EASILY ARRANGE THAT... IF YOU ARE REALLY WILLING TO GO!

WE NEED YOUR HELP, EARTHMAN! BUT WE CANNOT TAKE YOU WITH US AGAINST YOUR WILL! THIS *TELEPORTER* OPERATES *ONLY* ON A VOLUNTARY SUBJECT! WITH YOUR PERMISSION, I'LL PLACE IT AROUND YOUR HEAD...

YES! YES! GO AHEAD...

A MOMENT AFTER PALLAS VAN PLACED THE METAL CIRCLET ON MY FOREHEAD, I FELT A WEIGHTLESSNESS, AND THEN --

WH-WHERE AM I?

IN AN INSTANT, TAGAR MOR AND PALLAS VAN MATERIALIZED BESIDE ME...

WELCOME TO SATURN! FROM YOUR EXPERIENCE, YOU WILL UNDERSTAND OUR CIVILIZATION IS THOUSANDS OF YEARS AHEAD OF YOURS IN SCIENTIFIC DEVELOPMENT!

THEN HOW CAN *I* BE EXPECTED TO HELP YOU?

2

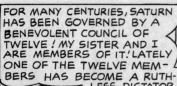

FOR MANY CENTURIES, SATURN HAS BEEN GOVERNED BY A BENEVOLENT COUNCIL OF TWELVE! MY SISTER AND I ARE MEMBERS OF IT! LATELY ONE OF THE TWELVE MEMBERS HAS BECOME A RUTHLESS DICTATOR!

"HE ISSUES ORDERS TO US THAT WE ARE FORCED TO OBEY BECAUSE OF A SECRET INVENTION THAT GIVES HIM ABSOLUTE MENTAL CONTROL OVER EVERYONE HE USES IT ON!"

FOLLOWING ARE THE NEW LAWS WE WILL ISSUE...

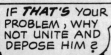

IF *THAT'S* YOUR PROBLEM, WHY NOT UNITE AND DEPOSE HIM?

FOR THE SIMPLE REASON THAT--*WE DON'T KNOW WHO HE IS!*

"AS SOON AS HE GIVES HIS ORDERS HE COMMANDS US TO FORGET HIS IDENTITY! THE DICTATOR COULD BE ANYONE--EXCEPT MY BROTHER AND ME! WE'RE SURE OF EACH OTHER!..."

YOU WILL FORGET WHO I AM! GO NOW!

OUR PLAN IS TO HAVE YOU SECRETLY MAKE A SKETCH OF THIS DICTATOR WHILE ATTENDING A COUNCIL MEETING!

HE'LL ORDER YOU TO FORGET HIS IDENTITY-- BUT WHEN YOU RETURN HERE WITH YOUR SKETCH, WE'LL KNOW WHO HE IS--AND EXPOSE HIM!

A MOMENT LATER, TAGAR MOR OPENED A DOOR TO A STRANGE ROOM...

YES, IT'S A CLEVER PLAN--*IF* YOU COULD SMUGGLE ME INTO THAT COUNCIL MEETING!

I'LL TAKE CARE OF *THAT* IN MY HOBBY ROOM! COME IN!

3

IN SECONDS, A SUPER-SCIENTIFIC PLASTIC MASK OVER MY FACE GAVE ME THE IDENTICAL FACE OF...

TAGAR MOR!

EXACTLY! *YOU* WILL GO IN MY PLACE TO THE COUNCIL MEETING!

NEXT DAY AT THE COUNCIL MEETING, MY PENCIL FLEW ACROSS THE SKETCH-PAD AS THE DICTATOR ISSUED HIS ORDERS...

YOU WILL OBEY MY COMMANDS AND FORGET WHO GAVE THEM TO YOU!

SILENTLY, PALLAS VAN AND I RETURNED TO HER HOME, WHERE TAGAR MOR AWAITED US...

DID YOU MAKE THAT SKETCH?

YES -- BUT AFTER I FINISHED IT, THE STRANGEST THING HAPPENED! MY MIND BLANKED OUT -- AND I CAN'T REMEMBER WHAT I DID WITH IT!

DESPAIR OVERCAME TAGAR MOR AND HIS SISTER...

EVIDENTLY THE DICTATOR'S ORDER TO FORGET HIS IDENTITY WAS POWERFUL ENOUGH TO MAKE ME FORGET WHERE I PUT THE SKETCH!

OUR PLAN FAILED...

WE'LL NEVER BE FREE!

SUDDENLY AN IDEA STRUCK ME --

NO -- *WAIT!* I HAVE ANOTHER PLAN TO EXPOSE HIS IDENTITY! LISTEN --

THE FOLLOWING MORNING AT ANOTHER COUNCIL MEETING...

FELLOW MEMBERS, I WISH TO REPORT AN IMPOSTOR AMONGST US! THAT MEMBER IS *NOT* MY BROTHER!

4

POWERFUL HANDS CAUGHT AND HELD ME HELPLESS WHILE FINGERS RIPPED THE PLASTIC MASK FROM MY FACE...

WHO IS HE?

WHERE DID HE COME FROM?

TAKE HIM TO THE *DETAIN CELLS!* WE'LL HOLD HIM FOR FURTHER INVESTIGATION!

IMPRISONED IN THE STRANGE TRANSPARENT TUBE THAT WAS THE SATURNIAN EQUIVALENT OF AN EARTH JAIL...

WILL MY PLAN SUCCEED? WILL THE *DICTATOR* COME HERE TO QUESTION ME PERSONALLY?

HOUR AFTER HOUR PASSED--AND THEN ALL OF A SUDDEN HE WAS THERE! BUT I HAD *NOT* COUNTED ON HIS BRINGING HIS MENTAL COMMANDER WITH HIM...

SPEAK, STRANGER! TELL ME HOW YOU CAME TO BE ON OUR COUNCIL! OMIT NOTHING!

I-I MUSN'T BETRAY MY SATURNIAN FRIENDS!

DESPERATELY I WAGED A MENTAL STRUGGLE AGAINST HIS ORDER...

MUST THINK OF *ANYTHING* BUT TAGAR MOR AND PALLAS VAN!

FOR LONG TERRIBLE MOMENTS THE UNEQUAL BATTLE WENT ON! I FOUGHT--BUT COULD NOT WIN! SOON I WAS POURING OUT THE WHOLE STORY--

TAGAR MOR AND PALLAS VAN BROUGHT ME FROM EARTH TO EXPOSE YOUR IDENTITY!

WHEN I CONFESSED THAT THIS WAS A TRAP TO LURE HIM TO ME, THE DICTATOR YANKED OUT A BLASTER-GUN... *I'LL BLAST YOU OUT OF EXISTENCE! AND AFTER I FINISH WITH YOU--I'LL DESTROY TAGAR MOR AND PALLAS VAN!*

BUT BEFORE THE DICTATOR COULD FIRE...

YOUR SCHEME WON'T WORK WITHOUT THIS COMMANDING DEVICE, KLAG JON! NOW I CAN FIGHT YOU ON EQUAL TERMS!

UNABLE TO HELP, I WATCHED TAGAR MOR FIGHT FOR HIS LIFE AND THE FREEDOM OF THE PLANET HE LOVED...

THEN, WITH A HOARSE CRY, KLAG JON CRUMPLED TO THE GROUND...

YOU CAN'T PROVE A THING! IT'S MY WORD AGAINST YOURS!

BUT I CAN PROVE YOUR GUILT!

PERPLEXED, I WATCHED TAGAR MOR REMOVE A STRANGE DEVICE FROM INSIDE MY CELL... *WE LAID THIS TRAP FOR YOU! UNKNOWN TO OUR EARTHMAN FRIEND, I TOOK THE ADDED PRECAUTION OF HIDING THIS RECORDER IN HIS CELL! EVERYTHING THE EARTHMAN SAID--EVERYTHING YOU SAID--IS DOWN HERE FOR EVIDENCE!*

AFTER KLAG JON WAS IMPRISONED, I SPENT HAPPY DAYS MAKING SKETCHES ALL OVER SATURN...

WHEN I RETURN, I'LL BE THE WORLD'S BEST SCIENCE-FICTION ARTIST-- AS FAR AS SATURN IS CONCERNED!

The End 6

The ICE-AGE MENACE!

STRANGELY ENOUGH, EVERYTIME WE BREATHE, WE HELP PREVENT ANOTHER ICE AGE FROM OCCURRING ON EARTH! THE *CARBON DIOXIDE* WE EXHALE INTO THE EARTH'S ATMOSPHERE ABSORBS THE SUN'S HEAT AND FORMS A WARM "BLANKET" AROUND THE WORLD! HOW LONG COULD OUR CIVILIZATION SURVIVE IF A MYSTERIOUS FORCE SUDDENLY STARTED TO DEPLETE THE EARTH OF ITS VITAL CARBON DIOXIDE?

THE WINDS ARE RUSHING DOWN INTO THAT EXTINCT VOLCANO-- AND CARRYING ME WITH THEM!

U.S. WEATHER BUREAU

31

AS ANXIOUS TELE-VIEWERS TUNE IN THE WEATHER REPORTS...

IF THE AVERAGE TEMPERATURE OF EARTH DROPPED ONLY A FEW DEGREES, CITIES WOULD SOON LOOK LIKE THIS!

ICEBERGS WOULD SMASH THEIR WAY THROUGH THE PANAMA CANAL IN THE TROPICS!

SNOWSTORMS IN EQUATORIAL AFRICA! GLACIERS ON THE MARCH! WATERFALLS-- FROZEN SOLID! THIS IS NO LONG-RANGE FORECAST! THE EARTH IS ENTERING ANOTHER *ICE AGE*

THE SIGNS OF COMING CATASTROPHE ARE ALREADY AT HAND! THOUGH IT IS MID-SUMMER, PEOPLE ARE FORCED TO HEAT THEIR COLD HOMES!

I WONDER WHAT'S CAUSED THE WORLD'S TEMPERATURE TO START DROPPING SO RAPIDLY IN RECENT WEEKS?

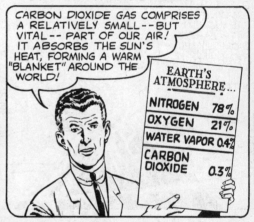

THE ANSWER IS PARTIALLY KNOWN BY THE WEATHER BUREAU...

CARBON DIOXIDE GAS COMPRISES A RELATIVELY SMALL--BUT VITAL-- PART OF OUR AIR! IT ABSORBS THE SUN'S HEAT, FORMING A WARM "BLANKET" AROUND THE WORLD!

EARTH'S ATMOSPHERE...	
NITROGEN	78%
OXYGEN	21%
WATER VAPOR	0.4%
CARBON DIOXIDE	0.3%

SCIENTIFIC THEORY SHOWS THAT IN PAST AGES, WHEN THE CO_2 PERCENTAGE FELL BELOW THE DANGER LINE, ICE AGES OCCURRED! WE HAVE ALREADY REACHED THAT DANGER POINT!

0.03% CARBON DIOXIDE... NORMAL
0.02% CARBON DIOXIDE... DANGER LINE
0.01% CARBON DIOXIDE... BRINGS SUB-ZERO CLIMATE

②

MEANWHILE, THE *CARBON DIOXIDE* MYSTERY HAS BAFFLED THE WORLD'S METEOROLOGISTS, INCLUDING JASON BOYD...

ANY SMALL DROP IN PERCENTAGE REPRESENTS MILLIONS OF CUBIC FEET OF CARBON DIOXIDE GAS! HOW ARE SUCH ENORMOUS QUANTITIES BEING DEPLETED FROM THE AIR?

0.02 DANGER LINE
.03   .01

AS HE CHECKS THE VARIOUS POSSIBILITIES...

PERHAPS SOME PROLIFIC NEW HYBRID PLANT SPRANG UP RECENTLY, USING UP CARBON DIOXIDE FASTER THAN IT IS REPLENISHED BY THE BREATHING OF ANIMALS AND MEN!

Each year, plant life on earth absorbs millions of tons of carbon dioxide from the air...

BUT AFTER SEEKING INFORMATION VIA RADIO...

BOTANICAL SOCIETY REPORTING... NO NEW PLANT LIFE REPORTED ANYWHERE ON EARTH!

CHECK THAT OFF! BUT THE WEATHER IS GETTING COLDER HOURLY! I MUST GET THE RIGHT ANSWER!

WEATHER BUREAU FIELD STATION 18

"COULD SOME CHAIN OF ERUPTING VOLCANOES BE PRODUCING GASES THAT COMBINE CHEMICALLY WITH CARBON DIOXIDE, THUS REMOVING IT FROM THE AIR?"

AGAIN, AFTER RADIO INQUIRY WITH VOLCANIC AUTHORITIES...

FEW VOLCANOES ACTIVE AT PRESENT... VOLCANIC GAS PRODUCTION LOW!

RULE THAT OUT! I'VE GOT TO KEEP TRACKING DOWN ALL OTHER NATURAL PHENOMENA THAT COULD ROB EARTH'S AIR OF CO_2!

BUT AFTER EXHAUSTIVE CHECKING...

ALL REPORTS NEGATIVE! BUT SOMETHING IS DRAWING CARBON DIOXIDE FROM THE ATMOSPHERE! IF ONLY I COULD FIND A CLUE--

THEN, WHILE FILING WEATHER CHARTS FOR THE PAST MONTH...

ODD! FOR THE PAST MONTH, HIGH WINDS HAVE BLOWN TOWARD MOUNT SHASTA FROM ALL DIRECTIONS, DAY AND NIGHT, WITHOUT ANY LET-UP!

DAILY WINDS NORTHERN CALIF.

MT. SHASTA

③

WIND CURRENTS DON'T NATURALLY ACT THAT WAY! I'LL FLY THERE IN MY HELICOPTER AND INVESTIGATE!

NEARING THE EXTINCT VOLCANO CALLED MOUNT SHASTA, UNEXPECTED DISASTER THREATENS!

THE WINDS ARE GOING STRAIGHT DOWN *INTO* THE CRATER! CAN'T BREAK OUT OF THEIR POWERFUL GRIP... I'M BEING DRAWN INTO THE VOLCANO TOO!

SKILLFULLY FIGHTING THE DOWN-DRAFT, BOYD PREVENTS A FATAL CRASH... TO MEET A SURPRISING REVELATION IN THE CRATER BOTTOM!

A *SPACE-SHIP* PARKED HERE! CREATURES FROM ANOTHER WORLD HAVE LANDED ON EARTH!

QUICKLY, BOYD IS SEIZED BY THE EXTRA-TERRESTRIALS...

WE MUST HOLD YOU PRISONER, EARTHMAN-- AND PREVENT YOU FROM WARNING THE OUTSIDE WORLD THAT *WE* ARE STEALING YOUR CARBON DIOXIDE!

HOW ARE YOU DOING IT?

AS THE ALIENS POINT OUT THE FANTASTIC MACHINERY THEY HAVE SET UP IN THE VOLCANO BOTTOM...

A GIANT FAN SUCTIONS HUGE QUANTITIES OF YOUR AIR DOWN INTO OUR REFRIGERATION CHAMBER! THIS EXTRACTS CARBON DIOXIDE GAS BY FREEZING IT INTO SOLID FORM!

JUST AS WE MAKE "DRY ICE," BUT ON A SMALLER SCALE!

4

LARGE VOLUMES OF CARBON DIOXIDE GAS, EXTRACTED FROM YOUR AIR, CONDENSE INTO SMALL CHUNKS, WHICH WE ARE LOADING INTO OUR SPACESHIP AS *GEMS!*

YOU MEAN IT IS *VALUABLE* TO YOU?

YES! WE ARE FROM A SUB-ZERO WORLD WHERE WHAT MINUTE QUANTITIES OF CARBON DIOXIDE EXIST ARE FROZEN SOLID! WE REGARD THEM AS PRECIOUS GEMS!

THAT'S NOT SO ODD! DIAMONDS ON EARTH ARE ACTUALLY A RARE CRYSTALLIZED FORM OF CHEAP CARBON OR COAL! ON THEIR WORLD, CARBON IN THE FORM OF CO_2, HAPPENS TO BE RARE!

BUT YOU'RE *ROBBING* EARTH OF ITS *VITAL* CARBON DIOXIDE, UNBALANCING THE NORMAL WEATHER PATTERN AND PRECIPITATING AN ICE AGE!

THAT IS NOT OUR CONCERN! WE'RE *SPACE-TREASURE HUNTERS* AND WE'VE FOUND OUR BIG *BONANZA!* GUARD THE EARTHMAN SO HE CAN'T ESCAPE AND WARN THE WORLD!

GOT TO THINK OF A PLAN TO ESCAPE!

NOT A CHANCE, EARTHMAN! I CAN EAVESDROP ON YOUR THOUGHTS!

MOMENTS LATER, THE ALIEN GUARD WHIRLS AROUND...

THE PRISONER IS THINKING OF *VENTRILO*-- I "HEAR" AN EARTHMAN'S TELEPATHIC VOICE BEHIND ME!

GRAB THAT ALIEN GUARD AND RESCUE BOYD!

INSTANTLY, BOYD LEAPS AT THE DISTRACTED GUARD...

I GOT THE IDEA OF USING A *VENTRILOQUISM* TRICK! BUT INSTEAD OF MY *VOICE,* I "THREW" MY *THOUGHTS* BEHIND ME! LUCKILY IT WORKED!

5

STEALING INTO THEIR SPACE-SHIP WHERE THE DRY-ICE JEWELS ARE STORED...

I'LL LET WARM CRATER AIR INSIDE THE SHIP! FROZEN CARBON DIOXIDE TURNS TO GAS AT ANY TEMPERATURE ABOVE *MINUS 78.5 DEGREES!* THE STOLEN CO_2 WILL SOON RETURN TO EARTH'S AIR!

THEN, AS THE EARTHMAN FLEES...

LOOK! OUR JEWELS ARE TURNING TO GAS! BUT WE CAN FREEZE MORE, IF WE CAN PREVENT THE EARTHMAN FROM ESCAPING AND WARNING HIS PEOPLE!

I TOOK A BAG OF JEWELS ALONG! POOLS OF HOT WATER USUALLY EXIST IN THE BOTTOMS OF CRATERS!

BRAMM! BRAMM!

AS HE PASSES A POOL HEATED BY UNDERGROUND LAVA, BOYD FLINGS THE GEMS INTO IT...

HOT WATER CAUSES DRY-ICE TO "BOIL" AWAY AS WHITE STEAM!

CAN'T SEE!

BEHIND THE COVER OF HIS INGEN-IOUS "SMOKESCREEN" BOYD REACHES HIS HELICOPTER...

THE EVAPORATING JEWELS CREATED AN UPDRAFT OF CARBON DIOXIDE-- PROPELLING ME OUT OF THE CRATER! GOT TO HOLD MY BREATH TILL I CAN BREATHE OXYGEN AGAIN!

SHORTLY AFTER, THE SPACE-SHIP ITSELF LEAVES...

ONCE I ESCAPED, THEY KNEW THEIR GAME WAS UP!

THE EARTH-MAN'S WARNING WILL BRING THEIR ARMED FORCES-- MORE POWERFUL THAN OURS! WE MUST LEAVE WITHOUT OUR CARBON DIOXIDE TREASURE!

LATER, BACK AT HIS METEOR-OLOGICAL JOB...

THE CARBON DIOXIDE CONTENT OF THE AIR IS BACK TO NORMAL AND WARMING THE EARTH AGAIN!

THE END

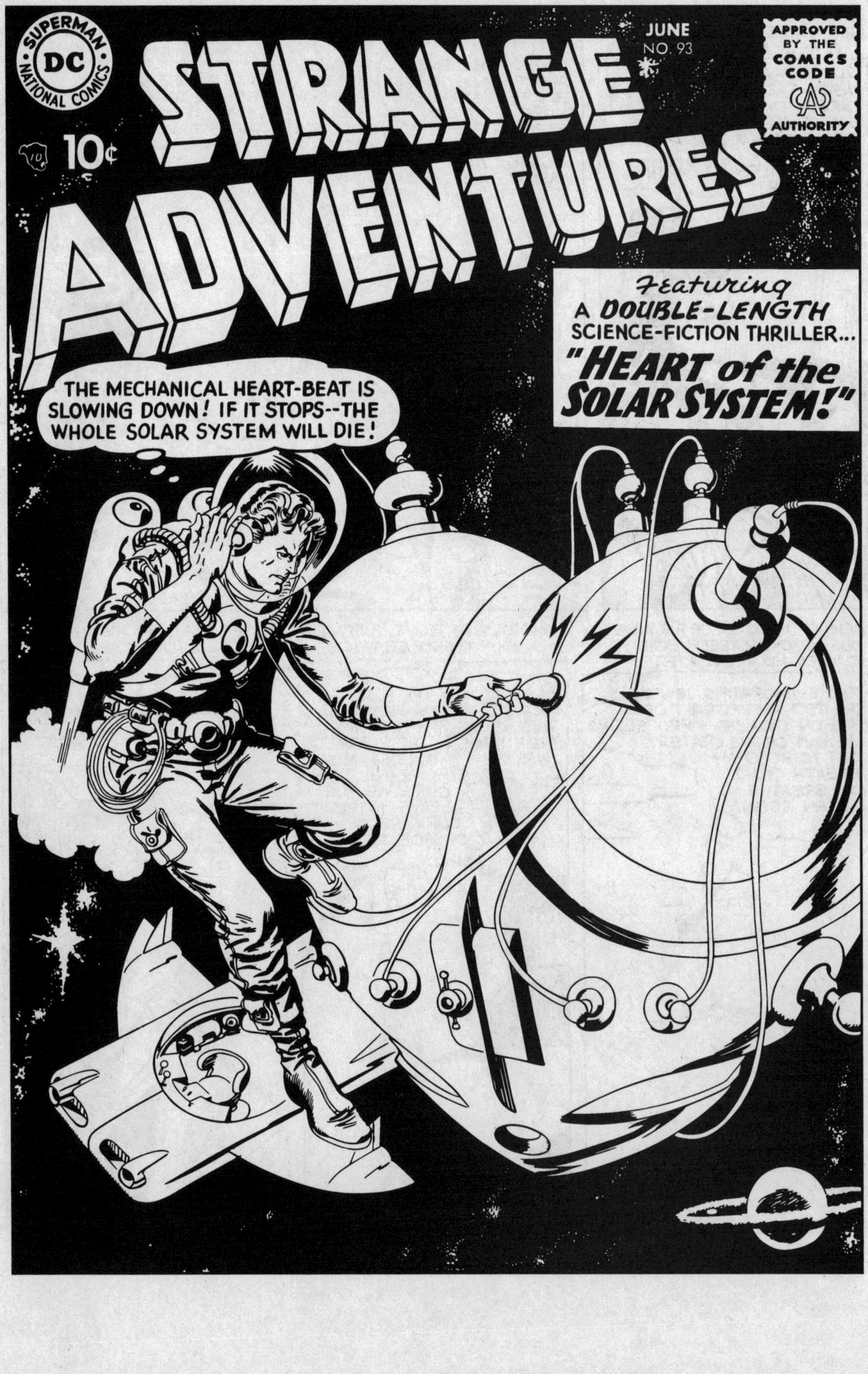
SUPERMAN DC NATIONAL COMICS
10¢
STRANGE ADVENTURES
JUNE
NO. 93
APPROVED BY THE COMICS CODE AUTHORITY
Featuring
A DOUBLE-LENGTH
SCIENCE-FICTION THRILLER...
"HEART of the SOLAR SYSTEM!"
THE MECHANICAL HEART-BEAT IS SLOWING DOWN! IF IT STOPS--THE WHOLE SOLAR SYSTEM WILL DIE!

HEART OF THE SOLAR SYSTEM!

THE PULSING HEART OF THE SOLAR SYSTEM WAS DYING! WHEN ITS BEAT STOPPED, VIOLENT CATACLYSMS WOULD SHATTER THE 9 PLANETS! WHO WAS DELIBERATELY DESTROYING THE SOLAR SYSTEM? TO FIND THE ANSWER BEFORE IT WAS TOO LATE, BOB CRANE HAD TO JOIN AN *INTERPLANETARY CIRCUS* IN THE MOST DANGEROUS IMPERSONATION OF HIS LIFE!

THE ENEMY WAR FLEET! IF THEY GET ME BEFORE I REPAIR THE HEART CONTROLS... THE SOLAR SYSTEM WILL DIE!

"I HAD SHOT PAST THE MOON WHEN MY RADIO SCREECHED LIKE A MARTIAN *MEEMEE* BIRD..."

OH-OH...THAT HOWLER WAVE IN MY RADIO MEANS BAD NEWS FROM THE *SPACE TRAFFIC PATROL!*

WWEEEEEEEEE!

TRAFFIC PATROL TO XZ702! CIRCUS LANDING AT TERRA SPACEPORT! ORBIT FOR 30 MINUTES UNTIL FIELD IS CLEAR!

BUT I MUST LAND! IT'S LIFE OR DEATH...!

"YOU DON'T ARGUE WITH SPACE PATROL! AFTER THEY CUT ME OFF, I TUNED IN FOR A LOOK AT WHAT WAS GOING ON BELOW!"

9 WORLDS CIRCUS

"I CUT IN MY RETARDER GEAR AND ORBITED ONCE AROUND EARTH, DOING A SLOW BURN..."

THE SOLAR SYSTEM IS DYING...WHILE I STOOGE AROUND TO LET A DIZZY CIRCUS LAND!

TRAFFIC CONTROL SATELLITE #11

OKAY TO LAND NOW, *XZ702!* USE VECTOR 3...

2

"COMING DOWN, I THOUGHT OF WHAT LAY AHEAD AND I WAS PLAIN SCARED..."

I HAVE TO TELL THE WORLD COUNCIL I'VE FAILED! I CAN'T FIND WHO'S DESTROYING THE SOLAR SYSTEM... OR HOW TO SAVE IT!

"MY MIND WENT BACK TO THE BEGINNING... WHEN THE SUN WENT BERSERK..."

IT'S ONLY SOME HUGE SUNSPOTS! THEY CAN'T HURT US!

"BUT WE SOON FOUND IT **COULD** HURT US..."

A DESTRUCTIVE FORCE FROM INSIDE THE SUN IS UPSETTING THE ENERGY BALANCE OF THE PLANETS!

"ALL THE PLANETS WERE AFFECTED... BUT STRANGELY ENOUGH, EACH OF THEM IN **DIFFERENT WAYS!** EARTH WAS ASSAULTED BY VIOLENT STORMS..."

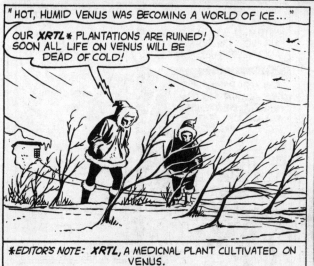

"HOT, HUMID VENUS WAS BECOMING A WORLD OF ICE..."

OUR **XRTL*** PLANTATIONS ARE RUINED! SOON ALL LIFE ON VENUS WILL BE DEAD OF COLD!

*EDITOR'S NOTE: **XRTL**, A MEDICNAL PLANT CULTIVATED ON VENUS.

"WHILE 3,671,000,000 MILES OUT ON FROZEN PLUTO, THE PLANET'S ICE SHELL WAS **MELTING!**"

WE'D BETTER GET THE PEOPLE AWAY BEFORE THE WHOLE CITY SINKS INTO THE MELTING SEA!

3

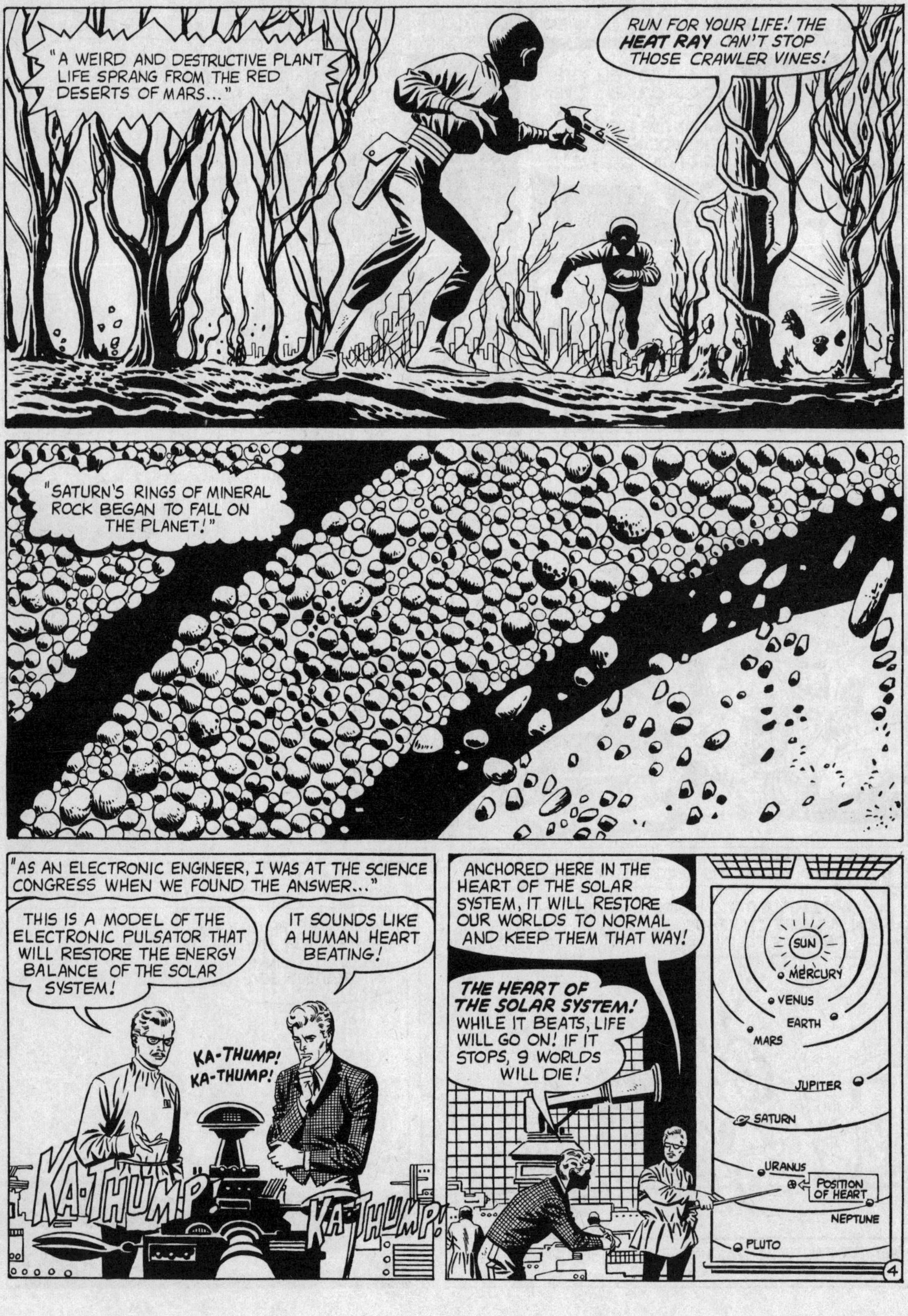
"A WEIRD AND DESTRUCTIVE PLANT LIFE SPRANG FROM THE RED DESERTS OF MARS..."
RUN FOR YOUR LIFE! THE HEAT RAY CAN'T STOP THOSE CRAWLER VINES!
"SATURN'S RINGS OF MINERAL ROCK BEGAN TO FALL ON THE PLANET!"
"AS AN ELECTRONIC ENGINEER, I WAS AT THE SCIENCE CONGRESS WHEN WE FOUND THE ANSWER..."
THIS IS A MODEL OF THE ELECTRONIC PULSATOR THAT WILL RESTORE THE ENERGY BALANCE OF THE SOLAR SYSTEM!
IT SOUNDS LIKE A HUMAN HEART BEATING!
KA-THUMP! KA-THUMP!
KA-THUMP
KA-THUMP!
ANCHORED HERE IN THE HEART OF THE SOLAR SYSTEM, IT WILL RESTORE OUR WORLDS TO NORMAL AND KEEP THEM THAT WAY!
THE HEART OF THE SOLAR SYSTEM! WHILE IT BEATS, LIFE WILL GO ON! IF IT STOPS, 9 WORLDS WILL DIE!
SUN
MERCURY
VENUS
EARTH
MARS
JUPITER
SATURN
URANUS
POSITION OF HEART
NEPTUNE
PLUTO
4

"IT WAS MADE HEART-SHAPED AS A SYMBOL AND TOWED TO ITS ANCHORAGE IN SPACE..."

KA-THUMP!

KA-THUMP!

"EACH PLANET HAD A RECEIVING STATION THAT CONVERTED THE HEART ENERGY INTO THE FORCE NEEDED TO KEEP THAT WORLD IN ELECTRONIC BALANCE!"

STATION EARTH REPORTING: SITUATION NORMAL!

"AND I--BOB CRANE--WAS MADE CHIEF TROUBLE-SHOOTER OF THE WHOLE HEART SYSTEM!"

THERE! I'VE REPLACED A TRANSISTOR AND THE OLD TICKER'LL BE AS SOUND AS A *BOTT* FOR ANOTHER YEAR!

*EDITOR'S NOTE: UNIT OF CURRENCY IN THE 22ND CENTURY!

"THEN, WITHOUT ANY WARNING..."

THE HEART-BEAT... IT'S SLOWING DOWN! BUT THE INSTRUMENTS CHECK OKAY!

KA-THUMP! KAAAA-THUMMMP!

KAAAA-THUMMMP!

"I BLASTED BACK TO MY SERVICE SHIP, WHICH WAS PACKED WITH TEST INSTRUMENTS..."

CAN'T UNDERSTAND IT! EVERYTHING IS WORKING FINE... YET THE HEART KEEPS SLOWING DOWN! IF IT STOPS...!

STATION EARTH CALLING CRANE! EMERGENCY!

THE HEART FORCE IS WEAKENING ON ALL PLANETS! FIND OUT WHAT IS WRONG!

I *HAVE* FOUND OUT! ONE OF THE 9 WORLDS IS SABOTAGING THE HEART TO DESTROY THE OTHER PLANETS!

5

"SO MUCH FOR PAST HISTORY! AND NOW AS I BLASTED DOWN TO EARTH, I GOT A NEW SCARE..."

STORM CLOUDS ALREADY FORMING OVER EARTH! AS THE HEART-BEAT SLOWS, THEY'LL GET WORSE...!

"I LANDED IN THE MIDDLE OF A THREE-RING MADHOUSE..."

HAVE TO FIGHT MY WAY THROUGH THIS CIRCUS!

HAVING TROUBLE, EARTHMAN?

DANGER DO NOT FEED THE VAM

CIRCUS TODAY

"THE NEPTUNIAN BIRDMAN SWOOPED DOWN..."

HEY! WHA--?!

RELAX, BOB CRANE! I'VE BEEN WAITING FOR YOU TO LAND!

CIRCUS TICKET

HOW DO YOU KNOW MY NAME? WHO ARE YOU?

OUTWARDLY, I'M A TICKET SELLER FOR THE CIRCUS! SECRETLY, I'M AGENT XOL-3, INTERPLANETARY BUREAU OF INVESTIGATION! THE CHIEF IS WAITING FOR A SECRET CONFERENCE WITH YOU!

TAKE THE THIRD TAXI! THE DRIVER'S ONE OF OUR AGENTS! AND BUY A CIRCUS TICKET FROM ME TO MAKE THIS LOOK GOOD!

OKAY, BUT THIS BETTER NOT BE A GAG TO SELL TICKETS!

TAXI

"IT WASN'T! MINUTES LATER I WAS FACE TO FACE WITH THE CHIEF OF IBI!"

ALL RIGHT-- WHAT HAVE I BEEN TAGGED FOR?

THE JOB OF SAVING THE DYING SOLAR SYSTEM!

6

"*SAVE* IT? I DIDN'T EVEN KNOW WHAT WAS *DESTROYING* IT!"

A STRANGE FORCE FROM *ONE* OF THESE NINE PLANETS IS STOPPING THE HEART...BUT MY INSTRUMENTS DON'T SHOW WHICH ONE!

IT ISN'T *EARTH!* *OUR* MEN ARE RUNNING THAT STATION! ONE OF THE OTHERS IS WRECKING OUR SOLAR SYSTEM IN ORDER TO PLUNDER IT!

MERCURY
VENUS
EARTH
MARS
JUPITER
SATURN
URANUS
NEPTUNE
PLUTO

YOU'D KNOW AT A GLANCE IF ONE OF THOSE STATIONS HAS BEEN ALTERED OR ANY UNUSUAL EQUIPMENT ADDED!

BUT EVERY-BODY KNOWS *ME!* THE MOMENT I SHOWED UP, THE GUILTY PLANET WOULD HIDE EVERY-THING!

EXACTLY! SO MEET DAN NOLAN, *ADVANCE MAN* FOR *NINE WORLDS CIRCUS!* YOU'LL TRAVEL AS *HIM* TO SAVE THE HEART!

WHAT? I DON'T EVEN LOOK LIKE HIM! BESIDES I DON'T KNOW ANY-THING ABOUT CIRCUSES OR WHAT AN *ADVANCE MAN* IS!

"THE CHIEF GRINNED AND OPENED A DOOR INTO A LABORATORY..."

YOU'LL BE DISGUISED AS NOLAN... AND THIS MEMORY-TRANSFER-ENCE MACHINE WILL PLANT HIS KNOW-LEDGE IN YOUR BRAIN!

AN *ADVANCE MAN* TRAVELS AHEAD OF THE CIRCUS TO DREAM UP PUBLICITY STUNTS!

"IT'S A PECULIAR FEELING... BORROWING ANOTHER GUY'S BRAIN AND FACE..."

ALL OF A SUDDEN I REMEMBER THINGS I NEVER KNEW AND PEOPLE I NEVER MET!

IT'S ONLY TEMPORARY! THE MEMORY WILL WEAR OFF SHORTLY... SO YOU'LL HAVE TO WORK DOUBLY FAST! NOW FOR THE DISGUISE!

"THIS WAS NO GREASE-PAINT JOB! THEY USED SYNTHETIC FLESH AND NATURAL PIGMENTS..."

GREAT SOL! I NOT ONLY LOOK LIKE DAN NOLAN... I REALLY *AM* DAN NOLAN!

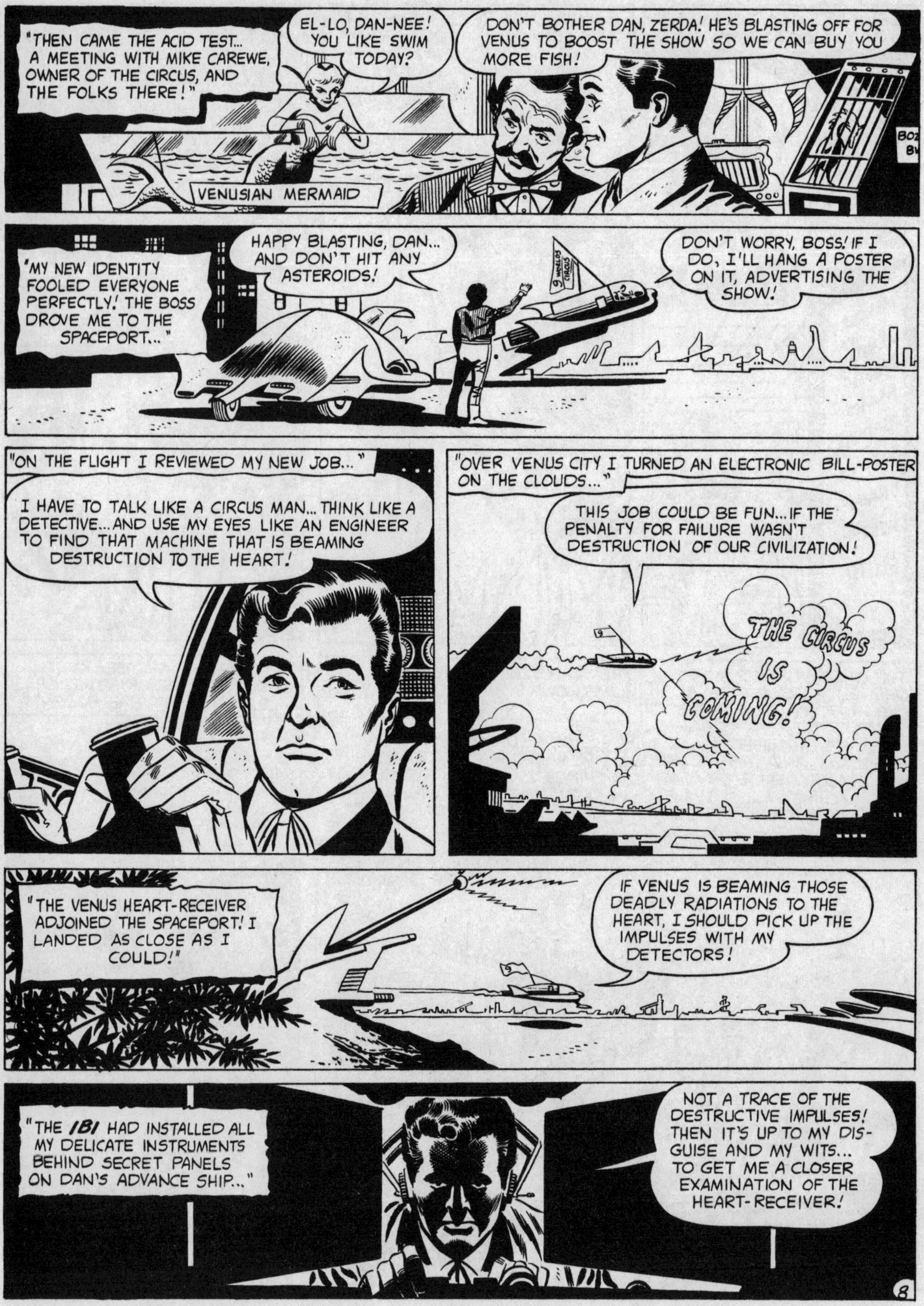
"THEN CAME THE ACID TEST... A MEETING WITH MIKE CAREWE, OWNER OF THE CIRCUS, AND THE FOLKS THERE!"
EL-LO, DAN-NEE! YOU LIKE SWIM TODAY?
DON'T BOTHER DAN, ZERDA! HE'S BLASTING OFF FOR VENUS TO BOOST THE SHOW SO WE CAN BUY YOU MORE FISH!
VENUSIAN MERMAID
"MY NEW IDENTITY FOOLED EVERYONE PERFECTLY! THE BOSS DROVE ME TO THE SPACEPORT..."
HAPPY BLASTING, DAN... AND DON'T HIT ANY ASTEROIDS!
DON'T WORRY, BOSS! IF I DO, I'LL HANG A POSTER ON IT, ADVERTISING THE SHOW!
"ON THE FLIGHT I REVIEWED MY NEW JOB..."
I HAVE TO TALK LIKE A CIRCUS MAN... THINK LIKE A DETECTIVE... AND USE MY EYES LIKE AN ENGINEER TO FIND THAT MACHINE THAT IS BEAMING DESTRUCTION TO THE HEART!
"OVER VENUS CITY I TURNED AN ELECTRONIC BILL-POSTER ON THE CLOUDS..."
THIS JOB COULD BE FUN... IF THE PENALTY FOR FAILURE WASN'T DESTRUCTION OF OUR CIVILIZATION!
THE CIRCUS IS COMING!
"THE VENUS HEART-RECEIVER ADJOINED THE SPACEPORT! I LANDED AS CLOSE AS I COULD!"
IF VENUS IS BEAMING THOSE DEADLY RADIATIONS TO THE HEART, I SHOULD PICK UP THE IMPULSES WITH MY DETECTORS!
"THE IBI HAD INSTALLED ALL MY DELICATE INSTRUMENTS BEHIND SECRET PANELS ON DAN'S ADVANCE SHIP..."
NOT A TRACE OF THE DESTRUCTIVE IMPULSES! THEN IT'S UP TO MY DISGUISE AND MY WITS... TO GET ME A CLOSER EXAMINATION OF THE HEART-RECEIVER!
8

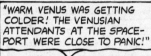

"WARM VENUS WAS GETTING COLDER! THE VENUSIAN ATTENDANTS AT THE SPACE-PORT WERE CLOSE TO PANIC!"

YOU GET AROUND SPACE, DAN! WHAT'S HAPPENING TO THE HEART?

DON'T ASK ME, SSZO! I'M ONLY A CIRCUS MAN! HERE'S A FREE PASS TO HELP YOU FORGET THE COLD!

EXIT →

"I TOOK AN AIR CAB TO THE HEART STATION! THEY KNEW DAN BUT I HAD TO DREAM UP AN EXCUSE TO EXAMINE THE MACHINERY!"

BOYS, I'VE GOT A TERRIFIC IDEA FOR PUBLICITY THAT'LL EARN YOU ALL FREE PASSES! LET ME LOOK AROUND A MINUTE...

WEL-L...OKAY, DAN! BUT DON'T TOUCH ANYTHING! NOBODY'S SUPPOSED TO GO NEAR THE RECEIVER EXCEPT CRANE!

NO ADMITTANCE

I CAN'T DETECT A THING WITH THIS POCKET IMPULSATOR! WITH THEM WATCHING, I CAN'T GET CLOSER... BUT IT LOOKS OKAY!

KAAA-THUMP!

"I WENT THROUGH DAN NOLAN'S USUAL PUBLICITY ROUTINE AND ASKED A LOT OF QUESTIONS..."

THE ELECTRONIC POSTER'LL FADE IN A FEW DAYS! ER-- WHAT DO YOU THINK IS WRONG WITH THE HEART SYSTEM?

IT'S THEM MARTIANS! THEY'VE HATED VENUS EVER SINCE WE LICKED 'EM IN THE LAST SPACE-WAR!

WORLDS CIRC

COMING

" I COVERED VENUS THE WAY DAN ALWAYS DID..."

YOU WIN, HONEY! WHAT DO *YOU* THINK IS WRONG WITH THE HEART?

EES NOSSING WRONG WITH *MY* HEART, HANDSOME!

BEAUTY CONT

FREE PASSES, MAYOR WLX! WHAT DO YOU THINK IS AFFECTING THE HEART?

HRRUMPH! *POLITICS*, YOUNG MAN!

AS LEADING EDITOR, WHAT IS YOUR OPINION?

THE MACHINE IS SIMPLY WEARING OUT AND SCIEN-TISTS ARE AFRAID TO ADMIT IT!

9

"I BLASTED OFF FOR MARS WITH MY HEAD SWIMMING!"

A DOZEN DIFFERENT GUESSES... AND NOT ONE SINGLE CLUE! I DON'T *THINK* VENUS IS DESTROYING THE HEART... BUT I CAN'T BE SURE!

"MARS WAS THE SAME...NO STRANGE RAYS...NO SUSPICIOUS MACHINES.."

UNLESS THE HEART IS FIXED FAST, WE'LL BE DRIVEN OUT BY THE CRAWLER VINES!

"HEADING FOR SATURN, I TRIED TO REASON OUT MY PROBLEM..."

THE GUILTY PLANET MUST HAVE DISCOVERED SOME WAY TO COUNTERACT THE CALAMITOUS EFFECTS THAT FOLLOW IF THE HEART STOPS! THAT WOULD TAKE MACHINERY...

THEY PLAN TO SIT BACK AND LET THE OTHER WORLDS GO TO RUIN! THEN THEY'LL STEP IN AND PLUNDER THE SOLAR SYSTEM! BUT WHICH PLANET IS IT?

"SATURN WAS THE SAME STORY OVER AGAIN..."

PEOPLE ARE ALREADY MOVING UNDERGROUND, DAN! SATURN'S MASS BEING 95 TIMES EARTH'S, IT TAKES LONGER FOR THE EFFECT TO GET REALLY GOING!

I WOULDN'T WANT TO BE HERE WHEN THOSE ROCKY RINGS SMASH DOWN!

10

"NOTHING SUSPICIOUS ON SATURN...NOTHING ON URANUS...I BLASTED PAST THE HEART TOWARD NEPTUNE..."

HALF THE PLANETS ACCOUNTED FOR-- AND NO NEARER A SOLUTION...

"SUDDENLY IT HAPPENED..."

WHA...? I'VE HIT A METEOR!

MY CONTROLS ARE OKAY BUT MY DETECTOR INSTRUMENTS ARE WRECKED AND I'M LOSING AIR FAST! GOT TO...GASP..GET INTO... GASP... SPACE SUIT!

HSSSSS!

I THINK I CAN MAKE IT TO NEPTUNE FOR REPAIRS! WHAT A BREAK...JUST WHEN EVERY WASTED MINUTE COULD MEAN THE END OF THE SOLAR SYSTEM!

"I FOUND OUT I WAS LOSING FUEL, TOO! IT RAN OUT OVER NEPTUNE SPACEPORT AND I THOUGHT I WAS A GONER WHEN..."

THOSE NEPTUNIAN BIRDMEN ARE EASING ME DOWN LIKE A FEATHER!

"I STUMBLED OUT AND GOT A FRESH SURPRISE..."

REMEMBER ME? AGENT *XOL-3, IBI!* I'VE BEEN WAITING TO GET YOUR REPORTS OR COOPERATE IN ANY WAY!

THIS IS TWICE YOU'VE GIVEN ME A LIFT, *XOL-3!* I WISH I HAD A REPORT TO GIVE YOU BUT I'M STILL DRAWING A BLANK!

"...AND THEN THAT HUNK OF SPACE HIT ME AND...HEY! *LOOK AT ITS COLORING!* NOW I KNOW WHO IS WRECKING THE HEART OF THE SOLAR SYSTEM!"

HUH...?

"*XOL-3* THOUGHT I WAS OFF MY ROCKET...BUT THERE IT WAS... THE *EVIDENCE* I'D BEEN SEEKING..."

THAT'S NO METEOR! THAT COLOR IS FOUND ONLY IN THE ROCKS THAT FORM THE *RINGS OF SATURN!*

SURE... EVERYBODY KNOWS THAT! BUT I DON'T GET THE POINT!

"I DRAGGED *XOL-3* INSIDE AND GOT OUT A CHART!"

THINK, XOL! SATURN'S RINGS ARE HELD IN PLACE BY CENTRIFUGAL FORCE! IF THE HEART STOPS, GRAVITY WILL PULL THE RINGS *IN ON THE PLANET!*

YES, BUT... *NOW I GET IT!* HOW COULD A PIECE OF SATURN'S RING GET OVER A BILLION MILES OUT IN SPACE TO HIT YOU?

JUPITER

SATURN

URANUS

"I WAS SO EXCITED I FORGOT ABOUT CAUTION..."

SATURN'S GOT AN ANTI-GRAVITY DEVICE TO HURL THE RINGS AWAY WHEN THE HEART STOPS! THEY'RE LETTING A FEW FALL NOW TO AVERT SUSPICION!

THE EARTHMAN KNOWS OUR SECRET! HE MUST BE STOPPED...

"WHILE I WAITED FOR MY SHIP TO BE REPAIRED, THE IDEA OF SPIES ON NEPTUNE NEVER OCCURRED TO ME!"

THE EARTHMAN KNOWS EVERYTHING! YOU MUST ACT AT ONCE! THE TIME FOR SECRECY IS PAST! DESTROY THE HEART OF THE SOLAR SYSTEM COMPLETELY!

12

"WE BLASTED OFF FOR SATURN--MY ONLY THOUGHT TO FIND AND DESTROY THEIR BEAM..."

ULP! I FORGOT THIS WAS CIRCUS DAY! I'LL TELL THEM I HAD TO COME BACK FOR BETTER REPAIRS TO THE SHIP!

GOOD! WE *CAN'T* LET ANY SATURNIANS GUESS WE'RE ON TO THEM NOW!

9 WORLDS CIRCUS

"BUT WHEN WE STEPPED DOWN..."

COME ALONG AND NO FUNNY STUFF, YOU TWO! YOU'RE NOT GOING TO STOP OUR PLANS NOW!

"IT WAS MADDENING, TO BE SO CLOSE AND LOSE!"

WAVE TO THE VENUSIAN MERMAID BUT DON'T TRY TO GIVE AN ALARM! OUR GUARDS ARE EVERY-WHERE!

HI, ZERDA! SEE YOU LATER!

"SUDDENLY I REMEMBERED THE OLD EARTH CIRCUS CALL FOR HELP... *HEY, RUBE!!*"

DAN, WHAT ARE YOU DOING BACK HERE? WHERE ARE YOU GOING?

HEY, RUBE, I'LL EXPLAIN LATER! I'M...ER...GOING WITH THESE CHAPS FOR A MEETING NOW, *HEY, RUBE!*

"MIKE AND THE CIRCUS CROWD GOT IT...AND WHAT HAPPENED TO THE SATURNIANS SHOULDN'T HAPPEN TO A PLUTONIAN *UTXL* *..."

XOL, GET ME TO OUR SHIP FAST! IF I CAN BEAT THE SATURNIANS TO THE HEART, I CAN SAVE THE SOLAR SYSTEM AND WRECK THEIR SCHEME!

*EDITOR'S NOTE: A DESPISED PLUTONIAN ANIMAL...LIKE AN EARTH JACKAL!

13

"IN THE MELEE, NOBODY SAW US BLAST OFF...OR SO I HOPED..."

I NEED 15 MINUTES TO GET INSIDE THE HEART AND CUT OFF THE SATURN BEAM! THAT WILL CUT OFF THE DESTRUCTIVE FORCE AND RETURN IT TO NORMAL BEAT!

HERE COME THREE SATURNIAN BATTLE-WAGONS... AND MY SHIP DOESN'T EVEN HAVE A SLING-SHOT FOR A DEFENSE WEAPON!

GET TO WORK ON THAT HEART! YOU HAVEN'T LIVED UNTIL YOU'VE SEEN A NEPTUNIAN BIRDMAN IN A SPACE-BATTLE!

"WHAT I SAW THEN, AS I WORKED AT THE HEART, WAS INCREDIBLE!"

XOL'S TERRIFIC! HE'S NOT ONLY DODGING THE SATURNIAN FIRE BUT MAKING THEM STAY AWAY TO KEEP FROM BEING RAMMED!

"THEN I WAS AT THE HEART CONTROL...CUTTING OFF THE SATURNIAN BEAM THAT WAS WRECKING IT!"

THAT DOES IT! THE HEART IS BACK TO NORMAL BEAT!

KA-THUMP! KA-THUMP! KA-THUMP! KA-THUMP!

"I WANTED TO YELL FOR JOY WHEN I SAW MY SHIP SWINGING IN... AND A SPACE GUARD FLEET CHASING THE SATURNIANS!"

COME ON BACK, DAN! THE WORLD FLEET GOT HERE IN TIME! THEY'VE TAKEN OVER SATURN AND THE MENACE IS OVER!

AS THEY USED TO SAY, BACK IN THE 20TH CENTURY... YIPPEEE!

The End

14

JOE BENTLEY WAS THE WORLD'S GREATEST AUTHORITY ON ALL KNOWLEDGE BEGINNING WITH THE LETTER A! BUT BEING AN "A EXPERT" HAD SURPRISING CONSEQUENCES--NOT ONLY ON JOE'S LIFE BUT ALL LIFE ON EARTH 1000 YEARS IN THE FUTURE!

The WIZARD of A!

AND NOW OUR PANEL OF EXPERTS WILL QUIZ JOE BENTLEY ON CATEGORIES BEGINNING WITH THE LETTER A!

ARTILLERY AGRICULTURE ARCHITECTURE AUTOMATION ANATOMY

AS JOE BENTLEY PREPARES TO START OUT ON A NEW JOB AT SANDERSON'S FURNITURE COMPANY...

THAT'S ODD--I DIDN'T NOTICE THAT BOOK THERE A MOMENT AGO! WHERE'D IT COME FROM?

A NOTE ATTACHED TO THE BOOK SAYS I'VE BEEN SINGLED OUT TO RECEIVE VOLUME A OF A NEW ENCYCLOPEDIA! THE NOTE CAUTIONS ME NOT TO TELL ANYONE ABOUT THE BOOK, OR IT'LL BE TAKEN AWAY FROM ME!

CURIOUSLY, JOE OPENS THE VOLUME AND...

VOLUME *A*, EH? WELL, A SMALL VOLUME LIKE THIS CAN'T SAY MUCH ABOUT *ATOMIC POWER*-- HEY, THE PAGES ARE ALL *BLANK*!

BUT THE NEXT MOMENT...

GOOD GOSH! ALL OF A SUDDEN, PRINTING APPEARED--AS IF MY *THINKING* OF ATOMIC POWER MADE IT APPEAR! YES--THERE'S A FOOTNOTE EXPLAINING THE BOOK IS PRINTED IN INVISIBLE *MENTO-TYPE*-- WHICH BECOMES VISIBLE AS I THINK OF A CERTAIN CATEGORY!

INTRIGUED, JOE READS THE CHAPTER ON ATOMIC POWER...

CAN'T UNDERSTAND MOST OF THIS-- *WAIT!* IT SAYS AN ATOMIC EXPLOSION WILL OCCUR IN TWIN FALLS APRIL 15, 1958! THAT'S TODAY-- THIS TOWN! I'VE GOT TO CALL BILL EVANS!

BILL, DON'T THROW THE SWITCH FOR THAT EXPERIMENT! ONE OF YOUR TUBULAR FUEL RODS IS FAULTY!

HOW CAN YOU POSSIBLY KNOW--? BUT I'LL CHECK IT AT ONCE!

SOMEWHAT LATER, AS BENTLEY APPROACHES THE SANDERSON FURNITURE COMPANY...

THERE HE IS!

COME ALONG WITH US, BENTLEY! THE TWIN FALLS TESTING LABORATORY WANTS TO LEARN HOW YOU KNEW THERE'D BE AN EXPLOSION THERE TODAY!

HOW DID SUCH A REMARKABLE BOOK COME INTO JOE BENTLEY'S HANDS, YOU ASK? TO ANSWER THAT, WE MUST GO INTO THE FUTURE-- ONE THOUSAND YEARS...

IN AN ELECTRONIC CONTROL ROOM--

EVER SINCE ABEL BENDEL INVENTED THE TIME-MACHINE, WE'VE BEEN AFRAID TO GO INTO THE PAST FOR FEAR WE MIGHT UNWITTINGLY DO SOMETHING TO CHANGE THE FUTURE-- *OUR PRESENT!*

2

AS A TEST CASE, WE SENT THE FIRST VOLUME OF AN ENCYCLOPEDIA TO JOSEPH BENTLEY OF 1000 YEARS AGO! IF BY USING THE INFORMATION IN THAT BOOK, BENTLEY DOES NOT DO ANYTHING THAT WILL ALTER OUR FUTURE TIME, IT'LL BE SAFE FOR US TO TRAVEL INTO THE PAST!

MEANWHILE, IN THE TWIN FALLS TESTING LABORATORY...

BUT, GENTLEMEN, I TELL YOU I DON'T KNOW *HOW* I KNEW THE TUBULAR FUEL WAS DEFECTIVE!

I DARE NOT TELL THEM ABOUT THE BOOK, OR IT'LL BE TAKEN AWAY FROM ME!

THEN YOU CLAIM TO BE AN EXPERT ON ATOMIC POWER? VERY WELL, SHOW US HOW WE COULD IMPROVE ON THIS ATOMIC POWER MOTOR!

I REMEMBER THE DIAGRAM OF A MOTOR LIKE THAT IN THE BOOK!

IF THE PRIMARY LOOP WERE PLACED INSIDE THE SECONDARY AND BOTH SUSPENDED MAGNETICALLY--AND THE TURBINE WERE CIRCULAR TO SURROUND THE REACTOR UNIT--

OF COURSE! IT'S THE PERFECT DESIGN! WHY DIDN'T *WE* THINK OF THAT?

EXCITED NEWSMEN GATHER AROUND THE NOW CONFIDENT JOE BENTLEY...

WHY DID YOU SPECIALIZE ON SUBJECTS JUST BEGINNING WITH *A*?

I'M AN EXPERT ON ANYTHING WITH THE LETTER *A*!

WE'LL PLAY UP THIS STORY AS *THE WIZARD OF A!*

I'VE BEEN SPEAKING TO THE PENTAGON! THEY WANT BENTLEY TO TAKE THE NEXT PLANE TO WASHINGTON!

GO BY PLANE? THAT'S TOO SLOW! I KNOW A *FASTER* WAY TO GET THERE!

3

AS THE **WIZARD OF A** STEPS INTO A TELEPHONE BOOTH...

WHAT'S HE DOING IN THAT PHONE BOOTH?

FASTER THAN A PLANE?

THE SECTION ON **ATOMIC TRANSMISSION** WILL TELEPORT ME TO WASHINGTON IN THE WINK OF AN EYE!

A GLOWING NIMBUS FORMS AROUND JOE BENTLEY'S BODY...

I DO THIS BY A METHOD OF MUSCULAR AND MENTAL CONTROL! I MUST REFER TO THE BOOK TO TELL ME HOW TO WORK THIS...

IN WASHINGTON, A MOMENT LATER...

GENTLEMEN, I'M HERE TO ANSWER YOUR QUESTIONS ON THE LETTER **A**!

BUT-BUT--I ONLY JUST HUNG UP THE PHONE!

QUERIES FLY FAST AND THICK--

TELL US ABOUT **AGRICULTURE**! **ANATOMY**!

ASTRONOMY! **ARCHITECTURE**!

"**AGRICULTURE** CAN BE IMPROVED BY A PROCESSED FORMULA I'LL GIVE YOU! VEGETABLES AND FRUIT WILL GROW SO LARGE, A SINGLE FARM WILL SERVE AN ENTIRE CITY..."

THIS POTATO WILL FEED A FAMILY FOR A WEEK!

"AS FOR **ANATOMY**, FUTURE HUMANS WILL BE TALLER, MORE POWERFULLY BUILT, AND HAVE A FAR GREATER BRAIN CAPACITY..."

4

"IN *ASTRONOMY*, THE SPACE-SATELLITES WE ARE SENDING OUT NOW WILL SOON BECOME SPACE-PLATFORMS--LAUNCHING SHIPS INTO SPACE. FIRST TO THE PLANETS, THEN TO THE STARS..."

WELCOME TO *ALPHA CENTAURI!*

"*ARCHITECTURE* WILL REACH AMAZING NEW HEIGHTS! MANEUVERABLE HOUSES WILL GO ABOVE OR BELOW THE GROUND--DEPENDING ON THE WEATHER...*"

TORNADO AHEAD! DOWN WE GO!

AT THAT MOMENT, IN THE YEAR 2958...

EVERYTHING IS PROCEEDING SMOOTHLY, SIR! WE'VE HAD BENTLEY UNDER CONSTANT CHECK! THE KNOWLEDGE HE'S GAINED IS NOT MATERIALLY AFFECTING THE FUTURE!

ALL HE IS DOING IS SPEEDING UP A NUMBER OF INVENTIONS AND SCIENTIFIC DISCOVERIES!

I DISAGREE! JOSEPH BENTLEY HAS ALREADY *DIGRESSED* FROM HIS *NORMAL LIFE PATTERN* IN AN *IMPORTANT DEGREE--BY NOT REPORTING FOR WORK THIS MORNING!* AS A HISTORIAN I'VE MADE A DETAILED STUDY OF HIS LIFE!

NORMALLY, BENTLEY WOULD HAVE GONE TO HIS NEW JOB AND MET A *LUCY PORTER*, HIS WIFE-TO-BE! I'VE TRACED THE DESCENDANTS OF THEIR CHILDREN, TOO! ONE OF THOSE DESCENDANTS IS OUR OWN ABEL BENDEL!

WITH NO ABEL BENDEL, THE GREATEST SCIENTIFIC GENIUS OF OUR AGE, MANY OF OUR MOST IMPORTANT ADVANCES WILL BE OBLITERATED!

THEN WE MUST GET THAT BOOK BACK IMMEDIATELY! I ONLY HOPE WE'RE NOT TOO LATE!

5

INSTANTLY, A TIMEBEAM TOUCHES THE *A* VOLUME, AND--

THEY WANT TO KNOW ABOUT *ARTILLERY*, NOW, AND-- THE BOOK! IT'S FADING-- *DISAPPEARING!*

WITHOUT THE BOOK, THE *WIZARD OF A* IS JUST ORDINARY JOE BENTLEY AGAIN...

MY--MY POWER IS GONE, GENTLEMEN!

YOU'VE PERFORMED WONDERS FOR US, BENTLEY! THANKS TO YOU, THE WORLD HAS BEEN ADVANCED SCIENTIFICALLY HUN- DREDS OF YEARS!

THAT NIGHT, JOE BENTLEY WALKS THE CITY STREETS, ALONE AND FORGOTTEN... *I'M A NOBODY AGAIN! AN UNEMPLOYED NOBODY, AT THAT!*

IN SHEER DESPERATION, HE PUTS IN A LONG-DISTANCE TELEPHONE CALL--

MR. SANDERSON, I WAS WONDERING IF THAT JOB IS STILL OPEN FOR ME? *IT IS?* I'LL REPORT FOR WORK AS SOON AS I CAN!

NEXT DAY, JOE BENTLEY APPEARS AT HIS NEW JOB...

GOLLY WHAT A PRETTY GIRL!

LUCY PORTER

IT'S A STRANGE THING, BUT THE MOMENT I SAW HER, I COULD TELL SHE'S THE GIRL I'M GOING TO MARRY!...

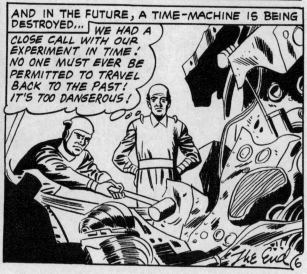

AND IN THE FUTURE, A TIME-MACHINE IS BEING DESTROYED... WE HAD A CLOSE CALL WITH OUR EXPERIMENT IN TIME! NO ONE MUST EVER BE PERMITTED TO TRAVEL BACK TO THE PAST! IT'S TOO DANGEROUS!

The End 6

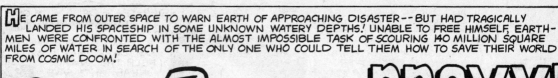

HE CAME FROM OUTER SPACE TO WARN EARTH OF APPROACHING DISASTER -- BUT HAD TRAGICALLY LANDED HIS SPACESHIP IN SOME UNKNOWN WATERY DEPTHS! UNABLE TO FREE HIMSELF, EARTHMEN WERE CONFRONTED WITH THE ALMOST IMPOSSIBLE TASK OF SCOURING 140 MILLION SQUARE MILES OF WATER IN SEARCH OF THE ONLY ONE WHO COULD TELL THEM HOW TO SAVE THEIR WORLD FROM COSMIC DOOM!

Space-Rescue by PROXY!

I DON'T KNOW WHERE ON EARTH I AM! UNLESS THE INHABITANTS OF THIS PLANET FIND ME IN TIME, WE'LL *ALL* PERISH!

IN A MID-WESTERN CITY, A PEDESTRIAN SUDDENLY CRIES OUT IN ALARM...

HELP! I'M TRAPPED UNDERWATER!

YOU'VE GOT TO LISTEN TO ME -- OR EVERYONE ON EARTH WILL DIE!

WHAT'S HE TALKING ABOUT?

SOMEONE CALL AN AMBULANCE!

IN THE HOSPITAL AND UNDER A SEDATIVE, BART SMITHERS SPEAKS IN A CLEAR, CRISP VOICE...

I AM SPEAKING TO YOU THROUGH THIS EARTHMAN! MY NAME IS *KRYLXT* FROM THE PLANET *ALPHA* OF THE STAR-SUN *RIGEL!* I'VE TRAVELED 540 LIGHT YEARS ACROSS SPACE TO WARN YOU--

"I TOOK OFF IN HYPER-SPACE DRIVE WITH ONE THOUGHT IN MIND..."

A COSMIC MENACE SWEEP-ING TOWARD EARTH! MUST HELP THE UNWARY INHABITANTS SAVE THEMSELVES--

"AN HOUR BEFORE LANDING TIME, I HIT A FOURTH-DIMENSIONAL SPACE-WARP! MY SHIP PLUMMETED EARTHWARD, OUT OF CONTROL..."

B-BLACKING OUT... GOING TO CRASH...

"WHEN I REGAINED CONSCIOUSNESS, I REALIZED MY SHIP WAS BURIED UNDERWATER, AND THERE WAS NO WAY OF ESCAPING IT ALIVE! BESIDES, I HAD LESS THAN TEN HOURS SUPPLY OF AIR LEFT..."

I DON'T KNOW WHERE ON EARTH I AM! EARTHMEN WILL NEVER FIND ME IN TIME!

"THOUGH I KNEW I COULDN'T SAVE MYSELF, I FIGURED I STILL HAD A CHANCE TO SAVE EARTH! WITH MY LIMITED TELEPATHIC POWERS, I TRIED TO CONTACT AN EARTHMAN MENTALLY..."

AT LAST! I'VE REACHED AN EARTH BEING WHOSE MENTAL WAVE LENGTH MATCHES MY OWN!

AS THE ALIEN FINISHES SPEAKING THROUGH BART SMITHERS...

THERE IS VERY LITTLE TIME LEFT! YOU MUST LISTEN TO MY INSTRUCTIONS AS I RELAY THEM THROUGH MY EARTHMAN PROXY! FOLLOW THEM EXACTLY IF YOU HOPE TO SAVE YOUR PLANET!

2

WITHIN AN HOUR, DARWIN JONES, CHIEF OF THE *DEPARTMENT OF SCIENTIFIC INVESTIGATION*, GATHERS THE COUNTRY'S FOREMOST SCIENTISTS TO THE HOSPITAL BED...

THE DANGER COMES FROM A VAST COSMIC CLOUD DUE TO ENVELOP EARTH IN-- EIGHT OF YOUR HOURS!

"THIS COSMIC CLOUD IS RADIOACTIVE, A MILLION TIMES MORE DEADLY THAN YOUR H-BOMBS!"

"ON EVERY PLANET IT TOUCHES, ALL LIFE DIES FROM THE HIGH CONCENTRATION OF LETHAL RADIO-ACTIVITY..."

INSIDE THE TRAPPED SPACESHIP...

YOU MUST BUILD A GREAT TOWER OF STEEL SURMOUNTED BY A ROD ONE THOUSAND FEET HIGH AND THREE FEET THICK-- TO ABSORB THE RADIOACTIVE CLOUD PARTICLES!

WORKING AT FRANTIC SPEED, EARTH ENGINEERS CONSTRUCT A MODEL TOWER...

CORRECT IN EVERY DETAIL! NOW-- BUILD IT!

KRYLXT, LISTEN-- WE'RE GOING TO MAKE AN ATTEMPT TO RESCUE YOU TOO!

73% OF YOUR PLANET IS COVERED WITH WATER! IT'S HOPELESS!

WE HAVE A SAYING-- "WHERE THERE'S LIFE, THERE'S HOPE!"

3

ALL WE NEED IS A CLUE OR TWO! TELL ME, HOW FAST WERE YOU TRAVELING WHEN YOU BLACKED OUT-- OVER WHAT PART OF EARTH WERE YOU--

"THE LAST THING I REMEMBER WAS APPROACHING EARTH FROM SPACE DIRECTLY ABOVE THE TALLEST BUILDING ON YOUR PLANET..."

MOMENTS LATER, AT EMERGENCY HEADQUARTERS...

KRYLXT WAS DIRECTLY OVER THE EMPIRE STATE BUILDING WHEN HE BLACKED OUT! HIS ESTIMATED TIME OF LANDING WAS ONE HOUR! AS HE PLUMMETED DOWNWARD THAT HOUR, EARTH ROTATED BENEATH HIM!

THE EARTH ROTATES EASTWARD ONE DEGREE OF LONGITUDE EVERY FOUR MINUTES! IN A HOUR, IT WOULD ROTATE 15 DEGREES! NEW YORK IS LOCATED AT 40° 42' LATITUDE, 74° LONGITUDE! AN HOUR'S ROTATION WOULD BRING THE SPACE-SHIP TO 89° LONGITUDE!

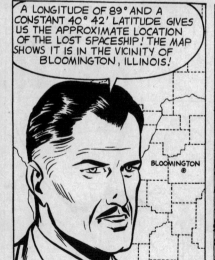

A LONGITUDE OF 89° AND A CONSTANT 40° 42' LATITUDE GIVES US THE APPROXIMATE LOCATION OF THE LOST SPACESHIP! THE MAP SHOWS IT IS IN THE VICINITY OF BLOOMINGTON, ILLINOIS!

BLOOMINGTON

WITHIN AN HOUR, A FLEET OF HELICOPTERS HOVERS OVER CENTRAL ILLINOIS, INSTRUMENTS VAINLY SEARCHING FOR THE MISSING SPACECRAFT...

NO LARGE BODY OF DEEP WATER AROUND HERE! AM HEADING FURTHER WEST!

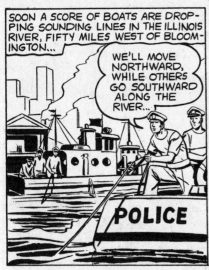

SOON A SCORE OF BOATS ARE DROPPING SOUNDING LINES IN THE ILLINOIS RIVER, FIFTY MILES WEST OF BLOOMINGTON...

WE'LL MOVE NORTHWARD, WHILE OTHERS GO SOUTHWARD ALONG THE RIVER...

POLICE

MEANWHILE, AN EMERGENCY ARMY OF CONSTRUCTION WORKERS ARE ASSEMBLING A GIGANTIC STEEL-WORK TOWER...

IT'S ALMOST COMPLETE! WE HAVE TWO HOURS LEFT IN WHICH TO PUT THE INTERCEPTOR ROD IN PLACE!

GIANT CABLES ARE LAID AND THE MASSIVE ROD HOISTED UPWARD...

KEEP IT RISING!

ONE HOUR AND THIRTY MINUTES LEFT! DARWIN JONES IS ON THE ILLINOIS RIVER WHERE IT WIDENS TO FORM LAKE PEORIA...

THE COSMIC DUST CLOUD HAS BEEN SPOTTED APPROACHING EARTH! IT'D BE GREAT IF WE COULD MAKE THIS A *DOUBLE RESCUE!*

POLICE

DESPERATE MEN SEARCH FRANTICALLY IN VAIN...

ONLY HALF AN HOUR LEFT NOW, MR. JONES! IF WE DON'T REACH HIM BY THEN, THE SPACEMAN WILL DIE!

HIS SHIP HAS TO BE IN LAKE PEORIA! KEEP SEARCHING!

IN THE MEANTIME, THE INTERCEPTOR ROD SETTLES INTO POSITION...

WE DID EVERYTHING THE ALIEN SAID! I JUST HOPE WE DID IT *RIGHT!*

5

FEVERISHLY HURRYING MEN STRUGGLE TO MAKE LAST-MOMENT HOOKUPS EVEN AS THE COSMIC CLOUD SWEEPS DOWN ONTO THE EARTH!

A HAND THRUST OVER A LEVER AND MILLIONS OF VOLTS OF ELECTRICITY HURL THE INTERCEPTOR ROD INTO QUIVERING LIFE!

AT THIS EXACT MOMENT, ON LAKE PEORIA...

LOCATED IT, SIR! RIGHT BENEATH OUR KEEL!

GET THE GRAPNELS AND HOISTS! THAT SHIP MUST BE RAISED IN LESS THAN TEN MINUTES!

POLICE

DIVERS DESCEND TO GUIDE THE PLACEMENT OF GRAPPLING IRONS...

WITHIN THE ALLOTED TEN MINUTES...

CONGRATULATIONS, EARTHMEN! YOU BROKE THE POWER OF THE COSMIC CLOUD AND ACHIEVED MY RESCUE AT THE SAME TIME!

6

THE LEAST WE COULD DO TO SHOW OUR APPRECIATION FOR SAVING US WAS TO ENABLE YOU TO RETURN TO YOUR WORLD AND ANNOUNCE-- *MISSION ACCOMPLISHED!*

The End

SHOWCASE
PRESENTS

**LOOK FOR THESE OTHER TITLES FEATURING
CLASSIC TALES OF DC SUPER HEROES!**

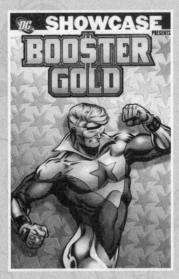

SHOWCASE
PRESENTS

**LOOK FOR THESE OTHER TITLES FEATURING
CLASSIC TALES THAT GO BEYOND DC SUPER HEROES!**

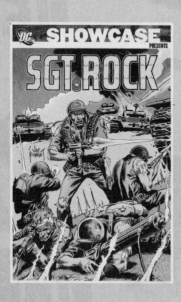